OUR DECLARATION TO THE WORLD

ALEXANDER HAMILTON: We declare that "societies of men are capable of ... establishing good government from reflection and choice," and need not be "forever destined to depend for their political constitutions on accident and force."

—Federalist 1:2

JAMES MADISON: We declare that "ambition must be made to counteract ambition. ... In framing a government which is to be administered by men over men ... you must first enable the government to control the governed; and in the next place oblige it to control itself."

—Federalist 51:6-7

JOHN JAY: We declare that "Providence has in a particular manner blessed America with a variety of soils and productions, and watered it with innumerable streams, for the delight and accommodation of its inhabitants. ... And, Providence has been pleased to give this one connected country to one united people."

—Federalist 2:8-9

FIVE-STAR REVIEWS*

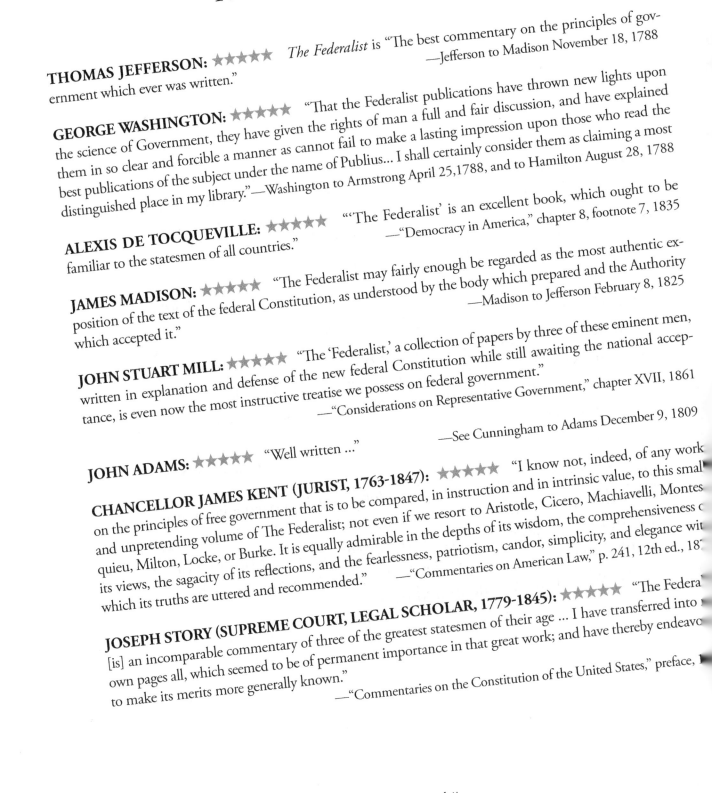

THOMAS JEFFERSON: ★★★★★ *The Federalist* is "The best commentary on the principles of government which ever was written."
—Jefferson to Madison November 18, 1788

GEORGE WASHINGTON: ★★★★★ "That the Federalist publications have thrown new lights upon
the science of Government, they have given the rights of man a full and fair discussion, and have explained
them in so clear and forcible a manner as cannot fail to make a lasting impression upon those who read the
best publications of the subject under the name of Publius... I shall certainly consider them as claiming a most
distinguished place in my library."—Washington to Armstrong April 25,1788, and to Hamilton August 28, 1788

ALEXIS DE TOCQUEVILLE: ★★★★★ "'The Federalist' is an excellent book, which ought to be
familiar to the statesmen of all countries."
—"Democracy in America," chapter 8, footnote 7, 1835

JAMES MADISON: ★★★★★ "The Federalist may fairly enough be regarded as the most authentic exposition of the text of the federal Constitution, as understood by the body which prepared and the Authority
which accepted it."
—Madison to Jefferson February 8, 1825

JOHN STUART MILL: ★★★★★ "The 'Federalist,' a collection of papers by three of these eminent men,
written in explanation and defense of the new federal Constitution while still awaiting the national acceptance, is even now the most instructive treatise we possess on federal government."
—"Considerations on Representative Government," chapter XVII, 1861

JOHN ADAMS: ★★★★★ "Well written ..."
—See Cunningham to Adams December 9, 1809

CHANCELLOR JAMES KENT (JURIST, 1763-1847): ★★★★★ "I know not, indeed, of any work
on the principles of free government that is to be compared, in instruction and in intrinsic value, to this small
and unpretending volume of The Federalist; not even if we resort to Aristotle, Cicero, Machiavelli, Montesquieu, Milton, Locke, or Burke. It is equally admirable in the depths of its wisdom, the comprehensiveness of
its views, the sagacity of its reflections, and the fearlessness, patriotism, candor, simplicity, and elegance with
which its truths are uttered and recommended."
—"Commentaries on American Law," p. 241, 12th ed., 18

JOSEPH STORY (SUPREME COURT, LEGAL SCHOLAR, 1779-1845): ★★★★★ "The Federa
[is] an incomparable commentary of three of the greatest statesmen of their age ... I have transferred into
own pages all, which seemed to be of permanent importance in that great work; and have thereby endeavo
to make its merits more generally known."
—"Commentaries on the Constitution of the United States," preface,

*Editors' Note: See end of book for quote sources for pages *i* and *ii*.

Hamilton • Madison • Jay

THE FEDERALIST PAPERS

Made Easier

THE COMPLETE AND ORIGINAL TEXT

SUBDIVIDED AND ANNOTATED

FOR EASIER UNDERSTANDING

PAUL B. SKOUSEN

IZZARD INK
PUBLISHING

IZZARD INK PUBLISHING COMPANY
PO Box 522251
Salt Lake City, Utah 84152
www.izzardink.com

First Edition published September 17, 2022

Contact Izzard Ink Publishing at info@izzardink.com
Contact the author at info@paulskousen.com

The Federalist Papers Made Easier paperback—ISBN 979-8-36204-285-1
The Federalist Papers Made Easier hardback—ISBN 978-1-64228-091-3
The Federalist Papers Made Easier eBook—ISBN 978-1-64228-092-0
The Federalist Papers Made Easier audiobook—ISBN 978-1-64228-093-7

CONTENTS

Below: *The Federalist* No. 50 (checks and balances) and No. 51 (elections in the House) by James Madison were published in the New York Packet, February 8, 1788. Four months later when all 85 essays were being published in two volumes, Hamilton divided No. 31 into two essays, which renumbered everything afterwards. That's why this text below became No. 51 and No. 52.*

*Image used under license from Shutterstock.com.

WHAT IS *THE FEDERALIST?*

The Federalist is one of America's three most important founding documents. The first, the *Declaration of Independence*, was a statement of beliefs undergirding America's separation from Britain.

The second, the *Constitution of the United States*, gave rise to the new form of government created specifically to protect those beliefs.

The third, *The Federalist*, is the most authoritative defense and explanation of the Constitution ever put in print, except for the Constitution itself.

The first two documents are products of the combined efforts of America's national representatives to address the immediate needs of the country.

The third document was a fortunate accident.

A FORTUNATE ACCIDENT

Within weeks of the release of the newly proposed Constitution in 1787, those opposed to it began an attack with anonymous opinion pieces in the local New York newspapers. Their primary complaint was that the new Constitution would give the federal government far too much power over the States. These critics later became known as Anti-Federalists.

When Alexander Hamilton saw this attack begin, he organized a defense and invited James Madison and John Jay to join him in writing a series of rebuttal opinion pieces.

What began as an effort to convince the people of New York to ratify the new Constitution ended up being the accidental creation of a detailed description of that entire document, examining the reasoning, logic, and principles of liberty constituting this new form of government—and showing why all other forms of human government always ended in dismal failure.

The *Federalist* project had a modest start. They planned to produce 25 or so essays for local newspapers. As the project got rolling, and as critics of the Constitution raised new arguments, their small project expanded to a total of 85 essays of more than 190,000 words. That's more words than in the New Testament (184,600 words).

The essays were produced at the blistering rate of three to four a week, an average of 2,200 words each. That's the modern-day equivalent of more than four typewritten pages of single-spaced lines.

WHEN WERE *THE FEDERALIST PAPERS* PUBLISHED?

The first Federalist paper appeared on October 27, 1787, in three New York newspapers—the *Independent Journal*, the *New-York Packet*, and the *Daily Advertiser*. The goal of Hamilton, Madison and Jay was to produce the papers at a pace so rapid as to overwhelm any effort by the Anti-Federalists to put up a challenge. The strategy worked, and the Anti-Federalists were unable to organize themselves and keep up.

By March 1788 demand was growing for a bound collection of the papers. The New York publishing firm, J&A McLean, announced it would take on the project and published the first thirty-six papers as *The Federalist Volume 1* on March 22, 1788. But this was not the end—Hamilton, Madison and Jay continued to pour out their essays at such a rate that a second volume was justified. Just two months later *The Federalist Volume II* was published on May 28, 1788. It included Nos. 37–77, plus eight new essays that had not yet appeared in the newspapers. Nos. 78–85 could be read for the first time in Volume II but were re-published in the newspapers over the following months, with the last, No. 85, appearing on August 16, 1788.

DID *THE FEDERALIST* INFLUENCE RATIFICATION?

The *Federalist* essays were published too late with too narrow of a distribution to influence many of the States and their decisions about ratifying the new Constitution. This chart shows that more than half the States had already ratified the Constitution before all of the essays were even published. Nine States were needed for the Constitution to become ratified, but George Washington expressed the hope that all thirteen States would ratify and join the Union.

	STATE	DATE OF RATIFICATION	PAPERS WRITTEN AND PUBLISHED
1	Delaware	December 7, 1787	17
2	Pennsylvania	December 12, 1787	20
3	New Jersey	December 18, 1787	22
4	Georgia	January 2, 1788	31
5	Connecticut	January 9, 1788	31
6	Massachusetts	February 6, 1788	49
7	Maryland	April 28, 1788	77
8	South Carolina	May 23, 1788	77
9	New Hampshire	June 21, 1788 – Constitution is ratified	85
10	Virginia	June 25, 1788	85
11	New York	July 26, 1788	85
12	North Carolina	November 21, 1789	85
13	Rhode Island	May 29, 1790	85

WHO WERE THE ANTI-FEDERALISTS?

Anti-Federalists were Americans who opposed this new federal form of government. Federalism is a mode of organization whereby the States surrender certain rights to a central power that could compel the States to obey its will regarding those certain rights. At the time, the States had just freed themselves of the King and were leery of any new central authority.

When the new Constitution was made public some leading citizens believed too much power was being given to the federal government and that one day, they would find themselves in the clutches of another monarchy—this time wearing not one crown but a thousand.

The nickname Anti-Federalists was given them by the Federalists to help cast them as against the new government. Some leading Anti-Federalists included George Mason, Patrick Henry, Samuel Adams, James Monroe, and Mercy Otis Warren.

THIRTY-FIVE OBJECTIONS

In 1788, a pro-Constitution pamphlet was published in Albany, New York, listing the Anti-Federalists' thirty-five main objections against the new Constitution. The list is revealing because it helps explain the selection of topics covered in *The Federalist*. The pamphlet also includes a rebuttal to each objection. See the full text of the pamphlet in the appendix.

NATURE OF *THE FEDERALIST* PAPERS

The eighty-five papers defend the principles of liberty with explanation and reasoning drawn from historical precedent and recent experiences. The writers refer to ideas gleaned from records covering thousands of years of human history: The Bible, Cicero, Polybius, Plutarch, Tacitus, Livy, John Locke, Thomas Hobbes, Adam Smith, Baron de Montesquieu, Sir William Blackstone, Immanuel Kant, David Hume, and so forth.

When the delegates to the Constitutional Convention first met to consider how to repair the many flaws in their government, they combined these timeless principles into careful order, unpacking them in a fashion that tightly governs political power in the presence of corruptible human nature. They placed in direct opposition power against power and jealousy against jealousy, and created a self-correcting and self-policing balance of political power that would ensure that the people's liberties were safe.

THE CONSTITUTION DOES NOT EXPLAIN ITSELF

The Constitution does not explain why its forms and powers and restrictions are arranged the way they are. That is where *The Federalist* plays such an important role. In the essays that follow, Hamilton, Madison, and Jay spell out the reasons for the Constitution's careful construction, its inclusions and exclusions of government powers, and its mechanisms for change as the need for change becomes necessary.

The authors' goal was straightforward: explain the Constitution with such clarity that future Americans could sufficiently understand its workings to successfully preserve and perpetuate true republican liberty into the ages.

WHO WROTE *THE FEDERALIST* PAPERS?

- **Alexander Hamilton** was a voracious reader in the law and economics, making him well suited to address those topics. He was a military commander in the War for Independence, a very successful and busy lawyer, politician, and banker. He was a delegate from New York, strong interpreter and promoter of the Constitution, and he later became the first secretary of the treasury. He married Elizabeth Schuyler, and they were parents of eight children. Hamilton wrote fifty-one papers: 1, 6–9, 11–13, 15–17, 21–36, 59–61, and 65–85.

- **James Madison** is considered the Father of the Constitution and the Bill of Rights, and one of the most influential delegates at the Constitutional Convention. He later became the fifth Secretary of State and the fourth president of the United States. He led the US through the War of 1812. Madison was an avid reader and a student of politics and history, and he was well equipped to discuss the political lessons learned by prior civilizations. For this Federalist project he had the advantage of access to the massive volume of notes that he took during the Constitutional Convention, equipping him to best convey the Framers' intentions expressed during the Convention. He married Dolley Todd and adopted her son John Payne Todd. Madison wrote twenty-nine papers: 10, 14, 18–20, 37–58, 62, and 63.[1]

- **John Jay** had long and solid experience in government. He served twice as a delegate to Congress, as well as ambassador to Spain, secretary of foreign affairs, and as the president of Congress during the war. He was the lead writer of New York's constitution and of the treaty ending the war with England. He had a sterling reputation as a man of deep and unyielding integrity, one with great faith in God, and he later became the first chief justice of the new Supreme Court. Unfortunately his contributions were limited to just five essays due to rheumatism and injuries from a brick thrown in his face during a New York street riot in 1788. He married Sarah Van Brugh Livingston, and they were parents of six children. Jay wrote papers 2–5 and 64.

QUESTIONS AND ANSWERS

Who is Publius?

The authors kept their identities secret to minimize partisan bickering and rejection, signing each essay with the pen name "Publius," from Publius Valerius Poplicola (died 503 BC). He was one of four leaders of the Roman revolution who orchestrated the overthrow of the Roman king in 509 BC and set up a republic in Rome.

Who were the essays intended to influence the most?

The essays were criticized for being much too complex for the common people. The real target audience were those "thought leaders" who commanded respect, those whose opinions could best influence the votes cast by delegates at the New York State ratifying convention.

What is the correct title, *The Federalist Papers* or *The Federalist*?

The correct form is *The Federalist*. When the various essays were published in the local New York newspapers, each essay had a numbered headline, "The Federalist, No. 1," and so

---

1 Authorship of twelve of the Federalist essays has been debated for 175 years. Madison said he was the author but Hamilton supporters challenged that, claiming Hamilton wrote them. For a summary of how this debate and mystery was finally resolved (they're all Madison's essays) see Ben Christopher, "How Statistics Solved a 175-Year-Old Mystery about Alexander Hamilton," Priceonomics, https://priceonomics.com/how-statistics-solved-a-175-year-old-mystery-about/, published October 31, 2016, accessed October 14, 2021.

forth (see the image of "The Federalist, No. 50" at the start of this introduction). When the essays were combined and published in book form in 1788 it was called *The Federalist*. Today's widely popular title, *The Federalist Papers*, gradually came into use over the following century.

What political slant does the collection follow?

None—not in the sense of being politically liberal or conservative as those terms are understood today. Putting partisan party politics aside, the collection is for all intents and purposes partisan toward the Constitution and the culture that is essential to perpetuating it.

How were the Papers received by the general public in 1787?

Many readers hated the essays, accusing the publishers of "cramming us" with too much, and making faithful readers "nauseous." Others called them too "elaborate" for the common people. Some of the subscribers even demanded a refund on their newspaper subscription.[2]

How did the Papers influence Supreme Court cases?

As of this writing, the Supreme Court has not based a finding on *The Federalist*, but in its published rulings it has referred to *The Federalist* at least 291 times. The most frequently cited totals are as follows:

First: No. 78, mentioned 37 times. This paper explains federal judicial powers, such as the power of judicial review.

Second: No. 42, mentioned 34 times. This paper explains the general scope of federal powers.

Third: No. 81, mentioned 27 times. This paper gives more explanation of the roles of the Supreme Court and inferior federal courts.

Fourth: No. 51, mentioned 26 times. This paper talks about checks and balances.

Fifth: No. 32, mentioned 25 times. This paper talks about the power to tax.

Sixth: No. 48 and No. 80, tied, mentioned 20 times each, discuss the separation of powers and powers of the Judiciary.

Seventh: No. 44, mentioned 18 times. This paper talks about restrictions on the authorities of the States.

Special Mention: No. 10 is mentioned 14 times with 13 of those mentions after 1980. This paper is widely respected for its discussion about factions and special interest groups that can give rise to tyranny by the majority, and how to manage that without destroying liberty.

Which version of *The Federalist* is the most authoritative?

Creating an exact original version of *The Federalist* remains elusive because of slight variations in the newspaper versions as well as in the published bound volumes. The authors made several corrections before they died, and some of these appeared in print in one or two versions but not the others. The text for this edition is the 1818 Gideon Edition, the version used most by historians and scholars. It is essentially the same as the original McLean edition.

What is the *Articles of Confederation*?

The *Articles of Confederation* is America's first constitution. It and its supporters are highly criticized throughout *The Federalist*. The many flaws and weaknesses in the *Articles* are the very reason Americans sent delegates to Philadelphia in 1787 to fix the problems.

The *Articles of Confederation* was a hastily written document designed to unite the thirteen

---

2 Dan T. Coenen, *The Story of the Federalist, How Hamilton and Madison Reconceived America*, (New York, Twelve Tables Press, 2007), 17-18.

original American States into an alliance, and having one central government. For our use here, the name is usually shortened to "the Articles." See the appendix for the complete text.

Who wrote the *Articles of Confederation?*

An effort to create America's first government started with a draft by Benjamin Franklin in 1775. This failed to win support. It was followed by a rejected proposal from Silas Deane of Connecticut. A third proposal by Deane's fellow delegates was also rejected. Lastly, a fourth proposal in 1776 by John Dickinson of Pennsylvania was accepted. Congress liked Dickinson's proposal and sent a revised version to the States in 1777. It wasn't ratified until 1781.

The Articles was a disaster. Because of its many weaknesses the Constitutional Convention was called to make all necessary corrections and changes to save the country from disintegrating into chaos.

What were the main problems in the *Articles of Confederation?*

In general, the Articles left the States too strong, similar to how a treaty among nations leaves the members sovereign and independent without a central authority strong enough to force everyone to obey the terms of their treaty. The Articles' flaws included the following:

Congress was left too weak with no power to enforce the law.

Congress could not effectively raise revenue for national needs or to fight the war.

Congress could not regulate commerce, leaving the States to guard their borders as if they were foreign enemies to each other.

There was no executive branch (President).

There was no judicial branch (Supreme Court).

Despite these serious problems, the Articles served as the law of the land during the opening four years of the Revolutionary War, and then formally for eight years until it was replaced by the new Constitution in 1789.

Is or *are* the Articles of Confederation a singular or plural noun?

When referring to the Articles as a complete document use the singular form. "The Articles of Confederation has thirteen Articles and is a constitution."

HOW DO I FIND SPECIFIC INFORMATION?

An exhaustive index at the back of the book provides direct access to more than 600 topics with more than 4,300 references. These references are spelled out and cited by paper/paragraph (Example: 37:44) and point the reader directly to the actual quote or discussion.

A second level of organization whereby general topics may be found is the table of contents entitled, "The Contents of the Federalist." A one-line summary of each paper is provided (Example, "Paper 18, All Confederacies Must Fail").

WHAT TO EXPECT WHEN READING THE FEDERALIST

The Federalist is delightfully insightful reading but it is not easy. The writing is very dense, complex, and quite often very difficult for the modern reader. Much of it is composed of compound sentences, fragments, double negatives, multi-layered parenthetical injections, referrals to "former" and "latter," and exhaustive streams of thought connected by semi-colons that sometimes don't unravel for an entire page. Dozens of antiquated vocabulary words are perfectly utilized but their meanings require a dictionary.

For the reader looking to better understand the Constitution there lies within these explanations, defenses, and arguments nothing short of pure constitutional gold. Though sometimes difficult, these nuggets are worth every effort to sift through the passages and mine them out. And that's where *The Federalist Papers Made Easier* can help.

To get the most out of *The Federalist*, approach each essay for what it is—an opinion piece published in the newspaper, responding to a criticism of the new Constitution. These 85 essays were not written to blend together as chapters in a book. They each stand alone as they were created, sometimes repeating, sometimes contradicting.

Second, the first few essays are especially verbose and difficult. As the authors delve more deeply into the various topics, the writing becomes more clear.

Third, the editors of this edition have added several comprehension aids. See those illustrated on the next page.

ADDITIONAL CLARIFICATIONS

Why all-caps in the original Federalist text? These capitalized words are actually part of the original version of *The Federalist*. The authors' purpose was to emphasize an important point. Some editions of *The Federalist* have changed the all-capitalized words to italicized words. The editors of this edition chose to retain the original form.

Lowercase letter at the start of a sentence: This indicates an artificial paragraph break by the editors between two thoughts in one sentence, or between many thoughts in a long series of fragments.

Capitalizing the word *convention*. Whenever Publius uses the word *convention* to mean the Constitutional Convention in Philadelphia that met from May 25 to September 17, 1787, the editors felt that this particular usage needed to stand apart from other uses of "convention." Each reference to that meeting in Philadelphia is capitalized as Convention.

Footnotes: All the footnotes prefaced with "Publius" are part of the original *Federalist*.

Brackets [...]: Some statements that are hard to follow have a clarification or a list number using brackets. These were added by the editors and are not part of the original text. All of the original parenthetical comments made by Hamilton, Madison and Jay appear in parentheses, (...), as originally published.

Strangely Spelled Words: Spelling corrections are rare except to help clarify a confusing word.

HOW THE FEDERALIST PAPERS ARE MADE EASIER

A dozen elements have been added to make easier the reading, understanding, and researching through *The Federalist*. The most helpful change was dividing the text into **shorter paragraphs** that can be more easily read and comprehended. Additional changes are indicated below.

THE FEDERALIST PAPERS MADE EASIER

6:34 This passage, at the same time, points out the EVIL and suggests the REMEDY.

—PUBLIUS

Review Questions written to highlight important ideas and principles are provided at the end of each *Paper*. The **paragraphs** with the answers are provided in parentheses. Complete answers are given in the appendix under "**Answers to Review Questions**."

REVIEW QUESTIONS

1. What are the additional dangers that will come from disunion? (6:1)
2. To think the disunited States would be kind to each other is to disregard what? (6:2)
3. What fantasy do Anti-Federalists believe about commerce? (6:13)
4. What passion is as domineering as power or glory"? (6:18)
5. What are some of the ancient republics or nations that fought for commercial power? (6:19–28)
6. Is "peace through commerce" a realistic expectation? (6:29–30)
7. What does nearness and close proximity of nations naturally create? (6:32–33)

FEDERALIST NO. 7

BENEFITS OF UNION, DANGERS OF SEPARATE CONFEDERACIES: Would the disunited States make war on each other? Hamilton points out that not only would the States squabble as in Europe, but such wars would spill out into war with other nations. The flash points for internal war could come from competition for commercial activities, fighting over Western territory, or squabbling over how to pay the national debt if the States chose to break apart into confederacies. Hamilton uses several hypothetical circumstances to relate these possibilities more intimately to the voters in New York.

By Alexander Hamilton
November 15, 1787

Introduction: A brief summary of each *Paper's* content is provided. The author's name and the date it was first published in the newspapers is also given.

REASONS FOR WAR BETWEEN DISUNITED STATES:
Can the people expect new hostilities if they become disunited?

7:1 IT IS sometimes asked, with an air of seeming triumph, <u>what inducements</u> could the <u>States</u> have, if disunited, to <u>make war upon each other</u>? It would be a full answer to this question to say — precisely the <u>same induce</u>-

<u>ments</u> which have, at different times, deluged in blood all the <u>nations</u> in the world.

REASONS FOR HOSTILITIES ARE ALREADY PRESENT:

7:2 But, unfortunately for us, the question admits of a more particular answer. There are causes of <u>differences</u> within our immediate contemplation, of the tendency of which, <u>even under</u> the restraints of a <u>federal constitution</u>, we have had <u>sufficient experience</u> to enable us to form a judgment of what <u>might be expected</u> if those <u>restraints</u> were <u>removed</u>.

TERRITORIAL DISPUTES:
What do nations frequently fight over? Are there such conflicts ongoing among the thirteen States?

7:3 <u>Territorial disputes</u> have at all times been found one of the most fertile sources of hostility among nations. Perhaps the <u>greatest</u> proportion of <u>wars</u> that have desolated the earth have sprung from this origin. This cause would exist among us in full force.

UNDECIDED LAND CLAIMS BETWEEN THE STATES:

7:4 We have a <u>vast tract of unsettled territory</u> within the boundaries of the United States. There still are discordant and <u>undecided claims</u> between several of them, and the <u>dissolution of the Union</u> would lay a foundation for similar claims between them all.

LAND DISPUTES BEFORE AND AFTER REVOLUTION:

7:5 It is well known that they have <u>heretofore had serious</u> and animated <u>discussion</u> concerning the <u>rights to the land</u> which were ungranted at the time of the <u>Revolution</u>, and which usually went under the name of <u>crown lands</u>. The <u>States</u> within the limits of whose co

Underlined Key Words: These underlines help draw out the main point of each paragraph, and are especially helpful for paragraphs that are difficult to understand. They also provide a valuable tool for later research. Instead of re-reading an entire paragraph, the reader can scan across the underlined words to locate key statements and topics.

Page Header: The *Paper's* number and author is given at the top of each page for faster navigation.

Paragraph Headline: The headlines tell the reader about the general content of a paragraph. This is especially helpful when scanning through a *Paper* for specific information.

NO. 7 – HAMILTON

lonial governments they were comprised have <u>claimed</u> <u>them</u> as their property, the <u>others</u> have <u>contended</u> that the rights of the crown in this article devolved upon the Union; especially as to all that part of the <u>Western territory</u> which, either by actual possession, or through the <u>submission of</u> <u>the Indian proprietors</u>, was <u>subjected to the jurisdiction</u> <u>of the king</u> of Great Britain, till it was relinquished in the treaty of peace. This, it has been said, was at all events an acquisition to the Confederacy by compact with a foreign power.

CONGRESS INTERVENES:
What policy did Congress implement to resolve land disputes? Is it a permanent arrangement?

7:6 It has been the <u>prudent policy of Congress</u> to appease this controversy, by prevailing upon the States to make <u>cessions</u> to the United States for the <u>benefit of the whole</u>. This has been so far accomplished as, under a continuation of the Union, to afford a decided prospect of an <u>amicable termination</u> of the dispute. A <u>dis-</u> <u>memberment</u> of the <u>Confederacy</u>, however, would <u>revive this dispute</u>, and would <u>create</u> <u>others</u> on the same subject.

RISK OF NEW TERRITORIAL DISPUTES:
The Northwest Ordinance (1787) demonstrates how to settle territorial disputes by admitting new States as equals instead of enlarging existing States.

7:7 At present, a large part of the vacant <u>West-</u> <u>ern territory</u> is, by cession at least, if not by any anterior right, the common <u>property of the</u> <u>Union</u>. If that were at an end, the States which made the cession, on a principle of federal compromise, would be apt when the motive of the grant had ceased, to <u>reclaim the lands as</u> <u>a reversion</u>. The other States would no doubt insist on a proportion, by right of representation. Their argument would be, that a grant, once made, could not be revoked; and that the justice of participating in territory acquired or

secured by the joint efforts of the Confederacy, remained undiminished.

SHARING LAND CREATES MANY NEW PROBLEMS:
A Union is necessary to resolve land disputes that individual States would handle unfairly.

7:8 If, contrary to probability, it should be admitted by all the States, that each had a right to a share of this common stock, there would still be a difficulty to be surmounted, as to a proper <u>rule of apportionment</u>. Different principles would be set up by different States for this purpose; and as they would affect the <u>opposite</u> <u>interests</u> of the parties, they might not easily be susceptible of a pacific adjustment.

WITH NO UMPIRE, HOSTILITIES WILL OCCUR:
What about future fighting over the great western territories?

7:9 In the wide <u>field</u> of <u>Western territory</u>, therefore, we perceive an <u>ample theatre</u> for <u>hostile pretensions</u>, without any <u>umpire</u> or common judge to interpose between the contending parties. To reason from the past to the future, we shall have good ground to apprehend, that the <u>sword</u> would sometimes be appealed to as the arbiter of their <u>differences</u>.

SETTLING DISPUTES IN COURT:
The dispute over the Wyoming land demonstrate how a national court can resolve national matters without States going to war.

7:10 The circumstances of the dispute between <u>Connecticut</u> and <u>Pennsylvania</u>, respecting the land at <u>Wyoming</u>, admonish us not to be **san-** **guine**[1] in expecting an easy accommodation of such differences. The articles of confederation obliged the parties to submit the matter to the decision of a federal court. The submission was made, and the court decided in favor of Pennsylvania. But Connecticut gave strong indicat-

---

1 *sanguine:* Eager hopefulness; confidently optimistic.

Paragraph Summary: The summary can be either a statement that explains the content of the paragraph, or it can be a question. The question can be answered from the words that follow, and is designed to reveal the intent of the writer, or encourage a more thoughtful consideration of the text.

Paragraph Numbers: The paragraphs are numbered according to chapter–verse like the Bible, except here it's Paper–Paragraph. These numbers also indicate paragraph breaks. Original breaks made by the three authors are shown in **Bold**. An artificial paragraph break made by the editors is not in bold. In a classroom using older versions of *The Federalist*, reference is often made to paragraphs (Example, "Turn to Paper 10, paragraph 6"). The **bold** paragraph numbers help both versions work together.

These paragraph numbers are used universally in the **index**. All index entries direct the reader to the precise paragraph instead of a general page number.

Vocabulary Words: Many unfamiliar words are defined in a footnote. To help the reader return to the place of interruption, the same word is in bold in the paragraph text. A **glossary** in the appendix lists these and other difficult words with brief definitions.

WORDS TO KNOW

Many vocabulary words in the *Federalist* are no longer commonly used. A few of those used repeatedly are explained below for convenience. The glossary at the back of the book defines many more such words.

popular. This doesn't mean trendy or prevailing or famous. *Popular* is used to mean "pertaining to the common people" as in *popular voice, popular vote, popular elections,* and *popular government* (which means both a representative republic and a pure democracy).

signal or signaling. This is not a misspelling of *single.* In context it means "unique, exceptional, remarkable, or striking," as in *signal advantage* (unique), *signalizes the genius* (exceptional), and *signal importance* (remarkable or striking).

faction. This refers to a dissenting group that rises up against the whole. A faction can be politicians within a government assembly, a group within a State, a whole State, or several States.

confederacy. This is a group of States that unite by agreement into a league or alliance. It was feared that if the thirteen States didn't unify they would divide into two or three weak confederacies that would always be quarreling, similar to the quarreling nations of Europe at that time.

embarrass. This is not like being ashamed but rather is used to mean hinder, entangle, confuse, or to make intricate: "Our public affairs are embarrassed."

energy. This word is frequently used to mean having sufficient political power to execute laws and perform the assigned duty. The Articles left the central government with too little *energy,* meaning, too little political power to forcefully impose itself on the States and compel them to fulfill their commitments. After the war, the Articles proved itself weak and seriously flawed, having granted too little *energy* (authority) to keep the peace between the States.

mutability. Think of "mutate," something that has changed from its original form. The Framers wanted a government that would not frequently change. Mutability (changeableness) in government discourages obedience to laws and makes lenders reluctant to lend because the people can't trust the laws to stay the same day to day.

electors. This is anyone who elects: The masses of the people, the electors choosing the president, representatives as electors, and senators as electors. It is confusing in places, so a careful reading in context helps reveal which particular elector is being referenced.

color. This word is used twenty times as both positive and negative to caste doubt or to establish the validity or meaning of a claim. Instances include "What colorable reason could be assigned" (what plausible reason), or "pretenses to color" (pretending to be legitimate), or "had some color" (had a little legitimacy), or "too highly colored" (exaggerated), or "destitute of color" (lacking any validity or proof).

SIGNIFICANT EVENTS IN THE HISTORY OF *THE FEDERALIST*

1787   **Twelve States approve** the new Constitution, September 17, 1787.

1787   **Congress receives** the new Constitution, September 20, 1787.

1787   **Congress votes to send** the Constitution to the States for approval or rejection, September 28, 1787.

1787   **The first of eighteen Anti-Federalist articles** by "Centinel" (Samuel Bryan) is printed in the *Philadelphia Independent Gazette.*

1787   **The first of five Anti-Federalist letters** by "The Federal Farmer" (possibly Melancton Smith) appears in a pamphlet. The letters were dated October 8–13, 1787, and were addressed to "The Republican" (New York state governor George Clinton).

1787   **The first of sixteen Anti-Federalist articles** by "Brutus" (perhaps Robert Yates of New York) is printed in the *New York Journal,* October 18, 1787.

1787   **The first of fifty-one Federalist papers** written by Publius (Alexander Hamilton) is published in New York's *Independent Journal*, October 27, 1787.

1787   **The second Federalist paper** is published October 31, 1787, by Publius (John Jay), the first of five papers Jay wrote before becoming ill and withdrawing due to an attack of rheumatism.

1787   **The tenth Federalist paper** is published November 22, 1787, by Publius (James Madison), the first of twenty-nine essays by Madison. No. 10 is often cited as the most highly regarded of all eighty-five essays.

1787   **Delaware becomes the first State** (December 7, 1787) to ratify the Constitution, by a vote of 30–0.

1787   **Pennsylvania ratifies** the Constitution by a vote of 46–23 (December 12, 1787).

1787   **New Jersey ratifies** the Constitution by a vote of 38–0 (December 18, 1787).

1788   **Georgia ratifies** the Constitution by a vote of 26–0 (January 2, 1788).

1788   **Connecticut ratifies** the Constitution by a vote of 128–40 (January 9, 1788).

1788   **Massachusetts ratifies** the Constitution by a vote of 187–168 (February 6, 1788). The close vote was secured after promises were made to include a bill of rights.

1788   **Volume I of The Federalist** is published by McLean and Company (New York City) on March 22, 1788. It reprinted the first thirty-six essays. These had already been printed in several New York newspapers.

1788   **Rhode Island rejects** the Constitution after a state-wide referendum, by a vote of 2,711–239 (March 24, 1788).

1788   **The Federalist No. 77** by Publius (Alexander Hamilton) is published (April 2, 1788).

1788   **Maryland ratifies** the Constitution by a vote of 63–11 (April 28, 1788).

1788   **South Carolina ratifies** the Constitution by a vote of 149–73 (May 23, 1788).

1788   **Volume II of The Federalist** is published by McLean and Company on May 28, 1788. It reprinted essays 37–85. Numbers 78–85 were eight new essays that had not yet appeared in the newspapers. The complete set of eighty-five essays was then available in the two volumes.

1788   **New Hampshire ratifies** the Constitution by a vote of 57–47 (June 21, 1788), reaching the milestone of nine states required to formally ratify the US Constitution. Washington expressed hope that all thirteen States would ratify.

1788   **Virginia ratifies** the Constitution by a vote of 89–77 (June 25, 1788).

1788   **Virginia Ratifying Convention** formally proposed amendments, including a bill of rights (June 27, 1788). Anti-Federalist leaders George Mason and Patrick Henry were particularly active in promoting the amendments. Several of the States ratifying with close votes made amendments a crucial factor in voting to ratify.

1788   **Ratification certified** on July 2, 1788, by Cyrus Griffin who served as president of Congress. He formally validated that nine States had ratified the Constitution, as required by Article VII of the Articles of Confederation, technically establishing the Constitution as the new ruling document of America.

1788   **New York ratifies** the Constitution by a vote of 30–27 (July 26, 1788), and formally asked for certain amendments to be added later.

1788   **North Carolina rejects** the Constitution by a vote of 184–83 (August 2, 1788). The biggest concern was the lack of a bill of rights.

1788   **Congress disbands** on its last day of existence (October 10, 1788), to make room for the new government.

1789   **The new House of Representatives meets** for the first time (April 1, 1789) and begins organizing itself.

1789   **The new Senate meets** for the first time (April 6, 1789), and begins organizing itself.

1789   **George Washington is inaugurated** as the first President under the new Constitution (April 30, 1789).

1789   **Nineteen amendments are introduced** by James Madison as the first formal draft of a bill of rights (June 8, 1789).

1789   **Congress distilled** Madison's amendments down to 12 and sent them to the States for ratification.

1789   **North Carolina ratifies** the Constitution by a vote of 194–77 (November 21, 1789).

1790   **Rhode Island ratifies** the Constitution by a vote of 34–32 (May 29, 1790). It was the last of the original thirteen States to finally ratify the new Constitution.

1791   **Virginia ratifies the Bill of Rights,** the first ten amendments (December 15, 1791), becoming the eleventh State to do so and fulfilling the requirement that three fourths of the States are needed to amend the Constitution. There were fourteen States at the time—Vermont had joined the Union on March 4, 1791.

1939   **Symbolic ratification:** Although ratification of the Bill of Rights by the remaining three States (Massachusetts, Connecticut, and Georgia), was not necessary, those three States eventually moved forward anyway. They symbolically ratified the Bill of Rights in 1939 during the 150th anniversary of Congressional approval of the Bill of Rights.

CONTENTS OF *THE FEDERALIST*

PART I
A MORE PERFECT UNION

SECTION 1 • BENEFITS OF A MORE PERFECT UNION

SECTION 2 • CONFEDERACY IS FATALLY FLAWED

SECTION 3 • GRANTING GOVERNMENT PROPER POWER

SECTION 4 • GIVING GOVERNMENT ENOUGH REVENUE

SECTION 5 • WRITING THE CONSTITUTION

SECTION 6 • PROTECTING THE STATES

SECTION 7 • CHECKS AND BALANCES

PART II
THE THREE BRANCHES

SECTION 8 • HOUSE OF REPRESENTATIVES

SECTION 9 • THE SENATE

SECTION 10 • EXECUTIVE BRANCH

SECTION 11 • JUDICIARY BRANCH SECTION

SECTION 12 • BILL OF RIGHTS, CONCLUDING REMARKS

THE FEDERALIST
HAMILTON • MADISON • JAY

PART I

A MORE

PERFECT

UNION

WORD COUNT AND PUBLISHING DATE OF EACH PAPER

We don't have the precise dates each paper was physically written but we do have the dates they were printed in the New York newspapers. The last eight papers were published first in book form on May 28, 1788 (designated with a "bk") and later republished in the newspapers (designated with "news").

PAPER	WORDS	DATE	AUTHOR	PAPER	WORDS	DATE	AUTHOR
1	1585	Oct. 27, 1787	Hamilton	48	1857	Feb. 1, 1788	Madison
2	1664	Oct. 31, 1787	Jay	49	1644	Feb. 2, 1788	Madison
3	1441	Nov. 3, 1787	Jay	50	1101	Feb. 5, 1788	Madison
4	1635	Nov. 7, 1787	Jay	51	1911	Feb. 6, 1788	Madison
5	1338	Nov. 10, 1787	Jay	52	1841	Feb. 8, 1788	Madison
6	2134	Nov. 14, 1787	Hamilton	53	2160	Feb. 9, 1788	Madison
7	2253	Nov. 15, 1787	Hamilton	54	1995	Feb. 12, 1788	Madison
8	1987	Nov. 20, 1787	Hamilton	55	2035	Feb. 13, 1788	Madison
9	1975	Nov. 21, 1787	Hamilton	56	1630	Feb. 16, 1788	Madison
10	2997	Nov. 22, 1787	Madison	57	2230	Feb. 19, 1788	Madison
11	2494	Nov. 24, 1787	Hamilton	58	2083	Feb. 20, 1788	Madison
12	2145	Nov. 27, 1787	Hamilton	59	1899	Feb. 22, 1788	Hamilton
13	960	Nov. 28, 1787	Hamilton	60	2233	Feb. 23, 1788	Hamilton
14	2138	Nov. 30, 1787	Madison	61	1515	Feb. 26, 1788	Hamilton
15	3075	Dec. 1, 1787	Hamilton	62	2381	Feb. 27, 1788	Madison
16	2033	Dec. 4, 1787	Hamilton	63	3032	Mar. 1, 1788	Madison
17	1564	Dec. 5, 1787	Hamilton	64	2304	Mar. 5, 1788	Jay
18	2086	Dec. 7, 1787	Madison	65	2014	Mar. 7, 1788	Hamilton
19	2020	Dec. 8, 1787	Madison	66	2220	Mar. 8, 1788	Hamilton
20	1522	Dec. 11, 1787	Madison	67	1636	Mar. 11, 1788	Hamilton
21	2000	Dec. 12, 1787	Hamilton	68	1496	Mar. 12, 1788	Hamilton
22	3481	Dec. 14, 1787	Hamilton	69	2739	Mar. 14, 1788	Hamilton
23	1804	Dec. 18, 1787	Hamilton	70	3290	Mar. 15, 1788	Hamilton
24	1826	Dec. 19, 1787	Hamilton	71	1701	Mar. 18, 1788	Hamilton
25	1990	Dec. 21, 1787	Hamilton	72	2034	Mar. 19, 1788	Hamilton
26	2387	Dec. 22, 1787	Hamilton	73	2343	Mar. 21, 1788	Hamilton
27	1425	Dec. 25, 1787	Hamilton	74	995	Mar. 25, 1788	Hamilton
28	1597	Dec. 26, 1787	Hamilton	75	1938	Mar. 26, 1788	Hamilton
29	2238	Jan. 9, 1788	Hamilton	76	1927	Apr. 1, 1788	Hamilton
30	1971	Dec. 28, 1787	Hamilton	77	1973	Apr. 2, 1788	Hamilton
31	1737	Jan. 1, 1788	Hamilton	78	3013	May 28, 1788 bk	Hamilton
32	1491	Jan. 2, 1788	Hamilton			Jun. 14, 1788 news	Hamilton
33	1693	Jan. 2, 1788	Hamilton	79	1019	May 28, 1788 bk	Hamilton
34	2218	Jan. 5, 1788	Hamilton			Jun. 18, 1788 news	Hamilton
35	2257	Jan. 5, 1788	Hamilton	80	2450	May 28, 1788 bk	Hamilton
36	2944	Jan. 8, 1788	Hamilton			Jun. 21, 1788 news	Hamilton
37	2718	Jan. 11, 1788	Madison	81	3781	May 28, 1788 bk	Hamilton
38	3324	Jan. 12, 1788	Madison			Jun. 28, 1788 news	Hamilton
39	2604	Jan. 16, 1788	Madison	82	1531	May 28, 1788 bk	Hamilton
40	3013	Jan. 18, 1788	Madison			Jul. 2, 1788 news	Hamilton
41	3548	Jan. 19, 1788	Madison	83	5707	May 28, 1788 bk	Hamilton
42	2776	Jan. 22, 1788	Madison			Jul. 5, 1788 news	Hamilton
43	3433	Jan. 23, 1788	Madison	84	3928	May 28, 1788 bk	Hamilton
44	2910	Jan. 25, 1788	Madison			Jul. 16, 1788 news	Hamilton
45	2115	Jan. 26, 1788	Madison	85	2657	May 28, 1788 bk	Hamilton
46	2610	Jan. 29 1788	Madison			Aug. 16, 1788 news	Hamilton
47	2735	Jan. 30, 1788	Madison				

SECTION 1 • BENEFITS OF A MORE PERFECT UNION

Papers 1–14

FEDERALIST NO. 1

INTRODUCTION: This is Hamilton's introduction to a series of papers defending and describing the new Constitution. He encourages people to honestly consider its merits and to answer that great question, Can a nation of free people thoughtfully create their own good government? Hamilton emphasizes that the Articles of Confederation is deeply flawed and that its defenders will use all manner of deceit and misleading tactics to destroy people's faith in the new Constitution. He intends to focus on the positive outcome of the Constitutional Convention and why their recommended Constitution should be supported. These eighty-five papers will cover six main topics that show why the new Constitution is best for America, and how it's a model for the entire world.

By Alexander Hamilton—October 27, 1787

ARTICLES OF CONFEDERATION HAS FAILED:
The Articles is a disaster and a stronger union is needed for the safety of all thirteen States.

1:1 AFTER an unequivocal experience of the inefficacy of the subsisting **federal**[3] government, you are called upon to deliberate on a new Constitution for the United States of America. The subject speaks its own importance; comprehending in its consequences nothing less than the existence of the UNION, the safety and welfare of the parts of which it is composed, the fate of an empire in many respects the most interesting in the world.

THE IMPORTANT QUESTION THAT MUST BE ANSWERED:
Good government is now within reach. What is the most important question that America is being asked to answer?

1:2 It has been frequently remarked that it seems to have been reserved to the people of this country, by their conduct and example, to decide the important question, whether societies of men are really capable or not of establishing good government from reflection and choice, or whether they are forever destined to depend for their political constitutions on accident and force. If there be any truth in the remark, the crisis at which we are arrived may with propriety be regarded as the era in which that decision is to be made; and a wrong election of the part we shall act may, in this view, deserve to be considered as the general misfortune of mankind.

WE MUST BE FREE OF BIAS TO DISCOVER THE TRUTH:
What must Americans set aside to give the new Constitution an honest consideration?

1:3 This idea will add the inducements of philanthropy to those of patriotism, to heighten the solicitude which all considerate and good men must feel for the event. Happy will it be if our choice should be directed by a judicious estimate of our true interests, unperplexed and unbiased by considerations not connected with the public good. But this is a thing more ardently to be wished than seriously to be expected. The plan offered to our deliberations affects too many particular interests, innovates upon too many local institutions, not to involve in its discussion a variety of objects foreign to its merits, and of views, passions and prejudices little favorable to the discovery of truth.

SELFISHNESS OBSTRUCTS POLITE DISCUSSION:
Political leaders always resist a new system that reduces their power. What two groups will be most offended by the new Constitution?

1:4 Among the most formidable of the obstacles which the new Constitution will have to encounter may readily be distinguished the obvious interest of a certain class of men in every State to resist all changes which may hazard a diminution of the power, emolument, and consequence of the offices they hold under the State establishments; and the perverted ambition of another class of men, who will either hope to aggrandize themselves by the confusions of their country, or will flatter themselves with fairer prospects of elevation from

---

3 **federal:** Latin, pertaining to a treaty, compact, contract, or agreement to unite independent entities or states.

the subdivision of the empire into several partial confederacies than from its union under one government.

GOOD PEOPLE ARE STANDING ON BOTH SIDES OF ISSUES:

Knowing this, how should Americans treat each other's viewpoints regarding the new Constitution?

1:5 It is not, however, my design to dwell upon observations of this nature. I am well aware that it would be disingenuous to resolve indiscriminately the opposition of any set of men (merely because their situations might subject them to suspicion) into interested or ambitious views. Candor will oblige us to admit that even such men may be actuated by upright intentions; and it cannot be doubted that much of the opposition which has made its appearance, or may hereafter make its appearance, will spring from sources, blameless at least, if not respectable—the honest errors of minds led astray by preconceived jealousies and fears.

PAST ERRORS UNDERSCORE NEED FOR OPEN-MINDEDNESS:

Wise people stand on both sides of these issues, so consider them carefully.

1:6 So numerous indeed and so powerful are the causes which serve to give a false bias to the judgment, that we, upon many occasions, see wise and good men on the wrong as well as on the right side of questions of the first magnitude to society. This circumstance, if duly attended to, would furnish a lesson of moderation to those who are ever so much persuaded of their being in the right in any controversy. And a further reason for caution, in this respect, might be drawn from the reflection that we are not always sure that those who advocate the truth are influenced by purer principles than their antagonists.

THE SAME HUMAN FLAWS OPERATE ON BOTH SIDES:

What human flaws harm both sides of controversies such as politics and religion?

1:7 Ambition, avarice, personal animosity, party opposition, and many other motives not more laudable than these, are apt to operate as well upon those who support as those who oppose the right side of a question. Were there not even these inducements to moderation, nothing could be more ill-judged than that intolerant spirit which has, at all times, characterized political parties. For in politics, as in religion, it is equally absurd to aim at making proselytes by fire and sword. Heresies in either can rarely be cured by persecution.

SHOUTING AND BITTERNESS WON'T PERSUADE:

To what extremes do antagonists typically resort when they lack a basis for their objections?

1:8 And yet, however just these sentiments will be allowed to be, we have already sufficient indications that it will happen in this as in all former cases of great national discussion. A torrent of angry and malignant passions will be let loose. To judge from the conduct of the opposite parties, we shall be led to conclude that they will mutually hope to evince the justness of their opinions, and to increase the number of their converts by the loudness of their declamations and the bitterness of their invectives.

POSITIVE CHANGES THWARTED BY FINGER POINTING:

Those supporting an active government working hard to keep the people free and moving forward will be tar-brushed as what?

1:9 An enlightened zeal for the energy and efficiency of government will be stigmatized as the offspring of a temper fond of despotic power and hostile to the principles of liberty. An over-scrupulous jealousy of danger to the rights of the people, which is more commonly the fault of the head than of the heart, will be represented as mere pretense and artifice, the stale bait for popularity at the expense of the public good.

DANGER TO RIGHTS SPRINGS FROM HEART NOT HEAD:

Behind what mask do the power-hungry often hide? What do the power-hungry really want in the end?

1:10 It will be forgotten, on the one hand, that jealousy is the usual concomitant of love, and that the noble enthusiasm of liberty is apt to be infected with a spirit of narrow and illiberal distrust.

DEMAGOGUES APPEAR AT FIRST BEHIND FRIENDLY MASKS:

Power-hungry people begin by appealing to the desires and prejudices of the people before taking their rights.

1:11 On the other hand, it will be equally forgotten that the vigor of government is essential to the security of liberty; that, in the contemplation of a sound and well-informed judgment, their interest can never be separated; and that a dangerous ambition more often lurks behind the specious mask of zeal for the rights of the people than under the forbidden appearance of zeal for the firmness and efficiency of government. History will teach us that the former has been found a much more certain road to the introduction of despotism than the latter, and that of those men who have overturned the liberties of republics, the greatest number have begun their career by paying an **obsequious**[4] court to the people; commencing **demagogues**[5], and ending tyrants.[6]

LET TRUTH BE THE GUIDE:
With many lies about the Constitution being spread around, what does Hamilton wish the people to always seek?

1:12 In the course of the preceding observations, I have had an eye, my fellow-citizens, to putting you upon your guard against all attempts, from whatever quarter, to influence your decision in a matter of the utmost moment to your welfare, by any impressions other than those which may result from the evidence of truth.

MY SUPPORT FOR THE NEW CONSTITUTION:
1:13 You will, no doubt, at the same time, have collected from the general scope of them, that they proceed from a source not unfriendly to the new Constitution. Yes, my countrymen, I own to you that, after having given it an attentive consideration, I am clearly of opinion it is your interest to adopt it. I am convinced that this is the safest course for your liberty, your dignity, and your happiness.

Does Hamilton intend to simply state his own reasons in support of the Constitution, or drill down deep into the opposition's viewpoints?

1:14 I affect not reserves which I do not feel. I will not amuse you with an appearance of deliberation when I have decided. I frankly acknowledge to you my convictions, and I will freely lay before you the reasons on which they are founded. The consciousness of good intentions disdains ambiguity. I shall not, however, multiply professions on this head. My motives must remain in the depository of my own breast.

MY ARGUMENTS ARE BASED ON TRUTH:
1:15 My arguments will be open to all, and may be judged of by all. They shall at least be offered in a spirit which will not disgrace the cause of truth.

SIX TOPICS FOR DISCUSSION:
Hamilton wishes to convince New York's future convention delegates that the new Constitution must not be feared, that it is quite comparable to New York's own constitution. What are the six topics Hamilton wants discussed in the eighty-five papers?

1:16 I propose, in a series of papers, to discuss the following interesting particulars:

[1.]—The utility of the union to your political prosperity

[2.]—The insufficiency of the present Confederation to preserve that Union

[3.]—The necessity of a government at least equally energetic with the one proposed, to the attainment of this object

[4.]—The conformity of the proposed constitution to the true principles of republican government

[5.]—Its analogy to your own state constitution

[6.]—and lastly, the additional security which its adoption will afford to the preservation of that species of government, to liberty, and to property.

1:17 In the progress of this discussion I shall endeavor to give a satisfactory answer to all the objections which shall have made their appearance, that may seem to have any claim to your attention.

MOST AMERICANS FAVOR CREATION OF ONE UNION:
1:18 It may perhaps be thought superfluous to offer arguments to prove the utility of the *union*, a point, no doubt, deeply engraved on the hearts of the great body of the people in every State, and one, which it may be imagined, has no adversaries. But the fact is, that we already hear it whispered in the private circles of those who oppose the new Constitution, that the thirteen States are of too great extent for any general system, and that we must of necessity resort to separate confederacies of distinct portions of the whole.[7]

CONSTITUTION PREVENTS DISMEMBERMENT:
The States will be bound together fairly and unitedly for their survival.

1:19 This doctrine will, in all probability, be gradually propagated, till it has votaries enough to countenance an open avowal of it. For nothing can be more evident, to those who are able to take an enlarged view of the subject, than the alternative of an adoption of the new Constitution or a dismemberment of the Union. It will therefore be of use to begin by examining the advantages of that Union, the certain evils, and the probable dangers, to which every State will be exposed from its dissolution. This shall accordingly constitute the subject of my next address.

—PUBLIUS

REVIEW QUESTIONS

1. What is the "important question" that needs answering?

---

4 **obsequious:** Excessive eagerness to please; a fawning attentiveness.

5 **demagogue:** A political leader seeking people's support by appealing to their desires rather than rational arguments..

6 Thomas Paine—Equal rights in all: "Rights are not gifts from one man to another, nor from one class of men to another ... It is impossible to discover any origin of rights otherwise than in the origin of man; it consequently follows that rights appertain to man in right of his existence, and must therefore be equal to every man." Paine, Dissertation on First Principles of Government, 1795.

7 *Publius:* The same idea, tracing the arguments to their consequences, is held out in several of the later publications against the new Constitution.

(1:2)

2. In both politics and religion, converts won't be made with what? (1:7–8)

3. Does Hamilton support or oppose the proposed Constitution? (1:13)

4. What are the six topics the papers will address? (1:16)

5. Do Americans favor one union? (1:18)

6. From what danger does the proposed Constitution save the States? (1:19)

FEDERALIST NO. 2

GOD BLESSED AMERICA: Jay highlights the positive reasons for government as the best security for liberty. He points out how Providence has already united the land and the people in so many ways, giving America an ideal foundation for which the new Constitution will prosper the nation. He also emphasizes that the Framers were extraordinary men whose Constitution is not being forced on the nation, but is offered as their best recommendation that deserves serious consideration. United we will stand, divided we will fall.

By John Jay—October 31, 1787

THE IMPORTANT QUESTION:
Are men capable or not of establishing good government from reflection and choice?

2:1 WHEN the people of America reflect that they are now called upon to decide a question, which, in its consequences, must prove one of the most important that ever engaged their attention, the propriety of their taking a very comprehensive, as well as a very serious, view of it, will be evident.

PEOPLE MUST DELEGATE NECESSARY POWER:
2:2 Nothing is more certain than the indispensable necessity of government, and it is equally undeniable, that whenever and however it is instituted, the people must cede to it some of their natural rights in order to vest it with requisite powers.

CHOOSE: ONE NATION OR SEPARATE CONFEDERACIES?
2:3 It is well worthy of consideration therefore, whether it would conduce more to the interest of the people of America that they should, to all general purposes, be one nation, under one federal government, or that they should divide themselves into separate confederacies, and give to the head of each the same kind of powers which they are advised to place in one national government.

A UNION IS STRONGER THAN MANY CONFEDERACIES:
Did Americans always prefer a Union over a Confederacy?

2:4 It has until lately been a received and uncontradicted opinion that the prosperity of the people of America depended on their continuing firmly united, and the wishes, prayers, and efforts of our best and wisest citizens have been constantly directed to that object.

SOME POLITICIANS ARE CALLING TO BREAK UNION:
2:5 But politicians now appear, who insist that this opinion is erroneous, and that instead of looking for safety and happiness in union, we ought to seek it in a division of the States into distinct confederacies or sovereignties.

OUR UNION FOUNDED IN TRUTH, NOT SPECULATION:
2:6 However extraordinary this new doctrine may appear, it nevertheless has its advocates; and certain characters who were much opposed to it formerly, are at present of the number. Whatever may be the arguments or inducements which have wrought this change in the sentiments and declarations of these gentlemen, it certainly would not be wise in the people at large to adopt these new political tenets without being fully convinced that they are founded in truth and sound policy.

AMERICA IS ALREADY UNITED GEOGRAPHICALLY:
What natural geographical advantages does America have?

2:7 It has often given me pleasure to observe that independent America was not composed of detached and distant territories, but that one connected, fertile, widespreading country was the portion of our western sons of liberty.

GOD BLESSED AMERICA IN MANY WAYS:
What natural resource already binds the nation together with many "highways"?

2:8 Providence has in a particular manner blessed it with a variety of soils and productions, and watered it with innumerable streams, for the delight and accommodation of its inhabitants. A succession of navigable waters forms a kind of chain round its borders, as if to bind it together; while the most noble rivers in the world, running at convenient distances, present them with highways for the easy communication of friendly aids, and the mutual transportation and exchange of their various commodities..

GOD WANTS THIS PEOPLE UNITED:
God wished to give this country to one united people with six common attributes. What are those six attributes?

2:9 With equal pleasure I have as often taken notice that Providence has been pleased to give this one connected country to one united people—a people descended from the same ancestors, speaking the same language, professing the same religion, attached to the same principles of government, very similar in their manners and customs, and who, by their joint counsels, arms, and efforts, fighting side by side throughout a long and bloody war, have nobly established general liberty and independence.

GOD UNITED THE LAND AND PEOPLE:
A tribute to the American character.

2:10 This country and this people seem to have been made for each other, and it appears as if it was the design of Providence, that an inheritance so proper and convenient for a band of brethren, united to each other by the strongest ties, should never be split into a number of unsocial, jealous, and alien sovereignties.

AMERICANS HAVE ACTED UNIFIED ALREADY:
What are some of the accomplishments Americans have achieved by working together as one nation, as one Union?

2:11 Similar sentiments have hitherto prevailed among all orders and denominations of men among us. To all general purposes we have uniformly been one people each individual citizen everywhere enjoying the same national rights, privileges, and protection. As a nation we have made peace and war; as a nation we have vanquished our common enemies; as a nation we have formed alliances, and made treaties, and entered into various compacts and conventions with foreign states.

FIRST CONSTITUTION WAS HASTILY WRITTEN:
Why was America's first constitution so imperfect at the outset?

2:12 A strong sense of the value and blessings of union induced the people, at a very early period, to institute a federal government to preserve and perpetuate it. They formed it almost as soon as they had a political existence; nay, at a time when their habitations were in flames, when many of their citizens were bleeding, and when the progress of hostility and desolation left little room for those calm and mature inquiries and reflections which must ever precede the formation of a wise and well balanced government for a free people.

NOT SURPRISING THERE ARE DEFECTS IN THE ARTICLES:
Why did the Articles of Confederation have so many flaws?

2:13 It is not to be wondered at, that a government instituted in times so inauspicious, should on experiment be found greatly deficient and inadequate to the purpose it was intended to answer.

STEPS WERE TAKEN TO REMEDY THE FLAWS:
What did Americans do to remedy their imperfect constitution?

2:14 This intelligent people perceived and regretted these defects. Still continuing no less attached to union than enamored of liberty, they observed the danger which immediately threatened the former and more remotely the latter; and being persuaded that ample security for both could only be found in a national government more wisely framed, they as with one voice, convened the late Convention at Philadelphia, to take that important subject under consideration.

WELL-DESERVED TRIBUTE TO THE FRAMERS:
What important traits did the Framers share in their personal lives?

2:15 This Convention composed of men who possessed the confidence of the people, and many of whom had become highly distinguished by their patriotism, virtue and wisdom, in times which tried the minds and hearts of men, undertook the arduous task. In the mild season of peace, with minds unoccupied by other subjects, they passed many months in cool, uninterrupted, and daily consultation; and finally, without having been awed by power, or influenced by any passions except love for their country, they presented and recommended to the people the plan produced by their joint and very unanimous councils.

CONSTITUTION BORN OF SERIOUS CONSIDERATION:
The urgency of the first constitution is replaced with sober and deliberate consideration. Is the new Constitution being forced and imposed on the States? Should it be blindly accepted?

2:16 Admit, for so is the fact, that this plan is only RECOMMENDED, not imposed, yet let it be remembered that it is neither recommended to BLIND approbation, nor to BLIND reprobation; but to that sedate and candid consideration which the magnitude and importance of the subject demand, and which it certainly ought to receive. But this (as was remarked in the foregoing number of this paper) is more to be wished than expected, that it may be so considered and examined. Experience on a former occasion teaches us not to be too sanguine in such hopes.

FIRST CONGRESS (1774) FORMED DUE TO DANGER:
What caused the people to form Congress in the first place?

2:17 It is not yet forgotten that well-grounded apprehensions of imminent danger induced the people of America to form the memorable Congress of 1774. That body recommended certain measures to their constituents, and the event proved their wisdom;

KNEE-JERK ANTAGONISTS:

What did the press and others start doing almost immediately after Congress took action?

2:18 yet it is fresh in our memories how soon the press began to teem with pamphlets and weekly papers against those very measures. Not only many of the officers of government, who obeyed the dictates of personal interest, but others, from a mistaken estimate of consequences, or the undue influence of former attachments, or whose ambition aimed at objects which did not correspond with the public good, were indefatigable in their efforts to persuade the people to reject the advice of that patriotic Congress.

Congress must do business by the voice of the people.

2:19 Many, indeed, were deceived and deluded, but the great majority of the people reasoned and decided judiciously; and happy they are in reflecting that they did so.

THE REASONS AMERICANS TRUSTED THEIR LEADERS:

2:20 They considered that the Congress was composed of many wise and experienced men. That, being convened from different parts of the country, they brought with them and communicated to each other a variety of useful information. That, in the course of the time they passed together in inquiring into and discussing the true interests of their country, they must have acquired very accurate knowledge on that head. That they were individually interested in the public liberty and prosperity, and therefore that it was not less their inclination than their duty to recommend only such measures as, after the most mature deliberation, they really thought prudent and advisable.

FRAMERS STEEPED IN EXPERIENCE, KNOWLEDGE:

The Framers had been tried and tested and found worthy on the first try, and therefore stood trusted for the second try.

2:21 These and similar considerations then induced the people to rely greatly on the judgment and integrity of the Congress; and they took their advice, notwithstanding the various arts and endeavors used to deter them from it. But if the people at large had reason to confide in the men of that Congress, few of whom had been fully tried or generally known, still greater reason have they now to respect the judgment and ad-

vice of the Convention, for it is well known that some of the most distinguished members of that Congress, who have been since tried and justly approved for patriotism and abilities, and who have grown old in acquiring political information, were also members of this Convention, and carried into it their accumulated knowledge and experience.

PROSPERITY DEPENDS ON THE STRENGTH OF THE UNION:

2:22 It is worthy of remark that not only the first, but every succeeding Congress, as well as the late Convention, have invariably joined with the people in thinking that the prosperity of America depended on its Union. To preserve and perpetuate it was the great object of the people in forming that Convention, and it is also the great object of the plan which the Convention has advised them to adopt.

Why, then, do some men attack the idea of Union?

2:23 With what propriety, therefore, or for what good purposes, are attempts at this particular period made by some men to depreciate the importance of the Union? Or why is it suggested that three or four confederacies would be better than one?

The people are wise, they have always favored the Union.

2:24 I am persuaded in my own mind that the people have always thought right on this subject, and that their universal and uniform attachment to the cause of the Union rests on great and weighty reasons, which I shall endeavor to develop and explain in some ensuing papers.

CONFEDERACIES WILL DESTROY AMERICA:

2:25 They who promote the idea of substituting a number of distinct confederacies in the room of the plan of the Convention, seem clearly to foresee that the rejection of it would put the continuance of the Union in the utmost jeopardy.

"FAREWELL TO ALL MY GREATNESS"

2:26 That certainly would be the case, and I sincerely wish that it may be as clearly foreseen by every good citizen, that whenever the dissolution of the Union arrives, America will have reason to exclaim, in the words of the poet: "FAREWELL! A LONG FAREWELL TO ALL MY GREATNESS."[8]

—PUBLIUS

REVIEW QUESTIONS

1. What must people give up to vest government with suffi-

---

8 "Farewell! A long farewell to all my greatness," is a quote is from William Shakespeare's play King Henry VIII, Act 3 Scene 2, Line 351.

cient power? (2:2)

2. On what do all Americans agree the people's prosperity rests? (2:4, 22–24)

3. How has God already united the land? (2:7–8)

4. With what six cultural attributes did God unite the American people? (2:9)

5. Was it God's design that the people unite under the Constitution? (2:10-11)

6. Why was the Articles of Confederation flawed from the start? (2:12–13)

7. Why was the Constitutional Convention called? (2:14)

8. What made the Constitutional Convention delegates so extraordinary? (2:15)

9. Was the Constitution forced on the people or just recommended? (2:16)

10. A confederacy system is certain to lead to what? (2:23–26)

FEDERALIST NO. 3

A STRONGER UNION IS A SAFER UNION: John Jay emphasizes that a strong unified nation stands a better chance against foreign nations in preventing war and protecting trade. But also important is protecting individuals from bullying by the majority. Factions that might rise up to oppress minority groups can be prevented by the same measure that will secure that nation against foreign invaders and tyrants at home and abroad. The new Constitution will best serve these ends.

By John Jay—November 3, 1787

AMERICANS WANT A UNION:
Proof of America's approval of their government is how long they retained it before looking to make changes. Did they prefer a single national government?

3:1 IT IS not a new observation that the people of any country (if, like the Americans, intelligent and well informed) seldom adopt and steadily persevere for many years in an erroneous opinion respecting their interests. That consideration naturally tends to create great respect for the high opinion which the people of America have so long and uniformly entertained of the importance of their continuing firmly united under one federal government, vested with sufficient powers for all general and national purposes.

3:2 The more attentively I consider and investigate the reasons which appear to have given birth to this opinion, the more I become convinced that they are cogent and conclusive.

GOVERNMENT'S FIRST PRIORITY IS SAFETY:
Among the many reasons for a national government, what ranks first?

3:3 Among the many objects to which a wise and free people find it necessary to direct their attention, that of providing for their safety seems to be the first. The SAFETY of the people doubtless has relation to a great variety of circumstances and considerations, and consequently affords great latitude to those who wish to define it precisely and comprehensively.

NATIONAL DEFENSE AND DOMESTIC TRANQUILITY:
Providing safety to America includes calming down what additional sources of strife?

3:4 At present I mean only to consider it as it respects security for the preservation of peace and tranquility, as well as against dangers from FOREIGN ARMS AND INFLUENCE, as from dangers of the LIKE KIND arising from domestic causes. As the former of these comes first in order, it is proper it should be the first discussed. Let us therefore proceed to examine whether the people are not right in their opinion that a cordial Union, under an efficient national government, affords them the best security that can be devised against *hostilities* from abroad.

PEACE IS PRESERVED WITH A UNION:
Are disunited States more vulnerable to wars with other nations?

3:5 The number of wars which have happened or will happen in the world will always be found to be in proportion to the number and weight of the causes, whether REAL or PRETENDED, which PROVOKE or INVITE them. If this remark be just, it becomes useful to inquire whether so many JUST causes of war are likely to be given by UNITED STATES as by DISUNITED America; for if it should turn out that United America will probably give the fewest, then it will follow that in this respect the Union tends most to preserve the people in a state of peace with other nations.

FOREIGN RELATIONS IMPROVED WITH A UNION:
Does a Union help secure international agreements and improve relations?

3:6 The *just* causes of war, for the most part, arise either from violation of treaties or from direct violence. America has already formed treaties with no less than six foreign nations, and All of them, except Prussia, are maritime, and therefore able to annoy and injure us. She has also extensive commerce with Portugal, Spain, and Britain, and, with respect to the two latter, has, in addition, the circumstance of neighborhood to attend to.

UNION HELPS AMERICA OBSERVE FOREIGN LAWS:

3:7 It is of high importance to the peace of America that she observe the laws of nations towards all these powers, and to me it appears evident that this will be more perfectly and punctually done by one national government than it could be either by thirteen separate States or by three or four distinct confederacies.

NATURAL ARISTOCRACY OF BEST MEN WILL RISE TO GOVERN:

A national government should attract the most talented and trusted leaders. See Deuteronomy 1:9–15, "Take you wise men..."

3:8 Because when once an efficient national government is established, the best men in the country will not only consent to serve, but also will generally be appointed to manage it; for, although town or country, or other contracted influence, may place men in State assemblies, or senates, or courts of justice, or executive departments, yet more general and extensive reputation for talents and other qualifications will be necessary to recommend men to offices under the national government – especially as it will have the widest field for choice, and never experience that want of proper persons which is not uncommon in some of the States.

NATIONAL LEADERS MORE APT TO SERVE ALL PEOPLE:

Will leaders considering the interests of the entire nation do better than thirteen local leaders considering their own States?

3:9 Hence, it will result that the administration, the political counsels, and the judicial decisions of the national government will be more wise, systematical, and judicious than those of individual States, and consequently more satisfactory with respect to other nations, as well as more *safe* with respect to us.

ONE GOVERNMENT BEST FOR TREATIES:

Which government(s) will best produce consistent foreign policy: One national government or thirteen State governments?

3:10 Because, under the national government, treaties and articles of treaties, as well as the laws of nations, will always be expounded in one sense and executed in the same manner,– whereas, adjudications on the same points and questions, in thirteen States, or in three or four confederacies, will not always accord or be consistent;

ONE GOVERNMENT BEST FOR COURTS:

Is one court or thirteen courts best for interpreting and enforcing treaties and laws?

3:11 and that, as well from the variety of independent courts and judges appointed by different and independent governments, as from the different local laws and interests which may affect and influence them. The wisdom of the Convention, in committing such questions to the jurisdiction and judgment of courts appointed by and responsible only to one national government, cannot be too much commended.

ONE GOVERNMENT TO NEGOTIATE INSTEAD OF THIRTEEN IS BEST:

The federal government has one interest only, and can't be tempted otherwise.

3:12 Because the prospect of present loss or advantage may often tempt the governing party in one or two States to swerve from good faith and justice; but those temptations, not reaching the other States, and consequently having little or no influence on the national government, the temptation will be fruitless, and good faith and justice be preserved. The case of the treaty of peace with Britain adds great weight to this reasoning.

NATIONAL GOVERNMENT LESS LIKELY TO ACT RASH:

Is a national government better situated to avoid mistakes brought on by isolated circumstances?

3:13 Because, even if the governing party in a State should be disposed to resist such temptations, yet as such temptations may, and commonly do, result from circumstances peculiar to the State, and may affect a great number of the inhabitants, the governing party may not always be able, if willing, to prevent the injustice meditated, or to punish the aggressors.

GOVERNMENT FOCUSED ON NATIONAL TASKS ONLY:

3:14 But the national government, not being affected by those local circumstances, will neither be induced to commit the wrong themselves, nor want power or inclination to prevent or punish its commission by others.

NATIONAL DEFENSE IS MORE SECURE:

If a cause of war is present, does one government or several best serve safety?

3:15 So far, therefore, as either designed or accidental violations of treaties and the laws of nations afford JUST causes of war, they are less to be apprehended under one general government than under several lesser ones, and in that respect the former most favors the SAFETY of the people.

INVASION BEST REPELLED BY ONE GOVERNMENT:

3:16 As to those just causes of war which proceed from direct and unlawful violence, it appears equally clear to me that <u>one good national government affords vastly more security against dangers of that sort than can be derived from any other quarter.</u>

STATES PROVOKED INDIAN WARS:

Did the federal government start any Indian wars? Have the States started any such wars?

3:17 Because such violences are more frequently caused by the passions and interests of a part than of the whole; of one or two States than of the Union. <u>Not a single Indian war has yet been occasioned by aggressions of the present federal government</u>, feeble as it is; but there are several instances of Indian hostilities having been provoked by the <u>improper conduct of individual States</u>, who, either unable or unwilling to restrain or punish offenses, have given occasion to the slaughter of many innocent inhabitants.

ONE GOVERNMENT BETTER AT PREVENTING WARS:

How does a national government prevent border wars with nations?

3:18 The neighborhood of <u>Spanish and British territories, bordering on some States and not on others, naturally confines the causes of quarrel more immediately to the borderers.</u> The bordering States, if any, will be those who, under the impulse of sudden irritation, and a quick sense of apparent interest or injury, will be most likely, by direct violence, to excite war with these nations; and <u>nothing can so effectually obviate that danger as a national government, whose wisdom and prudence will not be diminished by the passions</u> which actuate the parties immediately interested.

ONE GOVERNMENT BETTER AT MAKING PEACE:

3:19 But not only fewer just causes of war will be given by the national government, but it will also be more in their power to accommodate and settle them amicably. <u>They will be more temperate and cool</u>, and in that respect, as well as in others, will be more in capacity to act advisedly than the offending State.

PRIDE LEADS TO WAR:

National government is more likely to moderate conflict without magnifying the problem

3:20 The <u>pride of states, as well as of men, naturally disposes them to justify all their actions</u>, and opposes their acknowledging, correcting, or repairing their errors and offenses. The <u>national government, in such cases, will not be affected by</u> <u>this pride</u>, but will proceed with moderation and candor to consider and decide on the means most proper to extricate them from the difficulties which threaten them.

NATIONS CAN APOLOGIZE, STATES WON'T:

Is conflict resolution handled better on the state or national level?

3:21 Besides, it is well known that acknowledgments, explanations, and <u>compensations are often accepted as satisfactory from a strong united nation</u>, which would be <u>rejected as unsatisfactory if offered by a State</u> or confederacy of little consideration or power.

EXAMPLE OF THE WEAK RESPECTING THE STRONG:

How does Genoa demonstrate that in foreign relations the states are disrespected but strong nations are very much respected?

3:22 In the year 1685, <u>the state of Genoa having offended Louis XIV, endeavored to appease him. He demanded that they should send their Doge, or chief magistrate, accompanied by four of their senators, to *France*</u>, to ask his pardon and receive his terms. They were obliged to submit to it for the sake of peace. <u>Would he on any occasion either have demanded</u> or have received the like humiliation from Spain, or Britain, or any other *powerful* nation?

—PUBLIUS

REVIEW QUESTIONS

1. What great and universal opinion have Americans held about their desired and proper form of government? (3:1)

2. What should be government's first priority? (3:3)

3. Which govt best secures against insurrections and foreign invasion? (3:4–5)

4. Who will rise to govern if the government is stable? (3:8–9)

5. Who started the Indian wars? (3:17)

6. Opinion: How does the Union's superior ability to prevent war and bring peace also suggest a superior ability to ensure internal domestic peace?

FEDERALIST NO. 4

STRONG UNION IS BEST FOR SECURITY, PEACE AND PROSPERITY: John Jay proposes that a single Union will better serve the cause of security than several confederacies attempting these activities each on their own. As America's commercial influence grows, economic competitions and tensions will also grow. A single strong Union will better serve security than a few smaller, disunited confederacies.

By John Jay—November 7, 1787

A UNION PROVIDES BEST NATIONAL DEFENSE:

4:1 MY LAST paper assigned several reasons why the safety of the people would be <u>best secured by union</u> against the danger it may be exposed to by JUST causes of war given to other nations; and those reasons show that such causes would not only be more <u>rarely given</u>, but would also be more <u>easily accommodated</u>, by a national government than either by the State governments or the proposed little confederacies.

NATIONAL RESTRAINT PREVENTS WARS:
Americans must avoid placing themselves in a situation that creates war.

4:2 But the safety of the people of America against dangers from FOREIGN force depends not only on their forbearing to give JUST causes of war to other nations, but also on their placing and continuing themselves in such a situation as <u>not to INVITE hostility</u> or insult; for it need not be observed that there are PRETENDED as well as just causes of war.

REASONS WHY MONARCHS START WARS:
What are some motivations for international war?

4:3 It is too true, however disgraceful it may be to human nature, that nations in general will make war whenever they have a prospect of getting anything by it; nay, <u>absolute monarchs will often make war</u> when their nations are to get nothing by it, but for the purposes and objects merely personal, such as thirst for <u>military glory</u>, <u>revenge</u> for <u>personal affronts</u>, <u>ambition</u>, or <u>private compacts</u> to aggrandize or support their particular <u>families</u> or partisans.

MONARCHS LAUNCH WARS FOR SELFISH REASONS:

4:4 These and a variety of other motives, which affect only the mind of the sovereign, often lead him to engage in <u>wars not sanctified by justice</u> or the voice and interests of his people.

REASONS FOR WAR EXIST IN OUR SITUATION:

4:5 But, independent of these inducements to war, which are more prevalent in absolute monarchies, but which well deserve our attention, there are others which affect nations as often as kings; and some of them will on examination be found to grow out of our relative situation and circumstances.

RIVALRIES IN COMMERCE CAN LEAD TO WAR:
Character of American economy includes fishing, shipping, commodities.

4:6 With <u>France</u> and with <u>Britain</u> we are rivals in the <u>fisheries</u>, and can supply their markets cheaper than they can themselves, notwithstanding any efforts to prevent it by bounties on their own or **duties**[9] on foreign fish.

TRANSPORT OF CARGO CAN LEAD TO WAR:

4:7 With them and with most other European nations we are <u>rivals in navigation</u> and the carrying trade; and we shall deceive ourselves if we suppose that any of them will rejoice to see it flourish; for, as our carrying trade cannot increase without in some degree diminishing theirs, it is more their interest, and will be more their policy, to restrain than to promote it.

DIRECT TRADE IS CHEAPER:
This frustrates other nations.

4:8 In the <u>trade to China and India</u>, we interfere with more than one nation, inasmuch as it enables us to partake in advantages which they had in a manner <u>monopolized</u>, and as we thereby supply ourselves with commodities which we used to purchase from them.

AMERICAN COMMERCE IN THIS REGION IS STRONG:

4:9 The extension of our own commerce in our own vessels cannot give pleasure to any <u>nations who possess territories on or near this continent</u>, because the cheapness and <u>excellence</u> of our <u>productions</u>, added to the circumstance of <u>vicinity</u>, and the <u>enterprise</u> and address of <u>our **merchants**</u>[10] and navigators, will give us a greater share in the advantages which those territories afford, than consists with the wishes or policy of their respective sovereigns.

EUROPEAN CONTROL OF RIVERS:
Threats and tensions from Spain and Britain remain. What is a circumstance for war now brewing near our borders?

4:10 <u>Spain</u> thinks it convenient to shut the <u>Mississippi</u> against us on the one side, and <u>Britain</u> excludes us from the <u>Saint Lawrence</u> on the other; nor will either of them permit the other waters which are between them and us to become the means of mutual intercourse and traffic.

---

9 **duties:** Taxes collected by customs on imports, exports or the consumption of goods. An impost on land or other real estate, or on the stock of farmers in not called a duty, but a *direct tax*. (From Webster's *American Dictionary of the English Language*, 1828.)

10 **merchants:** Those buying and selling raw materials.

UNION, NATIONAL STRENGTH DISCOURAGE WAR:

Will other nations stand by and ignore America's economic growth?

4:11 From these and such like considerations, which might, if consistent with prudence, be more amplified and detailed, it is easy to see that jealousies and uneasinesses may gradually slide into the minds and cabinets of other nations, and that we are not to expect that they should regard our advancement in union, in power and consequence by land and by sea, with an eye of indifference and composure.

NATIONAL GOVERNMENT HELPS PREVENT WARS:

What does America need to discourage nations from waging war?

4:12 The people of America are aware that inducements to war may arise out of these circumstances, as well as from others not so obvious at present, and that whenever such inducements may find fit time and opportunity for operation, pretenses to color and justify them will not be wanting. Wisely, therefore, do they consider union and a good national government as necessary to put and keep them in SUCH A SITUATION as, instead of INVITING war, will tend to repress and discourage it. That situation consists in the best possible state of defense, and necessarily depends on the government, the arms, and the resources of the country.

ONE GOVERNMENT BETTER FOR SAFETY THAN MANY:

What is the main interest of all governments? Is one better at this than many?

4:13 As the safety of the whole is the interest of the whole, and cannot be provided for without government, either one or more or many, let us inquire whether one good government is not, relative to the object in question, more competent than any other given number whatever.

ONE GOVERNMENT CAN DRAW ON ALL RESOURCES:

What are some advantages of one national government?

4:14 One government can collect and avail itself of the talents and experience of the ablest men, in whatever part of the Union they may be found. It can move on uniform principles of policy. It can harmonize, assimilate, and protect the several parts and members, and extend the benefit of its foresight and precautions to each.

ONE GOVERNMENT IS EFFICIENT, MANY ARE NOT:

Why would many States fall short in a national call to arms?

4:15 In the formation of treaties, it will regard the interest of the whole, and the particular interests of the parts as connected with that of the whole. It can apply the resources and power of the whole to the defense of any particular part, and that more easily and expeditiously than State governments or separate confederacies can possibly do, for want of concert and unity of system.

ONE MILITIA UNDER PRESIDENT BETTER THAN THIRTEEN:

4:16 It can place the militia under one plan of discipline, and, by putting their officers in a proper line of subordination to the Chief Magistrate, will, as it were, consolidate them into one corps, and thereby render them more efficient than if divided into thirteen or into three or four distinct independent companies.

PROBLEM OF INDEPENDENT MILITIAS:

What are some disadvantages of many national governments?

4:17 What would the militia of Britain be if the English militia obeyed the government of England, if the Scotch militia obeyed the government of Scotland, and if the Welsh militia obeyed the government of Wales? Suppose an invasion; would those three governments (if they agreed at all) be able, with all their respective forces, to operate against the enemy so effectually as the single government of Great Britain would?

UNITED ENGLISH NAVAL FORCE VERY EFFECTIVE:

What if England, Wales, Scotland, and Ireland had built separate fleets for England?

4:18 We have heard much of the fleets of Britain, and the time may come, if we are wise, when the fleets of America may engage attention. But if one national government, had not so regulated the navigation of Britain as to make it a nursery for seamen–if one national government had not called forth all the national means and materials for forming fleets, their prowess and their thunder would never have been celebrated.

INDEPENDENT ENGLISH NAVIES WOULD DWINDLE:

4:19 Let England have its navigation and fleet – let Scotland have its navigation and fleet – let Wales have its navigation and fleet – let Ireland have its navigation and fleet – let those four of the constituent parts of the British empire be under four independent governments, and it is easy to perceive how soon they would each dwindle into comparative insignificance.

A CONFEDERATE GOVERNMENT WOULD NOT COOPERATE, EVEN IN SELF DEFENSE:

What fatal problems will arise if America is not united as one?

4:20 Apply these facts to our own case. Leave America divided into thirteen or, if you please, into three or four independent governments—what armies could they raise and pay—what fleets could they ever hope to have? If one was attacked, would the others fly to its succor, and spend their blood and money in its defense?

NATIONS WOULD FLATTER STATES INTO ALLIANCES:

If separate States felt threatened would they turn to foreign allies?

4:21 Would there be no danger of their being flattered into neutrality by its specious promises, or seduced by a too great fondness for peace to decline hazarding their tranquility and present safety for the sake of neighbors, of whom perhaps they have been jealous, and whose importance they are content to see diminished?

FOREIGN ALLIANCES ARE NOT WISE BUT OFTEN EMBRACED:

4:22 Although such conduct would not be wise, it would, nevertheless, be natural. The history of the states of Greece, and of other countries, abounds with such instances, and it is not improbable that what has so often happened would, under similar circumstances, happen again.

COMPLICATIONS OF DIS-UNITED DEFENSE EFFORTS:

How would a splintered America gather resources for defense?

4:23 But admit that they might be willing to help the invaded State or confederacy. How, and when, and in what proportion shall aids of men and money be afforded? Who shall command the allied armies, and from which of them shall he receive his orders? Who shall settle the terms of peace, and in case of disputes what umpire shall decide between them and compel acquiescence? Various difficulties and inconveniences would be inseparable from such a situation;

ONE AUTHORITY IS BEST AT NATIONAL DEFENSE:

4:24 whereas one government, watching over the general and common interests, and combining and directing the powers and resources of the whole, would be free from all these embarrassments, and conduce far more to the safety of the people.

DISUNION MEANS FOREIGN INTERVENTION:

If America breaks into three or four confederacies, France, Spain or England will move in. What will bring global respect to America?

4:25 But whatever may be our situation, whether firmly united under one national government, or split into a number of confederacies, certain it is, that foreign nations will know and view it exactly as it is; and they will act toward us accordingly. If they see that our national government is efficient and well administered, our trade prudently regulated, our militia properly organized and disciplined, our resources and finances discreetly managed, our credit re-established, our people free, contented, and united, they will be much more disposed to cultivate our friendship than provoke our resentment.

A STRONG AMERICA HAS MANY FRIENDS:

A splintered America would dilute its alliances and invite contempt.

4:26 If, on the other hand, they find us either destitute of an effectual government (each State doing right or wrong, as to its rulers may seem convenient), or split into three or four independent and probably discordant republics or confederacies, one inclining to Britain, another to France, and a third to Spain, and perhaps played off against each other by the three, what a poor, pitiful figure will America make in their eyes! How liable would she become not only to their contempt but to their outrage, and how soon would dear-bought experience proclaim that when a people or family so divide, it never fails to be against themselves.

—PUBLIUS

REVIEW QUESTIONS

1. Is a strong Union better at preventing war than individual States? (4:1)

2. What are some reasons why monarchs start wars? (4:3)

3. What can prevent future wars over foreign commercial activities? (4:12)

4. What can one government do better than individual States to preserve a nation? (4:14)

5. To where would disunited States turn to protect themselves from each other? (4:21–22)

6. How does a Union transform foreign enemies to foreign friends? (4:25)

7. To who would three or four confederacies eventually turn for security? (4:26)

FEDERALIST NO. 5

INDEPENDENT CONFEDERACIES CREATE NATURAL ENEMIES: The sad lessons of history show that dividing America into small independent confederacies will, without fail, end up in disaster. Queen Anne presents the case for union in England, a reasoned presentation that applies to America. Without a Union, we would become another Europe with each confederacy protecting its own borders with military might, and perhaps inviting foreign nations to help secure those borders. The result? Endless border skirmishes and wars.

By John Jay—November 10, 1787

QUEEN ANNE CALLS FOR UNITY WITH SCOTLAND:

5:1 QUEEN ANNE, in her letter of the 1st July, 1706, to the Scotch Parliament, makes some observations on the importance of the UNION then forming between England and Scotland, which merit our attention. I shall present the public with one or two extracts from it:

QUEEN ANNE: Advantages of an entire and perfect union.

5:2 "An entire and perfect union will be the solid foundation of lasting peace: It will secure your religion, liberty, and property; remove the animosities amongst yourselves, and the jealousies and differences betwixt our two kingdoms. It must increase your strength, riches, and trade; and by this union the whole island, being joined in affection and free from all apprehensions of different interest, will be ENABLED TO RESIST ALL ITS ENEMIES."

QUEEN ANNE: Common enemies don't want us to form a union.

5:3 "We most earnestly recommend to you calmness and unanimity in this great and weighty affair, that the union may be brought to a happy conclusion, being the only EFFECTUAL way to secure our present and future happiness, and disappoint the designs of our and your enemies, who will doubtless, on this occasion, USE THEIR UTMOST ENDEAVORS TO PREVENT OR DELAY THIS UNION."

WEAKNESS AT HOME INVITES DANGER FROM ABROAD:

Will dis-united States invite danger from abroad?

5:4 It was remarked in the preceding paper, that weakness and divisions at home would invite dangers from abroad; and that nothing would tend more to secure us from them than

union, strength, and good government within ourselves. This subject is copious and cannot easily be exhausted.

EXAMPLE OF BRITAIN SERVES BEST LESSON OF ALL:

What can America learn about unity from Great Britain?

5:5 The history of Great Britain is the one with which we are in general the best acquainted, and it gives us many useful lessons. We may profit by their experience without paying the price which it cost them.

DIS-UNITED BRITAIN WAS ALWAYS IN QUARRELS:

5:6 Although it seems obvious to common sense that the people of such an island should be but one nation, yet we find that they were for ages divided into three, and that those three were almost constantly embroiled in quarrels and wars with one another. Notwithstanding their true interest with respect to the continental nations was really the same, yet by the arts and policy and practices of those nations, their mutual jealousies were perpetually kept inflamed, and for a long series of years they were far more inconvenient and troublesome than they were useful and assisting to each other.

SIMILAR FATE AWAITS THE AMERICAN CONFEDERACIES:

Without a union would there rise jealousy and fighting?

5:7 Should the people of America divide themselves into three or four nations, would not the same thing happen? Would not similar jealousies arise, and be in like manner cherished?

ENVY AND JEALOUSY:

Bordering States would be in constant disputes and quarrels.

5:8 Instead of their being "joined in affection" and free from all apprehension of different "interests," envy and jealousy would soon extinguish confidence and affection, and the partial interests of each confederacy, instead of the general interests of all America, would be the only objects of their policy and pursuits. Hence, like most other BORDERING nations, they would always be either involved in disputes and war, or live in the constant apprehension of them.

EQUAL FOOTING IMPOSSIBLE AMONG THE STATES:

Without a union would the States remain equal?

5:9 The most sanguine advocates for three or four confederacies cannot reasonably suppose that they would long remain exactly on an equal footing in point of strength, even if it was possible to form them so at first; but, admitting that to be practicable, yet what human contrivance can secure the continuance of such equality? Independent of those local circumstances which tend to <u>beget and increase power</u> in one part and to impede its progress in another, we must advert to the effects of that superior policy and good management which would probably distinguish the government of one above the rest, and by which their relative equality in strength and consideration would be destroyed.

CONFEDERATE POLICIES ARE NEVER UNIFORM OR CONSTANT:

5:10 For <u>it cannot be presumed</u> that the <u>same degree of sound policy</u>, prudence, and foresight would uniformly be observed by each of these confederacies for a <u>long succession of years</u>.

ONE CONFEDERACY WOULD ALWAYS RISE ABOVE ANOTHER:

Without a Union would the differences in prosperity between the States soon create distrust, envy, and fear?

5:11 Whenever, and from whatever causes, it might happen, and happen it would, that any one of these nations or confederacies should <u>rise on the scale</u> of political importance much above the degree of her neighbors, that moment would those <u>neighbors behold her with envy and with fear</u>. Both those passions would lead them to countenance, if not to promote, whatever might promise to diminish her importance; and would also restrain them from measures calculated to advance or even to secure her prosperity. Much time would not be necessary to enable her to discern these unfriendly dispositions. She would soon begin, not only to <u>lose confidence in her neighbors</u>, but also to feel a disposition equally unfavorable to them.

DISTRUST CREATES MORE DISTRUST:

5:12 <u>Distrust</u> naturally <u>creates distrust</u>, and by nothing is good-will and kind conduct more speedily changed than by invidious jealousies and uncandid imputations, whether expressed or implied

INTERESTS OF NORTH AND SOUTH ARE VERY DIFFERENT:

Without a union would the North eventually dominate the others?

5:13 <u>The North</u> is generally the region of <u>strength</u>, and many local circumstances render it probable that the most Northern of the proposed confederacies would, at a period not very distant, be unquestionably more formidable than any of the others. No sooner would this become evident than the <u>northern hive</u> would excite the same ideas and sensations in the more southern parts of America which it formerly did in the southern parts of Europe. Nor does it appear to be a rash conjecture that its young swarms might often be tempted to <u>gather honey in the more blooming fields</u> and milder air of their luxurious and more delicate neighbors.

CONFEDERACIES CREATE UNNECESSARY ENEMIES:

What does history teach about splintered nations pretending to co-exist as one?

5:14 They who well consider the history of similar divisions and confederacies will find abundant reason to apprehend that those in contemplation would in no other sense be neighbors than as they would be borderers; that they would <u>neither love</u> nor <u>trust one another</u>, but on the contrary would be a <u>prey to discord</u>, jealousy, and mutual injuries; in short, that they would place us exactly in the situations in which some nations doubtless wish to see us, viz., <u>FORMIDABLE ONLY TO EACH OTHER</u>.

CONFEDERACIES WON'T UNITE IN COMMON DEFENSE:

5:15 From these considerations it appears that those gentlemen are greatly mistaken who suppose that <u>alliances</u> offensive and defensive might be formed between these <u>confederacies</u>, and would produce that combination and <u>union of wills</u> of arms and of resources, which would be necessary to put and keep them in a formidable state of defense against foreign enemies.

BRITAIN AND SPAIN CONFEDERACIES NEVER ALLIED:

If three or four confederacies are formed, they eventually will become independent nations with borders to defend.

5:16 <u>When did the independent states, into which Britain and Spain were formerly divided</u>, <u>combine</u> in such alliance, or unite their forces against a foreign enemy?

BECOME DISTINCT NATIONS:

5:17 The proposed confederacies will be <u>DISTINCT NATIONS</u>. Each of them would have its <u>commerce</u> with <u>foreigners</u> to regulate by distinct treaties; and as their <u>productions</u> and <u>commodities are different</u> and proper for different markets, so would those treaties be essentially different.

DIFFERENT COMMERCIAL CONCERNS:

5:18 <u>Different commercial concerns</u> must <u>create different interests</u>, and of course different degrees of political attachment to and connection with different foreign nations. Hence it might and probably would happen that the <u>foreign nation with whom the SOUTHERN confederacy might be at war</u> would be the one with whom the <u>NORTHERN confederacy</u> would be the most desirous of preserving peace and friendship. An alliance so contrary to their immediate interest would not therefore be easy to form, nor, if formed, would it be observed and fulfilled with perfect good faith.

OPPOSING STATES WOULD TAKE OPPOSING SIDES:

The confederacies would seek foreign help against their neighboring States.

5:19 Nay, it is <u>far more probable</u> that in America, as in Europe, <u>neighboring nations</u>, acting under the impulse of opposite interests and unfriendly passions, would frequently be found taking <u>different sides</u>.

STATES WOULD FEAR EACH OTHER THE MOST AND FORM FOREIGN ALLIANCES:

5:20 Considering our <u>distance from Europe</u>, it would be more natural for these confederacies to <u>apprehend danger from one another than from distant nations</u>, and therefore that each of them should be more desirous to guard against the others by the aid of foreign alliances, than to guard against foreign dangers by alliances between themselves.

EASY TO ACCEPT MILITARY HELP, DIFFICULT TO SEND IT AWAY:

5:21 And here let us not forget how much more easy it is to receive foreign fleets into our ports, and foreign armies into our country, than it is to persuade or compel them to depart. <u>How many conquests did the Romans and others make in the characters of allies</u>, and what innovations did they under the same character introduce into the governments of those whom they pretended to protect.

CONFEDERACIES WILL DESTROY AMERICA:

Without a union would the doors be opened to foreign control?

5:22 Let candid men judge, then, whether the division of America into any given number of independent sovereignties would <u>tend to secure us against the hostilities and improper interference of foreign nations</u>.

—Publius

Review Questions

1. What are some of the outcomes Queen Anne promised to Scotland if it would join England in a Union? (5:2)

2. What will internal weakness and division in America invite if a strong Union is not created? (5:4)

3. Did disunited Britain enjoy ages of peace? (5:6)

4. Are the interests between the northern and southern States similar to each other's? (5:13, 18)

5. Who should American confederacies fear the most? (5:20)

FEDERALIST NO. 6

GENIUS OF THE REPUBLICAN FORM OF GOVERNMENT: Hamilton warns that dissensions will arise between the States themselves if they are not bonded together in a complete and total Union. Any partial union or confederacy always unravels. He gives examples in history of the republics of Athens, Venice, Holland, Carthage, and even Britain frequently becoming embroiled in war over issues of commerce. The recent war should be proof enough of the importance of a strong Union of thirteen States.

By Alexander Hamilton—November 14, 1787

HOSTILITIES WILL RESULT FROM DISUNION:

What are some dangers that may come about because of thirteen disunited States?

6:1 THE three last numbers of this paper have been dedicated to an <u>enumeration of the dangers</u> to which we should be exposed, in a state of <u>disunion</u>, from the arms and arts of foreign nations. I shall <u>now proceed</u> to delineate <u>dangers of a different</u> and, perhaps, still more <u>alarming kind</u>—those which will in all probability flow from dissensions between the States themselves, and from <u>domestic factions</u> and convulsions. These have been already in some instances <u>slightly anticipated</u>; but they deserve a more particular and more full investigation.

PURE FANTASY TO THINK HUMAN NATURE WILL CHANGE:

Only a naive, deluded Utopian believer would doubt that the disunited States will explode in hostilities if they don't unite. Is it human nature to frequently engage in jealousies and fighting?

6:2 <u>A man must be far gone in Utopian speculations</u> who can seriously doubt that, if these States should either be wholly disunited, or only united in partial confederacies, the <u>subdivisions</u> into which they might be thrown would have <u>frequent and violent contests with each other</u>. To presume a want of motives for such contests as an argument against their existence, would be to forget that men are <u>ambitious</u>, <u>vindictive</u>, and <u>rapacious</u>. To look for a continuation of harmony between a number of independent, unconnected sovereignties in the same neighborhood, would be to <u>disregard</u> the uniform course of human events, and to set at defiance the accumulated <u>experience of ages</u>.

MANY REASONS FOR WAR:

What is the main cause of most wars?

6:3 The causes of hostility among nations are innumerable. There are some which have a general and almost constant operation upon the collective bodies of society. Of this description are the love of power or the desire of pre-eminence and dominion—the jealousy of power, or the desire of equality and safety.

COMMERCE CAN CAUSE WAR:
Simple competition for a marketplace or sales advantage can lead to war.

6:4 There are others which have a more circumscribed though an equally operative influence within their spheres. Such are the rivalships and competitions of commerce between commercial nations.

PRIVATE PASSIONS CAN LEAD TO WAR:
Does personal ego of a leader ever take nations into wars?

6:5 And there are others, not less numerous than either of the former, which take their origin entirely in private passions; in the attachments, enmities, interests, hopes, and fears of leading individuals in the communities of which they are members. Men of this class, whether the favorites of a king or of a people, have in too many instances abused the confidence they possessed; and assuming the pretext of some public motive, have not scrupled to sacrifice the national tranquility to personal advantage or personal gratification.

PERICLES' EGO WASTED NATIONAL TREASURE:
6:6 The celebrated Pericles, in compliance with the resentment of a prostitute,[11] at the expense of much of the blood and treasure of his countrymen, attacked, vanquished, and destroyed the city of the SAMNIANS.

PERICLES' PRIDE AND VANITY RUINED ATHENS:
6:7 The same man, stimulated by private pique against the MEGARENSIANS,[12] another nation of Greece, or to avoid a prosecution with which he was threatened as an accomplice of a supposed theft of the statuary Phidias,[13] or to get rid of the accusations prepared to be brought against him for dissipating the funds of the state in the purchase of popularity,[14] or from a combination of all these causes, was the primitive author of that famous and fatal war, distinguished in the Grecian annals by the name of the PELOPONNESIAN war; which, after various vicissitudes, intermissions, and renewals, terminated in the ruin of the Athenian commonwealth.

THOMAS WOLSEY'S PRIVATE AMBITION LED TO WAR:

6:8 The ambitious cardinal, who was prime minister to Henry VIII, permitting his vanity to aspire to the triple crown[15] entertained hopes of succeeding in the acquisition of that splendid prize by the influence of the Emperor Charles V. To secure the favor and interest of this enterprising and powerful monarch, he precipitated England into a war with France, contrary to the plainest dictates of policy, and at the hazard of the safety and independence, as well of the kingdom over which he presided by his counsels, as of Europe in general. For if there ever was a sovereign who bid fair to realize the project of universal monarchy, it was the Emperor Charles V, of whose intrigues Wolsey was at once the instrument and the dupe.

SEVERAL WOMEN HAVE STIRRED UP WARS:
6:9 The influence which the bigotry of one female,[16] the petulance of another,[17] and the **cabals**[18] of a third, [19]had in the contemporary policy, ferments, and pacifications, of a considerable part of Europe, are topics that have been too often descanted upon not to be generally known.[20]

PERSONAL PRIDE DRAGGED NATIONS TO WAR:
Are there other examples of personal pride leading to national ruin?

6:10 To multiply examples of the agency of personal considerations in the production of great national events, either foreign or domestic, according to their direction, would be an unnecessary waste of time. Those who have but a superficial acquaintance with the sources from which they are to be drawn, will themselves recollect a variety of instances; and those who have a tolerable knowledge of human nature will not stand in need of such lights to form their opinion either of the reality or extent of that agency.

---

11 *Publius:* Aspasia, vida Plutarch's *Life of Pericles.*

12 *Publius:* Ibid. *Editors' Note:* These are the inhabitants of Megara, a Greek city west of Athens. To punish Megara for an insult, Pericles excluded it from the Athenian market in 442 BC, ruining Megara's economy. Megara appealed to Sparta for help, and this is thought to have contributed to tensions that started the Peloponnesian War in 431 BC.

13 *Publius:* Ibid.

14 *Publius:* Ibid. Phidias, with Pericles, was supposed to have stolen some public gold for the embellishment of the statue of Minerva.

15 *Publius:* Worn by the popes.

16 *Publius:* Madame de Maintenon.

17 *Publius:* Duchess of Marlborough.

18 *cabal:* A secret political faction or clique.

19 *Publius:* Madame de Pompadour.

20 Identity of the three women in 6:9: The "bigot" refers to the wife of Louis XIV, Madame de Maintenon, so-called because she was so obstinate about her own opinion and prejudices. She helped influence the king to deal with non-Catholics in a harsh manner. The second, the Duchess of Marlborough, had a falling out with Queen Anne after trying to manipulate her for political matters. And the third, Madame de Pompadour, was the mistress of Louis XV and apparently involved herself deeply with national political events after the Seven Years War.

SHAYS' REBELLION
(AUGUST 1786–FEBRUARY 1787):
Was Shays' personal debt a cause for civil war?

6:11 Perhaps, however, a reference, tending to illustrate the general principle, may with propriety be made to a case which has lately happened among ourselves. If Shays had not been a DESPERATE DEBTOR, it is much to be doubted whether Massachusetts would have been plunged into a civil war.

ANTI-FEDERALISTS' FALSE PROMISE OF PEACE:
Peace between disunited States is impossible; history proves this.

6:12 But notwithstanding the concurring testimony of experience, in this particular, there are still to be found visionary or designing men, who stand ready to advocate the paradox of perpetual peace between the States, though dismembered and alienated from each other.

HISTORY PROVES COMMERCE WON'T
GUARANTEE PEACE:
The Anti-Federalists claim republics and commerce will encourage peace.

6:13 The genius of republics (say they) is pacific; the spirit of commerce has a tendency to soften the manners of men, and to extinguish those inflammable humors which have so often kindled into wars. Commercial republics, like ours, will never be disposed to waste themselves in ruinous contentions with each other. They will be governed by mutual interest, and will cultivate a spirit of mutual amity and concord.

ALL NATIONS WANT PEACE:
But do they really pursue it?

6:14 Is it not (we may ask these projectors in politics) the true interest of all nations to cultivate the same benevolent and philosophic spirit? If this be their true interest, have they in fact pursued it?

WARS START OVER COMMERCIAL DISPUTES:
Who is more inclined to war, the people or the monarchy?

6:15 Has it not, on the contrary, invariably been found that momentary passions, and immediate interest, have a more active and imperious control over human conduct than general or remote considerations of policy, utility or justice? Have republics in practice been less addicted to war than monarchies? Are not the former administered by MEN as well as the latter?

Popular assemblies are subject to jealousies just as are kings.

6:16 Are there not aversions, predilections, rivalships, and desires of unjust acquisitions, that affect nations as well as kings? Are not popular assemblies frequently subject to the impulses of rage, resentment, jealousy, avarice, and of other irregular and violent propensities?

Leaders are subject to passions over commerce.

6:17 Is it not well known that their determinations are often governed by a few individuals in whom they place confidence, and are, of course, liable to be tinctured by the passions and views of those individuals?

COMMERCIAL MOTIVES ARE OFTEN CAUSES OF
WAR:
Commercial and economic motives can be as greedy and evil as passion for power and glory.

6:18 Has commerce hitherto done anything more than change the objects of war? Is not the love of wealth as domineering and enterprising a passion as that of power or glory? Have there not been as many wars founded upon commercial motives since that has become the prevailing system of nations, as were before occasioned by the cupidity of territory or dominion? Has not the spirit of commerce, in many instances, administered new incentives to the appetite, both for the one and for the other? Let experience, the least fallible guide of human opinions, be appealed to for an answer to these inquiries.

WARS AMONG COMMERCIAL REPUBLICS:
Ancient republics let the pursuit of wealth drive them to war.

6:19 Sparta, Athens, Rome, and Carthage were all republics; two of them, Athens and Carthage, of the commercial kind. Yet were they as often engaged in wars, offensive and defensive, as the neighboring monarchies of the same times. Sparta was little better than a well regulated camp; and Rome was never sated of carnage and conquest.

Carthage let commercial ambition draw it into wars.

6:20 Carthage, though a commercial republic, was the aggressor in the very war that ended in her destruction. Hannibal had carried her arms into the heart of Italy and to the gates of Rome, before Scipio, in turn, gave him an overthrow in the territories of Carthage, and made a conquest of the commonwealth.

Venice let commercial ambition draw it into wars.

6:21 Venice, in later times, figured more than once in wars of ambition, till, becoming an object to the other Italian states, Pope Julius II found means to accomplish that formidable league[21] which gave a deadly blow to the power and pride of this haughty republic.

---

21 *Publius:* The League of Cambray, comprehending the Emperor, the King of France, the King of Arago, and most of the Italian princes and states.

Holland let commercial ambition draw it into wars.

6:22 The provinces of <u>Holland</u>, till they were overwhelmed in <u>debts</u> and <u>taxes</u>, took a leading and conspicuous part in the <u>wars of Europe</u>. They had <u>furious contests</u> with England for the dominion of the sea, and were among the most persevering and most implacable of the opponents of Louis XIV.

England let commercial ambition draw it into wars.

6:23 In the government of Britain the representatives of the people compose one branch of the national legislature. Commerce has been for ages the predominant pursuit of that country. Few nations, nevertheless, have been more frequently engaged in war; and the wars in which that kingdom has been engaged have, in numerous instances, <u>proceeded from the people</u>.

WARS OFTEN FOUGHT CONTRARY TO KING'S DESIRE:
Representatives have dragged their reluctant monarchs into war.

6:24 There have been, if I may so express it, <u>almost as many popular</u> as royal wars. The cries of the nation and the importunities of their representatives have, upon various occasions, <u>dragged their monarchs into war</u>, or continued them in it, contrary to their inclinations, and sometimes <u>contrary to the real interests of the State</u>.

Austria-Bourbon war was against the wishes of the royal court.

6:25 In that memorable struggle for superiority between the rival houses of <u>AUSTRIA</u> and **BOURBON,**[22] which so long kept Europe in a flame, it is well known that the antipathies of the English against the French, seconding the ambition, or rather the avarice, of a favorite leader,[23] protracted the war beyond the limits marked out by sound policy, and for a considerable time in opposition to the views of the court.

COMMERCIAL CONSIDERATIONS START WARS:
What triggered the many conflicts between Austria and Bourbon?

6:26 The wars of these two last-mentioned nations have in a great measure grown out of <u>commercial considerations</u>,—the desire of supplanting and the fear of being supplanted, either in particular branches of traffic or in the general advantages of <u>trade</u> and <u>navigation</u>.

What triggered the conflicts between Britain and Spain?

6:27 The last war but between Britain and Spain sprang from the attempts of the <u>British merchants to prosecute an illic-</u>it trade with the Spanish main. These unjustifiable practices on their part produced severity on the part of the Spaniards toward the subjects of Great Britain which were not more justifiable, because they exceeded the bounds of a just retaliation and were chargeable with inhumanity and cruelty. Many of the English who were taken on the Spanish coast were sent to dig in the mines of Potosi; and by the usual progress of a spirit of resentment, the innocent were, after a while, confounded with the guilty in indiscriminate punishment.

Merchants fomented violence against Spain.

6:28 <u>The complaints of the merchants kindled a violent flame</u> throughout the nation, which soon after broke out in the House of Commons, and was communicated from that body to the ministry. <u>Letters of reprisal were granted</u>, and a war ensued, which in its consequences overthrew all the alliances that but twenty years before had been formed with sanguine expectations of the most beneficial fruits.

PEACE THROUGH COMMERCE AMONG STATES?
History shows that "peace through commerce" is just an idle Utopian dream that is destined to fail if the States don't unite.

6:29 From this summary of what has taken place in other countries, whose situations have borne the nearest resemblance to our own, what reason can we have to confide in those reveries which would seduce us into an expectation of peace and cordiality between the members of the present confederacy, in a state of separation? <u>Have we not already seen enough of the fallacy and extravagance of those idle theories which have amused us with promises of an exemption from the imperfections, weaknesses and evils incident to society in every shape?</u>

AWAKE TO THE REALITIES OF IMPERFECTION:
Is the Utopian's commercial golden age just a deceitful dream?

6:30 Is it not time to <u>awake</u> from the <u>deceitful dream of a golden</u> age, and to adopt as a <u>practical maxim</u> for the direction of our political conduct that we, as well as the other inhabitants of the globe, are yet remote from the <u>happy empire</u> of <u>perfect wisdom</u> and perfect virtue?

AMERICA'S FAILINGS PROVE THE POINT:
Did the Articles of Confederation served our nation well, to build prosperity and improve our global credit, or have they miserably failed?

6:31 Let the point of extreme depression to which our national dignity and <u>credit have sunk</u>, let the inconveniences felt everywhere from a lax and <u>ill administration</u> of government,

---

22 ***House of Bourbon*** was a European dynasty of French origin that held thrones in Spain, Sicily, Naples, and Parma (in northern Italy).
23 *Publius:* The Duke of Marlborough.

let the revolt[24] of a part of the State of North Carolina, the late menacing disturbances in Pennsylvania, and the actual insurrections and rebellions in Massachusetts, declare—!

PROXIMITY CREATES ENEMIES:
A confederacy of disunited States requires borders that friendship will not respect when a crisis arises. What simple measure will prevent this?

6:32 So far is the general sense of mankind from corresponding with the tenets of those who endeavor to lull asleep our apprehensions of discord and hostility between the States, in the event of disunion, that it has from long observation of the progress of society become a sort of axiom in politics, that vicinity or nearness of situation, constitutes nations natural enemies.

NEIGHBORING STATES ARE NATURAL ENEMIES:
Forming a strong Union will solve the conflicts arising from interstate trade.

6:33 An intelligent writer expresses himself on this subject to this effect: "NEIGHBORING NATIONS (says he) are naturally enemies of each other unless their common weakness forces them to league in a CONFEDERATE REPUBLIC, and their constitution prevents the differences that neighborhood occasions, extinguishing that secret jealousy which disposes all states to aggrandize themselves at the expense of their neighbors." [25]

6:34 This passage, at the same time, points out the EVIL and suggests the REMEDY.

—PUBLIUS

REVIEW QUESTIONS

1. What are the additional dangers that will come from disunion? (6:1)

2. To think the disunited States would be kind to each other is to disregard what? (6:2)

3. What fantasy do Anti-Federalists believe about commerce? (6:13)

4. What passion is as domineering as power or glory"? (6:18)

5. What are some of the ancient republics or nations that fought for commercial power? (6:19–28)

6. Is "peace through commerce" a realistic expectation? (6:29–30)

7. What does nearness and close proximity of nations naturally create? (6:32–33)

FEDERALIST NO. 7

BENEFITS OF UNION, DANGERS OF SEPARATE CONFEDERACIES: Would the disunited States make war on each other? Hamilton points out that not only would the States squabble as in Europe, but such wars would spill out into war with other nations. The flash points for internal war could come from competition for commercial activities, fighting over Western territory, or squabbling over how to pay the national debt if the States chose to break apart into confederacies. Hamilton uses several hypothetical circumstances to relate these possibilities more intimately to the voters in New York.

By Alexander Hamilton—November 15, 1787

REASONS FOR WAR BETWEEN DISUNITED STATES:
Can the people expect new hostilities if they become disunited?

7:1 IT IS sometimes asked, with an air of seeming triumph, what inducements could the States have, if disunited, to make war upon each other? It would be a full answer to this question to say — precisely the same inducements which have, at different times, deluged in blood all the nations in the world.

REASONS FOR HOSTILITIES ARE ALREADY PRESENT:

7:2 But, unfortunately for us, the question admits of a more particular answer. There are causes of differences within our immediate contemplation, of the tendency of which, even under the restraints of a federal constitution, we have had sufficient experience to enable us to form a judgment of what might be expected if those restraints were removed.

TERRITORIAL DISPUTES:
What do nations frequently fight over? Are there such conflicts ongoing among the thirteen States?

7:3 Territorial disputes have at all times been found one of the most fertile sources of hostility among nations. Perhaps the greatest proportion of wars that have desolated the earth have sprung from this origin. This cause would exist among us in full force.

---

24 *Editors' note:* May 19, 1775, patriots in Mecklenburg County, North Carolina, led by local colonel Thomas Polk, met to consider the crumbling relationship with Britain. When a rider arrived with word that shots had been fired at the Battle of Lexington, the patriots drew up five proclamations in a declaration of independence and signed it the next day, May 20, 1775.

25 *Publius: Vide Principes des Negociations par L'Abbe de Mably.*

UNDECIDED LAND CLAIMS BETWEEN THE STATES:

7:4   We have a <u>vast tract of unsettled territory</u> within the boundaries of the United States. There still are discordant and <u>undecided claims</u> between several of them, and the <u>dissolution of the Union</u> would lay a foundation for similar claims between them all.

LAND DISPUTES BEFORE AND AFTER REVOLUTION:

7:5   It is well known that they have <u>heretofore had serious</u> and animated <u>discussion</u> concerning the <u>rights to the lands</u> which were ungranted at the time of the <u>Revolution</u>, and which usually went under the name of <u>crown lands</u>. The <u>States</u> within the limits of whose colonial governments they were comprised have <u>claimed them</u> as their property, the <u>others</u> have <u>contended</u> that the rights of the crown in this article devolved upon the Union; especially as to all that part of the <u>Western territory</u> which, either by actual possession, or through the <u>submission of the Indian proprietors</u>, was <u>subjected to the jurisdiction of the king</u> of Great Britain, till it was relinquished in the treaty of peace. This, it has been said, was at all events an acquisition to the Confederacy by compact with a foreign power.

CONGRESS INTERVENES:

What policy did Congress implement to resolve land disputes? Is it a permanent arrangement?

7:6   It has been the <u>prudent policy of Congress</u> to appease this controversy, by prevailing upon the States to make <u>cessions</u> to the United States for the <u>benefit of the whole</u>. This has been so far accomplished as, under a continuation of the Union, to afford a decided prospect of an <u>amicable termination</u> of the dispute. A <u>dismemberment</u> of the <u>Confederacy</u>, however, would <u>revive this dispute</u>, and would <u>create others</u> on the same subject.

RISK OF NEW TERRITORIAL DISPUTES:

The Northwest Ordinance (1787) demonstrates how to settle territorial disputes by admitting new States as equals instead of enlarging existing States.

7:7   At present, a large part of the vacant <u>Western territory</u> is, by cession at least, if not by any anterior right, the common <u>property of the Union</u>. If that were at an end, the States which made the cession, on a principle of federal compromise, would be apt when the motive of the grant had ceased, to <u>reclaim the lands as a reversion</u>. The other States would no doubt insist on a proportion, by right of representation. Their argument would be, that a grant, once made, could not be revoked; and that the justice of participating in territory

acquired or secured by the joint efforts of the Confederacy, remained undiminished.

SHARING LAND CREATES MANY NEW PROBLEMS:

Is dividing disputed territories among the States even possible?

7:8   If, contrary to probability, it should be admitted by all the States, that each had a right to a share of this common stock, there would still be a difficulty to be surmounted, as to a proper <u>rule of apportionment</u>. Different principles would be set up by different States for this purpose; and as they would affect the <u>opposite interests</u> of the parties, they might not easily be susceptible of a pacific adjustment.

WITH NO UMPIRE, HOSTILITIES WILL OCCUR:

What about future fighting over the great western territories?

7:9   In the wide <u>field of Western territory</u>, therefore, we perceive an <u>ample theatre for hostile pretensions</u>, without any umpire or common judge to interpose between the contending parties. To reason from the past to the future, we shall have good ground to apprehend, that the <u>sword</u> would sometimes be appealed to as the arbiter of their <u>differences</u>.

SETTLING DISPUTES IN COURT:

Did the dispute over the Wyoming land demonstrate how a national court can resolve national matters without States going to war?

7:10   The circumstances of the dispute between <u>Connecticut</u> and <u>Pennsylvania</u>, respecting the land at <u>Wyoming</u>, admonish us not to be **sanguine**[26] in expecting an easy accommodation of such differences. The articles of confederation obliged the parties to submit the matter to the decision of a federal court. The submission was made, and the <u>court decided in favor of Pennsylvania</u>. But Connecticut gave strong indications of dissatisfaction with that determination; nor did she appear to be entirely resigned to it, till, by negotiation and management, something like an equivalent was found for the loss she supposed herself to have sustained.

DIFFICULT TO REACH HAPPY MEDIUM AMONG STATES:

7:11   Nothing here said is intended to convey the slightest censure on the conduct of that State. She no doubt sincerely believed herself to have been injured by the decision; and <u>States, like individuals, acquiesce with great reluctance in determinations to their disadvantage</u>

---

26   *sanguine:* Eager hopefulness; confidently optimistic.

NEED FOR UNION PROVEN BY NEW YORK-VERMONT DISPUTE:

Did a dispute between New York and Vermont prove the value of a strong national Union?

7:12 Those who had an opportunity of seeing the inside of the transactions which attended the progress of the controversy between this State [New York] and the district of Vermont, can vouch the opposition we experienced, as well from States not interested as from those which were interested in the claim; and can attest the danger to which the peace of the Confederacy might have been exposed, had this State attempted to assert its rights by force.

Potential future power plus individual land grants caused conflict.

7:13 Two motives preponderated in that opposition: one, a jealousy entertained of our future power; and the other, the interest of certain individuals of influence in the neighboring States, who had obtained grants of lands under the actual government of that district.

Real motives were antagonistic to New York.

7:14 Even the States which brought forward claims, in contradiction to ours, seemed more solicitous to dismember this State, than to establish their own pretensions. These were New Hampshire, Massachusetts, and Connecticut. New Jersey and Rhode Island, upon all occasions, discovered a warm zeal for the independence of Vermont; and Maryland, till alarmed by the appearance of a connection between Canada and that State, entered deeply into the same views. These being small States, saw with an unfriendly eye the perspective of our growing greatness. In a review of these transactions we may trace some of the causes which would be likely to embroil the States with each other, if it should be their unpropitious destiny to become disunited.

COMPETITIONS OF COMMERCE:

The States stand to benefit by competing in commerce to resolve commercial weaknesses and gain advantages. Will this create friction if not united?

7:15 The competitions of commerce would be another fruitful source of contention. The States less favorably circumstanced would be desirous of escaping from the disadvantages of local situation, and of sharing in the advantages of their more fortunate neighbors.

Local commercial policies will add to contentions between the confederacies.

7:16 Each State, or separate confederacy, would pursue a system of commercial policy peculiar to itself. This would occasion distinctions, preferences, and exclusions, which would beget discontent. The habits of intercourse, on the basis of equal privileges, to which we have been accustomed since the earliest settlement of the country, would give a keener edge to those causes of discontent than they would naturally have independent of this circumstance.

RESULTING INJURIES NORMAL AMONG NATIONS:

A Union of States would avoid what nations normally encounter.

7:17 WE SHOULD BE READY TO DENOMINATE INJURIES THOSE THINGS WHICH WERE IN REALITY THE JUSTIFIABLE ACTS OF INDEPENDENT SOVEREIGNTIES CONSULTING A DISTINCT INTEREST.

DISUNITED STATES WON'T RESPECT RULES:

Is it likely the States would respect each other's trade laws?

7:18 The spirit of enterprise, which characterizes the commercial part of America, has left no occasion of displaying itself unimproved. It is not at all probable that this unbridled spirit would pay much respect to those regulations of trade by which particular States might endeavor to secure exclusive benefits to their own citizens. The infractions of these regulations, on one side, the efforts to prevent and repel them, on the other, would naturally lead to outrages, and these to reprisals and wars.

NEW YORK'S IMPORT DUTIES:

New York has trade laws that are creating friction with its neighboring States.

7:19 The opportunities which some States would have of rendering others tributary to them by commercial regulations would be impatiently submitted to by the tributary States. The relative situation of New York, Connecticut, and New Jersey would afford an example of this kind.

Connecticut and New Jersey must pay import duties.

7:20 New York, from the necessities of revenue, must lay duties on her importations. A great part of these duties must be paid by the inhabitants of the two other States in the capacity of consumers of what we import. New York would neither be willing nor able to forego this advantage. Her citizens would not consent that a duty paid by them should be remitted in favor of the citizens of her neighbors; nor would it be practicable, if there were not this impediment in the way, to distinguish the customers in our own markets.

STATES TAXING STATES:

States won't long endure one State taxing another. Forming a Union would resolve this.

7:21 Would Connecticut and New Jersey long submit to be taxed by New York for her exclusive benefit? Should we be long permitted to remain in the quiet and undisturbed enjoyment of a metropolis, from the possession of which we derived an advantage so odious to our neighbors, and, in their opinion, so oppressive? Should we be able to preserve it against the incumbent weight of Connecticut on the one side, and the co-operating pressure of New Jersey on the other? These are questions that temerity alone will answer in the affirmative.

SHARING THE PUBLIC DEBT:
Would outstanding public debt contribute to more fighting?

7:22   The public debt of the Union would be a further cause of collision between the separate States or confederacies. The apportionment, in the first instance, and the progressive extinguishment afterward, would be alike productive of ill-humor and animosity.

States would quarrel over who should pay or not pay.

7:23   How would it be possible to agree upon a rule of apportionment satisfactory to all? There is scarcely any that can be proposed which is entirely free from real objections. These, as usual, would be exaggerated by the adverse interest of the parties.

PUBLIC DEBT VIEWED AS ANOTHER'S PROBLEM:
Without a national arbitrator the states would not resolve their national indebtedness.

7:24   There are even dissimilar views among the States as to the general principle of discharging the public debt. Some of them, either less impressed with the importance of national credit, or because their citizens have little, if any, immediate interest in the question, feel an indifference, if not a repugnance, to the payment of the domestic debt at any rate. These would be inclined to magnify the difficulties of a distribution.

Some individuals are owed more than a State's fair share of the public debt. These people will demand fairness.

7:25   Others of them, a numerous body of whose citizens are creditors to the public beyond proportion of the State in the total amount of the national debt, would be strenuous for some equitable and effective provision.

Some States will be slow paying back their share of the debt, upsetting the rest.

7:26   The procrastinations of the former would excite the resentments of the latter. The settlement of a rule would, in the meantime, be postponed by real differences of opinion and affected delays.

On top of individual demands for repayment, foreign interest will make similar demands, further complicating the peace.

7:27   The citizens of the States interested would clamour; foreign powers would urge for the satisfaction of their just demands, and the peace of the States would be hazarded to the double contingency of external invasion and internal contention.

RULES FOR PAYING PUBLIC DEBT NOT WORKABLE:
Even if everyone agreed on the rules the disunited States wouldn't cooperate in paying their share.

7:28   Suppose the difficulties of agreeing upon a rule surmounted, and the apportionment made. Still there is great room to suppose that the rule agreed upon would, upon experiment, be found to bear harder upon some States than upon others. Those which were sufferers by it would naturally seek for a mitigation of the burden.

If one State refused to help pay off the public debt might other States use that as reason to withhold their own contributions?

7:29   The others would as naturally be disinclined to a revision, which was likely to end in an increase of their own encumbrances. Their refusal would be too plausible a pretext to the complaining States to withhold their contributions, not to be embraced with avidity; and the non-compliance of these States with their engagements would be a ground of bitter discussion and altercation.

ADDITIONAL PROBLEMS THWARTING PAYMENT OF DEBTS:
States usually have other internal problems that plague their ability to make payments. These, too, lead to quarrels.

7:30   If even the rule adopted should in practice justify the equality of its principle, still delinquencies in payments on the part of some of the States would result from a diversity of other causes—the real deficiency of resources; the mismanagement of their finances; accidental disorders in the management of the government; and, in addition to the rest, the reluctance with which men commonly part with money for purposes that have outlived the **exigencies**[27] which produced them, and interfere with the supply of immediate wants. Delinquencies, from whatever causes, would be productive of complaints, recriminations, and quarrels.

---

27   *exigencies:* Urgent needs and demands of a particular situation that require immediate relief.

COMMON DEBTS WITHOUT COMMON BENEFITS:

7:31   There is, perhaps, nothing more likely to disturb the tranquility of nations than their being bound to mutual contributions for any common object that does not yield an equal and coincident benefit. For it is an observation, as true as it is trite, that there is nothing men differ so readily about as the payment of money.

PRIVATE CONTRACTS:

Without a Union would States honor each other's contract laws?

7:32   Laws in violation of private contracts, as they amount to aggressions on the rights of those States whose citizens are injured by them, may be considered as another probable source of hostility. We are not authorized to expect that a more liberal or more equitable spirit would preside over the legislations of the individual States hereafter, if unrestrained by any additional checks, than we have heretofore seen in too many instances disgracing their several codes.

CONNECTICUT AND RHODE ISLAND:

Breaches of moral obligations between the States can lead to war.

7:33   We have observed the disposition to retaliation excited in Connecticut in consequence of the enormities perpetrated by the Legislature of Rhode Island; and we reasonably infer that, in similar cases, under other circumstances, a war, not of PARCHMENT, but of the sword, would chastise such atrocious breaches of moral obligation and social justice.

STATE ALLIANCES WITH FOREIGN POWERS:

If all thirteen of the States don't form a strong inclusive Union, a foreign alliance by some is a real danger. What is the motto of every nation that hates or fears America?

7:34   The probability of incompatible alliances between the different States or confederacies and different foreign nations, and the effects of this situation upon the peace of the whole, have been sufficiently unfolded in some preceding papers. From the view they have exhibited of this part of the subject, this conclusion is to be drawn, that America, if not connected at all, or only by the feeble tie of a simple league, offensive and defensive, would, by the operation of such jarring alliances, be gradually entangled in all the pernicious labyrinths of European politics and wars; and by the destructive contentions of the parts into which she was divided, would be likely to become a prey to the artifices and machinations of powers equally the enemies of them all. **Divide et impera**[28] [divide and command] must be the motto of every nation that either hates or fears us.

—PUBLIUS

28   *Publius*: Divide and command.

REVIEW QUESTIONS

1.   What is one of the most fertile sources of hostility between States? (7:3–4)

2.   What are some of the causes of land disputes? (7:5)

3.   What is needed for the States to settle land disputes? (7:9-10)

4.   Are the States likely to surrender any of their existing advantages? (7:11)

5.   Would paying public debts work under a confederacy? (7:22–31)

6.   What is the motto of nations that hate America? Does a confederacy of States make that a very real possibility? (7:34)

FEDERALIST NO. 8

NATIONAL DEFENSE IS GOVERNMENT'S FIRST PRIORITY: War between the States without a strong Union is inevitable. It would be made more disastrous because the land is largely flat with no natural geographic boundaries to defend as in Europe. Weaker States under constant threat of invasion would resort to establishing standing armies, and that would lead to a monarchy because a strong executive is always needed in war. Greece and Britain are good examples of what can happen without a strong Union.

By Alexander Hamilton—November 20, 1787

DISUNITED STATES WOULD BE IN CYCLES OF PEACE AND WAR:

Without a Union, could the States confidently anticipate peace?

8:1   ASSUMING it therefore as an established truth that the several States, in case of disunion, or such combinations of them as might happen to be formed out of the wreck of the general Confederacy, would be subject to those vicissitudes of peace and war, of friendship and enmity, with each other, which have fallen to the lot of all neighboring nations not united under one government, let us enter into a concise detail of some of the consequences that would attend such a situation.

EUROPE IS BETTER SITUATED WITH FORTS AND ARMIES:

Why would war and war preparations among the disunited States be so much more devastating and difficult than in Europe?

8:2 War between the States, in the first period of their separate existence, would be accompanied with much greater distresses than it commonly is in those countries where regular military establishments have long obtained. The disciplined armies always kept on foot on the continent of Europe, though they bear a malignant aspect to liberty and economy, have, notwithstanding, been productive of the **signal**[29] advantage of rendering sudden conquests impracticable, and of preventing that rapid desolation which used to mark the progress of war prior to their introduction.

Forts already exist in Europe, but not in every America State.

8:3 The art of fortification has contributed to the same ends. The nations of Europe are encircled with chains of fortified places, which mutually obstruct invasion. Campaigns are wasted in reducing two or three frontier garrisons, to gain admittance into an enemy's country.

Fortifications reduce the required defensive forces.

8:4 Similar impediments occur at every step, to exhaust the strength and delay the progress of an invader. Formerly, an invading army would penetrate into the heart of a neighboring country almost as soon as intelligence of its approach could be received; but now a comparatively small force of disciplined troops, acting on the defensive, with the aid of posts, is able to impede, and finally to frustrate, the enterprises of one much more considerable.

Europe has been the battleground of countless and fruitless wars.

8:5 The history of war, in that quarter of the globe, is no longer a history of nations subdued and empires overturned, but of towns taken and retaken; of battles that decide nothing; of retreats more beneficial than victories; of much effort and little acquisition.

HOSTILITIES AMONG STATES WILL BE DEVASTATING:

Why would war between the States be worse than wars in Europe?

8:6 In this country the scene would be altogether reversed. The jealousy of military establishments would postpone them

as long as possible. The want of fortifications, leaving the frontiers of one state open to another, would facilitate inroads. The populous States would, with little difficulty, overrun their less populous neighbors. Conquests would be as easy to be made as difficult to be retained. War, therefore, would be desultory and predatory. Plunder and devastation ever march in the train of irregulars. The calamities of individuals would make the principal figure in the events which would characterize our military exploits.

DISUNION INVITES MILITARY DICTATORSHIPS:

Without a Union, would the States give up freedom to be more safe?

8:7 This picture is not too highly wrought; though, I confess, it would not long remain a just one. Safety from external danger is the most powerful director of national conduct. Even the ardent love of liberty will, after a time, give way to its dictates. The violent destruction of life and property incident to war, the continual effort and alarm attendant on a state of continual danger, will compel nations the most attached to liberty to resort for repose and security to institutions which have a tendency to destroy their civil and political rights. To be more safe, they at length become willing to run the risk of being less free.

INTRODUCING THE TOPIC OF STANDING ARMIES:

Without a Union, would the States need standing armies and forts?

8:8 The institutions chiefly alluded to are STANDING ARMIES and the correspondent appendages of military establishments. Standing armies, it is said, are not provided against in the new Constitution; and it is therefore inferred that they may exist under it. Their existence, however, from the very terms of the proposition, is, at most, problematical and uncertain.[30]

EVERY DISUNITED STATE MUST ARM AND FORTIFY ITSELF:

Each disunited State would need to have its own standing army to survive.

8:9 But standing armies, it may be replied, must inevitably result from a dissolution of the Confederacy. Frequent war and constant apprehension, which require a state of as constant preparation, will infallibly produce them.

---

29 *signal*: Eminent, remarkable, memorable, in a distinguished manner.

30 *Publius*: This objection will be fully examined in its proper place, and it will be shown that the only rational precaution which could have been taken on this subject has been taken; and a much better one than is to be found in any constitution that has been heretofore framed in America, most of which contain no guard at all on this subject.

Weaker States would build even greater defensive forces.

8:10   The weaker States or confederacies would first have recourse to them, to put themselves upon an equality with their more potent neighbors. They would endeavor to supply the inferiority of population and resources by a more regular and effective system of defense, by disciplined troops, and by fortifications.

WAR STRENGTHENS EXECUTIVE:
How could constant war preparations lead to installing a king?

8:11   They would, at the same time, be necessitated to strengthen the executive arm of government, in doing which their constitutions would acquire a progressive direction toward monarchy. It is of the nature of war to increase the executive at the expense of the legislative authority.

THE WEAK OVERCOME THE POWERFUL:
How would preparations for war between the States start and continue conflicts as in Europe?

8:12   The expedients which have been mentioned would soon give the States or confederacies that made use of them a superiority over their neighbors. Small states, or states of less natural strength, under vigorous governments, and with the assistance of disciplined armies, have often triumphed over large states, or states of greater natural strength, which have been destitute of these advantages.

STATES TRIGGER RETALIATORY PREPARATIONS, A CHAIN REACTION:
If a State heavily arms itself, other States would as well—out of fear.

8:13   Neither the pride nor the safety of the more important States or confederacies would permit them long to submit to this mortifying and adventitious superiority. They would quickly resort to means similar to those by which it had been effected, to reinstate themselves in their lost pre-eminence. Thus, we should, in a little time, see established in every part of this country the same engines of despotism which have been the scourge of the Old World. This, at least, would be the natural course of things; and our reasonings will be the more likely to be just, in proportion as they are accommodated to this standard.

WAR IN DISUNITED AMERICA IS INEVITABLE:
Future war between the disunited States is not mere speculation and warning—it is expected based on the proven experiences of Europe.

8:14   These are not vague inferences drawn from supposed or speculative defects in a Constitution, the whole power of which is lodged in the hands of a people, or their representatives and delegates, but they are solid conclusions, drawn from the natural and necessary progress of human affairs.

GREECE WAS A NATION OF SOLDIERS:
Modern prosperity has caused war preparations to become less of a priority.

8:15   It may, perhaps, be asked, by way of objection to this, why did not standing armies spring up out of the contentions which so often distracted the ancient republics of Greece? Different answers, equally satisfactory, may be given to this question. The industrious habits of the people of the present day, absorbed in the pursuits of gain, and devoted to the improvements of agriculture and commerce, are incompatible with the condition of a nation of soldiers, which was the true condition of the people of those republics.

MODERN PROSPERITY MADE CAREER SOLDIERS POSSIBLE:
Professional armies eventually become a way of life.

8:16   The means of revenue, which have been so greatly multiplied by the increase of gold and silver and of the arts of industry, and the science of finance, which is the offspring of modern times, concurring with the habits of nations, have produced an entire revolution in the system of war, and have rendered disciplined armies, distinct from the body of the citizens, the inseparable companions of frequent hostility.

PEACETIME ARMIES:
Armies in countries not at risk pose less threat to the people than armies always armed and on alert.

8:17   There is a wide difference, also, between military establishments in a country seldom exposed by its situation to internal invasions, and in one which is often subject to them, and always apprehensive of them. The rulers of the former can have a good pretext, if they are even so inclined, to keep on foot armies so numerous as must of necessity be maintained in the latter.

Armies rarely needed in countries not at risk.

8:18   These armies being, in the first case, rarely, if at all, called into activity for interior defense, the people are in no danger of being broken to military subordination. The laws are not accustomed to relaxations, in favor of military exigencies; the civil state remains in full vigor, neither corrupted, nor confounded with the principles or propensities of the other state.

ARMED CITIZENS PREVENT MILITARY TAKEOVER:
Small government armies are not to be feared where the population is an over match.

8:19   The smallness of the army renders the natural strength of the community an over-match for it; and the citizens, not habituated to look up to the military power for protection, or to submit to its oppressions, neither love nor fear the soldiery; they view them with a spirit of jealous acquiescence in a necessary evil, and stand ready to resist a power which they suppose may be exerted to the prejudice of their rights.

ARMIES ARE BEST FOR SMALL UPRISINGS:
The President could use a standing army to put down small uprisings but could not withstand a majority of the people pushing back.

8:20   The army under such circumstances may usefully aid the magistrate to suppress a small faction, or an occasional mob, or insurrection; but it will be unable to enforce encroachments against the united efforts of the great body of the people.

LARGE ARMIES DECREASE CITIZENS' RIGHTS:
Why is a strong standing army important? Without a strong Union could such an army eventually lead to a police state?

8:21   In a country in the predicament last described, the contrary of all this happens. The perpetual menacings of danger oblige the government to be always prepared to repel it; its armies must be numerous enough for instant defense. The continual necessity for their services enhances the importance of the soldier, and proportionably degrades the condition of the citizen. The military state becomes elevated above the civil.

SUPPRESSING RIGHTS BECOMES A WAY OF LIFE:
When the military supports political decisions, the people eventually become victims to a new tyranny without even realizing it.

8:22   The inhabitants of territories, often the theatre of war, are unavoidably subjected to frequent infringements on their rights, which serve to weaken their sense of those rights; and by degrees the people are brought to consider the soldiery not only as their protectors, but as their superiors. The transition from this disposition to that of considering them masters, is neither remote nor difficult; but it is very difficult to prevail upon a people under such impressions, to make a bold or effectual resistance to usurpations supported by the military power.

BRITAIN DOESN'T REQUIRE A LARGE ARMY:
Britain's naval strength and internal security precludes the need for a standing army in spite of its corruption.

8:23   The kingdom of Great Britain falls within the first description. An insular situation, and a powerful marine, guarding it in a great measure against the possibility of foreign invasion, supersede the necessity of a numerous army within the kingdom. A sufficient force to make head against a sudden descent, till the militia could have time to rally and embody, is all that has been deemed requisite.

People would refuse needless expense.

8:24   No motive of national policy has demanded, nor would public opinion have tolerated, a larger number of troops upon its domestic establishment. There has been, for a long time past, little room for the operation of the other causes, which have been enumerated as the consequences of internal war.

BRITAIN WOULD NEED MORE MILITARY ESTABLISHMENTS IF IT WASN'T AN ISLAND:
What advantage does Britain have for self-defense? If it was on the European continent how would Britain's circumstances change?

8:25   This peculiar felicity of situation has, in a great degree, contributed to preserve the liberty which that country to this day enjoys, in spite of the prevalent venality and corruption. If, on the contrary, Britain had been situated on the continent, and had been compelled, as she would have been, by that situation, to make her military establishments at home coextensive with those of the other great powers of Europe, she, like them, would in all probability be, at this day, a victim to the absolute power of a single man.

Enslavement in Britain possible but not from their army.

8:26   'Tis possible, though not easy, that the people of that island may be enslaved from other causes; but it cannot be by the prowess of an army so inconsiderable as that which has been usually kept up within the kingdom.

UNITED AMERICA COULD ENJOY PEACE FOR THE AGES:
Could America enjoy Britain's peace if it formed one Union?

8:27   If we are wise enough to preserve the Union we may for ages enjoy an advantage similar to that of an insulated situation. Europe is at a great distance from us. Her colonies in our vicinity will be likely to continue too much disproportioned in strength to be able to give us any dangerous annoyance. Extensive military establishments cannot, in this position, be necessary to our security.

DISUNITED AMERICA WOULD MIMIC EUROPE:
Without a Union, America could become embroiled in quarrels like Europe.

8:28   But if we should be disunited, and the integral parts should either remain separated, or, which is most probable, should be thrown together into two or three confederacies, we should be, in a short course of time, in the predicament of the continental powers of Europe—our liberties would be a prey to the means of defending ourselves against the ambition and jealousy of each other.

DANGERS TO AMERICA ARE VERY REAL WITHOUT THE CONSTITUTION:
Setting aside partisan bickering, if this new Constitution is not adopted, would all of the trauma, dissolution, and war-making be the predictable outcome?

8:29 This is an idea not superficial or futile, but solid and weighty. It deserves the most serious and mature consideration of every prudent and honest man of whatever party.

A STRONG UNION IS OUR HIGHEST PRIORITY:
Trivial objections to the Constitution pale in importance to the dangers of not adopting it.

8:30 If such men will make a firm and solemn pause, and meditate dispassionately on the importance of this interesting idea; if they will contemplate it in all its attitudes, and trace it to all its consequences, they will not hesitate to part with trivial objections to a Constitution, the rejection of which would in all probability put a final period to the Union. The airy phantoms that flit before the distempered imaginations of some of its adversaries would quickly give place to the more substantial forms of dangers, real, certain, and formidable.

—PUBLIUS

REVIEW QUESTIONS

1. What does Europe have that the States do not that discourages war? (8:2–5)

2. What would the States be willing to surrender to be safe? (8:7)

3. What would the disunited States want to create to protect themselves? (8:8–10)

4. Why does war strengthen the executive authority in a nation? (8:11)

5. What chain reaction starts when one State arms itself? (8:12–13)

6. How does an on-going state of war hurt the people's liberty? (8:21–22)

7. As a Union, would America have European-type conflicts? (8:28)

8. What does Publius call the Anti-Federalist's objections to the Constitution? (8:30)

9. Setting aside trivial alarmist claims what is the real critical issue at hand? (8:29–30)

FEDERALIST NO. 9

A UNION IS BEST TO COMBAT FACTIONS: History offers examples of republics and unions that teetered on the brink of tyranny and at the opposite, the chaos of anarchy. The new Constitution is the balanced center between those failed models. The Constitution creates a self-defending and self-correcting republic that will best protect the liberties of all. The critics of this new form make several claims that can't be defended. Montesquieu himself supports what we're doing and shouldn't be misquoted. Bottom line is that all confederacies are too weak to self-govern and go too far toward anarchy, or no government.

By Alexander Hamilton—November 21, 1787

LIFE WITHOUT A FIRM UNION OF 13 STATES:
How have nations in ancient times fared without strong Unions?

9:1 A FIRM Union will be of the utmost moment to the peace and liberty of the States, as a barrier against domestic faction and insurrection.

ANCIENT GREECE AND ITALY FAILED TO FIND THE BALANCED POLITICAL CENTER:
On the spectrum of political power, tyranny is at the far left and anarchy is at the far right. The Constitution serves in the best place of all: The balanced center.

9:2 It is impossible to read the history of the petty republics of Greece and Italy without feeling sensations of horror and disgust at the distractions with which they were continually agitated, and at the rapid succession of revolutions by which they were kept in a state of perpetual vibration between the extremes of tyranny and anarchy. If they exhibit occasional calms, these only serve as short-lived contrast to the furious storms that are to succeed.

Moments of blissful liberty always spoiled by vices and rage.

9:3 If now and then intervals of felicity open to view, we behold them with a mixture of regret, arising from the reflection that the pleasing scenes before us are soon to be overwhelmed by the tempestuous waves of sedition and party rage. If momentary rays of glory break forth from the gloom, while they dazzle us with a transient and fleeting brilliancy, they at the same time admonish us to lament that the vices of government should pervert the direction and tarnish the lustre of those bright talents and exalted endowments for which the favored soils that produced them have been so justly celebrated.

DESPOTS DESPISE FREE GOVERNMENT:
Critics of self-government desire a return to ruling monarchs.

9:4 From the disorders that disfigure the annals of those republics the advocates of despotism have drawn arguments, not only <u>against the forms of republican government</u>, but against the very principles of civil liberty. They have <u>decried all free government</u> as <u>inconsistent</u> with the <u>order</u> of society, and have indulged themselves in malicious exultation over its friends and partisans.

HISTORIC MOMENTS OF LIBERTY SHINE AS EXAMPLES:

9:5 Happily for mankind, <u>stupendous fabrics reared on the basis of liberty</u>, which have <u>flourished for ages, have, in a few glorious instances</u>, refuted their gloomy sophisms. And, I trust, America will be the broad and solid foundation of other edifices, not less magnificent, which will be equally permanent monuments of their errors.

MODERN CONCEPTS IN POLITICS:
Have the principles of good government always been known and understood?

9:6 But it is not to be denied that the portraits they have sketched of republican government were too just copies of the originals from which they were taken. If it had been found impracticable to have devised models of a more perfect structure, the enlightened friends to liberty would have been obliged to abandon the cause of that species of government as indefensible. <u>The science of politics</u>, however, like most other sciences, has received <u>great improvement</u>. The efficacy of various principles is now well understood, which were either not known at all, or <u>imperfectly known to the ancients</u>.

NEW DISCOVERIES BY THE CONVENTION:
What limits did the Framers put on the new form of republican government?

9:7 The regular <u>distribution of power</u> into distinct departments; the introduction of <u>legislative balances and checks</u>; the institution of <u>courts composed of judges</u> holding their offices during <u>good behavior</u>; the <u>representation</u> of the people in the legislature by <u>deputies</u> of their own election: these are wholly <u>new discoveries</u>, or have made their principal progress towards perfection in <u>modern times</u>. They are means, and powerful means, by which the excellences of republican government may be retained and its <u>imperfections lessened</u> or avoided.

REPUBLICAN FORM IS EASILY EXPANDABLE:
The new Constitution allows for expansion of the republican system over a larger territory.

9:8 To this catalogue of circumstances that tend to the amelioration of **popular**[31] systems of civil government, I shall venture, however novel it may appear to some, to add one more, on a principle which has been made the foundation of an objection to the new Constitution; I mean the <u>ENLARGEMENT of the ORBIT</u> within which such systems are to revolve, either in respect to the dimensions of a single State or to the consolidation of several smaller States into one great Confederacy. The latter is that which immediately concerns the object under consideration. It will, however, be of use to examine the principle in its application to a single State, which shall be attended to in another place.

MONTESQUIEU SAYS SMALL TERRITORIES ARE BEST:
What size of territories did Montesquieu say worked best for representative governments? Was this all he said?

9:9 The <u>utility of a Confederacy</u>, as well to suppress faction and to guard the internal tranquility of States, as to increase their external force and security, is in reality <u>not a new idea</u>. It has been practiced upon in different countries and ages, and has received the sanction of the most approved writers on the subject of politics. The opponents of the plan proposed have, with great assiduity, cited and circulated the <u>observations of Montesquieu on the necessity of a contracted territory for a republican government</u>. But they seem not to have been apprised of the sentiments of that great man expressed in another part of his work, nor to have adverted to the consequences of the principle to which they subscribe with such ready acquiescence.

MONTESQUIEU'S THEORY NOT LIMITED TO GEOGRAPHICAL SIZE:
Montesquieu's theory about republics being small —in fact, smaller than most States—would lead to what kinds of problems?

9:10 When <u>Montesquieu</u> recommends a small extent for republics, the standards he had in view were of dimensions far short of the limits of almost every one of these States. Neither Virginia, Massachusetts, Pennsylvania, New York, North Carolina, nor Georgia can by any means be compared with the models from which he reasoned and to which the terms of his description apply.

"DISTANCE GOVERNMENT"
Claim: Central government managing numerous small communities would lead to needing a king, or otherwise they'd fall into chaos.

9:11 If we therefore take his ideas on this point as the criterion of truth, we shall be driven to the alternative either of

---

31 *popular:* This term is used repeatedly to refer to the authority of government that is created, sustained, and controlled by the consent of the people through the election of executives and legislators

taking refuge at once in the arms of monarchy, or of splitting ourselves into an infinity of little, jealous, clashing, tumultuous commonwealths, the wretched nurseries of unceasing discord, and the miserable objects of universal pity or contempt.

Some Anti-Federalists suggest breaking large States into small.

9:12 Some of the writers who have come forward on the other side of the question seem to have been aware of the dilemma; and have even been bold enough to hint at the division of the larger States as a desirable thing.

PETTY POLITICS WOULD THWART GREATNESS:
A nation of small units would never gain advantage of finding great leaders.

9:13 Such an infatuated policy, such a desperate expedient, might, by the multiplication of petty offices, answer the views of men who possess not qualifications to extend their influence beyond the narrow circles of personal intrigue, but it could never promote the greatness or happiness of the people of America.

MONTESQUIEU SUPPORTED A SINGLE UNION:
Although Montesquieu suggested a reduction in the size of territories, did he still support a single all-inclusive Union?

9:14 Referring the examination of the principle itself to another place, as has been already mentioned, it will be sufficient to remark here that, in the sense of the author who has been most emphatically quoted upon the occasion, it would only dictate a reduction of the SIZE of the more considerable MEMBERS of the Union, but would not militate against their being all comprehended in one confederate government. And this is the true question, in the discussion of which we are at present interested.

UNION PROMOTED BY MONTESQUIEU:
Montesquieu's description of a confederate republic is a close description of the strengths of the new Union. Montesquieu lists the advantages of republican governments united in a strong Union in 9:15–22.

9:15 So far are the suggestions of Montesquieu from standing in opposition to a general Union of the States, that he explicitly treats of a CONFEDERATE REPUBLIC as the expedient for extending the sphere of popular government, and reconciling the advantages of monarchy with those of republicanism.

QUOTING MONTESQUIEU:
Combining the best of a republic's internal and external forms is best of all.

9:16 "It is very probable," (says he[32]) "that mankind would have been obliged at length to live constantly under the government of a single person, had they not contrived a kind of constitution that has all the internal advantages of a republican, together with the external force of a monarchical government. I mean a CONFEDERATE REPUBLIC.

MONTESQUIEU:
Adding new States to a confederate Union can best provide for the national security.

9:17 "This form of government is a convention by which several smaller STATES agree to become members of a larger ONE, which they intend to form. It is a kind of assemblage of societies that constitute a new one, capable of increasing, by means of new associations, till they arrive to such a degree of power as to be able to provide for the security of the united body.

MONTESQUIEU:
Built-in protection against attack, insurrection, corruption.

9:18 "A republic of this kind, able to withstand an external force, may support itself without any internal corruptions. The form of this society prevents all manner of inconveniences.

MONTESQUIEU:
Insurrections quickly resolved by the majority of States.

9:19 "If a single member should attempt to usurp the supreme authority, he could not be supposed to have an equal authority and credit in all the confederate states. Were he to have too great influence over one, this would alarm the rest. Were he to subdue a part, that which would still remain free might oppose him with forces independent of those which he had usurped and overpower him before he could be settled in his usurpation.

MONTESQUIEU:
Majority able to put down minority abuses and corruptions.

9:20 "Should a popular insurrection happen in one of the confederate states the others are able to quell it. Should abuses creep into one part, they are reformed by those that remain sound. The state may be destroyed on one side, and not on the other; the confederacy may be dissolved, and the confederates preserve their sovereignty.

MONTESQUIEU:
If the States remain sovereign and united, a strong Union of all the States becomes formidable.

---

32 *Publius:* Spirit of Laws, Vol. I, Book ix, Chapter i

9:21 "As this government is composed of small republics, it enjoys the internal happiness of each; and with respect to its external situation, it is possessed, by means of the association, of all the advantages of large monarchies."

MONTESQUIEU SUPPORTS UNIONS:
What did Hamilton find so helpful in Montesquieu's comments?

9:22 I have thought it proper to quote at length these interesting passages, because they contain a luminous abridgment of the principal arguments in favor of the Union, and must effectually remove the false impressions which a misapplication of other parts of the work was calculated to make. They have, at the same time, an intimate connection with the more immediate design of this paper; which is, to illustrate the tendency of the Union to repress domestic faction and insurrection.

CONFEDERACY VERSUS CONSOLIDATION:
A confederacy is a league of sovereign States. A consolidation is a massive republic where the states lose their sovereignty (See 32:3).

9:23 A distinction, more subtle than accurate, has been raised between a CONFEDERACY and a CONSOLIDATION of the States. The essential characteristic of the first is said to be, the restriction of its authority to the members in their collective capacities, without reaching to the individuals of whom they are composed. It is contended that the national council ought to have no concern with any object of internal administration. An exact equality of suffrage between the members has also been insisted upon as a leading feature of a confederate government.

ARBITRARY DISTINCTIONS CONFUSE THE TWO FORMS:
The two forms have always had many exceptions to the practice.

9:24 These positions are, in the main, arbitrary; they are supported neither by principle nor precedent. It has indeed happened, that governments of this kind have generally operated in the manner which the distinction taken notice of, supposes to be inherent in their nature; but there have been in most of them extensive exceptions to the practice, which serve to prove, as far as example will go, that there is no absolute rule on the subject.

And where these two forms have existed, terrible disorder has followed.

9:25 And it will be clearly shown in the course of this investigation that as far as the principle contended for has prevailed, it has been the cause of incurable disorder and imbecility in the government.

DEFINITION OF CONFEDERATE REPUBLIC:
What elements of good government are present in a confederate republic?

9:26 The definition of a CONFEDERATE REPUBLIC seems simply to be "an assemblage of societies," or an association of two or more states into one state. The extent, modifications, and objects of the federal authority are mere matters of discretion. So long as the separate organization of the members be not abolished; so long as it exists, by a constitutional necessity, for local purposes; though it should be in perfect subordination to the general authority of the union, it would still be, in fact and in theory, an association of states, or a confederacy.

SENATE MUST BE SELECTED BY LEGISLATURES:
The States' legislatures should have direct representative in the Senate. This critical link is what the Seventeenth Amendment diluted when Senators could be elected popularly.

9:27 The proposed Constitution, so far from implying an **abolition**[33] of the State governments, makes them constituent parts of the national sovereignty, by allowing them a direct representation in the Senate,[34] and leaves in their possession certain exclusive and very important portions of sovereign power. This fully corresponds, in every rational import of the terms, with the idea of a federal government.

MONTESQUIEU APPROVES OF THE LYCIAN CONFEDERACY:
This describes the States under the Articles, where sovereign republics form a league, a confederation. Is there an example of a successful confederacy from ancient history?

9:28 In the Lycian confederacy, which consisted of twenty-three CITIES or republics, the largest were entitled to THREE votes in the COMMON COUNCIL, those of the middle class to TWO, and the smallest to ONE. The COMMON COUNCIL had the appointment of all the judges and magistrates of the respective CITIES. This was certainly the most, delicate species of interference in their internal administration; for if there be any thing that seems exclusively appropriated to the local jurisdictions, it is the appointment of their own officers. Yet Montesquieu, speaking of this association, says: "Were I to give a model of an excellent Confederate Republic, it would be that of Lycia."

---

33 **abolition:** The act of officially ending or stopping something; abolishing a system, practice, or institution.

34 *Editors' Note:* See comments and context about the emasculation of State sovereignty in 26:22 footnote and 59:18 footnote.

DETRACTORS HAVE DISTORTED MONTESQUIEU:

9:29 Thus we perceive that the distinctions insisted upon were not within the contemplation of this enlightened civilian; and we shall be led to conclude, that they are the novel refinements of an erroneous theory.

—PUBLIUS

REVIEW QUESTIONS

1. What are the two extremes of the political spectrum? (9:2)

2. According to despots what does self-government run counter to? (9:4)

3. What new principles of political science did the Convention discover? (9:6–8)

4. What did Montesquieu mean by "confederate republic"? (9:14–26)

5. How is a State's sovereignty protected under the new Constitution? (9:27)

6. How did the Seventeenth Amendment weaken the States' sovereignty? (9:27)

7. What example of a confederate republic does Montesquieu praise? (9:28)

Editors' note: The Lycian Confederation (Lycian League) just referenced in paper No. 9 is the first known democratic-republican union in history. This unique achievement was mentioned by Montesquieu, Hamilton (see papers No. 9 and No. 16), Madison (see paper No. 45), and others, as an example of how to make a national government work using the principles of fair representation.

The Lycians flourished in a mountainous region of Turkey along its southern Mediterranean coast. They loved their freedom and independence, and they defended it fiercely.

In 205 BC, twenty-three Lycian towns agreed to form a League for their common defense. They invited each town to elect one, two, or three representatives, according to the size of their populations, to form a central assembly. Smaller towns combined together to send one representative. The costs of the assembly were borne in the same proportion, the largest towns carrying the heaviest financial load.

Each year the assembly elected a leader, federal officers, judges, and magistrates. Their business included trade rights, communal lands, religious and economic issues, marriage laws, and legal matters. The league was highly successful and kept their political affairs stabilized even when they were occupied by foreign invaders.

The success of the Lycian League was known to the Founding Fathers and it impacted the US Constitution in three ways.

First, it showed that a Union of independent, self-governing states could be formed using a representative form of government.

Second, it showed that when the number of representatives was kept proportional to their individual populations, a sense of fairness prevailed.

Third, it showed that with the consent of the governed they could create a strong central government with the power to make its own laws, have its own official officers, and make laws that applied to each individual regardless of the town to which that person belonged.

Madison and Hamilton pointed out one reason the league succeeded is because they didn't form a democracy (one man, one vote). Government by all the people leads to factions, tyranny, and anarchy, they said. In Montesquieu's words, "The great advantage of representatives is that they are able to discuss public business. The people are not at all appropriate for such discussion... The People should not enter the government except to choose their representatives" (Montesquieu, Book XI of *The Spirit of the Laws*).

FEDERALIST NO. 10

REPUBLICS PREVENT FACTIONS FROM BULLYING MINORITY GROUPS: Madison defines "faction." He points out that given the ever-present challenges of human nature, factions will always form because of the natural inequality from differing opinions, different amounts of property, and party loyalty. He defines democracy. Pure democracies always crumble under the onslaught of various factions. Political parties are a main cause of factions, and a strong Union is best suited to contain and control the damages from such factions. While factions can't be stopped from forming, their effects can be minimized. He defines a republic. A republican form of government as anticipated in the new Constitution is the very best at protecting minority viewpoints and universal liberties, while at the same time preventing conspiracies and factions from gaining strength. Madison accurately predicts that the large and growing size of America and the preservation of its variety of interests will guarantee stability, justice, and liberty (see 10:38-51).Any form of socialism (in those days called "leveling") that calls for having property in common, opinions in common, refusing to pay legal debts, legalizing unsecured paper money, for example—is called out as "wicked" (see 10:50). The modern word "socialist" is first recorded in 1827, and means one who advocates socialism, from the French *socialiste*. (See 10:9 footnote)

By James Madison—November 22, 1787

UNION HELPS SOLVE PROBLEMS CAUSED BY FACTIONS:

10:1　AMONG the numerous advantages promised by a well-constructed Union, none deserves to be more accurately developed than its tendency to break and control the violence of faction.[35] The friend of popular governments never finds himself so much alarmed for their character and fate, as when he contemplates their propensity to this dangerous vice. He will not fail, therefore, to set a due value on any plan which, without violating the principles to which he is attached, provides a proper cure for it.

POPULAR GOVERNMENTS FAIL FOR THE SAME REASONS:

There are three diseases of past popular governments (elected by the people). These failures give ammunition to opponents of self-government.

10:2　The instability, injustice, and confusion introduced into the public councils, have, in truth, been the mortal diseases under which popular governments have everywhere perished; as they continue to be the favorite and fruitful topics from which the adversaries to liberty derive their most specious declamations.

PRIOR CONSTITUTIONS WERE BETTER BUT STILL FELL SHORT:

Many experiments in self-government had been tried in America, from the Mayflower Compact to the individual State constitutions. While some were improvements, did any of them correct the weaknesses inherent to democratic forms of government?

10:3　The valuable improvements made by the American constitutions on the popular models, both ancient and modern, cannot certainly be too much admired; but it would be an unwarrantable partiality, to contend that they have as effectually obviated the danger on this side, as was wished and expected.

UNSTABLE GOVERNMENTS VIOLATE RIGHTS:

An "interested majority" makes selfish decisions instead of what's best for the nation. Have the various American governments descended into overbearing majorities?

10:4　Complaints are everywhere heard from our most considerate and virtuous citizens, equally the friends of public and private faith, and of public and personal liberty, that our governments are too unstable, that the public good is disregarded in the conflicts of rival parties, and that measures are too often decided, not according to the rules of justice and the rights of the minor party, but by the superior force of an interested and overbearing majority.

Sadly, the records show that there is truth to these complaints.

10:5　However anxiously we may wish that these complaints had no foundation, the evidence, of known facts will not permit us to deny that they are in some degree true.

FACTIONS CREATE DISTRUST:

Imperfect government has increased distrust among the people who fear for their rights. Like-minded people want to break away into factions.

10:6　It will be found, indeed, on a candid review of our situation, that some of the distresses under which we labor have been erroneously charged on the operation of our governments; but it will be found, at the same time, that other causes will not alone account for many of our heaviest misfortunes; and, particularly, for that prevailing and increasing distrust of public engagements, and alarm for private rights, which are echoed from one end of the continent to the other. These must be chiefly, if not wholly, effects of the unsteadiness and injustice with which a factious spirit has tainted our public administrations.

FACTION DEFINED:

A faction acts in violation of the rights and interests of others. How does Madison define a faction?

10:7　By a faction, I understand a number of citizens, whether amounting to a majority or a minority of the whole, who are united and actuated by some common impulse of passion, or of interest, adverse to the rights of other citizens, or to the permanent and aggregate interests of the community.

TWO WAYS TO CURE FACTIONS:

10:8　There are two methods of curing the mischiefs of faction: the one, by removing its causes; the other, by controlling its effects.

REMOVING THE ROOT CAUSE:

Either destroy liberty or force everyone to think the same. Neither is good.

10:9　There are again two methods of removing the causes of faction: the one, by destroying the liberty which is essential to its existence; the other, by giving to every citizen the same opinions, the same passions, and the same interests.[36]

35　*faction:* Small group of people within a larger group that is contentious and self-serving against the rules, authority or rights of the whole.

36　*Editors' Note:* Presented here (10:9-13) is an argument against the ideas of socialism or government force to control and change the people. Such top-down control seeks to nullify the natural diversity of ability and desire in humans from which inequalities emerge. Governments that force equality, especially

CAN'T DESTROY LIBERTY:

Destroying liberty is not a viable solution. It is as needful to political life as air is to fire.

10:10 It could never be more truly said than of the first remedy, that it was worse than the disease. Liberty is to faction what air is to fire, an aliment without which it instantly expires. But it could not be less folly to abolish liberty, which is essential to political life, because it nourishes faction, than it would be to wish the annihilation of air, which is essential to animal life, because it imparts to fire its destructive agency.

HUMAN NATURE: CAN'T FORCE ALL TO THINK THE SAME:

Government cannot force people to be all alike. Is changing people's opinions, passions, and interests even possible?

10:11 The second expedient is as impracticable as the first would be unwise. As long as the reason of man continues fallible, and he is at liberty to exercise it, different opinions will be formed. As long as the connection subsists between his reason and his self-love, his opinions and his passions will have a reciprocal influence on each other; and the former will be objects to which the latter will attach themselves.

PROTECT LIVES, PROPERTY, MATERIAL WELL BEING:

This "first object" of government constrains it from violating people's rights.

10:12 The diversity in the faculties of men, from which the rights of property originate, is not less an insuperable obstacle to a uniformity of interests. The protection of these faculties is the first object of government.

UNEQUAL ABILITIES LEAD TO UNEQUAL OUTCOMES:

Self-interest and views will differ from man to man, thereby ensuring perpetual divisions in society.

10:13 From the protection of different and unequal faculties of acquiring property, the possession of different degrees and kinds of property immediately results; and from the influence of these on the sentiments and views of the respective proprietors, ensues a division of the society into different interests and parties.

CAUSES OF FACTION ARE PART OF HUMAN NATURE:

Factions are part of human nature. Is it a natural human tendency to align with one faction or another?

10:14 The latent causes of faction are thus sown in the nature of man; and we see them everywhere brought into different degrees of activity, according to the different circumstances of civil society.

FAMOUS MADISON QUOTE—REASONS FOR FACTIONS AND PARTIES:

10:15 A zeal for different opinions concerning religion, concerning government, and many other points, as well of speculation as of practice; an attachment to different leaders ambitiously contending for pre-eminence and power; or to persons of other descriptions whose fortunes have been interesting to the human passions, have, in turn, divided mankind into parties, inflamed them with mutual animosity, and rendered them much more disposed to vex and oppress each other than to co-operate for their common good.

SO STRONG IS THIS THAT LITTLE THINGS SET IT OFF:

10:16 So strong is this propensity of mankind to fall into mutual animosities, that where no substantial occasion presents itself, the most frivolous and fanciful distinctions have been sufficient to kindle their unfriendly passions and excite their most violent conflicts.

TRUE LIBERTY CREATES UNEQUAL PROPERTY— UNEQUAL PROPERTY CREATES JEALOUSIES:

The main reason for the uprising of angry factions is the unequal distribution of property.

10:17 But the most common and durable source of factions has been the various and unequal distribution of property. Those who hold and those who are without property have ever formed distinct interests in society. Those who are creditors, and those who are debtors, fall under a like discrimination. A landed interest, a **manufacturing**[37] interest, a mercantile interest, a moneyed interest, with many lesser interests, grow up of necessity in civilized nations, and divide them into different classes, actuated by different sentiments and views.

GOVERNMENTS ARE CREATED TO PROTECT THE COMMON-LAW RIGHTS OF ALL PARTIES:

10:18 The regulation of these various and interfering interests forms the principal task of modern legislation, and involves the spirit of party and faction in the necessary and ordinary operations of the government.

---

economic equality, are adhering to the doctrines of socialism or communism. Sam Adams said of these, "The Utopian schemes of levelling [take from the haves, give to the have nots], and a community of goods [all property is shared], are as visionary and impracticable as those which vest all property in the Crown, are arbitrary, despotic, and in our government, unconstitutional. Now, what property can the colonists be conceived to have, if their money may be granted away by others, without their consent?" (Letter to Dennys De Berdt, January 12, 1768).

37 *manufacturing:* Using raw materials to create finished goods.

UNBIASED GOVERNMENT NEEDED TO MANAGE FACTIONS:

No man can be his own judge. A body of many men is better suited for general tasks to prevent self-interested legislation.

10:19 No man is allowed to be a judge in his own cause, because his interest would certainly bias his, and, not improbably, corrupt his integrity.

Whose interests should government protect first?

10:20 With equal, nay with greater reason, a body of men are unfit to be both judges and parties at the same time; yet what are many of the most important acts of legislation, but so many judicial determinations, not indeed concerning the rights of single persons, but concerning the rights of large bodies of citizens? And what are the different classes of legislators but advocates and parties to the causes which they determine?

FACTIONS AND PRIVATE DEBTS:

Factions in the form of bodies of men should not be judges and defendants at the same time. Should the most powerful faction prevail over justice?

10:21 Is a law proposed concerning private debts? It is a question to which the creditors are parties on one side and the debtors on the other. Justice ought to hold the balance between them. Yet the parties are, and must be, themselves the judges; and the most numerous party, or, in other words, the most powerful faction must be expected to prevail.

COMPETING FACTIONS:

Factions often form from intervention into free trade by the various classes or by the government.

10:22 Shall domestic manufactures be encouraged, and in what degree, by restrictions on foreign manufactures? are questions which would be differently decided by the landed and the manufacturing classes, and probably by neither with a sole regard to justice and the public good.

UNFAIR TAXATION:

Unfair taxation is the major source of unfair government force. Do property taxes secure fairness, or help inflame the conflicts?

10:23 The apportionment of taxes on the various descriptions of property is an act which seems to require the most exact impartiality; yet there is, perhaps, no legislative act in which greater opportunity and temptation are given to a predominant party to trample on the rules of justice. Every shilling with which they overburden the inferior number, is a shilling saved to their own pockets

POLITICAL FACTIONS ARE EVER PRESENT:

Can we trust that good political leadership will always be present to support the best interests of the whole?

10:24 It is in vain to say that enlightened statesmen will be able to adjust these clashing interests, and render them all subservient to the public good. Enlightened statesmen will not always be at the helm. Nor, in many cases, can such an adjustment be made at all without taking into view indirect and remote considerations, which will rarely prevail over the immediate interest which one party may find in disregarding the rights of another or the good of the whole.

CONCLUSION: CAUSE OF FACTIONS IS HERE TO STAY

The *cause* of faction can't be removed. What, then, can be controlled?

10:25 The inference to which we are brought is, that the CAUSES of faction cannot be removed, and that relief is only to be sought in the means of controlling its EFFECTS.

THE EFFECT OF FACTION MUST BE CONTROLLED:

Factions in the minority are defeated by republican principles (being outvoted by the majority).

10:26 If a faction consists of less than a majority, relief is supplied by the republican principle, which enables the majority to defeat its sinister views by regular vote. It may clog the administration, it may convulse the society; but it will be unable to execute and mask its violence under the forms of the Constitution.

MAJORITY COULD TRAMPLE RIGHTS OF MINORITY:

Could the largest faction destroy the people's rights to achieve its own projects and goals?

10:27 When a majority is included in a faction, the form of popular government, on the other hand, enables it to sacrifice to its ruling passion or interest both the public good and the rights of other citizens.

CORRECT PRINCIPLES WILL PREVAIL REGARDING FACTIONS:

The great object of government is to prevent majority rule to trample rights, or to act in violation of correct principles. Private rights must be secured.

10:28 To secure the public good and private rights against the danger of such a faction, and at the same time to preserve the spirit and the form of popular government, is then the great object to which our inquiries are directed. Let me add that it is the great **desideratum**[38] by which this form of government can be rescued from the opprobrium under which it has so

---

38 *desideratum:* Something that is needed, wanted, or required.

long labored, and be recommended to the esteem and adoption of mankind.

TWO WAYS TO PREVENT ABUSE BY MAJORITY:

10:29 By what means is this object attainable? Evidently by one of two only. Either the existence of the same passion or interest in a majority at the same time must be prevented, or the majority, having such coexistent passion or interest, must be rendered, by their number and local situation, unable to concert and carry into effect schemes of oppression.

MORALS AND RELIGION CAN'T TEMPER HOSTILE FACTIONS:

10:30 If the impulse and the opportunity be suffered to coincide, we well know that neither moral nor religious motives can be relied on as an adequate control. They are not found to be such on the injustice and violence of individuals, and lose their efficacy in proportion to the number combined together, that is, in proportion as their efficacy becomes needful.

DEMOCRACY DEFINED— CAN'T STOP EVIL FACTIONS:

A democracy is rule by the majority. Can we conclude that pure democracies are not able to protect minority rights?

10:31 From this view of the subject it may be concluded that a pure democracy, by which I mean a society consisting of a small number of citizens, who assemble and administer the government in person, can admit of no cure for the mischiefs of faction. A common passion or interest will, in almost every case, be felt by a majority of the whole; a communication and concert result from the form of government itself; and there is nothing to check the inducements to sacrifice the weaker party or an obnoxious individual.

PURE DEMOCRACY CAN'T AND WON'T WORK:

Democracies are spectacles of turbulence that don't last very long.

10:32 Hence it is that such democracies have ever been spectacles of turbulence and contention; have ever been found incompatible with personal security or the rights of property; and have in general been as short in their lives as they have been violent in their deaths.[39]

"ONE SIZE FITS ALL" NEVER WORKS:

Equal rights does not lead to a natural adoption of group-think where everyone suddenly has equal interests, passions, abilities, and opinions.

10:33 Theoretic politicians, who have patronized this species of government, have erroneously supposed that by reducing mankind to a perfect equality in their political rights, they would, at the same time, be perfectly equalized and assimilated in their possessions, their opinions, and their passions.

REPUBLICAN FORM DEFINED—PROMISES THE CURE:

10:34 A republic, by which I mean a government in which the scheme of representation takes place, opens a different prospect, and promises the cure for which we are seeking. Let us examine the points in which it varies from pure democracy, and we shall comprehend both the nature of the cure and the efficacy which it must derive from the Union.

DIFFERENCE BETWEEN DEMOCRACY AND REPUBLIC:

Two points: Political power is delegated to small numbers elected to do the job. Second, this pattern or system can be duplicated with effectiveness over large areas and nations.

10:35 The two great points of difference between a democracy and a republic are: first, the delegation of the government, in the latter, to a small number of citizens elected by the rest; secondly, the greater number of citizens, and greater sphere of country, over which the latter may be extended.

REPUBLIC BENEFITS ALL:

Elected representatives seek what is good for the people, hoping to build the society and win reelection. In democracies the leaders seek what will keep them in power at the expense of minority viewpoints.

10:36 The effect of the first difference is, on the one hand, to refine and enlarge the public views, by passing them through the medium of a chosen body of citizens, whose wisdom may best discern the true interest of their country, and whose patriotism and love of justice will be least likely to sacrifice it to temporary or partial considerations. Under such a regulation, it may well happen that the public voice, pronounced by the representatives of the people, will be more consonant to the public good than if pronounced by the people themselves, convened for the purpose.

Sinister representatives have a harder time being elected, so their rise to power must be built on lies and deceit.

10:37 On the other hand, the effect may be inverted. Men of factious tempers, of local prejudices, or of sinister designs, may, by intrigue, by corruption, or by other means, first obtain the suffrages, and then betray the interests, of the people.

LARGE NATION BEST FOR REPUBLICAN FORM:

A large nation has more qualified people to choose from for public office.

---

39 *Editors' Note:* John Adams said it succinctly—"There never was a democracy yet that did not commit suicide." Letter to John Taylor (1814).

10:38 The question resulting is, whether small or extensive republics are more favorable to the election of proper guardians of the public weal;[40] and it is clearly decided in favor of the latter by two obvious considerations:

FINDING THE RIGHT RATIO:
The number of representatives needs be large enough to prevent conspiracies but sufficiently restricted to prevent confusion or outright manipulation from having too many.

10:39 In the first place, it is to be remarked that, however small the republic may be, the representatives must be raised to a certain number, in order to guard against the cabals of a few; and that, however large it may be, they must be limited to a certain number, in order to guard against the confusion of a multitude.

RATIO OF REPRESENTATIVE TO VOTERS:
In 1789 the ratio was set at one member of the House for every 30,000 people in a State. Today it is one representative for about 760,000.

10:40 Hence, the number of representatives in the two cases not being in proportion to that of the two constituents, and being proportionally greater in the small republic, it follows that, if the proportion of fit characters be not less in the large than in the small republic, the former will present a greater option, and consequently a greater probability of a fit choice.

UNWORTHY MEN HAVE HARDER TIME IN LARGE REPUBLIC:
The people are more likely to elect good leaders when the people's power to vote is secure.

10:41 In the next place, as each representative will be chosen by a greater number of citizens in the large than in the small republic, it will be more difficult for unworthy candidates to practice with success the vicious arts by which elections are too often carried; and the suffrages of the people being more free, will be more likely to centre in men who possess the most attractive merit and the most diffusive and established characters.

PROBLEMS ENCOUNTERED WHEN SETTING THE NUMBER OF REPRESENTATIVES:
Too many representatives means too little knowledge about local issues. Too few means inability to deal with national issues.

10:42 It must be confessed that in this, as in most other cases, there is a mean, on both sides of which inconveniences will be found to lie. By enlarging too much the number of electors, you render the too little acquainted with all their local circumstances and lesser interests; as by reducing it too much,

you render him unduly attached to these, and too little fit to comprehend and pursue great and national objects.

BALANCING BURDENS BETWEEN FEDERAL AND STATE:
The Constitution puts the more broad and national burdens on the federal representatives and leaves the local issues to the State legislatures.

10:43 The federal Constitution forms a happy combination in this respect; the great and aggregate interests being referred to the national, the local and particular to the State legislatures.

FACTIONS LESS DANGEROUS IN LARGE NATION:
A large republic spread over a large area is less vulnerable to factions.

10:44 The other point of difference is, the greater number of citizens and extent of territory which may be brought within the compass of republican than of democratic government; and it is this circumstance principally which renders factious combinations less to be dreaded in the former than in the latter.

SMALLER SOCIETIES WILL OPPRESS MORE EASILY:
A small society tends to have more one-sided majorities in same party.

10:45 The smaller the society, the fewer probably will be the distinct parties and interests composing it; the fewer the distinct parties and interests, the more frequently will a majority be found of the same party; and the smaller the number of individuals composing a majority, and the smaller the compass within which they are placed, the more easily will they concert and execute their plans of oppression.

HAVING MORE PEOPLE AND INTERESTS PROTECTS RIGHTS:
10:46 Extend the sphere, and you take in a greater variety of parties and interests; you make it less probable that a majority of the whole will have a common motive to invade the rights of other citizens; or if such a common motive exists, it will be more difficult for all who feel it to discover their own strength, and to act in unison with each other.

GREATER NUMBERS INCREASES COMPLEXITY OF CONSPIRACY:
Conspiring people have a harder time plotting when so many more people are involved in every step of their dishonorable purposes.

---

40 *weal:* The well-being, prosperity or happiness of a people or person.

10:47   Besides other impediments, it may be remarked that, where there is a <u>consciousness of unjust</u> or dishonorable <u>purposes</u>, communication is always checked by <u>distrust</u> in proportion to the <u>number</u> whose concurrence is necessary.

CONCLUSION: FACTIONS ARE BEST CONTROLLED IN A REPUBLIC:

As a republic is better over a democracy to control factions, so is a Union better over the States, and many parties over a few.

10:48   Hence, it clearly appears, that the <u>same advantage which a republic has over a democracy</u>, in controlling the effects of faction, is enjoyed by a large [republic] over a small republic,—is <u>enjoyed by the Union</u> <u>over</u> the <u>States</u> composing it. Does the advantage consist in the substitution of representatives whose enlightened views and virtuous sentiments render them superior to local prejudices and schemes of injustice? It will not be denied that the <u>representation of the Union</u> will be <u>most likely</u> to possess these requisite endowments. <u>Does it consist in the greater security afforded by a greater variety of parties</u>, against the event of any one party being able to outnumber and oppress the rest? In an <u>equal degree does the increased variety of parties comprised within the Union, increase this security</u>. Does it, in fine, consist in the greater obstacles opposed to the concert and accomplishment of the <u>secret wishes</u> of an <u>unjust</u> and interested majority? Here, again, the extent of the <u>Union gives it the most palpable advantage</u>.

VARIETY OF SECTS PREVENTS RELIGIOUS FACTIONS:

A large republic can prevent factious leaders from using religion to make demands on the government.

10:49   The influence of <u>factious leaders</u> may kindle a flame within their particular States, but will be <u>unable</u> to <u>spread</u> a general <u>conflagration</u> through the other States. A religious sect may degenerate into a political faction in a part of the Confederacy; but the <u>variety of sects</u> dispersed over the entire face of it must <u>secure the national councils</u> against any danger from that source.

"WICKED PROJECTS" THAT FACTIONS MIGHT DEMAND:

What are some of the outrageous demands a faction might make?

10:50   A <u>rage for paper money</u>, for an <u>abolition of debts</u>, for an <u>equal division of property</u>, or for any other improper or wicked project, will be less apt to pervade the whole body of the Union than a particular member of it; in the same proportion as such a malady is more likely to taint a particular county or district, than an entire State.

CONSTITUTION IS BEST REMEDY FOR DISEASES OF REPUBLIC:

The new Constitution is the best prevention and remedy for factions and diseases likely to infect a republican form of government.

10:51   In the extent and proper structure of the Union, therefore, we <u>behold a republican remedy for the diseases</u> most incident to republican <u>government</u>. And according to the degree of pleasure and pride we feel in being republicans, ought to be our <u>zeal in cherishing the spirit and</u> supporting the character of <u>Federalists</u>.

—Publius

Review Questions

1. What is the definition of faction? (10:7)

2. What are the two methods to remove the cause of factions? (10:9)

3. Is either of the prior two processes a workable option? (10:10–11)

4. What is the first object of government? (10:12)

5. Can government compel unequal people to work, create and produce equally? (10:13)

6. Are the causes of faction part of human nature? (10:14)

7. What are some causes of factions? (10:15–17, 19–23, 49)

8. Can the cause of faction be removed? (10:25)

9. Can the majority constitute a faction? Would this allow rights of the minority to be trampled? (10:27–28)

10. What are two ways to prevent bullying and abuse by the majority? (10:29)

11. Can morals, religion, or democracy prevent abuse? (10:30–33)

12. What is the definition of pure democracy? (10:31–32)

13. What is the definition of a republic? (10:34)

14. What promises the cure for bullying by the majority? (10:34)

15. What is the difference between a republic and a democracy? (10:36)

16. When it comes to a republic, is more land and more people better? (10:44–47)

17. What form of government is best suited to control factions? (10:51)

FEDERALIST NO. 11

NAVAL POWER WITH PROTECT THE UNION: A strong navy will protect the Union and commerce both locally and internationally. Protecting the waterways will help America grow into a superpower. The disunited States are incapable of establishing themselves in this manner. Likewise, without the strength of a Union the individual States will be vulnerable to the dictates of the more powerful nations of Europe. These nations already reign supreme over the American, Asian, and African nations.

By Alexander Hamilton—November 24, 1787

A UNION BENEFITS LOCAL AND FOREIGN TRADE:

11:1 THE importance of the Union, in a commercial light, is one of those points about which there is least room to entertain a difference of opinion, and which has, in fact, commanded the most general assent of men who have any acquaintance with the subject. This applies as well to our intercourse with foreign countries as with each other.

EUROPEAN DOMINATION OF AMERICAN FOREIGN TRADE:

Europe is aware of the growth of American trade overseas. So long as America is weak, Europe could interfere. How did they try to hamper America's trade?

11:2 There are appearances to authorize a supposition that the adventurous spirit, which distinguishes the commercial character of America, has already excited uneasy sensations in several of the maritime powers of Europe. They seem to be apprehensive of our too great interference in that carrying trade, which is the support of their navigation and the foundation of their naval strength. Those of them which have colonies in America look forward to what this country is capable of becoming, with painful solicitude. They foresee the dangers that may threaten their American dominions from the neighborhood of States, which have all the dispositions, and would possess all the means, requisite to the creation of a powerful marine.

EUROPE PROMOTES DIVISION IN AMERICA:

Division keeps the nation weak in its own waters and internationally.

11:3 Impressions of this kind will naturally indicate the policy of fostering divisions among us, and of depriving us, as far as possible, of an ACTIVE COMMERCE in our own bottoms.

This would answer the threefold purpose of preventing our interference in their navigation, of monopolizing the profits of our trade, and of clipping the wings by which we might soar to a dangerous greatness.

EASY TO PROVE POLITICAL MANEUVERINGS:

Europe's control over our commerce can be blamed on their ministers.

11:4 Did not prudence forbid the detail, it would not be difficult to trace, by facts, the workings of this policy to the cabinets of ministers.

A strong Union can force positive change.

11:5 If we continue united, we may counteract a policy so unfriendly to our prosperity in a variety of ways.

AMERICA'S HOME MARKET OF THREE MILLION CONSUMERS:

Unified trade polices would entice foreign trade to our shores.

11:6 By prohibitory regulations, extending, at the same time, throughout the States, we may oblige foreign countries to bid against each other, for the privileges of our markets. This assertion will not appear **chimerical**[41] to those who are able to appreciate the importance of the markets of three millions of people—increasing in rapid progression, for the most part exclusively addicted to agriculture, and likely from local circumstances to remain so—to any manufacturing nation; and the immense difference there would be to the trade and navigation of such a nation, between a direct communication in its own ships, and an indirect conveyance of its products and returns, to and from America, in the ships of another country.

GREAT ADVANTAGES OVER BRITAIN IF UNITED:

A strong Union can help America negotiate better trade deals with Britain. What role would the Dutch play in that?

11:7 Suppose, for instance, we had a government in America, capable of excluding Great Britain (with whom we have at present no treaty of commerce) from all our ports; what would be the probable operation of this step upon her politics? Would it not enable us to negotiate, with the fairest prospect of success, for commercial privileges of the most valuable and extensive kind, in the dominions of that kingdom?

WOULD BRITAIN TRULY BENEFIT FROM THE DUTCH?

11:8 When these questions have been asked, upon other occasions, they have received a plausible, but not a solid or satisfactory answer. It has been said that prohibitions on our part would produce no change in the system of Britain, because

---

41 *chimerical:* Imaginary, vainly conceived, can have no existence except in thought.

she could prosecute her trade with us through the medium of the Dutch, who would be her immediate customers and paymasters for those articles which were wanted for the supply of our markets.

Britain loses advantages by hiring the Dutch as the carrier.

11:9 But would not her navigation be materially injured by the loss of the important advantage of being her own carrier in that trade?

The Dutch would profit more than the British.

11:10 Would not the principal part of its profits be intercepted by the Dutch, as a compensation for their agency and risk?

Hiring the Dutch further reduces British profits.

11:11 Would not the mere circumstance of freight occasion a considerable deduction?

Increased competition would also reduce Britain's profits.

11:12 Would not so circuitous an intercourse facilitate the competitions of other nations, by enhancing the price of British commodities in our markets, and by transferring to other hands the management of this interesting branch of the British commerce?

BRITAIN WON'T RISK LOSING TRADE:
Pressuring Britain to relax its trade policies gives America greater access to the West Indies.

11:13 A mature consideration of the objects suggested by these questions will justify a belief that the real disadvantages to Great Britain from such a state of things, conspiring with the pre-possessions of a great part of the nation in favor of the American trade, and with the importunities of the West India islands, would produce a relaxation in her present system, and would let us into the enjoyment of privileges in the markets of those islands elsewhere, from which our trade would derive the most substantial benefits.

Relaxed British system would have good impact on other nations. They will offer concessions for good trade deals as well.

11:14 Such a point gained from the British government, and which could not be expected without an equivalent in exemptions and immunities in our markets, would be likely to have a correspondent effect on the conduct of other nations, who would not be inclined to see themselves altogether supplanted in our trade.

NEED FOR A FEDERAL NAVY:
A navy will strengthen American influence at home and overseas. Where would a navy have particular influence?

11:15 A further resource for influencing the conduct of European nations toward us, in this respect, would arise from the establishment of a federal navy. There can be no doubt that the continuance of the Union under an efficient government would put it in our power, at a period not very distant, to create a navy which, if it could not vie with those of the great maritime powers, would at least be of respectable weight if thrown into the scale of either of two contending parties. This would be more peculiarly the case in relation to operations in the West Indies.

SHIFTING THE BALANCE OF POWER:
A merchant marine will secure our foreign trade.

11:16 A few ships of the line, sent opportunely to the reinforcement of either side, would often be sufficient to decide the fate of a campaign, on the event of which interests of the greatest magnitude were suspended. Our position is, in this respect, a most commanding one.

PRACTICAL POLITICS MADE POSSIBLE:
American power consolidated into a strong Union will dictate European trade in this hemisphere.

11:17 And if to this consideration we add that of the usefulness of supplies from this country, in the prosecution of military operations in the West Indies, it will readily be perceived that a situation so favorable would enable us to bargain with great advantage for commercial privileges. A price would be set not only upon our friendship, but upon our neutrality. By a steady adherence to the Union we may hope, erelong, to become the arbiter of Europe in America, and to be able to incline the balance of European competitions in this part of the world as our interest may dictate.

WEAK NATIONS COMPELLED TO TAKE SIDES:
Without a united America could foreign nations pull us into their wars and prevent us from being neutral?

11:18 But in the reverse of this eligible situation, we shall discover that the rivalships of the parts would make them checks upon each other, and would frustrate all the tempting advantages which nature has kindly placed within our reach. In a state so insignificant our commerce would be a prey to the wanton intermeddlings of all nations at war with each other; who, having nothing to fear from us, would with little scruple or remorse, supply their wants by depredations on our property as often as it fell in their way.

CAN'T BE NEUTRAL:
A weak nation forfeits the privilege of being neutral.

11:19 The rights of neutrality will only be respected when they are defended by an adequate power. A nation, despicable by its weakness, forfeits even the privilege of being neutral.

STRONG UNION DISRUPTS FOREIGN MONOPOLIES:

How does a strong Union of States and navy protect America from monopolies by other nations?

11:20   Under a vigorous national government, the natural strength and resources of the country, directed to a common interest, would baffle all the combinations of European jealousy to restrain our growth. This situation would even take away the motive to such combinations, by inducing an impracticability of success. An active commerce, an extensive navigation, and a flourishing marine would then be the offspring of moral and physical necessity. We might defy the little arts of the little politicians to control or vary the irresistible and unchangeable course of nature.

COMMERCIAL POWER WILL DIE WITHOUT UNION:

Free enterprise that thrived even under disunion under the Confederation would be lost. A disunited America will be weak.

11:21   But in a state of disunion, these combinations might exist and might operate with success. It would be in the power of the maritime nations, availing themselves of our universal impotence, to prescribe the conditions of our political existence; and as they have a common interest in being our carriers, and still more in preventing our becoming theirs, they would in all probability combine to embarrass our navigation in such a manner as would in effect destroy it, and confine us to a PASSIVE COMMERCE. We should then be compelled to content ourselves with the first price of our commodities, and to see the profits of our trade snatched from us to enrich our enemies and persecutors.

SPIRIT OF ENTERPRISE CANNOT BE SAVED WITHOUT A UNION:

11:22   That unequaled spirit of enterprise, which signalizes the genius of the American merchants and navigators, and which is in itself an inexhaustible mine of national wealth, would be stifled and lost, and poverty and disgrace would overspread a country which, with wisdom, might make herself the admiration and envy of the world.

UNION GUARDS WATER RIGHTS:

Fishing and navigation rights could be lost under disunion. Without a Union, how might others nations take advantage of America?

11:23   There are rights of great moment to the trade of America which are rights of the Union—I allude to the fisheries, to the navigation of the lakes, and to that of the Mississippi. The dissolution of the Confederacy would give room for delicate questions concerning the future existence of these rights; which the interest of more powerful partners would hardly fail to solve to our disadvantage.

EUROPEAN CONTROL OVER WATERWAYS:

11:24   The disposition of Spain with regard to the Mississippi needs no comment. France and Britain are concerned with us in the fisheries, and view them as of the utmost moment to their navigation. They, of course, would hardly remain long indifferent to that decided mastery, of which experience has shown us to be possessed in this valuable branch of traffic, and by which we are able to undersell those nations in their own markets. What more natural than that they should be disposed to exclude from the lists such dangerous competitors?

STRONG NAVY HELPS INTERSTATE COMMERCE:

11:25   This branch of trade ought not to be considered as a partial benefit. All the navigating States may, in different degrees, advantageously participate in it, and under circumstances of a greater extension of mercantile capital, would not be unlikely to do it. As a nursery of seamen, it now is, or when time shall have more nearly assimilated the principles of navigation in the several States, will become, a universal resource. To the establishment of a navy, it must be indispensable.

STRONG NAVY NEEDED TO PROTECT RIGHTS:

A protected coast helps America in many ways. Individual States not well equipped to do this.

11:26   To this great national object, a NAVY, union will contribute in various ways. Every institution will grow and flourish in proportion to the quantity and extent of the means concentred towards its formation and support.

NATIONAL NAVY BETTER IN EVERY WAY:

Each section of the country is needed to equip a strong navy, and each would benefit.

11:27   A navy of the United States, as it would embrace the resources of all, is an object far less remote than a navy of any single State or partial confederacy, which would only embrace the resources of a single part. It happens, indeed, that different portions of confederated America possess each some peculiar advantage for this essential establishment.

Southern wood and products are the best.

11:28   The more southern States furnish in greater abundance certain kinds of naval stores—tar, pitch, and turpentine. Their wood for the construction of ships is also of a more solid and lasting texture. The difference in the duration of the ships of which the navy might be composed, if chiefly constructed of Southern wood, would be of signal importance, either in the view of naval strength or of national economy.

Middle States good for iron, Northern States good for seamen.

11:29   Some of the Southern and of the Middle States yield a greater plenty of iron, and of better quality. Seamen must chiefly be drawn from the Northern hive.

11:30   The necessity of naval protection to external or maritime commerce does not require a particular elucidation, no more than the conduciveness of that species of commerce to the prosperity of a navy.

INTERSTATE FLOW OF GOODS BENEFITS ALL:
Free trade between the States will prosper them all. What are some advantages of free interstate commerce?

11:31   An unrestrained intercourse between the States themselves will advance the trade of each by an interchange of their respective productions, not only for the supply of reciprocal wants at home, but for exportation to foreign markets. The veins of commerce in every part will be replenished, and will acquire additional motion and vigor from a free circulation of the commodities of every part. Commercial enterprise will have much greater scope, from the diversity in the productions of different States. When the staple of one fails from a bad harvest or unproductive crop, it can call to its aid the staple of another.

GREATER VARIETY OF GOODS OFFERED WITH UNION:
A variety of goods improves foreign trade, and a united States will secure more reliability and competitive power than single States.

11:32   The variety, not less than the value, of products for exportation contributes to the activity of foreign commerce. It can be conducted upon much better terms with a large number of materials of a given value than with a small number of materials of the same value; arising from the competitions of trade and from the fluctuations of markets. Particular articles may be in great demand at certain periods, and unsalable at others; but if there be a variety of articles, it can scarcely happen that they should all be at one time in the latter predicament, and on this account the operations of the merchant would be less liable to any considerable obstruction or stagnation.

MERCHANTS GIVEN WIDER ZONE OF TRADE:
Without a Union there will remain trade barriers. Is fair trade even possible under a disunited States?

11:33   The speculative trader will at once perceive the force of these observations, and will acknowledge that the aggregate balance of the commerce of the United States would bid fair to be much more favorable than that of the thirteen States without union or with partial unions.

UNDER DISUNITED STATES, COMMERCE WON'T FLOW:

11:34   It may perhaps be replied to this, that whether the States are united or disunited, there would still be an intimate intercourse between them which would answer the same ends; this intercourse would be fettered, interrupted, and narrowed by a multiplicity of causes, which in the course of these papers have been amply detailed. A unity of commercial, as well as political, interests, can only result from a unity of government.

A Union would eliminate European domination. How much of the world trade does Europe actually control?

11:35   There are other points of view in which this subject might be placed, of a striking and animating kind. But they would lead us too far into the regions of futurity, and would involve topics not proper for a newspaper discussion. I shall briefly observe, that our situation invites and our interests prompt us to aim at an ascendant in the system of American affairs.

WORLD DIVIDED INTO FOUR REGIONS OF COMMERCE:
Europe has dominated America, Africa, and Asia.

11:36   The world may politically, as well as geographically, be divided into four parts, each having a distinct set of interests. Unhappily for the other three, Europe, by her arms and by her negotiations, by force and by fraud, has, in different degrees, extended her dominion over them all. Africa, Asia, and America, have successively felt her domination. The superiority she has long maintained has tempted her to plume herself as the Mistress of the World, and to consider the rest of mankind as created for her benefit.

EUROPEAN'S DISDAIN FOR AMERICA:
They assert that "even dogs cease to bark" after living here for a while.

11:37   Men admired as profound philosophers have, in direct terms, attributed to her inhabitants a physical superiority, and have gravely asserted that all animals, and with them the human species, degenerate in America—that even dogs cease to bark after having breathed awhile in our atmosphere.

A strong Union will erase extravagances and create moderation.

11:38   Facts have too long supported these arrogant pretensions of the Europeans. It belongs to us to vindicate the honor of the human race, and to teach that assuming brother, moderation.

A UNION GIVES POWER, A DISUNION WILL DESTROY:

11:39 Union will enable us to do it. Disunion will add another victim to his triumphs.

STRONG UNION COULD BALANCE WORLD POWER:

11:40 <u>Let Americans disdain to be the instruments of European greatness</u>! Let the thirteen States, bound together in a strict and indissoluble Union, concur in erecting one <u>great American system</u>, superior to the control of all <u>transatlantic force or</u> influence, and able to dictate the <u>terms of the connection</u> between the old and the new world!

—PUBLIUS

REVIEW QUESTIONS

1. What does Europe already fear from the growth of America? (11:2)

2. Who has been fostering division in America to weaken its commerce? (11:3–4)

3. What might a Union with stronger trade policies force other trading partners to do in America? (11:6)

4. What trading advantages does a Union bring? (11:7–14)

5. What resource should America build to enhance its foreign commerce? (11:15–16)

6. What ability does a weak nation lose in a world at war? (11:18–19)

7. What are some advantages of a navy? (11:25–26)

8. How would different parts of the country help to build a navy? (11:27–30)

9. How does forming a Union help interstate commerce? (11:31–32)

10. How did Europe take control of world trade? What are the four parts? (11:36)

11. What can a strong Union do for the old and new world? (11:39–40)

FEDERALIST NO. 12

A UNION IS BEST FOR COMMERCE: One of the problems of having the States collect their own import taxes is that it pushes smugglers to bypass those checkpoints in any way they can. That loss of revenue forces the States to create revenue by some other form, even taxing the people directly. However, with a strong Union with uniform commerce rules in place, there are no advantages to smuggling between the States. Only foreign traders would seek to smuggle through the more easily defensible sea coast ports. With the Union encouraging an increase in profitable trade, its revenue will grow, increasing the nation's power and influence, which will in turn create even more prosperity and growth.

By Alexander Hamilton—November 27, 1787

A UNION IS BEST FOR BUILDING PROSPERITY:

12:1 THE effects of <u>Union</u> upon the commercial prosperity of the States have been sufficiently delineated. Its tendency to <u>promote</u> the <u>interests of revenue</u> will be the subject of our present inquiry.

COMMERCE GROWS STRONGER IN A UNION:
A Union has more to draw from to grow its wealth than do individual States. Does energetic commerce improve a nation's wealth?

12:2 The <u>prosperity of commerce</u> is now perceived and acknowledged by all enlightened statesmen to be the most useful as well as the most <u>productive source of national wealth</u>, and has accordingly become a primary object of their political cares.

PROFITS DRIVE NATIONAL ECONOMY FORWARD:
Free trade with precious metals is the key to prosperity for both agriculture and commerce The universal appeal of precious metals makes it the most stable form of currency.

12:3 By <u>multiplying</u> the <u>means</u> of <u>gratification</u>, by promoting the introduction and <u>circulation</u> of the <u>precious metals</u>, those darling objects of human avarice and enterprise, it serves to **vivify**[42] and <u>invigorate</u> the <u>channels of industry</u>, and to make them <u>flow with greater activity</u> and copiousness. The assiduous merchant, the laborious husbandman, the active mechanic, and the industrious manufacturer,—all orders of men, look forward with <u>eager expectation</u> and growing alacrity to this <u>pleasing reward of their toils</u>.

VALUE OF LAND GROWS IN A FREE MARKET:
Agriculture and commerce are not jealous rivals in a free market. As commerce flourishes what happens to land values?

12:4 The often-agitated question between <u>agriculture</u> and <u>commerce</u> has, from indubitable experience, received a decision which has silenced the rivalship that once subsisted between them, and has <u>proved</u>, to the satisfaction of their

---

42 *vivify:* Enliven or animate.

friends, that their <u>interests</u> are <u>intimately blended</u> and inter-woven. It has been found in various countries that, in propor-tion as <u>commerce has flourished</u>, <u>land</u> has <u>risen in value</u>. And how could it have happened otherwise?

FREE MARKET IS NATION'S BEST ECONOMIC TOOL:

The free market is a nation's most powerful economic tool. What does it help accomplish?

12:5   Could that which procures a freer vent for the prod-ucts of the earth, which furnishes new incitements to the <u>cul-tivation of land</u>, which is the most powerful instrument in <u>increasing the quantity of money in a state</u>—could that, in fine, which is the faithful handmaid of labor and industry, in every shape, fail to augment that article, which is the prolific parent of far the greatest part of the objects upon which they are exerted?

GREEDINESS BLINDS MEN TO BENEFITS OF FREEDOM:

Does free enterprise have enemies? Why?

12:6   It is <u>astonishing</u> that so simple a truth should <u>ever have had</u> an <u>adversary</u>; and it is one, among a multitude of proofs, how apt a spirit of <u>ill-informed jealousy</u>, or of too great ab-straction and refinement, is to lead men astray from the <u>plain-est truths</u> of reason and conviction.

ABILITY TO PAY TAXES DEPENDENT ON MONEY FLOW:

The free market keeps money moving quickly through the economy. Does this increase revenue? Why not in Germany?

12:7   The <u>ability</u> of a <u>country to pay taxes</u> must always be <u>proportioned</u>, in a great degree, to the <u>quantity of money in circulation</u>, and to the celerity with which it circulates. Com-merce, contributing to both these objects, must of necessity <u>render</u> the <u>payment of taxes easier</u>, and facilitate the requisite supplies to the treasury.

FLOURISHING BUSINESSES ENRICH A NATION:

However, inhibiting a free market, or excess taxation, thwarts prosperity.

12:8   The hereditary dominions of the <u>Emperor of Germa-ny</u> contain a great extent of fertile, cultivated, and populous territory, a large proportion of which is situated in mild and luxuriant climates. In some parts of this territory are to be found the <u>best gold and silver mines in Europe</u>. And yet, from the <u>want</u> of the fostering influence of <u>commerce</u>, that mon-arch can boast but <u>slender revenues</u>. He has several times been compelled to owe obligations to the pecuniary succors of oth-er nations for the preservation of his essential interests, and is <u>unable</u>, upon the strength of his own resources, to <u>sustain</u> a long or <u>continued war</u>.

DIRECT TAXATION HAS NOT SUCCEEDED:

More tax laws don't bring in more tax dollars. What has America learned about direct taxation?

12:9   But it is not in this aspect of the subject alone that Union will be seen to **conduce**[43] to the purpose of revenue. There are other points of view, in which its influence will ap-pear more immediate and decisive. It is evident from the state of the country, from the habits of the people, from the experi-ence we have had on the point itself, that it is <u>impracticable to raise any</u> very <u>considerable sums by direct taxation</u>.

STATES' DIRECT TAX EXPERIMENTS HAVE FAILED:

12:10   <u>Tax laws</u> have in vain been multiplied; <u>new methods</u> to enforce the collection have in vain been tried; the public expectation has been uniformly <u>disappointed</u>, and the <u>trea-suries</u> of the States have remained <u>empty</u>. The popular system of administration inherent in the nature of popular govern-ment, coinciding with the real scarcity of money incident to a <u>languid and mutilated state of trade</u>, has hitherto <u>defeated</u> every experiment for <u>extensive collections</u>, and has at length taught the different legislatures the folly of attempting them.

BRITISH SYSTEM BASED ON IMPOSTS AND EXCISE:

There are two forms of taxing: direct (on the people) or indirect (on products and services). Which form works the best?

12:11   No person acquainted with what happens in other countries will be surprised at this circumstance. In so opulent a nation as that of <u>Britain</u>, where <u>direct taxes</u> from <u>superior wealth</u> must be much <u>more tolerable</u>, and, from the vigor of the government, much more practicable, than in America, far the <u>greatest part</u> of the <u>national</u> revenue is <u>derived</u> from taxes of the <u>indirect</u> kind, from <u>imposts</u>, and from **excises**.[44] Duties on imported articles form a large branch of this latter description.

AMERICA MUST DEPEND ON DUTIES:

Vibrant commercial activity is the best source of tax revenue. The people won't tolerate intrusive taxes.

12:12   In America it is evident that <u>we must a long time de-pend</u> for the means of revenue chiefly <u>on such duties</u>. In most parts of it, excises must be confined within a narrow compass.

---

43   *conduce:* Help bring about a desirable result.

44   *excise taxes:* Taxes put on the manufacture, sale or consumption of articles that are consumed by the family such as soap, coffee, candles, gas, alcohol, tobacco, and so forth.

The genius of the people will ill brook the inquisitive and peremptory spirit of excise laws.

PERSONAL PROPERTY NEARLY IMPOSSIBLE TO TAX FAIRLY:

What activity is easier to tax?

12:13 The pockets of the farmers, on the other hand, will reluctantly yield but scanty supplies, in the unwelcome shape of <u>impositions</u> on <u>their houses</u> and <u>lands</u>; and <u>personal property is too precarious</u> and invisible a fund to be laid hold of in any other way than by the imperceptible agency of <u>taxes on consumption</u>.

REVENUE SYSTEMS BEST MANAGED IN A UNION:

Raising revenue is difficult for many reasons, and a disunion creates needless hardships. Is a Union best for a fair tax system?

12:14 If these remarks have any foundation, that state of things which will best enable us to improve and extend so valuable a resource must be best adapted to our <u>political welfare</u>. And it cannot admit of a serious doubt, that this state of things must rest on the <u>basis of a general Union</u>. As far as this would be conducive to the interests of commerce, so far it must tend to the extension of the revenue to be drawn from that source.

TAX RATES AND COLLECTION UNIFORM IN UNION:

A single government would manage rate increases on duties, and collect them, better than individual States.

12:15 As far as it would <u>contribute to rendering regulations for the collection of the duties more simple and efficacious</u>, so far it must serve to answer the purposes of making the same rate of duties more productive, and of putting it into the power of the government to increase the rate without prejudice to trade.

DISUNITED STATES MAKES SMUGGLING EASY:

Illicit trade reduces revenue. Without a Union will smuggling across State borders become easy and commonplace?

12:16 The <u>relative situation</u> of these States; <u>the number of rivers</u> with which they are intersected, and of bays that wash there shores; the facility of <u>communication</u> in every direction; the affinity of <u>language</u> and manners; the familiar <u>habits of intercourse</u>;—all these are circumstances that would conspire to render an illicit trade between them a matter of little difficulty, and would insure frequent <u>evasions of the commercial regulations</u> of <u>each other</u>.

STATES WILL REJECT OPPRESSIVE MONITORING:

A disunited States would not tolerate the loss of liberties in exchange for intense patrolling against smuggling.

12:17 The separate States or confederacies would be necessitated by <u>mutual jealousy</u> to avoid the temptations to that kind of trade by the lowness of their duties. The temper of our governments, for a long time to come, would not permit those rigorous precautions by which the European nations guard the avenues into their respective countries, as well by land as by water; and which, even there, are found insufficient obstacles to the adventurous <u>stratagems of avarice</u>.

FRENCH PATROLS THWART SMUGGLERS:

Border patrols help restrict smuggling. Would such an armed force be necessary in a disunited States?

12:18 In <u>France</u>, there is an army of <u>patrols</u> (as they are called) constantly employed to secure their fiscal regulations against the inroads of the dealers in contraband trade. Mr. Neckar computes the number of these patrols at upwards of <u>twenty thousand</u>. This shows the immense difficulty in preventing that species of traffic, where there is an inland communication, and places in a strong light the disadvantages with which the collection of duties in this country would be encumbered, if by disunion the States should be placed in a situation, with respect to each other, resembling that of France with respect to her neighbors. The arbitrary and vexatious powers with which the <u>patrols are necessarily armed</u>, would be <u>intolerable in a free country</u>.

ONE UNION HAS ONLY ONE COAST TO GUARD—THE ATLANTIC COAST:

A Union would have only one coast to protect from smuggling. Would creating a coast guard for this purpose be expensive?

12:19 If, on the contrary, there be but <u>one government</u> pervading all the States, there will be, as to the principal part of our commerce, but <u>ONE SIDE to guard</u>—the <u>ATLANTIC COAST</u>. Vessels arriving directly from foreign countries, laden with valuable cargoes, would rarely choose to hazard themselves to the complicated and critical perils which would attend attempts to unlade prior to their coming into port.

ESTABLISHING A COAST GUARD:

A few armed vessels would do the job to stop smuggling.

12:20 They would have to dread both the dangers of the coast, and of detection, as well after as before their arrival at the places of their final destination. An ordinary degree of vigilance would be competent to the prevention of any material infractions upon the rights of the revenue. A few armed vessels, judiciously stationed at the entrances of our ports, might at a small expense be made useful sentinels of the laws. And the government having the same interest to provide against violations everywhere, the co-operation of its measures in each State would have a powerful tendency to render them effectual.

ADVANTAGE OF AMERICA IS HER DISTANCE FROM EUROPE:
A Union would have natural geographical boundaries to prevent foreign smuggling. Could an individual State secure the same?

12:21   Here also we should preserve by Union, an advantage which nature holds out to us, and which would be relinquished by separation. The United States lie at a great distance from Europe, and at a considerable distance from all other places with which they would have extensive connections of foreign trade. The passage from them to us, in a few hours, or in a single night, as between the coasts of France and Britain, and of other neighboring nations, would be impracticable. This is a prodigious security against a direct contraband with foreign countries; but a circuitous contraband to one State, through the medium of another, would be both easy and safe. The difference between a direct importation from abroad, and an indirect importation through the channel of a neighboring State, in small parcels, according to time and opportunity, with the additional facilities of inland communication, must be palpable to every man of discernment.

UNION BETTER MANAGES IMPORT DUTIES:
A Union can manage import fees better than individual State governments.

12:22   It is therefore evident, that one national government would be able, at much less expense, to extend the duties on imports, beyond comparison, further than would be practicable to the States separately, or to any partial confederacies. Hitherto, I believe, it may safely be asserted, that these duties have not upon an average exceeded in any State three percent. In France they are estimated to be about fifteen percent, and in Britain the proportion is even greater.

WHISKEY TAX AS SOURCE OF REVENUE:
Taxing spirits could reduce consumption, and help improve morals and health.

12:23   There seems to be nothing to hinder their being increased in this country to at least treble their present amount. The single article of ardent spirits, under federal regulation, might be made to furnish a considerable revenue. Upon a ratio to the importation into this State, the whole quantity imported into the United States may be estimated at four millions of gallons; which, at a shilling per gallon, would produce two hundred thousand pounds. That article would well bear this rate of duty; and if it should tend to diminish the consumption of it, such an effect would be equally favorable to the agriculture, to the economy, to the morals, and to the health of the society. There is, perhaps, nothing so much a subject of national extravagance as these spirits.

INDEPENDENCE IS LOST WITHOUT REVENUE:
A nation cannot exist without revenue. Without revenue what is the outcome? Are excise taxes going to be enough?

12:24   What will be the consequence, if we are not able to avail ourselves of the resource in question in its full extent? A nation cannot long exist without revenues. Destitute of this essential support, it must resign its independence, and sink into the degraded condition of a province. This is an extremity to which no government will of choice accede.

REVENUE IS BEST RAISED FROM COMMERCIAL ACTIVITIES:
Excise taxes are very unpopular; property taxes too hard to calculate.

12:25   Revenue, therefore, must be had at all events. In this country, if the principal part be not drawn from commerce, it must fall with oppressive weight upon land. It has been already intimated that excises, in their true signification, are too little in unison with the feelings of the people, to admit of great use being made of that mode of taxation; nor, indeed, in the States where almost the sole employment is agriculture, are the objects proper for excise sufficiently numerous to permit very ample collections in that way.

CONSUMPTION TAXES:
Personal estates cannot be assessed accurately for taxing. What, then, is the only practical way to raise revenue?

12:26   Personal estate (as has been before remarked), from the difficulty in tracing it, cannot be subjected to large contributions, by any other means than by taxes on consumption. In populous cities, it may be enough the subject of conjecture, to occasion the oppression of individuals, without much aggregate benefit to the State; but beyond these circles, it must, in a great measure, escape the eye and the hand of the tax-gatherer.

LAND OWNERS WOULD END UP CARRYING REVENUE BURDEN:
If the States are not united, they won't have as many resources to draw from to raise revenue. Where would the revenue burden then fall?

12:27   As the necessities of the State, nevertheless, must be satisfied in some mode or other, the defect of other resources must throw the principal weight of public burdens on the possessors of land.

UNION OPENS ALL SOURCES OF REVENUE:
Only in a Union can the necessary revenue be realized without oppression.

12:28   And as, on the other hand, the wants of the government can never obtain an adequate supply, unless all the sources of revenue are open to its demands, the finances of the community, under such embarrassments, cannot be put into a situation consistent with its respectability or its security.

DISUNITED STATES WOULD OPPRESS FARMERS:

12:29   Thus we shall not even have the consolations of a full treasury, to atone for the oppression of that valuable class of the citizens who are employed in the cultivation of the soil. But public and private distress will keep pace with each other in gloomy concert; and unite in deploring the infatuation of those counsels which led to disunion.

—PUBLIUS

REVIEW QUESTIONS

1.   What builds national wealth better than any other kind of revenue scheme such as taxes or duties on imports? (12:1–3)

2.   What does increased commerce do for land values? (12:4–5)

3.   What does prosperity help citizens do? (12:7–8)

4.   Have new tax laws and collections helped make direct taxation succeed? (12:9–10)

5.   What illicit activity do high taxes and lengthy borders encourage? (12:16–21)

6.   Does national revenue best come from direct taxes or consumption taxes? (12:11, 25–26)

7.   Which part of society will carry the greatest tax burden if there is no Union? (12:27–29)

FEDERALIST NO. 13

A SINGLE UNION IS LESS COSTLY THAN THIRTEEN GOVERNMENTS: From a financial viewpoint it is less costly to have one national system to manage public affairs than thirteen that duplicate each other. A single national government with a single military that can expand to cover large areas is more efficient and less wasteful than thirteen State-level bureaucracies copying each other for the same ends.

By Alexander Hamilton—November 28, 1787

A UNION IS LESS COSTLY TO OPERATE:
What is least costly, shouldering the expenses of a central government as a Union, or as thirteen individual States?

13:1   AS CONNECTED with the subject of revenue, we may with propriety consider that of economy. The money saved from one object may be usefully applied to another, and there will be so much the less to be drawn from the pockets of the people. If the States are united under one government, there will be but one national **civil list**[45] to support; if they are divided into several confederacies, there will be as many different national civil lists to be provided for—and each of them, as to the principal departments, coextensive with that which would be necessary for a government of the whole.

DIVISION OF STATES INTO THREE CONFEDERACIES:
Would it take more or less effort to govern each confederacy as it would the Union?

13:2   The entire separation of the States into thirteen unconnected sovereignties is a project too extravagant and too replete with danger to have many advocates. The ideas of men who speculate upon the dismemberment of the empire seem generally turned toward three confederacies—one consisting of the four Northern, another of the four Middle, and a third of the five Southern States. There is little probability that there would be a greater number.

EACH CONFEDERACY NEEDS LARGE GOVERNMENT:
Each requires as much energy as is needed to run Britain.

13:3   According to this distribution, each confederacy would comprise an extent of territory larger than that of the kingdom of Great Britain. No well-informed man will suppose that the affairs of such a confederacy can be properly regulated by a government less comprehensive in its organs or institutions than that which has been proposed by the Convention. When the dimensions of a State attain to a certain magnitude, it requires the same energy of government and the same forms of administration which are requisite in one of much greater extent.

REPUBLICAN MODEL REPRODUCES ITSELF, WORKS FOR ALL SIZES:
A Union utilizes all the advantages offered by good government based on the republican model.

13:4   This idea admits not of precise demonstration, because there is no rule by which we can measure the momentum of

---

45   *civil list:* A list of people or funds authorized annually to fulfill the legal duties of the civil government (such as salaries for judges, secretaries, civil servants.)

civil power necessary to the government of any given number of individuals; but when we consider that the island of Britain, nearly commensurate with each of the supposed confederacies, contains about eight millions of people, and when we reflect upon the degree of authority required to direct the passions of so large a society to the public good, we shall see no reason to doubt that the like portion of power would be sufficient to perform the same task in a society far more numerous. Civil power, properly organized and exerted, is capable of diffusing its force to a very great extent; and can, in a manner, reproduce itself in every part of a great empire by a judicious arrangement of subordinate institutions.

COMMERCIAL AND GEOGRAPHICAL BOUNDARIES:
If the States fail to form a Union, what confederacies are they most likely to form?

13:5 The supposition that each confederacy into which the States would be likely to be divided would require a government not less comprehensive than the one proposed, will be strengthened by another supposition, more probable than that which presents us with three confederacies as the alternative to a general Union. If we attend carefully to geographical and commercial considerations, in conjunction with the habits and prejudices of the different States, we shall be led to conclude that in case of disunion they will most naturally league themselves under two governments.

LIKELY TO END UP AS TWO CONFEDERACIES:
13:6 The four Eastern States, from all the causes that form the links of national sympathy and connection, may with certainty be expected to unite. New York, situated as she is, would never be unwise enough to oppose a feeble and unsupported flank to the weight of that confederacy. There are other obvious reasons that would facilitate her accession to it. New Jersey is too small a State to think of being a frontier, in opposition to this still more powerful combination; nor do there appear to be any obstacles to her admission into it. Even Pennsylvania would have strong inducements to join the Northern league. An active foreign commerce, on the basis of her own navigation, is her true policy, and coincides with the opinions and dispositions of her citizens.

SOUTHERN STATES AND FOREIGN TRADE:
13:7 The more Southern States, from various circumstances, may not think themselves much interested in the encouragement of navigation. They may prefer a system which would give unlimited scope to all nations to be the carriers as well as the purchasers of their commodities.

PENNSYLVANIA BEST ALLIED WITH SOUTH:
13:8 Pennsylvania may not choose to confound her interests in a connection so adverse to her policy. As she must at all events be a frontier, she may deem it most consistent with her safety to have her exposed side turned towards the weaker power of the Southern, rather than towards the stronger power of the Northern, Confederacy. This would give her the fairest chance to avoid being the Flanders of America.[46]

13:9 Whatever may be the determination of Pennsylvania, if the Northern Confederacy includes New Jersey, there is no likelihood of more than one confederacy to the south of that State.

LESS COSTLY TO SUPPORT ONE MAIN GOVERNMENT:
It is less costly and more simple for the thirteen States to support one national government than to support thirteen individual governments.

13:10 Nothing can be more evident than that the thirteen States will be able to support a national government better than one half, or one third, or any number less than the whole. This reflection must have great weight in obviating that objection to the proposed plan, which is founded on the principle of expense; an objection, however, which, when we come to take a nearer view of it, will appear in every light to stand on mistaken ground.

DUPLICATED SERVICES ARE HARMFUL TO STATES:
Separate confederacies create many difficulties. What are some other ways a disunited States would hurt the States?

13:11 If, in addition to the consideration of a plurality of civil lists, we take into view the number of persons who must necessarily be employed to guard the inland communication between the different confederacies against illicit trade, and who in time will infallibly spring up out of the necessities of revenue; and if we also take into view the military establishments which it has been shown would unavoidably result from the jealousies and conflicts of the several nations into which the States would be divided, we shall clearly discover that a separation would be not less injurious to the economy, than to the tranquility, commerce, revenue, and liberty of every part.
—Publius

REVIEW QUESTIONS

1. What impact does a Union have on the overall cost of gov-

---

46 ***Flanders of America:*** This makes reference to an independent feudal state in the European Low Countries. It was famous for textile production and enjoyed independence and prosperity for many centuries — but it was vulnerable to invasion. When regional fighting ended in the late 1500s Flanders was split between the Dutch-held north (the leading province of the Netherlands), and the Spanish-held south.

ernment? (13:1)

2. If the States don't form a single Union, how might the States divide into confederacies? (13:2)

3. A republic can reproduce itself in which parts of a great empire? (13:4)

4. Which government is easier to support financially, one Union or three confederacies? (13:10)

5. What are the five parts of society that would be injured without a Union? (13:11)

FEDERALIST NO. 14

A REPUBLICAN FORM WORKS BEST FOR LARGE POPULATIONS: Even a nation as large as America works best with a representative government instead of a democracy. The people are secure because the general powers are very restricted, and the more intimate concerns are left to the States themselves. Advances in transportation and communication will make republicanism even more efficient and satisfactory. This path is made possible because of the courage and spirit of an exceptional and innovative people who trust their common sense more than the security of the tired old ways of the past. This paper concludes the first discussion topic by Publius, "The utility of the union to your political prosperity."

By James Madison—November 30, 1787

SUMMARY OF PREVIOUS *PAPERS*:
Factions have proven fatal to other representative or military governments. A strong Union is the best cure. Can this solution also work for a very large geographic area?

14:1 WE HAVE seen the necessity of the Union, as our bulwark against foreign danger [*see* Nos. 3, 4, 5], as the conservator of peace among ourselves [*see* Nos. 5, 6, 7, 8], as the guardian of our commerce [*see* No. 11] and other common interests, as the only substitute for those military establishments which have subverted the liberties of the Old World, and as the proper antidote for the diseases of faction, which have proved fatal to other popular governments, and of which alarming symptoms have been betrayed by our own.

DOES A REPUBLICAN FORM FAIL IN A LARGE NATION?
Critics claim a republican form won't work for America's large territory.

14:2 All that remains, within this branch of our inquiries, is to take notice of an objection that may be drawn from the great extent of country which the Union embraces. A few observations on this subject will be the more proper, as it is perceived that the adversaries of the new Constitution are availing themselves of the prevailing prejudice with regard to the <u>practicable sphere</u> of republican administration, in order to supply, by <u>imaginary difficulties</u>, the want of those solid objections which they endeavor in vain to find.

CRITICS HAVE CONFUSED THE TERMS:
Mixing up the terms "republic" and "democracy" forces false conclusions.

14:3 The error which limits republican government to a narrow district has been unfolded and refuted in preceding papers [No. 9]. I remark here only that it seems to owe its rise and prevalence chiefly to the <u>confounding of a republic</u> with a <u>democracy</u>, applying to the former reasonings drawn from the nature of the latter.

DEMOCRACY DEFINED—COMPARED TO REPUBLIC:
A republic relies on representatives to vote for the people. A democracy means everyone is present, in person, for all actions. Therefore, a democracy works best for relatively small groups.

14:4 The true distinction between these forms was also adverted to on a former occasion [No. 10]. It is, that in a <u>democracy</u>, the people meet and exercise the government <u>in person</u>; in a <u>republic</u>, they assemble and administer it by their <u>representatives</u> and agents. A <u>democracy</u>, consequently, will be confined to a <u>small spot</u>. A <u>republic</u> may be extended over a <u>large region</u>.

BLAMING A REPUBLIC FOR THE FLAWS OF A DEMOCRACY:
For lack of clear understanding, people will falsely attribute to republics many of the worst failures of democracies and monarchies.

14:5 To this accidental source of the error may be added the artifice of some celebrated authors, whose writings have had a great share in forming the modern standard of political opinions. Being subjects either of an <u>absolute</u> or <u>limited monarchy</u>, they have endeavored to heighten the advantages, or **palliate**[47] the evils of those forms, by placing in comparison the vices and defects of the republican, and by citing as specimens of the latter the <u>turbulent democracies of ancient Greece</u> and modern Italy.

---

47 **palliate:** Hide the seriousness of something.

FALSELY BLAMING REPUBLICS FOR THE MANY FLAWS OF A DEMOCRACY IS COMMON:
It's easy to attribute the flaws of democracy to a republic if the terms are confused.

14:6 Under the confusion of names, it has been an easy task to transfer to a republic observations applicable to a democracy only; and among others, the observation that it can never be established but among a small number of people, living within a small compass of territory.

TRUE REPUBLICAN GOVERNMENTS IN ANCIENT TIMES WERE VERY RARE:
Most ancient governments are thought to be republics (of the people) but are actually various failed democracies.

14:7 Such a fallacy may have been the less perceived, as most of the popular governments of antiquity were of the democratic species; and even in modern Europe, to which we owe the great principle of representation, no example is seen of a government wholly popular, and founded, at the same time, wholly on that principle.

AMERICANS DISCOVERED THE BEST REPUBLICAN FORM:
While Europe boasts about its use of democracy, American can claim its discovery of the superior republic.

14:8 If Europe has the merit of discovering this great mechanical power in government, by the simple agency of which the will of the largest political body may be concentred, and its force directed to any object which the public good requires, America can claim the merit of making the discovery the basis of unmixed and extensive republics. It is only to be lamented that any of her citizens should wish to deprive her of the additional merit of displaying its full efficacy in the establishment of the comprehensive system now under her consideration.

GEOGRAPHICAL LIMITS OF A DEMOCRACY:
A pure democracy must be small so all the people can frequently and conveniently gather to vote and act.

14:9 As the natural limit of a democracy is that distance from the central point which will just permit the most remote citizens to assemble as often as their public functions demand, and will include no greater number than can join in those functions;

GEOGRAPHICAL LIMITS OF A REPUBLIC:
A representative form must accommodate travel by the representatives to vote and act.

14:10 so the natural limit of a republic is that distance from the center which will barely allow the representatives of the people to meet as often as may be necessary for the administration of public affairs.

AMERICA'S SIZE DOES NOT HAMPER THE REPUBLICAN FORM:
For the past thirteen years representatives from the most remote States were always present for the various needs of Congress.

14:11 Can it be said that the limits of the United States exceed this distance? It will not be said by those who recollect that the Atlantic coast is the longest side of the Union, that during the term of thirteen years, the representatives of the States have been almost continually assembled, and that the members from the most distant States are not chargeable with greater intermissions of attendance than those from the States in the neighborhood of Congress.

MEASURING THE ACTUAL DIMENSIONS OF AMERICA:
Geographic distance for American representatives to travel is not very different from European governments.

14:12 That we may form a juster estimate with regard to this interesting subject, let us resort to the actual dimensions of the Union. The limits, as fixed by the treaty of peace [September 3, 1783], are: on the east the Atlantic, on the south the latitude of thirty-one degrees, on the west the Mississippi, and on the north an irregular line running in some instances beyond the forty-fifth degree, in others falling as low as the forty-second. The southern shore of Lake Erie lies below that latitude.

AVERAGE DISTANCE IS ABOUT 800 MILES:
America measures between 765 and 973 miles tall (north to south) and about 750 miles east to west (the east coast to the Mississippi River).

14:13 Computing the distance between the thirty-first and forty-fifth degrees, it amounts to nine hundred and seventy-three common miles; computing it from thirty-one to forty-two degrees, to seven hundred and sixty-four miles and a half. Taking the mean for the distance, the amount will be eight hundred and sixty-eight miles and three-fourths. The mean distance from the Atlantic to the Mississippi does not probably exceed seven hundred and fifty miles.

EUROPEAN NATIONS ABOUT THE SAME GEOGRAPHICAL SIZE:
America's geographical size is not much different than Europe's. Do Europe's various representatives have problems attending to their national government needs? Will America's?

14:14 On a comparison of this extent with that of several countries in Europe, the practicability of rendering our system commensurate to it appears to be demonstrable. It is not a great deal larger than Germany, where a diet representing the whole empire is <u>continually assembled</u>; or than <u>Poland</u> before the late dismemberment, where another national diet was the depositary of the supreme power. Passing by <u>France</u> and <u>Spain</u>, we find that in <u>Great Britain</u>, inferior as it may be in size, the representatives of the northern extremity of the island have as far to travel to the national council as will be required of those of the most remote parts of the Union.

REPUBLIC OFFERS ADDITIONAL ADVANTAGES:

14:15   Favorable as this view of the subject may be, some observations remain which will place it in a light still more satisfactory.

FEDERAL GOVERNMENT HAS LIMITED JURISDICTION OVER NATION:

The federal government is tasked with managing national issues only. Should the central government be involved in the local affairs of an American union of States?

14:16   <u>In the first place it is to be remembered that the general government is not to be charged with the whole power of making and administering laws.</u> Its is limited to certain enumerated objects, which concern all the members of the republic, but which are not to be attained by the separate provisions of any.

STATES RETAIN AUTHORITY AND ACTIVITY:

State and local governments must be retained to attend to local issues. The Union could not survive without this ruling power on the local levels. Who really should tend to the local issues?

14:17   The <u>subordinate [State] governments</u>, which can extend their care to all those other subjects which can be <u>separately provided</u> for, will retain their due <u>authority and activity</u>.

CONVENTION DIDN'T ABOLISH STATE GOVERNMENTS:

14:18   Were it proposed by the plan of the Convention to abolish the governments of the particular States, its adversaries would have some ground for their objection; though it would not be difficult to show that if they were abolished the general government would be compelled, by the principle of self-preservation, to reinstate them in their proper jurisdiction.

UNION CAN PROTECT CURRENT STATES AND ADD NEW STATES:

The Union must protect itself from dissolution but provide a way to allow growth and expansion.

14:19   A <u>second observation</u> to be made is that the immediate <u>object of the federal Constitution is to secure the union of the thirteen primitive States</u>, which we know to be practicable; and to <u>add</u> to them such <u>other States</u> as may arise in their own

bosoms, or in their neighborhoods, which we cannot doubt to be equally practicable. The arrangements that may be necessary for those angles and fractions of our territory which lie on our northwestern frontier, must be left to those whom further discoveries and experience will render more equal to the task.

A UNION LINKS THE NATION TOGETHER IN MANY WAYS:

In a Union, commerce and communications will always improve. What improvements can be expected if a strong Union is created?

14:20   Let it be remarked, in the <u>third place</u>, that the intercourse throughout the Union will be facilitated by new improvements. <u>Roads will everywhere be shortened</u>, and kept in <u>better order</u>; accommodations for <u>travelers</u> will be <u>multiplied</u> and <u>meliorated</u>; an <u>interior navigation</u> on our eastern side will be opened throughout, or nearly throughout, the whole extent of the thirteen States. The <u>communication</u> between the Western and Atlantic districts, and between different parts of each, will be rendered more and more easy by those numerous canals with which the beneficence of nature has intersected our country, and which art finds it so little difficult to connect and complete.

UNION GIVES BORDER SAFETY AND DEFENSE:

The frontier States will benefit from the Union defending their weak borders. How will the Union help the most distant and frontier states?

14:21   A <u>fourth</u> and still more important consideration is, that as <u>almost every State will, on one side or other, be a frontier</u>, and will thus find, in regard to its safety, an inducement to make <u>some sacrifices</u> for the sake of the general <u>protection</u>; so the States which lie at the greatest distance from the heart of the Union, and which, of course, may partake least of the ordinary circulation of its benefits, will be at the same time <u>immediately contiguous to foreign nations</u>, and will consequently stand, on particular occasions, in <u>greatest need of its strength</u> and resources.

WHICH IS WORSE, INVASION OR INCONVENIENCE?

14:22   It may be <u>inconvenient for Georgia</u>, or the States forming our western or northeastern borders, to <u>send their representatives</u> to the seat of government; but they would find <u>it more so to struggle alone</u> against an <u>invading enemy</u>, or even to support alone the whole expense of those precautions which may be dictated by the neighborhood of continual danger. If they should derive less benefit, therefore, from the Union in some respects than the less distant States, they will derive <u>greater benefit</u> from it in <u>other respects</u>, and thus the <u>proper equilibrium</u> will be maintained throughout.

AMERICANS ARE A UNIQUE AND UNITED PEOPLE:

America is united because of love and respect for each other in its common cause of liberty. What are the gloomy voices predicting about forming a Union under the new Constitution?

14:23 I submit to you, my fellow-citizens, these considerations, in full confidence that the good sense which has so often marked your decisions will allow them their due weight and effect; and that you will never suffer difficulties, however formidable in appearance, or however fashionable the error on which they may be founded, to drive you into the gloomy and perilous scene into which the advocates for disunion would conduct you.

IGNORE THE DECEPTIVE LIARS, WE AMERICANS ARE FAMILY:

14:24 Hearken not to the unnatural voice which tells you that the people of America, knit together as they are by so many cords of affection, can no longer live together as members of the same family; can no longer continue the mutual guardians of their mutual happiness; can no longer be fellow citizens of one great, respectable, and flourishing empire.

IGNORE THE LIES ABOUT THE NEW CONSTITUTION:

The Constitution is a new invention, brilliantly based on ancient principles, whose time has finally come. Why even listen to the naive criticisms against the Constitution?

14:25 Hearken not to the voice which petulantly tells you that the form of government recommended for your adoption is a novelty in the political world; that it has never yet had a place in the theories of the wildest projectors; that it rashly attempts what it is impossible to accomplish.

TRUE PRINCIPLES CONSECRATED WITH BLOOD:

14:26 No, my countrymen, shut your ears against this unhallowed language. Shut your hearts against the poison which it conveys; the kindred blood which flows in the veins of American citizens, the mingled blood which they have shed in defense of their sacred rights, consecrate their Union, and excite horror at the idea of their becoming aliens, rivals, enemies.

DISUNION LEADS TO DESTRUCTION NOT LIBERTY:

A strong Union may be a novelty but it is clearly the best means to guard and protect human rights and liberty. In truth, which novelty really deserves to be shunned?

14:27 And if novelties are to be shunned, believe me, the most alarming of all novelties, the most wild of all projects, the most rash of all attempts, is that of rendering us in pieces, in order to preserve our liberties and promote our happiness.

MANIFEST DESTINY—LET GOOD SENSE, KNOWLEDGE, AND EXPERIENCE LEAD:

Don't allow old ideas of the past to override good sense. Experience is the best teacher.

14:28 But why is the experiment of an extended republic to be rejected, merely because it may comprise what is new? Is it not the glory of the people of America, that, whilst they have paid a decent regard to the opinions of former times and other nations, they have not suffered a blind veneration for antiquity, for custom, or for names, to overrule the suggestions of their own good sense, the knowledge of their own situation, and the lessons of their own experience?

MANIFEST DESTINY—FAVORING PRIVATE RIGHTS AND PUBLIC HAPPINESS:

The Constitution establishes the first form of government in history that provides for private rights and public happiness.

14:29 To this manly spirit, posterity will be indebted for the possession, and the world for the example, of the numerous innovations displayed on the American theatre, in favor of private rights and public happiness.

MANIFEST DESTINY—COMPLETELY NEW FORM WITHOUT MODEL TO COPY:

The Constitution is a new form for which there is no model to mimic.

14:30 Had no important step been taken by the leaders of the Revolution for which a precedent could not be discovered, no government established of which an exact model did not present itself, the people of the United States might, at this moment have been numbered among the melancholy victims of misguided councils, must at best have been laboring under the weight of some of those forms which have crushed the liberties of the rest of mankind.

MANIFEST DESTINY—HAPPILY FOR AMERICA, HAPPILY FOR THE HUMAN RACE:

The Constitution is the fruit of a new and more noble course. And this, with so few imperfections—happily for the whole human race.

14:31 Happily for America, happily, we trust, for the whole human race, they pursued a new and more noble course. They accomplished a revolution which has no parallel in the annals of human society. They reared the fabrics of governments which have no model on the face of the globe. They formed the design of a great Confederacy, which it is incumbent on their successors to improve and perpetuate. If their works betray imperfections, we wonder at the fewness of them. If they erred most in the structure of the Union, this was the work <u>most difficult to be executed</u>; this is the work which has been new modeled by the act of your Convention, and it is that act on which you are now to deliberate and to decide.

—Publius

Review Questions

1. What is the difference between a republic and a democracy? (14:4)

2. Why do republics have a negative reputation in history? (14:5–7)

3. What political system did America discover? (14:8)

4. What is the geographical limit of democracy? (14:9)

5. What is the geographical limit of s republic? (14:10-11)

6. According to the 1783 Paris Peace Treaty, what is the geographical size of America? (14:12–13)

7. Is the new federal government given power to oversee the making and administering all of the laws in America? (14:16)

8. What kind of laws is the federal government authorized to manage? (14:16)

9. What kinds of laws do the States manage? (14:17)

10. What did American innovations stand in favor of? (14:29)

11. Did the Framers have any model of constitution to copy? (14:30–31)

12. Who has the job of perpetuating the Constitution? (14:31)

13. Happily for America and the world, the Framers did what? (14:31)

SECTION 2 • CONFEDERACY IS FATALLY FLAWED

Papers 15–22

FEDERALIST NO. 15

ARTICLES ARE FLAWED BEYOND REPAIR: Governing State governments is like managing without power a group of several nations through unenforceable treaties. It just doesn't work. All men agree the Articles can't solve America's most serious problems, and to continue down that path will lead to ruin for all. This demise wasn't sudden, but is the accumulation of improper choices made on bad principles.

By Alexander Hamilton
December 1, 1787

THE SACRED KNOT THAT BINDS:
The sense of *Union* is what holds the nation together, but it is very fragile under the Articles of Confederation. What is the sacred knot to which Hamilton refers?

15:1 IN THE course of the preceding papers, I have endeavored, my fellow-citizens, to place before you, in a clear and convincing light, the importance of Union to your political safety and happiness. I have unfolded to you a complication of dangers to which you would be exposed, should you permit that sacred knot which binds the people of America together be severed or dissolved by ambition or by avarice, by jealousy or by misrepresentation.

15:2 In the sequel of the inquiry through which I propose to accompany you, the truths intended to be inculcated will receive further confirmation from facts and arguments hitherto unnoticed.

CLARIFYING THE ISSUES:
The Anti-Federalists have confused many Americans about true principles embodied in the new Constitution.

15:3 If the road over which you will still have to pass should in some places appear to you tedious or irksome, you will recollect that you are in quest of information on a subject the most momentous which can engage the attention of a free people, that the field through which you have to travel is in itself spacious, and that the difficulties of the journey have been unnecessarily increased by the mazes with which sophistry has beset the way. It will be my aim to remove the obstacles from your progress in as compendious a manner as it can be done, without sacrificing utility to dispatch.

CONSENSUS IS THAT THE ARTICLES ARE FLAWED:
The weaknesses of the Articles of Confederation were criticized by both Federalists and Anti-Federalists.

15:4 In pursuance of the plan which I have laid down for the discussion of the subject, the point next in order to be examined is the "insufficiency of the present Confederation to the preservation of the Union."

WHY SHOW PROOF WHEN EVERYONE AGREES?
15:5 It may perhaps be asked what need there is of reasoning or proof to illustrate a position which is not either controverted or doubted, to which the understandings and feelings of all classes of men assent, and which in substance is admitted by the opponents as well as by the friends of the new Constitution.

ARTICLES OF CONFEDERATION SERIOUSLY FLAWED:
15:6 It must in truth be acknowledged that, however these may differ in other respects, they in general appear to harmonize in this sentiment, at least, that there are material imperfections in our national system, and that something is necessary to be done to rescue us from impending anarchy.

SUPPORTERS OF THE ARTICLES ADMIT DEFECTS:
15:7 The facts that support this opinion are no longer objects of speculation. They have forced themselves upon the sensibility of the people at large, and have at length extorted from those, whose mistaken policy has had the principal share in precipitating the extremity at which we are arrived, a reluctant confession of the reality of those defects in the scheme of our

federal government, which have been long pointed out and regretted by the intelligent friends of the Union.

ARTICLES CAN'T SOLVE PROBLEMS:
America has been humiliated on almost every front because of the flawed Articles. What are some examples of how the Articles are not working?

15:8 We may indeed with propriety be said to have reached almost the last stage of national humiliation. There is scarcely anything that can wound the pride or degrade the character of an independent nation which we do not experience. Are there engagements to the performance of which we are held by every tie respectable among men? These are the subjects of constant and unblushing violation.

Can't pay foreign debts.

15:9 Do we owe debts to foreigners and to our own citizens contracted in a time of imminent peril for the preservation of our political existence? These remain without any proper or satisfactory provision for their discharge.

Still suffer from foreign occupation.

15:10 Have we valuable territories and important posts in the possession of a foreign power which, by express stipulations, ought long since to have been surrendered? These are still retained, to the prejudice of our interests, not less than of our rights.

Can't enforce the peace treaty.

15:11 Are we in a condition to resent or to repel the aggression? We have neither troops, nor treasury, nor government (I mean for the Union). Are we even in a condition to remonstrate with dignity? The just imputations on our own faith, in respect to the same treaty, ought first to be removed.

Can't access the Mississippi.

15:12 Are we entitled by nature and compact to a free participation in the navigation of the Mississippi? Spain excludes us from it.

Poor public credit.

15:13 Is public credit an indispensable resource in time of public danger? We seem to have abandoned its cause as desperate and irretrievable.

Sluggish commerce.

15:14 Is commerce of importance to national wealth? Ours is at the lowest point of declension.

No foreign respect.

15:15 Is respectability in the eyes of foreign powers a safeguard against foreign encroachments? The imbecility of our

government even forbids them to treat with us. Our ambassadors abroad are the mere pageants of mimic sovereignty.

Land value is dropping.

15:16 Is a violent and unnatural decrease in the value of land a symptom of national distress? The price of improved land in most parts of the country is much lower than can be accounted for by the quantity of waste land at market, and can only be fully explained by that want of private and public confidence, which are so alarmingly prevalent among all ranks, and which have a direct tendency to depreciate property of every kind.

Poor private credit.

15:17 Is private credit the friend and patron of industry? That most useful kind which relates to borrowing and lending is reduced within the narrowest limits, and this still more from an opinion of insecurity than from the scarcity of money.

WITH SO MANY BLESSINGS WHY DO WE EXPERIENCE DISORDER?
In such a blessed land why is there so much disorder and poverty?

15:18 To shorten an enumeration of particulars which can afford neither pleasure nor instruction, it may in general be demanded, what indication is there of national disorder, poverty, and insignificance that could befall a community so peculiarly blessed with natural advantages as we are, which does not form a part of the dark catalogue of our public misfortunes?

THOSE CULPABLE ARE FIGHTING THE SOLUTION:
Those responsible for America's many problems are the same people opposed to the new Constitution that will correct them.

15:19 This is the melancholy situation to which we have been brought by those very maxims and councils which would now deter us from adopting the proposed Constitution; and which, not content with having conducted us to the brink of a precipice, seem resolved to plunge us into the abyss that awaits us below.

LET US NOW REPLACE THE ARTICLES:

15:20 Here, my countrymen, impelled by every motive that ought to influence an enlightened people, let us make a firm stand for our safety, our tranquility, our dignity, our reputation. Let us at last break the fatal charm which has too long seduced us from the paths of felicity and prosperity.

CRITICS ADMIT DEFECTS BUT REFUSE THE REPAIRS:

The Articles are a failure because they made the national government too weak. The States would not delegate enough power to remedy the problems. Can these Articles be repaired?

15:21 It is true, as has been before observed that facts, too stubborn to be resisted, have produced a species of general assent to the abstract proposition that there exist material defects in our national system; but the usefulness of the concession, on the part of the old adversaries of federal measures, is destroyed by a strenuous opposition to a remedy, upon the only principles that can give it a chance of success. While they admit that the government of the United States is destitute of energy, they contend against conferring upon it those powers which are requisite to supply that energy.

CRITICS REFUSE TO DIMINISH STATE POWER:

15:22 They seem still to aim at things repugnant and irreconcilable; at an augmentation of federal authority, without a diminution of State authority; at sovereignty in the Union, and complete independence in the members. They still, in fine, seem to cherish with blind devotion the political monster of an **imperium in imperio**.[48]

ARTICLES ARE FUNDAMENTALLY FLAWED:

15:23 This renders a full display of the principal defects of the Confederation necessary, in order to show that the evils we experience do not proceed from minute or partial imperfections, but from fundamental errors in the structure of the building, which cannot be amended otherwise than by an alteration in the first principles and main pillars of the fabric.

BIGGEST FLAW WAS ATTEMPTING TO GOVERN THE STATES AS SOVEREIGN ENTITIES:

Congress made legislation for the States, not for individuals. States could ignore any federal law because the Articles gave no power to force the States to obey.

15:24 The great and radical vice in the construction of the existing Confederation is in the principle of LEGISLATION for STATES or GOVERNMENTS, in their CORPORATE or COLLECTIVE CAPACITIES, and as contradistinguished from the INDIVIDUALS of which they consist.

ARTICLES HAD NO FEDERAL POWER TO ACT ON INDIVIDUALS:

15:25 Though this principle does not run through all the powers delegated to the Union, yet it pervades and governs those on which the efficacy of the rest depends. Except as to the rule of appointment, the United States has an indefinite discretion to make requisitions for men and money; but they have no authority to raise either, by regulations extending to the individual citizens of America.

CONGRESS'S REQUISITIONS WERE RECEIVED AS MERE RECOMMENDATIONS:

There was no written authority in the Articles for Congress to demand taxes, men, and supplies. Therefore it could only recommend or request those items, and the States could obey or not.

15:26 The consequence of this is, that though in theory their resolutions concerning those objects are laws, constitutionally binding on the members of the Union, yet in practice they are mere recommendations which the States observe or disregard at their option.

ANTI-FEDERALISTS ARE IRRATIONAL:

They worry about abandoning the same bad ideas that made the Articles a failure. If the essence of the Articles is retained to what will this lead?

15:27 It is a singular instance of the capriciousness of the human mind, that after all the admonitions we have had from experience on this head, there should still be found men who object to the new Constitution, for deviating from a principle which has been found the bane of the old, and which is in itself evidently incompatible with the idea of GOVERNMENT; a principle, in short, which, if it is to be executed at all, must substitute the violent and sanguinary agency of the sword to the mild influence of the magistracy.

ARTICLES, LIKE TREATIES, ARE INADEQUATE TO GOVERN:

Treaties are good if they have a precise, defined purpose. Ill-defined treaties are fragile and easily broken. Which has a stronger bond, one of a treaty or one of a formal Union?

15:28 There is nothing absurd or impracticable in the idea of a league or alliance between independent nations for certain defined purposes precisely stated in a treaty regulating all the details of time, place, circumstance, and quantity; leaving nothing to future discretion; and depending for its execution on the good faith of the parties.

Compacts and treaties last so long as does good will.

15:29 Compacts of this kind exist among all civilized nations, subject to the usual vicissitudes of peace and war, of observance and non-observance, as the interests or passions of the contracting powers dictate.

TREATIES BASED ON GOOD FAITH NEVER LAST LONG:

15:30 In the early part of the present century there was an epidemical rage in Europe for this species of compacts, from

---

48 **imperium in imperio:** An empire within an empire, like a two-headed monster.

which the politicians of the times fondly hoped for benefits which were never realized. With a view to establishing the equilibrium of power and the peace of that part of the world, all the resources of negotiation were exhausted, and triple and quadruple alliances were formed; but they were scarcely formed before they were broken, giving an instructive but afflicting lesson to mankind, how little dependence is to be placed on treaties which have no other sanction than the obligations of good faith, and which oppose general considerations of peace and justice to the impulse of any immediate interest or passion.

TREATIES EVENTUALLY FAIL:
History shows that neighboring nations bound only by treaties and compacts eventually become enemies. Would this happen to America if it didn't form a Union?

15:31   If the particular States in this country are disposed to stand in a similar relation to each other, and to drop the project of a general DISCRETIONARY SUPERINTENDENCE, the scheme would indeed be pernicious, and would entail upon us all the mischiefs which have been enumerated under the first head; but it would have the merit of being, at least, consistent and practicable Abandoning all views towards a confederate government, this would bring us to a simple alliance offensive and defensive;

Confederacies would expose the States to many intrigues of foreign nations.

15:32   and would place us in a situation to be alternate friends and enemies of each other, as our mutual jealousies and rivalships, nourished by the intrigues of foreign nations, should prescribe to us.

GOVERNMENT MUST EXTEND DIRECTLY TO CITIZENS:
A national government works only when its power extends to the people themselves.

15:33   But if we are unwilling to be placed in this perilous situation; if we still will adhere to the design of a national government, or, which is the same thing, of a superintending power, under the direction of a common council, we must resolve to incorporate into our plan those ingredients which may be considered as forming the characteristic difference between a league and a government; we must extend the authority of the Union to the persons of the citizens, —the only proper objects of government.

LAW IS MEANINGLESS WITHOUT A PENALTY:
A government of the people must have power to make laws and punish disobedience. What do laws become if there is no punishment attached to disobedience?

15:34   Government implies the power of making laws. It is essential to the idea of a law, that it be attended with a sanction; or, in other words, a penalty or punishment for disobedience. If there be no penalty annexed to disobedience, the resolutions or commands which pretend to be laws will, in fact, amount to nothing more than advice or recommendation.

Only two punishments for disobedience.

15:35   This penalty, whatever it may be, can only be inflicted in two ways: by the agency of the courts and ministers of justice, or by military force; by the COERCION of the magistracy, or by the COERCION of arms. The first kind can evidently apply only to men; the last kind must of necessity, be employed against bodies politic, or communities, or States.

COURTS HAVE NO MEANS TO ENFORCE THE LAWS:
15:36   It is evident that there is no process of a court by which the observance of the laws can, in the last resort, be enforced. Sentences may be denounced against them for violations of their duty; but these sentences can only be carried into execution by the sword.

ENFORCEMENT MEANS WAR:
The Articles could not be enforced without precipitating a war.

15:37   In an association where the general authority is confined to the collective bodies of the communities, that compose it, every breach of the laws must involve a state of war; and military execution must become the only instrument of civil obedience. Such a state of things can certainly not deserve the name of government, nor would any prudent man choose to commit his happiness to it.

LASTING COMPLIANCE NOT REALISTIC:
We once believed our common interests would create obedience to federal authority. Experience has taught us this won't work.

15:38   There was a time when we were told that breaches, by the States, of the regulations of the federal authority were not to be expected; that a sense of common interest would preside over the conduct of the respective members, and would beget a full compliance with all the constitutional requisitions of the Union.

Human nature can't be trusted.

15:39   This language, at the present day, would appear as wild as a great part of what we now hear from the same quarter will be thought, when we shall have received further lessons from that best oracle of wisdom, experience. It at all times betrayed an ignorance of the true springs by which human conduct is actuated, and belied the original inducements to the establishment of civil power.

GOVERNMENT MUST CONTROL MOB AND FACTION VIOLENCE:

Factions and mobs will do what an individual will not. Without strong enforcement of the law, to what extremes does passion often lead?

15:40   Why has government been instituted at all? Because the passions of men will not conform to the dictates of reason and justice, without constraint. Has it been found that bodies of men act with more rectitude or greater disinterestedness than individuals?

Personal responsibility can be deflected when blame can be spread across many others.

15:41   The contrary of this has been inferred by all accurate observers of the conduct of mankind; and the inference is founded upon obvious reasons. Regard to reputation has a less active influence, when the infamy of a bad action is to be divided among a number than when it is to fall singly upon one.

SPIRIT OF FACTION AGITATES INDIVIDUALS TO ACT BADLY:

15:42   A spirit of faction, which is apt to mingle its poison in the deliberations of all bodies of men, will often hurry the persons of whom they are composed into improprieties and excesses, for which they would blush in a private capacity.

POLITICIANS RESIST OUTSIDE AUTHORITY:

Legislative bodies hate being controlled by outside forces.

15:43   In addition to all this, there is, in the nature of sovereign power, an impatience of control, that disposes those who are invested with the exercise of it, to look with an evil eye upon all external attempts to restrain or direct its operations.

LOVE OF POWER IS ALWAYS A PROBLEM:

Human nature prevents a peaceful cooperation from a Confederacy of States. States tend to go their own way when they disagree with authority.

15:44   From this spirit it happens, that in every political association which is formed upon the principle of uniting in a common interest a number of lesser sovereignties, there will be found a kind of eccentric tendency in the subordinate or inferior orbs, by the operation of which there will be a perpetual effort in each to fly off from the common center. This tendency is not difficult to be accounted for. It has its origin in the love of power. Power controlled or abridged is almost always the rival and enemy of that power by which it is controlled or abridged.

It is human nature to resist submitting to authority.

15:45   This simple proposition will teach us how little reason there is to expect, that the persons intrusted with the administration of the affairs of the particular members of a confederacy will at all times be ready, with perfect good-humor, and an unbiased regard to the public weal, to execute the resolutions or decrees of the general authority. The reverse of this results from the constitution of man.

NO ENFORCEMENT POWER MEANS NO OBEDIENCE TO LAW:

Laws without any authority won't be obeyed. What do rulers often do with such laws if they can get away with it?

15:46   If, therefore, the measures of the Confederacy cannot be executed without the intervention of the particular administrations, there will be little prospect of their being executed at all. The rulers of the respective members, whether they have a constitutional right to do it or not, will undertake to judge of the propriety of the measures themselves. They will consider the conformity of the thing proposed or required to their immediate interests or aims; the momentary conveniences or inconveniences that would attend its adoption.

CENTRAL AUTHORITY ENSURES CONSISTENCY:

With no central authority, a confederacy of States will always fail.

15:47   All this will be done; and in a spirit of interested and suspicious scrutiny, without that knowledge of national circumstances and reasons of state, which is essential to a right judgment, and with that strong predilection in favor of local objects, which can hardly fail to mislead the decision. The same process must be repeated in every member of which the body is constituted; and the execution of the plans, framed by the councils of the whole, will always fluctuate on the discretion of the ill-informed and prejudiced opinion of every part.

ONE CENTRAL POWER NEEDED TO FOCUS ALL PARTS:

15:48   Those who have been conversant in the proceedings of popular assemblies; who have seen how difficult it often is, where there is no exterior pressure of circumstances, to bring them to harmonious resolutions on important points, will readily conceive how impossible it must be to induce a number of such assemblies, deliberating at a distance from each other, at different times, and under different impressions, long to co-operate in the same views and pursuits.

ONE STATE COULD BRING UNION TO A STANDSTILL:

There was no enforcement power in the Articles. Could any single State bring the whole government to a dead standstill?

15:49 In our case, the <u>concurrence of thirteen distinct</u> sovereign wills is requisite, under the Confederation, to the complete execution of every important measure that proceeds from the Union. It has happened as was to have been foreseen. The <u>measures of the Union have not been executed</u>; the <u>delinquencies of the States</u> have, step by step, matured themselves to an extreme, which has, at length, <u>arrested</u> all the <u>wheels of the national government</u>, and brought them to an awful stand.

THIS DESPERATE SITUATION DIDN'T COME ALL AT ONCE:

15:50 Congress at this time scarcely possess the means of keeping up the forms of administration, till the States can have time to agree upon a more substantial substitute for the present <u>shadow of a federal government</u>. Things did not come to this desperate extremity at once.

STRONG STATES GREW WEARY OF CARRYING THE WEAK STATES:

Some States became delinquent because of the shirking of duty by others.

15:51 The causes which have been specified produced <u>at first</u> only unequal and disproportionate degrees of compliance with the requisitions of the Union. The greater deficiencies of some States furnished the pretext of example and the temptation of interest to the complying, or to the least delinquent States. <u>Why should we do more in proportion than those who are embarked with us</u> in the same political voyage? Why should we consent to bear more than our proper share of the common burden? These were suggestions which human selfishness could not withstand, and which even speculative men, who looked forward to remote consequences, could not, without hesitation, combat.

FROM SUCH FATIGUE, EACH STATE WITHDREW ITS SUPPORT:

All of the above demonstrates the breakdown of governmental function under the Articles of Confederation. The frail and suffering Confederacy is ready to fall.

15:52 Each State, yielding to the persuasive voice of immediate interest or convenience, has successively withdrawn its support, <u>till the frail and tottering edifice seems ready to fall upon our heads</u>, and to crush us beneath its ruins.

—PUBLIUS

REVIEW QUESTIONS

1. Did everyone agree the Articles of Confederation was seriously flawed? (15:4–7)

2. What are the main problems and flaws in the Articles? (15:9–18)

3. Critics admit the Articles don't give the government enough power, but what do they "contend against conferring" to fix the problem? (15:21)

4. To raise men and money for the war, did the Articles act on the States as a corporate collective, or on individual citizens? (15:24–25)

5. In practice, did the Articles have power to compel obedience, or only to recommend obedience? (15:26)

6. Have leagues and alliances such as that created by the Articles existed in recent and ancient history? Did they last very long? (15:28-30)

7. Is it accurate to say the resolutions of Congress did not have the power of law but were more like treaties that the States could accept or reject however they chose? (15:31-32)

8. Must government have power to extend its authority to individual citizens? (15:33)

9. For government to make laws that will be obeyed, must it also have the power to punish or penalize the disobedient? (15:34)

10. Was "common interest" a strong enough bond to make the States fully comply with the Articles of Confederation? (15:38)

11. If there is no power in government to enforce laws can there really exist any laws at all? (15:46)

12. Under the Articles could one State extort from the other twelve certain favors for its vote? (15:49–52)

FEDERALIST NO. 16

LEGISLATING THE STATES ALWAYS FAILS BUT IS SOLVED WITH POWER OVER THE INDIVIDUAL: Discord, jealousies and fear will destroy the nation without a strong standing army, national government, and Union. The strongest States would prevail in any conflict, and like the wars in Europe, would destroy any hope of Union. The new federal government must have power over the individual citizen to protect the rights of all. Hamilton argues in Nos. 15, 16, and 17 the need for the federal government to rule over individuals in each State instead of over the State legislatures as sovereign entities. Madison gives authority to that same principle in Nos. 18, 29, and 20, using examples in history.

By Alexander Hamilton—December 4, 1787

LEGISLATING THE STATES NEVER WORKS:

Experiments with our own Articles, and from examples in history, prove that legislating sovereign States instead of individuals doesn't work.

16:1 THE tendency of the principle of legislation for States, or communities, in their political capacities, as it has been exemplified by the experiment we have made of it, is equally attested by the events which have befallen all other governments of the confederate kind, of which we have any account, in exact proportion to its prevalence in those systems.

ANCIENT CONFEDERACIES AVOIDED GOVERNING STATES:

Ancient confederacies that avoided governing their member states did better.

16:2 The confirmations of this fact will be worthy of a distinct and particular examination. I shall content myself with barely observing here, that of all the confederacies of antiquity, which history has handed down to us, the Lycian and Achaean leagues, as far as there remain vestiges of them, appear to have been most free from the fetters of that mistaken principle, and were accordingly those which have best deserved, and have most liberally received, the applauding suffrages of political writers.

CONFEDERATE FORCE FAILS:

Trying to legislate a State is inviting anarchy. If a State in a confederacy refuses to obey legislation, force must be used.

16:3 This exceptionable principle may, as truly as emphatically, be styled the parent of anarchy: It has been seen that delinquencies in the members of the Union are its natural and necessary offspring; and that whenever they happen, the only constitutional remedy is force, and the immediate effect of the use of it, civil war.

LARGE ARMY NEEDED IN CONFEDERACY:

To rectify any delinquency in a confederacy, a large army would always be needed to enforce the law. Whether the general authority won or lost, who would be left in charge?

16:4 It remains to inquire how far so odious an engine of government, in its application to us, would even be capable of answering its end. If there should not be a large army constantly at the disposal of the national government it would either not be able to employ force at all, or, when this could be done, it would amount to a war between parts of the Confederacy concerning the infractions of a league, in which the strongest combination would be most likely to prevail, whether it consisted of those who supported or of those who resisted the general authority.

DELINQUENT STATES WOULD UNITE WITH EACH OTHER IN COMMON DEFENSE:

16:5 It would rarely happen that the delinquency to be redressed would be confined to a single member, and if there were more than one who had neglected their duty, similarity of situation would induce them to unite for common defense.

CONFEDERACIES SUSCEPTIBLE TO PROPAGANDA:

A State refusing to obey a national government would likely attract allies in an uprising.

16:6 Independent of this motive of sympathy, if a large and influential State should happen to be the aggressing member, it would commonly have weight enough with its neighbors to win over some of them as associates to its cause. Specious arguments of danger to the common liberty could easily be contrived; plausible excuses for the deficiencies of the party could, without difficulty, be invented to alarm the apprehensions, inflame the passions, and conciliate the good-will, even of those States which were not chargeable with any violation or omission of duty.

A REBELLIOUS STATE WOULD FIRST SOLICIT AID FROM OTHER STATES:

Left to themselves would State rulers seek help from neighboring States or foreign help?

16:7 This would be the more likely to take place, as the delinquencies of the larger members might be expected sometimes to proceed from an ambitious premeditation in their rulers, with a view to getting rid of all external control upon their designs of personal aggrandizement; the better to effect which it is presumable they would tamper beforehand with leading individuals in the adjacent States.

STATES ASKING FOREIGN POWERS TO HELP:

16:8 If associates could not be found at home, recourse would be had to the aid of foreign powers, who would seldom be disinclined to encouraging the dissensions of a Confederacy, from the firm union of which they had so much to fear.

IF REBELLION SPREADS, THE UNION WILL END:

If war between the States broke out, it would be all out war, nothing withheld. Could the Union survive such a full scale war?

16:9 When the sword is once drawn, the passions of men observe no bounds of moderation. The suggestions of wounded pride, the instigations of irritated resentment, would be apt to carry the States against which the arms of the Union were exerted, to any extremes necessary to avenge the affront or to avoid the disgrace of submission. The first war of this kind would probably terminate in a dissolution of the Union.

CONFEDERACY IS DYING, NEW FEDERAL FORM NEEDED NOW:

The Articles are defined as a federal system, meaning, a compact among States as entities, not with the people. We've learned that complying States will resist supporting Union authority.

16:10 This may be considered as the violent death of the Confederacy. Its more natural death is what we now seem to be on the point of experiencing, if the federal system be not speedily renovated in a more substantial form. It is not probable, considering the genius of this country, that the complying States would often be inclined to support the authority of the Union by engaging in a war against the non-complying States. They would always be more ready to pursue the milder course of putting themselves upon an equal footing with the delinquent members by an imitation of their example. And the guilt of all would thus become the security of all.

DIFFICULT TO KNOW WHEN TO USE FORCE:

It is nearly impossible to know for certain why a State would be delinquent in its obligations, or if forcing obedience was the best resolution.

16:11 Our past experience has exhibited the operation of this spirit in its full light. There would, in fact, be an insuperable difficulty in ascertaining when force could with propriety be employed. In the article of pecuniary contribution, which would be the most usual source of delinquency, it would often be impossible to decide whether it had proceeded from disinclination or inability. The pretense of the latter would always be at hand. And the case must be very flagrant in which its fallacy could be detected with sufficient certainty to justify the harsh expedient of compulsion.

EVERY VIOLATION WOULD BECOME A MASSIVE CRISIS:

16:12 It is easy to see that this problem alone, as often as it should occur, would open a wide field for the exercise of factious views, of partiality, and of oppression, in the majority that happened to prevail in the national council.

STATES DON'T WANT GOVERNMENT BY ARMY:

The new Constitution does not require an army because it can exert influence over individuals. Without that, an army would be needed.

16:13 It seems to require no pains to prove that the States ought not to prefer a national Constitution which could only be kept in motion by the instrumentality of a large army continually on foot to execute the ordinary requisitions or decrees of the government. And yet this is the plain alternative involved by those who wish to deny it the power of extending its operations to individuals.

CONFEDERACY WOULD BECOME A MILITARY DESPOT:

Denying a central government its needed power would create a military despotism. Would there be sufficient resources for such an army?

16:14 Such a scheme, if practicable at all, would instantly degenerate into a military despotism; but it will be found in every light impracticable. The resources of the Union would not be equal to the maintenance of an army considerable enough to confine the larger States within the limits of their duty; nor would the means ever be furnished of forming such an army in the first instance.

FORCING THE STATES TO OBEY WILL FAIL:

Using an army to force member states is not proper government.

16:15 Whoever considers the populousness and strength of several of these States singly at the present juncture, and looks forward to what they will become, even at the distance of half a century, will at once dismiss as idle and visionary any scheme which aims at regulating their movements by laws to operate upon them in their collective capacities, and to be executed by a coercion applicable to them in the same capacities. A project of this kind is little less romantic than the monster-taming spirit which is attributed to the fabulous heroes and demigods of antiquity.

MILITARY COERCION HAS NEVER WORKED:

Legislation that is enforced by military coercion has never worked. What has been the outcome where that has been used?

16:16 Even in those confederacies which have been composed of members smaller than many of our counties, the principle of legislation for sovereign States, supported by military coercion, has never been found effectual. It has rarely been attempted to be employed, but against the weaker members; and in most instances attempts to coerce the refractory and disobedient have been the signals of bloody wars, in which one half of the confederacy has displayed its banners against the other half.

ENFORCEMENT THROUGH FEDERAL COURTS:

The national government must have access to the individual and enforce laws on them through ordinary courts.

16:17 The result of these observations to an intelligent mind must be clearly this, that if it be possible at any rate to construct a federal government capable of regulating the common concerns and preserving the general tranquility, it must be founded, as to the objects committed to its care, upon the reverse of the principle contended for by the opponents of the proposed Constitution. It must carry its agency to the persons of the citizens. It must stand in need of <u>no intermediate legislations</u>; but must itself be empowered to employ the <u>arm of the ordinary magistrate</u> to <u>execute its own resolutions</u>. The <u>majesty</u> of the national authority must be manifested through the medium of the <u>courts of justice</u>.

GOVERNMENTS EXERCISE POWER THROUGH ALL MEANS—COURTS, MILITARY, SO FORTH:

16:18 The government of the Union, like that of each State, must be able to address itself immediately to the <u>hopes and fears</u> of individuals; and to attract to its support those passions which have the strongest influence upon the human heart. It must, in short, possess all the means, and have a <u>right to resort to all the methods</u>, of executing the powers with which it is intrusted, that are possessed and exercised by the government of the particular States.

COULD THE STATES BLOCK LAWS?

The States must not have the power to thwart execution of the federal government's lawful duties. Could a State prevent passage of a federal law?

16:19 To this reasoning it may perhaps be objected, that if any State should be disaffected to the authority of the Union, it could at any time obstruct the execution of its laws, and bring the matter to the same issue of force, with the necessity of which the opposite scheme is reproached.

IS IT "NON-COMPLIANCE" OR "ACTIVE RESISTANCE"?

16:20 The plausibility of this objection will vanish the moment we advert to the essential difference between a mere <u>NON-COMPLIANCE</u> and a DIRECT and <u>ACTIVE RESISTANCE</u>.

STATES COULD DEFEAT ANY FEDERAL ACTION:

If States played a role in the execution of federal laws, any single State could easily defeat every measure put forward.

16:21 If the interposition of the State legislatures be necessary to give effect to a measure of the Union, they have only NOT TO ACT, or TO ACT EVASIVELY, and the measure is defeated.

NUMEROUS EXCUSES FOR THE STATES' DISOBEDIENCE:

16:22 This <u>neglect of duty</u> may be disguised under affected but unsubstantial provisions, so as not to appear, and of course not to excite any alarm in the people for the safety of the Constitution. The State leaders may even make a merit of their surreptitious invasions of it on the ground of some temporary <u>convenience</u>, <u>exemption</u>, or <u>advantage</u>.

STATES CAN'T STOP CONGRESS' CONSTITUTIONALLY-LEGAL LAWS:

States have no power to stop enforcement of federal laws. If they tried what would such attempts be labeled?

16:23 But if the execution of the laws of the national government should <u>not require the intervention of the State legislatures</u>, if they were to pass into immediate operation upon the <u>citizens</u> themselves, the particular governments could <u>not interrupt their progress</u> without an open and violent exertion of an <u>unconstitutional power</u>. No omissions nor evasions would answer the end.

There would be no doubt if a State acted unconstitutionally.

16:24 They would be <u>obliged to act</u>, and in such a manner as would leave no doubt that they had encroached on the national rights.

REBELLION LESS LIKELY WITH NEW CONSTITUTION:

16:25 An experiment of this nature would always be hazardous in the <u>face of a constitution</u> in any degree competent to its own defense, and of a people enlightened enough to distinguish between a legal exercise and an illegal <u>usurpation of authority</u>.

VIOLATING CONSTITUTION MADE DIFFICULT:

If a State tried to ignore federal law, such action could be stopped by the Constitution through the process of judicial review.

16:26 The success of it would require not merely a factious majority in the legislature, but the concurrence of the courts of justice and of the body of the people. If the <u>judges</u> were not embarked in a conspiracy with the legislature, they would <u>pronounce</u> the resolutions of such a majority to be contrary to the supreme law of the land, <u>unconstitutional</u>, and void.

PEOPLE WILL SIDE WITH CONSTITUTION:

Under a national Constitution the sympathies of the people are more likely to support common goals as expressed in the Constitution.

16:27 If the <u>people</u> were not tainted with the spirit of their State representatives, they, as the natural guardians of the Constitution, would <u>throw their weight into</u> the <u>national scale</u> and give it a decided preponderancy in the contest. Attempts of this kind would not often be made with levity or rashness, because they could seldom be made without danger to the authors, unless in cases of a tyrannical exercise of the federal authority.

NATIONAL AND STATE LAWS SIMILARLY ENFORCED:

Which government has the greater power to deal with insurrection?

16:28 If opposition to the national government should arise from the <u>disorderly conduct of refractory or seditious individuals</u>, it could be overcome by the same means which are daily employed against the same evil under the State governments. The <u>magistracy</u>, being equally the ministers of the law of the land, from whatever source it might emanate, would doubtless be as ready to guard the national as the local regulations from the inroads of private licentiousness.

NATIONAL GOVERNMENT BETTER EQUIPPED:

Emergencies will be better managed by the new federal government because it could command more resources.

16:29   As to those partial commotions and insurrections, which sometimes disquiet society, from the intrigues of an inconsiderable faction, or from sudden or occasional ill humors that do not infect the great body of the community the <u>general government</u> could command more extensive resources for the suppression of disturbances of that kind than would be in the power of any single member.

EVEN THE NEW CONSTITUTION CAN'T DO THE IMPOSSIBLE:

In the face of insurmountable civil war, no government can do the impossible to end such wars. Is that a good enough reason to reject the Constitution, simply because it can't perform the impossible?

16:30   And as to those mortal feuds which, in certain conjunctures, spread a conflagration through a whole nation, or through a very large proportion of it, proceeding either from weighty causes of discontent given by the government or from the contagion of some violent popular **paroxysm**,[49] they do not fall within any ordinary rules of calculation. When they happen, they commonly <u>amount to revolutions</u> and <u>dismemberments of empire</u>. No form of government can always either avoid or control them. It is in vain to hope to guard against events <u>too mighty for human foresight</u> or precaution, and it would be idle to object to a government because it could not <u>perform impossibilities</u>.

—PUBLIUS

REVIEW QUESTIONS

1. Has legislating sovereign states instead of individuals ever worked? (16:2–3)

2. What does legislating sovereign states always invite? (16:3)

3. In a confederacy where governments are managing governments, what would the general government always need at its immediate disposal? (16:4)

4. What was the outcome when military coercion supported confederate governments? (16:16)

5. What does the Constitution establish to resolve injustices and inequalities in society? (16:17–18)

6. Should the national laws operate on the States and their governments, or without interruption on their citizens? (16:23)

7. Under the new Constitution can States block federal laws? What recourse do they have? 16:23–25; 26)

8. Under the Constitution, which part of government is best equipped to handle insurrections and emergencies? (16:29)

9. What part of America's 230-plus year history proves Publius's declaration that no government is able to calm all mortal feuds? (16:30)

FEDERALIST NO. 17

FEDERAL DUTIES ARE FEW, STATE DUTIES ARE MANY, AND ARE KEPT SEPARATE: Local governments that do not abuse the people enjoy more loyalty from the people than do the national leaders. This loyalty protects the States from an overpowering central government. The European feudal societies are good examples of how the kings had difficulties controlling their local barons. The States are the guardians of the people's rights and would quickly rise up against any form of monarchy in the Union. In such a situation, anarchy is more likely than tyranny.

By Alexander Hamilton—December 5, 1787

FEAR OF CENTRALIZATION:

The federal government has no incentive and is not equipped to meddle in local affairs. Could the federal government become too powerful?

17:1   AN OBJECTION, of a nature different from that which has been stated and answered, in my last address, may perhaps be likewise urged <u>against the principle of legislation for the individual citizens of America</u>. It may be said that it would tend to render the government of the Union <u>too powerful</u>, and to enable it to <u>absorb those residuary authorities</u>, which it might be judged proper to leave with the States for local purposes.

---

49 ***paroxysm:*** A sudden outburst, attack, violent expression, or exacerbation of an emotion or activity.

LOVE OF POWER ON FEDERAL LEVEL WOULDN'T FLOW DOWN TO STATE LEVEL:

17:2 Allowing the utmost latitude to the love of power which any reasonable man can require, I confess I am at a loss to discover what temptation the persons intrusted with the administration of the general government could ever feel to divest the States of the authorities of that description. The regulation of the mere domestic police of a State appears to me to hold out slender allurements to ambition.

FOUR BASIC CONCERNS OF NATIONAL INTEREST:

What are the four main federal duties?

17:3 Commerce, finance, negotiation, and war seem to comprehend all the objects which have charms for minds governed by that passion; and all the powers necessary to those objects ought, in the first instance, to be lodged in the national depository.

LOCAL AFFAIRS ARE TOO NUMEROUS AND BURDENSOME FOR USURPERS:

Local affairs are far too numerous, burdensome, and widespread to concern the national government. What, for example, should be of local concern only and not national?

17:4 The administration of private justice between the citizens of the same State, the supervision of agriculture and of other concerns of a similar nature, all those things, in short, which are proper to be provided for by local legislation, can never be desirable cares of a general jurisdiction.

FEDERAL CONTROL OF STATE ISSUES IS POINTLESS:

Should any federal officer really want to be so burdened?

17:5 It is therefore improbable that there should exist a disposition in the federal councils to usurp the powers with which they are connected; because the attempt to exercise those powers would be as troublesome as it would be **nugatory**;[50] and the possession of them, for that reason, would contribute nothing to the dignity, to the importance, or to the splendor of the national government.

CONGRESS CAN CONTROL THE APPETITE FOR EXTRAVAGANCE:

Congress can control overly ambitious federal officers.

17:6 But let it be admitted, for argument's sake, that mere wantonness and lust of domination would be sufficient to beget that disposition; still it may be safely affirmed, that the sense of the constituent body of the national representatives, or, in other words, the people of the several States, would control the indulgence of so extravagant an appetite.

EASIER FOR STATES TO ENCROACH:

There is a danger from the States having power to disrupt the national authorities. Is this power greater than the federal government's?

17:7 It will always be far more easy for the State governments to encroach upon the national authorities than for the national government to encroach upon the State authorities.

PEOPLE SUPPORT WELL-RUN LOCAL GOVERNMENTS:

State governments that are well run have the support of the people. Does such intimacy exist with the national government?

17:8 The proof of this proposition turns upon the greater degree of influence which the State governments if they administer their affairs with uprightness and prudence, will generally possess over the people; a circumstance which at the same time teaches us that there is an inherent and intrinsic weakness in all federal constitutions; and that too much pains cannot be taken in their organization, to give them all the force which is compatible with the principles of liberty.

LOCAL GOVERNMENTS ARE MORE INFLUENTIAL:

Local governments have more influence because of the more intimate issues they deal with, unlike the national government.

17:9 The superiority of influence in favor of the particular governments would result partly from the diffusive construction of the national government, but chiefly from the nature of the objects to which the attention of the State administrations would be directed.

TRUST IN LOCAL LEADERS IS STRONGEST UNLESS RIGHTS ARE VIOLATED:

An inherent weakness in federalism is bias by people toward their own State and local concerns. Under what condition might the people turn to the national government for protection?

17:10 It is a known fact in human nature, that its affections are commonly weak in proportion to the distance or diffusiveness of the object. Upon the same principle that a man is more attached to his family than to his neighborhood, to his neighborhood than to the community at large, the people of each State would be apt to feel a stronger bias towards their local governments than towards the government of the Union; unless the force of that principle should be destroyed by a much better administration of the latter.

---

50 **nugatory:** Of no value or importance; of no force or consequence.

State concerns naturally attract more local attention.

17:11 This strong propensity of the human heart would find powerful auxiliaries in the objects of State regulation.

LOCAL INTERESTS TOO TEDIOUS FOR FEDERAL:

In regards to local issues and challenges, what advantage does local government have over federal?

17:12 The variety of more <u>minute interests</u>, which will necessarily fall under the superintendence of the local administrations, and which will form so many <u>rivulets of influence</u>, running through every part of the society, cannot be particularized, without involving a <u>detail too tedious</u> and uninteresting to <u>compensate</u> for the instruction it might afford.

LOCAL CONTROL OF POLICE AND COURTS:

The States' greatest advantage over the central government is their administration of criminal and civil justice. How is this so?

17:13 There is one transcendent advantage belonging to the province of the State governments, which alone suffices to place the matter in a clear and satisfactory light,—I mean the <u>ordinary administration of criminal and civil justice</u>. This, of all others, is the most powerful, most universal, and most attractive source of popular obedience and attachment. It is that which, being the immediate and visible <u>guardian of life and property</u>, having its benefits and its terrors in constant activity before the public eye, regulating all those personal interests and familiar concerns to which the sensibility of individuals is more immediately awake, contributes, more than any other circumstance, to <u>impressing</u> upon the minds of the <u>people</u>, <u>affection</u>, <u>esteem</u>, and <u>reverence towards the government</u>.

CONTROL OVER JUSTICE BINDS PEOPLE TOGETHER:

17:14 This great cement of society, which will diffuse itself almost wholly through the channels of the particular governments, independent of all other causes of influence, would insure them so decided an empire over their respective citizens as to render them at all times a complete counterpoise, and, not unfrequently, <u>dangerous rivals to the power of the Union</u>.

NATIONAL CONCERNS OF LESS INTEREST:

Both the workings and the benefits of the central government usually lack local impact, making them less obvious to the people.

17:15 The operations of the <u>national government</u>, on the other hand, falling <u>less immediately</u> under the observation of the <u>mass of the citizens</u>, the benefits derived from it will chiefly be perceived and attended to <u>by speculative men</u>. Relating to more general interests, they will be less apt to come home to the feelings of the people; and, in proportion, less likely to inspire an habitual sense of obligation, and an active sentiment of attachment.

All federal governments help prove this point.

17:16 The reasoning on this head has been abundantly exemplified by the experience of all federal constitutions with which we are acquainted, and of all others which have borne the least analogy to them.

FEUDAL SYSTEMS SIMILAR TO CONFEDERACIES:

What was the basic structure of the feudal systems?

17:17 Though the <u>ancient feudal systems</u> were not, strictly speaking, <u>confederacies</u>, yet they partook of the nature of that species of association. There was a common <u>head</u>, chieftain, or sovereign, whose <u>authority extended</u> over the <u>whole nation</u>; and a number of subordinate vassals, or feudatories, who had large portions of land allotted to them, and numerous trains of INFERIOR vassals or retainers, who occupied and cultivated that land upon the tenure of fealty or obedience, to the persons of whom they held it.

FEUDAL ANARCHY:

The various feudatories were frequently at war with each other, and the monarch was too weak to do anything about it. The monarchs did not have the people's support as well as did the lower-level leaders (barons).

17:18 <u>Each principal vassal was a kind of sovereign</u>, within his particular demesnes. <u>The consequences</u> of this situation were a <u>continual opposition to authority of the sovereign</u>, and frequent <u>wars between</u> the great barons or chief feudatories themselves. The power of the head of the nation was <u>commonly too weak</u>, either to preserve the public peace, or to <u>protect the people</u> against the oppressions of their <u>immediate lords</u>. This period of European affairs is emphatically styled by historians, the times of <u>feudal anarchy</u>.

FEUDALISM NATURALLY DESTROYS NATIONAL SPIRIT:

Even when national leaders were strong, those more connected to the people usually prevailed.

17:19 When the sovereign happened to be a man of vigorous and warlike temper and of superior abilities, he would acquire a personal weight and influence, which answered, for the time, the purpose of a more regular authority. But in general, the <u>power of the barons triumphed over that of the prince</u>; and in many instances his dominion was entirely thrown off, and the great fiefs were erected into <u>independent principalities</u> or States.

MONARCH'S SUCCESS BUILT ON BARON'S TYRANNY:

On the other hand, if local leaders became tyrants, the monarch usually won over the allegiance of the people and prevailed.

17:20 In those instances in which the monarch finally prevailed over his vassals, his success was chiefly owing to the tyranny of those vassals over their dependents. The barons, or nobles, equally the enemies of the sovereign and the oppressors of the common people, were dreaded and detested by both; till mutual danger and mutual interest effected a union between them fatal to the power of the aristocracy.

TRUST WAS THE MEANS TO CONTROL KING:

If the nobles preserved the trust, might the king have been toppled?

17:21 Had the nobles, by a conduct of clemency and justice, preserved the fidelity and devotion of their retainers and followers, the contests between them and the prince must almost always have ended in their favor, and in the abridgment or subversion of the royal authority.

FEUDAL SCOTLAND FURNISHES AN EXAMPLE:

Ages of "clanship" forged a unity that kings could not conquer.

17:22 This is not an assertion founded merely in speculation or conjecture. Among other illustrations of its truth which might be cited, Scotland will furnish a cogent example. The spirit of clanship which was, at an early day, introduced into that kingdom, uniting the nobles and their dependents by ties equivalent to those of kindred, rendered the aristocracy a constant overmatch for the power of the monarch, till the incorporation with England subdued its fierce and ungovernable spirit, and reduced it within those rules of subordination which a more rational and more energetic system of civil polity had previously established in the latter kingdom.

STATE GOVERNMENTS ARE MUCH LIKE FEUDAL BARONS:

They both will generally retain the trust and support of the people to resist encroachment by the national government.

17:23 The separate governments in a confederacy may aptly be compared with the feudal baronies; with this advantage in their favor, that from the reasons already explained, they will generally possess the confidence and good-will of the people, and with so important a support, will be able effectually to oppose all encroachments of the national government. It will be well if they are not able to counteract its legitimate and necessary authority.

BOTH HAVE RIVALRY FOR POWER AND AUTHORITY:

17:24 The points of similitude consist in the rivalship of power, applicable to both, and in the CONCENTRATION of large portions of the strength of the community into particular DEPOSITORIES, in one case at the disposal of individuals, in the other case at the disposal of political bodies.

HISTORICAL EXAMPLES:

A study of historical confederacies will demonstrate why confederacies don't work. Is the Articles of Confederation a failure because its writers didn't learn from the past?

17:25 A concise review of the events that have attended confederate governments will further illustrate this important doctrine; an inattention to which has been the great source of our political mistakes, and has given our jealousy a direction to the wrong side. This review shall form the subject of some ensuing papers.

—PUBLIUS

REVIEW QUESTIONS

1. What are the four basic objects of a national government? (17:3)

2. What are four examples of social and political issues that are best left to the States? (17:4–5, 13)

3. Why is it easier for States to encroach on national authorities? (17:7–10)

4. Which level of government do citizens trust the most? What can drive people to another level? (17:10–11)

5. How was the feudal system like a confederacy? (17:17–21)

6. Why were "political mistakes" made in drafting the Articles of Confederation? (17:25)

FEDERALIST NO. 18

ALL CONFEDERACIES MUST FAIL: The Articles of Confederation was fundamentally broken because it didn't give enough power to the central government to rule over thirteen sovereign and jealous States. This pattern is not new and can be demonstrated by the Greek republics that were united under the Amphyctionic Council. The problem with that Greek system is that the republics didn't surrender enough power to the council. In contrast, the Achaean League did much better because they did surrender sovereignty to the League.

By James Madison—December 7, 1787

ANCIENT FAILURES FORESHADOW TODAY'S:

The largest confederacy of ancient times was in Greece. Its grand failure foreshadows the end place for America under the Articles of Confederation.

18:1 AMONG the confederacies of antiquity, the most considerable was that of the <u>Grecian republics</u>, associated under the <u>Amphictyonic Council</u>.[51] From the best accounts transmitted of this celebrated institution, it bore a very instructive analogy to the present Confederation of the American States.

MEMBER STATES WERE LEFT TOO STRONG:

The ancient Greek city-states were independent and formed a league with representatives who had equal votes. The central council had power to resolve problems and wage war, but the states' failure to form a true republican system led to their eventual collapse (see 18:6-9).

18:2 The members retained the character of <u>independent</u> and <u>sovereign states</u>, and had <u>equal votes</u> in the federal council. This council had a <u>general authority</u> to propose and resolve whatever it judged necessary for the common welfare of Greece; to <u>declare</u> and <u>carry on war</u>; to <u>decide</u>, in the last resort, all <u>controversies between the members</u>; to <u>fine the aggressing</u> party; to employ the whole <u>force of the confederacy</u> against the disobedient; to <u>admit new members</u>.

GUARDIANS OF RELIGION AND WEALTH:

18:3 The Amphictyons were the guardians of <u>religion</u>, and of the <u>immense riches</u> belonging to the <u>temple of Delphos</u>, where they had the right of jurisdiction in controversies between the inhabitants and those who came to consult the <u>oracle</u>.

AN OATH IS NOT ENOUGH TO HOLD A UNION TOGETHER:

18:4 As a further provision for the efficacy of the federal powers, they took an <u>oath mutually</u> to defend and protect the <u>united cities</u>, to <u>punish the violators of this oath</u>, and to inflict vengeance on sacrilegious despoilers of the temple.

A CONFEDERATION APPEARED VERY PLAUSIBLE IN THEORY:

In comparison to the Articles of Confederation, did the Amphictyonic Council have more power than the States?

18:5 In <u>theory</u>, and upon paper, this apparatus of powers <u>seems amply sufficient</u> for all general purposes. In several material instances, they exceed the powers enumerated in the articles of confederation. The Amphictyons had in their hands the <u>superstition of the times</u>, one of the principal <u>engines by which government was then maintained</u>; they had a declared authority to <u>use coercion</u> against refractory cities, and were bound by oath to exert this authority on the necessary occasions.

CONFEDERACIES HAVE SAME FATAL FLAWS THEN AS NOW:

The council's enforcement power was not strong enough over the whole. How did the most powerful members seek control?

18:6 Very <u>different</u>, nevertheless, was the experiment from the <u>theory</u>. The powers, like those of the present Congress, were <u>administered by deputies</u> appointed wholly by the <u>cities</u> in their political capacities; and exercised over them in the same capacities. Hence the <u>weakness</u>, the disorders, and finally the <u>destruction of the confederacy</u>.

IT IS A FLAW OF HUMAN NATURE TO TYRANNIZE THE WEAK:

18:7 The <u>more powerful members</u>, instead of being kept in awe and subordination, <u>tyrannized</u> successively over all the rest. <u>Athens</u>, as we learn from Demosthenes, was the <u>arbiter of Greece seventy-three years</u>. The **Lacedaemonians**[52] next governed it <u>twenty-nine years</u>; at a subsequent period, after the battle of Leuctra, the <u>Thebans had their turn of domination</u>.

GREEK CITY-STATES COULDN'T COORDINATE IN WAR:

The strongest city-states used their influences to overpower the weaker. How were the weaker cities overpowered internally?

18:8 It happened but too often, according to <u>Plutarch</u>, that the deputies of the <u>strongest cities</u> awed and corrupted those of the weaker; and that judgment went in favor of the most powerful party.

The Greeks' league could not bring about a unified effort to defend itself. What contributed to losses during the ongoing wars?

18:9 Even in the midst of defensive and dangerous wars with <u>Persia</u> and <u>Macedon</u>, the members <u>never acted in concert</u>, and were, more or fewer of them, eternally the <u>dupes or the hirelings of the common enemy</u>. The intervals of foreign war were filled up by domestic vicissitudes, <u>convulsions</u>, and <u>carnage</u>.

---

51 ***Amphictyonic Council (pronounced "am-FIC-tea-onic"):*** A religious "league of neighbors" among neighboring city-states in ancient Greece formed to protect their religious, cultural, and political union. Founded around 1100 BC, it reached its peak of power around 500 BC.

52 ***Lacedaemon (pronounced "LASSA-demon"; Lacaedaemonians pronounced "LASSA-dee-moan-ians"):*** A prominent city-state in ancient Greece with Sparta as its main settlement. Sparta's social system and constitution promoted military preparedness as part of its culture, making it the dominant and uniting military power in Greece.

WEAK UNION FAILED TO CLEANSE ITSELF OF WEAKNESS:

After the wars an attempt to shift political power was made, but failed. What happened to the weaker and smaller members?

18:10 After the conclusion of the war with Xerxes, it appears that the Lacedaemonians required that a number of the cities should be turned out of the confederacy for the unfaithful part they had acted. The Athenians, finding that the Lacedaemonians would lose fewer partisans by such a measure than themselves, and would become masters of the public deliberations, vigorously opposed and defeated the attempt.

Weak confederacies pull all members down.

18:11 This piece of history proves at once the inefficiency of the union, the ambition and jealousy of its most powerful members, and the dependent and degraded condition of the rest. The smaller members, though entitled by the theory of their system to revolve in equal pride and majesty around the common center, had become, in fact, satellites of the orbs of primary magnitude.

WHY THE GREEK CONFEDERACY FAILED:

The Greeks did not learn from their experiences and failed to adopt critically-needed reforms and a closer union. What became of the two remaining powerhouses?

18:12 Had the Greeks, says the **Abbe Milot**,[53] been as wise as they were courageous, they would have been admonished by experience of the necessity of a closer union, and would have availed themselves of the peace which followed their success against the Persian arms, to establish such a reformation.

RIVALS FIRST, ENEMIES SECOND:

18:13 Instead of this obvious policy, Athens and Sparta, inflated with the victories and the glory they had acquired, became first rivals and then enemies; and did each other infinitely more mischief than they had suffered from Xerxes. Their mutual jealousies, fears, hatreds, and injuries ended in the celebrated Peloponnesian war; which itself ended in the ruin and slavery of the Athenians who had begun it.

FACTIONS GROW IN POWER:

What happens inside a country when the government is weak?

18:14 As a weak government, when not at war, is ever agitated by internal dissensions, so these never fail to bring on fresh calamities from abroad.

FOREIGN ALLIES BETRAY:

Foreign allies invited to help a weaker member of a league will stay as conquerer.

18:15 The Phocians having ploughed up some consecrated ground belonging to the temple of Apollo, the Amphictyonic council, according to the superstition of the age, imposed a fine on the sacrilegious offenders. The Phocians, being abetted by Athens and Sparta, refused to submit to the decree. The Thebans, with others of the cities, undertook to maintain the authority of the Amphictyons, and to avenge the violated god.

HOW PHILIP OF MACEDON CONQUERED THE PEOPLE:

18:16 The latter, being the weaker party, invited the assistance of Philip of Macedon, who had secretly fostered the contest. Philip gladly seized the opportunity of executing the designs he had long planned against the liberties of Greece. By his intrigues and bribes he won over to his interests the popular leaders of several cities; by their influence and votes, gained admission into the Amphictyonic council; and by his arts and his arms, made himself master of the confederacy.

HOW TO REPEL A TAKEOVER:

A closer union would have served best to repel foreign influences. How could Greece have prevented its take over?

18:17 Such were the consequences of the fallacious principle on which this interesting establishment was founded. Had Greece, says a judicious observer on her fate, been united by a stricter confederation, and persevered in her union, she would never have worn the chains of Macedon; and might have proved a barrier to the vast projects of Rome.

BEST EXAMPLE OF ANCIENT CONSTITUTIONS:

The Greece Achaean[54] league was better organized and took better steps to ensure equality among the member cities. How were the members made equal in politics?

18:18 The Achaean league, as it is called, was another society of Grecian republics, which supplies us with valuable instruction.

Organization was wise and intimate.

18:19 The Union here was far more intimate, and its organization much wiser, than in the preceding instance. It will accordingly appear, that though not exempt from a similar catastrophe, it by no means equally deserved it.

---

53 **Abbe Milot:** French Jesuit and historian, 1726-1785.
54 **Achaean** is pronounced "a-KEY-un."

Local control retained.

18:20 The cities composing this league retained their municipal jurisdiction, appointed their own officers, and enjoyed a perfect equality.

Senate was representative of all, with national duties only.

18:21 The senate, in which they were represented, had the sole and exclusive right of peace and war; of sending and receiving ambassadors; of entering into treaties and alliances; of appointing a chief magistrate or praetor, as he was called, who commanded their armies, and who, with the advice and consent of ten of the senators, not only administered the government in the recess of the senate, but had a great share in its deliberations, when assembled.

Two praetors ruled together, but at a formal trial it was only one at a time.

18:22 According to the primitive constitution, there were two praetors associated in the administration; but on trial a single one was preferred.

Common mediums of commerce.

18:23 It appears that the cities had all the same laws and customs, the same weights and measures, and the same money. But how far this effect proceeded from the authority of the federal council is left in uncertainty. It is said only that the cities were in a manner compelled to receive the same laws and usages.

SELF-GOVERNMENT KEY TO NATIONAL STRENGTH:

18:24 When Lacedaemon was brought into the league by Philopoemen, it was attended with an abolition of the institutions and laws of Lycurgus, and an adoption of those of the Achaeans. The Amphictyonic confederacy, of which she had been a member, left her in the full exercise of her government and her legislation. This circumstance alone proves a very material difference in the genius of the two systems.

ACHAEAN'S EXAMPLE IS BEST BUT LACKS RELIABLE RECORD:

For lack of a good historical record of the Greek leagues, no one knows the complete reasons for their successes and failures.

18:25 It is much to be regretted that such imperfect monuments remain of this curious political fabric. Could its interior structure and regular operation be ascertained, it is probable that more light would be thrown by it on the science of federal government, than by any of the like experiments with which we are acquainted.

THE ACHAEAN LEAGUE WAS MORE JUST:

The Achaean league enjoyed more peace because its laws were more fair and the people were likewise cooperative and peaceful. Were their leaders popularly elected? Did that help?

18:26 One important fact seems to be witnessed by all the historians who take notice of Achaean affairs. It is, that as well after the renovation of the league by Aratus, as before its dissolution by the arts of Macedon, there was infinitely more of moderation and justice in the administration of its government, and less of violence and sedition in the people, than were to be found in any of the cities exercising singly all the prerogatives of sovereignty. The **Abbe Mably,**[55] in his observations on Greece, says that the popular government, which was so tempestuous elsewhere, caused no disorders in the members of the Achaean republic, BECAUSE IT WAS THERE TEMPERED BY THE GENERAL AUTHORITY AND LAWS OF THE CONFEDERACY.

FACTIONS CAUSED DIFFICULTIES:

All was not peaceful, however. Factions still existed.

18:27 We are not to conclude too hastily, however, that faction did not, in a certain degree, agitate the particular cities; much less that a due subordination and harmony reigned in the general system. The contrary is sufficiently displayed in the vicissitudes and fate of the republic.

FOREIGN ALLIES BECOME CONQUERORS:

Foreigners were invited into the Achaean league and turned on them to become conquerers. What became of the union?

18:28 Whilst the Amphictyonic confederacy remained, that of the Achaeans, which comprehended the less important cities only, made little figure on the theatre of Greece. When the former became a victim to Macedon, the latter was spared by the policy of Philip and Alexander. Under the successors of these princes, however, a different policy prevailed. The arts of division were practiced among the Achaeans. Each city was seduced into a separate interest; the union was dissolved. Some of the cities fell under the tyranny of Macedonian garrisons; others under that of usurpers springing out of their own confusions.

OPPRESSED PEOPLE SOON LONG FOR LIBERTY:

A movement for liberty started to unite the Greek cities. Could Macedon stop this re-unification?

18:29 Shame and oppression erelong awaken their love of liberty. A few cities reunited. Their example was followed by others, as opportunities were found of cutting off their tyrants. The league soon embraced almost the whole Pelopon-

---

55   *Abbe Mably:* French philosopher, historian and write, 1709-1785.

nesus. Macedon saw its progress; but was hindered by internal dissensions from stopping it.

GREECE FAILED TO UNIFY:

When Greece failed to fully unify, they turned, once again, to foreign allies to save them. Whose help did they seek? Did it work?

18:30   All Greece caught the enthusiasm and seemed ready to unite in one confederacy, when the jealousy and envy in Sparta and Athens, of the rising glory of the Achaeans, threw a fatal damp on the enterprise. The dread of the Macedonian power induced the league to court the alliance of the Kings of Egypt and Syria, who, as successors of Alexander, were rivals of the king of Macedon.

ALLIANCE WAS ESSENTIALLY SABOTAGED:

18:31 This policy was defeated by Cleomenes, king of Sparta, who was led by his ambition to make an unprovoked attack on his neighbors, the Achaeans, and who, as an enemy to Macedon, had interest enough with the Egyptian and Syrian princes to effect a breach of their engagements with the league.

ACHAEANS SUBMIT TO FORMER OPPRESSOR:

Because Greece didn't unite independently it was thrown into chaos, dependent again on foreign help. Who did they turn to in an effort to overthrow the overzealous King Cleomenes?

18:32   The Achaeans were now reduced to the dilemma of submitting to Cleomenes, or of supplicating the aid of Macedon, its former oppressor. The latter expedient was adopted. The contests of the Greeks always afforded a pleasing opportunity to that powerful neighbor of intermeddling in their affairs. A Macedonian army quickly appeared. Cleomenes was vanquished.

THE ALLY BECOMES THE CONQUERER:

Were the Macedonians liberators or conquerers of the Acheans?

18:33 The Achaeans soon experienced, as often happens, that a victorious and powerful ally is but another name for a master. All that their most abject compliances could obtain from him was a toleration of the exercise of their laws.

Discord and dissension ruined the Greeks' effort to unify against their enemies. To what did they turn to resist Macedon?

18:34 Philip, who was now on the throne of Macedon, soon provoked by his tyrannies, fresh combinations among the

Greeks. The Achaeans, though weakened by internal dissensions and by the revolt of Messene, one of its members, being joined by the Aetolians and Athenians, erected the standard of opposition. The Romans, to whom the invitation was made, eagerly embraced it. Philip was conquered; Macedon subdued.

GREEKS FATEFULLY TURN, AGAIN, TO FOREIGN HELP:

18:35   Finding themselves, though thus supported, unequal to the undertaking, they once more had recourse to the dangerous expedient of introducing the succor of foreign arms. The Romans, to whom the invitation was made, eagerly embraced it. Philip was conquered; Macedon subdued.

What did Rome do to the Achaean league when they got the opportunity?

18:36 A new crisis ensued to the league. Dissensions broke out among it members. These the Romans fostered **Callicrates**[56] and other popular leaders became mercenary instruments for **inveigling**[57] their countrymen. The more effectually to nourish discord and disorder the Romans had, to the astonishment of those who confided in their sincerity, already proclaimed universal liberty.[58] With the same insidious views, they now seduced the members from the league, by representing to their pride the violation it committed on their sovereignty.

Was Greece able to keep its liberty after Rome entered the scene?

18:37   By these arts this union, the last hope of Greece, the last hope of ancient liberty, was torn into pieces; and such imbecility and distraction introduced, that the arms of Rome found little difficulty in completing the ruin which their arts had commenced. The Achaeans were cut to pieces, and Achaia loaded with chains, under which it is groaning at this hour.

FEDERAL GOVERNMENT TENDS TOWARD ANARCHY:

The lesson to be learned is that federal bodies not properly organized or controlled will ultimately ignite anarchy rather than unify their forces of tyranny.

18:38   I have thought it not superfluous to give the outlines of this important portion of history; both because it teaches more than one lesson, and because, as a supplement to the outlines of the Achaean constitution, it emphatically illustrates the tendency of federal bodies rather to anarchy among the members, than to tyranny in the head.

—PUBLIUS

---

56 **Callicrates:** ("Ca-lick-ra-tease") Achaean politician (died 149 BC) who helped Rome infiltrate Greek states. He betrayed Polybius who was a prominent Greek historian, and 1,000 other nobles, whom he identified to be transported to Rome as hostages.

57 *inveigling:* Persuasion by deception or flattery.

58 *Publius:* This was but another name more specious for the independence of the members of the federal head throughout Greece

REVIEW QUESTIONS

1. To what ancient confederacy does Madison compare the Articles of Confederation? (18:1)

2. What fatal flaw eventually tore the Amphyctionic council apart? (18:2–4)

3. What destroys a confederacy? (18:6–11)

4. What lesson did the Greeks fail to learn from their wars? (18:12)

5. What relationship developed between Athens and Sparta that led to their destruction? Does this accurately exemplify Publius's assertion that neighbors in a confederacy eventually turn on each other? (18:13)

6. What happens inside a country when the government is weak? (18:14)

7. What was the Achaean league? (18:18–25)

8. Why was peace better maintained in the Achaean republic? (18:25)

9. As shown by the ancient Grecian republics, do federal governments tend toward tyranny or anarchy? (18:37)

FEDERALIST NO. 19

THE GERMAN, POLISH, AND SWISS CONFEDERA-CIES FAILED: Germany and Poland are good examples of how confederacies under a weak central government will dissolve into civil war, roaming gangs and militias, killings, confiscations, and violations of human rights. The breakdowns are brought about by ethnic or religious tyranny, corruption at the top levels, the rise of and rule by guerrilla and militia groups, civil wars and coups, and poorly supported successions in government. America is not immune from these collapses.

By James Madison—December 8, 1787

EXISTING INSTITUTIONS ILLUSTRATE THE PROBLEM OF CONFEDERACIES:

19:1 THE examples of ancient confederacies, cited in my last paper, have not exhausted the source of experimental instruction on this subject. There are existing institutions, founded on a similar principle, which merit particular consideration. The first which presents itself is the Germanic body.

THE GERMAN CONFEDERACY:
It underwent decades of major change. Was Germany always a single nation under a single ruler?

19:2 In the early ages of Christianity, Germany was occupied by seven distinct nations, who had no common chief. The Franks, one of the number, having conquered the Gauls, established the kingdom which has taken its name from them.

CHARLEMAGNE ADDS GERMANY TO HIS EMPIRE:

19:3 In the ninth century Charlemagne, its warlike monarch, carried his victorious arms in every direction; and Germany became a part of his vast dominions. On the dismemberment, which took place under his sons, this part was erected into a separate and independent empire. Charlemagne and his immediate descendants possessed the reality, as well as the ensigns and dignity of imperial power.

CHARLEMAGNE'S EMPIRE BEGINS TO DECLINE:
The main parts of Charlemagne's empire gradually broke away to become sovereign and independent.

19:4 But the principal vassals, whose fiefs had become hereditary, and who composed the national **diets**[59] which Charlemagne had not abolished, gradually threw off the yoke and advanced to sovereign jurisdiction and independence. The force of imperial sovereignty was insufficient to restrain such powerful dependents; or to preserve the unity and tranquility of the empire. The most furious private wars, accompanied with every species of calamity, were carried on between the different princes and states.

Monarchs started to lose control.

19:5 The imperial authority, unable to maintain the public order, declined by degrees till it was almost extinct in the anarchy, which agitated the long interval between the death of the last emperor of the Suabian, and the accession of the first emperor of the Austrian lines.

Emperors took over but eventually became mere figureheads.

19:6 In the eleventh century the emperors enjoyed full sovereignty: In the fifteenth they had little more than the symbols and decorations of power.

NEW GERMAN FEDERAL SYSTEM SIMILAR TO FEUDALISM:
The resulting feudal system in the Germanic empire had many similar features of a confederacy. Who was the executive authority in Germany?

---

59 **diet:** An ancient Greek/Latin term meaning "an assembly." In politics it's used to mean a deliberative assembly, a gathering of members who make political decisions.

19:7 Out of this feudal system, which has itself many of the important features of a confederacy, has grown the federal system which constitutes the Germanic empire.

The Germanic's legislature, emperor, and judiciary tribunals.

19:8 Its powers are vested in a diet representing the component members of the confederacy; in the emperor, who is the executive magistrate, with a **negative**[60] on the decrees of the diet; and in the imperial chamber and the **aulic council**,[61] two judiciary tribunals having supreme jurisdiction in controversies which concern the empire, or which happen among its members.

DUTIES OF THE DIET:
The central authority of the Germanic empire managed and controlled the various groups in the confederacy.

19:9 The diet possesses the general power of legislating for the empire; of making war and peace; contracting alliances; assessing quotas of troops and money; constructing fortresses; regulating coin; admitting new members; and subjecting disobedient members to the ban of the empire, by which the party is degraded from his sovereign rights and his possessions forfeited.

RESTRICTIONS ON MEMBERS OF THE CONFEDERACY:
19:10 The members of the confederacy are expressly restricted from entering into compacts prejudicial to the empire; from imposing tolls and duties on their mutual intercourse, without the consent of the emperor and diet; from altering the value of money; from doing injustice to one another; or from affording assistance or retreat to disturbers of the public peace. And the ban is denounced against such as shall violate any of these restrictions.

A JUDICIARY:
19:11 The members of the diet, as such, are subject in all cases to be judged by the emperor and diet, and in their private capacities by the aulic council and imperial chamber.

THE EMPEROR:
The emperor owned no territory and wasn't paid, but he was one of the most powerful leaders in Europe.

19:12 The prerogatives of the emperor are numerous. The most important of them are: his exclusive right to make propositions to the diet; to negative its resolutions; to name ambassadors; to confer dignities and titles; to fill vacant electorates; to found universities; to grant privileges not injurious to the states of the empire; to receive and apply the public revenues; and generally to watch over the public safety.

COUNCIL TO THE EMPEROR:
19:13 In certain cases, the electors form a council to him. In quality of emperor, he possesses no territory within the empire, nor receives any revenue for his support. But his revenue and dominions, in other qualities, constitute him one of the most powerful princes in Europe.

GERMAN CONFEDERACY SIMILAR TO ARTICLES:
The German diet could not regulate its own members, as is the case for today's Congress under the Articles of Confederation.

19:14 From such a parade of constitutional powers, in the representatives and head of this confederacy, the natural supposition would be, that it must form an exception to the general character which belongs to its kindred systems. Nothing would be further from the reality. The fundamental principle on which it rests, that the empire is a community of sovereigns, that the diet is a representation of sovereigns and that the laws are addressed to sovereigns, renders the empire a nerveless body, incapable of regulating its own members, insecure against external dangers, and agitated with unceasing fermentations in its own bowels.

MADISON'S INDICTMENT OF THE GERMAN SYSTEM:
Germany was in constant conflict between the emperor, the states, and foreign invaders. Did the various states fail to comply with requests for military support, similar to America?

19:15 The history of Germany is a history of wars between the emperor and the princes and states; of wars among the princes and states themselves; of the licentiousness of the strong, and the oppression of the weak; of foreign intrusions, and foreign intrigues; of requisitions of men and money disregarded, or partially complied with; of attempts to enforce them, altogether abortive, or attended with slaughter and desolation, involving the innocent with the guilty; of general imbecility, confusion, and misery.

ON-GOING CIVIL WAR:
Thirty years of war, conflict, confusion, and chaos marked Germany's history during this period. Who finally came along and brought peace to the infighting?

19:16 In the sixteenth century, the emperor, with one part of the empire on his side, was seen engaged against the other

---

60 **negative:** To veto or cancel; the power or right vested in one part of government to cancel or postpone decisions or enactments of another.

61 **Aulic Council (pronounced "OWL-ic," or "ALL-ic")** was an executive organ of the Holy Roman Empire from 1407–1806. This was an official counsel of paid, permanent members who handled petitions to the emperor, and served as the private court of the emperor.

princes and states. In one of the conflicts, the emperor himself was put to flight, and very near being made prisoner by the elector of Saxony. The late king of Prussia was more than once pitted against his imperial sovereign; and commonly proved an overmatch for him.

CONSTANT BLOODSHED:

19:17   Controversies and wars among the members themselves have been so common, that the German annals are crowded with the bloody pages which describe them.

PEACE TREATIES IN GERMANY'S CONSTITUTION:

19:18   Previous to the peace of Westphalia, Germany was desolated by a war of thirty years, in which the emperor, with one half of the empire, was on one side, and Sweden, with the other half, on the opposite side. Peace was at length negotiated, and dictated by foreign powers; and the articles of it, to which foreign powers are parties, made a fundamental part of the Germanic constitution.

PANIC WON'T SOLVE CORE PROBLEMS OF CONFEDERACY:

A new crisis won't necessarily unify and pacify a confederacy already in conflict among its members.

19:19   If the nation happens, on any emergency, to be more united by the necessity of self-defense, its situation is still deplorable. Military preparations must be preceded by so many tedious discussions, arising from the jealousies, pride, separate views, and clashing pretensions of sovereign bodies, that before the diet can settle the arrangements, the enemy are in the field; and before the federal troops are ready to take it, are retiring into winter quarters.

GERMAN ARMY IS INADEQUATE:

19:20   The small body of national troops, which has been judged necessary in time of peace, is defectively kept up, badly paid, infected with local prejudices, and supported by irregular and disproportionate contributions to the treasury.

INTERNAL WARS DUE TO DELINQUENT MEMBERS:

Failing to overcome the weaknesses of its confederacy, Germany was in a constant state of internal strife and civil war.

19:21   The impossibility of maintaining order and dispensing justice among these sovereign subjects, produced the experiment of dividing the empire into nine or ten circles or districts; of giving them an interior organization, and of charging them with the military execution of the laws against delinquent and contumacious members. This experiment has

only served to demonstrate more fully the radical vice of the constitution. Each circle is the miniature picture of the deformities of this political monster. They either fail to execute their commissions, or they do it with all the devastation and carnage of civil war. Sometimes whole circles are defaulters; and then they increase the mischief which they were instituted to remedy.

USE OF INTERNAL MILITARY INTERVENTION:

In the German confederacy one member was sent to quell disorder by another member and ended up conquering and annexing the rebellious section to himself.

19:22   We may form some judgment of this scheme of military coercion from a sample given by Thuanus. In Donawerth, a free and imperial city of the circle of Suabia, the Abbe de St. Croix enjoyed certain immunities which had been reserved to him. In the exercise of these, on some public occasions, outrages were committed on him by the people of the city.

BAVARIAN DUKE TAKES OVER ABBE DE ST. CROIX:

19:23   The consequence was that the city was put under the ban of the empire, and the Duke of Bavaria, though director of another circle, obtained an appointment to enforce it. He soon appeared before the city with a corps of ten thousand troops, and finding it a fit occasion, as he had secretly intended from the beginning, to revive an antiquated claim, on the pretext that his ancestors had suffered the place to be dismembered from his territory,[62] he took possession of it in his own name, disarmed, and punished the inhabitants, and reannexed the city to his domains.

WEAKNESS OF MEMBER STATES MAINTAINS THE STATUS QUO:

19:24   It may be asked, perhaps, what has so long kept this disjointed machine from falling entirely to pieces? The answer is obvious: The weakness of most of the members, who are unwilling to expose themselves to the mercy of foreign powers; the weakness of most of the principal members, compared with the formidable powers all around them; the vast weight and influence which the emperor derives from his separate and hereditary dominions; and the interest he feels in preserving a system with which his family pride is connected, and which constitutes him the first prince in Europe;

CIRCUMSTANCES DISCOURAGE PROPER REFORMS:

19:25   —these causes support a feeble and precarious Union; whilst the repellant quality, incident to the nature of sovereignty, and which time continually strengthens, prevents any reform whatever, founded on a proper consolidation.

---

62   *Publius:* (Pfeffel, "Nouvel Abreg. Chronol. de l'Hist., etc., d'Allemagne," says the pretext was to indemnify himself for the expense of the expedition.)

NEIGHBORING NATIONS WANT GERMANY WEAK:

Germany is kept weak by being in a state of disorder.

19:26　Nor is it to be imagined, if this obstacle could be surmounted, that the neighboring powers would suffer a revolution to take place which would give to the empire the force and preeminence to which it is entitled. Foreign nations have long considered themselves as interested in the changes made by events in this constitution; and have, on various occasions, betrayed their policy of perpetuating its anarchy and weakness.

POLAND—AN EXAMPLE OF A DISJOINTED CONFEDERACY:

Poland is also unprepared to defend or govern itself. What kind of relationship does Poland have with its neighbors?

19:27　If more direct examples were wanting, Poland, as a government over local sovereigns, might not improperly be taken notice of. Nor could any proof more striking be given of the calamities flowing from such institutions. Equally unfit for self-government and self-defense, it has long been at the mercy of its powerful neighbors; who have lately had the mercy to disburden it of one third of its people and territories.

SWISS STATES NOT AN ACTUAL CONFEDERACY:

The members of the Swiss cantons are even more disjointed. What institutions normally found in a confederacy missing?

19:28　The connection among the Swiss **cantons**[63] scarcely amounts to a confederacy; though it is sometimes cited as an instance of the stability of such institutions.

No common or shared marks of sovereignty.

19:29　They have no common treasury; no common troops even in war; no common coin; no common judicatory; nor any other common mark of sovereignty.

SWISS UNITED BY GEOGRAPHY, FEAR, AND INTERESTS:

19:30　They are kept together by the peculiarity of their topographical position; by their individual weakness and insignificancy; by the fear of powerful neighbors, to one of which they were formerly subject; by the few sources of contention among a people of such simple and homogeneous manners; by their joint interest in their dependent possessions; by the mutual aid they stand in need of, for suppressing insurrections and rebellions, an aid expressly stipulated and often required and afforded; and by the necessity of some regular and permanent provision for accommodating disputes among the cantons.

CHOOSING JUDGES AND UMPIRE:

The Swiss settled their disputes by electing judges, one of whom was the umpire of all. What was his duty?

19:31　The provision is, that the parties at variance shall each choose four judges out of the neutral cantons, who, in case of disagreement, choose an umpire. This tribunal, under an oath of impartiality, pronounces definitive sentence, which all the cantons are bound to enforce. The competency of this regulation may be estimated by a clause in their treaty of 1683, with [Duke] Victor Amadeus of Savoy; in which he obliges himself to interpose as mediator in disputes between the cantons, and to employ force, if necessary, against the contumacious party.

ANY CONTROVERSY DESTROYED THE CONNECTIONS:

Though the Swiss confederacy is much different from the US confederacy, how did fighting over religion contribute to the breakup of the Swiss confederacy?

19:32　So far as the peculiarity of their case will admit of comparison with that of the United States, it serves to confirm the principle intended to be established. Whatever efficacy the union may have had in ordinary cases, it appears that the moment a cause of difference sprang up, capable of trying its strength, it failed. The controversies on the subject of religion, which in three instances have kindled violent and bloody contests, may be said, in fact, to have severed the league.

PROTESTANTS AND CATHOLICS FORMED DIETS:

19:33　The Protestant and Catholic cantons have since had their separate diets, where all the most important concerns are adjusted, and which have left the general diet little other business than to take care of the common **bailages**.[64]

ALLIANCES FORMED ON BASIS OF RELIGION:

19:34　That separation had another consequence, which merits attention. It produced opposite alliances with foreign powers: of Berne, at the head of the Protestant association, with the United Provinces; and of Luzerne, at the head of the Catholic association, with France.

—Publius

Review Questions

1. Which confederacies does Madison talk about in No. 19? (19:1, 27, 30)

2. Who was the leader who conquered the regions of

63　*canton:* A small territorial district or state of a larger country or confederation.

64　*bailage:* A duty imposed upon the delivery of goods, (See Oxford English Dictionary, 1913 ed., Vol. 1 (a–b), James A. H. Murray, et al., eds., p. 625).

Germany and made them part of his empire? (19:3)

3. What kinds of government formed after Charlemagne's empire declined in power? (19:3–6)

4. From what did Germany's federal system grow or develop out of? (19:7-8)

5. What powers did their confederacy's emperor have? (19:12)

6. What are some of the disruptions the territory experienced from its confederate members? (19:15)

7. Was panic a strong enough motivation to unite the confederacy in their common effort at self defense? (19:19)

8. With each German district armed to enforce the law, what actually happened when these forces were used? (19:21)

9. What factions broke up the Swiss confederacy? (19:32–34)

FEDERALIST NO. 20

THE NETHERLANDS CONFEDERACY IS ANOTHER EXAMPLE OF FAILURE: As shown in the Netherlands, attempting to govern other governments is inefficient and always ends in weakness, civil wars, and foreign attacks or invasions. Tyranny results when weak central governments are compelled to exceed their authorities and extract by force the necessary obedience from the States. The only solution is to give the central government power to impose laws directly on individuals, where it can take them to court for disobedience instead of summoning the entire army as was needed under the Articles.

By James Madison—December 11, 1787

THE NETHERLANDS IS A CONFEDERACY OF REPUBLICS:

20:1 THE United Netherlands are a confederacy of republics, or rather of aristocracies of a very remarkable texture, yet confirming all the lessons derived from those which we have already reviewed.

SEVEN MEMBERS:
The Netherlands confederacy consists of seven equal states.

20:2 The union is composed of seven coequal and sovereign states, and each state or province is a composition of equal and independent cities. In all important cases, not only the provinces but the cities must be unanimous.

CENTRAL AUTHORITY:
The states' representatives have widely varying terms.

20:3 The sovereignty of the Union is represented by the States-General, consisting usually of about fifty deputies appointed by the provinces. They hold their seats, some for life, some for six, three, and one year; from two provinces they continue in appointment during pleasure.

DUTIES OF CENTRAL AUTHORITY:
All actions must be approved by unanimous affirmation and approval of the people.

20:4 The States-General have authority to enter into treaties and alliances; to make war and peace; to raise armies and equip fleets; to ascertain quotas and demand contributions. In all these cases, however, unanimity and the sanction of their constituents are requisite.

Foreign relations, revenue, sovereignty.

20:5 They have authority to appoint and receive ambassadors; to execute treaties and alliances already formed; to provide for the collection of duties on imports and exports; to regulate the mint, with a saving to the provincial rights; to govern as sovereigns the dependent territories.

Restraints on the members.

20:6 The provinces are restrained, unless with the general consent, from entering into foreign treaties; from establishing imposts injurious to others, or charging their neighbors with higher duties than their own subjects.

Administrative councils.

20:7 A council of state, a chamber of accounts, with five colleges of admiralty, aid and fortify the federal administration.

Executive magistrate.

20:8 The executive magistrate of the union is the stadtholder, who is now an hereditary prince. His principal weight and influence in the republic are derived from this independent title; from his great patrimonial estates; from his family connections with some of the chief potentates of Europe; and, more than all, perhaps, from his being stadtholder in the several provinces, as well as for the union; in which provincial quality he has the appointment of town magistrates under certain regulations, executes provincial decrees, presides when he pleases in the provincial tribunals, and has throughout the power of pardon.

20:9 As stadtholder of the union, he has, however, considerable prerogatives.

MAGISTRATE'S AUTHORITY OVER THE MEMBERS:

20:10 In his political capacity he has authority to settle disputes between the provinces, when other methods fail; to assist at the deliberations of the States-General, and at their particular conferences; to give audiences to foreign ambassadors, and to keep agents for his particular affairs at foreign courts.

Control over the military.

20:11 In his military capacity he commands the federal troops, provides for garrisons, and in general regulates military affairs; disposes of all appointments, from colonels to ensigns, and of the governments and posts of fortified towns.

Control over the navy

20:12 In his marine capacity he is admiral-general, and superintends and directs every thing relative to naval forces and other naval affairs; presides in the admiralties in person or by proxy; appoints lieutenant-admirals and other officers; and establishes councils of war, whose sentences are not executed till he approves them.

Magistrate's salary and standing army.

20:13 His revenue, exclusive of his private income, amounts to 300,000 florins. The standing army which he commands consists of about 40,000 men.

BELGIC CONFEDERACY:

Did the confederacy prosper or suffer from this arrangement?

20:14 Such is the nature of the celebrated **Belgic confederacy**,[65] as delineated on parchment. What are the characters which practice has stamped upon it? **Imbecility**[66] in the government; discord among the provinces; foreign influence and indignities; a precarious existence in peace, and peculiar calamities from war.

HATRED KEPT THE CONFEDERACY WHOLE:

20:15 It was long ago remarked by **Grotius**,[67] that nothing but the hatred of his countrymen to the house of Austria kept them from being ruined by the vices of their constitution.

STRONG GOVERNMENT CAN'T BRING HARMONY:

Why didn't the provinces get along?

20:16 The union of Utrecht, says another respectable writer, reposes an authority in the States-General, seemingly sufficient to secure harmony, but the jealousy in each province renders the practice very different from the theory.

SOME MEMBERS CAN'T PAY EQUAL SHARES:

Why didn't fair contributions by each province work out?

20:17 The same instrument, says another, obliges each province to levy certain contributions; but this article never could, and probably never will, be executed; because the inland provinces, who have little commerce, cannot pay an equal quota.

CONSTITUTION HAD TO BE IGNORED:

If some provinces couldn't keep up, which province carried the financial load?

20:18 In matters of contribution, it is the practice to waive the articles of the constitution. The danger of delay obliges the consenting provinces to furnish their quotas, without waiting for the others; and then to obtain reimbursement from the others, by deputations, which are frequent, or otherwise, as they can. The great wealth and influence of the province of Holland enable her to effect both these purposes.

TAXES COLLECTED BY MILITARY FORCE:

How did the strongest provinces get reimbursed?

20:19 It has more than once happened, that the deficiencies had to be ultimately collected at the point of the bayonet; a thing practicable, though dreadful, in a confederacy where one of the members exceeds in force all the rest, and where several of them are too small to meditate resistance; but utterly impracticable in one composed of members, several of which are equal to each other in strength and resources, and equal singly to a vigorous and persevering defense.

FOREIGN MINISTERS TAKE MATTERS INTO THEIR OWN HANDS:

How did foreign ministers bypass matters agreed to by the other members?

20:20 Foreign ministers, says Sir William Temple, who was himself a foreign minister, elude matters taken ad referendum, by tampering with the provinces and cities. In 1726, the treaty of Hanover was delayed by these means a whole year. Instances of a like nature are numerous and notorious.

CONSTITUTIONAL UNANIMITY MANDATE HAD TO BE OCCASIONALLY BE IGNORED:

Did various weak constitutions open the door to tyranny?

20:21 In critical emergencies, the States-General are often compelled to overleap their constitutional bounds. In 1688, they concluded a treaty of themselves at the risk of their heads. The treaty of Westphalia, in 1648, by which their independence was formerly and finally recognized, was concluded without the consent of Zealand. Even as recently as the last

---

65 **Belgic confederacy:** A group of the northern provinces of the Netherlands that united to resist Spanish domination in 1579.

66 **imbecility:** The state of behaving very stupidly, foolishly, feebly, or incapably.

67 **Hugo Grotius:** A Dutch jurist, politician, theologian, and scholar in natural law and international law (1583-1645).

treaty of peace with Great Britain, the constitutional principle of <u>unanimity was departed from</u>.

TYRANNY GROWS FROM A WEAK CONSTITUTION:

Does tyranny come mainly from a crisis more than mere bullying?

20:22   A <u>weak constitution</u> must necessarily terminate in <u>dissolution</u>, for want of proper powers, or the <u>usurpation</u> of powers <u>requisite for the public safety</u>. Whether the usurpation, when once begun, will stop at the **salutary**[68] point, or go forward to the dangerous extreme, must depend on the contingencies of the moment. Tyranny has perhaps oftener grown out of the assumptions of power, called for, on pressing exigencies, by a defective constitution, than out of the full exercise of the largest constitutional authorities.

MAGISTRATE KEPT CONFEDERACY INTACT:

What kept these issues from blowing the confederacy apart?

20:23   Notwithstanding the calamities produced by the stadtholdership, it has been supposed that without his influence in the individual provinces, the causes of anarchy manifest in the confederacy would long ago have dissolved it.

Magistrate personally intervened.

20:24 "Under such a government," says the Abbe Mably, "the Union could never have subsisted, if the provinces had not a spring within themselves, capable of quickening their tardiness, and compelling them to the same way of thinking. This spring is the stadtholder."

Holland, the richest member, kept the confederacy financially afloat, but in that process made the others dependent on it.

20:25 It is remarked by Sir William Temple, "that in the intermissions of the stadtholdership, Holland, by her riches and her authority, which drew the others into a sort of dependence, supplied the place."

SURROUNDING NATIONS CREATED URGENCY:

Were other means used to keep the confederacy intact?

20:26   These are not the only circumstances which have controlled the tendency to anarchy and dissolution. The surrounding powers impose an absolute necessity of union to a certain degree, at the same time that they nourish by their intrigues the constitutional vices which keep the republic in some degree always at their mercy.

COULD NOT REPAIR THE FAILED CONFEDERACY:

They can't agree on how to fix their own problems. Did any of the people ever conspire to obtain a better union?

20:27   <u>The true patriots</u> have long bewailed the fatal tendency of these vices, and have made no less than four regular experiments by EXTRAORDINARY ASSEMBLIES, convened for the special purpose, to apply a remedy. As many times has their laudable zeal found it impossible to UNITE THE PUBLIC COUNCILS in reforming the known, the acknowledged, the fatal evils of the existing constitution.

CONFEDERACIES FAIL, CONSTITUTION INSPIRED:

Isn't America's Constitution by comparison truly heaven sent?

20:28 Let us pause, my fellow-citizens, for one moment, over this melancholy and monitory <u>lesson of history</u>; and with the <u>tear that drops</u> for the calamities brought on mankind by their adverse opinions and selfish passions, let our gratitude mingle an ejaculation to <u>Heaven</u>, for the <u>propitious</u> **concord**[69] which has distinguished the consultations for <u>our political happiness</u>.

GENERAL TAX FAILED:

While a federal tax didn't work in the confederacy, that advantage built into America's new Constitution was abandoned by the Sixteenth Amendment.

20:29 A design was also conceived of establishing a general tax to be administered by the <u>federal authority</u>. This also had its adversaries and failed.

CURRENT CRISES MIGHT FORGE STRONGER UNION:

The problems in the Netherlands' confederacy can serve as a warning to America to avoid the same traps that gave rise to Shays' Rebellion (1786–1787).

20:30 <u>This unhappy people seem</u> to be now suffering from <u>popular convulsions</u>, from <u>dissensions among</u> the states, and from the <u>actual invasion</u> of <u>foreign arms</u>, the crisis of their destiny. <u>All nations</u> have their <u>eyes fixed</u> on the awful spectacle. The first wish prompted by humanity is, that this severe trial may issue in such a revolution of their government as will establish their union, and render it the <u>parent of tranquility</u>, <u>freedom</u> and <u>happiness</u>: The next, that the asylum under which, we trust, the enjoyment of these blessings will speedily be <u>secured</u> in <u>this country</u>, may receive and console them for the catastrophe of <u>their own</u>.

---

68 **salutary:** Producing good effects; beneficial.

69 **concord:** Agreement or harmony between people or groups.

EXPERIENCE IS THE ORACLE OF TRUTH:
When truth is discovered to be unambiguous, it must be accepted as conclusive.

20:31   I make no apology for having dwelt so long on the contemplation of these federal precedents. Experience is the oracle of truth; and where its responses are unequivocal, they ought to be conclusive and sacred.

SOVEREIGNTY OVER SOVEREIGNS NEVER WORKS:
The Articles never succeeded. As shown, attempting to legislate over States instead of individuals puts the government in a place where it must use violence to enforce the law instead of the court system.

20:32   The important truth, which it unequivocally pronounces in the present case, is that a sovereignty over sovereigns, a government over governments, a legislation for communities, as contradistinguished from individuals, as it is a solecism in theory, so in practice it is subversive of the order and ends of civil polity, by substituting VIOLENCE in place of LAW, or the destructive coercion of the SWORD in place of the mild and salutary COERCION of the MAGISTRACY.

—Publius

Review Questions

1. What lessons does Madison say are confirmed by the demise of the confederacy of the Netherlands? (20:1)

2. On important issues, how many governments in The Netherlands must vote in the affirmative for a bill to pass? (20:2)

3. If a province didn't pay its fair share how were those funds ultimately collected? (20:19)

4. Did a weak constitution in the Netherlands lead to tyranny? (20:21–22)

5. For what does Madison thank heaven? (20:28)

6. What is the oracle of truth that teaches so much in the political development of a country? (20:31)

7. What does "sovereignty over sovereigns" mean? (20:32)

8. Because the Netherlands' central government couldn't turn to a court to resolve conflicts, what was it forced to use? (20:32)

FEDERALIST NO. 21

THREE WEAKNESSES OF THE ARTICLES OF CONFEDERATION: First, there was no authority granted to enforce its own laws. Second, there was no protection of the States from internal rebellion or takeover. Third, power was not granted to compel the States to pay taxes and carry their share of the national needs. The new Constitution resolves these fatal weaknesses.

By Alexander Hamilton—December 12, 1787

WHY DID THE ARTICLES OF CONFEDERATION FAIL?
The prior papers have illustrated why confederacies don't last very long and what flaws they have in common (see No. 12).

21:1   HAVING in the three last numbers taken a summary review of the principal circumstances and events which have depicted the genius and fate of other confederate governments, I shall now proceed in the enumeration of the most important of those defects which have hitherto disappointed our hopes from the system established among ourselves. To form a safe and satisfactory judgment of the proper remedy, it is absolutely necessary that we should be well acquainted with the extent and malignity of the disease.

THE ARTICLES HAD NO POWER TO FORCE OBEDIENCE:
The Articles gave no power to enforce federal laws, and it lacked an official penalty to punish violators.

21:2   The next most palpable defect of the subsisting Confederation, is the total want of a SANCTION to its laws. The United States, as now composed, have no powers to exact obedience, or punish disobedience to their resolutions, either by pecuniary **mulcts**,[70] by a suspension or divestiture of privileges, or by any other constitutional mode. There is no express delegation of authority to them to use force against delinquent members;

SOCIAL CONTRACT DEFINED:
The Articles established that the States retained all rights not specifically delegated to Congress.

21:3   and if such a right should be ascribed to the federal head, as resulting from the nature of the **social compact**[71] between the States, it must be by inference and construction,

---

70   *mulcts:* A fine or compulsory payment.

71   *social compact:* An unofficial agreement between the States to cooperate on issues that work best if shared in common, such as basic laws and rules of trade.

in the face of that part of the second article, by which it is declared, "that each State shall retain every power, jurisdiction, and right, not EXPRESSLY delegated to the United States in Congress assembled."[72]

CORRECTING CRITICS' FALSE CLAIMS:
The new Constitution corrects the enforcement flaw, allowing it to enforce its own laws.

21:4 There is, doubtless, a striking absurdity in supposing that a right of this kind does not exist, but we are reduced to the dilemma either of embracing that supposition, preposterous as it may seem, or of contravening or explaining away a provision, which has been of late a repeated theme of the eulogies of those who oppose the new Constitution;

STATE POWER CURTAILED:
The new Constitution lacks a States' Rights clause because giving too much back to the States results in the same federal weakness now in the Articles.

21:5 and the want of which, in that plan, has been the subject of much plausible **animadversion**,[73] and severe criticism. If we are unwilling to impair the force of this applauded provision, we shall be obliged to conclude, that the United States afford the extraordinary spectacle of a government destitute even of the shadow of constitutional power to enforce the execution of its own laws.

ENFORCEMENT POWER MISSING FROM ARTICLES:

21:6 It will appear, from the specimens which have been cited, that the American Confederacy, in this particular, stands discriminated from every other institution of a similar kind, and exhibits a new and unexampled phenomenon in the political world.

ARTICLES DID NOT GUARANTEE PROTECTION OF THE STATES:
The Articles failed to grant any provision whereby the States may come to the aid of one another to suppress insurrection or attack. This flaw is corrected by Article IV, Section 4 of the new Constitution.

21:7 The want of a mutual guaranty of the State governments is another capital imperfection in the federal plan. There is nothing of this kind declared in the articles that compose it; and to imply a tacit guaranty from considerations of utility, would be a still more flagrant departure from the clause which has been mentioned, than to imply a tacit power of coercion from the like considerations.

21:8 The want of a guaranty, though it might in its consequences endanger the Union, does not so immediately attack its existence as the want of a constitutional sanction to its laws.

WEAK ARTICLES LEFT STATES VULNERABLE:
Under the Articles, the States must defend themselves and cannot count on the help of other States in case of domestic insurrection or invasion.

21:9 Without a guaranty the assistance to be derived from the Union in repelling those domestic dangers which may sometimes threaten the existence of the State constitutions, must be renounced. Usurpation may rear its crest in each State, and trample upon the liberties of the people, while the national government could legally do nothing more than behold its encroachments with indignation and regret. A successful faction may erect a tyranny on the ruins of order and law, while no succor could constitutionally be afforded by the Union to the friends and supporters of the government.

SHAYS' REBELLION PROVES STATES NOT PROTECTED:
Had the rebellion of 1786–1787 been led by a more competent leader, the insurrection might have drawn in neighboring States.

21:10 The tempestuous situation from which Massachusetts has scarcely emerged, evinces that dangers of this kind are not merely speculative. Who can determine what might have been the issue of her late convulsions, if the malcontents had been headed by a Caesar or by a **Cromwell**?[74] Who can predict what effect a despotism, established in Massachusetts, would have upon the liberties of New Hampshire or Rhode Island, of Connecticut or New York?

CENTRAL AUTHORITY IS THE STRENGTH OF UNION:
The main purpose of a Union is to stop insurrection and not interfere in a State's sovereign and constitutional activities.

21:11 The inordinate pride of State importance has suggested to some minds an objection to the principle of a guaranty in the federal government, as involving an officious interference in the domestic concerns of the members.

A UNION PROTECTS STATES FROM VIOLENCE:
A Union would not override the will of the people in the States; it would come into play only when usurpations or violence erupted.

21:12 A scruple of this kind would deprive us of one of the principal advantages to be expected from union, and can only

---

72 See Articles of Confederation, Article II.
73 *animadversion:* A harsh, critical remark.
74 *Oliver Cromwell:* An English general and statesman famous for his leadership skills, 1599–1658,.

flow from a misapprehension of the nature of the provision itself. It could be no impediment to reforms of the State constitution by a <u>majority of the people</u> in a <u>legal and peaceable mode</u>. This right would remain undiminished. <u>The guaranty could only operate against changes to be effected by violence.</u>

PEACE DEPENDS ON EFFICACY OF PRECAUTIONS:

21:13   Towards the preventions of calamities of this kind, too many checks cannot be provided. <u>The peace of society and the stability of government depend absolutely on the **efficacy**</u>[75] of the precautions adopted on this head.

ELECTIONS ARE THE NATURAL CURE FOR INFERIOR LEADERS:

There is much less of a chance of military intervention in a government that is controlled by the people through representatives.

21:14   Where the whole power of the government is in the hands of the people, there is the less pretense for the use of violent remedies in partial or occasional distempers of the State. The natural cure for an ill-administration, in a popular or representative constitution, is a change of men. <u>A guaranty by the national authority</u> would be as much leveled against the usurpations of rulers as against the <u>ferments</u> and outrages of <u>faction</u> and <u>sedition in the community.</u>

QUOTAS DON'T WORK, STATES HATE THEM:

Raising revenues by making requisitions on the states has been inequitable and inefficient. Quotas on the States are impossible to assign and manage.

21:15   The principle of regulating the <u>contributions of the States to the common treasury by QUOTAS</u> is another fundamental error in the Confederation. Its repugnancy to an adequate supply of the national exigencies has been already pointed out, and has sufficiently appeared from the trial which has been made of it. I speak of it now solely with a view to equality among the States.

NO STANDARD WAY TO MEASURE AND TAX WEALTH:

21:16   Those who have been accustomed to contemplate the circumstances which produce and constitute national wealth, must be satisfied that there is no common standard or barometer by which the degrees of it can be ascertained. <u>Neither the value of lands</u>, nor the <u>numbers of the people</u>, which have been successively proposed as the rule of State contributions, has any pretension to being a just representative.

NATIONAL WEALTH CAN'T BE COMPARED:

Europe as an example shows that there is no way to compare wealth, land, and populations for the purposes of setting quotas.

21:17   If we compare the <u>wealth</u> of the United <u>Netherlands</u> with that of <u>Russia</u> or <u>Germany</u>, or even of <u>France</u>, and if we at the same time compare the total value of the lands and the aggregate population of that contracted district with the total value of the lands and the aggregate population of the immense regions of either of the three last-mentioned countries, we shall at once discover that there is <u>no comparison</u> between <u>the proportion of either of these</u> two objects and that of the relative wealth of those nations.

STATES' WEALTH CAN'T BE COMPARED:

The same problem is present in trying to compare the wealth of one state to another using size or population.

21:18   If the like parallel were to be run between several of the American States, it would furnish a like result. Let Virginia be contrasted with North Carolina, Pennsylvania with Connecticut, or Maryland with New Jersey, and we shall be convinced that the <u>respective abilities of those States, in relation to revenue, bear little or no analogy to their comparative stock in lands or to their comparative population.</u>

COUNTIES' WEALTH CAN'T BE COMPARED:

The problem isn't resolved by trying to compare cities or counties to determine their respective wealth.

21:19   The position may be equally illustrated by a similar process between the counties of the same State. No man who is acquainted with the State of New York will doubt that the active wealth of Kings County bears a much greater proportion to that of Montgomery than it would appear to be if we should take either the total value of the lands or the total number of the people as a criterion!

WEALTH OF NATION HAS INFINITE VARIABLES:

The wealth of a nation depends on an infinite number of variables that make unfair any attempt to regulate contributions.

21:20   The <u>wealth of nations depends upon an infinite variety of causes</u>. Situation, soil, climate, the nature of the productions, the nature of the government, the genius of the citizens, the degree of information they possess, the state of commerce, of arts, of industry, these circumstances and many more, too complex, minute, or adventitious to admit of a particular specification, occasion differences hardly conceivable in the relative opulence and riches of different countries.

---

75   *efficacy:* The power to produce effects.

NO COMMON MEASURE OF NATIONAL OR STATE WEALTH:

Therefore, there is no common measure to tax the States based on wealth.

21:21　The consequence clearly is that there can be <u>no common measure of national wealth</u>, and, of course, no general or stationary rule by which the ability of a state to pay taxes can be determined. The attempt, therefore, to regulate the contributions of the members of a confederacy by any such rule, cannot fail to be productive of <u>glaring inequality</u> and extreme oppression.

QUOTAS DON'T CONSIDER STATES' ABILITIES:

If the States were forced to comply with paying taxes based on quotas, the inequalities alone would be enough to blast the Union to pieces.

21:22　This <u>inequality</u> would of itself be sufficient in America to work the <u>eventual destruction of the Union</u>, if any mode of enforcing a compliance with its requisitions could be devised. The <u>suffering States</u> would <u>not long consent to remain associated</u> upon a principle which distributes the public burdens with so unequal a hand, and which was calculated to <u>impoverish</u> and oppress the citizens of <u>some States</u>, while those of <u>others</u> would <u>scarcely be conscious</u> of the small proportion of the weight they were required to sustain. This, however, is an evil inseparable from the principle of quotas and requisitions.

THE PEOPLE MUST ALLOW THEIR GOVERNMENT TO RAISE REVENUE:

There is only one way to avoid inequality that comes from taxing at the State level, and that is for the national government to raise its own revenue.

21:23　There is no method of steering clear of this inconvenience, but by authorizing the <u>national government to raise its own revenues in its own way</u>.

CONSUMPTION TAXES:

Imposts (a tax on imported goods), excises (a sales tax on specific items such as luxuries, or tobacco, alcohol, gambling, gasoline), consumption (sales tax on all items sold for consumption) are taxes that can be avoided by not making purchases.

21:24　Imposts, excises, and, in general, all duties upon articles of consumption, may be compared to a fluid, which will, in time, find its level with the means of paying them. <u>The amount to be contributed by each citizen will in a degree be at his own option</u>, and can be regulated by an attention to his resources. The <u>rich may be extravagant</u>, the <u>poor can be frugal</u>; and private oppression may always be avoided by a <u>judicious selection of objects proper for such impositions</u>.

INEQUALITIES ON IMPORT DUTIES WILL EXIST BUT EVENTUALLY BALANCE OUT:

The free market will sort out assorted import duties that are higher or lower depending on the object and the State.

21:25　If inequalities should arise in some States from duties on particular objects, these will, in all probability, be counterbalanced by proportional inequalities in other States, from the duties on other objects. In the course of time and things, <u>an equilibrium, as far as it is attainable</u> in so complicated a subject, will be established everywhere. Or, if inequalities should still exist, they would neither be so great in their degree, so uniform in their operation, nor so odious in their appearance, as those which would necessarily spring from quotas, upon any scale that can possibly be devised.

HOW TO PROTECT AGAINST EXCESS:

Consumption taxes are best because they are self-regulating. If they are too high, consumption decreases, and revenue drops.

21:26　It is a <u>signal advantage of taxes on articles of consumption, that they contain in their own nature a security against excess</u>. They prescribe their own limit; which cannot be exceeded without defeating the end proposed, that is, an extension of the revenue.

HIGH DUTIES CREATE LESS CONSUMPTION, RESULTING IN LOWER REVENUE:

21:27　When applied to this object, the saying is as just as it is witty, that, "in political arithmetic, two and two do not always make four." If duties are too high, they lessen the consumption; the collection is eluded; and the product to the treasury is not so great as when they are confined within proper and moderate bounds. This forms a complete barrier against any material oppression of the citizens by taxes of this class, and is itself a natural limitation of the power of imposing them.

INDIRECT TAXES SHOULD BE MAIN SOURCE:

Consumption taxes are indirect taxes. Upon these the nation should rely for a long time to come.

21:28　<u>Impositions of this kind usually fall under the denomination of indirect taxes</u>, and <u>must for a long time constitute</u> the <u>chief part of the revenue</u> raised in this country.

DIRECT TAXES ON LAND SHOULD BE LIMITED:

21:29　Those of the <u>direct kind</u>, which principally <u>relate to land and buildings</u>, may admit of a rule of apportionment. Either the <u>value of land</u>, or the <u>number of the people</u>, <u>may serve as a standard</u>. The state of agriculture and the populousness of a country have been considered as nearly connected with each other. And, as a rule, for the purpose intended, numbers, in the view of simplicity and certainty, are entitled to a preference.

DIFFICULT TO ASSESS DIRECT TAXES:
Direct taxes are hard to assess and require some set of arbitrary rules.

21:30 In every country it is a herculean task to obtain a valuation of the land; in a country imperfectly settled and progressive in improvement, the difficulties are increased almost to impracticability. The expense of an accurate valuation is, in all situations, a formidable objection.

ATTENDING TO TAXES AND PRIVACY RIGHTS:
Collecting taxes must invade a person's privacy to determine values and personal wealth.

21:31 In a branch of taxation <u>where no limits to the discretion of the government are to be found in the nature of the thing</u>, the establishment of a fixed rule, not incompatible with the end, may be <u>attended with fewer inconveniences</u> than to leave that discretion altogether at large.

—PUBLIUS

REVIEW QUESTIONS

1. Could the Articles of Confederation enforce its own laws? Why? (21:2)

2. Which section of the Articles is violated if Congress tried to enforce new laws (see full text of the Articles in the appendix)? (21:3)

3. Could the Articles protect the States from domestic dangers? (21:7–9)

4. What rebellion proved the inability of the Articles to protect the States? (21:10)

5. Did raising revenue with quotas on each State succeed? Why? (21:15–17)

6. To raise revenue, what sources of wealth cannot be utilized for comparison and measurement? (21:17–19)

7. Which form of taxation seems to work best because it is self-regulating? (21:24–26)

8. Which form of taxation should be the Union's main source? (21:28)

FEDERALIST NO. 22

EXAMPLES OF THE FAILURES IN THE ARTICLES: Additional problems in the Articles include no power to regulate commerce among the States, no power to raise armies, no equal representation as will now exist in the Senate under the new Constitution, and no Supreme Court. The process of ratifying the Articles by the State legislatures should have been done by the consent of the people directly (12:46). This paper concludes the second discussion topic by Publius, "The insufficiency of the present Confederation to preserve that Union." *See appendix for the complete text of the Articles of Confederation.*

By Alexander Hamilton—December 14, 1787

OTHER DEFECTS IN ARTICLES OF CONFEDERATION:

22:1 IN ADDITION to the <u>defects</u> already <u>enumerated</u> in the existing federal system, there are <u>others</u> of not less importance, which concur in rendering it altogether unfit for the administration of the affairs of the Union.

NO REGULATION OF INTERSTATE COMMERCE:
Central power to keep the rules of commerce fair for the States and foreign markets is necessary in order to make trade treaties. Did the lack of this power hurt America's foreign trade?

22:2 The want of a <u>power to regulate commerce</u> is by all parties allowed to be of the number. The utility of such a power has been anticipated under the first head of our inquiries; and for this reason, as well as from the universal conviction entertained upon the subject, little need be added in this place.

FEDERAL MANAGEMENT OF COMMERCE IS CRITICAL:

22:3 It is indeed evident, on the most superficial view, that there is no object, either as it respects the interests of trade or finance, that more strongly demands a <u>federal superintendence</u>. <u>The want of it</u> has already operated as a <u>bar to the formation of beneficial treaties with foreign powers</u>, and has given occasions of dissatisfaction between the States.

LACK OF UNITY IS HURTING OUR FOREIGN RELATIONS:
Nations recognize weakness and will take advantage of it whenever possible.

22:4 No nation acquainted with the nature of our political association would be unwise enough to enter into stipulations with the United States, by which they conceded privileges of any importance to them, while they were apprised that the <u>engagements on the part of the Union might at any moment be violated by its members</u>, and while they found from experience that they might enjoy every advantage they desired in our markets, without granting us any return but such as their momentary convenience might suggest.

BRITAIN TOOK ADVANTAGE OF THIS WEAKNESS:

22:5 It is not, therefore, to be wondered at that Mr. Jenkinson, in ushering into the House of Commons a bill for regulating the temporary <u>intercourse</u> between the <u>two countries</u>, should preface its introduction by a declaration that similar provisions in former bills had been found to answer every purpose to the commerce of Great Britain, and that it would be prudent to persist in the plan until it should appear <u>whether</u> the <u>American government</u> was likely or not to acquire <u>greater consistency</u>.[76]

STATES POWERLESS IN FACE OF BRITAIN:
Without a strong central government, individual States were unable to compel Great Britain to be more fair in its trade. Can the States ever expect fairness as a disjointed confederation?

22:6 <u>Several States</u> have endeavored, by separate prohibitions, restrictions, and exclusions, to influence the conduct of that kingdom in this particular, but the <u>want of concert</u>, arising from the <u>want</u> of a <u>general authority</u> and from clashing and <u>dissimilar views</u> in the State, has hitherto <u>frustrated</u> every experiment of the kind, and will <u>continue</u> to do so as long as the <u>same obstacles</u> to a uniformity of measures <u>continue to exist</u>.

STATES INTERFERING WITH STATES:
Several States under the Articles treated each other unfairly. The Articles needed to be reformed with a central government empowered to stop this squabbling. What happened in Germany?

22:7 The interfering and <u>unneighborly regulations</u> of some States, <u>contrary to the true spirit of the Union</u>, have, in different instances, given just cause of **umbrage**[77] and complaint to others, and it is to be feared that examples of this nature, if not restrained by a national control, would be multiplied and extended till they became not less serious sources of animosity and discord than injurious impediments to the intercourse between the different parts of the Confederacy.

GERMANY'S COMMERCE RUINED BY EXCESSIVE DUTIES:
Hamilton quotes from an encyclopedia article on empires.

22:8 "<u>The commerce of the German empire</u>[78] is in <u>continual trammels</u> from the <u>multiplicity</u> of the <u>duties which</u> the <u>several princes</u> and <u>states</u> exact upon the merchandises <u>passing through their territories</u>, by means of which the <u>fine streams</u> and navigable rivers with which Germany is so happily watered are rendered almost <u>useless</u>."

STATE AGAINST STATE WILL CREATE ENEMIES OF CITIZENS:

22:9 Though the genius of the people of this country might never permit this description to be strictly applicable to us, yet we may reasonably <u>expect</u>, from the gradual conflicts of State regulations, that the citizens of each would at length come to be considered and treated by the others in no better light than that of foreigners and aliens.

RAISING ARMIES FAILED UNDER ARTICLES:
Federal authority to raise troops is essential, but making the requisitions directly upon the States was extremely inefficient. What were some of the terrible outcomes of this process?

22:10 <u>The power of raising armies</u>, by the most obvious construction of the articles of the Confederation, is merely a <u>power of making requisitions</u> upon the States for <u>quotas of men</u>. This practice in the course of the late war, was found replete with <u>obstructions</u> to a vigorous and to an economical system of defense.

The scarcity of men willing to fight led to ever-increasing incentives, almost an auction.

22:11 It gave birth to a competition between the States which created a kind of <u>auction for men</u>. In order to furnish the quotas required of them, they <u>outbid each other</u> till <u>bounties grew</u> to an enormous and <u>insupportable size</u>. The hope of a still further increase afforded an inducement to those who were disposed to serve to <u>procrastinate their enlistment</u>, and disinclined them from engaging for any considerable periods.

Anemic support from the States created a crisis during the War.

22:12 Hence, <u>slow and scanty levies of men</u>, in the most critical emergencies of our affairs; <u>short enlistments</u> at an unparalleled expense; continual <u>fluctuations</u> in the <u>troops</u>, <u>ruinous</u> to their discipline and <u>subjecting the public safety</u> frequently to the perilous <u>crisis of a disbanded</u> army. Hence, also, those oppressive expedients for raising men which were upon several occasions practiced, and which nothing but the enthusiasm of liberty would have induced the <u>people</u> to <u>endure</u>.

STATES NOT CONSISTENT IN SUPPORT OF WAR:
The States most vulnerable sacrificed the most, while distant States were shamefully irresponsible. Making quota demands on the State governments was at fault—these demands couldn't be enforced.

22:13 This method of raising troops is not more unfriendly to economy and vigor than it is to an equal distribution of the

---

76 *Publius:* This, as nearly as I can recollect, was the sense of his speech on introducing the last bill.

77 **umbrage:** A feeling of resentment, offense, or annoyance.

78 *Publius:* Encyclopedia, article "Empire." [A French encyclopedia with essays by Rousseau, Montesquieu, Voltaire, and other notable authors, edited by Denis Diderot, et al, 1745-1772]

burden. The States near the seat of war, influenced by motives of self-preservation, made efforts to furnish their quotas, which even exceeded their abilities; while those at a distance from danger were, for the most part, as remiss as the others were diligent, in their exertions.

MONEY DEBT PALES COMPARED TO BLOOD DEBT (SOLDIERS):

States that failed to supply men owe a debt that can't be paid.

22:14   The immediate pressure of this inequality was not in this case, as in that of the contributions of money, alleviated by the hope of a final liquidation. The States which did not pay their proportions of money might at least be charged with their deficiencies; but no account could be formed of the deficiencies in the supplies of men. We shall not, however, see much reason to regret the want of this hope, when we consider how little prospect there is, that the most delinquent States will ever be able to make compensation for their pecuniary failures.

QUOTA SYSTEM IS DEFICIENT:

What did Hamilton call the Articles' system for quotas for defense and raising federal revenue?

22:15   The system of quotas and requisitions, whether it be applied to men or money, is, in every view, a system of imbecility in the Union, and of inequality and injustice among the members.

MAJORITY SHOULD PREVAIL:

An equal vote for States is not the same as equal representation. A majority of States does not always mean a majority of Americans. A single vote for each State violates the principle of majority rule.

22:16   The right of equal suffrage among the States is another exceptionable part of the Confederation. Every idea of proportion and every rule of fair representation conspire to condemn a principle, which gives to Rhode Island an equal weight in the scale of power with Massachusetts, or Connecticut, or New York; and to Delaware an equal voice in the national deliberations with Pennsylvania, or Virginia, or North Carolina. Its operation contradicts the fundamental maxim of republican government, which requires that the sense of the majority should prevail.

MAJORITY OF STATES IS NOT ALWAYS A MAJORITY OF THE PEOPLE:

Some States were scantily populated yet they carried an equal vote in government. Would the larger States revolt against the smaller States trying to force law on them?

22:17   Sophistry may reply, that sovereigns are equal, and that a majority of the votes of the States will be a majority of confederated America. But this kind of logical **legerdemain**[79] will never counteract the plain suggestions of justice and common-sense.

PROBLEMS OF POPULATION VS REPRESENTATION:

What if a controlling number of States is also a minority of population?

22:18   It may happen that this majority of States is a small minority of the people of America;[80] and two thirds of the people of America could not long be persuaded, upon the credit of artificial distinctions and syllogistic subtleties, to submit their interests to the management and disposal of one third. The larger States would after a while revolt from the idea of receiving the law from the smaller. To acquiesce in such a privation of their due importance in the political scale, would be not merely to be insensible to the love of power, but even to sacrifice the desire of equality. It is neither rational to expect the first, nor just to require the last.

Safety and welfare of smaller States depend on a Union.

22:19   The smaller States, considering how peculiarly their safety and welfare depend on union, ought readily to renounce a pretension which, if not relinquished, would prove fatal to its duration.

REQUIRING NINE STATES TO PASS LAWS WAS HARMFUL IDEA:

Requiring such a high percentage gives the minority States power to tell that super majority, "Give me what I want or I'll kill this bill."

22:20   It may be objected to this, that not seven but nine States, or two thirds of the whole number, must consent to the most important resolutions; and it may be thence inferred that nine States would always comprehend a majority of the Union. But this does not obviate the impropriety of an equal vote between States of the most unequal dimensions and populousness; nor is the inference accurate in point of fact; for we can enumerate nine States which contain less than a majority of the people; and it is constitutionally possible that these nine may give the vote.[81]

---

79   *legerdemain:* Trickery, cunning, sleight of hand.

80   *Publius:* New Hampshire, Rhode Island, New Jersey, Delaware, Georgia, South Carolina, and Maryland are a majority of the whole number of the States, but they do not contain one third of the people.

81   *Publius:* Add New York and Connecticut to the foregoing seven, and they will be less than a majority.

A BARE MAJORITY OF SEVEN STATES ELIMINATES THE HOLDOUTS:

States must work more effectively together when a bare majority is all that's needed. With nine of thirteen, any one State can just sit back and if the voting is tight, be a holdout for favors.

22:21 Besides, there are matters of considerable moment determinable by a bare majority; and there are others, concerning which doubts have been entertained, which, if interpreted in favor of the sufficiency of a vote of seven States, would extend its operation to interests of the first magnitude.

THE SET NUMBER OF NINE STATES IGNORES FUTURE GROWTH:

22:22 In addition to this, it is to be observed that there is a probability of an increase in the number of States, and no provision for a proportional augmentation of the ratio of votes.

THE PROBLEMS OF A SUPER MAJORITY (TWO THIRDS) OF STATES:

This provision allowed two of the very smallest states, Delaware and Rhode Island, to frequently bring government to a standstill.

22:23 But this is not all: what at first sight may seem a remedy, is, in reality, a poison. To give a minority a negative upon the majority (which is always the case where more than a majority is requisite to a decision), is, in its tendency, to subject the sense of the greater number to that of the lesser.[82]

A single vote can bring government to a dead stop.

22:24 Congress, from the nonattendance of a few States, have been frequently in the situation of a Polish diet, where a single VOTE has been sufficient to put a stop to all their movements. A sixtieth part of the Union, which is about the proportion of Delaware and Rhode Island, has several times been able to oppose an entire bar to its operations. This is one of those refinements which, in practice, has an effect the reverse of what is expected from it in theory.

UNANIMITY DOESN'T CREATE GREATER SECURITY:

In theory, unanimous approval for a political cause encourages greater success. Is this really true when a single voice can thwart the desires of the overwhelming majority?

22:25 The necessity of unanimity in public bodies, or of something approaching towards it, has been founded upon a supposition that it would contribute to security. But its real operation is to embarrass the administration, to destroy the energy of the government, and to substitute the pleasure,

caprice, or artifices of an insignificant, turbulent, or corrupt junto, to the regular deliberations and decisions of a respectable majority.

SINGLE PERSON CAN CONTROL THE MAJORITY:

When power is given so that a single voice can prevent the majority from prevailing, the will of the single voice actually controls everyone.

22:26 In those emergencies of a nation, in which the goodness or badness, the weakness or strength of its government, is of the greatest importance, there is commonly a necessity for action. The public business must, in some way or other, go forward.

The majority is woefully compelled to conform to the minority.

22:27 If a **pertinacious**[83] minority can control the opinion of a majority, respecting the best mode of conducting it, the majority, in order that something may be done, must conform to the views of the minority; and thus the sense of the smaller number will overrule that of the greater, and give a tone to the national proceedings. Hence, tedious delays; continual negotiation and intrigue; contemptible compromises of the public good.

Compromise is necessary at times, but when compromise is wrong and a position must be secured for the betterment of the whole nation, a factious minority can ruin it.

22:28 And yet, in such a system, it is even happy when such compromises can take place: for upon some occasions things will not admit of accommodation; and then the measures of government must be injuriously suspended, or fatally defeated. It is often, by the impracticability of obtaining the concurrence of the necessary number of votes, kept in a state of inaction. Its situation must always savor of weakness, sometimes border upon anarchy.

THE ARTICLES' VOTING RATIO INVITED FOREIGN CORRUPTION:

Foreign and domestic corruption is much easier when a single voice can be utilized to stop the wheels of progress.

22:29 It is not difficult to discover, that a principle of this kind gives greater scope to foreign corruption, as well as to domestic faction, than that which permits the sense of the majority to decide; though the contrary of this has been presumed. The mistake has proceeded from not attending with due care to the mischiefs that may be occasioned by obstructing the progress of government at certain critical seasons.

---

82 *Editors' Note:* Equal suffrage among sovereign states is the same weakness incorporated into the United Nations Security Council. The UN gives veto power to five prominent nations. One negative can thwart the whole council (fifteen total). That is an unjust and primitive device. The American Founding Fathers eliminated this problem by making voting power equal, and using simple majorities (51 percent).

83 *pertinacious:* Determined, dogged, persistent, tenacious, stubborn.

SINGLE VOTE CAN PREVENT MUCH GOODNESS:
22:30 When the concurrence of a large number is required by the Constitution to the doing of any national act, we are apt to rest satisfied that all is safe, because <u>nothing improper will be likely TO BE DONE</u>, but we forget how <u>much good may be prevented</u>, and how much ill may be produced, by the power of hindering <u>that which is necessary to be done</u>, and of keeping affairs in the same unfavorable posture in which they may happen to stand at particular periods.

SIMPLE MAJORITY HARDER TO CORRUPT:
Where only 51 percent is required to pass law, no single State could hold much sway. But when 66 percent leans one way, a single vote could demand big favors to reach 67 percent.

22:31 Suppose, for instance, we were <u>engaged in a war</u>, in conjunction with one foreign nation, against another. Suppose the necessity of our situation <u>demanded peace</u>, and the interest or ambition of our ally led him to seek the prosecution of the war, with views that might justify us in making <u>separate terms</u>. In such a state of things, this ally of ours would evidently find it much easier, by his <u>bribes</u> and <u>intrigues</u>, to <u>tie up the hands of government</u> from making peace, where <u>two thirds</u> of all the votes were <u>requisite</u> to that object, than where a simple majority would suffice. In the first case, he would have to <u>corrupt a smaller number</u>; in the last, a greater number.

ENEMIES COULD PERPLEX AND PARALYZE:
22:32 Upon the same principle, it would be much easier for a foreign power with which we were at war to perplex our councils and embarrass our exertions.

SAME INCONVENIENCES APPLY TO INTERNATIONAL TRADE:
22:33 And, in a <u>commercial view</u>, we may be subjected to <u>similar inconveniences</u>. A nation, with which we might have a <u>treaty of commerce</u>, could with much greater facility prevent our forming a connection with her <u>competitor in trade</u>, though such a connection should be ever so beneficial to ourselves.

REPUBLICAN SYSTEM VULNERABLE TO FOREIGNERS:
Republican governments have many strengths but their chief weakness is susceptibility to foreign corruption.

22:34 <u>Evils</u> of this description ought <u>not</u> to be regarded as <u>imaginary</u>. One of the weak sides of republics, among their numerous advantages, is that they afford <u>too easy an inlet to foreign corruption</u>.

KINGS LESS VULNERABLE DUE TO PRIDE IN KINGDOM:
22:35 An hereditary monarch, though often disposed to <u>sacrifice his subjects</u> to his ambition, has so great a personal interest in the government and in the external glory of the nation, that it is not easy for a foreign power to give him an equivalent for what he would sacrifice by treachery to the state. The world has accordingly been witness to few examples of this species of <u>royal prostitution</u>, though there have been abundant specimens of every other kind.

REPUBLICS SUSCEPTIBLE TO FOREIGN CORRUPTION:
Some people elevated from inferior levels to positions of elected office may see added personal benefit by betraying their trust.

22:36 <u>In republics</u>, <u>persons elevated</u> from the mass of the community, by the suffrages of their fellow-citizens, to stations of great pre-eminence and <u>power may find compensations for betraying their trust</u>, which, to any but minds animated and guided by superior virtue, may appear to exceed the proportion of interest they have in the common stock, and to overbalance the obligations of <u>duty</u>. Hence it is that <u>history</u> furnishes us with so many <u>mortifying examples</u> of the <u>prevalency of foreign corruption in republican governments</u>. How much this contributed to the ruin of the ancient commonwealths has been already delineated.

BRIBING FOREIGN NEIGHBORS:
This practice was a well-known corruption in Europe. Which monarch went from abject weakness to all-powerful in a single day?

22:37 It is <u>well known</u> that the <u>deputies</u> of the United Provinces have, in various instances, been <u>purchased</u> by the <u>emissaries</u> of the <u>neighboring kingdoms</u>. The Earl of <u>Chesterfield</u> (if my memory serves me right), in a letter to his court, intimates that <u>his success</u> in an important negotiation must <u>depend on</u> his obtaining a major's <u>commission for one of those deputies</u>. And in <u>Sweden</u> the parties were <u>alternately bought</u> by <u>France</u> and <u>England</u> in so barefaced and notorious a manner that it excited universal disgust in the nation, and was a <u>principal cause</u> that the <u>most limited monarch</u> <u>in Europe</u>, in a single day, without tumult, violence, or opposition, became one of the <u>most absolute and uncontrolled</u>.

CROWNING DEFECT OF ARTICLES—NO JUDICIARY:
The lack of judicial power in the Articles created massive problems.

22:38 A circumstance which crowns the defects of the Confederation remains yet to be mentioned, the <u>want of a judi-</u>

ciary power. Laws are a dead letter without <u>courts to expound and define</u> their true meaning and operation.

22:39 The <u>treaties</u> of the United States, to have any force at all, must be considered as part of the law of the land. Their true import, as far as respects individuals, must, like all other laws, be ascertained by judicial determinations. To produce uniformity in these determinations, they ought to be submitted, in the last resort, to <u>one SUPREME TRIBUNAL</u>. And this tribunal ought to be instituted under the <u>same authority</u> which forms the <u>treaties themselves</u>. These ingredients are both indispensable.

ONE COURT SUPERIOR TO ALL OTHERS IS CRITICAL:
A separate court in each member of a confederacy will render as many different decisions as there are numbers of States.

22:40 If there is in each <u>State a court of final jurisdiction</u>, there may be as many different final determinations on the same point as there are courts. There are endless diversities in the <u>opinions of men</u>. We often see not only different courts but the judges of the came court differing from each other. <u>To avoid the confusion</u> which would unavoidably result from the contradictory decisions of a number of independent judicatories, all nations have found it necessary to establish one court paramount to the rest, possessing a general superintendence, and authorized to settle and declare in the last resort a <u>uniform rule of civil justice</u>.

STATE COURTS ARE SUBJECT TO LOCAL BIASES ABOUT MEANING OF THE LAW:
A supreme court is particularly critical in a republic where the federal laws are in danger of being overpowered by the varying laws of the States.

22:41 This is the more necessary where the frame of the government is so compounded that the <u>laws of the whole</u> are in danger of being <u>contravened by the laws of the parts</u>. In this case, <u>if the particular</u> tribunals are invested with a right of <u>ultimate jurisdiction</u>, besides the contradictions to be expected from difference of opinion, there will be much to fear from the <u>bias of local views</u> and <u>prejudices</u>, and from the <u>interference</u> of <u>local regulations</u>. As often as such an interference was to happen, there would be reason to apprehend that the provisions of the particular laws might be preferred to those of the general laws; for nothing is more natural to men in office than to look with peculiar deference towards that authority to which they owe their official existence.

TREATIES MORE CORRUPTIBLE UNDER ARTICLES:
Treaties created under the Articles could be violated by thirteen different legislatures and just as many courts.

22:42 <u>The treaties</u> of the United States, under the present Constitution, <u>are liable to the infractions of thirteen different legislatures</u>, and as many different courts of final jurisdiction, acting under the authority of those legislatures. The faith, the reputation, the peace of the whole Union, are thus continually at the mercy of the prejudices, the passions, and the interests of every member of which it is composed. Is it possible that foreign nations can either respect or confide in such a government? Is it possible that <u>the people</u> of America will longer consent to trust their honor, their happiness, their safety, on so <u>precarious a foundation</u>?

THE ARTICLES ARE SO WEAK NO AMENDMENT COULD FIX THEM:
The Articles of Confederation is so radically broken and beyond repair there is no other option than to replace it.

22:43 In this review of the Confederation, I have <u>confined myself</u> to the exhibition of its <u>most material defects</u>; passing over those <u>imperfections in its details</u> by which even a great part of the <u>power</u> intended to be conferred upon it has been in a great measure rendered <u>abortive</u>. It must be by this time evident to all men of reflection, who can divest themselves of the prepossessions of preconceived opinions, that it is a system so radically vicious and unsound, as to admit <u>not of amendment</u> but by an <u>entire change</u> in its leading features and characters.

CONGRESS UNDER ARTICLES IS INADEQUATE:
Congress as now constituted can't repair the flaws in the Articles. Some suggest it be given more powers for that very purpose.

22:44 The <u>organization of Congress is itself utterly improper for the exercise of those powers</u> which are necessary to be deposited in the Union. A single assembly may be a proper receptacle of those slender, or rather fettered, authorities, which have been heretofore delegated to the federal head; but it would be <u>inconsistent with all the principles of good government</u>, to intrust it with those <u>additional powers which</u>, <u>even the moderate and more rational adversaries</u> of the proposed Constitution admit, ought to reside in the United States.

TRYING TO FIX ARTICLES ONLY MAKES THEM WORSE:
22:45 If that plan should not be adopted, and if the necessity of the Union should be able to withstand the ambitious aims of those men who may indulge magnificent schemes of personal aggrandizement from its dissolution, the probability would be, that we should run into the project of <u>conferring supplementary powers upon Congress, as they are now con-</u>

stituted; and either the machine, from the intrinsic feebleness of its structure, will moulder into pieces, in spite of our ill-judged efforts to prop it; or, by successive augmentations of its force an energy, as necessity might prompt, we shall finally accumulate, in a single body, all the most important preroga-tives of sovereignty, and thus entail upon our posterity one of the most **execrable**[84] forms of government that human infat-uation ever contrived. Thus, we should create in reality that very tyranny which the adversaries of the new Constitution either are, or affect to be, solicitous to avert.

PEOPLE THEMSELVES NOT ALLOWED TO RATIFY ARTICLES:

The States ratified the Articles, which has raised an unend-ing stream of questions about its legitimate authority to govern. The people themselves never adopted the Articles.

22:46 It has not a little contributed to the infirmities of the existing federal system, that it never had a ratification by the PEOPLE. Resting on no better foundation than the consent of the several legislatures, it has been exposed to frequent and intricate questions concerning the validity of its powers, and has, in some instances, given birth to the enormous doctrine of a right of legislative repeal. Owing its ratification to the law of a State, it has been contended that the same authority might repeal the law by which it was ratified. However gross a heresy it may be to maintain that a PARTY to a COMPACT has a right to revoke that COMPACT, the doctrine itself has had respectable advocates.

DELEGATED AUTHORITY NOT THE PRIME ISSUE:

22:47 The possibility of a question of this nature proves the necessity of laying the foundations of our national govern-ment deeper than in the mere sanction of delegated authority.

FOUNTAIN OF AMERICA'S AUTHORITY IS THE CONSENT OF THE PEOPLE:

As amplified in the preamble, "We the People," not "We the States."

22:48 The fabric of American empire ought to rest on the solid basis of THE CONSENT OF THE PEOPLE. The streams of national power ought to flow immediately from that pure, original fountain of all legitimate authority.

—PUBLIUS

REVIEW QUESTIONS

1. Does this paper promote the Constitution or highlight the flaws in the Articles of Confederation? (22:1–48)

2. Does the Articles grant power to Congress to regulate commerce? (22:2)

3. Why did that lack of regulation over commerce hurt foreign relations? (22:3–4)

4. Could America develop a favorable trade balance or build diplomatic relations under the current Articles? Why? (22:4–7)

5. How did the States hurt each other when it came to pros-perous commerce? (22:5–7)

6. How did excessive duties among the states of Germany ruin its commerce? (22:8)

7. How did America raise troops for the war? Did it work? (22:10–11)

8. What enthusiasm ultimately led to raising an army? (22:12)

9. Which States supported the war the most? The least? (22:13–14)

10. How is a majority of States not a majority of people? Is this fair? (22:16–19)

11. Why is a nine-State rule to pass a resolution a bad idea? (22:20–22)

12. Can a single vote prevent much goodness or create much evil? (22:30)

13. Why is a simple majority harder to corrupt? (22:31)

14. What is the crowning defect of the Confederation? (22:38)

15. What could happen if each State had its own final juris-diction? (22:40)

16. Can the Articles be repaired with amendments? Why? (22:43)

17. Who ratified the Articles? Who really should ratify the new Constitution? Why? (22:46–48)

---

84 **execrable:** Extremely bad, wretched, or unpleasant.

SECTION 3 • GRANTING GOVERNMENT PROPER POWER

Papers 23–29

FEDERALIST NO. 23

THE FEDERAL GOVERNMENT MUST HAVE SUFFI-CIENT POWER: This paper is a reminder that the authors did not write these essays to be read like a book, and assumed many readers were not familiar with their earlier writings. That's why there appears a lot of repetition, as follows. The new Constitution provides enough energy to the federal government so that it can preserve the Union. Among its duties are to provide for the common defense at home and abroad, to ensure that interstate commerce is fair, and to deal with foreign countries. The national government must be strong enough to care for national interests, but the powers given it must not exceed what is necessary to carry forward that primary purpose. See No. 51 for more information about the federal government's role and its powers.

By Alexander Hamilton—December 18, 1787

ARTICLES DON'T HAVE ENOUGH POWER:
The Articles don't have sufficient political power or energy to fulfill its responsibilities. What are the three critical parts of an energetic government?

23:1 THE necessity of a Constitution, at least equally **energetic**[85] with the one proposed, to the preservation of the Union, is the point at the examination of which we are now arrived.

23:2 This inquiry will naturally divide itself into three branches [1] the objects to be provided for by the federal government, [2] the quantity of power necessary to the accomplishment of those objects, [3] the persons upon whom that power ought to operate. Its distribution and organization will more properly claim our attention under the succeeding head.

FOUR JOBS OF THE UNION:
The are four primary jobs the government is expected to perform. What is the first?

23:3 The principal purposes to be answered by union are these [1] the common defense of the members; [2] the preservation of the public peace as well against internal convulsions as external attacks; [3] the regulation of commerce with other nations and between the States; [4] the superintendence of our intercourse, political and commercial, with foreign countries.

POWER MUST BE UNLIMITED FOR NATIONAL DEFENSE:
War powers by the federal government must be unlimited. Why?

23:4 The authorities essential to the common defense are these: to raise armies; to build and equip fleets; to prescribe rules for the government of both; to direct their operations; to provide for their support.

IMPOSSIBLE TO PREDICT FUTURE WAR NEEDS:
23:5 These powers ought to exist without limitation, BECAUSE IT IS IMPOSSIBLE TO FORESEE OR DEFINE THE EXTENT AND VARIETY OF NATIONAL EXIGENCIES, OR THE CORRESPONDENT EXTENT AND VARIETY OF THE MEANS WHICH MAY BE NECESSARY TO SATISFY THEM.

ANY CONSTITUTIONAL SHACKLES FOR WAR IS UNWISE:
23:6 The circumstances that endanger the safety of nations are infinite, and for this reason no constitutional shackles can wisely be imposed on the power to which the care of it is committed. This power ought to be coextensive with all the possible combinations of such circumstances; and ought to be under the direction of the same councils which are appointed to preside over the common defense.

GOVERNMENT MUST HAVE ENOUGH POWER:
Enough power must be delegated for the government to achieve its stated purposes. This includes sufficient power granted to the officers themselves.

---

85 *energetic:* Powerful. A frequently used term meaning that the government must have *all* the necessary political, enforcement, and taxing power to fulfill its assigned tasks. The Articles of Confederation did not grant this power, so the government was not energetic.

23:7 This is one of those <u>truths</u> which, to a correct and un-prejudiced mind, carries its own evidence along with it; and may be obscured, but <u>cannot</u> be made <u>plainer</u> by argument or reasoning. It rests upon axioms as <u>simple</u> as they are <u>universal</u>; the <u>MEANS</u> ought to be <u>proportioned</u> to the <u>END</u>; the persons, from whose agency the attainment of any <u>END</u> <u>is expected</u>, ought to possess the <u>MEANS</u> by which it is to be <u>attained</u>.

GIVE GOVERNMENT ENOUGH POWER TO DEFEND THE NATION:
The government's war powers must not be limited.

23:8 Whether there ought to be a federal government intrusted with the care of the common defense, is a question in the first instance, open for discussion; but the moment it is decided in the affirmative, it will follow, that that <u>government</u> <u>ought to be clothed with all the powers requisite to complete</u> <u>execution of its trust</u>. And unless it can be shown that the circumstances which may affect the public safety are reducible within certain determinate limits; unless the contrary of this position can be fairly and rationally disputed, it must be admitted, as a necessary consequence, that there <u>can be no</u> <u>limitation of that authority</u> which is to provide for the defense and protection of the community, in any matter essential to its efficacy that is, in any matter essential to the <u>FORMATION</u>, <u>DIRECTION</u>, or <u>SUPPORT</u> of the <u>NATIONAL</u> <u>FORCES</u>.

GOOD WILL IS A WEAK POWER OF ENFORCEMENT:
The Confederacy depended on the good will of the States to perform their obligations for quotas (troops) and requisitions (supplies). The Constitution grants Congress power to demand such help.

23:9 <u>Defective</u> as the present <u>Confederation</u> has been proved to be, this principle appears to have been fully recognized by the framers of it; though they have <u>not made</u> proper or <u>adequate provision</u> for its exercise. <u>Congress have an unlimited</u> <u>discretion to</u> make <u>requisitions</u> of men and money; to govern the army and navy; to direct their operations. <u>As their requisitions</u> are made <u>constitutionally binding</u> upon the <u>States</u>, who are in fact under the most solemn obligations to furnish the supplies required of them, the intention evidently was that the United States should <u>command whatever resources</u> were by them judged <u>requisite to the</u> "<u>common defense and general</u> <u>welfare</u>." It was <u>presumed</u> that a <u>sense</u> of their <u>true interests</u>, and a regard to the dictates of good faith, would be found <u>sufficient</u> pledges for the punctual performance of the duty of the members to the federal head.

UNION MUST HAVE DIRECT AUTHORITY OVER PEOPLE:
Were "good faith" and "legally binding" sufficient inducements to compel the States to materially support the war? Legislating the States is a dismal failure. The federal government must be able to extend laws directly to the individual citizen.

23:10 The experiment has, however, demonstrated that this <u>expectation was ill-founded</u> and illusory; and the observations, made under the last head, will, I imagine, have sufficed to convince the impartial and discerning, that there is <u>an absolute necessity for an entire change in the first principles of</u> <u>the system</u>; that if we are in earnest about giving the Union energy and duration, we must abandon the vain project of legislating upon the States in their collective capacities; we must <u>extend the laws of the federal government to the individual</u> <u>citizens</u> of America; we must discard the fallacious scheme of <u>quotas and requisitions</u>, as equally impracticable and unjust.

DEFENSE IS STRICTLY A FEDERAL RESPONSIBILITY:
No state should have the discretion or power to impede the profound responsibility of the Union to provide the security of the people.

23:11 The result from all this is that the Union ought to be invested with full power to levy troops; to build and equip fleets; and to raise the revenues which will be required for the formation and support of an army and navy, in the customary and ordinary modes practiced in other governments.

GOVERNMENT MUST BE FULLY EMPOWERED TO DEFEND US:
It must have the authority to pass all necessary and proper laws for each of its departments to fulfill their responsibilities.

23:12 If the circumstances of our country are such as to demand a compound instead of a simple, a confederate instead of a sole, government, the essential point which will remain to be adjusted will be to discriminate the <u>OBJECTS</u>, as far as it can be done, which shall appertain to the different provinces or departments of power; allowing to each the most ample authority for fulfilling the objects committed to its charge.

Fleets and armies managed better by the Union.

23:13 Shall the Union be constituted the guardian of the <u>common safety</u>? Are fleets and armies and revenues necessary to this purpose? <u>The government of the Union must be empowered to pass all laws, and to make all regulations which</u> <u>have relation to them</u>.

IMPLIED POWERS NEEDED TO BE SUFFICIENT AND EFFICIENT.

Could justice, for example, be fully exercised and examined if those departments didn't have proper authority?

23:14 The same must be the case in respect to <u>commerce</u>, and to every other matter to which its jurisdiction is permitted to extend.

States need enough power to deliver justice.

23:15 Is the administration of <u>justice</u> between the citizens of the same State the proper department of the local governments? These must <u>possess all the authorities</u> which are connected with this object, and with every other that may be allotted to their particular cognizance and direction.

Withholding the necessary power to get the job done defeats the whole purpose.

23:16 <u>Not to confer in each case a degree of power commensurate to the end, would be to violate</u> the most obvious rules of prudence and propriety, and improvidently to trust the great interests of the nation to hands which are disabled from managing them with vigor and success.

War powers must be a federal responsibility. Can the States be trusted to provide suitable public defense?

23:17 Who is likely to make suitable provisions for the public defense, as that body to which the guardianship of the public safety is confided; which, as the center of information, will best understand the extent and urgency of the dangers that threaten; as the representative of <u>the WHOLE</u>, will feel itself most deeply interested in the preservation of <u>every part</u>; which, from the responsibility implied in the duty assigned to it, will be most sensibly impressed with the <u>necessity</u> of <u>proper exertions</u>; and which, by the extension of its authority throughout the States, can alone establish uniformity and concert in the plans and measures by which the common safety is to be secured?

GIVE POWERS THAT CAN BE SAFELY ENTRUSTED:

23:18 <u>Is there not a manifest inconsistency in devolving upon the federal government the care of the general defense, and leaving in the State governments the EFFECTIVE powers by which it is to be provided for?</u> Is not a <u>want of co-operation</u> the infallible consequence of such a system? And will not <u>weakness</u>, <u>disorder</u>, an undue distribution of the burdens and calamities of war, an unnecessary and intolerable <u>increase of expense</u>, be its natural and inevitable concomitants? Have we not had unequivocal experience of its effects in the course of the revolution which we have just accomplished?

CONSTITUTION PROVIDES SAFE GOVERNMENT:

A government must be empowered to fulfill its sacred duties. Its powers are dependent on the consent of the people.

23:19 Every view we may take of the subject, as candid inquirers after truth, will serve to convince us, that it is both <u>unwise and dangerous to deny the federal government an unconfined authority, as to all those objects which are intrusted to its management</u>. It will indeed deserve the most vigilant and careful attention of the people, to see that it be modeled in such a manner as to admit of its being safely vested with the requisite powers. If any plan which has been, or may be, offered to our consideration, should not, upon a dispassionate inspection, be found to answer this description, it ought to be rejected.

Government should have only those powers which can be safely entrusted to it by a free people.

23:20 <u>A government, the constitution of which renders it unfit to be trusted with all the powers which a free people OUGHT TO DELEGATE TO ANY GOVERNMENT, would be an unsafe and improper depository of the NATIONAL INTERESTS</u>. Wherever THESE can with propriety be confided, the coincident powers may safely accompany them. This is the true result of all just reasoning upon the subject.

CRITICS SHOULD RESTRAIN INFLAMMATORY ATTACKS:

How did the adversaries of the Constitution ruin their own arguments against the proposed changes?

23:21 And the adversaries of the plan promulgated by the Convention would given a better impression of their candor <u>if they had confined</u> themselves to showing that the <u>internal structure</u> of the proposed government was such as to render it <u>unworthy of the confidence</u> of the people. <u>They ought not</u> to have wandered into <u>inflammatory declamations</u> and unmeaning cavils about the extent of the powers.

POWERS MUST BE KEPT EQUAL TO THE TASK:

If such powers have the potential to hurt the liberties of the people, what is the better alternative?

23:22 <u>The POWERS are not too extensive for the OBJECTS of federal administration</u>, or, in other words, for the management of our <u>NATIONAL INTERESTS</u>; nor can any satisfactory argument be framed to show that they are chargeable with such an excess. If it be true, as has been insinuated by some of the writers on the <u>other side</u>, that the difficulty arises from the nature of the thing, and that the <u>extent of the country will not permit us to form a government</u> in which such ample powers can safely be reposed, it would prove that we ought to contract our views, and resort to the expedient of separate confederacies, which will move within more practicable spheres.

IT IS FOOLISH TO WITHHOLD POWER TO DO THE JOB:

23:23   For the absurdity must continually stare us in the face of confiding to a government the direction of the most essential national interests, without daring to trust it to the authorities which are indispensable to their proper and efficient management. Let us not attempt to reconcile contradictions, but firmly embrace a rational alternative.

NO OTHER FORM CAN WORK:
All governments of lesser energy must eventually fail.

23:24 I trust, however, that the impracticability of one general system cannot be shown. I am greatly mistaken if any thing of weight has yet been advanced of this tendency; and I flatter myself, that the observations which have been made in the course of these papers have served to place the reverse of that position in as clear a light as any matter still in the womb of time and experience can be susceptible of. This, at all events, must be evident, that the very difficulty itself, drawn from the extent of the country, is the strongest argument in favor of an energetic government; for any other can certainly never preserve the Union of so large an empire.

Without the new Constitution, all of the gloomy predictions and known failures will indeed unfold and ruin the country.

23:25   If we embrace the tenets of those who oppose the adoption of the proposed Constitution, as the standard of our political creed, we cannot fail to verify the gloomy doctrines which predict the impracticability of a national system pervading entire limits of the present Confederacy.

—Publius

Review Questions

1. What is meant by "energetic" government? (23:1–2, see footnote)

2. What are the four jobs of the Union? (23:3)

3. Why must war powers for the federal government be unlimited? (23:5–6)

4. What does it mean to give government the means "proportional to the end"? (23:7)

5. Did the Articles give Congress unlimited power for self defense? (23:9)

6. What was the mistake in the Articles that gutted and made

pointless this unlimited war power? (23:9–10).

7. To whom, then, must the federal laws be extended to ensure proper execution of the law? (23:10)

8. Why should the States be given all power necessary to render justice? (23:13–16)

FEDERALIST NO. 24

STANDING ARMIES ARE SAFE: Standing armies are necessary but must be kept under the control of the Congress, not the President alone, or the States. The Constitution grants sufficient power and control for this important responsibility. With military threats posed by Indians, Spain, and Britain, a professional army is already needed. The militias are not well-suited for these long-term assignments. A safety switch to prevent any attempt to build a dangerously large military is built into the Constitution by requiring that military budgets be renewed every two years.

By Alexander Hamilton—December 19, 1787

STANDING ARMIES IN TIMES OF PEACE ARE SAFE:
Critics worry about such an army; I will show the concern is groundless.

24:1 To THE powers proposed to be conferred upon the federal government, in respect to the creation and direction of the national forces, I have met with but one specific objection, which, if I understand it right, is this, that proper provision has not been made against the existence of standing armies in time of peace; an objection which, I shall now endeavor to show, rests on weak and unsubstantial foundations.

ARMY ISN'T DANGEROUS IF CONGRESS HAS CONTROL:
The only worry about standing armies in peacetime is the attempt to curtail Congress's control over the military.

24:2 It has indeed been brought forward in the most vague and general form, supported only by bold assertions, without the appearance of argument; without even the sanction of theoretical opinions; in contradiction to the practice of other free nations, and to the general sense of America, as expressed in most of the existing constitutions. The propriety of this remark will appear, the moment it is recollected that the objection under consideration turns upon a supposed necessity of restraining the LEGISLATIVE authority of the nation, in the article of military establishments; a principle unheard of, except in one or two of our State constitutions, and rejected in all the rest.

FALSE REPRESENTATION OF THIS ISSUE IN THE MEDIA:

24:3 A stranger to our politics, who was to read our newspapers at the present juncture, without having previously inspected the plan reported by the Convention, would be naturally led to one of two conclusions: either that it contained a positive injunction, that standing armies should be kept up in time of peace; or that it vested in the EXECUTIVE the whole power of levying troops, without subjecting his discretion, in any shape, to the control of the legislature.

CORRECTING MYTH #1: *EXECUTIVE IS IN CONTROL.*

The executive can militarily respond to emergencies but he has no power to raise armies. Only the legislature may raise armies.

24:4 If he came afterwards to peruse the plan itself, he would be surprised to discover, that neither the one nor the other was the case; that the whole power of raising armies was lodged in the LEGISLATURE, not in the EXECUTIVE; that this legislature was to be a popular body, consisting of the representatives of the people periodically elected;

CORRECTING MYTH #2: *CAN'T STAND ARMY DOWN.*

The Constitution requires that funding an army must be renewed every two years. If the money stops, the army must disband.

24:5 and that instead of the provision he had supposed in favor of standing armies, there was to be found, in respect to this object, an important qualification even of the legislative discretion, in that clause which forbids the appropriation of money for the support of an army for any longer period than two years a precaution which, upon a nearer view of it, will appear to be a great and real security against the keeping up of troops without evident necessity.

CORRECTING MYTH #3: *PROTECTION IS NOW MISSING.*

The States' constitutions make no specific mention of standing armies, so the people's great concern over such armies doesn't really exist except in the minds of the Anti-Federalists.

24:6 Disappointed in his first surmise, the person I have supposed would be apt to pursue his conjectures a little further. He would naturally say to himself, it is impossible that all this vehement and pathetic declamation can be without some colorable pretext. It must needs be that this people, so jealous of their liberties, have, in all the preceding models of the constitutions which they have established, inserted the most precise and rigid precautions on this point, the omission of which, in the new plan, has given birth to all this apprehension and clamor.

CORRECTING MYTH #4: *STATES ARE AGAINST IT.*

Only two States actually forbid standing armies in peacetime. Eleven States left the matter up to the legislature or were silent.

24:7 If, under this impression, he proceeded to pass in review the several State constitutions, how great would be his disappointment to find that TWO ONLY of them[86] contained an interdiction of standing armies in time of peace; that the other eleven had either observed a profound silence on the subject, or had in express terms admitted the right of the Legislature to authorize their existence.

CORRECTING MYTH #5: *ARTICLES ARE OPPOSED TO IT.*

The Articles don't address restricting standing armies. They simply outline Congress's role in national defense.

24:8 Still, however he would be persuaded that there must be some plausible foundation for the cry raised on this head. He would never be able to imagine, while any source of information remained unexplored, that it was nothing more than an experiment upon the public credulity, dictated either by a deliberate intention to deceive, or by the overflowings of a zeal too intemperate to be ingenuous.

---

86 *Publius:* This statement of the matter is taken from the printed collection of State constitutions. Pennsylvania and North Carolina are the two which contain the interdiction in these words: "As standing armies in time of peace are dangerous to liberty, THEY OUGHT NOT to be kept up." This is, in truth, rather a CAUTION than a PROHIBITION. New Hampshire, Massachusetts, Delaware, and Maryland have, in each of their bills of rights, a clause to this effect: "Standing armies are dangerous to liberty, and ought not to be raised or kept up WITHOUT THE CONSENT OF THE LEGISLATURE"; which is a formal admission of the authority of the Legislature. New York has no bills of her rights, and her constitution says not a word about the matter. No bills of rights appear annexed to the constitutions of the other States, except the foregoing, and their constitutions are equally silent. I am told, however that one or two States have bills of rights which do not appear in this collection; but that those also recognize the right of the legislative authority in this respect. (Underlining added by the editors)

There is no precaution against standing armies in the Articles.

24:9 It would probably occur to him, that he would be likely to find the <u>precautions he was in search of in the primitive compact between the States</u>. Here, at length, he would expect to meet with a solution of the enigma. No doubt, he would observe to himself, the existing Confederation must contain the most <u>explicit provisions</u> against <u>military establishments</u> in time of <u>peace</u>; and a departure from this model, in a favorite point, has occasioned the discontent which appears to influence these political champions.

TRUTH BECOMES CLEAR, IT IS A BASELESS CRITICISM:

24:10 If he should now apply himself to a careful and critical survey of the <u>articles of Confederation</u>, his <u>astonishment</u> would not only be increased, but would <u>acquire a mixture of indignation</u>, at the unexpected <u>discovery</u>, that these articles, instead of containing the prohibition he looked for, and though they had, with jealous circumspection, restricted the authority of the State legislatures in this particular, <u>had not imposed a single restraint on that of the United States</u>.

ANTI-FEDERALIST'S STRATEGY EXPOSED AS A FULL-SCALE LIE.

24:11 If he happened to be a man of quick sensibility, or ardent temper, he could now no longer refrain from regarding these clamors as the dishonest artifices of a <u>sinister</u> and unprincipled <u>opposition</u> to a plan which ought at least to receive a fair and candid examination from all sincere lovers of their country!

CRITICS IGNORE NEW SECURITY MEASURES:

24:12 How else, he would say, could the authors of them have been tempted to vent such loud censures upon that <u>plan</u>, about a point in which it seems to have conformed itself to the general sense of America as declared in its different forms of government, and in which it has even super-added a new and <u>powerful guard unknown</u> to <u>any of them</u>?

NO ATTEMPT TO PERSUADE:

Critics' arguments are easily dismissed for lack of any sincere attempt to use reasoning.

24:13 If, on the contrary, he happened to be a man of calm and dispassionate feelings, he would indulge a sigh for the frailty of human nature, and would lament, that in a matter so interesting to the happiness of millions, the <u>true merits</u> of the <u>question</u> should be perplexed and <u>entangled</u> by expedients so <u>unfriendly</u> to an impartial and right determination. Even such a man could hardly forbear remarking, that a conduct of this kind has too much the appearance of an <u>intention</u> to <u>mis-</u><u>lead</u> the people by alarming their passions, rather than to convince them by arguments addressed to their understandings.

RESTRAINING CONGRESS IN PEACE TIME IS DANGEROUS:

24:14 But however little this objection may be countenanced, even by precedents among ourselves, it may be satisfactory to take a nearer view of its intrinsic merits. From a close examination it will appear that <u>restraints</u> upon the <u>discretion of the legislature</u> in respect to military establishments in <u>time of peace</u>, would be <u>improper</u> to be imposed, and if imposed, from the <u>necessities</u> of society, would be <u>unlikely</u> to be <u>observed</u>.

MANY INTERNATIONAL DANGERS LURK UNSEEN:

Despite the barrier of the ocean, threats from Europe and the Indians remain.

24:15 Though a <u>wide ocean</u> separates the United States from Europe, yet there are <u>various considerations</u> that <u>warn us</u> against an <u>excess of confidence</u> or <u>security</u>. On one side of us, and stretching far into <u>our rear</u>, are growing settlements subject to the <u>dominion of Britain</u>. On the other side, and extending to meet the British settlements, are colonies and establishments subject to the dominion of <u>Spain</u>. This situation and the vicinity of the <u>West India Islands</u>, belonging to these two powers create between them, in respect to their American possessions and in relation to us, a common interest. The <u>savage tribes</u> on our Western frontier ought to be regarded as our <u>natural enemies</u>, their natural allies, because they have most to fear from us, and most to hope from them.

SHRINKING WORLD:

Improved navigation makes America's shores easier to reach.

24:16 The improvements in the <u>art of navigation</u> have, as to the facility of communication, rendered distant nations, in a great measure, neighbors. Britain and Spain are among the <u>principal maritime powers</u> of Europe. A future concert of views between these nations ought not to be regarded as improbable.

DON'T TRUST CONNECTIONS WITH FRANCE AND SPAIN:

24:17 The increasing remoteness of consanguinity is every day diminishing the force of the family compact between France and Spain. And politicians have ever with great reason considered the <u>ties of blood as feeble</u> and precarious links of <u>political connection</u>.

NEVER BE OVER-CONFIDENT ABOUT SECURITY:

24:18 These circumstances combined, admonish us <u>not to be too sanguine</u> in considering ourselves as entirely out of the reach of danger.

PROTECTING WESTERN BORDER STILL NEEDED:

24:19 <u>Previous to the Revolution</u>, and <u>ever since the peace</u>, there has been a <u>constant necessity for keeping small garrisons</u> on our <u>Western frontier</u>. No person can doubt that these will continue to be <u>indispensable</u>, if it should only be against the ravages and depredations of the Indians.

MILITIA NOT GOOD FOR FRONTIER:

Standing armies on the frontier are better, and Congress should pay for that.

24:20 These <u>garrisons must either be furnished</u> by occasional detachments from the <u>militia</u>, or by <u>permanent corps</u> in the pay of the government. The first is impracticable; and if practicable, would be pernicious. The <u>militia</u> would <u>not long</u>, if at all, <u>submit</u> to be dragged from their <u>occupations</u> and <u>families</u> to perform that most disagreeable duty in times of <u>profound</u> peace. And if they could be prevailed upon or compelled to do it, the increased <u>expense of a frequent rotation of service</u>, and the loss of labor and disconcertion of the industrious pursuits of individuals, would form conclusive objections to the scheme. It would be as <u>burdensome</u> and <u>injurious</u> to the <u>public</u> as <u>ruinous to private citizens</u>.

STANDING ARMY NEEDED RIGHT NOW:

24:21 The latter resource of <u>permanent corps</u> in the pay of the government amounts to <u>a standing army</u> in <u>time of peace</u>; a small one, indeed, but not the less real for being small.

LET CONGRESS DECIDE WHEN TO HAVE STANDING ARMY:

Whether a standing army in peacetime is needed or not, leave the option up to Congress and don't block it in the Constitution.

24:22 Here is a simple view of the subject, that shows us at once the <u>impropriety of a constitutional interdiction of such establishments</u>, and the necessity of <u>leaving the matter</u> to the discretion and <u>prudence</u> of the <u>legislature</u>.

AS WE ARM SO WILL BRITAIN AND SPAIN ARM THEMSELVES:

As the western frontier is fortified, Britain and Spain will increase their own forces. A standing army becomes important to prevent hostilities and protect trade, even trade with the Indian nations.

24:23 In proportion to our increase in strength, it is probable, nay, it may be said certain, that Britain and Spain would augment their military establishments in our neighborhood. If we should not be willing to be exposed, in a <u>naked</u> and <u>defenseless</u> condition, to their <u>insults</u> and <u>encroachments</u>, we should find it expedient to <u>increase</u> our <u>frontier garrisons</u> in some ratio to the force by which our Western settlements might be annoyed. There are, and will be, particular posts, the possession of which will include the command of large districts of territory, and facilitate future invasions of the remainder. It may be added that some of those <u>posts</u> will be <u>keys to the trade with the Indian nations</u>.

Does it make any sense to just leave those frontier posts unprotected?

24:24 Can any man think it would be wise to leave such posts in a situation to be at any instant seized by one or the other of two neighboring and formidable powers? To act this part would be to desert all the usual maxims of prudence and policy.

A NAVY PROTECTS COUNTRY AND COMMERCE:

Until we acquire a strong navy, local garrisons will be needed.

24:25 If we mean to be a <u>commercial people</u>, or even to be secure on our Atlantic side, we must endeavor, as soon as possible, to have a <u>navy</u>. To this purpose there must be <u>dockyards</u> and <u>arsenals</u>; and for the <u>defense of these, fortifications, and probably garrisons</u>. When a nation has become so powerful by sea that it can protect its dock-yards by its fleets, this supersedes the necessity of garrisons for that purpose; but where naval establishments are in their infancy, moderate garrisons will, in all likelihood, be found an indispensable security against descents for the destruction of the arsenals and dock-yards, and sometimes of the fleet itself.

—PUBLIUS

REVIEW QUESTIONS

1. What concern does Publius address about standing armies in times of peace? (24:1)

2. Is the executive in charge of raising armies? (24:3-4)

3. Can a standing army be forced to stand down? (24:5)

4. If people had been greatly concerned about a standing army, would it be fair to expect to see restrictions to that end written out in their State constitutions? (24:6-7)

5. How many States forbade standing armies in times of

peace? (24:7)

6. Do the Articles prohibit a standing army? (24:8–9)

7. Where is a standing army needed right now? (24:19–23)

8. Would the militia adequately meet the needs of self-defense? Why? (24:20)

FEDERALIST NO. 25

PEACE THROUGH STRENGTH IS A FEDERAL RE-SPONSIBILITY: If national defense is left to the States, they would be tempted to misuse that power to forcefully resolve tensions with other States. States most vulnerable to foreign aggression would also be dependent on other States for help, a cooperation poorly exemplified under the Articles. State militias are useful but ill-prepared compared to a full-time army. A standing army is a necessary risk America must take, but State-created armies would be much more dangerous to liberty. If a standing army is forbidden, then in times of need such forces will be established anyway, in violation of the written law. And with that violation, more violations will later be justified until the whole Constitution unravels.

By Alexander Hamilton—December 21, 1787

NATIONAL DEFENSE IS FEDERAL JOB:
Providing for the common defense is best done by the central government. Are the States equipped to handle that burden?

25:1 IT MAY perhaps be urged that the objects enumerated in the preceding number ought to be provided for by the State governments, under the direction of the Union. But this would be, in reality, an inversion of the primary principle of our political association, as it would in practice transfer the care of the common defense from the federal head to the individual members: a project oppressive to some States, dangerous to all, and baneful to the Confederacy.

DISUNION INVITES INVASION:
Border States have direct exposure to border threats, and none of them are able to protect themselves.

25:2 The territories of Britain, Spain, and of the Indian nations in our neighborhood do not border on particular States, but encircle the Union from Maine to Georgia. The danger, though in different degrees, is therefore common. And the

means of guarding against it ought, in like manner, to be the objects of common councils and of a common treasury.

NEW YORK HAS LARGE DEFENSE NEEDS:
If maintaining defense is left to the States, New York will carry a very large and unfair share of that, because of its unique situation.

25:3 It happens that some States, from local situation, are more directly exposed. New York is of this class. Upon the plan of separate provisions, New York would have to sustain the whole weight of the establishments requisite to her immediate safety, and to the mediate or ultimate protection of her neighbors. This would neither be equitable as it respected New York nor safe as it respected the other States.

STATES CAN'T AFFORD COMPLETE PROTECTION:
If the States most threatened could summon Union forces for protection, or build their own, other States would be left feeling vulnerable and obligated to arm themselves.

25:4 Various inconveniences would attend such a system. The States, to whose lot it might fall to support the necessary establishments, would be as little able as willing, for a considerable time to come, to bear the burden of competent provisions. The security of all would thus be subjected to the **parsimony**,[87] **improvidence**,[88] or inability of a part.

STATES WOULD COMPETE OVER LOPSIDED DEFENSES:
25:5 If the resources of such part becoming more abundant and extensive, its provisions should be proportionally enlarged, the other States would quickly take the alarm at seeing the whole military force of the Union in the hands of two or three of its members, and those probably amongst the most powerful. They would each choose to have some counterpoise, and pretenses could easily be contrived.

STATE JEALOUSIES COULD RUIN NATIONAL TRUST:
25:6 In this situation, military establishments, nourished by mutual jealousy, would be apt to swell beyond their natural or proper size; and being at the separate disposal of the members, they would be engines for the abridgment or demolition of the national authority.

STATES WOULD COMPETE TO DOMINATE:
States' armies cannot be trusted to unify in a common cause such as national defense. Which level of government would the citizens align to if their security is threatened?

25:7 Reasons have been already given to induce a supposition that the State governments will too naturally be prone to

---

87 ***parsimony:*** Extreme frugality, excessive caution, stingy.

88 ***improvidence:*** Without foresight or adequate consideration; rash; acting on mistaken assumptions.

a rivalship with that of the Union, the foundation of which will be the love of power; and that in any contest between the federal head and one of its members the people will be most apt to unite with their local government.

STATE DEFENSE WOULD FAIL:
Would the people's liberty be safer under State armies or federal armies?

25:8 If, in addition to this immense advantage, the ambition of the members should be stimulated by the separate and independent possession of military forces, it would afford too strong a temptation and too great a facility to them to make enterprises upon, and finally to subvert, the constitutional authority of the Union. On the other hand, the liberty of the people would be less safe in this state of things than in that which left the national forces in the hands of the national government.

GREATEST THREAT FROM LEAST SUSPECTED:
The people's rights are more secure when the people are leery and suspicious of the powers that protect their rights.

25:9 As far as an army may be considered as a dangerous weapon of power, it had better be in those hands of which the people are most likely to be jealous than in those of which they are least likely to be jealous. For it is a truth, which the experience of ages has attested, that the people are always most in danger when the means of injuring their rights are in the possession of those of whom they entertain the least suspicion.

ARMIES IN STATES ARE DANGEROUS FOR LIBERTY:
The framers of the Articles of Confederation knew it was dangerous to allow States to have their own armies. Under what conditions could a State have an army or navy?

25:10 The framers of the existing Confederation, fully aware of the danger to the Union from the separate possession of military forces by the States, have, in express terms, prohibited them from having either ships or troops, unless with the consent of Congress. The truth is, that the existence of a federal government and military establishments under State authority are not less at variance with each other than a due supply of the federal treasury and the system of quotas and requisitions.

RESTRAINING CONGRESS'S ROLE IN DEFENSE IS FOOLISH:

25:11 There are other lights besides those already taken notice of, in which the impropriety of restraints on the discretion of the national legislature will be equally manifest. The design of the objection, which has been mentioned, is to preclude standing armies in time of peace, though we have never been informed how far it is designed the prohibition should extend;

whether to raising armies as well as to KEEPING THEM UP in a season of tranquility or not.

NO STRONG DEFINITION OF "KEEPING THEM UP"

25:12 If it be confined to the latter it will have no precise signification, and it will be ineffectual for the purpose intended. When armies are once raised what shall be denominated "keeping them up," contrary to the sense of the Constitution? What time shall be requisite to ascertain the violation? Shall it be a week, a month, a year?

NO STRONG TIME FRAME FOR "KEEPING UP" ARMY:

25:13 Or shall we say they may be continued as long as the danger which occasioned their being raised continues? This would be to admit that they might be kept up IN TIME OF PEACE, against threatening or impending danger, which would be at once to deviate from the literal meaning of the prohibition, and to introduce an extensive latitude of construction.

CENTRAL GOVERNMENT IS BEST JUDGE OF ALL:
Only a national government could equitably decide if armies must stand in times of danger, and after that danger has passed. Could any written law remove all ambiguity and describe with precision the conditions when "all danger has passed"?

25:14 Who shall judge of the continuance of the danger? This must undoubtedly be submitted to the national government, and the matter would then be brought to this issue, that the national government, to provide against apprehended danger, might in the first instance raise troops, and might afterwards keep them on foot as long as they supposed the peace or safety of the community was in any degree of jeopardy. It is easy to perceive that a discretion so latitudinary as this would afford ample room for eluding the force of the provision.

CONSPIRACY TO OVERTHROW GOVERNMENT:
A standing army opens the door to the branches of government conspiring to seize control. Those fearing such a collusion raise this possibility of eliminating this power from the Constitution.

25:15 The supposed utility of a provision of this kind can only be founded on the supposed probability, or at least possibility, of a combination between the executive and the legislative, in some scheme of usurpation. Should this at any time happen, how easy would it be to fabricate pretenses of approaching danger! Indian hostilities, instigated by Spain or Britain, would always be at hand. Provocations to produce the desired appearances might even be given to some foreign power, and appeased again by timely concessions.

CONSPIRATORS COULD BENEFIT FROM ARMY:

25:16 If we can reasonably presume such a combination to have been formed, and that the enterprise is warranted by a sufficient prospect of success, the army, when once raised, from whatever cause, or on whatever pretext, may be applied to the execution of the project.

PEACE THROUGH STRENGTH:

Any legal restrictions that prevent the government from raising and maintaining standing armies would leave America open to attack and invasion.

25:17 If, to obviate this consequence, it should be resolved to extend the prohibition to the RAISING of armies in time of peace, the United States would then exhibit the most extraordinary spectacle which the world has yet seen, that of a nation incapacitated by its Constitution to prepare for defense, before it was actually invaded.

INTENTIONAL HESITATION COULD PROVE FATAL:

25:18 As the ceremony of a formal denunciation of war has of late fallen into disuse, the presence of an enemy within our territories must be waited for, as the legal warrant to the government to begin its levies of men for the protection of the State. We must receive the blow, before we could even prepare to return it. All that kind of policy by which nations anticipate distant danger, and meet the gathering storm, must be abstained from, as contrary to the genuine maxims of a free government.

FOOLISH TO TRUST FANTASY MORE THAN REALITY:

Which is worse, utter defenselessness or dealing with elected leaders who might abuse their political powers?

25:19 We must expose our property and liberty to the mercy of foreign invaders, and invite them by our weakness to seize the naked and defenseless prey, because we are afraid that rulers, created by our choice, dependent on our will, might endanger that liberty, by an abuse of the means necessary to its preservation.

STATE MILITIAS NOT A RELIABLE SAFETY NET:

State militias are not up to the task of national defense. Were the militias expensive?

25:20 Here I expect we shall be told that the militia of the country is its natural bulwark, and would be at all times equal to the national defense. This doctrine, in substance, had like to have lost us our independence. It cost millions to the United States that might have been saved.

PROFESSIONAL ARMY AGAINST PROFESSIONAL FOE:

25:21 The facts which, from our own experience, forbid a reliance of this kind, are too recent to permit us to be the dupes of such a suggestion. The steady operations of war against a regular and disciplined army can only be successfully conducted by a force of the same kind. Considerations of economy, not less than of stability and vigor, confirm this position.

MILITIA WAS GOOD, AMERICAN ARMY WAS BETTER:

A disciplined enemy must be met by an equally disciplined army. Did the bravest of men admit their militias were inadequate to advance the cause without a trained army?

25:22 The American militia, in the course of the late war, have, by their valor on numerous occasions, erected eternal monuments to their fame; but the bravest of them feel and know that the liberty of their country could not have been established by their efforts alone, however great and valuable they were. War, like most other things, is a science to be acquired and perfected by diligence, by perseverance, by time, and by practice.

STATES RAISED ARMIES DESPITE THE ARTICLES:

The States have openly declared that standing armies are dangerous, yet some of them are building their own armies because the national government is too weak to help.

25:23 All violent policy, as it is contrary to the natural and experienced course of human affairs, defeats itself. Pennsylvania, at this instant, affords an example of the truth of this remark. The Bill of Rights of that State declares that standing armies are dangerous to liberty, and ought not to be kept up in time of peace. Pennsylvania, nevertheless, in a time of profound peace, from the existence of partial disorders in one or two of her counties, has resolved to raise a body of troops; and in all probability will keep them up as long as there is any appearance of danger to the public peace.

MASSACHUSETTS ILLUSTRATES NEED FOR STANDING ARMY:

25:24 The conduct of Massachusetts affords a lesson on the same subject, though on different ground. That State (without waiting for the sanction of Congress, as the articles of the Confederation require) was compelled to raise troops to quell a domestic insurrection, and still keeps a corps in pay to prevent a revival of the spirit of revolt. The particular constitution of Massachusetts opposed no obstacle to the measure; but the instance is still of use to instruct us that cases are likely to occur under our government, as well as under those of other nations, which will sometimes render a military force in time of peace essential to the security of the society, and that it is therefore improper in this respect to control the legislative discretion.

FEEBLE GOVERNMENT ISN'T RESPECTED:

25:25 It also teaches us, in its application to the United States, how little the rights of a feeble government are likely to be respected, even by its own constituents. And it teaches us, in addition to the rest, how unequal parchment provisions are to a struggle with public necessity.

EXAMPLE OF GREECE SUFFERING UNDER WEAK LAWS:
Nations pay little regard to rules that run counter to their immediate needs.

25:26 It was a fundamental maxim of the Lacedaemonian commonwealth, that the post of admiral should not be conferred twice on the same person. The Peloponnesian confederates, having suffered a severe defeat at sea from the Athenians, demanded Lysander, who had before served with success in that capacity, to command the combined fleets. The Lacedaemonians, to gratify their allies, and yet preserve the semblance of an adherence to their ancient institutions, had recourse to the flimsy subterfuge of investing Lysander with the real power of <u>admiral</u>, under the nominal title of <u>vice-admiral</u>.

NATIONS WILL DISCARD RULES THAT WEAKEN THEM:

25:27 This instance is selected from among a multitude that might be cited to confirm the truth already advanced and illustrated by domestic examples; which is, that nations pay little regard to rules and maxims calculated in their very nature to run counter to the necessities of society.

WISE LEADERS WILL PREVENT FOOLISH LAWS:
Foolish restrictions should never be adopted as law. It fosters widespread disobedience.

25:28 <u>Wise politicians will be cautious about fettering the government with restrictions that cannot be observed, because they know that every breach of the fundamental laws, though dictated by necessity, impairs that sacred reverence which ought to be maintained in the breast of rulers towards the constitution</u> of a country, and forms a precedent for other breaches where the same plea of necessity does not exist at all, or is less urgent and palpable.

—Publius

Review Questions

1. Why is it a bad idea for the States to provide a standing army, even if under the direction of the Union? (25:1–3)

2. If defense was in the State's hands, what could competition and jealousy lead to? (25:4–6)

3. When are the people most in danger? (25:9)

4. Are people more suspicious of a national standing army than that of a State? How does that suspicion help protect liberty? (25:9)

5. What are some of the problems that come with restraining Congress from keeping up a standing army in peacetime? (25:11–13)

6. If the executive and legislature wanted to conspire to take over the country, what might they use as a pretense to raise a standing army? (25:15–16)

7. If Congress cannot raise an army, what primary government role will it be constitutionally prevented from fulfilling? (25:17)

8. Without a standing army what would America be forced to receive before it could respond? (25:18)

9. Why is the militia not a sufficiently prepared force to render quick national defense? (25:20–22)

10. Why is it important to avoid laws that won't be obeyed? (25:25–28)

FEDERALIST NO. 26

STANDING ARMIES ARE NECESSARY: Standing armies are necessary for peace. Historically speaking, it's an unusual outcome of a revolution against a monarchy to slow down a new nation's reorganization process long enough to consider a more proper form of government that protects individual rights. The new Constitution is well organized to protect rights. The great concern that must be addressed is how to prepare against internal and external threats without giving away too much power so that the government could turn on the people as a new monarchy or dictatorship. As part of this balance under the new Constitution, the federal government must have power to raise and control the military, but there must also exist a safety check against abuse. That check is in the power of the people to release money every two years to fund the military. While there is a risk associated with maintaining a standing army in times of peace, being caught without one in times of foreign attack or internal insurrection would be much worse.

By Alexander Hamilton—December 22, 1787

THE BOUNDARY BETWEEN LIBERTY AND AUTHORITY:

The Framers' goal was to find the right balance between too much political power and none at all—between ruler's law and people's law.

26:1 IT WAS a thing hardly to be expected that in a popular revolution the minds of men should stop at that happy mean which marks the salutary boundary between POWER and PRIVILEGE, and combines the energy of government with the security of private rights.

ARTICLES LEANED TOO FAR TOWARD "NO LAW" OR ANARCHY:

26:2 A failure in this delicate and important point is the great source of the inconveniences we experience, and if we are not cautious to avoid a repetition of the error, in our future attempts to rectify and ameliorate our system, we may travel from one **chimerical**[89] project to another; we may try change after change; but we shall never be likely to make any material change for the better.

IT IS "UNENLIGHTENED" TO RESTRAIN CONGRESS IN AREAS OF SELF DEFENSE:

26:3 The idea of restraining the legislative authority, in the means of providing for the national defense, is one of those refinements which owe their origin to a zeal for liberty more ardent than enlightened.

BETTER TO SUFFER ABUSE THAN SUFFER DEFEAT:

What two States formally limited their legislatures from providing proper defense?

26:4 We have seen, however, that it has not had thus far an extensive prevalency; that even in this country, where it made its first appearance, Pennsylvania and North Carolina are the only two States by which it has been in any degree patronized; and that all the others have refused to give it the least countenance; wisely judging that confidence must be placed somewhere; that the necessity of doing it, is implied in the very act of delegating power; and that it is better to hazard the abuse of that confidence than to embarrass the government and endanger the public safety by impolitic restrictions on the legislative authority.

STRONGER GOVERNMENT IS NEEDED TO PROSPER US:

The new Constitution is an expression of lessons learned under Britain's king. Those refusing to acknowledge those lessons are leading the country into additional error. Are the Anti-Federalists now supporting what they originally were totally against?

26:5 The opponents of the proposed Constitution combat, in this respect, the general decision of America; and instead of being taught by experience the propriety of correcting any extremes into which we may have heretofore run, they appear disposed to conduct us into others still more dangerous, and more extravagant. As if the tone of government had been found too high, or too rigid, the doctrines they teach are calculated to induce us to depress or to relax it, by expedients which, upon other occasions, have been condemned or forborne.

DANGER OF SWAYING PUBLIC AWAY FROM CONSTITUTION:

If enemies of the new Constitution successfully turn Americans away, the people are not worthy of any government whatsoever.

26:6 It may be affirmed without the imputation of invective, that if the principles they inculcate, on various points, could so far obtain as to become the popular creed, they would utterly unfit the people of this country for any species of government whatever.

The American public now realizes the Confederacy was too weak, lacked authority, and had failed them. The citizens won't be fooled into anarchy.

26:7 But a danger of this kind is not to be apprehended. The citizens of America have too much discernment to be argued into anarchy. And I am much mistaken, if experience has not wrought a deep and solemn conviction in the public mind, that greater energy of government is essential to the welfare and prosperity of the community.

FEAR OF STANDING ARMIES:

Where did Americans get the idea that standing armies in peacetime was bad?

26:8 It may not be amiss in this place concisely to remark the origin and progress of the idea, which aims at the exclusion of military establishments in time of peace. Though in speculative minds it may arise from a contemplation of the nature and tendency of such institutions, fortified by the events that have happened in other ages and countries, yet as a national sentiment, it must be traced to those habits of thinking which we derive from the nation from whom the inhabitants of these States have in general sprung.

ARMIES KEPT BRITAIN'S KING IN POWER:

The deep-seated worry about standing armies in peace can be traced to England.

26:9 In England, for a long time after the Norman Conquest, the authority of the monarch was almost unlimited. Inroads were gradually made upon the prerogative, in favor of liberty,

---

89 *chimerical:* Imaginary, vainly conceived, can have no existence except in thought.

first by the barons, and afterwards by the people, till the greatest part of its most formidable pretensions became extinct. But it was not till the revolution in 1688, which elevated the Prince of Orange to the throne of Great Britain, that English liberty was completely triumphant.

STANDING ARMIES UNDER CHARLES II AND JAMES II:

26:10 As incident to the undefined power of making war, an acknowledged prerogative of the crown, Charles II had, by his own authority, kept on foot in time of peace a body of 5,000 regular troops. And this number James II increased to 30,000; who were paid out of his civil list. At the revolution, to abolish the exercise of so dangerous an authority, it became an article of the Bill of Rights then framed, that "the raising or keeping a standing army within the kingdom in time of peace, UNLESS WITH THE CONSENT OF PARLIAMENT, was against law."

LIMITS WERE PUT ON THE KING NOT ON PARLIAMENT:

26:11 In that kingdom, when the pulse of liberty was at its highest pitch, no security against the danger of standing armies was thought requisite, beyond a prohibition of their being raised or kept up by the mere authority of the executive magistrate.

British patriots knew that Parliament was the safest place for military control.

26:12 The patriots, who effected that memorable revolution, were too temperate, too well-informed, to think of any restraint on the legislative discretion. They were aware that a certain number of troops for guards and garrisons were indispensable; that no precise bounds could be set to the national exigencies; that a power equal to every possible contingency must exist somewhere in the government: and that when they referred the exercise of that power to the judgment of the legislature, they had arrived at the ultimate point of precaution which was reconcilable with the safety of the community.

AMERICANS SAW WHAT HAPPENED IN BRITAIN:
How many States moved to restrict legislative control over the army?

26:13 From the same source, the people of America may be said to have derived an hereditary impression of danger to liberty, from standing armies in time of peace. The circumstances of a revolution quickened the public sensibility on every point connected with the security of popular rights, and in some instances raise the warmth of our zeal beyond the degree which consisted with the due temperature of the body politic. The attempts of two of the States to restrict the authority of

the legislature in the article of military establishments, are of the number of these instances.

SOME STATES LEFT ISSUE OF ARMIES TO LEGISLATURES:
Did some states overreact by passing unnecessary restrictions?

26:14 The principles which had taught us to be jealous of the power of an hereditary monarch were by an injudicious excess extended to the representatives of the people in their popular assemblies. Even in some of the States, where this error was not adopted, we find unnecessary declarations that standing armies ought not to be kept up, in time of peace, WITHOUT THE CONSENT OF THE LEGISLATURE.

ENGLISH MODEL NOT APPLICABLE TO STATES:
It was absurd to require permission from the only body possessing the power to raise armies.

26:15 I call them unnecessary, because the reason which had introduced a similar provision into the English Bill of Rights is not applicable to any of the State constitutions. The power of raising armies at all, under those constitutions, can by no construction be deemed to reside anywhere else, than in the legislatures themselves; and it was superfluous, if not absurd, to declare that a matter should not be done without the consent of a body, which alone had the power of doing it.

The point is so well understood that New York's constitution makes no mention.

26:16 Accordingly, in some of these constitutions, and among others, in that of this State of New York, which has been justly celebrated, both in Europe and America, as one of the best of the forms of government established in this country, there is a total silence upon the subject.

Even those States opposed to a standing army in peacetime retained the option should the emergency occasion arise.

26:17 It is remarkable, that even in the two States which seem to have meditated an interdiction of military establishments in time of peace, the mode of expression made use of is rather cautionary than prohibitory. It is not said, that standing armies SHALL NOT BE kept up, but that they OUGHT NOT to be kept up, in time of peace. This ambiguity of terms appears to have been the result of a conflict between jealousy and conviction; between the desire of excluding such establishments at all events, and the persuasion that an absolute exclusion would be unwise and unsafe.

RESTRICTIONS WOULD BE IGNORED IN CRISIS:
A State fearing for its safety would certainly ignore any ban on raising an army in peacetime.

26:18 Can it be doubted that such a provision, whenever the situation of public affairs was understood to require a departure from it, would be interpreted by the legislature into a mere admonition, and would be made to yield to the necessities or supposed necessities of the State? Let the fact already mentioned, with respect to Pennsylvania, decide. What then (it may be asked) is the use of such a provision, if it cease to operate the moment there is an inclination to disregard it?

TWO-YEAR FEDERAL FUNDING LIMIT ON MILITARY IS GOOD CONTROL:

26:19 Let us examine whether there be any comparison, in point of efficacy, between the provision alluded to and that which is contained in the new Constitution, for restraining the appropriations of money for military purposes to the period of two years. The former, by aiming at too much, is calculated to effect nothing; the latter, by steering clear of an imprudent extreme, and by being perfectly compatible with a proper provision for the exigencies of the nation, will have a salutary and powerful operation.

JUSTIFICATION FOR A STANDING ARMY MUST BE REVIEWED EVERY TWO YEARS:

The two-year sunset clause serves the positive purpose of regularly alerting the public to the utility of a standing army each time that deadline approaches.

26:20 The legislature of the United States will be OBLIGED, by this provision, once at least in every two years, to deliberate upon the propriety of keeping a military force on foot; to come to a new resolution on the point; and to declare their sense of the matter, by a formal vote in the face of their constituents. They are not AT LIBERTY to vest in the executive department permanent funds for the support of an army, if they were even incautious enough to be willing to repose in it so improper a confidence.

MILITARY SPENDING IS ALWAYS CONTROVERSIAL:

26:21 As the spirit of party, in different degrees, must be expected to infect all political bodies, there will be, no doubt, persons in the national legislature willing enough to arraign the measures and criminate the views of the majority. The provision for the support of a military force will always be a favorable topic for declamation. As often as the question comes forward, the public attention will be roused and attracted to the subject, by the party in opposition; and if the majority should be really disposed to exceed the proper limits, the community will be warned of the danger, and will have an opportunity of taking measures to guard against it.

SENATORS ARE EYES AND EARS FOR THEIR LEGISLATURES:

The State legislators are the best watchdogs over their State's rights because of their two senators (This critical link favorable to the people's control of the government has been lost. See footnote.)

26:22 Independent of parties in the national legislature itself, as often as the period of discussion arrived, the State legislatures, who will always be not only vigilant but suspicious and jealous guardians of the rights of the citizens against encroachments from the federal government, will constantly have their attention awake to the conduct of the national rulers, and will be ready enough, if any thing improper appears, to sound the alarm to the people, and not only to be the VOICE, but, if necessary, the ARM of their discontent.[90]

CONSPIRACIES ARE COMPLEX PROCESSES:

26:23 Schemes to subvert the liberties of a great community REQUIRE TIME to mature them for execution. An army, so large as seriously to menace those liberties, could only be formed by progressive augmentations; which would suppose, not merely a temporary combination between the legislature and executive, but a continued conspiracy for a series of time.

FREQUENT TURNOVER DISRUPTS CONSPIRACY:

What impact would frequent elections have on conspiracy?

26:24 Is it probable that such a combination would exist at all? Is it probable that it would be persevered in, and transmitted along through all the successive variations in a representative body, which biennial elections would naturally produce in both houses?

NOT REASONABLE THAT A CONSPIRACY WOULD ARISE:

Newly elected representatives are naturally passionate about the reasons that got them elected. Is it reasonable to expect that they would expose any conspiracies they happened to discover?

26:25 Is it presumable, that every man, the instant he took his seat in the national Senate or House of Representatives, would commence a traitor to his constituents and to his country? Can it be supposed that there would not be found one man,

---

90 *Editors' Note:* The State legislatures were the "vigilant but suspicious and jealous guardians" (26:22) who sent their elected representatives, the Senators, to directly influence the federal government, protect States' rights and sovereignty, and be a check on excesses by the federal government. The Seventeenth Amendment mutated that representative process and changed Senators into just another form of popularly elected representatives. Today, support for passionate, popular issues has become the primary reason why Senators are elected instead of their quality of being "informed, vigilant and jealous guardians" of States' rights. It was a step down onto the failed path of pure democracy, a danger against which the Framers vehemently warned (see No. 10, especially 10:32–34; and see "Seventeenth Amendment," "Democracy," and "Senate" in index).

discerning enough to detect so atrocious a conspiracy, or <u>bold or honest enough to apprise his constituents</u> of their danger?

END CONSPIRACY BY REVOKING DELEGATED POWER:

Deal with abused power by revoking that very power from the federal government.

26:26   If such presumptions can fairly be made, there ought at once to be an end of all delegated authority. The people should resolve to recall all the powers they have heretofore parted with out of their own hands, and to divide themselves into as many States as there are counties, in order that they may be able to <u>manage their own concerns in person</u>.

CONSPIRACIES HARD TO HIDE:

A conspiracy against the new Constitution would encompass such vast resources and people, it could not long be hidden from view.

26:27   If such suppositions could even be reasonably made, still the <u>concealment of the design</u>, for <u>any duration</u>, would be <u>impracticable</u>. It would be announced, by the very circumstance of augmenting the army to so great an extent in time of profound peace. What colorable reason could be assigned, in a country so situated, for such vast augmentations of the military force? <u>It is impossible that the people could be long deceived; and the destruction of the project, and of the projectors, would quickly follow the discovery</u>.

CAN PRESIDENT BYPASS CONGRESS TO RAISE AN ARMY?

26:28   It has been <u>said that</u> the provision which <u>limits the appropriation of money</u> for the support of an army to the period of <u>two years</u> would be unavailing, because the <u>Executive</u>, when once possessed of a force large enough to awe the people into submission, would find resources in that very force <u>sufficient to enable him</u> to dispense with supplies from the <u>acts of the legislature</u>.

ARMY FOR INSURRECTION OR FOR TIMES OF PEACE?

26:29   But the question again recurs, upon what pretense could he be put in possession of a force of that magnitude in time of peace? If we suppose it to have been created in consequence of <u>some domestic insurrection</u> or foreign war, then it becomes a case not within the principles of the objection; for this is leveled against the power of keeping up troops in time of peace.

STANDING ARMY IS NECESSARY:

Handling rebellion and invasion is a natural use of a standing army.

26:30   <u>Few persons will be so visionary as seriously to contend that military forces ought not to be raised to quell a rebellion or resist an invasion</u>; and if the defense of the community under such circumstances should make it necessary to have an army so numerous as to hazard its liberty, this is one of those calamities for which there is neither preventative nor cure. It cannot be provided against by any possible form of government; it might even result from a simple league offensive and defensive, if it should ever be necessary for the confederates or allies to form an army for <u>common defense</u>.

STANDING ARMY SAFER IN A UNION THAN IN A CONFEDERACY OF DISUNION:

26:31   But it is an evil infinitely less likely to attend us in a united than in a disunited state; nay, it may be safely asserted that it is an evil altogether unlikely to attend us in the latter situation. <u>It is not easy to conceive a possibility that dangers so formidable can assail the whole Union, as to demand a force considerable enough to place our liberties in the least jeopardy, especially if we take into our view the aid to be derived from the militia</u>, which ought always to be counted upon as a valuable and powerful auxiliary. But in a <u>state of disunion</u> (as has been fully shown in another place), the <u>contrary</u> of this supposition would become <u>not only probable</u>, but almost <u>unavoidable</u>.

—PUBLIUS

REVIEW QUESTIONS

1. Was it a surprise that after the American Revolution the people stopped short of national anarchy and gave thoughtfully consideration to a better form of government that protected individual rights? (26:1)

2. What form of government do you suppose already existed that the people wanted to preserve? (26:1)

3. What did Publius warn the people about regarding experimenting with different modes of political organization? (26:1)

4. Was it a surprise the American people decided to keep a central government to protect rights? (26:1)

5. Did the Articles go far enough to protect rights? (26:2)

6. What did Hamilton mean when he said that critics of Congress's war powers show "a zeal for liberty more ardent than enlightened"? (26:3)

7. Why is it wise that "confidence must be placed somewhere"? (26:4)

8. Why is it better to suffer abuse than defeat? (26:4)

9. Did the American public realize that too little energy in government would lead to anarchy? (26:7)

10. Where did Americans get the idea that standing armies in

times of peace was a bad idea? (26:8–10, 13)

11. What year was the revolution in England? (26:9)

12. As an outcome of England's revolution, who gained the power to control standing armies? (26:9–10)

13. Were restraints on standing armies put on the king or on the legislative branch? (26:11–12)

14. Did Americans take their wariness of standing armies to an extreme under the Articles? (26:13–16)

15. Did some States that were opposed to standing armies still leave room for them in their constitutions? (26:17)

16. In times of crisis would restrictions on standing armies be ignored? (26:18)

17. Who are the State legislatures' direct and first-hand eyes and ears in Congress to watch for protection of State sovereignty and safety, and conspiracy by others? (26:22)

18. Which Amendment severed and destroyed the State legislatures' first-hand eyes and ears in Congress? (26:22 footnote)

FEDERALIST NO. 27

FEDERAL AUTHORITY MUST REACH INDIVIDUAL CITIZENS: The Articles of Confederation failed because it could not compel individual citizens to obey its laws and decrees. The best it could do was use military authority against a State and force the State to obey. The Constitution grants federal power to create laws that individual citizens must obey. Such laws are enforceable using the courts of the land instead of troops. This same arrangement discourages uprisings. Factions and sedition are discouraged because it's much harder to rebel against the whole Union than a single State, as was the case under the Articles. Good people who are in office with good laws being passed will work to build trust between the government and the governed.

By Alexander Hamilton—December 25, 1787

MILITARY NOT NEEDED TO ENFORCE LAW:
The people will obey national laws so long as the laws are fair, prudent, and were created with the people's consent.

27:1 IT HAS been urged, in different shapes, that a Constitution of the kind proposed by the Convention cannot operate without the aid of a military force to execute its laws. This, however, like most other things that have been alleged on that side, rests on mere general assertion, unsupported by any pre-

cise or intelligible designation of the reasons upon which it is founded.

WILL AMERICANS HATE FEDERAL MEDDLING?
Critics claim that the people will hate the idea of any federal jurisdiction over internal affairs of the States.

27:2 As far as I have been able to divine the latent meaning of the objectors, it seems to originate in a presupposition that the people will be disinclined to the exercise of federal authority in any matter of an internal nature. Waiving any exception that might be taken to the inaccuracy or inexplicitness of the distinction between internal and external, let us inquire what ground there is to presuppose that disinclination in the people.

FEDERAL EFFICIENCY NO WORSE THAN STATES':
Well-run federal laws will not be resisted by the people.

27:3 Unless we presume at the same time that the powers of the general government will be worse administered than those of the State governments, there seems to be no room for the presumption of ill-will, disaffection, or opposition in the people. I believe it may be laid down as a general rule that their confidence in and obedience to a government will commonly be proportioned to the goodness or badness of its administration.

CONSTITUTION NOT PERFECT:
The people will support the new Constitution, and where a technical problem arises, it is accidental and doesn't reflect on the core principles.

27:4 It must be admitted that there are exceptions to this rule; but these exceptions depend so entirely on accidental causes, that they cannot be considered as having any relation to the intrinsic merits or demerits of a constitution. These can only be judged of by general principles and maxims.

NEW GOVERNMENT WILL BE MORE DIVERSE:
The electorate will have a broader range of choices for their national government.

27:5 Various reasons have been suggested, in the course of these papers, to induce a probability that the general government will be better administered than the particular governments; the principal of which reasons are that the extension of the spheres of election will present a greater option, or latitude of choice, to the people;

CRITICAL ROLE OF SENATE:
The general government is of a higher quality and less apt to factions than State governments because the legislatures will appoint only their wisest and most knowledgeable to the national Senate.

27:6 that through the medium of the State legislatures which are select bodies of men, and which are to <u>appoint the members of the national</u>[91] there is reason to expect that this branch will generally <u>be composed with peculiar care and judgment</u>; that these circumstances promise greater knowledge and more extensive information in the national councils, and that they will be <u>less apt to be tainted by the spirit of faction</u>, and more out of the reach of those occasional ill-humors, or temporary prejudices and propensities, which, in <u>smaller societies</u>, frequently contaminate the public councils, beget injustice and oppression of a <u>part of the community</u>, and engender <u>schemes</u> which, though they gratify a <u>momentary</u> <u>inclination</u> or desire, terminate in <u>general distress</u>, dissatisfaction, and disgust.

FEDERAL LAWS NOT EXTREME:
There is no evidence to the claim the Constitution will become odious in its operation, enforcement, and control than current State laws.

27:7 Several additional reasons of considerable force, to fortify that probability, will occur when we come to survey, with a more critical eye, the interior structure of the edifice which we are invited to erect. It will be sufficient here to remark, that until satisfactory reasons can be assigned to justify an opinion, that the federal government is likely to be administered in such a manner as to render it odious or contemptible to the people, there can be <u>no reasonable foundation</u> for the <u>supposition</u> that the <u>laws of the Union will</u> meet with any greater <u>obstruction from them, or will stand in need of any other methods to enforce their execution</u>, than the <u>laws of the particular members</u>.

STRONG UNION MEANS MORE RESOURCES TO PUT DOWN INSURRECTIONS:
Individual States can't face down factions and insurrections as well as can a strong Union.

27:8 The hope of **impunity**[92] is a strong incitement to sedition; the <u>dread of punishment, a proportionably strong discouragement to</u> it. Will not the government of the Union, which, if possessed of a due degree of power, can call to its aid the <u>collective resources of the whole Confederacy, be more likely to repress the FORMER sentiment and to inspire the LATTER</u>, than that of a single State, which can only command the resources within itself?

FACTIONS OUTMATCHED BY COMBINED EFFORTS OF UNION:
27:9 A turbulent faction in a State may easily suppose itself able to contend with the friends to the government in that State; but it can hardly be so infatuated as to imagine itself a <u>match for the combined efforts of the Union</u>. If this reflection be just, there is less danger of resistance from irregular combinations of individuals to the authority of the Confederacy than to that of a single member.

OUT OF SIGHT, OUT OF MIND:
The more a national government can function quietly in the background the more its citizens will look upon it favorably.

27:10 I will, in this place, hazard <u>an observation</u>, which will not be the less just because to some it <u>may appear new</u>; which is, that the more the operations of the national authority are intermingled in the ordinary exercise of government, the more the citizens are accustomed to meet with it in the common occurrences of their political life, the more it is familiarized to their sight and to their feelings, the <u>further it enters into those objects which touch the most sensible chords and put</u> in motion the <u>most active springs of the human heart</u>, the greater will be the probability that it will <u>conciliate the respect and attachment of the community</u>.

MAN IS A CREATURE OF HABIT:
A government tending to its proper duties and becoming a common part of life will gain appreciation and respect of the people.

27:11 Man is very much a creature of <u>habit</u>. A thing that rarely strikes his senses will generally have but little influence upon his mind. A government continually at a distance and out of sight can hardly be expected to interest the sensations of the people. The inference is, that the <u>authority of the Union</u>, and the affections of the citizens towards it, will be strengthened, rather than weakened, by its extension to what are called matters of <u>internal concern</u>;

GOVERNMENT OF NATURAL LAWS IS MORE CONDUCIVE:
Government acting in harmony with the people has less occasion to use force.

27:12 and will have less occasion to recur to force, in proportion to the familiarity and comprehensiveness of its agency. The <u>more it circulates</u> through those channels and currents in which the passions of mankind naturally flow, the <u>less</u> will it require the aid of the violent and perilous expedients of <u>compulsion</u>.

CONSTITUTION DOESN'T GOVERN GOVERNMENT:
New Constitution won't trigger the use of force to exert its authority. States retain sovereignty pertaining to their most logical role in the nation.

---

91 *Editors' Note:* The original design of the Senate as described here by Hamilton was destroyed by the Seventeenth Amendment.
92 **impunity:** Free from punishment; exemption from the injurious consequences of an action.

27:13 One thing, at all events, must be evident, that a government like the one <u>proposed</u> would bid much fairer to <u>avoid</u> the necessity of <u>using force</u>, than that species of <u>league</u> contend for by most of its opponents; the authority of which should only <u>operate upon the States</u> in their political or collective capacities. It has been shown that in <u>such a Confederacy there can be no sanction</u> for the laws but force; that <u>frequent delinquencies</u> in the members are the natural offspring of the <u>very frame of the government</u>; and that as often as these happen, they can only be <u>redressed</u>, if at all, by <u>war and violence</u>.

PARTIAL CONSOLIDATION USES COURT SYSTEM:

The federal machinery can obtain obedience to laws through the governors and court systems without resorting to military intervention.

27:14 The plan reported by the Convention, <u>by extending the authority of the federal</u> head to the individual citizens of the <u>several States</u>, will enable the government to employ the <u>ordinary magistracy</u> of each, in the execution of its laws. It is easy to perceive that this will tend to destroy, in the common apprehension, all distinction between the sources from which they might proceed; and will give the <u>federal government</u> the same <u>advantage</u> for <u>securing a due obedience to its authority</u> which is enjoyed by the <u>government of each State</u>, in addition to the influence on public opinion which will result from the important consideration of its having power to call to its assistance and support the resources of the whole Union.

CONSTITUTION WILL BE SUPREME LAW OF THE LAND:

The act of federal officers taking an oath to sustain the Constitution makes them legally liable for their actions.

27:15 It merits particular attention in this place, that the <u>laws of the Confederacy,</u>[93] as to the ENUMERATED and LEGITIMATE objects of its jurisdiction, will become the SUPREME LAW of the land; to the observance of which All officers, legislative, executive, and judicial, in each State, will be <u>bound</u> by the <u>sanctity of an oath</u>. Thus the legislatures, courts, and magistrates, of the respective members, will be incorporated into the operations of the national government AS FAR AS ITS JUST AND CONSTITUTIONAL AUTHORITY EXTENDS; and will be rendered auxiliary to the enforcement of its laws.[94]

PEACEFUL EXECUTION OF LAWS UNDER UNION:

If federal law is administered with common share of prudence there will be peaceable execution of those laws.

27:16 Any man who will pursue, by his own reflections, the consequences of this situation, will perceive that there is good ground to calculate upon <u>a regular and peaceable execution of the laws of the Union</u>, if its powers are administered with a common share of prudence.

NEW SYSTEM DISCOURAGES AMBITION, USURPATION:

27:17 If we will arbitrarily suppose the contrary, we may deduce any inferences we please from the supposition; for it is certainly possible, by an **injudicious**[95] <u>exercise of the authorities of the best government that ever was</u>, or ever can be instituted, to provoke and precipitate the people into the <u>wildest excesses</u>. But though the adversaries of the proposed Constitution should presume that the national rulers would be insensible to the motives of public good, or to the obligations of duty, I would still ask them <u>how the interests of ambition</u>, or the views of encroachment, <u>can be promoted</u> by such a conduct?

—PUBLIUS

REVIEW QUESTIONS

1. What do critics believe will be needed to enforce law under the Constitution? (27:1)

2. Is there any reason to believe the federal government will be any better or worse than State governments? (27:3, 7)

3. Upon what is the people's trust in government based? (27:3)

4. Why would the federal government be better administered under the Constitution? (27:5-6)

5. Why will the federal Senate be composed of the best of the best? (27:6)

6. Why was military force the only option to get obedience under the Articles? (27:14)

7. What clever mechanism prevents the proposed government from using military force to gain obedience? (27:14)

8. Does Hamilton acknowledge that even the best government on earth cannot prevent tyranny or factions? (27:17)

9. All speculation aside, is the Constitution really the best bet for America to fix its problems and live in peace and prosperity? (27:15–16)

---

93 *Editors' Note:* The use of *Confederacy* in this instance means a Union of thirteen States.

94 *Publius:* The sophistry which has been employed to show that this will tend to the destruction of the State governments will, in its proper place, be fully detected.

95 *injudicious:* Unwise, showing lack of judgment. Hamilton here issues a warning that a minimum standard of good behavior is necessary for the new Constitution.

FEDERALIST NO. 28

NATIONAL FORCE BALANCED BY STATE FORCE: It is in the nature of all nations that the central government will need to use force in some instances. A standing army will help ensure peace and safety internally, but also against external threats. If the military was turned against the people, the States would become immediate centers of resistance. This check and balance works both ways. A State violating the people's rights would not have sufficient means to organize against the powers of the combined States or the central government.

By Alexander Hamilton—December 26, 1787

FEDERAL FORCE IS INEVITABLE:

28:1 THAT there may happen cases in which the national government may be necessitated to resort to force, cannot be denied.

All national governments must have standing armies to maintain law and order. Upheavals are, unhappily, a part of humanity.

28:2 Our own experience has corroborated the lessons taught by the examples of other nations; that emergencies of this sort will sometimes arise in all societies, however constituted; that seditions and insurrections are, unhappily, maladies as inseparable from the body politic as tumors and eruptions from the natural body;

FORCE OF LAW NOT ALWAYS THE PERFECT ANSWER:

Representative governments are structured so that the force of law will prevail. However, does force of law always work?

28:3 that the idea of governing at all times by the simple force of law (which we have been told is the only admissible principle of republican government), has no place but in the reveries of those political doctors whose sagacity disdains the admonitions of experimental instruction.

KEEP FORCE PROPORTIONAL TO THE THREAT:

28:4 Should such emergencies at any time happen under the national government, there could be no remedy but force. The means to be employed must be proportioned to the extent of the mischief.

USE MILITIAS FOR LOCAL UPRISINGS:

When would federal intervention be needed?

28:5 If it should be a slight commotion in a small part of a State, the militia of the residue would be adequate to its suppression; and the national presumption is that they would be ready to do their duty. An insurrection, whatever may be its immediate cause, eventually endangers all government. Regard to the public peace, if not to the rights of the Union, would engage the citizens to whom the contagion had not communicated itself to oppose the insurgents; and if the general government should be found in practice conducive to the prosperity and felicity of the people, it were irrational to believe that they would be disinclined to its support.

INSTANCES WHEN MILITIA IS NOT ENOUGH:

28:6 If, on the contrary, the insurrection should pervade a whole State, or a principal part of it, the employment of a different kind of force might become unavoidable.

Massachusetts and Pennsylvania.

28:7 It appears that Massachusetts found it necessary to raise troops for repressing the disorders within that State; that Pennsylvania, from the mere apprehension of commotion among a part of her citizens, has thought proper to have recourse to the same measure.

New York and Vermont.

28:8 Suppose the State of New York had been inclined to re-establish her lost jurisdiction over the inhabitants of Vermont, could she have hoped for success in such an enterprise from the efforts of the militia alone? Would she not have been compelled to raise and to maintain a more regular force for the execution of her design?

FEDERAL GOVERNMENT MIGHT NEED TROOPS:

Which is better, occasional use of force for peace, or being unprepared and suffering from frequent revolutions or even a civil war?

28:9 If it must then be admitted that the necessity of recurring to a force different from the militia, in cases of this extraordinary nature, is applicable to the State governments themselves, why should the possibility, that the national government might be under a like necessity, in similar extremities, be made an objection to its existence?

In the same way that States might need extra protection, so might the national government.

28:10 Is it not surprising that men who declare an attachment to the Union in the abstract, should urge as an objection to the proposed Constitution what applies with tenfold weight to the plan for which they contend; and what, as far as it has any foundation in truth, is an inevitable consequence of civil society upon an enlarged scale? Who would not prefer that possibility to the unceasing agitations and frequent revolutions which are the continual scourges of petty republics?

CONFEDERACIES WOULD ALSO REQUIRE THEIR SEPARATE MILITARY:
The tendency toward disorder is the same with one large Union as with several smaller confederacies.

28:11 Let us pursue this examination in another light. Suppose, in lieu of one general system, two, or three, or even four Confederacies were to be formed, would not the same difficulty oppose itself to the operations of either of these Confederacies? Would not each of them be exposed to the same casualties; and when these happened, be obliged to have recourse to the same expedients for upholding its authority which are objected to in a government for all the States?

LOCAL MILITIA NOT STRONG ENOUGH ON ITS OWN:
Are the State militias strong enough to resist all rebellions?

28:12 Would the militia, in this supposition, be more ready or more able to support the federal authority than in the case of a general union? All candid and intelligent men must, upon due consideration, acknowledge that the principle of the objection is equally applicable to either of the two cases; and that whether we have one government for all the States, or different governments for different parcels of them, or even if there should be an entire separation of the States, there might sometimes be a necessity to make use of a force constituted differently from the militia, to preserve the peace of the community and to maintain the just authority of the laws against those violent invasions of them which amount to insurrections and rebellions.

POWERS OF GOVERNMENT IN HANDS OF THE PEOPLE:
Does this power include the control of a standing federal army?

28:13 Independent of all other reasonings upon the subject, it is a full answer to those who require a more peremptory provision against military establishments in time of peace, to say that the whole powers of the proposed government is to be in the hands of the representatives of the people. This is the essential, and, after all, only efficacious security for the rights and privileges of the people, which is attainable in civil society.[96]

IF LEADERS BETRAY US, THE PEOPLE HAVE A DEFENSE:
For this emergency the people must retain their right to bear arms. Will they be able to resist if the government takes their guns? The right to bear arms is their last resort.

28:14 If the representatives of the people betray their constituents, there is then no resource left but in the exertion of that original right of self-defense which is paramount to all positive forms of government, and which against the usurpations of the national rulers, may be exerted with infinitely better prospect of success than against those of the rulers of an individual state.

HARDER TO TOPPLE STATE GOVERNMENTS:
The people must able to go "to arms" to protect themselves from State betrayal.

28:15 In a single state, if the persons intrusted with supreme power become usurpers, the different parcels, subdivisions, or districts of which it consists, having no distinct government in each, can take no regular measures for defense. The citizens must rush tumultuously to arms, without concert, without system, without resource; except in their courage and despair. The usurpers, clothed with the forms of legal authority, can too often crush the opposition in embryo.

SMALLER TERRITORIES EASIER TO CONTROL:
A tyrannical government can more easily crush the people in small areas.

28:16 The smaller the extent of the territory, the more difficult will it be for the people to form a regular or systematic plan of opposition, and the more easy will it be to defeat their early efforts. Intelligence can be more speedily obtained of their preparations and movements, and the military force in the possession of the usurpers can be more rapidly directed against the part where the opposition has begun. In this situation there must be a peculiar coincidence of circumstances to insure success to the popular resistance.

STATE SOVEREIGNTY PREVENTS USURPATION:
If the people know their rights and are willing to defend them, they can overcome any federal tyranny.

28:17 The obstacles to usurpation and the facilities of resistance increase with the increased extent of the state, provided the citizens understand their rights and are disposed to defend them. The natural strength of the people in a large community, in proportion to the artificial strength of the government, is greater than in a small, and of course more competent to a struggle with the attempts of the government to establish a tyranny.

In a Union the States and federal government will check each other.

28:18 But in a confederacy the people, without exaggeration, may be said to be entirely the masters of their own fate. Power being almost always the rival of power, the general government will at all times stand ready to check the usurpations of

---

96 *Publius:* Its full efficacy will be examined hereafter

the state governments, and these will have the same disposition towards the general government.

A Union helps people fight usurpers on State or federal levels.

28:19 The people, by throwing themselves into either scale, will infallibly make it preponderate. <u>If</u> their <u>rights</u> are <u>invaded</u> by either, they can make <u>use</u> of the <u>other</u> as the instrument of <u>redress</u>. How wise will it be in them by cherishing the union to preserve to themselves an advantage which can never be too highly prized!

STATES WILL BE ABLE TO RESIST FEDERAL INVASION:

28:20 It may safely be received as an axiom in our political system, that the <u>State governments will</u>, in all possible contingencies, <u>afford complete security against invasions of the public liberty</u> by the <u>national authority</u>.

The legislators enjoy the allegiance of the local people and can combine with other States to protect common liberty.

28:21 Projects of usurpation cannot be masked under pretenses so likely to escape the penetration of select bodies of men, as of the people at large. The <u>legislatures</u> will have better means of <u>information</u>. They can discover the danger at a distance; and possessing all the organs of civil power, and the confidence of the people, they can at once <u>adopt a regular plan of opposition</u>, in which they can combine <u>all the resources of the community</u>. They can readily communicate with each other in the different States, and unite their common forces for the protection of their common liberty.

VAST SIZE OF AMERICA IMPEDES FEDERAL INVASION:

Any number of States rising up to regain their liberties would be difficult to subdue.

28:22 The <u>great extent</u> of the <u>country</u> is a <u>further security</u>. We have already experienced its utility against the attacks of a foreign power. And it would have precisely the same effect against the enterprises of ambitious rulers in the national councils.

STATES WOULD RISE UP AGAINST FEDERAL ASSAULT:

Those States that are put down would rebuild while the federal focus is moved to another State.

28:23 <u>If the federal army</u> should be able to <u>quell the resistance of one State</u>, the <u>distant States</u> would have it in their power to make head with fresh forces. The <u>advantages</u> obtained in <u>one place</u> must be abandoned to <u>subdue</u> the <u>opposition in others</u>; and the moment the part which had been reduced to

submission was left to itself, its efforts would be renewed, and its resistance revive.

COULD THE MILITARY TAKE OVER AMERICA? This question is impossible to answer, although as the nation grows so does the peoples' ability to prevent such a desperate act of despotism.

28:24 We should recollect that the <u>extent of the military force</u> must, at all events, be <u>regulated</u> by the <u>resources of the country</u>. For a long time to come, it will <u>not be possible</u> to maintain a <u>large army</u>; and as the means of doing this increase, the population and natural strength of the community will proportionally increase. When will the time arrive that the federal government can raise and maintain an <u>army capable of erecting a despotism</u> over the great body of the people of an immense empire, who are in a situation, through the medium of their <u>State governments</u>, to take measures for their <u>own defense</u>, with all the celerity, regularity, and system of independent nations? The apprehension may be considered as a <u>disease</u>, for which there can be found no cure in the resources of <u>argument</u> and <u>reasoning</u>.

—PUBLIUS

REVIEW QUESTIONS

1. Can America expect times when the use of military force becomes necessary? From what causes? (28:1–2)

2. Could the militia handle slight commotions among the people? (28:5)

3. If an emergency was too big for the militia what would a State do? (28:6)

4. In what States was the militia deemed insufficient and troops were raised? (28:7)

5. Would the need for troops be any different among several confederacies or States than in the Union? (28:11–12)

6. Who ultimately controls the military in times of peace? (28:13)

7. What does "power being almost always the rival of power" mean? (28:17–20)

8. How could the States prevent an attempted takeover by the federal government? (28:20–23)

FEDERALIST NO. 29

MILITIA SHOULD BE UNDER FEDERAL CONTROL: Militias are a formidable force to deal with and therefore must be properly trained. This is a role the federal government must play. Putting militias under federal authority empowers Congress to put down uprisings anywhere in the nation where a State's defensive abilities are overwhelmed. Militias can carry the heavy burdens of defensive action that smaller States are unable to afford. This can delay or eliminate the need to deploy the Army to such skirmishes, an act the people avoid because the Army could threaten liberty. Allowing the States to select officers who are homegrown and loyal will help ensure that the control over these militia forces remains in the States' favor.

By Alexander Hamilton—January 9, 1788

MILITIA HAS A ROLE IN NATIONAL DEFENSE:[97]

29:1 THE power of regulating the militia, and of commanding its services in times of insurrection and invasion are natural incidents to the duties of superintending the common defense, and of watching over the internal peace of the Confederacy.

MILITIA IS BENEFICIAL IF SUFFICIENTLY TRAINED:

The militia will be an asset to the regular army if they are professionally trained in a manner consistent with standards set by Congress.

29:2 It requires no skill in the science of war to discern that uniformity in the organization and discipline of the militia would be attended with the most beneficial effects, whenever they were called into service for the public defense. It would enable them to discharge the duties of the camp and of the field with mutual intelligence and concert an advantage of peculiar moment in the operations of an army; and it would fit them much sooner to acquire the degree of proficiency in military functions which would be essential to their usefulness.

As a protection to the States, who can appoint militia officers?

29:3 This desirable uniformity can only be accomplished by confiding the regulation of the militia to the direction of the national authority. It is, therefore, with the most evident propriety, that the plan of the Convention proposes to empower the Union "to provide for organizing, arming, and disciplining the militia, and for governing such part of them as may be employed in the service of the United States, RESERVING TO THE STATES RESPECTIVELY THE APPOINTMENT OF THE OFFICERS, AND THE AUTHORITY OF TRAINING THE MILITIA ACCORDING TO THE DISCIPLINE PRESCRIBED BY CONGRESS."

ISSUE OF CHOOSING LEADERSHIP OF THE MILITIA IS WEAKEST OF ALL CRITICISMS:

29:4 Of the different grounds which have been taken in opposition to the plan of the Convention, there is none that was so little to have been expected, or is so untenable in itself, as the one from which this particular provision has been attacked.

MILITIA WILL BE UNDER CONGRESSIONAL CONTROL:

29:5 If a well-regulated militia be the most natural defense of a free country, it ought certainly to be under the regulation and at the disposal of that body which is constituted the guardian of the national security.

MILITIA HELPS AVOID DEPLOYMENT OF ARMY:
A standing army is perceived as dangerous and militias are not.

29:6 If standing armies are dangerous to liberty, an efficacious power over the militia, in the body to whose care the protection of the State is committed, ought, as far as possible, to take away the inducement and the pretext to such unfriendly institutions. If the federal government can command the aid of the militia in those emergencies which call for the military arm in support of the civil magistrate, it can the better dispense with the employment of a different kind of force. If it cannot avail itself of the former, it will be obliged to recur to the latter. To render an army unnecessary, will be a more certain method of preventing its existence than a thousand prohibitions upon paper.

POSSES AS AN ALTERNATIVE TO MILITIA ARE NOT MENTIONED IN CONSTITUTION:
Does this automatically mean that the standing army is the only way the government will enforce its will?

29:7 In order to cast an odium upon the power of calling forth the militia to execute the laws of the Union, it has been remarked that there is nowhere any provision in the proposed Constitution for calling out the [POSSE] **COMITATUS**,[98] to assist the magistrate in the execution of his duty, whence it has been inferred, that military force was intended to be his only auxiliary.

---

97 *Editors' Note:* The militia is composed of regular citizens, males ages seventeen through forty-five, with regular jobs and a home life not on a military base, who can be called up immediately to respond to emergencies. In contrast, a standing army lives on base and trains as a full-time job. The members of the militia are rarely standing ready at arms.

98 **POSSE COMITATUS** (Latin for "power of the county"): A town's able-bodied males over age fifteen who could be mobilized by the local sheriff to keep the peace or catch a culprit. While the militia was trained for police or military action, the posse comitatus was not. It included anyone the sheriff might call, regardless of their role in the militia.

ANTI-FEDERALISTS ARE FOOLISHLY INCONSISTENT:

They claim the new government will be all powerful and despotic, but at the same time too weak to martial the citizens into a posse.

29:8   There is a striking incoherence in the objections which have appeared, and sometimes even from the same quarter, not much calculated to inspire a very favorable opinion of the sincerity or fair dealing of their authors. The <u>same persons</u> who tell us in one breath, that the powers of the <u>federal government</u> will be <u>despotic</u> and unlimited, inform us in the next, that it has <u>not authority</u> sufficient even to call out the POSSE COMITATUS. The latter, fortunately, is as much short of the truth as the former exceeds it.

ALL POWER INCLUDES POWER TO CALL UP CITIZENS:

All laws necessary and proper for a government to execute a power include requiring the help of citizens.

29:9   It would be as absurd to doubt, that a right to pass all laws NECESSARY AND PROPER to execute its declared powers, would include that of requiring the <u>assistance of the citizens</u> to the officers who may be intrusted with the <u>execution of those laws</u>, as it would be to believe, that a right to <u>enact laws necessary and proper</u> for the imposition and collection of taxes would involve that of varying the rules of descent and of the alienation of landed property, or of abolishing the trial by jury in cases relating to it.

MILITIA IS NOT THE ONLY SOURCE OF ENFORCEMENT—POSSES ARE ALSO AVAILABLE:

Federal authority over the militia does not mean military force is intended to be the first response to enforce law.

29:10   It being therefore evident that the supposition of a <u>want of power</u> to require the aid of the POSSE COMITATUS is entirely <u>destitute of color</u>, it will follow, that the conclusion which has been drawn from it, in its application to the authority of the federal government over the militia, is as uncandid as it is illogical. What reason could there be to <u>infer</u>, that force was intended to be the <u>sole instrument</u> of authority, merely because there is a power to make use of it when necessary? What shall we think of the motives which could induce men of sense to reason in this manner? How shall we prevent a conflict between <u>charity</u> and <u>judgment</u>?

MILITIA IS PEOPLE'S MOST VIRTUOUS DEFENSE:

Just because it's under federal control doesn't make it dangerous. Does a clear plan for regulating the militia yet exist?

29:11   By a curious refinement upon the spirit of republican jealousy, we are even taught to apprehend <u>danger from the militia itself</u>, in the hands of the <u>federal government</u>. It is observed that select corps may be formed, composed of the <u>young</u> and <u>ardent</u>, who may be rendered <u>subservient</u> to the views of <u>arbitrary power</u>. What plan for the regulation of the militia may be pursued by the national government, is impossible to be foreseen.

HAMILTON'S ADVICE:

29:12   But so far from viewing the matter in the same light with those who object to select corps as dangerous, were the Constitution ratified, and <u>were I to deliver my sentiments</u> to a member of the federal legislature from this State on the subject of a militia establishment, I should hold to him, in substance, <u>the following discourse</u>:

Hamilton's discourse begins: Universal militia training is not practical.

29:13   "The project of <u>disciplining all the militia</u> of the United States is as <u>futile</u> as it would be injurious, if it were capable of being carried into execution. A tolerable <u>expertness</u> in military movements is a business that <u>requires time and practice</u>. It is not a day, or even a week, that will suffice for the attainment of it. <u>To oblige</u> the great body of the **yeomanry**,[99] and of the <u>other</u> classes of the <u>citizens</u>, to be <u>under arms</u> for the purpose of going through military exercises and evolutions, as often as might be necessary <u>to acquire</u> the degree of perfection which would entitle them to the character of a well-regulated militia, would be a real <u>grievance</u> to the <u>people</u>, and a serious <u>public inconvenience</u> and loss. It would form an annual <u>deduction</u> from the <u>productive labor</u> of the country, to an amount which, calculating upon the present numbers of the people, would not fall far short of the whole expense of the civil establishments of all the States.

Universal training would not be worth the cost, although annual local training is good.

29:14   "To attempt a thing which would <u>abridge</u> the <u>mass of labor</u> and industry to so considerable an extent, would be unwise: and the experiment, if made, could not succeed, because it would <u>not long be endured</u>. Little more can reasonably be aimed at, with respect to the people at large, than to have them properly <u>armed</u> and <u>equipped</u>; and in order to see that this be not neglected, it will be necessary to <u>assemble</u> them <u>once or twice</u> in the course of a <u>year</u>.

Some level of universal establishment of the State militias is important.

29:15   "But though the scheme of <u>disciplining the whole nation must be abandoned</u> as mischievous or impracticable; yet

---

99   **yeomanry:** Small landowning family farmers.

it is a matter of the utmost importance that a well-digested plan should, as soon as possible, be adopted for the proper establishment of the militia. The attention of the government ought particularly to be directed to the formation of a select corps of moderate extent, upon such principles as will really fit them for service in case of need. By thus circumscribing the plan, it will be possible to have an excellent body of well-trained militia, ready to take the field whenever the defense of the State shall require it.

The State militias serve to prevent a standing army from abusing the people.

29:16 "This will not only lessen the call for military establishments, but if circumstances should at any time oblige the government to form an army of any magnitude that army can never be formidable to the liberties of the people while there is a large body of citizens, little, if at all, inferior to them in discipline and the use of arms, who stand ready to defend their own rights and those of their fellow-citizens. This appears to me the only substitute that can be devised for a standing army, and the best possible security against it, if it should exist."

THERE IS SAFETY IN THE FRAMEWORK:
Properly construed, the militia under the authority of Congress will be safe and beneficial.

29:17 Thus differently from the adversaries of the proposed Constitution should I reason on the same subject, deducing arguments of safety from the very sources which they represent as fraught with danger and perdition. But how the national legislature may reason on the point, is a thing which neither they nor I can foresee.

MILITIA WON'T HURT LIBERTY:

29:18 There is something so far-fetched and so extravagant in the idea of danger to liberty from the militia, that one is at a loss whether to treat it with gravity or with raillery; whether to consider it as a mere trial of skill, like the paradoxes of rhetoricians; as a disingenuous artifice to instill prejudices at any price; or as the serious offspring of political fanaticism.

MILITIA MADE UP OF KNOWN PEOPLE:
There is no danger from a militia of sons, brothers, neighbors, and fellow citizens.

29:19 Where in the name of common-sense, are our fears to end if we may not trust our sons, our brothers, our neighbors, our fellow-citizens? What shadow of danger can there be from men who are daily mingling with the rest of their countrymen and who participate with them in the same feelings, sentiments, habits and interests?

STATES APPOINT MILITIA OFFICERS:
The States have the exclusive right to appoint officers who would be faithful to their neighbors.

29:20 What reasonable cause of apprehension can be inferred from a power in the Union to prescribe regulations for the militia, and to command its services when necessary, while the particular States are to have the SOLE AND EXCLUSIVE APPOINTMENT OF THE OFFICERS?

Militia leaders' allegiance will always be to States.

29:21 If it were possible seriously to indulge a jealousy of the militia upon any conceivable establishment under the federal government, the circumstance of the officers being in the appointment of the States ought at once to extinguish it. There can be no doubt that this circumstance will always secure to them a preponderating influence over the militia.

ANTI-CONSTITUTION LITERATURE IS LAUGHABLE:
Do these publications give an honest consideration of the militia?

29:22 In reading many of the publications against the Constitution, a man is apt to imagine that he is perusing some ill-written tale or romance, which instead of natural and agreeable images, exhibits to the mind nothing but frightful and distorted shapes "Gorgons, hydras, and chimeras dire"; discoloring and disfiguring whatever it represents, and transforming everything it touches into a monster.

CRITICISMS OF MILITIA ARE DESIGNED TO INSTILL FEAR:
The critics' goal is fear instead of understanding and factual knowledge.

29:23 A sample of this is to be observed in the exaggerated and improbable suggestions which have taken place respecting the power of calling for the services of the militia. That of New Hampshire is to be marched to Georgia, of Georgia to New Hampshire, of New York to Kentucky, and of Kentucky to Lake Champlain. Nay, the debts due to the French and Dutch are to be paid in militiamen instead of **louis d'ors**[100] and **ducats**.[101]

EXAMPLE OF CRITICS' LIES:

29:24 At one moment there is to be a large army to lay prostrate the liberties of the people; at another moment the militia of Virginia are to be dragged from their homes five or six hundred miles, to tame the republican **contumacy**[102] of Massachusetts; and that of Massachusetts is to be transported

---

100 *Louis d'or:* A French gold coin first struck in 1640 and issued until the French Revolution in 1789.
101 *ducat:* A gold or silver trade coin, sometimes diluted or coated to deceive, traded in Europe beginning in the 1100s AD.
102 *contumacy:* Stubborn resistance to authority; refusal to obey or comply with a court order or summons.

an equal distance to subdue the refractory haughtiness of the aristocratic Virginians.

AMERICAN PEOPLE TOO SMART TO FALL FOR LIES:

29:25 Do the persons who rave at this rate imagine that their art or their eloquence can impose any conceits or upon the people of America for infallible truths?

MILITIA WOULD BE LOYAL TO PEOPLE NOT TYRANTS:

Such groups of armed men would not betray their families and neighbors and would not follow federal orders that betray the trust of their families.

29:26 If there should be an army to be made use of as the engine of despotism, what need of the militia? If there should be <u>no army</u>, whither would the <u>militia</u>, <u>irritated</u> by being called upon to <u>undertake</u> a distant and hopeless <u>expedition</u>, for the purpose of riveting the chains of slavery upon a part of their countrymen, direct their course, but to the seat of the tyrants, who had meditated so foolish as well as <u>so wicked a project</u>, to crush them in their imagined intrenchments of power, and to make them an example of the just vengeance of an <u>abused</u> and <u>incensed people</u>? Is this the way in which usurpers stride to dominion over a <u>numerous and enlightened nation</u>? Do they begin by exciting the detestation of the very instruments of their intended usurpations? Do they usually commence their career by wanton and disgustful acts of power, calculated to answer no end, but to draw upon themselves universal hatred and execration?

THESE IMAGINED THREATS ARE INFLAMMATORY:

29:27 <u>Are suppositions of this sort</u> the sober admonitions of discerning patriots to a discerning people? Or are they the <u>inflammatory ravings</u> of incendiaries or distempered enthusiasts?

DESPOTS MIGHT TRY TO ENLIST THE MILITIA:

29:28 If we were even to suppose the national rulers actuated by the most ungovernable ambition, it is impossible to believe that they would employ such preposterous means to accomplish their designs.

MILITIAS CAN HELP OTHER STATES:

There is a legitimate need for a militia to cross State borders to put down an insurrection. With a strong Union managing these activities there is no fear militias would be used to attack other States.

29:29 In times of <u>insurrection</u>, or <u>invasion</u>, it would be natural and proper that the <u>militia of a neighboring State</u> should

be <u>marched into another</u>, <u>to resist a</u> <u>common enemy</u>, or to guard the republic against the <u>violence of faction</u> or sedition. This was frequently <u>the case</u>, in respect to the first object, in the course of the <u>late war</u>; and this mutual succor is, indeed, a principal end of our political association. If the power of affording it be placed under the direction of the Union, there will be <u>no danger</u> of a <u>supine</u> and <u>listless inattention</u> to the <u>dangers</u> of a <u>neighbor</u>, till its near approach had **superadded**[103] the incitements of self-preservation to the too feeble impulses of duty and sympathy.

—PUBLIUS

REVIEW QUESTIONS

1. What topic does Hamilton address with No. 29? (29:1)

2. What is the value of "organizing, arming and disciplining" the militia on the federal level? (2:2)

3. How can States prevent the federal government from using the militia to usurp power? (29:3)

4. Does a militia reduce the need for a standing army? (29:6)

5. What does the term *posse comitatus* mean? (29:7, see footnote)

6. What warning did the Anti-Federalists raise about there being no mention of posse comitatus in the Constitution? (29:7–8)

7. What provision in the Constitution allows for the assembly of posse comitatus or any other needful thing not specifically named in the Constitution? (29:9-10)

8. Why is universal training of the militia not practical? (29:14)

9. How frequently should the militia assemble? (29:14)

10. Does the militia prevent a standing army from abusing the people? (29:16)

11. Who is the militia made up of? Should this make it more trustworthy? (20:19)

12. To whom will the militia always have allegiance? (29:21)

13. Could the militia be used against insurrection in a neighboring State? Did this happen during the War for Independence? (29:29)

---

103 **superadded:** To add, especially in a way that magnifies an effect.

SECTION 4 • GIVING GOVERNMENT ENOUGH REVENUE

Papers 30–36

FEDERALIST NO. 30

DIRECT TAXATION BY THE FEDERAL GOVERN-MENT IS CRITICAL: A single national government strong enough to carry out its duties is critical to the survival of the United States. One reason the Articles failed was its inability to tax the people directly. It had to request funds from the States, and the States frequently failed to deliver. For lack of reliable funding, lenders would not be able to trust the government to pay back loans. In wartime this could prove disastrous. Americans feared the power to tax as a power to oppress. Hamilton assures his readers that this necessary power can be controlled through other means outlined in the Constitution.

By Alexander Hamilton—December 28, 1787

FEDERAL GOVERNMENT PAYS FOR ALL NATIONAL DEFENSE:

People hate taxes but how else are these responsibilities to be paid?

30:1 IT HAS been already observed that the federal government ought to possess the power of providing for the support of the national forces; in which proposition was intended to be included the expense of raising troops, of building and equipping fleets, and all other expenses in any wise connected with military arrangements and operations.

REVENUE NEEDED FOR THE CIVIL LIST IN ADDITION TO DEFENSE AND DEBTS:

A national government can't do its job without revenue.

30:2 But these are not the only objects to which the jurisdiction of the Union, in respect to revenue, must necessarily be empowered to extend. It must embrace a provision for the support of the national civil list;[104] for the payment of the national debts contracted, or that may be contracted; and, in general, for all those matters which will call for disbursements out of the national treasury.

FEDERAL GOVERNMENT MUST HAVE THE MEANS TO TAX:

30:3 The conclusion is, that there must be interwoven, in the frame of the government, a general power of taxation, in one shape or another.

FEDERAL TAXING POWER IS MISSING IN THE ARTICLES:

The Articles' major weakness was making the general government dependent on the assorted political intrigues of the States for its necessary revenue.

30:4 Money is, with propriety, considered as the vital principle of the body politic; as that which sustains its life and motion, and enables it to perform its most essential functions. A complete power, therefore, to procure a regular and adequate supply of it, as far as the resources of the community will permit, may be regarded as an indispensable ingredient in every constitution.

TWO EVILS IF FEDERAL CAN'T TAX THE PEOPLE:

30:5 From a deficiency in this particular, one of two evils must ensue; either the people must be subjected to continual plunder, as a substitute for a more eligible mode of supplying the public wants, or the government must sink into a fatal atrophy, and, in a short course of time, perish.

OTTOMAN EMPIRE HAD PILLAGING PROBLEMS DUE TO NO AUTHORITY TO TAX:

They left local authorities free to pillage the people as needed.

30:6 In the Ottoman or Turkish empire, the sovereign, though in other respects absolute master of the lives and fortunes of his subjects, has no right to impose a new tax. The consequence is that he permits the bashaws or governors of provinces to pillage the people without mercy; and, in turn, squeezes out of them the sums of which he stands in need, to satisfy his own exigencies and those of the state.

---

104 *civil list:* A list of expenses budgeted annually for the support of the civil government (judges, secretaries, civil servants).

A SIMILAR DECAY IS SPREADING IN AMERICA:

30:7   In America, from a like cause, the government of the Union has gradually dwindled into a state of decay, approaching nearly to annihilation. Who can doubt, that the happiness of the people in both countries would be promoted by competent authorities in the proper hands, to provide the revenues which the necessities of the public might require?

THE ARTICLES ALLOWED TAXATION BUT IN WRONG WAY:

30:8   The present Confederation, feeble as it is intended to repose in the United States, an unlimited power of providing for the pecuniary wants of the Union. But proceeding upon an erroneous principle, it has been done in such a manner as entirely to have frustrated the intention.

STATES HAD NO SAY IN USE OF FEDERAL REVENUE:

The Articles had no mechanism whereby the States could question the use or quantity of funds demanded of them.

30:9   Congress, by the articles which compose that compact (as has already been stated), are authorized to ascertain and call for any sums of money necessary, in their judgment, to the service of the United States; and their requisitions, if conformable to the rule of apportionment, are in every constitutional sense obligatory upon the States. These have no right to question the propriety of the demand; no discretion beyond that of devising the ways and means of furnishing the sums demanded.

ARTICLES WERE OFTEN VIOLATED TO MEET URGENT NEEDS OF THE MOMENT:

30:10   But though this be strictly and truly the case; though the assumption of such a right would be an infringement of the articles of Union; though it may seldom or never have been avowedly claimed, yet in practice it has been constantly exercised, and would continue to be so, as long as the revenues of the Confederacy should remain dependent on the intermediate agency of its members.

Without a power of enforcement, the whole nation is dwindling into failure.

30:11   What the consequences of this system have been, is within the knowledge of every man the least conversant in our public affairs, and has been amply unfolded in different parts of these inquiries. It is this which has chiefly contributed to reduce us to a situation, which affords ample cause both of mortification to ourselves, and of triumph to our enemies.

BEST REMEDY IS DIRECT TAXATION OF CITIZENS:

Quotas and requisitions don't work to raise revenue.

30:12   What remedy can there be for this situation, but in a change of the system which has produced it in a change of the fallacious and delusive system of quotas and requisitions? What substitute can there be imagined for this **ignis fatuus**[105] in finance, but that of permitting the national government to raise its own revenues by the ordinary methods of taxation authorized in every well-ordered constitution of civil government? Ingenious men may declaim with plausibility on any subject; but no human ingenuity can point out any other expedient to rescue us from the inconveniences and embarrassments naturally resulting from defective supplies of the public treasury.

DIVIDING INTERNAL AND EXTERNAL TAXATION POWERS WITH THE STATES:

30:13   The more intelligent adversaries of the new Constitution admit the force of **this reasoning**;[106] but they qualify their admission by a distinction between what they call INTERNAL and EXTERNAL taxation. The former they would reserve to the State governments; the latter, which they explain into commercial imposts, or rather duties on imported articles, they declare themselves willing to concede to the federal head.

POWER MUST BE IN PROPORTION TO ITS PURPOSE:

This division would still leave the federal level in short supply.

30:14   This distinction, however, would violate the maxim of good sense and sound policy, which dictates that every POWER ought to be in proportion to its OBJECT; and would still leave the general government in a kind of tutelage to the State governments, inconsistent with every idea of vigor or efficiency.

IMPOSTS NOT ENOUGH FOR FEDERAL DUTIES:

Commercial imposts are not predictable or sufficient for the federal level.

30:15   Who can pretend that commercial imposts are, or would be, alone equal to the present and future exigencies of the Union? Taking into the account the existing debt, foreign and domestic, upon any plan of extinguishment which a man moderately impressed with the importance of public justice and public credit could approve, in addition to the establishments which all parties will acknowledge to be necessary, we could not reasonably flatter ourselves, that this resource alone,

---

105   **ignis fatuus:** Latin for "foolish fire," or a deceptive goal or misleading in one form or another.
106   *Editors' Note:* "this reasoning," refers to the need for federal taxation.

upon the most improved scale, would even suffice for its present necessities.

FUTURE NECESSITIES CANNOT BE CALCULATED:

30:16   Its future necessities admit not of calculation or limitation; and upon the principle, more than once adverted to, the power of making provision for them as they arise ought to be equally unconfined.

NATIONAL NECESSITIES ARE EQUAL TO RESOURCES:

30:17   I believe it may be regarded as a position warranted by the history of mankind, that, IN THE USUAL PROGRESS OF THINGS, THE NECESSITIES OF A NATION, IN EVERY STAGE OF ITS EXISTENCE, WILL BE FOUND AT LEAST EQUAL TO ITS RESOURCES.

RELYING ON STATES IN ANY WAY HASN'T WORKED:

30:18   To say that deficiencies may be provided for by requisitions upon the States, is on the one hand to acknowledge that this system cannot be depended upon, and on the other hand to depend upon it for every thing beyond a certain limit. Those who have carefully attended to its vices and deformities as they have been exhibited by experience or delineated in the course of these papers, must feel invincible repugnancy to trusting the national interests in any degree to its operation. Its inevitable tendency, whenever it is brought into activity, must be to enfeeble the Union, and sow the seeds of discord and contention between the federal head and its members, and between the members themselves.

PARTIAL DEPENDENCY NO BETTER THAN TOTAL:

30:19   Can it be expected that the deficiencies would be better supplied in this mode than the total wants of the Union have heretofore been supplied in the same mode? It ought to be recollected that if less will be required from the States, they will have proportionably less means to answer the demand.

NO ONE CAN PREDICT FUTURE NEEDS:
The shortfalls would be impossible to calculate or predict.

30:20   If the opinions of those who contend for the distinction which has been mentioned were to be received as evidence of truth, one would be led to conclude that there was some known point in the economy of national affairs at which it would be safe to stop and to say: Thus far the ends of public happiness will be promoted by supplying the wants of government, and all beyond this is unworthy of our care or anxiety.

CONTINUOUS SHORTFALLS PREVENT FULFILLMENT:

30:21   How is it possible that a government half supplied and always necessitous, can fulfill the purposes of its institution, can provide for the security, advance the prosperity, or support the reputation of the commonwealth? How can it ever possess either energy or stability, dignity or credit, confidence at home or respectability abroad?

Would result in panic and shortcuts.

30:22   How can its administration be any thing else than a succession of expedients temporizing, impotent, disgraceful? How will it be able to avoid a frequent sacrifice of its engagements to immediate necessity? How can it undertake or execute any liberal or enlarged plans of public good?

LET WAR PROVE THE FUTILITY OF FAITH IN IMPOST DUTIES:

30:23   Let us attend to what would be the effects of this situation in the very first war in which we should happen to be engaged. We will presume, for argument's sake, that the revenue arising from the impost duties answers the purposes of a provision for the public debt and of a peace establishment for the Union. Thus circumstanced, a war breaks out. What would be the probable conduct of the government in such an emergency?

FEDERAL GOVERNMENT WILL DIVERT FUNDS:
This would instantly destroy public credit at the very moment it needs it the most.

30:24   Taught by experience that proper dependence could not be placed on the success of requisitions, unable by its own authority to lay hold of fresh resources, and urged by considerations of national danger, would it not be driven to the expedient of diverting the funds already appropriated from their proper objects to the defense of the State? It is not easy to see how a step of this kind could be avoided; and if it should be taken, it is evident that it would prove the destruction of public credit at the very moment that it was becoming essential to the public safety. To imagine that at such a crisis credit might be dispensed with, would be the extreme of infatuation.

WITH POOR CREDIT, LENDERS WOULD TAKE ADVANTAGE OF THE AMERICAN PEOPLE:

30:25   In the modern system of war, nations the most wealthy are obliged to have recourse to large loans. A country so little opulent as ours must feel this necessity in a much stronger degree. But who would lend to a government that prefaced its overtures for borrowing by an act which demonstrated that no reliance could be placed on the steadiness of its measures for paying? The loans it might be able to procure would be as limited in their extent as burdensome in their conditions.

They would be made upon the same principles that <u>usurers</u> commonly lend to bankrupt and fraudulent debtors, with a sparing hand and at <u>enormous premiums</u>.

DIVERTING FUNDS MAY BE UNAVOIDABLE:

30:26 It may perhaps be imagined that, from the scantiness of the resources of the country, the necessity of diverting the established funds in the case supposed would exist, though the national government should possess an <u>unrestrained power of taxation</u>.

TWO REMEDIES THAT WE CAN COUNT ON:

30:27 But two considerations will serve to quiet all apprehension on this head: [1] one is, that we are sure the <u>resources of the community</u>, in their full extent, will be brought into activity for the benefit of the Union; [2] the other is, that whatever deficiencies there may be, can without difficulty be supplied by <u>loans</u>.

ONE TAXING POWER BETTER THAN INDIVIDUAL STATES:

Nations would be more willing to lend if the States, as unreliable middlemen, were removed from the federal power to tax.

30:28 The <u>power of creating new funds</u> upon new objects of taxation, by its own authority, would <u>enable</u> the national <u>government to borrow</u> as far as its necessities might require. <u>Foreigners</u>, as well as the <u>citizens of America</u>, could then reasonably repose <u>confidence</u> in its engagements; but to depend upon a government that must itself depend upon <u>thirteen</u> other governments for the means of fulfilling its contracts, when once its situation is clearly understood, would require a degree of credulity not often to be met with in the pecuniary transactions of mankind, and little reconcilable with the usual sharp-sightedness of avarice.

UTOPIAN VISIONARIES DON'T SEE THE RISKS:

There are risks inherent to liberty and self-government. Americans must hope for the best and prepare for the worst.

30:29 Reflections of this kind may have trifling weight with men who hope to see realized in America the halcyon scenes of the poetic or fabulous age; but to those who believe we are likely to experience a common portion of the vicissitudes and calamities which have fallen to the lot of other nations, they must appear entitled to serious attention. Such men must behold the <u>actual situation</u> of their country with painful solicitude, and deprecate the evils which <u>ambition or revenge might</u>, with too much facility, <u>inflict upon it</u>.

—PUBLIUS

REVIEW QUESTIONS

1. Why does the federal government need the general power of taxation? (30:1–3)

2. What is the outcome if the government can't tax the people? (30:6)

3. The Articles allowed federal taxation but why did that fail? (30:8–11)

4. Did quotas and requisitions succeed in raising federal revenue? (30:12–13)

5. Why couldn't the federal government share its revenue collection efforts with the States? (30:13–14, 18–19)

6. How could irregular and insufficient federal revenue hurt the country? (30:20–25)

FEDERALIST NO. 31

UNLIMITED FEDERAL TAXING POWER WON'T WEAKEN STATE POWERS: The government must have sufficient power and revenue to accomplish its objectives and fulfill all of its duties and responsibilities. The federal power to tax the people directly won't weaken the States or pave the way for tyranny because the structure of government and shared power will prevent such abuse. Checks and balances with the States and the people will regulate the power to tax.

By Alexander Hamilton—January 1, 1788

EXPLORING TRUTH STARTS WITH PRIMARY TRUTHS:

If first principles cannot be agreed upon there must exist corruptions of misunderstanding or prejudice or blind passion.

31:1 IN **DISQUISITIONS**[107] of every kind, there are certain <u>primary truths</u>, or <u>first principles</u>, upon which all subsequent reasonings must depend. These contain an internal evidence which, antecedent to all reflection or combination, <u>commands</u> the <u>assent</u> of the <u>mind</u>. Where it produces not this effect, it must proceed either from some <u>defect</u> or disorder in the organs of perception, or from the influence of some strong interest, or passion, or <u>prejudice</u>.

---

107 ***disquisition:*** A formal inquiry or investigation of a subject, often in writing.

GEOMETRY, LIKE POLITICS, HAS IMMUTABLE FACTS:

31:2 Of this nature are the maxims in geometry, that "the whole is greater than its part; things equal to the same are equal to one another; two straight lines cannot enclose a space; and all right angles are equal to each other."

CANNOT BE AN EFFECT WITHOUT A CAUSE:

In politics the power granted government must be proportionate to the end goal. If the goal is boundless then the power to achieve it must be boundless.

31:3 Of the same nature are these other maxims in ethics and politics, that there <u>cannot</u> be an <u>effect</u> without a <u>cause</u>; that the means ought to be proportioned to the end; that every <u>power</u> ought to be <u>commensurate</u> with its <u>object</u>; that there ought to be <u>no limitation of</u> a power destined to effect a <u>purpose</u> which is itself <u>incapable</u> of <u>limitation</u>.

SOME TRUTHS ARE CLEARLY SELF-EVIDENT:

When people refuse to see absolute and simple truths, they must be irrational or have a deeply-seat prejudice against them.

31:4 And there are other truths in the two latter sciences which, if they cannot pretend to rank in the class of axioms, are yet such direct inferences from them, and so obvious in themselves, and so agreeable to the natural and unsophisticated dictates of <u>common-sense</u>, that they challenge the assent of a sound and unbiased mind, with a degree of force and conviction almost equally irresistible.

GEOMETRY IS SO BASIC IT IS READILY ACCEPTED:

31:5 The objects of geometrical inquiry are so entirely abstracted from those pursuits which stir up and put in motion the unruly passions of the human heart, that mankind, without difficulty, adopt not only the more simple theorems of the science, but even those abstruse paradoxes which, however they may appear susceptible of demonstration, are at variance with the natural conceptions which the mind, without the aid of philosophy, would be led to entertain upon the subject.

EVEN THE COMPLEX IS ACCEPTABLE:

31:6 The <u>INFINITE DIVISIBILITY</u> of matter, or, in other words, the INFINITE divisibility of a <u>FINITE thing</u>, extending even to the minutest atom, is a point agreed among geometricians, though not less incomprehensible to common-sense than any of those mysteries in religion, against which the batteries of infidelity have been so industriously leveled.

MORALS AND POLITICS NOT AS ACCEPTABLE AS MATH :

Men won't as easily accept facts in politics and ethics on the same basis.

31:7 But in the sciences of <u>morals</u> and <u>politics</u>, men are found <u>far less</u> **tractable**.[108] To a certain degree, it is right and useful that this should be the case. Caution and investigation are a necessary armor against error and imposition. But this untractableness may be carried too far, and may degenerate into obstinacy, perverseness, or disingenuity.

MORALS AND POLITICS DON'T HAVE SAME CERTAINTY:

31:8 Though it cannot be pretended that the principles of <u>moral</u> and <u>political</u> <u>knowledge</u> have, in general, the <u>same degree of certainty</u> with those of the <u>mathematics</u>, yet they have much better claims in this respect than, to judge from the conduct of men in particular situations, we should be disposed to allow them. The obscurity is much oftener in the <u>passions</u> and <u>prejudices</u> of the reasoner than in the subject. <u>Men</u>, upon too many occasions, <u>do not give</u> their <u>own understandings</u> <u>fair play</u>; but, yielding to some untoward bias, they entangle themselves in words and confound themselves in subtleties.

PERSONAL BIAS MASKS TRUTH OF TAXATION:

Personal bias must be the only reason for objectors to miss the logic of giving unlimited power of taxation to the federal government.

31:9 How else could it happen (if we admit the objectors to be sincere in their opposition), that positions so clear as those which manifest the necessity of a general power of taxation in the government of the Union, should have to encounter any adversaries among men of discernment?

TO SUMMARIZE...

31:10 Though these positions have been elsewhere fully stated, they will perhaps not be improperly recapitulated in this place, as introductory to an <u>examination</u> of what may have been offered by way of <u>objection to them</u>. They are in substance as follows:

GOVERNMENT NEEDS ALL POWER NECESSARY:

A government must have every power needed to fulfill its roles.

31:11 A government ought to contain in itself <u>every power requisite</u> to the full accomplishment of the <u>objects committed to its</u> care, and to the complete <u>execution</u> of the trusts for which it is responsible, free from every other control but a regard to the <u>public good</u> and to the sense of the people.

---

108 *tractable:* Easy to control or influence.

THE VARIOUS COSTS OF WAR CANNOT BE MEASURED:

31:12 As the duties of superintending the <u>national defense</u> and of securing the <u>public peace</u> against foreign or domestic violence involve a provision for casualties and dangers to which <u>no possible limits</u> can be assigned,

ONLY TWO LIMITS ON AFFORDING NATIONAL DEFENSE:

A nation's needs and a nation's resources.

31:13 the power of making that provision ought to know no other bounds than the **exigencies**[109] of the nation and the <u>resources</u> of the community.

REVENUE ESSENTIAL TO GOVERNING:

The ability to acquire the necessary resources must be unrestricted.

31:14 As <u>revenue</u> is the <u>essential</u> engine by which the means of answering the national exigencies must be procured, the <u>power of procuring</u> that article in its full extent must <u>necessarily</u> be comprehended in that of providing for those exigencies.

TAXING THE STATES DIDN'T WORK:

Therefore, only direct and unlimited taxation of the people will work.

31:15 As theory and practice conspire to prove that the power of procuring revenue is unavailing when exercised over the States in their collective capacities, the <u>federal government</u> <u>must</u> of necessity be <u>invested</u> with an <u>unqualified</u> power of <u>taxation</u> in the ordinary modes.

CRITICS WON'T ADMIT THE TRUTH:

Taxation seems to be their greatest complaint. Let us examine their arguments.

31:16 Did not experience evince the contrary, it would be natural to conclude that the propriety of a general power of taxation in the national government might safely be permitted to rest on the evidence of these propositions, unassisted by any additional arguments or illustrations. But we find, in fact, that the <u>antagonists</u> of the proposed <u>Constitution</u>, so far from acquiescing in their justness or truth, seem to make their principal and most zealous effort against this part of the plan. It may therefore be satisfactory to analyze the <u>arguments</u> with which they <u>combat it</u>.

FIRST ARGUMENT AGAINST TAXING POWERS:

Giving the Union limitless power to tax could deprive the States of revenue needed to run local affairs.

31:17 Those of them which have been most labored with that view, seem in substance to amount to this: "It is not true, because the exigencies of the Union may not be susceptible

of limitation, that its power of laying taxes ought to be unconfined. Revenue is as requisite to the purposes of the local administrations as to those of the Union; and the former are at least of equal importance with the latter to the happiness of the people.

SECOND ARGUMENT AGAINST:

States should likewise have limitless power to tax, but the Union might take away everything.

31:18 "It is, therefore, as necessary that the <u>State governments</u> <u>should be able to command the means of supplying their</u> <u>wants</u>, as that the national government should possess the like faculty in respect to the wants of the Union. But an indefinite power of taxation in the LATTER might, and probably would in time, <u>deprive the FORMER</u> of the means of providing for their <u>own necessities</u>; and would subject them entirely to the mercy of the national legislature.

THIRD ARGUMENT AGAINST:

The Union has all power and this would let it tell the States they cannot tax the people because it interferes with Union needs.

31:19 "As the laws of the Union are to become the <u>supreme</u> <u>law of the land</u>, as it is to have power to pass all laws that may be NECESSARY for carrying into execution the authorities with which it is proposed to vest it, the national government might at any time abolish the taxes imposed for State objects upon the pretense of an interference with its own. It might allege a necessity of doing this in order to give efficacy to the national revenues. And thus <u>all the resources</u> of taxation might by degrees become the subjects of <u>federal monopoly</u>, to the entire exclusion and destruction of the State governments."

OPPONENTS SUGGEST TWO COURSES OF ACTION:

First, limiting the Union's taxing power to prevent it from taking over the country, or second, taking away constitutional powers.

31:20 <u>This mode of reasoning</u> appears sometimes to turn upon the supposition of usurpation in the national government; at other times it seems to be designed only as a deduction from the constitutional operation of its intended powers.

ONLY THE SECOND OPTION HAS PRETENSE OF FAIRNESS:

Usurpation by the federal government can be prevented by the people with amendments curtailing the government's powers.

31:21 It is only in the latter light that it can be admitted to have any pretensions to fairness. The moment we launch into <u>conjectures</u> about the <u>usurpations</u> of the federal government,

---

109 ***exigencies:*** An urgent need or demand, or a special situation in the current state of affairs.

we get into an <u>unfathomable abyss</u>, and fairly put ourselves out of the reach of all reasoning.

CONSPIRACY THEORIES DESTROY CREDIBILITY:
Wild imaginations about the worst possible scenario can freeze progress.

31:22 <u>Imagination</u> may range at pleasure till it gets <u>bewildered</u> amidst the labyrinths of an enchanted castle, and knows not on which side to turn to extricate itself from the perplexities into which it has so rashly adventured. <u>Whatever</u> may be the <u>limits</u> or modifications of the <u>powers of the</u> Union, it is easy to imagine an endless train of <u>possible dangers</u>; and by indulging an excess of jealousy and timidity, we may bring ourselves to a state of absolute skepticism and irresolution.

FOCUS FEARS OF USURPATION ON STRUCTURE:
And not on the nature or extent of delegated powers.

31:23 I repeat here what I have observed in substance in another place, that all observations founded upon the <u>danger of usurpation</u> ought to be referred to the composition and <u>structure of the government</u>, not to the nature or extent of its powers.

UNION IS SAFE DUE TO STRUCTURE OF GOVERNMENT:
Similar to the States, the Union will be dependent on the election process and balance of powers to prevent usurpation.

31:24 The <u>State governments</u>, by their original constitutions, are invested with <u>complete sovereignty</u>. In <u>what does our security</u> consist against <u>usurpation</u> from <u>that quarter</u>? Doubtless in the manner of their formation, and in a due dependence of those who are to administer them upon the people. If the proposed construction of the federal government be found, upon an impartial examination of it, to be such as to afford, to a proper extent, the same species of security, all <u>apprehensions</u> on the score of <u>usurpation</u> ought to be <u>discarded</u>.

STATES COULD ENCROACH ON UNION RIGHTS:
In such a contest the States are more likely to win the upper hand. Why?

31:25 It should not be forgotten that a <u>disposition</u> in the <u>State governments</u> to <u>encroach</u> upon the rights of the <u>Union</u> is quite as probable as a disposition in the <u>Union</u> to encroach upon the <u>rights</u> of the <u>State</u> governments. What side would be likely to prevail in such a conflict, must depend on the means which the contending parties could employ toward insuring success. As <u>in republics strength</u> is always on the <u>side of the people</u>, and as there are weighty reasons to induce a belief that the <u>State governments</u> will commonly possess most influence over them, the natural conclusion is that such contests will be most apt to end to the <u>disadvantage</u> of <u>the Union</u>; and that there is greater probability of encroachments by the members upon the federal head, than by the federal head upon the members.

WILD CONJECTURES ARE TOO VAGUE TO PROVE:
A better use of time is focusing on the nature and extent of powers given the general government by the new Constitution. The people must learn to preserve that constitutional equilibrium.

31:26 But it is evident that all <u>conjectures</u> of this kind must be extremely <u>vague and fallible</u>: and that it is by far the safest course to lay them altogether aside, and to confine our attention wholly to the <u>nature and extent</u> of the <u>powers</u> as they are delineated in the Constitution. Every thing beyond this must be left to the <u>prudence</u> and <u>firmness</u> of the <u>people</u>; who, as they will hold the scales in their own hands, it is to be hoped, will always take care to <u>preserve the constitutional equilibrium</u> between the <u>general</u> and the <u>State governments</u>. Upon this ground, which is evidently the <u>true one</u>, it will not be difficult to obviate the objections which have been made to an indefinite power of taxation in the United States.

—PUBLIUS

REVIEW QUESTIONS

1. How much power should a government be given? (31:11)

2. Should government's powers for national defense be controlled in any way? Why? (31:12)

3. What two natural processes automatically moderate the government's national defense powers? (31:13)

4. What must the federal government have to meet these national exigencies? (31:14)

5. What is taxation "in the ordinary mode"? (31:14–15)

6. On what should our fear of usurpation be focused, on the *structure* of government or on its *power*? (31:23)

7. If one side of government begins to encroach on another's powers, to which government will the people most likely throw their support? Why? (31:25)

FEDERALIST NO. 32

FEDERAL AND STATE TAXING AUTHORITY IS UNLIMITED: The fact that Congress can impose taxes doesn't interfere or restrict the States' power to do the same. It is up to the prudent discretion of leaders not to double tax or overtax the people. To raise revenue the States may not trespass on federal responsibilities. For example, the States may not levy taxes on exports and imports without permission from Congress. The States remain constitutionally empowered to directly tax their own citizens.

By Alexander Hamilton—January 2, 1788

FEDERAL POWER TO TAX WON'T HARM THE STATES:
The people's good sense will prevent abuses by Congress.

32:1   ALTHOUGH I am of opinion that there would be no real danger of the consequences which seem to be apprehended to the State governments from a power in the Union to control them in the levies of money, because I am persuaded that the sense of the people, the <u>extreme hazard of provoking</u> the resentments of the <u>State governments</u>, and a conviction of the utility and necessity of local administrations for local purposes, would be a complete barrier against the oppressive use of such a power;

STATES' TAXING AUTHORITY IS INDEPENDENT:
Congress has no authority to interfere with State taxing power.

32:2   yet I am willing here to allow, in its full extent, the justness of the reasoning which requires that the individual States should possess an independent and uncontrollable authority to raise their own revenues for the supply of their own wants. And making this concession, I affirm that (with the <u>sole exception</u> of duties on <u>imports</u> and <u>exports</u>) they would, under the plan of the Convention, retain that authority in the most absolute and unqualified sense; and that an attempt on the part of the national government to abridge them in the exercise of it, would be a violent assumption of power, unwarranted by any article or clause of its Constitution.

PARTIAL CONSOLIDATION OF STATES:
The States retain the rights and powers they had under the Articles, except those delegated.

32:3   An entire <u>consolidation</u> of the <u>States</u> into one <u>complete national sovereignty</u> would <u>imply</u> an entire <u>subordination of the parts</u>; and whatever powers might remain in them, would be altogether dependent on the general will. But as the plan of the Convention aims only at a partial union or consolidation, the State governments would clearly retain <u>all the rights of sovereignty</u> which they before had, and which were <u>not</u>, by that act, <u>EXCLUSIVELY</u> <u>delegated</u> to the United States.

THREE DELEGATED RIGHTS AND RESPONSIBILITIES:
The States lose only three varieties of powers under the new Constitution.

32:4   This exclusive delegation, or rather this alienation, of State sovereignty, would only exist in <u>three cases</u>: [1] where the <u>Constitution</u> in express terms <u>granted</u> an <u>exclusive authority</u> to the <u>Union</u>; [2] where it granted in one instance an authority to the Union, and in another <u>prohibited the States from exercising the like authority</u>; and [3] where it granted an authority to the Union, to which a <u>similar authority in the States</u> would be absolutely and totally <u>CONTRADICTORY and REPUGNANT</u>.

CONCURRENT JURISDICTION AND INTERFERENCE:

32:5   I use these terms to distinguish this last case from another which might appear to resemble it, but which would, in fact, be essentially different; I mean where the exercise of a **concurrent**[110] jurisdiction might be productive of occasional interferences in the POLICY of any branch of administration, but would not imply any direct contradiction or **repugnancy**[111] in point of constitutional authority.

THREE EXAMPLES OF EXCLUSIVE JURISDICTION:

32:6   These <u>three cases</u> of <u>exclusive jurisdiction</u> in the federal government may be exemplified by the following instances:

Article I Section 8: The Seat of Government to be established at Washington, DC.

32:7   The last clause but one in the <u>eighth section</u> of the first article provides expressly that Congress shall exercise "<u>EXCLUSIVE LEGISLATION</u>" over the district to be appropriated as the <u>seat of government</u>. This answers to the first case.

Duties, Imposts, and Excises.

32:8   The first clause of the same section empowers Congress "<u>TO LAY AND COLLECT TAXES, DUTIES, IMPOSTS AND EXCISES</u>"; and the second clause of the tenth section of the same article declares that, "NO STATE SHALL, without the consent of Congress, LAY ANY IMPOSTS OR DUTIES ON IMPORTS OR EXPORTS, except for the purpose of executing its inspection laws."

States are free to export goods without paying a tax.

32:9   Hence would result an exclusive power in the Union to lay duties on <u>imports</u> and <u>exports</u>, with the particular <u>exception mentioned</u>; but this power is abridged by another clause, which declares that <u>no tax or duty</u> shall be laid on articles ex-

---

110   *concurrent:* Existing, happening, or done at the same time.
111   *repugnancy:* Contradiction or inconsistency between clauses of the same document or contract.

ported from any State; in consequence of which qualification, it now only extends to the DUTIES ON IMPORTS. This answers to the second case.

Rules of naturalization.

32:10   The third will be found in that clause which declares that Congress shall have power "to establish an UNIFORM RULE of naturalization throughout the United States." This must necessarily be exclusive; because if each State had power to prescribe a DISTINCT RULE, there could not be a UNIFORM RULE.

STATES AND UNION MAY TAX MOST ARTICLES:
The power to impose taxes on articles that are not exported or imported is shared equally by both levels of government.

32:11   A case which may perhaps be thought to resemble the latter, but which is in fact widely different, affects the question immediately under consideration. I mean the power of imposing taxes on all articles other than exports and imports. This, I contend, is manifestly a concurrent and coequal authority in the United States and in the individual States.

Taxing other articles is not exclusive to the Union or States.

32:12   There is plainly no expression in the granting clause which makes that power EXCLUSIVE in the Union. There is no independent clause or sentence which prohibits the States from exercising it. So far is this from being the case, that a plain and conclusive argument to the contrary is to be deduced from the restraint laid upon the States in relation to duties on imports and exports.

That States may tax anything they require except those issues that are solely the duty of the federal government.

32:13   This restriction implies an admission that, if it were not inserted, the States would possess the power it excludes; and it implies a further admission, that as to all other taxes, the authority of the States remains undiminished.

Any other view is unnecessary and dangerous.

32:14   In any other view it would be both unnecessary and dangerous; it would be unnecessary, because if the grant to the Union of the power of laying such duties implied the exclusion of the States, or even their subordination in this particular, there could be no need of such a restriction; it would be dangerous, because the introduction of it leads directly to the conclusion which has been mentioned, and which, if the reasoning of the objectors be just, could not have been intended; I mean that the States, in all cases to which the restriction did

not apply, would have a concurrent power of taxation with the Union.

STATES ARE RESTRICTED AND AUTHORIZED:
What is a "negative pregnant"?

32:15   The restriction in question amounts to what lawyers call a **NEGATIVE PREGNANT**[112] that is, a NEGATION of one thing, and an AFFIRMANCE of another; a negation of the authority of the States to impose taxes on imports and exports, and an affirmance of their authority to impose them on all other articles.

STATES CAN LEVY TAXES, BUT LIMITED:
The States can tax imports and exports only if Congress gives them permission to do so.

32:16   It would be mere sophistry to argue that it was meant to exclude them ABSOLUTELY from the imposition of taxes of the former kind, and to leave them at liberty to lay others SUBJECT TO THE CONTROL of the national legislature.

STATES CAN'T TAX IMPORTS:

32:17   The restraining or prohibitory clause only says, that they shall not, WITHOUT THE CONSENT OF CONGRESS, lay such duties; and if we are to understand this in the sense last mentioned, the Constitution would then be made to introduce a formal provision for the sake of a very absurd conclusion; which is, that the States, WITH THE CONSENT of the national legislature, might tax imports and exports; and that they might tax every other article, UNLESS CONTROLLED by the same body.

ARGUMENT SUGGESTS ONLY UNION CAN TAX:

32:18   If this was the intention, why not leave it, in the first instance, to what is alleged to be the natural operation of the original clause, conferring a general power of taxation upon the Union? It is evident that this could not have been the intention, and that it will not bear a construction of the kind.

SAME OBJECTS MAY BE TAXED BY STATES AND UNION:
The fact that Congress and the States can tax the same items, and the federal declines because State tax makes costs too high, doesn't mean federal has surrendered right. It still has the right.

32:19   As to a supposition of repugnancy between the power of taxation in the States and in the Union, it cannot be supported in that sense which would be requisite to work an exclusion of the States. It is, indeed, possible that a tax might be laid on a particular article by a State which might render

---

112   **Negative pregnant:** Also called a pregnant denial, is being intentionally misleading and ambiguous. It is when a person makes it difficult to determine if a fact is being denied, or if the qualification of the fact is being denied. Denying part of an assertion implies that the rest of the assertion is admitted. Example: "I deny selling him cocaine on Tuesday" implies he *did* sell him cocaine on another day. The better denial is, "I never sell illegal drugs." Another: "I deny the existence of a birth certificate." But being the baby's father was not denied.

it **INEXPEDIENT**[113] that thus a further tax should be laid on the same article by the Union; but it would not imply a constitutional inability to impose a further tax.

TIMING AND AMOUNT IS MATTER OF PRUDENCE:

32:20 The quantity of the imposition, the expediency or inexpediency of an increase on either side, would be mutually questions of prudence; but there would be involved no direct contradiction of power. The particular policy of the national and of the State systems of finance might now and then not exactly coincide, and might require reciprocal forbearances. It is not, however a mere possibility of inconvenience in the exercise of powers, but an immediate constitutional repugnancy that can by implication alienate and extinguish a pre-existing right of sovereignty.

ALL STATE POWERS NOT DELEGATED MUST REMAIN:

Any State power that is not specifically removed by a clause in the Constitution remain a State power.

32:21 The necessity of a concurrent jurisdiction in certain cases results from the division of the sovereign power; and the rule that all authorities, of which the States are not explicitly divested in favor of the Union, remain with them in full vigor, is not a theoretical consequence of that division, but is clearly admitted by the whole tenor of the instrument which contains the articles of the proposed Constitution. We there find that, notwithstanding the affirmative grants of general authorities, there has been the most pointed care in those cases where it was deemed improper that the like authorities should reside in the States, to insert negative clauses prohibiting the exercise of them by the States.

THREE GROUPS OF DELEGATED STATE POWERS:

What are the powers specifically removed from the States as listed in Article I, Section 10?

32:22 The tenth section of the first article consists altogether of such provisions. This circumstance is a clear indication of the sense of the Convention, and furnishes a rule of interpretation out of the body of the act, which justifies the position I have advanced and refutes every hypothesis to the contrary.
—PUBLIUS

REVIEW QUESTIONS

1. What powers of taxation do the States retain under the Constitution? (32:1–2)

2. What form of revenue gathering may the States not exercise? (32:2)

3. What three varieties of rights do the States lose under the Constitution? (32:4)

4. What does concurrent mean? (32:5)

5. What does repugnancy mean? (32:5)

6. What are three examples of exclusive jurisdiction for the Union? (32:7–10)

7. Do the States keep their powers to tax? (32:13, 16, 19)

8. What is a negative pregnant? (32:15, and footnote)

9. Is it a direct contradiction of power to allow both State and Union governments to tax the same item? (32:20)

FEDERALIST NO. 33

CONGRESS MAY PASS NECESSARY AND PROPER LAWS: These are common-sense laws that every country has so their governments can fulfill the responsibilities given them. Just because Congress has the authority to pass necessary and proper laws, and these are supreme over State laws, does not mean it may pass laws that violate the Constitution. And without such laws the end result would be the same place where the Articles had left them—an ineffective and powerless government of interstate treaties that are easily broken or ignored. While these common-sense laws didn't need to be included, they were added anyway as a guard against people's attempting to dilute federal authority.

By Alexander Hamilton—January 2, 1788

ALL LAWS "NECESSARY AND PROPER" ARE SUPREME:

33:1 THE residue of the argument against the provisions of the Constitution in respect to taxation is ingrafted upon the following clause. The last clause of the eighth section of the first article of the plan under consideration authorizes the national legislature "to make all laws which shall be NECESSARY and PROPER for carrying into execution THE POWERS by that Constitution vested in the government of the United States, or in any department or officer thereof"; and the second clause of the sixth article declares, "that the Constitution and the laws of the United States made IN PURSUANCE THEREOF, and the treaties made by their authority shall be the SUPREME LAW of the land, any thing

---

113 *inexpedient:* Not practical, suitable, judicious, or advisable

in the constitution or laws of any State to the contrary notwithstanding."

MUCH MISINFORMATION ABOUT THESE SUPREMACY CLAUSES:

33:2 These two clauses [Art. I Sec. 8 last clause; and, Art. VI Sec. 2] have been the source of much virulent invective and petulant declamation against the proposed Constitution. They have been held up to the people in all the exaggerated colors of misrepresentation as the pernicious engines by which their local governments were to be destroyed and their liberties exterminated; as the hideous monster whose devouring jaws would spare neither sex nor age, nor high nor low, nor sacred nor profane;

SUPREME LAWMAKING IS JOB OF FEDERAL GOVERNMENT:

A central government is pointless if its laws are not supreme. Would those principles have remained supreme even if they were not written down?

33:3 and yet, strange as it may appear, after all this clamor, to those who may not have happened to contemplate them in the same light, it may be affirmed with perfect confidence that the constitutional operation of the intended government would be precisely the same, if these clauses were entirely obliterated, as if they were repeated in every article. They are only declaratory of a truth which would have resulted by necessary and unavoidable implication from the very act of constituting a federal government, and vesting it with certain specified powers. This is so clear a proposition, that moderation itself can scarcely listen to the railings which have been so copiously vented against this part of the plan, without emotions that disturb its equanimity.

A POLITICAL "POWER" IS THE ABILITY TO MAKE LAWS:

Legislative power once granted may not be transferred to another body without approval of the founding source.

33:4 What is a power, but the ability or faculty of doing a thing? What is the ability to do a thing, but the power of employing the MEANS necessary to its execution? What is a LEGISLATIVE power, but a power of making LAWS? What are the MEANS to execute a LEGISLATIVE power but LAWS? What is the power of laying and collecting taxes, but a LEGISLATIVE POWER, or a power of MAKING LAWS,

to lay and collect taxes? What are the proper means of executing such a power, but NECESSARY and PROPER laws?[114]

POWER TO LAY AND COLLECT TAXES IS NECESSARY AND PROPER:

33:5 This simple train of inquiry furnishes us at once with a test by which to judge of the true nature of the clause complained of. It conducts us to this palpable truth, that a power to lay and collect taxes must be a power to pass all laws NECESSARY and PROPER for the execution of that power;

LEGISLATURE MUST POSSESS LAW-MAKING POWERS:

33:6 and what does the unfortunate and calumniated[115] provision in question do more than declare the same truth, to wit, that the national legislature, to whom the power of laying and collecting taxes had been previously given, might, in the execution of that power, pass all laws NECESSARY and PROPER to carry it into effect?

SPECIFIC LAWS MADE FOR SPECIFIC DUTIES:

The act of executing the powers given to the government means also the act of passing such necessary laws.

33:7 I have applied these observations thus particularly to the power of taxation, because it is the immediate subject under consideration, and because it is the most important of the authorities proposed to be conferred upon the Union. But the same process will lead to the same result, in relation to all other powers declared in the Constitution. And it is EXPRESSLY to execute these powers that the **sweeping clause**,[116] as it has been affectedly called, authorizes the national legislature to pass all NECESSARY and PROPER laws.

CLAUSES ARE HARMLESS AND REDUNDANT:

33:8 If there is any thing exceptionable, it must be sought for in the specific powers upon which this general declaration is predicated. The declaration itself, though it may be chargeable with **tautology**[117] or redundancy, is at least perfectly harmless.

STATES MIGHT SAP THE FOUNDATIONS OF THE UNION:

Physically writing down the Necessary and Proper clause and the Supremacy clause is an additional protection of the Union's authority.

33:9 But SUSPICION may ask, Why then was it introduced? The answer is, that it could only have been done for

---

114 John Locke— "The legislative cannot transfer the power of making laws to any other hands, for it being but a delegated power from the people, they who have it cannot pass it over to others. The people alone can appoint the form of the commonwealth, which is by constituting the legislative, and appointing in whose hands that shall be. And when the people have said, "We will submit, and be governed by laws made by such men, and in such forms," nobody else can say other men shall make laws for them; nor can they be bound by any laws but such as are enacted by those whom they have chosen and authorized to make laws for them." Locke, Second Essay on Civil Government, para. 141; See A.L.A. Schechter Poultry Corp. v. United States, 295 U.S. 495 (1935).

115 *calumniated:* To speak about falsely with malicious intent to defame and damage.

116 *sweeping clause:* Anti-Federalists called the "The Necessary and Proper Clause" the "Sweeping Clause" to imply that it allowed all loose ends and unidentified needs to be swept up into a little pile of unrestricted power.

117 *tautology:* Needless repetition using different words. Examples: global pandemic, dry desert, dead corpse.

greater caution, and to guard against all **cavilling**[118] refinements in those who might hereafter feel a disposition to curtail and evade the legitimate authorities of the Union. The Convention probably foresaw, what it has been a principal aim of these papers to inculcate, that the danger which most threatens our political welfare is that the State governments will finally sap the foundations of the Union; and might therefore think it necessary, in so cardinal a point, to leave nothing to construction.

LOUD PROTESTING VALIDATES WISDOM OF CAUTION:

33:10   Whatever may have been the inducement to it, the wisdom of the precaution is evident from the cry which has been raised against it; as that very cry betrays a disposition to question the great and essential truth which it is manifestly the object of that provision to declare.

WHO DECIDES IF LAWS ARE NECESSARY OR PROPER?

33:11   But it may be again asked, Who is to judge of the NECESSITY and PROPRIETY of the laws to be passed for executing the powers of the Union?

GOVERNMENT AND CONSTITUENTS ARE JUDGES:

33:12   I answer, first, that this question arises as well and as fully upon the simple grant of those powers as upon the declaratory clause; and I answer, in the second place, that the national government, like every other, must judge, in the first instance, of the proper exercise of its powers, and its constituents in the last.

CITIZENS SHOULD APPEAL TO THE CONSTITUTION:

If the federal government exceeds its authorities, the people must challenge it to preserve their liberties.

33:13   If the federal government should overpass the just bounds of its authority and make a tyrannical use of its powers, the people, whose creature it is, must appeal to the standard they have formed, and take such measures to redress the injury done to the Constitution as the exigency may suggest and prudence justify. The propriety of a law, in a constitutional light, must always be determined by the nature of the powers upon which it is founded.

EXAMPLE OF CONGRESS OVERSTEPPING BOUNDS:

What if the federal government attempted to interfere with a State's inheritance laws?

33:14   Suppose, by some forced constructions of its authority (which, indeed, cannot easily be imagined), the federal legislature should attempt to vary the **law of descent**[119] in any State, would it not be evident that, in making such an attempt, it had exceeded its jurisdiction, and infringed upon that of the State?

ANOTHER EXAMPLE, ABOLISHING STATE TAX:

What if Congress claimed a State interfered with collecting revenue?

33:15   Suppose, again, that upon the pretense of an interference with its revenues, it should undertake to abrogate a land-tax imposed by the authority of a State; would it not be equally evident that this was an invasion of that concurrent jurisdiction in respect to this species of tax, which its Constitution plainly supposes to exist in the State governments? If there ever should be a doubt on this head, the credit of it will be entirely due to those reasoners who, in the imprudent zeal of their animosity to the plan of the Convention, have labored to envelop it in a cloud calculated to obscure the plainest and simplest truths.

NATIONAL LAW IN ITS PROPER REALM IS SUPREME:

33:16   But it is said that the laws of the Union are to be the SUPREME LAW of the land. But what inference can be drawn from this, or what would they amount to, if they were not to be supreme? It is evident they would amount to nothing. A LAW, by the very meaning of the term, includes supremacy. It is a rule which those to whom it is prescribed are bound to observe. This results from every political association.

IF NOT SUPREME, THE LAW IS MERELY A TREATY:

Are treaties and compacts as binding as supreme law?

33:17   If individuals enter into a state of society, the laws of that society must be the supreme regulator of their conduct. If a number of political societies enter into a larger political society, the laws which the latter may enact, pursuant to the powers intrusted to it by its constitution, must necessarily be supreme over those societies, and the individuals of whom they are composed. It would otherwise be a mere treaty, dependent on the good faith of the parties, and not a government, which is only another word for POLITICAL POWER AND SUPREMACY.

UNCONSTITUTIONAL LAWS ARE NOT SUPREME:

The supremacy law applies only to what is written into the Constitution.

---

118   *cavil:* To grumble, carp, complain, and make petty and unnecessary objections; to find fault over trivial matters.
119   *law of descent:* How property is inherited by another when the original owner dies.

33:18 But it will not follow from this doctrine that acts of the large society which are NOT PURSUANT[120] to its constitutional powers, but which are invasions of the residuary authorities of the smaller societies, will become the supreme law of the land. These will be merely acts of usurpation, and will deserve to be treated as such.

SUPREMACY CLAUSE DOESN'T MEAN LAWS MAY VIOLATE CONSTITUTION:

33:19 Hence we perceive that the clause which declares the supremacy of the laws of the Union, like the one we have just before considered, only declares a truth, which flows immediately and necessarily from the institution of a federal government. It will not, I presume, have escaped observation, that it EXPRESSLY confines this supremacy to laws made PURSUANT TO THE CONSTITUTION; which I mention merely as an instance of caution in the Convention; since that limitation would have been to be understood, though it had not been expressed.

OVERRULING STATE TAX LAWS IS NOT LEGAL:
Congress trying to change State tax laws is abuse of power.

33:20 Though a law, therefore, laying a tax for the use of the United States would be supreme in its nature, and could not legally be opposed or controlled, yet a law for abrogating or preventing the collection of a tax laid by the authority of the State, (unless upon imports and exports), would not be the supreme law of the land, but a usurpation of power not granted by the Constitution.

COOPERATION PREVENTS ABUSE OR CONFLICTS:
Is the power to abuse the supremacy law a weakness in the Constitution or proof of illegal actions by dishonest leaders?

33:21 As far as an improper accumulation of taxes on the same object might tend to render the collection difficult or precarious, this would be a mutual inconvenience, not arising from a superiority or defect of power on either side, but from an injudicious exercise of power by one or the other, in a manner equally disadvantageous to both. It is to be hoped and presumed, however, that mutual interest would dictate a concert in this respect which would avoid any material inconvenience.

CONCURRENT JURISDICTION IS THE BEST SUBSTITUTE:
Without this system of mutual taxation powers, who might have gained all power to tax?

33:22 The inference from the whole is, that the individual States would, under the proposed Constitution, retain an in-

dependent and uncontrollable authority to raise revenue to any extent of which they may stand in need, by every kind of taxation, except duties on imports and exports. It will be shown in the next paper that this CONCURRENT JURISDICTION in the article of taxation was the only admissible substitute for an entire subordination, in respect to this branch of power, of the State authority to that of the Union.

—PUBLIUS

REVIEW QUESTIONS

1. Where in the Constitution are the two controversial clauses, "necessary and proper" laws, and "supreme law of the land"? (33:1; see also the US Constitution)

2. Are these powers a natural part of a supreme government? (33:3)

3. What are the three elements present that demonstrate that "necessary and proper" are already built in to the new law? (33:4–6)

4. What is the Sweeping Clause? (33:7, see footnote)

5. If these controversial clauses are already built into the concept of a federal government, why mention them again— is that not redundant? (33:8–9)

6. Who decides if laws are necessary and proper? (33:11–12)

7. If the government oversteps its bounds, what can the people do? (33:13)

8. A federal law by its very meaning includes what? (33:16)

9. If a law isn't supreme, what does it amount to? What does it rely on? (33:17)

10. Are unconstitutional laws supreme? (33:18–19)

FEDERALIST NO. 34

TAXATION MUST BE A SHARED POWER: The States and the government have co-equal authorities. One of them, the unlimited authority to tax, must not be restricted because future emergencies could require more resources and revenues than the law allows. Wars and rebellions will come to America just as in other countries, so the government must have the powers necessary to fully defend the country. As co-equals in making laws relative to their legal boundaries, the State and federal governments may not reject the constitutionally proper acts of the other. Surrendering some State power to the federal government is valuable and critical to national defense and peace.

---

120 ***pursuant:*** In accordance with a law or legal document or resolution.

By Alexander Hamilton—January 5, 1788

STATES COEQUAL WITH UNION TO RAISE REVENUE:

34:1 I FLATTER myself [that] it has been clearly shown in my last number that the particular <u>States</u>, under the proposed Constitution, would have <u>COEQUAL</u> authority with the <u>Union</u> in the article of <u>revenue</u>, <u>except</u> as to <u>duties on imports</u>. <u>As this leaves open to the States far the greatest part of the resources of the community</u>, there can be no color for the assertion that they would not possess means as abundant as could be desired for the <u>supply of</u> their own <u>wants</u>, <u>independent of all external control</u>. That the field is sufficiently wide will more fully appear when we come to advert to the inconsiderable share of the public expenses for which it will fall to the lot of the State governments to provide.

FACTS PROVE THAT SHARED AUTHORITY WORKS FINE:

34:2 To argue upon abstract principles that this co-ordinate authority cannot exist, is to set up supposition and theory against fact and reality. However proper such reasonings might be to show that a <u>thing OUGHT NOT TO EXIST</u>, they are wholly to be rejected when they are made use of to prove that it <u>does not exist</u> contrary to the evidence of the fact itself.

SHARED AUTHORITY WORKED WELL FOR ROME:

The Senate and Assembly were separate bodies with competing interests.

34:3 It is well known that <u>in the Roman republic</u> the <u>legislative authority</u>, in the last resort, resided for ages <u>in two different political bodies</u> <u>not</u> as <u>branches of the same legislature</u>, but as distinct and <u>independent legislatures</u>, in each of which an opposite interest prevailed: in one the **patrician**;[121] in the other, the **plebian**.[122] Many arguments might have been adduced to prove the unfitness of two such seemingly contradictory authorities, <u>each having power to ANNUL or REPEAL the acts of the other</u>. But a man would have been regarded as frantic who should have attempted at Rome to disprove their existence.

ROME PROSPERED WITH SHARED POWERS:

34:4 It will be readily understood that I allude to the **COMITIA CENTURIATA**[123] and the **COMITIA TRIBUTA.**[124]

The former, in which the <u>people voted by centuries</u>, was so arranged as to give a superiority to the <u>patrician interest</u>; in the latter, in which numbers prevailed, the <u>plebian</u> interest had an <u>entire predominancy</u>. And yet these two legislatures coexisted for ages, and the Roman republic attained to the utmost height of human greatness.

AMERICA'S FEDERAL-STATE RELATIONSHIP:

The Union system is less confrontational than Rome's, and over time it will settle into well-defined roles.

34:5 In the case particularly under consideration, there is <u>no such contradiction</u> as appears in the example cited; there is <u>no power on either side to annul the acts of the other</u>. And in practice there is little reason to apprehend any inconvenience; because, in a short course of time, the <u>wants of the States</u> will naturally reduce themselves within A <u>VERY NARROW COMPASS</u>; and in the interim, the United States will, in all probability, find it convenient to <u>abstain wholly</u> from <u>those objects</u> to which the particular <u>States</u> would be <u>inclined to resort</u>.

COMPARING FEDERAL AND STATE REVENUE:

Federal needs are unlimited, the States' needs are moderate.

34:6 To form a more precise judgment of the true merits of this question, it will be well to advert to the proportion between the objects that will require a <u>federal provision</u> in respect to revenue, and those which will <u>require a State provision</u>. We shall discover that the former are <u>altogether unlimited</u>, and that the latter are <u>circumscribed</u> within very <u>moderate bounds</u>.

TAX POLICIES MUST BE BASED ON NATURAL LAWS, NOT CURRENT EVENTS:

They must be written according to correct principles and not according to current circumstances.

34:7 In pursuing this inquiry, we must bear in mind that we are not to confine our view to the present period, but to look forward to <u>remote futurity</u>. <u>Constitutions of civil government are not to be framed upon a calculation of existing exigencies</u>, but upon a combination of these with the <u>probable exigencies of ages</u>, according to the natural and tried course of human affairs.[125]

---

121 *Patrician:* An aristocrat or nobleman.

122 *Plebian:* A commoner or general citizen.

123 *Comitia Centuriata:* A military assembly that decided on war, passed laws, elected consuls, and considered appeals.

124 *Comitia Tributa: A nonmi*litary civilian assembly that did most of the legislating and dealt with the most serious public offenses.

125 John Locke—Statutory law is void if it violates God's law: "Thus the law of Nature stands as an eternal rule to all men, legislators as well others. The rules that they make for other men's actions must...be conformable to the law of Nature—i.e., to the will of God, of which that is a declaration, and the fundamental law of Nature being the preservation of mankind, no human sanction can be good or valid against it." Locke, Second Essay Concerning Civil

NEVER MEASURE FUTURE NEEDS BY THE PRESENT NECESSITIES:
True principles endure the ages. Can the revenue needs for the future accurately be limited by the judgments of the present?

34:8 Nothing, therefore, can be more fallacious than to infer the extent of any power, proper to be lodged in the national government, from an estimate of its immediate necessities. There ought to be a CAPACITY to provide for future contingencies as they may happen; and as these are illimitable in their nature, it is impossible safely to limit that capacity.

MANAGE THE KNOWN, PREPARE FOR THE UNKNOWN:
Government must have unlimited powers for emergencies.

34:9 It is true, perhaps, that a computation might be made with sufficient accuracy to answer the purpose of the quantity of revenue requisite to discharge the subsisting engagements of the Union, and to maintain those establishments which, for some time to come, would suffice in time of peace.

CAPPING FUTURE DEFENSE NEEDS IS FOOLISH:
Is it wise to limit today the Union's ability to defend the country tomorrow?

34:10 But would it be wise, or would it not rather be the extreme of folly, to stop at this point, and to leave the government intrusted with the care of the national defense in a state of absolute incapacity to provide for the protection of the community against future invasions of the public peace, by foreign war or domestic convulsions?

WHERE DO WE DRAW THE LINE SO WE DON'T FALL SHORT?

34:11 If, on the contrary, we ought to exceed this point, where can we stop, short of an indefinite power of providing for emergencies as they may arise?

IMPOSSIBLE TO PREDICT FUTURE DEFENSE NEEDS:
It's as impossible as predicting when the world will end.

34:12 Though it is easy to assert, in general terms, the possibility of forming a rational judgment of a due provision against probable dangers, yet we may safely challenge those who make the assertion to bring forward their data, and may affirm that they would be found as vague and uncertain as any that could be produced to establish the probable duration of the world.

DON'T LIMIT DEFENSE NEEDS TO INTERNAL DEFENSE ONLY:
Foreign trade and aggression will demand we have a strong navy.

34:13 Observations confined to the mere prospects of internal attacks can deserve no weight; though even these will admit of no satisfactory calculation: but if we mean to be a commercial people, it must form a part of our policy to be able one day to defend that commerce. The support of a navy and of naval wars would involve contingencies that must baffle all the efforts of political arithmetic.

FOREIGN WARS COULD SPILL OVER INTO AMERICA:
Even if we were foolish enough to tie our own hands, what if Europe's stormy scenes somehow engulfed our new nation?

34:14 Admitting that we ought to try the novel and absurd experiment in politics of tying up the hands of government from offensive war founded upon reasons of state, yet certainly we ought not to disable it from guarding the community against the ambition or enmity of other nations. A cloud has been for some time hanging over the European world. If it should break forth into a storm, who can insure us that in its progress a part of its fury would not be spent upon us? No reasonable man would hastily pronounce that we are entirely out of its reach.

EUROPE ASIDE, OTHER NATIONS MIGHT GO TO WAR:

34:15 Or if the combustible materials that now seem to be collecting should be dissipated without coming to maturity, or if a flame should be kindled without extending to us, what security can we have that our tranquility will long remain undisturbed from some other cause or from some other quarter?

WE CAN'T CONTROL THE AMBITIONS OF OTHERS:

34:16 Let us recollect that peace or war will not always be left to our option; that however moderate or unambitious we may be, we cannot count upon the moderation, or hope to extinguish the ambition of others.

PEACE THROUGH STRENGTH IS ONLY OPTION:
The human character turns to war if that becomes its last option.

34:17 Who could have imagined at the conclusion of the last war that France and Britain, wearied and exhausted as they both were, would so soon have looked with so hostile an aspect upon each other? To judge from the history of mankind, we shall be compelled to conclude that the fiery and destruc-

---

Government, para 135.

tive passions of war reign in the human breast with much more powerful sway than the mild and beneficent sentiments of peace; and that to model our political systems upon speculations of lasting tranquility, is to calculate on the weaker springs of the human character.

WAR IS GREATEST DRAIN ON NATIONAL RESOURCES:
Taxation is mostly for government's greatest expense—national defense

34:18 What are the chief sources of expense in every government? What has occasioned that enormous accumulation of debts with which several of the European nations are oppressed? The answers plainly is, wars and rebellions; the support of those institutions which are necessary to guard the body politic against these two most mortal diseases of society.

COST OF INTERNAL POLICING PALES IN COMPARISON:

34:19　The expenses arising from those institutions which are relative to the mere domestic police of a state, to the support of its legislative, executive, and judicial departments, with their different appendages, and to the encouragement of agriculture and manufactures (which will comprehend almost all the objects of state expenditure), are insignificant in comparison with those which relate to the national defense.

93 PERCENT OF BRITAIN'S REVENUE SPENT FOR DEFENSE:

34:20 In the kingdom of Great Britain, where all the ostentatious apparatus of monarchy is to be provided for, not above a fifteenth part of the annual income of the nation is appropriated to the class of expenses last mentioned; the other fourteen fifteenths are absorbed in the payment of the interest of debts contracted for carrying on the wars in which that country has been engaged, and in the maintenance of fleets and armies.

COST OF EXTRAVAGANT MONARCHY COMPARED:
The republican form is more simple, modest, and inexpensive to run.

34:21　If, on the one hand, it should be observed that the expenses incurred in the prosecution of the ambitious enterprises and vainglorious pursuits of a monarchy are not a proper standard by which to judge of those which might be necessary in a republic, it ought, on the other hand, to be remarked that there should be as great a disproportion between the profusion and extravagance of a wealthy kingdom in its domestic administration, and the frugality and economy which in that particular become the modest simplicity of republican

government. If we balance a proper deduction from one side against that which it is supposed ought to be made from the other, the proportion may still be considered as holding good.

FEDERAL GOVERNMENT WILL ALWAYS CARRY THE MOST COSTLY BURDENS:
The State's expenses are easier to calculate and predict.

34:22 But let us **advert**[126] to the large debt which we have ourselves contracted in a single war, and let us only calculate on a common share of the events which disturb the peace of nations, and we shall instantly perceive, without the aid of any elaborate illustration, that there must always be an immense disproportion between the objects of federal and state expenditures. It is true that several of the States, separately, are encumbered with considerable debts, which are an excrescence of the late war.

STATES' FINANCIAL DEMANDS MUCH LESS THAN FEDERAL:
Under the Constitution the States' biggest expenses are running their governments.

34:23　But this cannot happen again, if the proposed system be adopted; and when these debts are discharged, the only call for revenue of any consequence, which the State governments will continue to experience, will be for the mere support of their respective civil lists, to which, if we add all contingencies, the total amount in every State ought to fall considerably short of two hundred thousand pounds.

THE CONSTITUTION IS DESIGNED TO LAST THE AGES:
"Framing a government for posterity" repeats the Framer's desire to create a Constitution that would stand forever, founded on true principles.

34:24　In framing a government for posterity as well as ourselves, we ought, in those provisions which are designed to be permanent, to calculate, not on temporary, but on permanent causes of expense. If this principle be a just one our attention would be directed to a provision in favor of the State governments for an annual sum of about 200,000 pounds; while the exigencies of the Union could be susceptible of no limits, even in imagination.

UNWISE TO GIVE STATES EXCLUSIVE TAXING POWER:
That would deprive the Union of necessary funds.

34:25　In this view of the subject, by what logic can it be maintained that the local governments ought to command, in perpetuity, an EXCLUSIVE source of revenue for any sum beyond the extent of 200,000 pounds? To extend its power further, in EXCLUSION of the authority of the Union,

---

126　*advert:* Take a view of the; to turn our attention to.

would be to take the resources of the community out of those hands which stood in need of them for the <u>public welfare</u>, in order to put them into <u>other hands</u> which could have <u>no just or proper occasion for them</u>.

NO FORMULA WILL WORK TO RESOLVE ALL NEEDS:

34:26 Suppose, then, the Convention had been inclined to proceed upon the principle of a <u>repartition</u> of the <u>objects of revenue</u>, between <u>the Union</u> and its <u>members</u>, in PROPOR-TION to their comparative necessities; what particular fund could have been selected for the use of the States, that would not either have been <u>too much or too little</u>—too little for their present, too much for their future wants?

TRYING TO DIVIDE EXTERNAL AND INTERNAL NEEDS:

Such a formula would give States too much, the Union too little.

34:27 As to the line of separation between <u>external</u> and <u>internal taxes</u>, this would <u>leave to the States</u>, at a rough computation, the command of <u>two thirds</u> of the resources of the community to defray from a <u>tenth</u> to a <u>twentieth part of its expenses</u>; and to the <u>Union</u>, <u>one third</u> of the resources of the community, to defray from nine tenths to <u>nineteen twentieths</u> of its <u>expenses</u>.

LIMITING THE STATES' TAXING OPTIONS ALSO FAILS:

34:28 If we desert this boundary and content ourselves with <u>leaving to the States an exclusive power of taxing houses and lands</u>, there would still be a great disproportion between the MEANS and the END; the <u>possession of one third of the resources</u> of the community to supply, at most, <u>one tenth of its wants</u>.

STATES' DEBTS COULD NOT BE PAID BACK:

34:29 If any fund could have been selected and appropriated, equal to and not greater than the object, it would have been inadequate to the discharge of the existing debts of the particular States, and would have left them dependent on the Union for a provision for this purpose.

CONCURRENT JURISDICTION OVER TAXATION:

Sharing the power to tax is better than putting the Union at the mercy of the capricious States—a painful lesson learned with the Articles.

34:30 The preceding train of observation will justify the position which has been elsewhere laid down, that "<u>A CONCURRENT JURISDICTION</u> in the article of taxation was the only admissible substitute for an entire subordination, in respect to this branch of power, of State authority to that of the Union."

ANY SCHEME BESIDES CONCURRENT WON'T WORK:

34:31 Any separation of the objects of revenue that could have been fallen upon, would have amounted to a <u>sacrifice</u> of the great INTERESTS of the <u>Union</u> to the POWER of the individual <u>States</u>. The Convention thought the <u>concurrent jurisdiction preferable to that subordination</u>; and it is evident that it has at least the merit of reconciling an indefinite constitutional power of taxation in the federal government with an adequate and independent power in the States to provide for their own necessities. There remain a few other lights, in which this important subject of taxation will claim a further consideration.

—PUBLIUS

REVIEW QUESTIONS

1. The States and the Union have coequal taxing authority except pertaining to what? (34:1)

2. Explain the example of Rome that shows that coequal powers have worked in the past. (34:3–4)

3. Regarding the revenue required to do its job, which government requires the most, the Union or the States? (34:6)

4. On what time basis should revenue requirements be measured? (34:7–8)

5. Trying to limit the Union's resources for proper defense is the "extreme of" what? (34:10)

6. Can international peace and war be controlled by America? (34:16)

7. What is the worst assumption on which America should build its defense policies? (34:17)

8. What is the greatest expense of every government? (34:18)

9. For whom was the Constitution framed? (34:24)

10. If any other taxing arrangement was attempted between the Union and the States, what would be the outcome? (34:31)

FEDERALIST NO. 35

REVENUE FROM IMPORT TAXES IS NOT ENOUGH: The Union's power to tax must go beyond imports alone if it is to distribute the tax burden fairly and without favoritism. In a similar vein, membership in the House of Representatives must be open to all (not the elitist or well-connected). However, it is impractical and unnecessary to include people from every social class. All classes of people depend in one way or another upon all the other classes because economic and political interests rise above social class. A poor man's dollar and vote is just as wanted as a rich man's dollar and vote. Representatives therefore will be concerned with all interests and needs. And, being accountable to voters, the representatives will have that additional motivation to understand all classes and concerns.

By Alexander Hamilton—January 5, 1788

UNEQUAL TAXATION CREATES OPPRESSION:
Unequal tax burdens would be forced among the people.

35:1 BEFORE we proceed to examine any other objections to an indefinite power of taxation in the Union, I shall make one general remark; which is, that if the jurisdiction of the national government, in the article of revenue, should be restricted to particular objects, it would naturally occasion an undue proportion of the public burdens to fall upon those objects. Two evils would spring from this source: the oppression of particular branches of industry; and an unequal distribution of the taxes, as well among the several States as among the citizens of the same State.

LACK OF TAXING OPTIONS WOULD RESULT IN INCREASING IMPORT DUTY CHARGES:
If the Union's revenues are strictly confined to duties on imports, the Union's increasing needs will result in ever-increasing duties.

35:2 Suppose, as has been contended for, the federal power of taxation were to be confined to duties on imports, it is evident that the government, for want of being able to command other resources, would frequently be tempted to extend these duties to an injurious excess. There are persons who imagine that they can never be carried to too great a length; since the higher they are, the more it is alleged they will tend to discourage an extravagant consumption, to produce a favorable balance of trade, and to promote domestic manufactures.

HIGH IMPORT DUTIES ENCOURAGE SMUGGLING:
High duties inhibit the free flow of goods due to the higher costs and put merchants out of business.

35:3 But all extremes are pernicious in various ways. Exorbitant duties on imported articles would beget a general spirit of smuggling; which is always prejudicial to the fair trader, and eventually to the revenue itself: they tend to render other classes of the community tributary, in an improper degree, to the manufacturing classes, to whom they give a premature monopoly of the markets; they sometimes force industry out of its more natural channels into others in which it flows with less advantage;

MERCHANTS ARE OFTEN FORCED TO PAY IMPORT DUTIES:

35:4 and in the last place, they oppress the merchant, who is often obliged to pay them himself without any retribution from the consumer. When the demand is equal to the quantity of goods at market, the consumer generally pays the duty; but when the markets happen to be overstocked, a great proportion falls upon the merchant, and sometimes not only exhausts his profits, but breaks in upon his capital.

MERCHANTS CAN'T ALWAYS SPLIT DUTY WITH CONSUMERS:
Why would merchants sometimes absorb payment of those duties?

35:5 I am apt to think that a division of the duty, between the seller and the buyer, more often happens than is commonly imagined. It is not always possible to raise the price of a commodity in exact proportion to every additional imposition laid upon it. The merchant, especially in a country of small commercial capital, is often under a necessity of keeping prices down in order to a more expeditious sale.

IMPORT DUTIES SHOULD NOT BE THE ONLY SOURCE OF FEDERAL REVENUE:
Even so, such duties should not be the only revenue for federal government.

35:6 The maxim that the consumer is the payer, is so much oftener true than the reverse of the proposition, that it is far more equitable that the duties on imports should go into a common stock, than that they should redound to the exclusive benefit of the importing States. But it is not so generally true as to render it equitable, that those duties should form the only national fund.

IMPORTING STATES END UP PAYING MORE TAX:

35:7 When they are paid by the merchant they operate as an additional tax upon the importing State, whose citizens pay their proportion of them in the character of consumers. In this view they are productive of inequality among the States; which inequality would be increased with the increased extent of the duties.

DUTIES ALSO UNFAIR FOR MANUFACTURING STATES:

35:8 The confinement of the national revenues to this species of imposts would be attended with inequality, from a different cause, between the manufacturing and the non-manufacturing States.

SELF-SUFFICIENT STATES WON'T IMPORT AS MUCH:

Taxing these States with tailor-made excise taxes could be used to compel such States to carry their fair share of taxes.

35:9　The States which can go farthest towards the supply of their own wants, by their <u>own manufactures</u>, will not, according to their numbers or wealth, consume so great a proportion of imported articles as those States which are not in the same favorable situation. They would not, therefore, in this mode alone <u>contribute to the public treasury in a ratio to their abilities</u>. To make them do this it is necessary that recourse be had to <u>excises</u>, the proper objects of which are particular kinds of manufactures.

NEW YORK WOULD SUFFER UNDER IMPORT TAXES:

New York citizens may not realize how hard such taxes will hit.

35:10　New York is more deeply interested in these considerations than such of her citizens as contend for limiting the power of the Union to external taxation may be aware of. <u>New York</u> is an <u>importing State</u>, and is not likely speedily to be, to any great extent, a manufacturing State. She would, of course, suffer in a double light from restraining the jurisdiction of the Union to commercial imposts.

HIGHER CONSUMPTION TAXES WILL SLOW DOWN CONSUMER BUYING:

To avoid paying higher import or consumption taxes people will simply stop buying goods. Is this, then, a reliable source of government revenue?

35:11　So far as these observations tend to inculcate a danger of the import duties being extended to an injurious extreme it may be observed, **conformably**[127] to a remark made in another part of these papers, that the <u>interest of the revenue itself would be a sufficient guard against such an extreme</u>. I readily admit that this would be the case, as long as other resources were open; but if the avenues to them were closed, HOPE, stimulated by necessity, would beget <u>experiments</u>, fortified by rigorous precautions and additional penalties, which, for a time, would have the intended effect, till there had been leisure to contrive expedients to elude these new precautions. The first success would be apt to inspire <u>false opinions</u>, which it might require a <u>long course of subsequent experience to correct</u>. Necessity, especially in politics, often occasions false hopes, false reasonings, and a system of measures correspondingly erroneous.

NO MATTER THE OUTCOME, INEQUALITIES WILL REMAIN:

35:12　But even if this supposed excess should not be a consequence of the limitation of the federal power of taxation, the inequalities spoken of would still ensue, though not in the same degree, from the other causes that have been noticed. Let us now return to the examination of objections.

TAXATION WITHOUT FULL REPRESENTATION:

Another argument is that there are not enough members in the House to represent the many different classes of people.

35:13　One which, if we may judge from the frequency of its repetition, seems most to be relied on, is, that the <u>House of Representatives</u> is <u>not sufficiently numerous</u> for the reception of all the <u>different classes of citizens</u>, in order to combine the interests and feelings of <u>every part</u> of the <u>community</u>, and to produce a <u>due sympathy</u> between the representative body and its constituents. This argument presents itself under a very specious and seducing form; and is well calculated to lay hold of the prejudices of those to whom it is addressed. But when we come to dissect it with attention, it will appear to be made up of nothing but fair-sounding words. The object it seems to aim at is, in the first place, impracticable, and in the sense in which it is contended for, is unnecessary.

HAMILTON WILL DISCUSS REPRESENTATION LATER:

35:14　I reserve for <u>another place</u> the discussion of the question which relates to the <u>sufficiency</u> of the <u>representative</u> body in respect to numbers, and shall content myself with examining here the particular use which has been made of a contrary supposition, in reference to the immediate subject of our inquiries.

IMPOSSIBLE TO REPRESENT ALL CLASSES:

35:15　The idea of an <u>actual representation of all classes of the people</u>, by <u>persons of each</u> class, is altogether <u>visionary</u>. Unless it were expressly provided in the Constitution, that each different occupation should send one or more members, the thing would never take place in practice.

CLASSES WOULD PROMOTE THEIR OWN INTERESTS:

A Congress of class representatives would always vote to favor their specific class instead of considering what would benefit the greater whole.

35:16　Mechanics and manufacturers will always be inclined, with few exceptions, to give their votes to merchants, in preference to persons of their own professions or trades. Those discerning citizens are well aware that the mechanic and man-

---

127　*conformably:* Similar in form, consistent.

ufacturing arts furnish the materials of mercantile enterprise and industry. Many of them, indeed, are <u>immediately connected</u> with the operations of <u>commerce</u>.

THE PRODUCING CLASSES WOULD ELECT MERCHANTS:

35:17 They know that the merchant is their natural patron and friend; and they are aware, that however great the confidence they may justly feel in their own good sense, their interests can be more effectually promoted by the merchant than by themselves. They are sensible that their habits in life have not been such as to give them those acquired endowments, without which, in a deliberative assembly, the greatest natural abilities are for the most part useless; and that the influence and weight, and superior acquirements of the merchants render them more equal to a contest with any spirit which might happen to infuse itself into the public councils, unfriendly to the manufacturing and trading interests.

MERCHANTS ARE NATURAL REPRESENTATIVES:
These people would seem the best representatives of all classes.

35:18 These considerations, and many others that might be mentioned prove, and experience confirms it, that artisans and manufacturers will commonly be disposed to bestow their votes upon merchants and those whom they recommend. We must therefore consider merchants as the natural representatives of all these classes of the community.

LEARNED PROFESSIONS WILL ALSO BE ELECTED:
These cross all cultural lines and have no natural representative.

35:19 With regard to the **learned professions**,[128] little need be observed; they truly form <u>no distinct interest</u> in society, and according to their situation and talents, will be indiscriminately the objects of the confidence and choice of each other, and of other parts of the community.

LANDOWNERS AS REPRESENTATIVES WILL SHARE DESIRE FOR LOW LAND TAXES:

35:20 Nothing remains but the **landed interest**;[129] and this, in a political view, and particularly in relation to taxes, I take to be perfectly united, from the wealthiest landlord down to the poorest tenant. <u>No tax</u> can be laid on land which will <u>not affect the proprietor of millions</u> of acres as well as the proprietor of a single acre. <u>Every landholder</u> will therefore have a <u>common interest</u> to keep the <u>taxes on land</u> as low as possible;

and common interest may always be reckoned upon as the surest bond of sympathy.

LAND WEALTH IS NOT AN AUTOMATIC ADVANTAGE:
Many posts in New York's government are held by "middling farmers."

35:21   But if we even could suppose a distinction of interest between the opulent landholder and the middling farmer, what reason is there to conclude, that the first would stand a better chance of being deputed to the national legislature than the last? If we take fact as our guide, and look into our own senate and assembly, we shall find that moderate proprietors of land prevail in both; nor is this less the case in the senate, which consists of a smaller number, than in the assembly, which is composed of a greater number.

VOTERS SUPPORT THOSE THEY TRUST:
This is always true regardless of the person's status or wealth.

35:22   Where the qualifications of the electors are the same, whether they have to choose a small or a large number, their <u>votes will fall</u> upon those in <u>whom they have most confidence</u>; whether these happen to be men of large fortunes, or of moderate property, or of no property at all.

REPRESENTING ALL CLASSES IS NOT LIKELY:
People don't vote to be fair, they vote for the person they trust.

35:23   It is said to be necessary, that all classes of citizens should have some of <u>their own number in the representative</u> body, in order that their feelings and interests may be the better understood and attended to. But we have seen that this will never happen under any arrangement that leaves the votes of the people free. Where this is the case, the representative body, with too few exceptions to have any influence on the spirit of the government, will be composed of <u>landholders</u>, <u>merchants</u>, and men of the <u>learned professions</u>.

CONGRESS WILL HAVE THREE MAIN TYPES:
Landholders, merchants, and men of the learned professions.

35:24   But where is the danger that the interests and feelings of the different classes of citizens will not be understood or attended to by these three descriptions of men?

Landholders will vote to protect the land.

35:25   Will not the landholder know and feel whatever will promote or insure the interest of landed property? And will he not, from his own interest in that species of property, be

---

128 *learned professions:* Skilled vocations requiring a high degree of education (doctor, lawyer, theologian, engineer, and so forth).
129 *landed interest* (or landholders): Landowners who makes a living off the land or rents it out to others.

sufficiently prone to resist every attempt to prejudice or encumber it?

Merchants will vote to protect mechanics and manufacturers.

35:26 Will not the merchant understand and be disposed to cultivate, as far as may be proper, the interests of the mechanic and manufacturing arts, to which his commerce is so nearly allied?

The learned will vote to promote the nation's interests.

35:27 Will not the man of the learned profession, who will feel a neutrality to the rivalships between the different branches of industry, be likely to prove an impartial arbiter between them, ready to promote either, so far as it shall appear to him conducive to the general interests of the society?

REPRESENTATIVES SHOULD ALLOW VOTER INPUT:

Representatives should not simply win election and disappear in Congress for two years, they should touch base with home so voters can have their say.

35:28 If we take into the account the <u>momentary humors or dispositions</u> which may happen to prevail in particular parts of the society, and to which a wise administration will never be inattentive, is the man whose situation leads to extensive inquiry and information less likely to be a competent judge of their nature, extent, and foundation than one whose observation does not travel beyond the circle of his neighbors and acquaintances? Is it not natural that a man who is a candidate for the favor of the people, and who is dependent on the suffrages of his fellow-citizens for the continuance of his public honors, should <u>take care to inform himself</u> of their dispositions and inclinations, and should be willing to <u>allow them their proper degree of influence</u> upon his conduct? This dependence, and the necessity of being bound himself, and his posterity, by the laws to which he gives his assent, are the true, and they are the <u>strong chords</u> of sympathy between the <u>representative</u> and the <u>constituent</u>.

TAXATION IS MOST COMPLEX ISSUE OF ALL:

Representatives should know well the people being taxed, and the resources available so that taxation policies meet the needs of America.

35:29 There is no part of the administration of government that requires extensive information and a thorough knowledge of the principles of political economy, so much as the <u>business of taxation</u>. The man who understands those principles best will be least likely to resort to oppressive expedients, or sacrifice any particular class of citizens to the procurement of revenue.

LET QUALIFIED MEN DECIDE:

The most productive systems of taxation are also the least burdensome.

35:30 It might be demonstrated that the most productive system of finance will always be the least burdensome. There can be no doubt that in order to a judicious exercise of the power of taxation, it is necessary that the person in whose hands it should be should be acquainted with the general genius, habits, and modes of thinking of the people at large, and with the resources of the country. And this is all that can be reasonably meant by a knowledge of the interests and feelings of the people. In any other sense the proposition has either no meaning, or an absurd one. And in that sense let every considerate citizen judge for himself where the requisite <u>qualification</u> is most likely to be <u>found</u>.

—PUBLIUS

REVIEW QUESTIONS

1. What would happen if the Union's taxing power was restricted to certain objects? (35:1)

2. If Union revenue is restricted to duties on imports, and duties must rise, what does that growing expense for the importers suddenly encourage? (35:2–3)

3. Under what instance might the merchant end up paying the duties instead of being able to pass those costs to the consumer? (35:4–5)

4. Which States would pay most of the duties? And which the least? (35:7–8)

5. Why is seeking Congressional representatives of all classes of society a foolish pursuit? (35:13–16)

6. What is a "learned profession"? (35:19, see footnote)

7. What main characteristic wins the most votes for representatives regardless of wealth or status? (35:22)

8. What are the three main types of people the voters tend toward the most? (35:23–24)

9. What principles are most important for a Representative to understand? Why? (35:29)

FEDERALIST NO. 36

STATE AND FEDERAL GOVERNMENTS HAVE COMPETING TAXATION NEEDS: The Union needs revenue to do its job. The federal and State governments must recognize the people's fear of double taxation, and must avoid taxing the same items. Congress may save money by using the States' internal tax collectors. These officers will be local and will know enough about their own district to value things fairly. A poll tax is a harmful idea but a necessary one in times of national crisis.

By Alexander Hamilton—January 8, 1788

REPRESENTATIVES FROM THREE MAIN CLASSES:
The people will naturally choose landowners, merchants, and those of the learned professions as the truest representatives of all.

36:1 WE HAVE seen that the result of the observations, to which the foregoing number has been principally devoted, is, that from the natural operation of the different interests and views of the various classes of the community, whether the representation of the people be more or less numerous, it will consist almost entirely of <u>proprietors of land</u>, of <u>merchants</u>, and of members of the <u>learned professions</u>, who will truly represent all those different interests and views.

MINOR EXCEPTIONS WON'T CHANGE MUCH:
36:2 If it should be objected that we have seen other descriptions of men in the local legislatures, I answer that it is admitted there are exceptions to the rule, but not in sufficient number to influence the general complexion or character of the government.

NATURAL ARISTOCRACY IS IN ALL CULTURES:
There are always strong minds among all people who will rise to leadership.

36:3 There are <u>strong</u> minds in <u>every walk</u> of life that will rise <u>superior</u> to the disadvantages of situation, and will <u>command the tribute due to their merit</u>, not only from the classes to which they particularly belong, <u>but from the society in general</u>. The <u>door ought</u> to be equally <u>open to all</u>; and I trust, for the credit of human nature, that we shall see examples of such vigorous plants flourishing in the soil of federal as well as of State legislation; but <u>occasional instances</u> of this sort will not <u>render the reasoning</u> founded upon the <u>general course of things</u>, less conclusive.

A REPRESENTATIVE BODY MUST BE LIMITED IN SIZE:
Every variable of class that exists realistically can't be represented in Congress or it would become too massive to function.

36:4 The subject might be placed in several other lights that would all lead to the same result; and in particular it might be asked, <u>What greater affinity</u> or relation of interest can be conceived between the <u>carpenter</u> and <u>blacksmith</u>, and the <u>lin</u>-en manufacturer or <u>stocking weaver</u>, than between the <u>merchant</u> and either of them? It is notorious that there are often as great <u>rivalships</u> between different branches of the mechanic or manufacturing arts as there are between any of the departments of <u>labor</u> and <u>industry</u>; so that, unless the representative body were to be far more numerous than would be consistent with any idea of regularity or wisdom in its deliberations, it is impossible that what seems to be the spirit of the objection we have been considering should ever be realized in practice.

OPTIMAL SIZE OF CONGRESS ALREADY DISCUSSED:
36:5 But I forbear to dwell any longer on a matter which has hitherto worn too loose a garb to admit even of an accurate inspection of its real shape or tendency.

CRITICS SAY CONGRESS CAN'T ACCESS ENOUGH INFORMATION:
Knowledge of local affairs will be lacking to fairly assess taxes.

36:6 There is another <u>objection</u> of a somewhat <u>more precise</u> nature that claims our attention. It has been asserted that a power of <u>internal taxation</u> in the <u>national legislature</u> could never be exercised with advantage, as well from the want of a sufficient knowledge of local circumstances, as from an interference between the revenue laws of the Union and of the particular States.

CONGRESS AND STATES ACQUIRE KNOWLEDGE IN THE SAME WAY:
The States' representatives will be generally acquainted already.

36:7 The supposition of a <u>want of proper knowledge</u> seems to be entirely destitute of foundation. If any question is depending in a State legislature respecting one of the counties, which demands a knowledge of local details, <u>how is it acquired</u>? No doubt from the information of the members of the county. Cannot the like knowledge be obtained in the national legislature from the <u>representatives of each State</u>? And is it not to be presumed that the men who will generally be sent there will be possessed of the necessary degree of intelligence to be able to communicate that information?

GENERAL KNOWLEDGE IS SUFFICIENT FOR TAXATION:
36:8 Is the knowledge of local circumstances, as applied to taxation, a minute topographical acquaintance with all the mountains, rivers, streams, highways, and bypaths in each State; or is it a <u>general acquaintance</u> with its <u>situation</u> and <u>resources</u>, with the state of its <u>agriculture</u>, <u>commerce</u>, <u>manufactures</u>, with the nature of its products and consumptions,

with the different degrees and kinds of its <u>wealth</u>, <u>property</u>, and <u>industry</u>?

GOVERNMENTS RELY ON SMALL GROUPS:
Tax plans are best prepared by experts. Legislatures then pass them into law.

36:9 Nations in general, even under governments of the more popular kind, usually commit the <u>administration of their finances</u> to <u>single men</u> or to boards composed of a <u>few individuals</u>, who digest and prepare, in the first instance, the <u>plans of taxation</u>, which are afterwards <u>passed into laws</u> by the authority of the <u>sovereign or legislature</u>.

KNOWLEDGEABLE STATESMEN ARE BEST QUALIFIED:
Such men have enough local knowledge to design proper tax codes.

36:10 Inquisitive and enlightened statesmen are deemed everywhere best qualified to make a judicious selection of the objects proper for revenue; which is a clear indication, as far as the sense of mankind can have weight in the question, of the species of <u>knowledge of local circumstances</u> requisite to the purposes of <u>taxation</u>.

INTERNAL TAXES ARE DIRECT OR INDIRECT:
Direct taxation is the Anti-Federalists' issue of greatest concern.

36:11 The taxes intended to be comprised under the general denomination of <u>internal</u> taxes may be subdivided into those of the <u>DIRECT and those of the INDIRECT kind</u>. Though the <u>objection be made to both</u>, yet the reasoning upon it <u>seems to be confined to the</u> former branch.

INDIRECT TAXES ARE EASIER TO COMPREHEND:
The details of duties and excises are not difficult to discover.

36:12 And indeed, <u>as to the latter</u>, by which must be understood <u>duties</u> and <u>excises</u> on <u>articles of consumption</u>, one is at a loss to conceive what can be the nature of the difficulties apprehended. The knowledge relating to them must evidently be of a kind that will either be suggested by the nature of the article itself, or can easily be procured from any well-informed man, especially of the mercantile class. The circumstances that may distinguish its situation in one State from its situation in another must be few, simple, and easy to be comprehended.

STATE EXCEPTIONS:
Federal taxing should avoid items unique to a particular State's needs.

36:13 The principal thing to be attended to, would be to <u>avoid those articles which had been previously appropriated</u> <u>to the use of a particular State</u>; and there could be no difficulty in ascertaining the revenue system of each. This could always be known from the respective codes of laws, as well as from the information of the members from the several States.

TAXING REAL PROPERTY:

36:14 The objection, when applied to <u>real property</u> or to <u>houses</u> and <u>lands</u>, appears to have, at first sight, more foundation, but even in this view it will not bear a close examination.

TAXES ON LAND BEST DONE BY LOCAL ASSESSORS:

36:15 Land <u>taxes</u> are commonly <u>laid</u> in one of two modes, either by <u>ACTUAL</u> valuations, permanent or periodical, or by <u>OCCASIONAL assessments</u>, at the discretion, or according to the best judgment, of certain officers whose duty it is to make them. In either case, the <u>EXECUTION of the business, which alone requires the knowledge of local details, must be devolved upon discreet persons in the character of commissioners or assessors, elected by the people or appointed by the government for the purpose</u>.

GOVERNMENT CAN'T AND SHOULDN'T MICRO-MANAGE:

36:16 All that the law can do must be to name the persons or to prescribe the manner of their election or appointment, to fix their numbers and qualifications and to draw the general outlines of their powers and duties.

FEDERAL AND STATE DON'T KNOW LOCAL DETAILS:

36:17 And what is there in all this that cannot as <u>well be performed</u> by the <u>national legislature</u> as by a <u>State legislature</u>? The attention of either can only reach to general principles; <u>local details, as already observed, must be referred to those who are to execute the plan</u>.

CONGRESS CAN MAKE USE OF LOCAL AND STATE EXPERTISE:

36:18 But there is a simple point of view in which this matter may be placed that must be altogether satisfactory. <u>The national legislature can make use of the SYSTEM OF EACH STATE WITHIN THAT STATE. The method of laying and collecting this species of taxes in each State can, in all its parts, be adopted and employed by the federal government</u>.

PROPORTION OF TAXES DECIDED BY CENSUS:
Congress can't set the amount of taxes; they must depend on State populations.

36:19 <u>Let it be recollected that the proportion of these taxes is not to be left to the discretion of the national legislature, but is to be determined by the numbers</u> of each State, as described in the second section of the first article. An <u>actual</u>

census or enumeration of the people must furnish the rule, a circumstance which effectually shuts the door to partiality or oppression.

UNIFORMITY HELPS PREVENT ABUSE IN LEVYING DUTIES.

36:20 The abuse of this power of taxation seems to have been provided against with guarded circumspection. In addition to the precaution just mentioned, there is a provision that "all duties, imposts, and excises shall be UNIFORM throughout the United States."

SOME ASK, WHY NOT SIMPLY REQUISITION IT (TAKE IT)?

36:21 It has been very properly observed by different speakers and writers on the side of the Constitution, that if the exercise of the power of internal taxation by the Union should be discovered on experiment to be really inconvenient, the federal government may then forbear the use of it, and have recourse to requisitions in its stead.

36:22 By way of answer to this, it has been triumphantly asked, Why not in the first instance omit that ambiguous power, and rely upon the latter resource?

REQUISITION IS CONVENIENT AND THUS PREFERABLE:
It's impossible to prove it works or not except by experimenting.

36:23 Two solid answers may be given. The first is, that the exercise of that power, if convenient, will be preferable, because it will be more effectual; and it is impossible to prove in theory, or otherwise than by the experiment, that it cannot be advantageously exercised. The contrary, indeed, appears most probable.

STATES WILL WORK TO PREVENT DIRECT TAXATION:

36:24 The second answer is, that the existence of such a power in the Constitution will have a strong influence in giving efficacy to requisitions. When the States know that the Union can apply itself without their agency, it will be a powerful motive for exertion on their part.

FEDERAL AND STATE TAX LAWS CANNOT INTERFERE:

36:25 As to the interference of the revenue laws of the Union, and of its members, we have already seen that there can be no clashing or repugnancy of authority. The laws cannot, therefore, in a legal sense, interfere with each other; and it is far from impossible to avoid an interference even in the policy of their different systems.

JOINT FEDERAL AND STATE TAXING POWER:
(**Editors' note: An example of joint taxing power is modern gasoline taxes taken at the pump, alcohol, tobacco, and income taxes.**)

36:26 An effectual expedient for this purpose will be, mutually, to abstain from those objects which either side may have first had recourse to. As neither can CONTROL the other, each will have an obvious and sensible interest in this reciprocal forbearance. And where there is an IMMEDIATE common interest, we may safely count upon its operation.

MOST CONFLICTS WILL END WHEN STATE DEBTS ARE PAID:

36:27 When the particular debts of the States are done away, and their expenses come to be limited within their natural compass, the possibility almost of interference will vanish. A small land tax will answer the purpose of the States, and will be their most simple and most fit resource.

CRITICS RAISE MANY FEARS ABOUT TAXING POWER:

36:28 Many spectres have been raised out of this power of internal taxation, to excite the apprehensions of the people: double sets of revenue officers, a duplication of their burdens by double taxations, and the frightful forms of odious and oppressive poll-taxes, have been played off with all the ingenious dexterity of political legerdemain.

TWO CASES WHERE THERE IS NO ROOM FOR DOUBLE SETS OF OFFICERS:

36:29 As to the first point, there are two cases in which there can be no room for double sets of officers: one, where the right of imposing the tax is exclusively vested in the Union, which applies to the duties on imports; the other, where the object has not fallen under any State regulation or provision, which may be applicable to a variety of objects.

CONGRESS CAN USE EXISTING STATE PROCESSES:

36:30 In other cases, the probability is that the United States will either wholly abstain from the objects preoccupied for local purposes, or will make use of the State officers and State regulations for collecting the additional imposition. This will best answer the views of revenue, because it will save expense in the collection, and will best avoid any occasion of disgust to the State governments and to the people.

Predictions of pending disaster are unfounded.

36:31 At all events, here is a practicable expedient for avoiding such an inconvenience; and nothing more can be required than to show that evils predicted to not necessarily result from the plan.

FEAR OF FEDERAL CRONYISM:[130]
To steer revenue away from State coffers and into the federal government's, Congress would have to directly hire as many State employees as it could and win their loyalty with generous compensation and pay.

36:32 As to any argument derived from a supposed system of influence, it is a sufficient answer to say that it ought not to be presumed; but the supposition is susceptible of a more precise answer. If such a spirit should infest the councils of the Union, the most certain road to the accomplishment of its aim would be to employ the State officers as much as possible, and to attach them to the Union by an accumulation of their emoluments. This would serve to turn the tide of State influence into the channels of the national government, instead of making federal influence flow in an opposite and adverse current.

FEAR OF CRONYISM IS A MERE SUPPOSITION THAT OBSCURES TRUTH:

36:33 But all suppositions of this kind are invidious, and ought to be banished from the consideration of the great question before the people. They can answer no other end than to cast a mist over the truth.

DOUBLE TAXATION:
The Union will acquire funding one way or the other, and if the funding is for the federal level, it won't be paid for by the States.

36:34 As to the suggestion of double taxation, the answer is plain. The wants of the Union are to be supplied in one way or another; if to be done by the authority of the federal government, it will not be to be done by that of the State government. The quantity of taxes to be paid by the community must be the same in either case;

COMMERCIAL TAXES EASIEST FOR FEDERAL:

36:35 with this advantage, if the provision is to be made by the Union that the capital resource of commercial imposts, which is the most convenient branch of revenue, can be prudently improved to a much greater extent under federal than under State regulation, and of course will render it less necessary to recur to more inconvenient methods;

LUXURY TAXES PUT BURDEN ON RICH, NOT POOR:

36:36 and with this further advantage, that as far as there may be any real difficulty in the exercise of the power of internal taxation, it will impose a disposition to greater care in the choice and arrangement of the means; and must naturally tend to make it a fixed point of policy in the national administration to go as far as may be practicable in making

the luxury of the rich tributary to the public treasury, in order to diminish the necessity of those impositions which might create dissatisfaction in the poorer and most numerous classes of the society.

BEST BALANCE IS TO MEET NATIONAL NEEDS WHILE PROTECTING THE POOR:

36:37 Happy it is when the interest which the government has in the preservation of its own power, coincides with a proper distribution of the public burdens, and tends to guard the least wealthy part of the community from oppression!

POLL TAXES:
Hamilton hates these direct individual taxes.

36:38 As to **poll taxes**,[131] I, without scruple, confess my disapprobation of them; and though they have prevailed from an early period in those States[132] which have uniformly been the most tenacious of their rights, I should lament to see them introduced into practice under the national government.

STATES HAVE POLL-TAXING POWER BUT DON'T USE IT:

36:39 But does it follow because there is a power to lay them that they will actually be laid? Every State in the Union has power to impose taxes of this kind; and yet in several of them they are unknown in practice. Are the State governments to be stigmatized as tyrannies, because they possess this power? If they are not, with what propriety can the like power justify such a charge against the national government, or even` be urged as an obstacle to its adoption?

POLL TAXES ARE A NECESSARY EVIL FOR EMERGENCIES:

36:40 As little friendly as I am to the species of imposition, I still feel a thorough conviction that the power of having recourse to it ought to exist in the federal government. There are certain emergencies of nations, in which expedients, that in the ordinary state of things ought to be forborne, become essential to the public weal. And the government, from the possibility of such emergencies, ought ever to have the option of making use of them.

THERE ARE FEW THINGS TO TAX IN AMERICA:
An emergency could make a poll tax a highly valued resource.

36:41 The real scarcity of objects in this country, which may be considered as productive sources of revenue, is a reason peculiar to itself, for not abridging the discretion of the national councils in this respect. There may exist certain critical and tempestuous conjunctures of the State, in which a poll tax

---

130 *cronyism:* Appointing friends to positions of authority without proper regard to their qualifications.
131 *poll tax:* A tax of a fixed amount levied on everyone in a described area, sometimes as a condition of voting.
132 *Publius:* The New England States.

may become an inestimable resource. And as I know nothing to exempt this portion of the globe from the common calamities that have befallen other parts of it, I acknowledge my aversion to every project that is calculated to disarm the government of a single weapon, which in any possible contingency might be usefully employed for the general defense and security.

NEW POWERS GIVE GOVERNMENT NEEDED ENERGY:

36:42 I have now gone through the examination of such of the powers proposed to be conferred upon the federal government which relate more peculiarly to its energy, and to its efficiency for answering the great and primary objects of union. There are others which, though omitted here, will, in order to render the view of the subject more complete, be taken notice of under the next head of our inquiries.[133]

WE'VE SHOWN THAT THE CRITICS' CLAIMS ARE POINTLESS:

36:43 I flatter myself the progress already made will have sufficed to satisfy the candid and judicious part of the community that some of the objections which have been most strenuously urged against the Constitution, and which were most formidable in their first appearance, are not only destitute of substance, but if they had operated in the formation of the plan, would have rendered it incompetent to the great ends of public happiness and national prosperity.

MORE EXPLANATION WILL PROVE EVEN BETTER:

Does Hamilton believe the Constitution sets an example of good government for the entire world?

36:44 I equally flatter myself that a further and more critical investigation of the system will serve to recommend it still more to every sincere and disinterested advocate for good government and will leave no doubt with men of this character of the propriety and expediency of adopting it. Happy will it be for ourselves, and more honorable for human nature, if we have wisdom and virtue enough to set so glorious an example to mankind!

—PUBLIUS

REVIEW QUESTIONS

1. Repeating from the prior paper, from what classes of people will most representatives come? (36:1)

2. The Framers envisioned an America where it didn't matter into what walk of life a person was born. There are strong minds in all that will rise superior using their natural faculties to get ahead. America, therefore, should be a country where

the "____ ought to be equally ____ to ____." (36:3)

3. Who makes up the natural aristocracy that will rise to lead and govern the people? (36:3)

4. All of the different classes of human activities listed in 36:4 share the goal of trading their goods or services to make a profit and get ahead. What class of market activity is listed that has a close relation with "either of them"? Why is this class so integral? (36:4)

5. How will Congress acquire enough information to assess taxes fairly? (36:7–8)

6. Are tax plans best created by a single person or even by a very small group, as opposed to a large assembly? Why? (36:9–10)

7. What is an indirect tax? (36:12)

8. Will the States work hard to prevent direct taxation by the Union? Why? (36:24)

9. With both governments (State and federal) able to tax, isn't there a risk of double taxation? Why? (36:34)

10. Will there need to be a double set of tax collectors, one for the State, the other for the Union? Why? (36:29–30)

11. What is a poll tax? (36:38, see footnote)

12. How does Hamilton view poll taxes? (36:40–41)

---

133 *Editors' Note:* Paragraphs 36:42-44 appear in the McLean (1788) and Hopkins (1802) printed collections but do not appear in the newspaper versions.

SECTION 5 • WRITING THE CONSTITUTION

Papers 37–44

FEDERALIST NO. 37

THE MIRACLE THAT SOLVED THE IMPOSSIBLE PUZZLE: The new Constitution has no equal in history. Therefore, all issues had to be directly addressed and considered, and not swept out of sight. The Convention found a balanced center of political power and its proper distribution. Madison observes that the hand of God is clearly evident in the completion of this complex, arduous task. And those judging the final result should also examine the mighty obstacles and difficulties that had to be successfully resolved—and realize that all of this was accomplished without any ancient or modern guide or example or experience to direct the final formulation of the Constitution.

By James Madison—January 11, 1788

REVIEWING THE DEFECTS IN THE ARTICLES: Fixing them can't be done unless the new government has sufficient energy.

37:1 IN REVIEWING the defects of the existing Confederation, and showing that they cannot be supplied by a government of less energy than that before the public, several of the most important principles of the latter fell of course under consideration.

OUR OBJECT IS TO EXAMINE THE MERITS OF CONSTITUTION:

37:2 But as the ultimate object of these papers is to determine clearly and fully the merits of this Constitution, and the expediency of adopting it, our plan cannot be complete without taking a more critical and thorough survey of the work of the Convention, without examining it on all its sides, comparing it in all its parts, and calculating its probable effects.

37:3 That this remaining task may be executed under impressions conducive to a just and fair result, some reflections must in this place be indulged, which candor previously suggests.

PUBLIC AFFAIRS ARE RARELY EVALUATED FAIRLY:

37:4 It is a misfortune, inseparable from human affairs, that public measures are rarely investigated with that spirit of moderation which is essential to a just estimate of their real tendency to advance or obstruct the public good; and that this spirit is more apt to be diminished than promoted, by those occasions which require an unusual exercise of it.

NO SURPRISE THAT THERE IS MUCH CONTROVERSY:

37:5 To those who have been led by experience to attend to this consideration, it could not appear surprising, that the act of the Convention, which recommends so many important changes and innovations, which may be viewed in so many lights and relations, and which touches the springs of so many passions and interests, should find or excite dispositions unfriendly, both on one side and on the other, to a fair discussion and accurate judgment of its merits.

SOME CRITICS, SADLY, ARE TOO PREJUDICED:

37:6 In some, it has been too evident from their own publications, that they have scanned the proposed Constitution, not only with a predisposition to censure, but with a predetermination to condemn;

ANTI-FEDERALISTS' BIASED LANGUAGE RUINS THEIR CREDIBILITY:

37:7 as the language held by others betrays an opposite predetermination or bias, which must render their opinions also of little moment in the question.

FAIR TO SAY MOST HEARTS PROBABLY IN RIGHT PLACE:

37:8 In placing, however, these different characters on a level, with respect to the weight of their opinions, I wish not to insinuate that there may not be a material difference in the purity of their intentions. It is but just to remark in favor of the latter description, that as our situation is universally admitted to be peculiarly critical, and to require indispensably that something should be done for our relief, the predetermined patron of what has been actually done may have taken his bias from the weight of these considerations, as well as from considerations of a sinister nature.

INTENTIONS MAY BE GOOD, BUT SOME CLEARLY NOT:

37:9 The underlined adversary, on the other hand, can have been governed by no venial motive whatever. The intentions of the first may be upright, as they may on the contrary be culpable. The views of the last cannot be upright, and must be culpable.

FEDERALIST PAPERS WERE WRITTEN FOR THOSE WANTING BEST FOR AMERICA:

37:10 But the truth is, that these papers are not addressed to persons falling under either of these characters. They solicit the attention of those only, who add to a sincere zeal for the happiness of their country, a temper favorable to a just estimate of the means of promoting it.

HONEST PEOPLE WILL LOOK FOR GOOD NOT BAD:

Will such critics also appreciate the fact they too are imperfect judges?

37:11 Persons of this character will proceed to an examination of the plan submitted by the Convention, not only without a disposition to find or to magnify faults; but will see the propriety of reflecting, that a faultless plan was not to be expected. Nor will they barely make allowances for the errors which may be chargeable on the fallibility to which the Convention, as a body of men, were liable; but will keep in mind, that they themselves also are but men, and ought not to assume an infallibility in rejudging the fallible opinions of others.

MASSIVE CHALLENGES TO OVERCOME:

Correcting the Articles involved solving nearly impossible puzzles and blending in new creations.

37:12 With equal readiness will it be perceived, that besides these inducements to candor, many allowances ought to be made for the difficulties inherent in the very nature of the undertaking referred to the Convention.

FOUNDATION HAD TO BE CHANGED FIRST, THEN THE SUPERSTRUCTURE ATOP IT:

37:13 The novelty of the undertaking immediately strikes us. It has been shown in the course of these papers, that the existing Confederation is founded on principles which are fallacious; that we must consequently change this first foundation, and with it the superstructure resting upon it.

NO PRIOR GOVERNMENT TO PATTERN EXCEPT TO LEARN FROM THEIR ERRORS:

The new Constitution corrects the Articles, avoids past errors, and is open to amending.

37:14 It has been shown, that the other confederacies which could be consulted as precedents have been vitiated by the same erroneous principles, and can therefore furnish no other light than that of beacons, which give warning of the course to be shunned, without pointing out that which ought to be pursued. The most that the Convention could do in such a situation, was to avoid the errors suggested by the past experience of other countries, as well as of our own; and to provide a convenient mode of rectifying their own errors, as future experiences may unfold them.

FINDING THAT PERFECT BALANCE OF POWER AND STABILITY:

The Convention hunted for the balanced republican center between too much political power and none at all—between tyranny and anarchy.

37:15 Among the difficulties encountered by the Convention, a very important one must have lain in combining the requisite stability and energy in government, with the inviolable attention due to liberty and to the republican form. Without substantially accomplishing this part of their undertaking, they would have very imperfectly fulfilled the object of their appointment, or the expectation of the public; yet that it could not be easily accomplished, will be denied by no one who is unwilling to betray his ignorance of the subject.

ENERGY IN GOVERNMENT:

Having the power to execute the laws is necessary to protect the rights of the people.

37:16 Energy in government is essential to that security against external and internal danger, and to that prompt and salutary execution of the laws which enter into the very definition of good government.

STABILITY IN GOVERNMENT:

When trust reigns strong from the top to the bottom, prosperity will blossom.

37:17 Stability in government is essential to national character and to the advantages annexed to it, as well as to that repose and confidence in the minds of the people, which are among the chief blessings of civil society.

FREQUENTLY-CHANGING LAWS ARE RUINOUS:

The people insisted a remedy to the flaws in the Articles be found that would solve the severe problems they were facing.

37:18 An irregular and mutable legislation is not more an evil in itself than it is odious to the people; and it may be pronounced with assurance that the people of this country, enlightened as they are with regard to the nature, and interested, as the great body of them are, in the effects of good government, will never be satisfied till some remedy be applied to the vicissitudes and uncertainties which characterize the State administrations.[134]

FINDING BALANCE WAS DIFFICULT AND COMPLICATED:

37:19   On comparing, however, these valuable ingredients with the vital principles of liberty, we must perceive at once the difficulty of mingling them together in their due proportions.

GENIUS OF REPUBLICAN FORM:
While power is delegated from the people, those wielding that power are subject to frequent elections.

37:20   The genius of republican liberty seems to demand on one side, not only that all power should be derived from the people, but that those intrusted with it should be kept in independence on the people, by a short duration of their appointments; and that even during this short period the trust should be placed not in a few, but a number of hands.

REGULAR ELECTIONS BRINGS STABILITY:

37:21   Stability, on the contrary, requires that the hands in which power is lodged should continue for a length of time the same. A frequent change of men will result from a frequent return of elections; and a frequent change of measures from a frequent change of men: whilst energy in government requires not only a certain duration of power, but the execution of it by a single hand.

DIFFICULT TO MIX POWER AND ELECTIONS:
Avoiding both anarchy and monarchy was an arduous task for the Convention.

37:22   How far the Convention may have succeeded in this part of their work, will better appear on a more accurate view of it. From the cursory view here taken, it must clearly appear to have been an arduous part.

ARDUOUS TASK TO SEPARATE GOVERNMENT POWERS:
Separating general powers from the States' powers was grueling process.

37:23   Not less arduous must have been the task of marking the proper line of partition between the authority of the general and that of the State governments. Every man will be sensible of this difficulty, in proportion as he has been accustomed to contemplate and discriminate objects extensive and complicated in their nature.

FOR EXAMPLE, THE FACULTIES OF THE HUMAN MIND ARE NOT CLEARLY DEFINED:
A myriad of human capacities magnify the complication even more.

37:24   The faculties of the mind itself have never yet been distinguished and defined, with satisfactory precision, by all the efforts of the most acute and metaphysical philosophers. Sense, perception, judgment, desire, volition, memory, imagination, are found to be separated by such delicate shades and minute gradations that their boundaries have eluded the most subtle investigations, and remain a pregnant source of ingenious disquisition and controversy.

BEST MINDS CAN'T ACCURATELY DELINEATE NATURE:

37:25   The boundaries between the great kingdom of nature, and, still more, between the various provinces, and lesser portions, into which they are subdivided, afford another illustration of the same important truth. The most sagacious and laborious naturalists have never yet succeeded in tracing with certainty the line which separates the district of vegetable life from the neighboring region of unorganized matter, or which marks the termination of the former and the commencement of the animal empire. A still greater obscurity lies in the distinctive characters by which the objects in each of these great departments of nature have been arranged and assorted.

INSTITUTIONS OF MEN ARE MORE COMPLICATED:
The works of nature are perfect. The works or man are not, and perceiving their failings is further hampered by the flaws in the observers and judges.

37:26   When we pass from the works of nature, in which all the delineations are perfectly accurate, and appear to be otherwise only from the imperfection of the eye which surveys them, to the institutions of man, in which the obscurity arises as well from the object itself as from the organ by which it is contemplated, we must perceive the necessity of moderating still further our expectations and hopes from the efforts of human sagacity.

BOUNDARIES BETWEEN THREE BRANCHES WAS ARDUOUS TO PRECISELY DEFINE:

37:27   Experience has instructed us that no skill in the science of government has yet been able to discriminate and define,

---

134   John Adams said fixed law is crucial to liberty: "No man will contend, that a nation can be free, that is not governed by fixed laws. All other government than that of permanent known laws, is the government of mere will and pleasure." Adams, John, A Defence of the Constitutions of Government of the United States (Philadelphia: Budd and Bartram, 3rd ed., 1797) vol. 1, p 124.

with sufficient certainty, its **three**[135] great **provinces**[136] the legislative, executive, and judiciary; or even the privileges and powers of the different legislative branches. Questions daily occur in the course of practice, which prove the obscurity which reins in these subjects, and which puzzle the greatest adepts in political science.

AMBIGUOUS WORDS CAN OBSCURE CLEAR IDEAS:

Written laws never enjoy a perfect understanding.

37:28 The experience of ages, with the continued and combined labors of the most enlightened legislatures and jurists, has been equally unsuccessful in delineating the several objects and limits of different codes of laws and different tribunals of justice.

LONG-STANDING LAWS REMAIN SUBJECT TO DEBATE:

37:29 The precise extent of the common law, and the statute law, the maritime law, the ecclesiastical law, the law of corporations, and other local laws and customs, remains still to be clearly and finally established in Great Britain, where accuracy in such subjects has been more industriously pursued than in any other part of the world. The jurisdiction of her several courts, general and local, of law, of equity, of admiralty, etc., is not less a source of frequent and intricate discussions, sufficiently denoting the indeterminate limits by which they are respectively circumscribed.

BEST LAWS ARE OBSCURE AND EQUIVOCAL UNTIL TESTED:

Written law may lay out the initial purpose, intent, and meaning of its writers but its true applications won't be known until they are fleshed out in the courts.

37:30 All new laws, though penned with the greatest technical skill, and passed on the fullest and most mature deliberation, are considered as more or less obscure and equivocal, until their meaning be liquidated and ascertained by a series of particular discussions and adjudications.

THE MEDIUM OF EXCHANGE CAN COMPOUND TRUTH:

37:31 Besides the obscurity arising from the complexity of objects, and the imperfection of the human faculties, the medium through which the conceptions of men are conveyed to each other adds a fresh embarrassment.

WORDS EXPRESS THE IDEAS, SO THE ORIGINAL IDEAS MUST BE VERY CLEAR:

37:32 The use of words is to express ideas. **Perspicuity**,[137] therefore, requires not only that the ideas should be distinctly formed, but that they should be expressed by words distinctly and exclusively appropriate to them. But no language is so copious as to supply words and phrases for every complex idea, or so correct as not to include many equivocally denoting different ideas.

INACCURATE TERMS MEANS FAILED DEFINITION:

All too often the mediums of communication obscure a writer's original intent.

37:33 Hence it must happen that however accurately objects may be discriminated in themselves, and however accurately the discrimination may be considered, the definition of them may be rendered inaccurate by the inaccuracy of the terms in which it is delivered. And this unavoidable inaccuracy must be greater or less, according to the complexity and novelty of the objects defined.

GOD'S OWN MESSAGES ARE DIMMED BY WORDS:

37:34 When the Almighty himself condescends to address mankind in their own language, his meaning, luminous as it must be, is rendered dim and doubtful by the cloudy medium through which it is communicated.

THREE SOURCES OF VAGUE DEFINITIONS:

37:35 Here, then, are three sources of vague and incorrect definitions: indistinctness of the object, imperfection of the organ of conception, inadequateness of the vehicle of ideas.

FEDERAL AND STATE JURISDICTIONS ARE OBSCURED:

37:36 Any one of these must produce a certain degree of obscurity. The Convention, in delineating the boundary between the federal and State jurisdictions, must have experienced the full effect of them all.

CONFLICTING DEMANDS OF THE STATES:

The confusion that common language introduces into political discussions is made worse by conflicting demands made by the various States.

37:37 To the difficulties already mentioned may be added the interfering pretensions of the larger and smaller States. We cannot err in supposing that the former would contend for a

---

135 *Editors' Note:* The concept of three provinces of government is ancient. For example, the Prophet Isaiah (800-700 BC) identified the three branches of good government, "For the LORD is our judge [judicial], the LORD is our lawgiver [legislative], the LORD is our king [executive]; he will save us." (Isaiah 33:22 KJV) All three provinces are necessary to "save us," that is, necessary to preserve our freedom and liberty.

136 *province:* The proper office or area of responsibility.

137 *perspicuity:* Penetrating discernment; ability to see clearly with understanding and insight.

participation in the government, fully proportioned to their superior wealth and importance; and that the latter would not be less tenacious of the equality at present enjoyed by them. We may well suppose that <u>neither side</u> would <u>entirely yield to</u> the other, and consequently that the struggle could be terminated only <u>by compromise</u>.

AFTER THE GREAT COMPROMISE ON REPRESENTATION, DISCORD CONTINUED:

37:38   It is extremely probable, also, that after the <u>ratio of representation</u> had been adjusted, this very compromise must have produced a fresh struggle between the same parties, to give such a turn to the organization of the government, and to the distribution of its powers, as would <u>increase the importance of the branches</u>, in forming which they had respectively obtained the greatest share of <u>influence</u>.

COMPLEX ISSUES FORCED CREATIVITY AND EXPLORATION INTO NEW CONSIDERATIONS:

37:39   There are features in the Constitution which warrant each of these suppositions; and as far as either of them is well founded, it shows that the <u>Convention</u> must have been <u>compelled to sacrifice theoretical propriety</u> to the force of <u>extraneous considerations</u>.

MANY TYPES AND LEVELS OF SOCIAL ISSUES TO EXAMINE:

Various local issues also reared their heads to complicate matters.

37:40   Nor could it have been the large and small States only, which would marshal themselves in opposition to each other on various points. Other combinations, resulting from a <u>difference of local position and policy</u>, must have created additional <u>difficulties</u>.

MANY DIFFERENCES DIVIDE PEOPLE ON ALL LEVELS:

37:41   As every State may be divided into different <u>districts</u>, and its citizens into different <u>classes</u>, which give birth to <u>contending</u> <u>interests</u> and local jealousies, so the different parts of the United States are distinguished from each other by a variety of circumstances, which produce a like effect on a larger scale.

FORMING AND FORMED:

While one kind of pressure will influence the running of the newly formed government, a much different pressure exerted influence on the forming of it.

37:42   And although this variety of interests, for reasons sufficiently explained in a former paper, may have a salutary influence on the administration of the government when formed, yet every one must be sensible of the contrary influence, which must have been experienced in the task of forming it.

THE MANY DIFFICULTIES FORGED THE GOOD:

37:43   Would it be wonderful if, under the pressure of all these difficulties, the Convention should have been forced into some deviations from that artificial structure and regular symmetry which an abstract view of the subject might lead an ingenious theorist to bestow on a Constitution planned in his closet or in his imagination?

GOD INSPIRED THE CONSTITUTION:

It is a wonder and astonishment. There were so many complex issues worked out, resolved, and supported that it's obvious that God's hand was as present in this as during the many crisis periods of the recent war.

37:44   <u>The real</u> **wonder**[138] is that <u>so many difficulties</u> should have been <u>surmounted</u>, and surmounted with a <u>unanimity</u> almost as <u>unprecedented</u> as it must have been <u>unexpected</u>. <u>It is impossible for any man of candor to reflect on this circumstance without partaking of the astonishment. It is impossible for the man of pious reflection not to perceive in it a finger of that Almighty hand which has been so frequently and</u> **signally**[139] <u>extended to our relief in the critical stages of the revolution.</u>[140]

THE NETHERLANDS FAILED TO CORRECT FLAWS:

37:45   We had occasion, in a <u>former paper</u>, to take notice of the <u>repeated trials</u> which have been unsuccessfully made in the United Netherlands for reforming the baneful and notorious <u>vices of their constitution</u>.

TRADITIONAL REVIEW COUNCILS ALWAYS FAIL:

That the Convention did not fail is an historic achievement by itself.

37:46   The history of almost all the great councils and consultations held among mankind for reconciling their <u>discordant opinions</u>, assuaging their <u>mutual jealousies</u>, and adjusting their respective interests, is a history of factions, contentions, and disappointments, and may be classed among the <u>most dark and degraded</u> pictures which display the <u>infirmities</u> and <u>depravities</u> of the <u>human character</u>. If, in a <u>few scattered instances, a brighter aspect</u> is presented, they serve only as exceptions to admonish us of the general truth; and by their

---

138   *wonder:* Feeling of surprise mingled with admiration.

139   *signally:* Eminently, remarkably, memorably, in a distinguished manner.

140   *Editors' Note:* A similar comment is attributed to Alexander Hamilton under the pseudonym "Caesar," as the possible author of a letter published October 15, 1787 in the New York *Daily Advertiser* stating "For my own part, I sincerely esteem it a system which without the finger of God, never could have been suggested and agreed upon by such a diversity of interests."

lustre to darken the gloom of the adverse prospect to which they are contrasted.

TWO REASONS WHY THE CONVENTION WAS A SUCCESS:

First reason was the delegates came with no political partisanship to defend.

37:47   In revolving the causes from which these exceptions result, and applying them to the particular instances before us, we are necessarily led to two important conclusions. The first is, that the Convention must have enjoyed, in a very singular degree, an exemption from the pestilential influence of party animosities the disease most incident to deliberative bodies, and most apt to contaminate their proceedings.

PRIVATE INTERESTS SACRIFICED FOR PUBLIC GOOD:

Secondly, so great was their satisfaction with the final product that they put aside personal objections to avoid further delay.

37:48   The second conclusion is that all the deputations composing the Convention were satisfactorily accommodated by the final act, or were induced to accede to it by a deep conviction of the necessity of sacrificing private opinions and partial interests to the public good, and by a despair of seeing this necessity diminished by delays or by new experiments.

—PUBLIUS

REVIEW QUESTIONS

1. Can the flaws in the Articles be corrected by a government lacking the power or energy to do so? (37:1)

2. Did some critics of the Constitution simply scan it briefly, looking only for ways to censure and condemn it? (37:6–7)

3. For whom are these papers written? (37:10)

4. On what principles were the Articles founded? (37:13)

5. With no model of good government to follow, what was the most the Convention could do in forming a better government? (37:14)

6. What was the great difficulty the Convention had to solve? (37:15)

7. What four forms in the Constitution keep the genius of the republican system intact? (37:20–21)

8. What task for the Convention was particularly arduous but necessary? (37:23)

9. What examples does Madison provide to illustrate the difficulty of setting boundaries in other parts of the world and universe? (37:24–25)

10. Are the boundaries of nature set perfectly? Are boundaries of men set perfectly? (37:26)

11. What are some of the variables listed by Madison that make the act of separating powers so difficult? (37:27–33)

12. Can human words obscure God's truth, making truth debatable? (37:34)

13. What does Madison list as the three sources of obscurity in language? (37:35)

14. Upon what specific problem did these many variables of obscurity bear down with full effect? (37:36)

15. Even after the Convention thought it had resolved all of these issues did disagreements compel them to dig down deeper, over and over? (37:37–42)

16. Did anyone expect so many challenges to be resolved? (37:44)

17. Did anyone expect so many challenges to be resolved with such support, agreement, and consensus? (37:44)

18. Can any honest person look at this achievement and not be astonished? (37:44)

19. Can any devoutly religious person look at this achievement and not see the hand of God in its achievements? (37:44)

20. Does Madison give credit to God for his help in the critical stages of the revolution against Britain? (37:44)

21. What are the two reasons why the Convention was a success? (37:47–48)

FEDERALIST NO. 38

CONSTITUTION MUST GRANT THE MEANS TO REACH ENDS: Constitutions of ancient times were entrusted to single people because the fear of treachery of the writer was less than their fear of infighting among the group composing the instrument. A government's means must equal its ends. That is, there must be enough power to fulfill the task given it. That was the weakness in the Articles: it did not possess sufficient power or means to do its job. Arguments against the new Constitution cannot be defended. If the Anti-Federalists are so smart, where is their plan? Their hypocrisy and objections are easily exposed using their own words against them.

By James Madison—January 12, 1788

GOVERNMENTS OF THE PAST CREATED BY INDIVIDUALS:

And not created by assemblies of men, as might be expected.

38:1 IT IS not a little remarkable that in every case reported by ancient history, in which government has been established with deliberation and consent, the task of framing it has not been committed to an assembly of men, but has been performed by some individual citizen of preeminent wisdom and approved integrity.

EXAMPLES FROM GREECE AND ROME:

38:2 Minos, we learn, was the primitive founder of the government of Crete, as Zaleucus was of that of the Locrians. Theseus first, and after him Draco and Solon, instituted the government of Athens. Lycurgus was the lawgiver of Sparta.

BRUTUS ENDED ROYALTY IN GOVERNMENT:

38:3 The foundation of the original government of Rome was laid by Romulus, and the work completed by two of his elective successors, Numa and Tullius Hostilius. On the abolition of royalty the consular administration was substituted by Brutus, who stepped forward with a project for such a reform, which, he alleged, had been prepared by Tullius Hostilius, and to which his address obtained the assent and ratification of the senate and people.

SAME PROCESS USED TO CREATE ANCIENT CONFEDERACIES:

38:4 This remark is applicable to confederate governments also. Amphictyon, we are told, was the author of that which bore his name. The Achaean league received its first birth from Achaeus, and its second from Aratus.

DEGREE OF POWER IN LAWMAKERS IS UNCERTAIN:

It is not known in every instance how much liberty these men enjoyed to draft the constitution for their countries.

38:5 What degree of agency these reputed lawgivers might have in their respective establishments, or how far they might be clothed with the legitimate authority of the people, cannot in every instance be ascertained. In some, however, the proceeding was strictly regular.

SOME MEN WERE GRANTED ABSOLUTE POWER TO CREATE:

38:6 Draco appears to have been intrusted by the people of Athens with indefinite powers to reform its government and laws. And Solon, according to Plutarch, was in a manner compelled, by the universal suffrage of his fellow-citizens, to take upon him the sole and absolute power of new-modeling the constitution.

LYCURGUS WAS AMPLY RESPECTED TO DO THE JOB:

38:7 The proceedings under Lycurgus were less regular; but as far as the advocates for a regular reform could prevail, they all turned their eyes towards the single efforts of that celebrated patriot and sage, instead of seeking to bring about a revolution by the intervention of a deliberative body of citizens.

GREEKS PUT TRUST IN ONE PERSON:

38:8 Whence could it have proceeded, that a people, jealous as the Greeks were of their liberty, should so far abandon the rules of caution as to place their destiny in the hands of a single citizen?

HOW COULD THOSE SO DISTRUSTFUL FIND TRUST?

The Athenians rejected a body of select citizens and put their fate in the hands of a single man.

38:9 Whence could it have proceeded, that the Athenians, a people who would not suffer an army to be commanded by fewer than ten generals, and who required no other proof of danger to their liberties than the illustrious merit of a fellow-citizen, should consider one illustrious citizen as a more eligible depositary of the fortunes of themselves and their posterity, than a select body of citizens, from whose common deliberations more wisdom, as well as more safety, might have been expected?

DESIRE FOR INTERNAL PEACE WAS PARAMOUNT:

Infighting over who is in charge could be calmed by assigning one person to do the job.

38:10 These questions cannot be fully answered, without supposing that the fears of discord and disunion among a number of counselors exceeded the apprehension of treachery or incapacity in a single individual. History informs us, likewise, of the difficulties with which these celebrated reformers had to contend, as well as the expedients which they were obliged to employ in order to carry their reforms into effect.

SOLON CONCEDED TO THE PEOPLE'S PREJUDICES:

38:11 Solon, who seems to have indulged a more temporizing policy, confessed that he had not given to his countrymen the government best suited to their happiness, but most tolerable to their prejudices.

LYCURGUS SEALED HIS SINCERITY BY SUICIDE:

38:12 And Lycurgus, more true to his object, was under the necessity of mixing a portion of violence with the authority of superstition, and of securing his final success by a voluntary renunciation, first of his country, and then of his life.

AMERICAN FORM IS PROOF THERE IS A BETTER WAY:

The lessons of history stand in lowly contrast to the inspired genius of the Convention process.

38:13   If these lessons teach us, on one hand, to <u>admire</u> the <u>improvement</u> made by <u>America</u> on the ancient mode of preparing and establishing regular plans of government, they serve not less, on the other, to admonish us of the <u>hazards</u> and difficulties incident to such <u>experiments</u>, and of the great imprudence of unnecessarily multiplying them.

CONSTITUTION WRITTEN WITH GREATEST OF CARE:

Any flaws in the Constitution will be the fault of inexperience with such complexity, not from a lack of care and effort.

38:14   Is it an unreasonable conjecture, that the errors which may be contained in the plan of the Convention are such as have resulted rather from the defect of antecedent experience on this complicated and difficult subject, than from a want of accuracy or care in the investigation of it; and, consequently such as will not be <u>ascertained</u> until an <u>actual trial</u> shall have pointed them out?

NO ONE SAW THE MAJOR FLAWS IN THE ARTICLES:

Not until it was actually put into effect did the major flaws in the Articles of Confederation come to light. (Note: There were five fundamental flaws—no executive, no judiciary, no taxation power, no control over commerce, and no authority to force obedience.)

38:15   This conjecture is rendered probable, not only by many considerations of a general nature, but by the particular case of the Articles of Confederation. It is observable that among the numerous objections and <u>amendments</u> suggested by the <u>several States</u>, when these articles were submitted for their ratification [speaking here of the Articles of Confederation], not one is found which alludes to the great and radical error which on actual trial has discovered itself.

AT FIRST, NO REASON TO QUESTION THE ARTICLES :

Even if there was, the States were too preoccupied with themselves than to rally around the needs of the confederacy.

38:16   And if we except the observations which New Jersey was led to make, rather by her local situation, than by her peculiar foresight, it may be questioned whether a <u>single suggestion</u> was of <u>sufficient</u> moment to justify a <u>revision of the system</u>.

STATES TOO OBSTINATE TO WORK TOGETHER:

38:17   There is abundant reason, nevertheless, to suppose that immaterial as these objections were, they would have been adhered to with a very <u>dangerous inflexibility</u>, in some States, had not a zeal for their opinions and supposed interests been stifled by the more powerful sentiment of self-preservation. <u>One State</u>,[141] we may remember, persisted for several years in <u>refusing her concurrence</u>, although the enemy remained the whole period at our gates, or rather in the very bowels of our country.

MARYLAND DIDN'T WANT TO CARRY THE BLAME:

Maryland finally concurred—not for reasons of good principles, but to avoid being blamed for the possible disaster.

38:18   Nor was her pliancy in the end effected by a less motive, than the fear of being chargeable with protracting the public calamities, and endangering the event of the contest. Every candid reader will make the proper reflections on these important facts.

EXAMPLE OF A SICK MAN SEEKING HELP:

Madison puts forward a parable of a sick man confident about his recovery options because of harmony among his doctors.

38:19   <u>A patient</u> who finds his disorder daily growing worse, and that an efficacious remedy can no longer be delayed without extreme danger, after coolly revolving his situation, and the characters of different physicians, selects and <u>calls in</u> such of them as he judges <u>most capable</u> of administering relief, and best entitled to his confidence. The physicians attend; the case of the patient is carefully examined; a consultation is held; they are unanimously agreed that the symptoms are critical, but that the case, with proper and timely relief, is so far from being desperate, that it may be made to issue in an improvement of his constitution. They are equally unanimous in prescribing the remedy, by which this happy effect is to be produced.

CRITICS' OBJECTIONS ARE CONTRADICTORY:

If those opposed to the original doctors' plan can't unify, a prudent patient would ignore the contradictory group and choose the unanimous group.

38:20   The prescription is no sooner made known, however, than a <u>number of persons interpose</u>, and, without denying the reality or danger of the disorder, assure the patient that the prescription will be poison to his constitution, <u>and forbid him</u>, under pain of certain <u>death</u>, to make use of it. Might not the patient reasonably demand, before he ventured to follow this advice, that the authors of it should at <u>least agree among</u>

---

141   *Editors' Note:* Maryland withheld its ratification of the Articles of Confederation until March 1, 1781.

themselves on some <u>other remedy</u> to be substituted? And if he found them differing as much from one another as from his first counselors, would he not act prudently in trying the <u>experiment unanimously recommended</u> by the latter, rather than be hearkening to those who could <u>neither</u> deny the necessity of a speedy remedy, nor <u>agree in proposing</u> one?

THE SICK MAN IS AMERICA, THE DOCTORS ARE THE CONVENTION:
America has chosen wise doctors to fix her problems.

38:21 Such a patient and in such a situation is <u>America at this moment</u>. She has been <u>sensible of her malady</u>. She has obtained a regular and <u>unanimous advice</u> from men of her own deliberate choice. And she is warned by others <u>against following</u> this <u>advice</u> under <u>pain of the most fatal consequences</u>.

CRITICS REJECT REMEDIES FOR FLAWED ARTICLES:
But they reject the remedy and can't agree on why the new Constitution is so harmful and dangerous.

38:22 Do the monitors deny the reality of her danger? No. Do they deny the necessity of some speedy and powerful remedy? No. Are they agreed, are any two of them agreed, in their objections to the remedy proposed, or in the proper one to be substituted? Let them speak for themselves.

FEARFUL CRITICS CAN'T AGREE ON CONSTITUTION'S FLAWS:
One argument opposes the Constitution because it's a government over people.

38:23 This one tells us that the proposed <u>Constitution</u> ought to be <u>rejected</u>, because it is <u>not</u> a <u>confederation of the States</u>, but a <u>government over individuals</u>.

A second says power over the people is okay, just not so much.

38:24 <u>Another</u> admits that it ought to be a government over individuals to a certain extent, but by no means to the extent proposed.

A third says there's no bill of rights.

38:25 A <u>third</u> does not object to the government over individuals, or to the extent proposed, but to the want of a <u>bill of rights</u>.

A fourth says a bill of rights should be for States rights, not individual rights.

38:26 A <u>fourth</u> concurs in the absolute necessity of a bill of rights, but contends that it ought to be declaratory, <u>not</u> of the personal rights of <u>individuals</u>, but of the <u>rights reserved to the States</u> in their political capacity.

A fifth says a bill of rights is superfluous except for regulating elections.

38:27 A <u>fifth</u> is of opinion that a bill of rights of any sort would be superfluous and misplaced, and that the plan would be unexceptionable but for the <u>fatal power</u> of regulating the times and <u>places of election</u>.

A sixth opposes equal representation with small States.

38:28 An <u>objector</u> in a <u>large State</u> exclaims loudly against the <u>unreasonable equality of representation</u> in the <u>Senate</u>.

A seventh opposes proportional representation in the House.

38:29 An <u>objector</u> in a <u>small State</u> is equally loud against the <u>dangerous inequality</u> in the <u>House</u> of Representatives.

An eighth objects to the cost and limitations of Congress.

38:30 From this quarter, we are alarmed with the <u>amazing expense</u>, from the <u>number of persons</u> who are to administer the new government. From another quarter, and sometimes from the same quarter, on another occasion, the cry is that the <u>Congress</u> will be but a <u>shadow of a representation</u>, and that the government would be far less objectionable if the number and the expense were doubled.

A ninth objects to direct taxes and consumption taxes.

38:31 A <u>patriot</u> in a <u>State</u> that does <u>not import or export</u>, discerns insuperable objections against the power of <u>direct taxation</u>. The patriotic adversary in a <u>State</u> of <u>great exports and imports</u>, is not less dissatisfied that the whole burden of taxes may be thrown on <u>consumption</u>.

A tenth critic sees the installation of another monarch or aristocracy.

38:32 This politician discovers in the Constitution a direct and irresistible tendency to <u>monarchy</u>; that is equally sure it will end in <u>aristocracy</u>. Another is puzzled to say which of these shapes it will ultimately assume, but sees clearly it must be <u>one or other</u> of them; whilst a fourth is not wanting, who with no less confidence affirms that the Constitution is so far from having a bias towards either of these dangers, that the weight on that side will not be sufficient to keep it upright and firm against its opposite propensities.

An eleventh fears the three branches are too intermixed.

38:33 With another class of adversaries to the Constitution the language is that the <u>legislative</u>, <u>executive</u>, and <u>judiciary</u> departments <u>are intermixed</u> in such a manner as to contradict all the ideas of regular government and all the requisite precautions in favor of liberty. Whilst this objection circulates in vague and general expressions, there are but a <u>few who lend their sanction to it</u>.

LET THEM PRESENT THE DETAILS OF THEIR FEARS:

And because they have no foundation, none will agree.

38:34 Let each one come forward with his particular explanation, and scarce any two are exactly agreed upon the subject.

One will object to the President's appointment power.

38:35 In the eyes of one the junction of the Senate with the President in the responsible function of appointing to offices, instead of vesting this executive power in the Executive alone, is the vicious part of the organization.

One will object to scant involvement in appointments by the House.

38:36 To another, the exclusion of the House of Representatives, whose numbers alone could be a due security against corruption and partiality in the exercise of such a power, is equally obnoxious.

One will object to any power in the presidency, regardless.

38:37 With another, the admission of the President into any share of a power which ever must be a dangerous engine in the hands of the executive magistrate, is an unpardonable violation of the maxims of republican jealousy.

One will object to Senate's judiciary power in impeachments.

38:38 No part of the arrangement, according to some, is more inadmissible than the trial of impeachments by the Senate, which is alternately a member both of the legislative and executive departments, when this power so evidently belonged to the judiciary department.

Others will object to the Senate's overall powers.

38:39 "We concur fully," reply others, "in the objection to this part of the plan, but we can never agree that a reference of impeachments to the judiciary authority would be an amendment of the error. Our principal dislike to the organization arises from the extensive powers already lodged in that department."

Others will object to the rise and function of a State Department.

38:40 Even among the zealous patrons of a council of state the most irreconcilable variance is discovered concerning the mode in which it ought to be constituted. The demand of one gentleman is, that the council should consist of a small number to be appointed by the most numerous branch of the legislature. Another would prefer a larger number, and considers it as a fundamental condition that the appointment should be made by the President himself.

MOST ZEALOUS CRITICS MUST HAVE SUPERIOR JUDGMENT:

As such, they must be superior to the members and the ideas they brought forward at the recent Convention.

38:41 As it can give no umbrage to the writers against the plan of the federal Constitution, let us suppose, that as they are the most zealous, so they are also the most sagacious, of those who think the late Convention were unequal to the task assigned them, and that a wiser and better plan might and ought to be substituted.

WHAT IF CRITICS FORMED A SECOND CONVENTION?

38:42 Let us further suppose that their country should concur, both in this favorable opinion of their merits, and in their unfavorable opinion of the Convention; and should accordingly proceed to form them into a second convention, with full powers, and for the express purpose of revising and remoulding the work of the first.

CRITICS COULD NOT SOLVE THEIR OWN OBJECTIONS:

Their record of discord and enmity gives proof that they have no superior plan or what that plan might even look like.

38:43 Were the experiment to be seriously made, though it required some effort to view it seriously even in fiction, I leave it to be decided by the sample of opinions just exhibited, whether, with all their enmity to their predecessors, they would, in any one point, depart so widely from their example, as in the discord and ferment that would mark their own deliberations;

NEW CONSTITUTION WILL STAND IN IMMORTALITY:

The critics would not only fail at doing better, but fail in total.

38:44 and whether the Constitution, now before the public, would not stand as fair a chance for immortality, as Lycurgus gave to that of Sparta, by making its change to depend on his own return from exile and death, if it were to be immediately adopted, and were to continue in force, not until a BETTER, but until ANOTHER should be agreed upon by this new assembly of lawgivers.

CRITICS REFUSE TO SAY THE ARTICLES TEN TIMES WORSE:

They never address the horrible flaws in the Articles that are being corrected by the new Constitution.

38:45 It is a matter both of wonder and regret, that those who raise so many objections against the new Constitution should never call to mind the defects of that which is to be exchanged for it. It is not <u>necessary that the former should be perfect</u>; it is sufficient that the latter is more <u>imperfect</u>.

NO SANE PERSON REFUSES BETTER OVER WORSE:
Even if the better wasn't perfect, it remains preferable.

38:46 No man would refuse to give brass for silver or gold, because the latter had some alloy in it. No man would refuse to <u>quit a shattered and tottering habitation for a firm and commodious building, because the latter had not a porch</u> to it, or because some of the rooms might be a little larger or smaller, or the ceilings a little higher or lower than his fancy would have planned them.

OBJECTIONS SHOULD ALSO BE APPLIED TO ARTICLES:
The objections against the Constitution would weigh ten times heavier if the same were used to assess the Articles.

38:47 But waiving illustrations of this sort, is it not manifest that most of the capital objections urged against the new system lie with tenfold weight against the existing Confederation?

CONGRESS'S TAXING POWER IS ALREADY IN ARTICLES:

38:48 Is an <u>indefinite power to raise money</u> dangerous in the hands of the federal government? The present Congress <u>can make requisitions to any amount they please</u>, and the States are constitutionally bound to furnish them; they can emit bills of credit as long as they will pay for the paper; they can borrow, both abroad and at home, as long as a shilling will be lent.

ARTICLES ALREADY ALLOW THE RAISING OF TROOPS:

38:49 Is an indefinite power to raise <u>troops dangerous</u>? The Confederation gives to Congress that power also; and they have already begun to make use of it.

ARTICLES ALREADY CONCENTRATE ALL POWERS:

38:50 Is it improper and unsafe to <u>intermix</u> the different <u>powers of government</u> in the same body of men? Congress, a single body of men, are the sole depositary of all the federal powers.

ARTICLES GIVE TREASURY AND ARMY TO CONGRESS:

38:51 Is it particularly dangerous to give the <u>keys of the treasury</u>, and the <u>command of the army</u>, into the same hands? The Confederation places them both in the hands of Congress.

ARTICLES HAVE NO BILL OF RIGHTS

38:52 Is a <u>bill of rights essential</u> to liberty? The Confederation has no bill of rights.

ARTICLES ALREADY LET CONGRESS MAKE TREATIES:

38:53 Is it an objection against the new Constitution, that it empowers the <u>Senate</u>, with the concurrence of the Executive, to <u>make treaties</u> which are to be the laws of the land? The existing Congress, without any such control, can make treaties which they themselves have declared, and most of the States have recognized, to be the <u>supreme law of the land</u>.

ARTICLES DON'T STOP IMPORTATION OF SLAVES:
But the new Constitution does, with a phase-out period of twenty years.

38:54 Is the importation of slaves permitted by the new Constitution for twenty years? By the old it is <u>permitted forever</u>.

FEDERAL POWERS REST ON STATES AND PEOPLE:

38:55 I shall be told, that however dangerous this <u>mixture</u> of powers may be in theory, it is rendered harmless by the dependence of Congress on the State for the means of carrying them into practice; that however large the mass of <u>powers</u> may be, it is in fact a <u>lifeless mass</u>.

ARTICLES ARE TOOTHLESS ON FEDERAL DUTIES:

38:56 Then, say I, in the first place, that the <u>Confederation</u> is chargeable with the <u>still greater folly</u> of declaring certain powers in the federal government to be <u>absolutely necessary</u>, and at the same time rendering them <u>absolutely nugatory</u>;

IF ARTICLES REMAIN IN PLACE, MASSIVE CHANGES ARE NEEDED:

38:57 and, in the next place, that if the Union is to continue, and no better government be substituted, effective powers must either be granted to, or assumed by, the <u>existing Congress</u>; in either of which events, the contrast just stated will hold good.

VIOLATING THE ARTICLES:
Congress has already been violating the Articles and exercising many powers it was not given.

38:58 But this is not all. Out of this lifeless mass has already grown an **excrescent**[142] power, which tends to realize all the dangers that can be apprehended from a <u>defective construction</u> of the <u>supreme government</u> of the Union.

---

142 ***excrescent:*** An abnormal, excessive, or useless outgrowth.

LANDS WESTWARD OFFER HUGE POTENTIAL:
Under correct management these lands could pay off the national debt.

38:59   It is now no longer a point of speculation and hope, that the Western territory is a mine of vast wealth to the United States; and although it is not of such a nature as to extricate them from their present distresses, or for some time to come, to yield any regular supplies for the public expenses, yet must it hereafter be able, under proper management, both to effect a gradual discharge of the domestic debt, and to furnish, for a certain period, liberal tributes to the federal treasury.

STATES HAVE SURRENDERED CLAIMS TO WESTERN LANDS:

38:60   A very large proportion of this fund has been already surrendered by individual States; and it may with reason be expected that the remaining States will not persist in withholding similar proofs of their equity and generosity.

CONGRESS IS ILLEGALLY DEVELOPING THE WEST:
These actions are in direct violation of the Articles.

38:61   We may calculate, therefore, that a rich and fertile country, of an area equal to the inhabited extent of the United States, will soon become a national stock. Congress have assumed the administration of this stock. They have begun to render it productive.

CONGRESS IS ILLEGALLY FORMING NEW STATES:

38:62   Congress have undertaken to do more: they have proceeded to form new States, to erect temporary governments, to appoint officers for them, and to prescribe the conditions on which such States shall be admitted into the Confederacy.

MANY CONGRESSIONAL ACTS VIOLATE THE ARTICLES:

38:63   All this has been done; and done without the least color of constitutional authority. Yet no blame has been whispered; no alarm has been sounded.

SINGLE BODY OF MEN CAN BUILD MASSIVE ARMY:
Under the Articles, Congress could raise troops indefinitely.

38:64   A GREAT and INDEPENDENT fund of revenue is passing into the hands of a SINGLE BODY of men, who can RAISE TROOPS to an INDEFINITE NUMBER, and appropriate money to their support for an INDEFINITE PERIOD OF TIME.

CRITICS READILY DISREGARD THESE MANY ABUSES:
They are inconsistent regarding the violations of the Articles, and yet ridicule the necessary corrections offered by the Constitution.

38:65   And yet there are men, who have not only been silent spectators of this prospect, but who are advocates for the system which exhibits it; and, at the same time, urge against the new system the objections which we have heard. Would they not act with more consistency, in urging the establishment of the latter, as no less necessary to guard the Union against the future powers and resources of a body constructed like the existing Congress, than to save it from the dangers threatened by the present impotency of that Assembly?

CONGRESS EXCEEDS AUTHORITY OUT OF NECESSITY:
Usurping powers to properly serve the people is more proof that a government without power to do its job is unstable, dangerous, and needs to be replaced.

38:66   I mean not, by any thing here said, to throw censure on the measures which have been pursued by Congress. I am sensible they could not have done otherwise. The public interest, the necessity of the case, imposed upon them the task of overleaping their constitutional limits. But is not the fact an alarming proof of the danger resulting from a government which does not possess regular powers commensurate to its objects? A dissolution or usurpation is the dreadful dilemma to which it is continually exposed.

—PUBLIUS

REVIEW QUESTIONS

1. In free societies of the past, who usually got the job to write a constitution? (38:1)

2. Who were some of these solo creators of national law? (38:2–7)

3. Why was that important task of writing a constitution given to just one man? (38:10)

4. How was the American system of creating a constitution superior? (38:14)

5. What must happen to discern any flaws with the Constitution? (38:14)

6. Did anyone notice or look for flaws in the Articles? (38:15–17)

7. What does Madison's parable of a sick patient teach? (38:19–22)

8. How many complaints by the Anti-Federalists does

Madison list? (38:22–40)

9. Could the Anti-Federalists holding a second Convention do any better than the first? (38:41–44)

10. While critics of the new Constitution are happy to point out weaknesses, are they willing to apply the same level of criticism to the Articles of Confederation? (38:45–47)

11. Are the Articles being violated right now? Is that proof of their weakness? (38:60–66)

FEDERALIST NO. 39

EXAMINING THE FORMS OF REPUBLICAN, FEDERAL, STATE, AND NATIONAL GOVERNMENT: America is a republic with representatives, not a democracy with "one man, one vote." The government is partly national (over all the people individually regardless of State boundaries), and partly federal (over the several sovereign States). These distinctions are important because the people are leery of a strong federal government, of adopting another monarchy. The real form of republican government doesn't exist in countries claiming to be republics, but in America it does with direct or indirect control by the people, free elections, limited periods in office, and no favoritism or caste system.

By James Madison—January 16, 1788

HOW TO IMPLEMENT THE NEW CONSTITUTION:

39:1 THE last paper having concluded the observations which were meant to introduce a candid survey of the plan of government reported by the Convention, we now proceed to the execution of that part of our undertaking.

IS THE NEW GOVERNMENT STRICTLY REPUBLICAN?

A republican form of government (with representatives), not a democracy (one man, one vote), is the only kind of government America would have.

39:2 The first question that offers itself is, whether the general form and aspect of the government be strictly republican.

AMERICAN PEOPLE WOULD ACCEPT NO OTHER:

39:3 It is evident that no other form would be reconcilable with the genius of the people of America; with the funda-

mental principles of the Revolution; or with that honorable determination which animates every votary of freedom, to rest all our political experiments on the capacity of mankind for self-government.

REJECT CONSTITUTION IF NOT REPUBLICAN IN FORM:

39:4 If the plan of the Convention, therefore, be found to depart from the republican character, its advocates must abandon it as no longer defensible.

REPUBLICAN NOT DEFINED:

The meaning of the term "republican" has not been cleanly settled. Even John Adams said he wasn't sure exactly what it meant.[143]

39:5 What, then, are the distinctive characters of the republican form? Were an answer to this question to be sought, not by recurring to principles, but in the application of the term by political writers, to the constitution of different States, no satisfactory one would ever be found.

EXAMPLES OF REPUBLICS THAT ACTUALLY ARE NOT:

39:6 Holland, in which no particle of the supreme authority is derived from the people, has passed almost universally under the denomination of a republic. The same title has been bestowed on Venice, where absolute power over the great body of the people is exercised, in the most absolute manner, by a small body of hereditary nobles. Poland, which is a mixture of aristocracy and of monarchy in their worst forms, has been dignified with the same appellation.

ENGLAND'S REPUBLIC ALSO NOT A TRUE FORM:

39:7 The government of England, which has one republican branch only, combined with an hereditary aristocracy and monarchy, has, with equal impropriety, been frequently placed on the list of republics.

THE TERM *REPUBLIC* IS GENERALLY MISUSED:

39:8 These examples, which are nearly as dissimilar to each other as to a genuine republic, show the extreme inaccuracy with which the term has been used in political disquisitions.

DEFINITION OF REPUBLICAN GOVERNMENT:

39:9 If we resort for a criterion to the different principles on which different forms of government are established, we may define a republic to be, or at least may bestow that name on, a government which derives all its powers directly or indirectly from the great body of the people, and is administered

---

143 *Editors' Note:* John Adams defended his support of the republican form but admitted, "The word is so loose and indefinite that successive predominant factions will put glosses and constructions upon it as different as light and darkness." Letter from John Adams to Mercy Warren, July 20, 1807.

by persons holding their offices during pleasure, for a limited period, or during good behavior.

ELECTED BY ALL, NOT BY ELITES OR THE PRIVILEGED:
Government is derived from All of society, not special classes.

39:10   It is ESSENTIAL to such a government that it be derived from the great body of the society, not from an inconsiderable proportion, or a favored class of it; otherwise a handful of tyrannical nobles, exercising their oppressions by a delegation of their powers, might aspire to the rank of republicans, and claim for their government the honorable title of republic.

KEY STRENGTH: PEOPLE PICK TEMPORARY LEADERS:
Elected positions must be for terms, not for eternity.

39:11   It is SUFFICIENT for such a government that the persons administering it be appointed, either directly or indirectly, by the people; and that they hold their appointments by either of the tenures just specified;

REPUBLIC INCLUDES REGULAR AND FREE ELECTIONS:

39:12   otherwise every government in the United States, as well as every other popular government that has been or can be well organized or well executed, would be degraded from the republican character.

SOME LEADERS ELECTED INDIRECTLY:

39:13   According to the constitution of every State in the Union, some or other of the officers of government are appointed indirectly only by the people. According to most of them, the chief magistrate himself is so appointed. And according to one, this mode of appointment is extended to one of the co-ordinate branches of the legislature.

HIGHEST LEADER HAS A DEFINED, TEMPORARY TERM:
The judiciary, on the other hand, are in office for life.

39:14   According to all the constitutions, also, the tenure of the highest offices is extended to a definite period, and in many instances, both within the legislative and executive departments, to a period of years. According to the provisions of most of the constitutions, again, as well as according to the most respectable and received opinions on the subject, the members of the judiciary department are to retain their offices by the firm tenure of good behavior.

BY THIS MEASURE THE CONSTITUTION SETS UP A REPUBLIC:

39:15   On comparing the Constitution planned by the Convention with the standard here fixed, we perceive at once that it is, in the most rigid sense, conformable to it. The House of Representatives, like that of one branch at least of all the State legislatures, is elected immediately by the great body of the people. The Senate, like the present Congress, and the Senate of Maryland, derives its appointment indirectly from the people. The President is indirectly derived from the choice of the people, according to the example in most of the States. Even the judges, with all other officers of the Union, will, as in the several States, be the choice, though a remote choice, of the people themselves.

ANOTHER REPUBLICAN TRAIT IS LIMITED LENGTH OF TERMS:
This pattern is already common in America.

39:16   The duration of the appointments is equally conformable to the republican standard, and to the model of State constitutions The House of Representatives is periodically elective, as in all the States; and for the period of two years, as in the State of South Carolina. The Senate is elective, for the period of six years; which is but one year more than the period of the Senate of Maryland, and but two more than that of the Senates of New York and Virginia.

PRESIDENT'S TERM AND POWER TO REMOVE HIM:
These, too, are traits of a republican form of government.

39:17   The President is to continue in office for the period of four years; as in New York and Delaware, the chief magistrate is elected for three years, and in South Carolina for two years. In the other States the election is annual. In several of the States, however, no constitutional provision is made for the impeachment of the chief magistrate. And in Delaware and Virginia he is not impeachable till out of office. The President of the United States is impeachable at any time during his continuance in office.

APPOINTMENT FOR LIFE IS PROPER FOR JUDGES:

39:18   The tenure by which the judges are to hold their places, is, as it unquestionably ought to be, that of good behavior.

LOWER OFFICE TERMS SET BY STATE LEGISLATURES:

39:19   The tenure of the ministerial offices generally, will be a subject of legal regulation, conformably to the reason of the case and the example of the State constitutions.

TITLES OF NOBILITY STRICTLY FORBIDDEN:
Guarantee of a republican form on all other levels retains republican form.

39:20 Could any further proof be required of the republican complexion of this system, the most decisive one might be found in its <u>absolute prohibition</u> of <u>titles of **nobility**,</u>[144] both under the federal and the State governments; and in its express <u>guaranty</u> of the <u>republican form to each of the latter</u>.

CRITICS NOT SATISFIED:
They claim the Constitution fails to sustain a true republican form.

39:21 "But it was not sufficient," say the adversaries of the proposed Constitution, "for the Convention to adhere to the <u>republican form</u>. They ought, with equal care, to have preserved the <u>FEDERAL form</u>, which regards the Union as a <u>CONFEDERACY of sovereign</u> states; instead of which, they have framed a NATIONAL government, which regards the <u>Union as a CONSOLIDATION of the States</u>."

THE OBJECTION REQUIRES CLOSE EXAMINATION:
39:22 And it is asked by what authority this bold and radical innovation was undertaken? The handle which has been made of this objection requires that it should be examined with some precision.

THREE BASIC QUESTIONS ABOUT REPUBLICAN FORM:
The way to understand the new government is to first understand the answer to three basic questions.

39:23 Without inquiring into the accuracy of the distinction on which the objection is founded, it will be necessary to a just estimate of its force,

What is its real foundation? (See No. 39)

39:24 first, to ascertain the <u>real character of the government</u> in question;

Where does it get its powers? (See No. 40)

39:25 secondly, to inquire <u>how far the Convention were authorized to propose such a government</u>; and

What is the extent of its power and can it manage future growth? (See Nos. 41–58)

39:26 thirdly, <u>how far the duty they owed</u> to their country could supply any defect of regular authority.

FIRST QUESTION:
What is the foundation of power?

39:27 First. In order to ascertain the real character of the government, it may be considered in relation to the foundation on which it is to be established;

Sources of power.

39:28 to the <u>sources from which its ordinary powers</u> are to be drawn;

Operation of powers.

39:29 to the operation of those powers;

Extent of powers.

39:30 to the extent of them;

Future changes.

39:31 and to the authority by which future changes in the government are to be introduced.

CONSTITUTION RESTS ON ASSENT OF THE PEOPLE:
The people ratify this Constitution, not as a whole people but as citizens of sovereign States choosing deputies to cast the votes.

39:32 On examining the first relation, it appears, on one hand, that the Constitution is to be founded on the <u>assent and ratification of the people</u> of America, given by deputies elected for the special purpose; but, on the other, that this <u>assent</u> and <u>ratification</u> is to be given by <u>the people</u>, not as individuals composing one entire nation, but as composing the distinct and <u>independent States</u> to which they respectively belong. It is to be the assent and ratification of the several States, derived from the <u>supreme authority in each State</u>, the authority of the <u>people themselves</u>. The act, therefore, establishing the Constitution, will <u>not</u> be a <u>NATIONAL</u>, but <u>a FEDERAL act</u>.

MAJORITY OF STATES OR THE PEOPLE NOT ENOUGH:
Ratification by majority of people or States is not the goal. Ratification by unanimous consent of the thirteen States is the goal.

39:33 That it will be a federal and not a national act, as these terms are understood by the objectors; the act of the <u>people</u>, as forming so many <u>independent States</u>, <u>not</u> as forming <u>one aggregate nation</u>, is obvious from this single consideration, that it is to result neither from the decision of a MAJORITY of the people of the Union, nor from that of a MAJORITY of the States.

---

144 **nobility:** A class of people who receive privileges at the expense of the rest of the people.

EACH STATE MUST VOLUNTARILY RATIFY:
The will of the whole can't decide ratification because it is then rule by majority. Instead, each State sends deputies to represent their desire. The unanimous vote is by thirteen States, not three million people.

39:34 It must result from the UNANIMOUS assent of the several States that are parties to it, differing no otherwise from their ordinary assent than in its being expressed, not by the legislative authority, but by that of the people themselves. Were the people regarded in this transaction as forming one nation, the will of the majority of the whole people of the United States would bind the minority, in the same manner as the majority in each State must bind the minority; and the will of the majority must be determined either by a comparison of the individual votes, or by considering the will of the majority of the States as evidence of the will of a majority of the people of the United States. Neither of these rules have been adopted.[145]

CONSTITUTION IS PART FEDERAL, PART NATIONAL:
It is federal by the States as entities ratifying it, and national by the people electing delegates to a ratifying Convention.

39:35 Each State, in ratifying the Constitution, is considered as a sovereign body, independent of all others, and only to be bound by its own voluntary act. In this relation, then, the new Constitution will, if established, be a FEDERAL, and not a NATIONAL constitution.

SECOND QUESTION:
From where are the ordinary political powers derived?

39:36 The next relation is, to the sources from which the ordinary powers of government are to be derived.

GOVERNMENT IS NATIONAL:
The House of Representatives gives the government its national condition.

39:37 The House of Representatives will derive its powers from the people of America; and the people will be represented in the same proportion, and on the same principle, as they are in the legislature of a particular State. So far the government is NATIONAL, not FEDERAL.

GOVERNMENT IS FEDERAL:
Senate is a federal component (until the Seventeenth Amendment excluded the legislatures, making it more national).

39:38 The Senate, on the other hand, will derive its powers from the States, as political and coequal societies; and these will be represented on the principle of equality in the Senate, as they now are in the existing Congress. So far the government is FEDERAL, not NATIONAL.

EXECUTIVE POWER FROM COMPOUND SOURCE:
America's government is technically a mixed government containing elements of both federal and national features. The executive power comes from that mixed source.

39:39 The executive power will be derived from a very compound source. The immediate election of the President is to be made by the States in their political characters. The votes allotted to them are in a compound ratio, which considers them partly as distinct and coequal societies, partly as unequal members of the same society. The eventual election, again, is to be made by that branch of the legislature which consists of the national representatives; but in this particular act they are to be thrown into the form of individual delegations, from so many distinct and coequal bodies politic.

MIXED CHARACTER WHEN ELECTING PRESIDENT:
39:40 From this aspect of the government it appears to be of a mixed character, presenting at least as many FEDERAL as NATIONAL features.

GOVERNMENT IS MORE NATIONAL THAN FEDERAL:
The Constitution acts on the people as Americans more than on the States as sovereign political entities. Generally speaking, what is America's new government, federal or national?

39:41 The difference between a federal and national government, as it relates to the OPERATION OF THE GOVERNMENT, is supposed to consist in this,

ACTING ON STATES AS ENTITIES, AND ON INDIVIDUAL CITIZENS:
39:42 that in the former [federal] the powers operate on the political bodies composing the Confederacy, in their political capacities; in the latter [national], on the individual citizens composing the nation, in their individual capacities.

CONSTITUTION IS MOSTLY NATIONAL:
Federal traits appear, for example, when resolving disputes between the States.

---

145 *Editors' Note:* Thomas Jefferson said the majority must rule—"The first principle of republicanism is that the *lex majoris partis* is the fundamental law of every society of individuals of equal right; to consider the will of the society announced by the majority of a single vote as sacred as if unanimous is the first of all lessons of importance, yet the last which is thoroughly learned. This law once disregarded, no other remains but that of force, which ends necessarily in military despotism." Paul Leicester Ford, *Writings of Thomas Jefferson*, 10:89. (Underlining added)

39:43 On trying the Constitution by this criterion, it falls under the NATIONAL, not the FEDERAL character; though perhaps not so completely as has been understood. In several cases, and particularly in the trial of controversies to which States may be parties, they must be viewed and proceeded against in their collective and political capacities only.

SOME FEDERAL TRAITS MUST ALSO EXIST:
39:44 So far the national countenance of the government on this side seems to be disfigured by a few federal features. But this blemish is perhaps unavoidable in any plan; and the operation of the government on the people, in their individual capacities, in its ordinary and most essential proceedings, may, on the whole, designate it, in this relation, a NATIONAL government.

NATIONAL GOVERNMENT'S POWER IS FEDERAL:
The government is national because it can use its powers on individual citizens. It is federal because those powers are restricted on the federal level by mutual agreement among the States.

39:45 But if the government be national with regard to the OPERATION of its powers, it changes its aspect again when we contemplate it in relation to the EXTENT of its powers.

Purely national government has indefinite supreme authority.

39:46 The idea of a national government involves in it, not only an authority over the individual citizens, but an indefinite supremacy over all persons and things, so far as they are objects of lawful government.

National Congress reigns supreme. In a mixed system, supreme power is shared between federal government and States.

39:47 Among a people consolidated into one nation, this supremacy is completely vested in the national legislature. Among communities united for particular purposes, it is vested partly in the general and partly in the municipal legislatures.

A purely national government could abolish local leadership.

39:48 In the former case, all local authorities are subordinate to the supreme; and may be controlled, directed, or abolished by it at pleasure.

LOCAL GOVERNMENTS ARE PROTECTED:
39:49 In the latter, the local or municipal authorities form distinct and independent portions of the supremacy, no more subject, within their respective spheres, to the general authority, than the general authority is subject to them, within its own sphere.

POWERS RESERVED TO STATES AND PEOPLE:
Federal government has certain listed rights superior to the States as entities, and in that regard it is not a national government.

39:50 In this relation, then, the proposed government cannot be deemed a NATIONAL one; since its jurisdiction extends to certain enumerated objects only, and leaves to the several States a residuary and inviolable sovereignty over all other objects.

IMPARTIAL TRIBUNAL NEEDED TO PREVENT WAR:
A tribunal must be in the general government where national authority and force can safely reside.

39:51 It is true that in controversies relating to the boundary between the two jurisdictions, the tribunal which is ultimately to decide, is to be established under the general government. But this does not change the principle of the case. The decision is to be impartially made, according to the rules of the Constitution; and all the usual and most effectual precautions are taken to secure this impartiality. Some such tribunal is clearly essential to prevent an appeal to the sword and a dissolution of the compact; and that it ought to be established under the general rather than under the local governments, or, to speak more properly, that it could be safely established under the first alone, is a position not likely to be combated.

IF PEOPLE ALONE CAN RATIFY, IT IS NATIONAL:
More proof that the Constitution is a mixture of federal and national models is that the people alone could not ratify it.

39:52 If we try the Constitution by its last relation to the authority by which amendments are to be made, we find it neither wholly NATIONAL nor wholly FEDERAL.

WHOLLY NATIONAL AND MAJORITY OF PEOPLE RULES:
Such a majority could, if it wanted to, alter or abolish the Constitution.

39:53 Were it wholly national, the supreme and ultimate authority would reside in the MAJORITY of the people of the Union; and this authority would be competent at all times, like that of a majority of every national society, to alter or abolish its established government.

WHOLLY FEDERAL MEANS ALL STATES MUST CONCUR:

39:54 Were it wholly federal, on the other hand, the concurrence of each State in the Union would be essential to every alteration that would be binding on all.

NEITHER PRINCIPLE APPLIES COMPLETELY:

Depending on the duty it manages, the federal government is many things.

39:55 The mode provided by the plan of the Convention is not founded on either of these principles. In requiring more than a majority, and principles, in requiring more than a majority, and particularly in computing the proportion by STATES, not by CITIZENS, it departs from the NATIONAL and advances towards the FEDERAL character; in rendering the concurrence of less than the whole number of States sufficient, it loses again the FEDERAL and partakes of the NATIONAL character.

GOVERNMENT IS BOTH NATIONAL AND FEDERAL:

Technically speaking it is neither national nor federal.

39:56 The proposed Constitution, therefore, is, in strictness, neither a national nor a federal Constitution, but a composition of both.

Foundation is federal.

39:57 In its foundation it is federal, not national;

Sources of power are both.

39:58 in the sources from which the ordinary powers of the government are drawn, it is partly federal and partly national;

Use of powers is national.

39:59 in the operation of these powers, it is national, not federal;

Extent of powers is federal.

39:60 in the extent of them, again, it is federal, not national;

Introducing Amendments is both.

39:61 and, finally, in the authoritative mode of introducing amendments, it is neither wholly federal nor wholly national.

—PUBLIUS

REVIEW QUESTIONS

1. What is the first question this paper will discuss? (39:1–2)

2. What form of government did the American people fight for in the War for Independence? (39:2–3)

3. Is the term *republican government* frequently wrongly applied? (39:8)

4. What are the definition and characteristics of a Republic? (39:9–14)

5. What are some of the ways the Constitution conforms to these republican principles? (39:15–20)

6. On what foundation is the Constitution founded? (39:32)

7. In what respect is the Constitution a federal constitution? (39:35)

8. In what respect is the Constitution a national constitution? (39:37)

9. What does the government become when the Senate is appointed by the States? (39:38)

10. What then is the form of America's government? (39:56–61)

FEDERALIST NO. 40

THE CONVENTION DID NOT EXCEED ITS AUTHORITY: The Constitutional Convention was given two prime directives: Use the Articles to build a "national and adequate government," and make necessary "alterations and provisions in the Articles of Confederation" to meet the urgent demands and needs of the nation. Correcting the Articles' flaws and shortcomings required more than a few alterations. To answer the first directive, massive restructuring had to take place. This renovation process did not differ from that which produced the original Articles. In the end several dozen provisions in the Articles were retained in the Constitution. In performing its directives, the Convention did not exceed the authority given it by Congress.

James Madison—January 18, 1788

DID THE CONVENTION HAVE LEGAL AUTHORITY?

40:1 THE SECOND point to be examined is, whether the Convention were authorized to frame and propose this mixed Constitution.

GRANTING AUTHORITY TO CONVENTION DELEGATES:

The idea to fix the Articles was formalized at the Annapolis meeting and then was made official by Congress in 1787.

40:2 The powers of the Convention ought, in strictness, to be determined by an inspection of the commissions given to the members by their respective constituents. As All of these, however, had reference, either to the recommendation from the meeting at Annapolis, in September, 1786, or to that from Congress, in February, 1787, it will be sufficient to recur to these particular acts.

OFFICIAL ANNAPOLIS RECOMMENDATION:
This is a beautiful summary statement of the Convention's purpose.

40:3 The act from Annapolis recommends the "appointment of commissioners to take into consideration the situation of the United States; to devise SUCH FURTHER PROVISIONS as shall appear to them necessary to render the Constitution of the federal government ADEQUATE TO THE EXIGENCIES OF THE UNION; and to report[146] such an act for that purpose, to the United States in Congress assembled, as when agreed to by them, and afterwards confirmed by the legislature of every State, will effectually provide for the same."

THE FORMAL ACT OF CONGRESS:

40:4 The recommendatory act of Congress is in the words following: "WHEREAS, there is provision in the articles of Confederation and perpetual Union, for making alterations therein, by the assent of a Congress of the United States, and of the legislatures of the several States; and whereas experience hath evinced, that there are defects in the present Confederation; as a mean to remedy which, several of the States, and PARTICULARLY THE STATE OF NEW YORK, by express instructions to their delegates in Congress, have suggested a convention for the purposes expressed in the following resolution; and such convention appearing to be the most probable mean of establishing in these States A FIRM NATIONAL GOVERNMENT."

THE FORMAL ACT OF CONGRESS, CONTINUED:
40:5 "Resolved,—That in the opinion of Congress it is expedient, that on the second Monday of May next a convention of delegates, who shall have been appointed by the several States, be held at Philadelphia, for the sole and express purpose OF THE ARTICLES OF CONFEDERATION, and reporting to Congress and the several legislatures such ALTERATIONS AND PROVISIONS THEREIN, as shall, when agreed to in Congress, and confirmed by the States, render the federal Constitution ADEQUATE TO THE EXIGENCIES OF GOVERNMENT AND THE PRESERVATION OF THE UNION."

MADISON'S SUMMARY OF THE FOUR OBJECTIVES:

40:6 From these two acts, it appears,

First, form a stable government.

40:7 1st, that the object of the Convention was to establish, in these States, A FIRM NATIONAL GOVERNMENT;

Second, give it sufficient power to do the job.

40:8 2d, that this government was to be such as would be ADEQUATE TO THE EXIGENCIES OF GOVERNMENT and THE PRESERVATION OF THE UNION;

Third, make *all* necessary changes.

40:9 3d, that these purposes were to be effected by ALTERATIONS AND PROVISIONS IN THE ARTICLES OF CONFEDERATION, as it is expressed in the act of Congress, or by SUCH FURTHER PROVISIONS AS SHOULD APPEAR NECESSARY, as it stands in the recommendatory act from Annapolis;

Fourth, present it to the States and ratify.

40:10 4th, that the alterations and provisions were to be reported to Congress, and to the States, in order to be agreed to by the former and confirmed by the latter.

GOAL WAS TO DO WHAT WAS NEEDED TO CORRECT ARTICLES:

40:11 From a comparison and fair construction of these several modes of expression, is to be deduced the authority under which the Convention acted. They were to frame a NATIONAL GOVERNMENT, adequate to the EXIGENCIES OF GOVERNMENT, and OF THE UNION; and to reduce the articles of Confederation into such form as to accomplish these purposes.

MAKING SENSE OF THE CALL TO FIX THE PROBLEMS:

40:12 There are two rules of construction, dictated by plain reason, as well as founded on legal axioms.

Every part has meaning.

40:13 The one is, that every part of the expression ought, if possible, to be allowed some meaning, and be made to conspire to some common end.

End goal is most important of all, not the process.

40:14 The other is, that where the several parts cannot be made to coincide, the less important should give way to the more important part; the means should be sacrificed to the end, rather than the end to the means.

CONVENTION HAD A DILEMMA:
What if the Articles of Confederation could not be sufficiently altered to meet the objectives of an "adequate government" as established by Congress?

---

146 *exigencies:* An urgent need or demand, or a special situation in the current state of affairs.

40:15   Suppose, then, that the expressions defining the authority of the Convention were irreconcilably at variance with each other; that a NATIONAL and ADEQUATE GOVERNMENT could not possibly, in the judgment of the Convention, be affected by ALTERATIONS and PROVISIONS in the ARTICLES OF CONFEDERATION; which part of the definition ought to have been embraced, and which rejected? Which was the more important, which the less important part? Which the end; which the means?

LET THE CRITICS PROVE THEMSELVES:
40:16   Let the most scrupulous expositors of delegated powers; let the most inveterate objectors against those exercised by the Convention, answer these questions.

WHICH IS THE REAL GOAL, THE ENDS OR THE MEANS?
The critics wish to retain a flawed government.

40:17   Let them declare, whether it was of most importance to the happiness of the people of America, that the articles of Confederation should be disregarded, and an adequate government be provided, and the Union preserved; or that an adequate government should be omitted, and the articles of Confederation preserved.

WAS PRESERVATION OF ARTICLES THE REAL GOAL?
The end goal was a working government, not preserving Articles.

40:18   Let them declare, whether the preservation of these articles was the end, for securing which a reform of the government was to be introduced as the means; or whether the establishment of a government, adequate to the national happiness, was the end at which these articles themselves originally aimed, and to which they ought, as insufficient means, to have been sacrificed.

CAN THE ARTICLES BE SUFFICIENTLY ALTERED?
Critics must declare that no, they can't be adequately changed.

40:19   But is it necessary to suppose that these expressions are absolutely irreconcilable to each other; that no ALTERATIONS or PROVISIONS in THE ARTICLES OF THE CONFEDERATION could possibly mold them into a national and adequate government; into such a government as has been proposed by the Convention?

CHANGING THE NAME CAUSES NO GREAT HARM:
40:20   No stress, it is presumed, will, in this case, be laid on the TITLE; a change of that could never be deemed an exercise of ungranted power.

CHANGING THE BODY IS AUTHORIZED:
40:21   ALTERATIONS in the body of the instrument are expressly authorized.

NEW PROVISIONS ARE AUTHORIZED:
40:22   NEW PROVISIONS therein are also expressly authorized. Here then is a power to change the title; to insert new articles; to alter old ones.

WHERE IS LINE BETWEEN ALTERATION AND TRANSMUTATION?
The power to change the Articles is expressly granted in the Articles themselves. Where those powers are used and parts of the Articles remain, it was a legal and proper action. What must those objectors do who say that changing the Articles was illegal?

40:23   Must it of necessity be admitted that this power is infringed, so long as a part of the old articles remain? Those who maintain the affirmative ought at least to mark the boundary between authorized and usurped innovations; between that degree of change which lies within the compass of ALTERATIONS AND FURTHER PROVISIONS, and that which amounts to a **TRANSMUTATION**[147] of the government. Will it be said that the alterations ought not to have touched the substance of the Confederation?

SUBSTANTIAL REFORM WAS FULLY EXPECTED:
The fundamental principles of the Articles were expected to be examined and improved by the Convention.

40:24   The States would never have appointed a convention with so much solemnity, nor described its objects with so much latitude, if some SUBSTANTIAL reform had not been in contemplation. Will it be said that the FUNDAMENTAL PRINCIPLES of the Confederation were not within the purview of the Convention, and ought not to have been varied?

WHICH PRINCIPLES FROM ARTICLES ARE RETAINED?
40:25   I ask, What are these principles?

STATES REMAIN INDEPENDENT SOVEREIGNS:
40:26   Do they require that, in the establishment of the Constitution, the States should be regarded as distinct and independent sovereigns? They are so regarded by the Constitution proposed.

---

147 *transmutation:* The process of changing one thing into something completely different.

SENATORS ELECTED BY LEGISLATURES:

This distinction is important. In order to treat the States as entities, there needed to be representatives of the State entity. That was the senator appointed by the legislature. That chain on the federal government was broken with passage of the Seventeenth Amendment.

40:27 Do they require that the members of the government should derive their appointment from the legislatures, not from the people of the States? One branch of the new government is to be appointed by these legislatures; and under the Confederation, the delegates to Congress MAY ALL be appointed immediately by the people, and in two States[148] are actually so appointed.

POWER TO ACT DIRECTLY ON THE STATES IS RETAINED:

This is expanded to act on individuals as well—a necessary alteration.

40:28 Do they require that the powers of the government should act on the States, and not immediately on individuals? In some instances, as has been shown, the powers of the new government will act on the States in their collective characters. In some instances, also, those of the existing government act immediately on individuals.

FEDERAL POWER ON INDIVIDUALS IS RETAINED:

These Confederate powers are retained in Article I Section 8 of the new Constitution.

40:29 In cases of capture; of piracy; of the post office; of coins, weights, and measures; of trade with the Indians; of claims under grants of land by different States; and, above all, in the case of trials by courts-marshal in the army and navy, by which death may be inflicted without the intervention of a jury, or even of a civil magistrate; in all these cases the powers of the Confederation operate immediately on the persons and interests of individual citizens.

POWER TO TAX IS RETAINED AND ENLARGED:

States and the federal government both have unlimited power to tax.

40:30 Do these fundamental principles require, particularly, that no tax should be levied without the intermediate agency of the States? The Confederation itself authorizes a direct tax, to a certain extent, on the post office. The power of coinage has been so construed by Congress as to levy a tribute immediately from that source also.

REGULATION OF COMMERCE FINALLY AUTHORIZED:

Now, finally, this flaw in the Articles about which Congress repeatedly expressed concern, is now corrected.

40:31 But pretermitting these instances, was it not an acknowledged object of the Convention and the universal expectation of the people, that the regulation of trade should be submitted to the general government in such a form as would render it an immediate source of general revenue? Had not Congress repeatedly recommended this measure as not inconsistent with the fundamental principles of the Confederation? Had not every State but one; had not New York herself, so far complied with the plan of Congress as to recognize the PRINCIPLE of the innovation?

STATES RIGHTS ARE RETAINED:

In both the Articles and the new Constitution, the federal government's powers are enumerated and limited.

40:32 Do these principles, in fine, require that the powers of the general government should be limited, and that, beyond this limit, the States should be left in possession of their sovereignty and independence? We have seen that in the new government, as in the old, the general powers are limited; and that the States, in all unenumerated cases, are left in the enjoyment of their sovereign and independent jurisdiction.

CONSTITUTION EXPANDS PRINCIPLES IN ARTICLES:

The Constitution is more an enlargement of the Articles of Confederation than the creation of something absolutely new.

40:33 The truth is, that the great principles of the Constitution proposed by the Convention may be considered less as absolutely new, than as the expansion of principles which are found in the articles of Confederation. The misfortune under the latter system has been, that these principles are so feeble and confined as to justify all the charges of inefficiency which have been urged against it, and to require a degree of enlargement which gives to the new system the aspect of an entire transformation of the old.

FRAMERS EXCEEDED BOUNDS ONCE BUT IN A MINOR WAY, IN THE RATIFICATION PROCESS:

40:34 In one particular it is admitted that the Convention have departed from the tenor of their commission. Instead of reporting a plan requiring the confirmation OF THE LEGISLATURES OF ALL THE STATES, they have reported a plan which is to be confirmed by the PEOPLE, and may be carried into effect by NINE STATES ONLY.

---

148 *Publius:* Connecticut and Rhode Island.

RATIFICATION IS NOT A MAJOR OBJECTION:
Preventing a thirteenth State from stopping the twelve is well sustained.

40:35   It is worthy of remark that this objection, though the most plausible, has been the <u>least urged</u> in the publications which have swarmed against the Convention. The forbearance can only have proceeded from an irresistible conviction of the <u>absurdity</u> of <u>subjecting</u> the fate of <u>twelve States</u> to the perverseness or corruption of a <u>thirteenth</u>;[149]

OTHER STATES ANGRY AT RHODE ISLAND:

40:36   from the example of inflexible opposition given by a MAJORITY of one sixtieth of the people of America to a measure approved and called for by the voice of twelve States, comprising fifty-nine sixtieths of the people an example still fresh in the memory and indignation of every citizen who has felt for the wounded honor and prosperity of his country.

CRITICS DON'T SEEM TO CARE SO I'LL DISMISS IT:

40:37   As this objection, therefore, has been in a manner waived by those who have criticized the powers of the Convention, <u>I dismiss it without further observation</u>.

DID DUTY DISPLACE AUTHORITY?

40:38   The <u>THIRD</u> point to be inquired into is, how far considerations <u>of duty</u> arising out of the case itself <u>could have supplied any defect</u> of regular authority.

CRITICS MIS-CHARACTERIZED THE CONVENTION:
They criticized the Convention as if it had power to force a new government on America. It had no such power.

40:39   In the preceding inquiries the powers of the Convention have been analyzed and tried with the same rigor, and by the same rules, as if they had been real and final powers for the establishment of a Constitution for the United States. We have seen in what manner they have borne the trial even on that supposition.

CONSTITUTION WAS MERELY A RECOMMENDATION:
It was a harmless pieces of paper—until ratified into authority.

40:40   It is time now to recollect that the powers were merely <u>advisory</u> and <u>recommendatory</u>; that they were so meant by the States, and so understood by the Convention; and that the latter have accordingly planned and proposed a Constitution which is to be of <u>no more consequence</u> than the paper on which it is written, <u>unless it</u> be stamped with the approba-

tion of those to whom it is addressed. This reflection places the subject in a point of view altogether different, and will enable us to judge with propriety of the course taken by the Convention.

REVIEW OF CONVENTION IN PROPER CONTEXT:
The Convention understood the crisis facing America and that it was called upon to correct the errors.

40:41   Let us view the <u>ground</u> on which the <u>Convention stood</u>. It may be collected from their proceedings, that they were deeply and unanimously <u>impressed with the crisis</u>, which had led their country almost with one voice to make so singular and solemn an experiment for <u>correcting the errors</u> of a system by which this crisis had been produced; that they were no less deeply and unanimously convinced that such a reform as they have proposed was absolutely necessary to <u>effect the purposes of their appointment</u>.

FRAMERS KNEW THE NATION WAS COUNTING ON THEM:

40:42   It could not be unknown to them that the hopes and expectations of the great body of citizens, throughout this great empire, were turned with the keenest anxiety to the event of their deliberations.

FRAMERS KNEW CRITICS WORKED AGAINST THEM:

40:43   They had every reason to believe that the contrary sentiments agitated the minds and bosoms of every external and internal foe to the liberty and prosperity of the United States.

FRAMERS WERE QUICK TO CONSIDER IMPROVEMENTS:

40:44   They had seen in the origin and progress of the experiment, the alacrity with which the <u>PROPOSITION, made by a single State (Virginia)</u>, towards a partial amendment of the Confederation, had been attended to and promoted.

FRAMERS KNEW PUBLIC SUPPORTED CHANGES:

40:45   They had seen the <u>LIBERTY ASSUMED by a VERY FEW</u> deputies from a <u>VERY FEW States</u>, convened at Annapolis, of recommending a great and critical object, wholly foreign to their commission, not only justified by the public opinion, but actually carried into effect by twelve out of the thirteen States.

---

149 *Editors' Note:* Rhode Island's refusal to send delegates to the Convention, and being a single holdout on some critical votes under the Articles of Confederation, the Convention changed the ratification qualification from unanimous to only nine states to put the Constitution into operation.

FRAMERS SAW CONGRESS TAKE ILLEGAL AUTHORITY:

And these authorities were very much outside the powers granted to them in the Articles.

40:46 They had seen, in a variety of instances, assumptions by Congress, not only of recommendatory, but of operative, powers, warranted, in the public estimation, by occasions and objects infinitely less urgent than those by which their conduct was to be governed.

SUBSTANCE REIGNS SUPREME OVER FORM OF GOVERNMENT:

The *substance* of government is far more important than its *form*. Change is frequently dependent on informal and unauthorized groups of patriots to trigger needed corrections.

40:47 They must have reflected, that in all great changes of established governments, forms ought to give way to substance; that a rigid adherence in such cases to the former, would render nominal and nugatory the transcendent and precious right of the people to "abolish or alter their governments as to them shall seem most likely to effect their safety and happiness,"[150] since it is impossible for the people spontaneously and universally to move in concert towards their object; and it is therefore essential that such changes be instituted by some INFORMAL AND UNAUTHORIZED PROPOSITIONS, made by some patriotic and respectable citizen or number of citizens.

STATES TOOK INITIATIVES AGAINST BRITAIN:

When war was imminent, they formed their own State constitutions.

40:48 They must have recollected that it was by this irregular and assumed privilege of proposing to the people plans for their safety and happiness, that the States were first united against the danger with which they were threatened by their ancient government; that committees and congresses were formed for concentrating their efforts and defending their rights; and that CONVENTIONS were ELECTED in THE SEVERAL STATES for establishing the constitutions under which they are now governed;

STATES CHOSE SUBSTANCE OVER FORM:

40:49 nor could it have been forgotten that no little ill-timed scruples, no zeal for adhering to ordinary forms, were anywhere seen, except in those who wished to indulge, under these masks, their secret enmity to the substance contended for.

STATE CONSTITUTIONS APPROVED BY THE PEOPLE:

This important step shows that the people want substance more than form.

40:50 They must have borne in mind, that as the plan to be framed and proposed was to be submitted TO THE PEOPLE THEMSELVES, the disapprobation of this supreme authority would destroy it forever; its approbation blot out antecedent errors and irregularities. It might even have occurred to them, that where a disposition to cavil prevailed, their neglect to execute the degree of power vested in them, and still more their recommendation of any measure whatever, not warranted by their commission, would not less excite animadversion, than a recommendation at once of a measure fully commensurate to the national exigencies.

THE CONVENTION PUT THEIR TRUST IN THE PEOPLE:

The Convention's delegates proved brave, wise, and trustworthy.

40:51 Had the Convention, under all these impressions, and in the midst of all these considerations, instead of exercising a manly confidence in their country, by whose confidence they had been so peculiarly distinguished, and of pointing out a system capable, in their judgment, of securing its happiness, taken the cold and sullen resolution of disappointing its ardent hopes, of sacrificing substance to forms, of committing the dearest interests of their country to the uncertainties of delay and the hazard of events, let me ask the man who can raise his mind to one elevated conception, who can awaken in his bosom one patriotic emotion, what judgment ought to have been pronounced by the impartial world, by the friends of mankind, by every virtuous citizen, on the conduct and character of this assembly?

DID THE STATES USURP POWER?

Sending delegates to correct the Articles is not authorized in State constitutions. Was a crime committed?

40:52 Or if there be a man whose propensity to condemn is susceptible of no control, let me then ask what sentence he has in reserve for the twelve States who USURPED THE POWER of sending deputies to the Convention, a body utterly unknown to their constitutions; for Congress, who recommended the appointment of this body, equally unknown to the Confederation; and for the State of New York, in particular, which first urged and then complied with this unauthorized interposition?

---

150 *Publius:* Declaration of Independence.

IT IS POINTLESS TO CLAIM THE CONVENTION WAS ILLEGAL:

Even if pretending that the Convention was illegal, the product of their labors remains vastly superior to the current Articles of Confederation.

40:53 But that the objectors may be disarmed of every pretext, it shall be granted for a moment that the <u>Convention were neither authorized by their commission</u>, nor justified by circumstances in proposing a Constitution for their country: does it follow that the <u>Constitution</u> ought, for that reason alone, to be <u>rejected</u>?

GOOD ADVICE FROM BAD PEOPLE IS STILL GOOD:

40:54 If, according to the noble precept, it be lawful to <u>accept good</u> advice even from an enemy, shall we set the ignoble example of refusing such advice even when it is offered by our friends?

NOT *WHO* BUT *WHAT* IS MOST IMPORTANT:

40:55 The prudent inquiry, in all cases, ought surely to be, not so much <u>FROM WHOM the advice comes</u>, as whether the <u>advice be GOOD</u>.

NO PROOF THAT CONVENTION EXCEEDED ITS POWERS:

40:56 The sum of what has been here advanced and proved is, that the <u>charge against the Convention of exceeding their powers, except in one instance</u>[151] little urged by the objectors, <u>has no foundation to support</u> it;

IF CONVENTION DID EXCEED POWERS, IT'S JUSTIFIED:

40:57 that if they had exceeded their powers, they were not only warranted, but required, as the confidential servants of their country, by the circumstances in which they were placed, to exercise the liberty which they assume;

BOTTOM LINE IS— EMBRACE THE NEW CONSTITUTION.

40:58 and that finally, <u>if they had violated both their</u> powers and their <u>obligations</u>, in proposing a Constitution, this <u>ought nevertheless to be embraced</u>, if it be calculated to <u>accomplish</u> the views and happiness of the <u>people of America</u>. How far this character is due to the Constitution, is the subject under investigation.

—Publius

REVIEW QUESTIONS

1. What is the main point Madison wants to examine in paper No. 40? (40:1)

2. When was the meeting at Annapolis? What did it recommend to Congress? (40:3, see also "Significant Dates in the Founding of America")

3. When did Congress formally call for a Convention? (40:2, see also "Significant Dates in the Founding of America")

4. What are the four primary tasks given to the Convention? (40:5–10)

5. Are "alterations and provisions in the Articles of Confederation" sufficient to form a "national and adequate government?" Why? (40:15–19)

6. What was the real goal of the Convention? To preserve the Articles or to fix its problems? (40:17–22)

7. Which parts of the Articles are retained in the Constitution? (40:26–32)

8. Is the Constitution more of a new creation or more of an expansion of the Articles? (40:33)

9. What two weaknesses in the Articles drag it so far down that it makes the new Constitution appear, by contrast, a complete replacement? (40:33)

10. Where did the Framers exceed the Congressional mandate? (40:34)

11. Did the Convention force their new Constitution on the nation, or was it only advisory and recommended? (40:40)

12. Should the Constitution be judged for its own merits, or the means whereby it came into being? (40:56–58)

FEDERALIST NO. 41

THE FIRST FEDERAL POWER—NATIONAL DEFENSE: Government power is a necessary evil. A government with too little power must fail, as shown by the weak Articles of Confederation. Liberty is not possible without a strong government to sustain and protect it. Controlling such a strong government and preventing it from becoming tyrannical is solved by putting it under the direct control and authority of the people. The powers given to the federal government can be grouped into six major areas (see 41:8). This essay examines the first: security against foreign danger.

---

151 *Editors' Note:* The "one instance" (40:56) is when the Convention bypassed the stipulation in Article XIII of the Articles of Confederation that mandates all alterations to the Articles must be approved by Congress and the State legislatures. Since power was being taken from the State legislatures it made sense to bypass their likely "no" votes and go directly to the people for ratification. The stipulation was not actually violated because the Convention only recommended that action, it had no power to impose it.

James Madison—January 19, 1788

DISTRIBUTION OF NEW CONSTITUTIONAL POWERS:

The powers are spread out vertically and horizontally.

41:1 THE Constitution proposed by the Convention may be considered under two general points of view. The FIRST relates to the <u>sum or quantity of power</u> which it vests in <u>the government</u>, including the <u>restraints</u> imposed on the <u>States</u>. The SECOND, to the particular <u>structure of</u> the <u>government</u>, and the <u>distribution of this power</u> among its several branches.

TWO IMPORTANT QUESTIONS:

Are the delegated powers improper or dangerous to the Union or the States?

41:2 Under the FIRST view of the subject, two important questions arise: 1. <u>Whether any part</u> of the powers transferred to the general government be <u>unnecessary or improper</u>? 2. Whether the entire mass of them be <u>dangerous</u> to the portion of <u>jurisdiction</u> left in the several <u>States</u>?

FIRST QUESTION: ARE FEDERAL POWERS TOO GREAT?

Are there any powers in the Constitution that are improper?

41:3 Is the aggregate power of the general government greater than ought to have been vested in it? This is the FIRST question.

CRITICS IGNORE NECESSITY OF DELEGATED POWERS:

They focus too much on the unavoidable inconveniences.

41:4 It cannot have escaped those who have attended with candor to the arguments employed against the extensive powers of the government, that the authors of them have very little considered <u>how far these powers were necessary</u> means of attaining a <u>necessary end</u>. They have chosen rather to dwell on the <u>inconveniences</u> which must be <u>unavoidably blended</u> with all <u>political advantages</u>; and on the <u>possible abuses</u> which must be incident to every power or trust, of which a beneficial use can be made.

CONSTITUTION IS IMPERFECT BUT ALSO THE GREATER GOOD:

Americans realize no government is perfect so we will do the best we can.

41:5 This method of handling the <u>subject cannot impose on the good sense of the people</u> of America. It may display the subtlety of the writer; it may open a boundless field for rhet-

oric and declamation; it may inflame the passions of the unthinking, and may confirm the prejudices of the misthinking: but cool and candid people will at once reflect, that the <u>purest of human blessings</u> must have a portion of <u>alloy in them</u>; that the choice must always be made, if not of the <u>lesser evil</u>, at least of the <u>GREATER</u>, not the <u>PERFECT, good</u>;

EVERY HUMAN GOVERNMENT CAN BE ABUSED:

41:6 and that in every political institution, a power to advance the public happiness involves a discretion which may be misapplied and abused.

DELEGATED POWERS MUST BE GUARDED:

Power given to government must be tested in two ways: First, to ensure it serves the public good. Second, to guard against abuse.

41:7 They will see, therefore, that <u>in all cases</u> where <u>power is</u> to be <u>conferred</u>, the point first to be decided is, <u>whether</u> such a <u>power be necessary to the public good</u>; as the next will be, in case of an affirmative decision, to <u>guard as effectually</u> as possible against a <u>perversion of the power</u> to the public <u>detriment</u>.

SIX DUTIES OF A STRONG UNION:

41:8 That we may form a correct judgment on this subject, it will be proper to review the several powers conferred on the government of the Union; and that this may be the more conveniently done they may be reduced into different classes as they relate to the following different objects: 1. <u>Security against foreign danger</u>; 2. <u>Regulation</u> of the intercourse with <u>foreign nations</u>; 3. Maintenance of <u>harmony</u> and proper intercourse <u>among the States</u>; 4. Certain <u>miscellaneous objects</u> of general utility; 5. <u>Restraint of the States</u> from certain injurious acts; 6. Provisions for giving <u>due efficacy to all these powers</u>.

FIRST CLASS OF FEDERAL POWERS— NATIONAL DEFENSE.

41:9 The powers falling within the <u>FIRST</u> class are those of <u>declaring war</u> and granting **letters of marque**;[152] of providing <u>armies and fleets</u>; of regulating and calling forth the <u>militia</u>; of levying and borrowing <u>money</u>.

COMMON DEFENSE MUST BE A FEDERAL DUTY:

41:10 <u>Security</u> against foreign danger is one of the <u>primitive objects of civil society</u>. It is an avowed and essential object of the American Union. The powers requisite for attaining it <u>must be</u> effectually confided to the <u>federal councils</u>.

POWER TO DECLARE WAR IS NECESSARY:

41:11 <u>Is the power</u> of declaring <u>war necessary</u>? No man will answer this question in the negative. It would be superfluous,

---

152 *letters of marque:* Written authority granting a private person license to plunder the enemy. If captured, laws of war then apply. Without such a letter the person could instead be treated as a pirate and executed on the spot.

therefore, to enter into a proof of the affirmative. The existing Confederation establishes this power in the most ample form.

FEDERAL POWER TO RAISE ARMIES IS NECESSARY:

41:12 Is the power of raising armies and equipping fleets necessary? This is involved in the foregoing power. It is involved in the power of self-defense.

POWERS FOR SELF-DEFENSE MUST BE UNLIMITED:

41:13 But was it necessary to give an INDEFINITE POWER of raising TROOPS, as well as providing fleets; and of maintaining both in PEACE, as well as in war?

QUESTIONS ABOUT DEFENSE ARE EASILY ANSWERED:

41:14 The answer to these questions has been too far anticipated in another place to admit an extensive discussion of them in this place. The answer indeed seems to be so obvious and conclusive as scarcely to justify such a discussion in any place.

EXTENT OF THREAT DECIDES EXTENT OF PREPARATIONS:

The level of danger guides how much preparation is needed. Setting legal limits for self-defense is foolish.

41:15 With what color of propriety could the force necessary for defense be limited by those who cannot limit the force of offense? If a federal Constitution could chain the ambition or set bounds to the exertions of all other nations, then indeed might it prudently chain the discretion of its own government, and set bounds to the exertions for its own safety.

MADISON PROMOTES PEACE THROUGH STRENGTH:

Limiting an enemy's power is not possible.

41:16 How could a readiness for war in time of peace be safely prohibited, unless we could prohibit, in like manner, the preparations and establishments of every hostile nation?

SELF-PRESERVATION CAN'T BE CURBED IN A CRISIS:

Constitution facilitates all measures needed for self preservation.

41:17 The means of security can only be regulated by the means and the danger of attack. They will, in fact, be ever determined by these rules, and by no others. It is in vain to oppose constitutional barriers to the impulse of self-preservation. It is worse than in vain; because it plants in the Constitution itself necessary usurpations of power, every precedent of which is a germ of unnecessary and multiplied repetitions.

AMBITIOUS NATIONS PROVOKE OTHERS INTO ACTION:

41:18 If one nation maintains constantly a disciplined army, ready for the service of ambition or revenge, it obliges the most pacific nations who may be within the reach of its enterprises to take corresponding precautions.

EUROPE IS NOW ARMED TO SECURE ITSELF:

Had Europe not established standing armies during times of peace those nations today might all be subject to one crown.

41:19 The fifteenth century was the unhappy epoch of military establishments in the time of peace. They were introduced by Charles VII of France. All Europe has followed, or been forced into, the example. Had the example not been followed by other nations, all Europe must long ago have worn the chains of a universal monarch. Were every nation except France now to disband its peace establishments, the same event might follow. The veteran legions of Rome were an overmatch for the undisciplined valor of all other nations and rendered her the mistress of the world.

STANDING ARMY IS BOTH NEEDED AND DANGEROUS IF NOT MANAGED WELL:

Rome and Europe both sacrificed the people's liberties to maintain their standing armies.

41:20 Not the less true is it, that the liberties of Rome proved the final victim to her military triumphs; and that the liberties of Europe, as far as they ever existed, have, with few exceptions, been the price of her military establishments. A standing force, therefore, is a dangerous, at the same time that it may be a necessary, provision.

SELF-DEFENSE MUST BE CREATED WITH CAUTION:

41:21 On the smallest scale it has its inconveniences. On an extensive scale its consequences may be fatal. On any scale it is an object of laudable circumspection and precaution.

GOOD SELF-DEFENSE INCLUDES REDUCING DANGERS:

41:22 A wise nation will combine all these considerations; and, whilst it does not rashly preclude itself from any resource which may become essential to its safety, will exert all its prudence in diminishing both the necessity and the danger of resorting to one which may be inauspicious to its liberties.

UNITY PRESERVES LIBERTY AND PROMOTES DEFENSE:

The new Constitution solves the dangers of a standing army.

41:23 The clearest marks of this prudence are stamped on the proposed Constitution. The Union itself, which it cements and secures, destroys every pretext for a military establishment which could be dangerous. America united, with a handful of troops, or without a single soldier, exhibits a more forbidding posture to foreign ambition than America disunited, with a hundred thousand veterans ready for combat.

GEOGRAPHICAL ADVANTAGES FOR BRITAIN:
Being an island is an advantage for Britain's self-defense.

41:24 It was remarked, on a former occasion, that the want of this pretext had saved the liberties of one nation in Europe. Being rendered by her insular situation and her maritime resources impregnable to the armies of her neighbors, the rulers of Great Britain have never been able, by real or artificial dangers, to cheat the public into an extensive peace establishment.

GEOGRAPHICAL ADVANTAGES FOR AMERICA:
Being so far removed from foreign dangers is an advantage for America.

41:25 The distance of the United States from the powerful nations of the world gives them the same happy security. A dangerous establishment can never be necessary or plausible, so long as they continue a united people.

ONLY A STRONG UNION CAN PROVIDE THESE ADVANTAGES :

41:26 But let it never, for a moment, be forgotten that they are indebted for this advantage to the Union alone. The moment of its dissolution will be the date of a new order of things.

WITHOUT A UNION OUR LIBERTIES WILL BE CRUSHED:
A divided America would mirror Europe with many armies and taxes.

41:27 The fears of the weaker, or the ambition of the stronger States, or Confederacies, will set the same example in the New, as Charles VII did in the Old World. The example will be followed here from the same motives which produced universal imitation there. Instead of deriving from our situation the precious advantage which Great Britain has derived from hers, the face of America will be but a copy of that of the continent of Europe. It will present liberty everywhere crushed between standing armies and perpetual taxes.

DISUNITED AMERICA WOULD SUFFER WORSE:
Geography is the main limit in Europe, pitting neighbor against neighbor.

41:28 The fortunes of disunited America will be even more disastrous than those of Europe. The sources of evil in the latter are confined to her own limits. No superior powers of another quarter of the globe intrigue among her rival nations, inflame their mutual animosities, and render them the instruments of foreign ambition, jealousy, and revenge.

AMERICA'S INTERNAL CONFLICTS ARE COMPOUNDED BY EXTERNAL EVILS:
In America the worst culprit would rise from inside where no geographic boundaries exist to hold back contentions and wars.

41:29 In America the miseries springing from her internal jealousies, contentions, and wars, would form a part only of her lot. A plentiful addition of evils would have their source in that relation in which Europe stands to this quarter of the earth, and which no other quarter of the earth bears to Europe.

THOSE WHO LOVE LIBERTY ALSO LOVE A STRONG UNION:

41:30 This picture of the consequences of disunion cannot be too highly colored, or too often exhibited. Every man who loves peace, every man who loves his country, every man who loves liberty, ought to have it ever before his eyes, that he may cherish in his heart a due attachment to the Union of America, and be able to set a due value on the means of preserving it.

HOW TO PREVENT THE DANGERS OF A STANDING ARMY:
A two-year term for funding a standing army in peacetime is a strong protection from it becoming dangerous to the people.

41:31 Next to the effectual establishment of the Union, the best possible precaution against danger from standing armies is a limitation of the term for which revenue may be appropriated to their support. This precaution the Constitution has prudently added.

ANSWERING THE CRITICS WHO POINT TO BRITAIN:

41:32 I will not repeat here the observations which I flatter myself have placed this subject in a just and satisfactory light. But it may not be improper to take notice of an argument against this part of the Constitution, which has been drawn from the policy and practice of Great Britain.

BRITAIN'S AUTHORIZATION PROCESS FOR ARMY IS NOT THE SAME AS AMERICA'S:

41:33 It is said that the continuance of an army in that kingdom requires an annual vote of the legislature; whereas the American Constitution has lengthened this critical period to two years. This is the form in which the comparison is usually stated to the public: but is it a just form? Is it a fair comparison? Does the British Constitution restrain the parliamentary discretion to one year? Does the American impose on the Congress appropriations for two years?

MILITARY AUTHORIZATION IS TIED TO TWO-YEAR TERMS:

41:34   On the contrary, it cannot be unknown to the authors of the fallacy themselves, that the <u>British Constitution fixes no limit whatever to the discretion of the legislature</u>, and that the <u>American ties down the legislature</u> to <u>two years</u>, as the longest admissible term.

TECHNICALLY, BRITAIN'S TIME FOR MILITARY PROCUREMENTS IS UNLIMITED:

41:35   Had the argument from the <u>British example</u> been truly stated, it would have stood thus: The term for which supplies may be appropriated to the army establishment, though unlimited by the British Constitution, has nevertheless, in practice, been limited by parliamentary discretion to a single year.

AMERICAN SYSTEM OF CONTROL IS MORE SECURE:

The funding of the military, a process tied down by the Constitution, is vastly superior to that corrupted system in Britain.

41:36   Now, if in Great Britain, where the <u>House of Commons is elected for seven years</u>; where so great a proportion of the members are elected by so small a proportion of the people; where the electors are so corrupted by the representatives, and the representatives so corrupted by the Crown, the <u>representative body</u> can possess a power to make <u>appropriations</u> to the army for an <u>indefinite</u> term, without desiring, or without daring, to extend the term beyond a single year, ought not suspicion herself to blush, in pretending that the representatives of the United States, <u>elected FREELY by the WHOLE BODY of the people, every SECOND YEAR, cannot be safely intrusted with the discretion</u> over such appropriations, expressly limited to the short period of <u>TWO YEARS</u>?

STANDING ARMY CRITICISM IS WEAK ATTACK ON NEW GOVERNMENT:

The critics erred by using standing armies as reason to reject Constitution.

41:37   <u>A bad cause seldom fails to betray</u> itself. Of this truth, the management of the opposition to the federal government is an unvaried exemplification. But among all the blunders which have been committed, none is more striking than the attempt to enlist on that side the prudent <u>jealousy entertained by the people, of standing armies</u>.

CONTROVERSY OVER STANDING ARMIES ENHANCED SUPPORT FOR THE UNION:

Awakening the public to the issue of standing armies created in them a spirit of investigation that won their support for how the Constitution will handle that issue.

41:38   The attempt has awakened fully the public attention to that important subject; and has led to investigations which must terminate in a thorough and universal conviction, not only that the <u>Constitution has provided the most effectual guards against danger from that</u> quarter, but that nothing short of a Constitution <u>fully adequate</u> to the national <u>defense</u> and the <u>preservation</u> of the Union, can save America from <u>as many standing armies</u> as it may be split into <u>States or Confederacies, and</u> from such a progressive augmentation, of these establishments in each, as will render them as <u>burdensome to the properties</u> and ominous to the liberties of the people, as any establishment that can become necessary, under a united and efficient government, must be tolerable to the former and safe to the latter.

A STRONG UNION CAN BEST SUPPLY A NAVY:

The Framers all agreed we need a navy to protect commerce.

41:39   The palpable necessity of the power to provide and maintain a <u>navy</u> has protected that part of the Constitution against a spirit of censure, which has spared few other parts. It must, indeed, be numbered among the greatest blessings of America, that as her <u>Union will be the only source of her maritime strength</u>, so this will be a principal source of her <u>security against danger</u> from abroad.

NAVY IS MORE DIFFICULT TO USE AGAINST THE PEOPLE:

41:40   In this respect our situation bears another likeness to the insular advantage of <u>Great Britain</u>. The batteries most capable of repelling foreign enterprises on our safety, are happily such as can never be turned by a perfidious government against our liberties.

COASTAL STATES BENEFIT FROM NAVY THE MOST:

A navy is of special concern to New Yorkers and their unique dangers.

41:41   The inhabitants of the <u>Atlantic frontier</u> are All of them deeply interested in this provision for <u>naval protection</u>, and if they have hitherto been suffered to sleep quietly in their beds; if their property has remained safe against the predatory spirit of licentious adventurers; if their <u>maritime towns</u> have not yet been compelled to <u>ransom themselves from the terrors of a conflagration</u>, by <u>yielding to the exactions</u> of daring and sudden <u>invaders</u>, these instances of good fortune are not to be ascribed to the capacity of the existing government for the protection of those from whom it claims allegiance, but to causes that are fugitive and fallacious.

NEW YORK IS ESPECIALLY VULNERABLE TO ATTACK ON ITS COASTS:

41:42 If we except perhaps <u>Virginia</u> and <u>Maryland</u>, which are <u>peculiarly vulnerable</u> on their eastern frontiers, no part of the Union ought to feel more anxiety on this subject than <u>New York</u>. Her <u>seacoast is extensive</u>. A very important district of the State is an <u>island</u>. The State itself is penetrated by a large navigable river for more than fifty leagues. The great emporium of its commerce, the great reservoir of its wealth, lies every moment at the mercy of events, and may almost be regarded as a hostage for ignominious compliances with the dictates of a foreign enemy, or even with the rapacious demands of <u>pirates</u> and barbarians.

THE ARTICLES FAILED TO PROTECT AMERICA'S COASTS:

Any major European war that spills out into the oceans would certainly draw in the American States.

41:43 Should a war be the result of the precarious situation of European affairs, and all the unruly passions attending it be let loose on the ocean, our escape from insults and depredations, not only on that element, but every part of the other bordering on it, will be truly miraculous. In the present condition of America, the <u>States more immediately exposed</u> to these calamities have nothing to hope from the phantom of a general government which now exists; and if their single resources were equal to the task of fortifying themselves against the danger, the <u>object to be protected</u> would be almost <u>consumed</u> by the <u>means</u> of <u>protecting them</u>.

TOPIC OF THE MILITIA HAS ALREADY BEEN PRESENTED:

41:44 The power of <u>regulating and calling forth the militia</u> has been already sufficiently vindicated and <u>explained</u>.

FUNDING OF MILITARY IS HANDLED IN CONSTITUTION:

41:45 The <u>power of levying and borrowing money</u>, being the <u>sinew</u> of that which is to be exerted in the <u>national defense</u>, is properly thrown into the same class with it. This power, also, has been examined already with much attention, and has, I trust, been clearly shown to be <u>necessary</u>, both in the <u>extent</u> and form given to it by the Constitution.

OTHER MILITARY FUNDING:

41:46 I will address one additional reflection only to those who contend that the power ought to have been <u>restrained to external taxation</u> by which they mean, <u>taxes on articles imported</u> from other countries. It cannot be doubted that this will always be a valuable source of revenue; that for a considerable time it must be a principal source; that at this moment it is an essential one.

TAXING IMPORTS NOT SUFFICIENTLY RELIABLE:

41:47 But we may form very mistaken ideas on this subject, if we do not call to mind in our calculations, that the <u>extent of revenue</u> drawn from foreign commerce must <u>vary with the variations</u>, both in the extent and the kind of imports; and that these variations do not correspond with the <u>progress of population</u>, which must be the general measure of the <u>public wants</u>.

IMPORTS WILL SHRINK WITH SELF-SUFFICIENCY:

If the military funding was dependent on import taxes its revenue would shrink as the nation reduces its dependency on imports.

41:48 As long as agriculture continues the sole field of labor, the <u>importation of manufactures must increase</u> as the <u>consumers multiply</u>. As soon as domestic manufactures are begun by the hands not called for by agriculture, the imported manufactures will decrease as the numbers of <u>people increase</u>. In a more remote stage, the imports may consist in a considerable part of raw materials, which will be wrought into articles for exportation, and will, therefore, require rather the <u>encouragement of bounties</u>, than to be loaded with discouraging duties. A system of <u>government, meant for duration, ought to contemplate these revolutions</u>, and be able to accommodate itself to them.

CRITICS CLAIM POWER TO TAX IS LEFT RUDDERLESS:

The General Welfare clause limits government's spending power to only those twenty items listed in Article I Section 8.[153]

41:49 <u>Some</u> who have not <u>denied the necessity of the power of taxation</u> have grounded a very fierce <u>attack against the Constitution</u>, on the language in which it is defined. It has been urged and echoed, that the power "to lay and collect tax-

---

153 *Editors' Note:* The Anti-Federalists were correct in their fear of uncontrolled taxation. In the 1936 Butler Case the Supreme Court interpreted the General Welfare clause (Art. I, Sec. 8, Clause 1) exactly as that, as a grant of power, not a limitation on taxation. The Court granted power to Congress to raise money for any cause Congress deemed important for the national welfare. As Madison explains in No. 41, Congress was supposed to remain limited to the twenty powers or permissions listed in Article I, Section 8. Hamilton, on the other hand, supported letting Congress decide what is "national welfare" (see Nos. 30, 34) and spend money as it saw fit. Since that 1936 court ruling, Congress has taxed the nation for thousands of projects clearly unrelated to national welfare. It destroyed the founding concept of limited government. The result is a national debt exploding beyond $30 trillion. The Butler case opened the door to excessive taxing and spending that Madison, Jefferson, and the Framers wisely prepared against in Article I Section 8, and that Madison clarified and defended here in No. 41. See United States v. Butler, 297 US 1 (1936).

es, duties, imposts, and excises, to pay the debts, and provide for the common defense and general welfare of the United States," amounts to an unlimited commission to exercise every power which may be alleged to be necessary for the common defense or general welfare.

Critics are stooping to a new low.

41:50   No stronger proof could be given of the distress under which these writers labor for objections, than their stooping to such a misconstruction.

CONSTITUTION PROTECTS RIGHTS NOT YET LISTED:

The critics must really labor to pervert the term "raise money for general welfare" to somehow mean the destruction of freedoms.

41:51   Had no other enumeration or definition of the powers of the Congress been found in the Constitution, than the general expressions just cited, the authors of the objection might have had some color for it; though it would have been difficult to find a reason for so awkward a form of describing an authority to legislate in all possible cases. A power to destroy the freedom of the press, the trial by jury, or even to regulate the course of descents, or the forms of conveyances, must be very singularly expressed by the terms "to raise money for the general welfare."

GENERAL WELFARE POWERS (ART. I, SEC. 8) ARE LIMITED BY A SEMI-COLON:

The "general welfare" term means *only* the twenty powers that follow.

41:52   But what color can the objection have, when a specification of the objects alluded to by these general terms immediately follows, and is not even separated by a longer pause than a semicolon?

Madison explains the general welfare reference is a general phrase, an introduction to the detailed list that the term is meant to encompass.

41:53   If the different parts of the same instrument ought to be so expounded, as to give meaning to every part which will bear it, shall one part of the same sentence be excluded altogether from a share in the meaning; and shall the more doubtful and indefinite terms be retained in their full extent, and the clear and precise expressions be denied any signification whatsoever?

THE GENERAL WELFARE INTRODUCTION IS NOT A GRANT OF POWER

If the power to levy taxes was meant to extend beyond the permissions listed in Article I, Section 8, then why put that list there at all?

41:54   For what purpose could the enumeration of particular powers be inserted, if these and all others were meant to be included in the preceding general power? Nothing is more natural nor common than first to use a general phrase, and then to explain and qualify it by a recital of particulars. But the idea of an enumeration of particulars which neither explain nor qualify the general meaning, and can have no other effect than to confound and mislead, is an absurdity, which, as we are reduced to the dilemma of charging either on the authors of the objection or on the authors of the Constitution, we must take the liberty of supposing, had not its origin with the latter.

GENERAL WELFARE IS A LIMIT—NOT A POWER:

The true understanding of "General Welfare" is statement of limits not a grant of power.

41:55   The objection here is the more extraordinary, as it appears that the language used by the Convention is a copy from the Articles of Confederation. The objects of the Union among the States, as described in article third, are "their common defense, security of their liberties, and mutual and general welfare." The terms of article eighth are still more identical: "All charges of war and all other expenses that shall be incurred for the common defense or general welfare, and allowed by the United States in Congress, shall be defrayed out of a common treasury," etc. A similar language again occurs in article ninth.

Apply the same interpretation to the Articles and it gives Congress power to legislate in all cases.

41:56   Construe either of these articles by the rules which would justify the construction put on the new Constitution, and they vest in the existing Congress a power to legislate in all cases whatsoever.

CONGRESS MUST ABIDE BY SPECIFIC LIST:

By ignoring the twenty specific limitations in Art. I, Sec. 8, Congress will tax and spend on whatever it regards as "general welfare," which is *everything*.

41:57   But what would have been thought of that assembly, if, attaching themselves to these general expressions, and disregarding the specifications which ascertain and limit their import, they had exercised an unlimited power of providing for the common defense and general welfare?

CRITICS SHOULD APPLY SAME CRITICISM TO ARTICLES:

If the objectors applied the same accusation to the Articles, which they support, they would see their folly.

41:58   I appeal to the objectors themselves, whether they would in that case have employed the same reasoning in justification of Congress as they now make use of against the

Convention. <u>How difficult it is for error to escape its own condemnation</u>!

—PUBLIUS

REVIEW QUESTIONS

1. What are the two considerations Madison wishes to discuss next? (41:1)

2. Which of the two considerations will he focus on in this paper? (41:2)

3. Can the powers of government to do good also be used to do evil? (41:6–7)

4. What are the six powers conferred on the government of the Union? (41:8)

5. Should America anticipate every national defense threat by remaining so prepared? (41:16–17)

6. What presents a more "forbidding posture to foreign ambition" than 100,000 trained troops? (41:23)

7. Is it better to put up with the risks of a standing army than be caught totally defenseless in a surprise attack or invasion? (41:38)

8. What phrase in the Constitution implies Congress has unlimited permission to tax and spend on anything it deems necessary for the "general welfare"? (41:49)

9. Does that interpretation remain valid when a list of what those "general welfare" powers are is written down immediately after? (41:52)

10. What piece of punctuation seems to totally upset the true meaning of this limitation, the welfare clause? (41:52)

11. What is the intention of the introduction of the welfare clause (Art. I, Sec. 8, Clause 1)? (41:53–54)

12. Is abiding by a general statement (the introduction) and ignoring the particulars (the list that follows) in actuality giving unlimited power to Congress to do anything it pleases? (41:54, 57)

13. Is this flawed interpretation in harmony with the intent of the entire Constitution, to establish a balanced and *limited* government? (41:56–57)

FEDERALIST NO. 42

THE SECOND AND THIRD FEDERAL POWERS— REGULATION OF COMMERCE AND SLAVERY: The second power conferred on Congress is regulating commerce be- tween the States and with foreign nations. A single national voice is critical to successful diplomacy and fair trade regulations. The States were suspicious of any national authority and Madison explains how the Constitution can both secure State sovereignty while giving sufficient strength to the central government to se- cure the Union. The compromise on slavery was an anti-slavery compromise worked out to eventually ban all slavery, but at the same time to keep all thirteen States united in a single Union. The Anti-Federalists inflated that clause into a deceitful monster not worthy of a response. See all six federal powers listed in 41:8.

By James Madison—January 22, 1788

SECOND CLASS OF POWERS— INTERNATIONAL AFFAIRS:
The new federal government is charged with represent- ing the States when regulating relations with other coun- tries, to include regulating the importation of slaves after 1808.

42:1 THE <u>SECOND</u> <u>class of powers</u>, lodged in the gen- eral government, consists of those which <u>regulate</u> the inter- course with <u>foreign nations</u>, to wit: to make <u>treaties</u>; to send and receive <u>ambassadors</u>, other public <u>ministers</u>, and <u>consuls</u>; to define and <u>punish piracies</u> and <u>felonies</u> committed on the <u>high seas</u>, and <u>offenses</u> against the <u>law</u> of <u>nations</u>; to <u>regulate foreign commerce</u>, including a power to <u>prohibit</u>, <u>after</u> the year <u>1808</u>, the <u>importation of slaves</u>, and to lay an intermedi- ate duty of <u>ten dollars per head, as a discouragement to such importation</u>.

WE MUST BE ONE NATION TOWARD OTHER NATIONS:
42:2 This class of powers forms an obvious and essential branch of the federal administration. If we are to be <u>one na- tion</u> in any respect, it clearly ought to be in respect to <u>other nations</u>.

CONSTITUTION IMPROVES AND CORRECTS THE ARTICLES:
42:3 The powers to make <u>treaties</u> and to send and receive <u>ambassadors</u>, speak their own propriety. <u>Both</u> of them are comprised <u>in the articles</u> of <u>Confederation</u>, with this differ- ence only,

FIRST, THE STATES HAVE NO ROLE REGARDING TREATIES:
42:4 that the former is disembarrassed, by the plan of the Convention, of an exception, under which treaties might be substantially frustrated by regulations of the States;

SECOND, OTHER HIGH LEVEL-MINISTERS ARE MADE LEGAL:

42:5   and that a power of appointing and receiving "other public ministers and consuls," is expressly and very properly added to the former provision concerning ambassadors.

MOST FOREIGN RELATIONS ACTIVITY IS TRANSACTED BELOW AMBASSADOR:

Lower-level ministers and consuls were not authorized under the Articles.

42:6   The term ambassador, if taken strictly, as seems to be required by the second of the articles of Confederation, comprehends the highest grade only of public ministers, and excludes the grades which the United States will be most likely to prefer, where foreign embassies may be necessary. And under no latitude of construction will the term comprehend consuls. Yet it has been found expedient, and has been the practice of Congress, to employ the inferior grades of public ministers, and to send and receive consuls.

ARTICLES ALLOW RECEIVING FOREIGN CONSULS:

42:7   It is true, that where treaties of commerce stipulate for the mutual appointment of consuls, whose functions are connected with commerce, the admission of foreign consuls may fall within the power of making commercial treaties; and that where no such treaties exist, the mission of American consuls into foreign countries may PERHAPS be covered under the authority, given by the ninth article of the Confederation, to appoint all such civil officers as may be necessary for managing the general affairs of the United States.

WITHOUT A TREATY THE CONSULS ARE ILLEGAL:

42:8   But the admission of consuls into the United States, where no previous treaty has stipulated it, seems to have been nowhere provided for.

CONSTITUTION CORRECTS THESE MINOR FLAWS:

42:9   A supply of the omission is one of the lesser instances in which the Convention have improved on the model before them. But the most minute provisions become important when they tend to obviate the necessity or the pretext for gradual and unobserved usurpations of power.

ARTICLES OF CONFEDERATION INVITED NUMEROUS VIOLATIONS:

That alone gives strong reasons to support the new Constitution.

42:10   A list of the cases in which Congress have been betrayed, or forced by the defects of the Confederation, into violations of their chartered authorities, would not a little surprise those who have paid no attention to the subject; and would be no inconsiderable argument in favor of the new Constitution, which seems to have provided no less studiously for the lesser, than the more obvious and striking defects of the old.

ARTICLES ARE WEAK ON PIRACY AND LAWS OF NATIONS:

42:11   The power to define and punish piracies and **felonies**[154] committed on the high seas, and offenses against the law of nations, belongs with equal propriety to the general government, and is a still greater improvement on the articles of Confederation.

SINGLE STATE COULD PULL THE WHOLE NATION INTO WAR:

42:12   These articles contain no provision for the case of offenses against the law of nations; and consequently leave it in the power of any indiscreet member to embroil the Confederacy with foreign nations. The provision of the federal articles on the subject of piracies and felonies extends no further than to the establishment of courts for the trial of these offenses.

IS "PIRACY" PROPERLY DEFINED?

42:13   The definition of piracies might, perhaps, without inconveniency, be left to the law of nations; though a legislative definition of them is found in most municipal codes.

INTERNATIONAL DEFINITION OF FELONY:

42:14   A definition of felonies on the high seas is evidently requisite. Felony is a term of loose signification, even in the common law of England; and of various import in the statute law of that kingdom. But neither the common nor the statute law of that, or of any other nation, ought to be a standard for the proceedings of this, unless previously made its own by legislative adoption.

DEFINITION OF FELONY NOT UNIFORM IN THE STATES:

If felonies and misdemeanors are not uniformly defined among the various States, can there truly be any justice?

42:15   The meaning of the term, as defined in the codes of the several States, would be as impracticable as the former would be a dishonorable and illegitimate guide. It is not precisely the same in any two of the States; and varies in each with every revision of its criminal laws. For the sake of certainty and uniformity, therefore, the power of defining felonies in this case was in every respect necessary and proper.

---

154 *felony:* Any serious crime warranting prison or death. From the feudal period where a vassal failed in his fidelity to the lord by committing an offense for which he loses his feud or stewardship, such as being traitor or rebellious.

FOREIGN COMMERCE ALREADY DISCUSSED:

42:16 The regulation of foreign commerce, having fallen within several views which have been taken of this subject, has been too fully discussed to need additional proofs here of its being properly submitted to the federal administration.

IMPORTATION OF SLAVES ABOLISHED AFTER 1808:

A highlight of the Convention was setting a twenty-year adjustment period to stop importation of slaves (see Article I Sec. 9).

42:17 It were doubtless to be wished, that the power of prohibiting the importation of slaves had not been postponed until the year 1808, or rather that it had been suffered to have immediate operation. But it is not difficult to account, either for this restriction on the general government, or for the manner in which the whole clause is expressed.[155]

SLAVE STATES COULD ABOLISH SLAVERY BEFORE 1808 IF THEY SO DESIRED:

Did the Constitution mandate the end of slavery or just importation?

42:18 It ought to be considered as a great point gained in favor of humanity, that a period of twenty years may terminate forever, within these States, a traffic which has so long and so loudly upbraided the barbarism of modern policy; that within that period, it will receive a considerable discouragement from the federal government, and may be totally abolished, by a concurrence of the few States which continue the unnatural traffic, in the prohibitory example which has been given by so great a majority of the Union. Happy would it be for the unfortunate Africans, if an equal prospect lay before them of being redeemed from the oppressions of their European brethren!

ENDING A MYTH ABOUT SLAVERY AND IMMIGRATION:

Anti-Federalists twisted Art. I, Sec. 9, Clause 1 to mean criminal toleration of slavery.

42:19 Attempts have been made to pervert this clause into an objection against the Constitution, by representing it on one side as a criminal toleration of an illicit practice, and on another as calculated to prevent voluntary and beneficial emigrations from Europe to America. I mention these misconstructions, not with a view to give them an answer, for they deserve none, but as specimens of the manner and spirit in which some have thought fit to conduct their opposition to the proposed government.

THIRD CLASS OF POWERS—COMMERCE:

42:20 The powers included in the THIRD class are those which provide for the harmony and proper intercourse among the States.

INTERSTATE JUDICIAL ISSUES DISCUSSED LATER:

42:21 Under this head might be included the particular restraints imposed on the authority of the States, and certain powers of the judicial department; but the former are reserved for a distinct class, and the latter will be particularly examined when we arrive at the structure and organization of the government.

LIST OF ISSUES RELATED TO INTERSTATE COMMERCE:

42:22 I shall confine myself to a cursory review of the remaining powers comprehended under this third description, to wit: to regulate commerce among the several States and the Indian tribes; to coin money, regulate the value thereof, and of foreign coin; to provide for the punishment of counterfeiting the current coin and securities of the United States; to fix the standard of weights and measures; to establish a uniform rule of naturalization, and uniform laws of bankruptcy, to prescribe the manner in which the public acts, records, and judicial proceedings of each State shall be proved, and the effect they shall have in other States; and to establish post offices and post roads.

ARTICLES FAILED TO REGULATE TRADE:

Sad experience has proven that the Articles had no power to regulate fairly any interstate or foreign commerce.

42:23 The defect of power in the existing Confederacy to regulate the commerce between its several members, is in the number of those which have been clearly pointed out by experience. To the proofs and remarks which former papers have brought into view on this subject, it may be added that without this supplemental provision, the great and essential power of regulating foreign commerce would have been incomplete and ineffectual.

ARTICLES ALLOWED STATES TO TAX EACH OTHER:

If the States could charge import taxes they would surely abuse it.

42:24 A very material object of this power was the relief of the States which import and export through other States, from the improper contributions levied on them by the latter. Were

---

155 *Editors' Note:* The slave States made it clear they would refuse to join the Union if slavery was abolished in the new Constitution. They declared their intention to form their own confederacy of six or more States. The final outcome would be, first, slavery would have continued in those states. Second, the slave-state confederacy would protect its northern border by military means, most likely by an invitation to Spain to bring in troops, arms, and build forts. This would have led to European-style border skirmishes, leaving America a much weaker and vulnerable nation. The compromise to abolish importation of slaves in twenty years, and to retain the slave states in the Union was an ingenious anti-slavery compromise.

these at liberty to regulate the trade between State and State, it must be foreseen that ways would be found out to load the articles of import and export, during the passage through their jurisdiction, with duties which would fall on the makers of the latter and the consumers of the former.

EXORBITANT IMPORT TAXES COULD START FIGHTS:

Could this lead to border skirmishes between States? To war?

42:25   We may be assured by past experience, that such a practice would be introduced by future contrivances; and both by that and a common knowledge of human affairs, that it would nourish unceasing animosities, and not improbably terminate in serious interruptions of the public tranquillity.

UNFAIR TRADE PRACTICE PROMOTES SMUGGLING:

42:26   To those who do not view the question through the medium of passion or of interest, the desire of the commercial States to collect, in any form, an indirect revenue from their uncommercial neighbors, must appear not less impolitic than it is unfair; since it would stimulate the injured party, by resentment as well as interest, to resort to less convenient channels for their foreign trade. But the mild voice of reason, pleading the cause of an enlarged and permanent interest, is but too often drowned, before public bodies as well as individuals, by the clamors of an impatient avidity for immediate and immoderate gain.

THE NEED FOR TOP LEVEL REGULATION OF TRADE:

42:27   The necessity of a superintending authority over the reciprocal trade of confederated States, has been illustrated by other examples as well as our own.

Switzerland's cantons can't charge tolls.

42:28   In Switzerland, where the Union is so very slight, each canton is obliged to allow to merchandises a passage through its jurisdiction into other cantons, without an augmentation of the tolls.

Germany's princes and states can't charge tolls.

42:29   In Germany it is a law of the empire, that the princes and states shall not lay tolls or customs on bridges, rivers, or passages, without the consent of the emperor and the diet; though it appears from a quotation in an antecedent paper, that the practice in this, as in many other instances in that confederacy, has not followed the law, and has produced there the mischiefs which have been foreseen here.

The Netherlands' states can't charge tolls.

42:30   Among the restraints imposed by the Union of the Netherlands on its members, one is, that they shall not establish imposts disadvantageous to their neighbors, without the general permission.

TRADE RELATIONS WITH INDIAN TRIBES:

The Articles left Indian commerce and relations quite confusing.[156] The Constitution removes the confusion by giving Congress sole responsibility.

42:31   The regulation of commerce with the Indian tribes is very properly unfettered from two limitations in the Articles of Confederation, which render the provision obscure and contradictory. The power is there restrained to Indians, not members of any of the States, and is not to violate or infringe the legislative right of any State within its own limits.

STATUS OF INDIANS AS CITIZENS NOT YET RESOLVED:

Madison points out it hasn't been decided how to deem an Indian as a member of a State, or how Congress can regulate Indian trade inside a State without violating that State's rights of legislation.

42:32   What description of Indians are to be deemed members of a State, is not yet settled, and has been a question of frequent perplexity and contention in the federal councils. And how the trade with Indians, though not members of a State, yet residing within its legislative jurisdiction, can be regulated by an external authority, without so far intruding on the internal rights of legislation, is absolutely incomprehensible.

ARTICLES CAN'T TAKE A PART AND AT THE SAME TIME, ALSO LEAVE A WHOLE:

42:33   This is not the only case in which the articles of Confederation have inconsiderately endeavored to accomplish impossibilities; to reconcile a partial sovereignty in the Union, with complete sovereignty in the States; to subvert a mathematical axiom, by taking away a part, and letting the whole remain.

CONSTITUTION CORRECTS MANY OMISSIONS IN ARTICLES:

Articles allow regulating only the coins Congress creates. Uniformity is destroyed because of the States' different regulations.

42:34   All that need be remarked on the power to coin money, regulate the value thereof, and of foreign coin, is, that by providing for this last case, the Constitution has supplied a material omission in the Articles of Confederation. The authority of the existing Congress is restrained to the regulation of coin

---

156   *Editors' Note:* Article IX in the Articles of Confederation grants Congress power of "regulating the trade and managing all affairs with the Indians, not members of any of the states; provided that the legislative right of any state, within its own limits, be not infringed or violated. ..."

STRUCK by their own authority, or that of the respective States. It must be seen at once that the proposed uniformity in the VALUE of the current coin might be destroyed by subjecting that of foreign coin to the different regulations of the different States.

CONGRESS WILL PUNISH COUNTERFEITERS:

42:35 The punishment of counterfeiting the public securities, as well as the current coin, is submitted of course to that authority which is to secure the value of both.

WEIGHTS AND MEASURES IS RETAINED:

42:36 The regulation of weights and measures is transferred from the articles of Confederation, and is founded on like considerations with the preceding power of regulating coin.

RULES OF NATURALIZATION ARE CLARIFIED:

42:37 The dissimilarity in the rules of naturalization has long been remarked as a fault in our system, and as laying a foundation for intricate and delicate questions.

LAWS CREATED UNDER THE ARTICLES WERE OFTEN BASED ON ILL-DEFINED TERMS:
Free inhabitants, citizens, and people.

42:38 In the fourth article of the Confederation, it is declared "that the FREE INHABITANTS of each of these States, paupers, vagabonds, and fugitives from justice, excepted, shall be entitled to all privileges and immunities of FREE CITIZENS in the several States; and THE PEOPLE of each State shall, in every other, enjoy all the privileges of trade and commerce," etc.

ARTICLES MISUSED THESE TERMS FREQUENTLY AND INTERCHANGEABLY:

42:39 There is a confusion of language here, which is remarkable. Why the terms FREE INHABITANTS are used in one part of the article, FREE CITIZENS in another, and PEOPLE in another; or what was meant by superadding to "all privileges and immunities of free citizens," "all the privileges of trade and commerce," cannot easily be determined.

ARTICLES CONFUSED THE CONFERRING OF STATE RIGHTS:

42:40 It seems to be a construction scarcely avoidable, however, that those who come under the denomination of FREE INHABITANTS of a State, although not citizens of such State, are entitled, in every other State, to all the privileges of FREE CITIZENS of the latter; that is, to greater privileges than they may be entitled to in their own State: so that it may be in the power of a particular State, or rather every State is laid under a necessity, not only to confer the rights of citizenship in other States upon any whom it may admit to such rights within itself, but upon any whom it may allow to become inhabitants within its jurisdiction.

RIGHTS OF CITIZENSHIP NOT CLEARLY DEFINED IN THE ARTICLES:

42:41 But were an exposition of the term "inhabitants" to be admitted which would confine the stipulated privileges to citizens alone, the difficulty is diminished only, not removed. The very improper power would still be retained by each State, of naturalizing aliens in every other State. In one State, residence for a short term confirms all the rights of citizenship: in another, qualifications of greater importance are required.

ARTICLES FAILED TO MANAGE EQUAL RIGHTS FOR CITIZENS:

42:42 An alien, therefore, legally incapacitated for certain rights in the latter, may, by previous residence only in the former, elude his incapacity; and thus the law of one State be preposterously rendered paramount to the law of another, within the jurisdiction of the other.

CONFUSION OVER TERMS:
People failing a standard in one State could meet it in another State, then go to the first State and demand equal treatment.

42:43 We owe it to mere casualty, that very serious embarrassments on this subject have been hitherto escaped. By the laws of several States, certain descriptions of aliens, who had rendered themselves obnoxious, were laid under interdicts inconsistent not only with the rights of citizenship but with the privilege of residence. What would have been the consequence, if such persons, by residence or otherwise, had acquired the character of citizens under the laws of another State, and then asserted their rights as such, both to residence and citizenship, within the State proscribing them? Whatever the legal consequences might have been, other consequences would probably have resulted, of too serious a nature not to be provided against.

CONSTITUTION SOLVES ALL DIFFICULT ISSUES INCLUDING NATURALIZATION:

42:44 The new Constitution has accordingly, with great propriety, made provision against them, and all others proceeding from the defect of the Confederation on this head, by authorizing the general government to establish a uniform rule of naturalization throughout the United States.

UNIFORM LAWS REGARDING BANKRUPTCY:

42:45 The power of establishing uniform laws of bankruptcy is so intimately connected with the regulation of commerce, and will prevent so many frauds where the parties or their property may lie or be removed into different States, that the expediency of it seems not likely to be drawn into question.

CONGRESS WILL SET STANDARD FOR MEASURING LEGAL ACTS:
While the Articles gave all State proceedings equal weight in all States, there was no provision to prove or standardize them.

42:46 The power of prescribing by general laws, the manner in which the public acts, records and judicial proceedings of each State shall be proved, and the effect they shall have in other States, is an evident and valuable improvement on the clause relating to this subject in the articles of Confederation. The meaning of the latter is extremely indeterminate, and can be of little importance under any interpretation which it will bear.

CONGRESS SETS STANDARDS SO JUSTICE IS EQUAL FOR ALL:
42:47 The power here established may be rendered a very convenient instrument of justice, and be particularly beneficial on the borders of contiguous States, where the effects liable to justice may be suddenly and secretly translated, in any stage of the process, within a foreign jurisdiction.

MAKING POST ROADS WAS AN IMPORTANT IMPROVEMENT:
Building public post roads promotes the general welfare.

42:48 The power of establishing post roads must, in every view, be a harmless power, and may, perhaps, by judicious management, become productive of great public conveniency.

POST ROADS ALSO ENCOURAGE INTERSTATE COMMERCE:
42:49 Nothing which tends to facilitate the intercourse between the States can be deemed unworthy of the public care.

—PUBLIUS

REVIEW QUESTIONS

1. What two major topics does Madison discuss in paper No. 42? (42:1)

2. What aspect of slavery does he mention in 42:1? (42:1)

3. How long until trafficking in slavery will be ended in America? (42:17–18)

4. Does Madison call for abolishment of slavery in Europe? (42:18)

5. About slavery, what did the Anti-Federalists claim the Constitution supported in Art. I, Sec. 9, Clause 1? (42:19)

6. Which was the better choice: Postponing the end of slavery in twenty years or demanding slavery be stopped immediately and risk losing the slave states? Why? (See 42:17 footnote)

7. What are a few of the parts and pieces involved in interstate commerce that the Constitution regulates? (42:22)

8. How would the public tranquility be impacted if interstate commerce was not regulated by the Union? (42:24–25)

9. Without the Union, what would States impose on goods crossing their borders and lands? (42:24–25)

10. Why is the Indian issue so complicated? (42:31–32, see footnote; 42:37–41)

FEDERALIST NO. 43

FOURTH POWER—REPUBLICANISM, DEBTS, WASHINGTON DC, RATIFICATION: The fourth class of federal powers covers a broad range including copyrights, patents, government landholdings, treason, adding States, national defense, paying off national debts, insurrection, and issues surrounding ratification of the Constitution. The most important power discussed is the guarantee to each State to have a republican form of government which also protects suffrage of the minority, and that each State will be protected from internal violence and invasion. See all six federal powers listed in 41:8.

By James Madison—January 23, 1788

FOURTH CLASS OF POWERS—SEVERAL MISC.:
The miscellaneous powers, divided into nine major points.

43:1 THE FOURTH class comprises the following miscellaneous powers:

ENCOURAGE INVENTION AND PROGRESS:
43:2 **1.** A power "to promote the progress of science and useful arts, by securing, for a limited time,[157] to authors and inventors, the exclusive right to their respective writings and discoveries."

A UNION CAN BEST PROTECT COPYRIGHTS, PATENTS:
Could individual States do a better job of protecting intellectual property?

---

157 *Editors' Note:* "Limited time" allows a temporary monopoly but eventually is released to encourage more inventive ideas.

43:3 The utility of this power will scarcely be questioned. The copyright of authors has been solemnly adjudged, in Great Britain, to be a right of common law. The right to useful inventions seems with equal reason to belong to the inventors.

UNIFORM COPYRIGHT PROTECTION NOT SAFE WITHOUT A UNION:

43:4 The public good fully coincides in both cases with the claims of individuals. The States cannot separately make effectual provisions for either of the cases, and most of them have anticipated the decision of this point, by laws passed at the instance of Congress.

CREATION OF THE SEAT OF GOVERNMENT:
Washington DC is created. All other federal lands within the States may be taken only by the consent of the legislatures. Does this authorize federal wilderness areas and national parks?

43:5 2. "To exercise exclusive legislation, in all cases whatsoever, over such district (not exceeding ten miles square) as may, by cession of particular States and the acceptance of Congress, become the seat of the government of the United States; and to exercise like authority over all places purchased by the consent of the legislatures of the States in which the same shall be, for the erection of forts, magazines, arsenals, dockyards, and other needful buildings."

COMPLETE AUTHORITY OVER THE NATION'S CAPITAL ENSURES STABILITY:
Federal control over the seat of government ensures peace and safety for its ongoing proceedings.

43:6 The indispensable necessity of complete authority at the seat of government, carries its own evidence with it. It is a power exercised by every legislature of the Union, I might say of the world, by virtue of its general supremacy. Without it, not only the public authority might be insulted and its proceedings interrupted with impunity; but a dependence of the members of the general government on the State comprehending the seat of the government, for protection in the exercise of their duty, might bring on the national councils an imputation of awe or influence, equally dishonorable to the government and dissatisfactory to the other members of the Confederacy.

COSTS OF CAPITAL FACILITIES ARE TOO GREAT FOR A STATE:

43:7 This consideration has the more weight, as the gradual accumulation of public improvements at the stationary residence of the government would be both too great a public pledge to be left in the hands of a single State, and would create so many obstacles to a removal of the government, as still further to abridge its necessary independence.

PEOPLE AND THE STATE CONSENTED TO CEDING LAND FOR OUR CAPITOL:
The people living in Washington DC retain rights of citizens.

43:8 The extent of this federal district is sufficiently circumscribed to satisfy every jealousy of an opposite nature. And as it is to be appropriated to this use with the consent of the State ceding it; as the State will no doubt provide in the compact for the rights and the consent of the citizens inhabiting it; as the inhabitants will find sufficient inducements of interest to become willing parties to the cession; as they will have had their voice in the election of the government which is to exercise authority over them; as a municipal legislature for local purposes, derived from their own suffrages, will of course be allowed them; and as the authority of the legislature of the State, and of the inhabitants of the ceded part of it, to concur in the cession, will be derived from the whole people of the State in their adoption of the Constitution, every imaginable objection seems to be obviated.

STATES CAN'T MEDDLE WITH FEDERAL TERRITORIES:
The federal government has complete authority over the land it acquires from the States and facilities it builds.

43:9 The necessity of a like authority over forts, magazines, etc., established by the general government, is not less evident. The public money expended on such places, and the public property deposited in them, requires that they should be exempt from the authority of the particular State. Nor would it be proper for the places on which the security of the entire Union may depend, to be in any degree dependent on a particular member of it.

STATE CONSENT SATISFIES ALL OBJECTIONS:
43:10 All objections and scruples are here also obviated, by requiring the concurrence of the States concerned, in every such establishment.

DEFINITION OF TREASON:
Article 3 Section 3 Clause 1 of the Constitution defines treason. Clause 3 describing punishment is quoted below.

43:11 3. "To declare the punishment of treason, but no **attainder**[158] of treason shall work **corruption of blood**,[159] or forfeiture, except during the life of the person attained."

---

158 **bill of attainder:** A formal act of the government passed by majority vote that declares a specifically named person instantly guilty of a capital crime—without a trial—and simultaneously having his civil rights canceled, all property confiscated, and putting him in jail.

159 **corruption of blood:** This is a consequence of a bill of attainder. It involves punishing the innocent relatives of a felon. The punishment comes in the form of not allowing property to be inherited by the felon, owned by the felon, or passed along by the felon to his descendants. Also, any relative benefit-

TREASON NOT A CRIME UNTIL WAR IS DECLARED:

The act of treason is not an enforceable crime until after Congress declares war with the offending nation. Up to that time anyone may give aid or otherwise engage with an adversarial nation.

43:12   As treason may be committed against the United States, the authority of the United States ought to be enabled to <u>punish it</u>. But as new-fangled and <u>artificial treasons</u> have been the great engines by which violent <u>factions</u>, the natural offspring of free government, have usually wreaked their alternate malignity on each other, the Convention have, with great judgment, opposed a barrier to this peculiar danger, by inserting a <u>constitutional definition of the crime</u>, fixing the <u>proof</u> necessary for conviction of it, <u>and restraining the</u> Congress, even in punishing it, from extending the <u>consequences of guilt beyond the person of its author</u>.

LOCAL LEGISLATURES MUST BE INVOLVED TO CREATE STATES:

43:13   4. "To <u>admit new States</u> into the Union; but no new State shall be formed or erected within the jurisdiction of any other State; nor any State be formed by the junction of two or more States, or parts of States, without the consent of the <u>legislatures of the States concerned</u>, <u>as well as of the Congress</u>."

ARTICLES HAVE NO PROVISION FOR NEW STATES:

43:14   <u>In the articles of Confederation, no provision is found on this important subject. Canada was to be admitted of right, on her joining in the measures of the United States; and the other COLONIES</u>, by which were evidently meant the other British colonies, at the <u>discretion of nine</u> States.

CONSTITUTION CORRECTS THE OMISSION IN ARTICLE IV:

43:15   The eventual establishment of <u>NEW STATES</u> seems to have been overlooked by the compilers of that instrument. We have seen the inconvenience of this omission, and the assumption of power into which Congress have been led by it. With great propriety, therefore, has the new system supplied the defect.

STATE CONSENT REQUIRED TO PARTITION OR COMBINE IT:

State sovereignty is protected from federal overreach.

43:16   <u>The general precaution, that no new States shall be formed, without the concurrence of the federal authority, and that of the States concerned, is consonant to the principles which ought to govern such transactions. The particular precaution against the erection of new States, by the partition of</u> a State without its consent, quiets the jealousy of the larger States; as that of the smaller is quieted by a like precaution, against a junction of States without their consent.

GOVERNMENT-OWNED PROPERTY:

In Article IV of the new Constitution the federal government may own land within the States for the specific purposes listed.

43:17   5. "To <u>dispose of and make all needful rules</u> and regulations respecting the <u>territory</u> or other <u>property belonging to the United States</u>, with a proviso, that nothing in the Constitution shall be so construed as to prejudice any claims of the United States, or of any particular State."

OMITTED BY ARTICLES:

Federal land ownership in each State is very important. Because this was neglected by the Articles it had to be added as a new power by the Convention.

43:18   This is a power of <u>very great importance</u>, and required by considerations similar to those which show the propriety of the former. The proviso annexed is proper in itself, and was probably rendered absolutely necessary by <u>jealousies</u> and questions concerning the <u>Western territory</u> sufficiently known to the public.

CONSISTENT REPUBLICAN GOVERNMENT IN ALL STATES:

The form of government in one State can impact the entire Union. It is prudent to ensure member governments are patterned the same.

43:19   6. "To <u>guarantee to every State in the Union a republican form of government</u>; to protect each of them against invasion; and on application of the legislature, or of the executive (when the legislature cannot be convened), against domestic violence."

DEFENDING REPUBLICANISM:

The Constitution guarantees three things for the States: Their existence, their republican forms, and the maintenance of the federal system as a whole.

43:20   In a confederacy founded on republican principles, and composed of republican members, the <u>superintending government</u> ought clearly to possess authority to <u>defend the system</u> against aristocratic or monarchical innovations. The more intimate the nature of such a union may be, the greater interest have the members in the political institutions of each other; and the greater right to insist that the forms of government under which the compact was entered into should be <u>SUBSTANTIALLY</u> maintained.

---

ing from the felon's reputation, inheritance, government position, or prestige would be stripped of those advantages.

A RIGHT IMPLIES A REMEDY:

43:21 But a right implies a **remedy**;[160] and where else could the remedy be deposited, than where it is deposited by the Constitution?

STATES MUST REMAIN REPUBLICAN:

The specific makeup of a State's government is allowed to vary from State to State so long as it remains republican in form.

43:22 Governments of dissimilar principles and forms have been found less adapted to a federal coalition of any sort, than those of a kindred nature. "As the confederate republic of Germany," says Montesquieu, "consists of free cities and petty states, subject to different princes, experience shows us that it is more imperfect than that of Holland and Switzerland." "Greece was undone," he adds, "as soon as the king of Macedon obtained a seat among the Amphictyons." In the latter case, no doubt, the disproportionate force, as well as the monarchical form, of the new confederate, had its share of influence on the events.

FEDERAL INTERFERENCE WITH STATES IS LOCKED:

The federal government can't interfere in State governments except to ensure there's always a republican form.

43:23 It may possibly be asked, what need there could be of such a precaution, and whether it may not become a pretext for alterations in the State governments, without the concurrence of the States themselves. These questions admit of ready answers.

THIS PROVISION PROTECTS AGAINST INTRIGUES:

43:24 If the interposition of the general government should not be needed, the provision for such an event will be a harmless superfluity only in the Constitution. But who can say what experiments may be produced by the caprice of particular States, by the ambition of enterprising leaders, or by the intrigues and influence of foreign powers?

STATES CAN'T REJECT REPUBLICAN FORM:

The federal government won't impose itself on the specific form of republican government the States choose to adopt so long as it is republican in form.

43:25 To the second question it may be answered, that if the general government should interpose by virtue of this constitutional authority, it will be, of course, bound to pursue the authority. But the authority extends no further than to a GUARANTY of a republican form of government, which supposes a pre-existing government of the form which is to be guaranteed. As long, therefore, as the existing republican forms are continued by the States, they are guaranteed by the federal Constitution. Whenever the States may choose to substitute other republican forms, they have a right to do so, and to claim the federal guaranty for the latter. The only restriction imposed on them is, that they shall not exchange republican for anti-republican Constitutions; a restriction which, it is presumed, will hardly be considered as a grievance.

FEDERAL PROTECTION AGAINST INVASION:

The federal government will protect the Union from foreign invasion and also from the larger States exerting unwanted coercions and influences over the smaller States.

43:26 A protection against invasion is due from every society to the parts composing it. The latitude of the expression here used seems to secure each State, not only against foreign hostility, but against ambitious or vindictive enterprises of its more powerful neighbors. The history, both of ancient and modern confederacies, proves that the weaker members of the union ought not to be insensible to the policy of this article.

DOMESTIC VIOLENCE NOT UNUSUAL:

Giving member states a guarantee of safety is not unusual in other countries.

43:27 Protection against domestic violence is added with equal propriety. It has been remarked, that even among the Swiss cantons, which, properly speaking, are not under one government, provision is made for this object; and the history of that league informs us that mutual aid is frequently claimed and afforded; and as well by the most democratic, as the other cantons.

SHAYS' REBELLION:

43:28 A recent and well-known event among ourselves[161] has warned us to be prepared for emergencies of a like nature.

EVEN IN A REPUBLIC ENFORCEMENT IS NEEDED:

Any combination of people seeking to dismantle a republican government would be subject to federal intervention.

43:29 At first view, it might seem not to square with the republican theory, to suppose, either that a majority have not the right, or that a minority will have the force, to subvert a government; and consequently, that the federal interposition can never be required, but when it would be improper. But theoretic reasoning, in this as in most other cases, must be qualified by the lessons of practice. Why may not illicit combinations, for purposes of violence, be formed as well by

---

160 **remedy:** The guarantee that a right will be defended. The Constitution assigns the satisfaction of that guarantee in Congress to make proper laws protecting a right, and in the judicial system to grant relief when a right is violated.

161 *Editors' Note:* This reference is to Shays' Rebellion, an uprising in 1786–1787 in Massachusetts that spread to other States, to protest aggressive tax collection and corruption in the government.

a majority of a State, especially a <u>small State</u> as by a majority of a county, or a district of the same State; and if the authority of the <u>State</u> ought, in the latter case, to <u>protect</u> the <u>local magistracy</u>, <u>ought not</u> the <u>federal authority</u>, in the former, to <u>support the State authority</u>?

ISOLATED EVENTS CAN IMPACT WHOLE NATION:

43:30 Besides, there are certain parts of the State constitutions which are so interwoven with the federal Constitution, that a violent blow cannot be given to the one without communicating the wound to the other.

IDLE POWERS ARE ALSO A USEFUL DETERRENT:
The federal government has the power to put down insurrections. This would be rarely used. The mere existence of such power also creates a good deterrent against insurrections.

43:31 <u>Insurrections in a State</u> will <u>rarely</u> induce a <u>federal interposition</u>, unless the number concerned in them bear some proportion to the friends of government. It will be much better that the violence in such cases should be repressed by the superintending power, than that the majority should be left to maintain their cause by a bloody and obstinate contest. <u>The existence of a right to interpose</u>, will generally <u>prevent the necessity</u> of exerting it.

FORCE IS NOT ALWAYS ON THE GOOD SIDE:
Is armed force in a State always on the side of truth and liberty?

43:32 Is it true that <u>force and right are necessarily on the same side in republican governments</u>? May not the minor party possess such a superiority of <u>pecuniary resources</u>, of military talents and experience, or of secret succors from foreign powers, as will render it <u>superior also in an appeal to the sword</u>?

MINORITIES CAN OVERPOWER MAJORITIES:

43:33 May not a more compact and advantageous position turn the scale on the same side, against a superior number so situated as to be less capable of a prompt and collected exertion of its strength? Nothing can be more chimerical than to imagine that in a <u>trial of actual force</u>, victory may be calculated by the rules which prevail in a census of the inhabitants, or which determine the event of an election!

BUILDING A COALITION TO OVERPOWER A STATE:

43:34 May it not happen, in fine, that the <u>minority of CITIZENS</u> may become a <u>majority of PERSONS</u>, by the accession of <u>alien residents</u>, of a casual concourse of <u>adventurers</u>, or of those whom the constitution of the State has not <u>admitted to the rights of suffrage</u>?

REVOLT OF THE SLAVES DURING UNREST:

43:35 I take no notice of an unhappy species of population abounding in some of the States, who, during the calm of regular government, are <u>sunk below the level of men</u>; but who, in the tempestuous scenes of civil violence, may emerge into the human character, and give a <u>superiority of strength</u> to any party with which they may associate themselves.

NEIGHBORING STATES ARE BEST IMPARTIAL UMPIRES:

43:36 In cases where it may be doubtful on which side justice lies, what <u>better umpires</u> could be desired by two violent factions, flying to arms, and <u>tearing a State to pieces</u>, than the representatives of confederate States, not heated by the local flame? To the impartiality of judges, they would unite the affection of friends. Happy would it be if such a remedy for its infirmities could be enjoyed by all free governments; if a project equally effectual could be established for the universal peace of mankind!

LESS RISK OF INSURRECTION:
National rebellion is discouraged because Constitution contains ability to defend itself.

43:37 Should it be asked, what is to be the redress for an <u>insurrection pervading all the States</u>, and comprising a superiority of the entire force, though <u>not a constitutional</u> right? the answer must be, that such a case, as it would be without the compass of human remedies, so it is fortunately not within the compass of human probability; and that it is a sufficient recommendation of the federal Constitution, that it diminishes the risk of a calamity for which no possible constitution can provide a cure.

OTHER STATES IN A REPUBLIC CAN QUELL UPRISINGS:

43:38 Among the advantages of a <u>confederate republic</u> enumerated by <u>Montesquieu</u>, an important one is, "that should a popular insurrection happen in one of the States, the others <u>are able to quell it</u>. Should <u>abuses creep</u> into one part, they are reformed by those that remain sound."

PROMISE TO PAY ALL CONFEDERACY DEBTS:

43:39 7. "To consider all debts contracted, and engagements entered into, before the adoption of this Constitution, as being no less valid against the United States, under this Constitution, than under the Confederation."

NEW GOVERNMENTS USUALLY DISMISS OLD DEBTS:
Newly established governments regularly dismiss the debts incurred by the old, a violation of their moral obligation to lenders. In reality, is the excuse "we're starting over" actually dishonest?

43:40 This can only be considered as a <u>declaratory proposition</u>; and may have been inserted, among other reasons, for the satisfaction of the foreign creditors of the United States, who cannot be strangers to the <u>pretended doctrine</u>, that a <u>change in the political form of civil</u> society has the magical effect of <u>dissolving its moral</u> obligations.

SHOULD NEW CONGRESS IGNORE SOME DEBTS?

Critics of the Constitution argue that the promise to pay all debts doesn't go far enough. In truth, every aspect of borrowing and repayment has a moral obligation whether it is specified in writing or not.

43:41 Among the lesser criticisms which have been exercised on the Constitution, it has been remarked that the <u>validity of engagements</u> ought to have been asserted in <u>favor of the United States</u>, as well as against them; and in the spirit which usually characterizes little critics, the omission has been transformed and magnified into a plot against the national rights.

PAYING OLD DEBTS IS RIGHT THING TO DO:

43:42 The authors of this discovery may be told, what few others need to be informed of, that as <u>engagements</u> are in their nature <u>reciprocal</u>, an assertion of their validity on one side, necessarily involves a validity on the other side; and that as the article is merely declaratory, the establishment of the principle in one case is sufficient for every case. They may be further told, that <u>every constitution</u> must limit its precautions to dangers that are not altogether imaginary; and that no real danger can exist that the government would DARE, with, or even without, this constitutional declaration before it, to remit the debts justly due to the public, on the pretext here condemned.

POWERS TO AMEND THE CONSTITUTION:

43:43 8. "To <u>provide for amendments</u> to be ratified by <u>three fourths</u> of the <u>States</u> under two exceptions only."

CANNOT FORESEE ALL NEEDFUL ALTERATIONS:

43:44 That useful alterations will be suggested by experience, could not but be foreseen. It was requisite, therefore, that a mode for introducing them should be provided. The mode preferred by the Convention seems to be stamped with every mark of propriety.

AMENDING MADE DIFFICULT ON PURPOSE:

Constitution must not be easily changed because distrust and chaos results.

43:45 It <u>guards equally against that extreme facility</u>, which would render the Constitution <u>too mutable</u>; and that extreme difficulty, which might perpetuate its discovered faults.

BOTH FEDERAL AND STATES MAY PROPOSE:

Either level of government can propose an amendment (Article V convention) to point out errors.

43:46 It, moreover, equally enables the general and the State governments to originate the amendment of errors, as they may be pointed out by the experience on one side, or on the other.

CANNOT AMEND AWAY THE SENATE— EQUALITY AT THIS LEVEL IS GUARANTEED:

43:47 The exception in favor of the <u>equality of suffrage in the Senate</u>, was probably meant as a **palladium**[162] to the residuary sovereignty of the States, implied and secured by that principle of representation in one branch of the legislature; and was probably insisted on by the States particularly attached to that equality.

43:48 The <u>other exception</u> must have been admitted on the same considerations which produced the privilege defended by it.

RATIFYING BY NINE STATES:

The "conventions of the States" means the citizens of the States holding a convention, *not* their legislatures.

43:49 9. "The ratification of the conventions of <u>nine States</u> shall be sufficient for the establishment of this Constitution between the States, ratifying the same."

REQUIRING A UNANIMOUS VOTE LETS ONE MEMBER BE A HOLDOUT FOR FAVORS:

43:50 This article speaks for itself. The express authority of the people alone could give due validity to the Constitution. To have required the unanimous ratification of the thirteen States, would have subjected the essential interests of the whole to the <u>caprice</u> or <u>corruption</u> of a <u>member</u>. It would have marked a want of foresight in the Convention, which our own experience would have rendered inexcusable.

TWO QUESTIONS ABOUT ARTICLES:

What right is there to ignore the Articles without unanimous consent? And what's the relationship between States voting Yea or Nay for Constitution?

43:51 Two questions of a very delicate nature present themselves on this occasion: 1. On what principle the Confederation, which stands in the solemn form of a compact among the States, can be <u>superseded without the unanimous consent of the parties to it</u>? 2. What relation is to

---

162 *palladium:* A safeguard or protective measure.

subsist between the nine or more States ratifying the Constitution, and the remaining few who do not become parties to it?

FIRST QUESTION: IS SELF-PRESERVATION A RIGHT?

43:52   The first question is answered at once by recurring to the absolute necessity of the case; to the great principle of self-preservation; to the transcendent law of nature and of nature's God, which declares that the safety and happiness of society are the objects at which all political institutions aim, and to which all such institutions must be sacrificed.

THE ARTICLES ARE NOT UNIVERSALLY RESPECTED:

43:53   PERHAPS, also, an answer may be found without searching beyond the principles of the compact itself. It has been heretofore noted among the defects of the Confederation, that in many of the States it had received no higher sanction than a mere legislative ratification. The principle of **reciprocality**[163] seems to require that its obligation on the other States should be reduced to the same standard.

ARTICLES NO STRONGER THAN A TREATY:
One infraction by any one sovereign member and the whole agreement becomes void, if they so choose.

43:54   A compact between independent sovereigns, founded on ordinary acts of legislative authority, can pretend to no higher validity than a league or treaty between the parties. It is an established doctrine on the subject of treaties, that all the articles are mutually conditions of each other; that a breach of any one article is a breach of the whole treaty; and that a breach, committed by either of the parties, absolves the others, and authorizes them, if they please, to pronounce the compact violated and void.

COMPLAINING STATES ARE ALSO PARTIES TO MANY VIOLATIONS OF THE ARTICLES:
It will be hard to insist on unanimous consent to dissolve the Articles when many States have been violating Articles all along.

43:55   Should it unhappily be necessary to appeal to these delicate truths for a justification for dispensing with the consent of particular States to a dissolution of the federal pact, will not the complaining parties find it a difficult task to answer the MULTIPLIED and IMPORTANT infractions with which they may be confronted? The time has been when it was incumbent on us all to veil the ideas which this paragraph exhibits. The scene is now changed, and with it the part which the same motives dictate.

SECOND QUESTION: WHAT RELATION DO WE SEEK WITH DISSENTING STATES?

43:56   The second question is not less delicate; and the flattering prospect of its being merely hypothetical forbids an over-curious discussion of it. It is one of those cases which must be left to provide for itself.

DISSENTING STATES MUST BE RESPECTED:
Should some refuse to join the new Union they must be respected and encouraged to join.

43:57   In general, it may be observed, that although no political relation can subsist between the assenting and dissenting States, yet the moral relations will remain uncancelled. The claims of justice, both on one side and on the other, will be in force, and must be fulfilled; the rights of humanity must in all cases be duly and mutually respected; whilst considerations of a common interest, and, above all, the remembrance of the endearing scenes which are past, and the anticipation of a speedy triumph over the obstacles to reunion, will, it is hoped, not urge in vain MODERATION on one side, and PRUDENCE on the other.

—PUBLIUS

REVIEW QUESTIONS

1. Why is it important that the seat of government not be beholden to the States in any way? (43:6)

2. Why is it important that the federal government have total control over its authorized federal lands within a State? (43:9)

3. Where in the Constitution is treason defined and its punishment? (43:11–12)

4. Can a new State be formed without the consent of all States concerned? (43:16)

5. Can a State reject its republican form of government? (43:25)

6. Should new governments pay off the debts of the prior government? (43:39–42)

7. Why is amending the Constitution made difficult? (43:45)

8. Are the Articles much different than mere treaties? Are treaties easily broken? (43:54)

9. With only nine States needed to ratify the Constitution, how should the non-member States be treated? Why? (43:57)

---

163 ***reciprocality:*** A formal political or social agreement of mutual benefit, dependence, or influence.

FEDERALIST NO. 44

T HE FIFTH AND SIXTH FEDERAL POWERS—SU-
PREMACY, AND NECESSARY AND PROPER LAWS:
The States must be prevented from committing certain dangerous acts. A single State should not be acting on behalf of the
entire nation on either internal or external activities. The Constitution is supreme and Congress must have power to pass any
Constitutional law necessary to perform its duties. The sixth
power, giving proper powers to the government, is examined
starting in 44:19. See all six federal powers listed in 41:8.

By James Madison—January 25, 1788

FIFTH CLASS OF POWERS:
Restrictions on the authority of the several States.

44:1   A FIFTH class of provisions in favor of the federal authority consists of the following restrictions on the authority
of the several States:

FROM ARTICLE I SECTION 10 OF U.S. CONSTITUTION:

44:2   1. "No State shall enter into any treaty, alliance, or confederation; grant letters of marque and reprisal; coin money;
emit bills of credit; make any thing but gold and silver a legal tender in payment of debts; pass any **bill of attainder**,[164]
ex-post-facto law,[165] or law impairing the obligation of contracts; or grant any title of nobility."

STATES AND WAR:
The States may not start or end wars.

44:3   The prohibition against treaties, alliances, and confeder-
ations makes a part of the existing articles of Union; and for
reasons which need no explanation, is copied into the new
Constitution.

LETTERS OF MARQUE:
**The carrier must represent the united power of the Union,
not a single State.**

44:4   The prohibition of letters of marque is another part of
the old system, but is somewhat extended in the new. According to the former, letters of marque could be granted by the
States after a declaration of war; according to the latter, these
licenses must be obtained, as well during war as previous to its
declaration, from the government of the United States. This
alteration is fully justified by the advantage of uniformity in

all points which relate to foreign powers; and of immediate
responsibility to the nation in all those for whose conduct the
nation itself is to be responsible.

COINING MONEY:
**Under the Articles the individual States could coin their
own money. What problems did State-minted coins create
for the nation?**

44:5   The right of coining money, which is here taken from
the States, was left in their hands by the Confederation, as a
concurrent right with that of Congress, under an exception in
favor of the exclusive right of Congress to regulate the alloy
and value. In this instance, also, the new provision is an improvement on the old.

ONLY THE FEDERAL GOVERNMENT MAY DEAL WITH COINING AND VALUES:
Uniformity of money is critical to national prosperity.

44:6   Whilst the alloy and value depended on the general
authority, a right of coinage in the particular States could have
no other effect than to multiply expensive mints and diversi-
fy the forms and weights of the circulating pieces. The latter
inconveniency defeats one purpose for which the power was
originally submitted to the federal head; and as far as the former might prevent an inconvenient remittance of gold and
silver to the central mint for recoinage, the end can be as well
attained by local mints established under the general authority.

STATES CAN'T CREATE ANY FORM OF CURRENCY:
**Paper money is especially risky when issued by States that
lack deep resources to redeem them for gold or silver.**

44:7   The extension of the prohibition to **bills of credit**[166]
must give pleasure to every citizen, in proportion to his love
of justice and his knowledge of the true springs of public prosperity. The loss which America has sustained since the peace,
from the pestilent effects of paper money on the necessary
confidence between man and man, on the necessary confidence in the public councils, on the industry and morals of
the people, and on the character of republican government,
constitutes an enormous debt against the States chargeable
with this unadvised measure, which must long remain un-
satisfied; or rather an accumulation of guilt, which can be ex-
piated no otherwise than by a voluntary sacrifice on the altar
of justice, of the power which has been the instrument of it.

---

164   *bill of attainder:* A legislative act establishing new law of which someone is automatically guilty without a trial.
165   *ex-post-facto law:* A law that criminalizes conduct that was legal when originally performed.
166   *bill of credit:* A promissory note backed by the State (not a bank) to be circulated among the people as real money and redeemable on a future day.

WHAT IF STATES COULD COIN AND SET VALUES?

There would be as many different coins and values as there are States.

44:8 In addition to these persuasive considerations, it may be observed, that the same reasons which show the necessity of denying to the States the power of regulating coin, prove with equal force that they ought not to be at liberty to substitute a paper medium in the place of coin. Had every State a right to regulate the value of its coin, there might be as many different currencies as States, and thus the intercourse among them would be impeded; retrospective alterations in its value might be made, and thus the citizens of other States be injured, and animosities be kindled among the States themselves.

FOREIGN COINS WOULD SUFFER SAME CONFUSION:

44:9 The subjects of foreign powers might suffer from the same cause, and hence the Union be discredited and embroiled by the indiscretion of a single member. No one of these mischiefs is less incident to a power in the States to emit paper money, than to coin gold or silver.

PAYMENT OF DEBTS ONLY IN GOLD OR SILVER:

44:10 The power to make any thing but gold and silver a tender in payment of debts, is withdrawn from the States, on the same principle with that of issuing a paper currency.

UNIFORM LAWS:

State laws that impose on personal rights must be uniform. Therefore, these are a federal responsibility.

44:11 Bills of attainder, ex-post-facto laws, and laws impairing the obligation of contracts, are contrary to the first principles of the **social compact**,[167] and to every principle of sound legislation. The two former are expressly prohibited by the declarations prefixed to some of the State constitutions, and All of them are prohibited by the spirit and scope of these fundamental charters.

GUARDIANS ARE BUILT RIGHT INTO THE CONSTITUTION TO PROTECT RIGHTS:

44:12 Our own experience has taught us, nevertheless, that additional fences against these dangers ought not to be omitted. Very properly, therefore, have the Convention added this constitutional bulwark in favor of personal security and private rights; and I am much deceived if they have not, in so doing, as faithfully consulted the genuine sentiments as the undoubted interests of their constituents.

PEOPLE ARE WEARY OF NATIONAL FLUCTUATING POLICY:

44:13 The sober people of America are weary of the fluctuating policy which has directed the public councils. They have seen with regret and indignation that sudden changes and legislative interferences, in cases affecting personal rights, become jobs in the hands of enterprising and influential speculators, and snares to the more-industrious and less informed part of the community.

ONE VIOLATION OPENS DOOR TO MANY MORE:

44:14 They have seen, too, that one legislative interference is but the first link of a long chain of repetitions, every subsequent interference being naturally produced by the effects of the preceding. They very rightly infer, therefore, that some thorough reform is wanting, which will banish speculations on public measures, inspire a general prudence and industry, and give a regular course to the business of society.

TITLES OF NOBILITY:

44:15 The prohibition with respect to titles of nobility is copied from the articles of Confederation and needs no comment.

STATE'S POWER OF TAXATION:

Quoting the Constitution (Article I, Sec. 10, Clause 2), the States may lay a tax on imports and exports only with the permission of Congress.

44:16 2. "No State shall, without the consent of the Congress, lay any imposts or duties on imports or exports, except what may be absolutely necessary for executing its inspection laws, and the net produce of all duties and imposts laid by any State on imports or exports, shall be for the use of the treasury of the United States; and all such laws shall be subject to the revision and control of the Congress."

STATES FORBIDDEN TO HAVE STANDING ARMIES:

44:17 "No State shall, without the consent of Congress, lay any duty on tonnage, keep troops or ships of war in time of peace, enter into any agreement or compact with another State, or with a foreign power, or engage in war unless actually invaded, or in such imminent danger as will not admit of delay."

FOREIGN TRADE:

Federal regulation of imports and exports will help ensure a fair and standard process for all States.

44:18 The restraint on the power of the States over imports and exports is enforced by all the arguments which prove the

---

167 **social compact:** An unofficial agreement between the States to cooperate on issues that work best if shared in common such as basic laws and rules of trade.

necessity of submitting the regulation of trade to the federal councils. It is needless, therefore, to remark further on this head, than that the manner in which the restraint is qualified seems well calculated at once to secure to the States a reasonable discretion in providing for the conveniency of their imports and exports, and to the United States a reasonable check against the abuse of this discretion. The remaining particulars of this clause fall within reasonings which are either so obvious, or have been so fully developed, that they may be passed over without remark.

SIXTH CLASS OF POWERS:
These are powers given to do the job.

44:19 The SIXTH and last class consists of the several powers and provisions by which efficacy is given to all the rest.

NECESSARY AND PROPER:
This clause grants power to manage things unknown. It gave Congress the power to fulfill its duties without violating the Constitution.

44:20 **1.** Of these the first is, the "power to make all laws which shall be necessary and proper for carrying into execution the foregoing powers, and all other powers vested by this Constitution in the government of the United States, or in any department or officer thereof."

WITHOUT THIS "NECESSARY AND PROPER" CLAUSE THE CONSTITUTION IS DEAD:

44:21 Few parts of the Constitution have been assailed with more intemperance than this; yet on a fair investigation of it, no part can appear more completely invulnerable. Without the SUBSTANCE of this power, the whole Constitution would be a dead letter.

COULD ANY BETTER GRANT OF POWER BE CRAFTED?

44:22 Those who object to the article, therefore, as a part of the Constitution, can only mean that the FORM of the provision is improper. But have they considered whether a better form could have been substituted?

PROBLEM OF LISTING POWERS:
There are four alternatives to granting power aside from allowing laws "necessary and proper." Each alternative, however, would not contain or permit government action to the degree as does the simple term "necessary and proper."

44:23 There are four other possible methods which the Constitution might have taken on this subject.

ARTICLES CAN'T SOLVE THE PROBLEM:

44:24 [1] They might have copied the second article of the existing Confederation, which would have prohibited the exercise of any power not EXPRESSLY delegated;

MAKING AN ALL-INCLUSIVE LIST IS IMPOSSIBLE:

44:25 [2] they might have attempted a positive enumeration of the powers comprehended under the general terms "necessary and proper";

LISTING ALL DENIALS IS ALSO IMPOSSIBLE:

44:26 [3] they might have attempted a negative enumeration of them, by specifying the powers excepted from the general definition;

SILENCE ON THE MATTER WOULD BE TOO DANGEROUS:

44:27 [4] they might have been altogether silent on the subject, leaving these necessary and proper powers to construction and inference.

"EXPRESSLY" IS TOO VAGUE:
(For use of "expressly," see Article II of the Articles of Confederation.) Madison argued this term could be used so broadly there would be no control over Congress at all, or so narrowly as to disarm Congress of any power.

44:28 Had the Convention taken the first method of adopting the second article of Confederation,[168] it is evident that the new Congress would be continually exposed, as their predecessors have been,

Defining the word "expressly" too strongly.

44:29 to the alternative of construing the term "EXPRESSLY"[169] with so much rigor, as to disarm the government of all real authority whatever,

Defining the word "expressly" too weakly.

44:30 or with so much latitude as to destroy altogether the force of the restriction.

CONGRESS REGULARLY HAD TO VIOLATE THE ARTICLES:
No important power in the Articles could be exercised without Congress creating or implying powers they legally didn't have.

44:31 It would be easy to show, if it were necessary, that no important power, delegated by the articles of Confederation, has been or can be executed by Congress, without recurring

---

168 *Publius:* "Article II. Each state retains its sovereignty, freedom, and independence, and every Power, Jurisdiction and right, which is not by this confederation expressly delegated to the United States, in Congress assembled."

169 *expressly:* For a specific purpose. That word created havoc because it was too open to interpretation and argument.

more or less to the doctrine of <u>CONSTRUCTION or IM-PLICATION</u>.

CONGRESS WILL VIOLATE LAW WITHOUT THIS CLAUSE:

Congress under the new Constitution would also be guilty of violating the law without a specific clause granting necessary but unknown powers.

44:32 As the powers delegated under the new system are more extensive, the government which is to administer it would find itself still more distressed with the alternative of betraying the public interests by doing nothing, or of violating the Constitution by exercising powers indispensably necessary and proper, but, at the same time, <u>not EXPRESSLY granted</u>.

LISTING ALL POWERS ALSO AN IMPOSSIBLE TASK:

44:33 Had the Convention attempted a positive enumeration of the powers necessary and proper for carrying their other powers into effect, the attempt would have involved a <u>complete digest of laws on every subject</u> to which the Constitution relates; accommodated too, not only to the existing state of things, but to <u>all the possible changes</u> which <u>futurity</u> may produce; for in every new application of a general power, the <u>PARTICULAR POWERS</u>, which are the means of <u>attaining the OBJECT</u> of the general power, must <u>always</u> necessarily <u>vary</u> with that object, and be often properly varied whilst the object remains the same.

LISTING POWERS NOT NEEDED ALSO IMPOSSIBLE:

44:34 Had they attempted to <u>enumerate</u> the particular <u>powers</u> or means <u>not necessary</u> or proper for carrying the general powers into execution, the task would have been <u>no less **chimerical**</u>;[170] and would have been liable to this further objection, that <u>every defect in the enumeration</u> would have been equivalent to a <u>positive grant of authority</u>.

EVEN A PARTIAL LIST OF POWERS WOULD HAVE FAILED TO ENCOMPASS THE ISSUES:

44:35 If, to avoid this consequence, they had attempted a partial enumeration of the exceptions, and described the residue by the general terms, <u>NOT NECESSARY OR PROPER</u>, it must have happened that the enumeration would comprehend a few of the excepted powers only; that these would be such as would be least likely to be assumed or tolerated, because the enumeration would of course select such as would be least necessary or proper; and that the unnecessary and improper powers included in the residuum, would be less forcibly excepted, than if no partial enumeration had been made.

WITHOUT "SWEEPING CLAUSE," THE SAME POWERS WOULD BE IMPLIED ANYWAY:

The Constitution's power to make all laws that are "necessary and proper" was assumed to be a power under the Articles. What would have happened if the Constitution was silent on powers?

44:36 Had the Constitution been silent on this head, there can be no doubt that all the particular powers requisite as means of executing the <u>general powers</u> would have resulted to the government, by <u>unavoidable implication</u>.

IF RESULTS ARE REQUIRED, POWERS ARE IMPLIED:

44:37 No axiom is more clearly established in law, or in reason, than that wherever the <u>end</u> is <u>required</u>, the means are <u>authorized</u>; wherever a general power to do a thing is given, every <u>particular power necessary</u> for doing it is included.

WITHOUT THIS CLAUSE EVERY OBJECTION REMAINS:

44:38 Had this last method, therefore, been pursued by the Convention, every objection now urged against their plan would remain in all its plausibility; and the real inconveniency would be incurred of not removing a <u>pretext</u> which may be seized on <u>critical occasions</u> for drawing into question the <u>essential powers</u> of the Union.

CONSEQUENCES IF CONGRESS OVERSTEPS BOUNDS:

44:39 If it be asked <u>what is</u> to be the <u>consequence</u>, in case the Congress shall misconstrue this part of the Constitution, and <u>exercise powers</u> not warranted by its true meaning, I answer, the same as if they should misconstrue or enlarge any other power vested in them; as if the general power had been reduced to particulars, and any one of these were to be violated; the same, in short, as if the State legislatures should violate the irrespective constitutional authorities.

JUDICIAL, EXECUTIVE, AND THE PEOPLE NEED TO BE A CHECK:

44:40 In the first instance, the <u>success of the usurpation will depend</u> on the <u>executive</u> and <u>judiciary departments</u>, which are to <u>expound and give effect to the legislative acts</u>; and in the last resort a <u>remedy must be obtained from the people</u> who can, by the <u>election of more faithful representatives</u>, <u>annul the acts of the usurpers</u>.

STATES ALSO ACT AS A CHECK:

The State legislators will watch for federal overreach, and react at any trespass.

---

170 ***chimerical:*** Imaginary, vainly conceived, can have no existence except in thought.

44:41 The truth is that this ultimate redress may be more confided in against unconstitutional acts of the federal than of the State legislatures, for this plain reason, that as every such act of the former will be an invasion of the rights of the latter, these will be ever ready to mark the innovation, to sound the alarm to the people, and to exert their local influence in effecting a change of federal representatives.

THERE IS NO INTERMEDIATE CHECK ON STATE LEVEL:

44:42 There being no such intermediate body between the State legislatures and the people interested in watching the conduct of the former, violations of the State constitutions are more likely to remain unnoticed and unredressed.

CONSTITUTION IS SUPREME:

Quoting from Article VI Clause 2, the supremacy clause says the Constitution is supreme in its delegations over the States' laws and constitutions.

44:43 2. "This Constitution and the laws of the United States which shall be made in pursuance thereof, and all treaties made, or which shall be made, under the authority of the United States, shall be the supreme law of the land, and the judges in every State shall be bound thereby, any thing in the constitution or laws of any State to the contrary notwithstanding."

WHAT IF STATES WERE SUPREME?

There would be four negative outcomes if the States could remain supreme.

44:44 The indiscreet zeal of the adversaries to the Constitution has betrayed them into an attack on this part of it also, without which it would have been evidently and radically defective. To be fully sensible of this, we need only suppose for a moment that the supremacy of the State constitutions had been left complete by a saving clause in their favor.

FIRST, NO POWER IN FEDERAL:

Constitution would not have power to fix the flaws in the Articles of Confederation.

44:45 In the first place, as these constitutions invest the State legislatures with absolute sovereignty, in all cases not excepted by the existing articles of Confederation, all the authorities contained in the proposed Constitution, so far as they exceed those enumerated in the Confederation, would have been annulled, and the new Congress would have been reduced to the same impotent condition with their predecessors.

SECOND, STATES WOULD IGNORE CONGRESS:

The various States could ignore the Constitution as a mere compact instead of solid, enforceable law, and rendering Congress as impotent as before.

44:46 In the next place, as the constitutions of some of the States do not even expressly and fully recognize the existing powers of the Confederacy, an express saving of the supremacy of the former would, in such States, have brought into question every power contained in the proposed Constitution.

THIRD, NO CONSISTENCY AMONG THE STATES:

The various States could randomly interpret laws and treaties, and void them if desired.

44:47 In the third place, as the constitutions of the States differ much from each other, it might happen that a treaty or national law, of great and equal importance to the States, would interfere with some and not with other constitutions, and would consequently be valid in some of the States, at the same time that it would have no effect in others.

FOURTH, TAIL WAGGING THE DOG:

If the general government was not supreme, then the States would control it to their demise, in the same way as they did with the Articles.

44:48 In fine, the world would have seen, for the first time, a system of government founded on an inversion of the fundamental principles of all government; it would have seen the authority of the whole society every where subordinate to the authority of the parts; it would have seen a monster, in which the head was under the direction of the members.

SWEARING OATH TO CONSTITUTION:

Why must government officers take an oath to support the Constitution and not take an oath to support the States' constitutions?

44:49 3. "The Senators and Representatives, and the members of the several State legislatures, and all executive and judicial officers, both of the United States and the several States, shall be bound by oath or affirmation to support this Constitution."

CAN'T SERVE TWO MASTERS:

44:50 It has been asked why it was thought necessary, that the State magistracy should be bound to support the federal Constitution, and unnecessary that a like oath should be imposed on the officers of the United States, in favor of the State constitutions.

FEDERAL OFFICERS NOT BOUND TO STATE GOVERNMENTS:

Wherever the federal is supreme, officers from the various States must support what's best for entire nation.

44:51 Several reasons might be assigned for the distinction. I content myself with one, which is obvious and conclusive.

The members of the federal government will have no agency in carrying the State constitutions into effect.

ELECTING PRESIDENT, CHOOSING SENATORS:
The State legislatures play a direct role in choosing senators and electors for the President. *Note: The direct dependence mentioned below was stripped away by the Seventeenth Amendment.*

44:52 The members and officers of the State governments, on the contrary, will have an <u>essential agency</u> in giving effect to the <u>federal Constitution</u>. <u>The election of the President and Senate will depend, in all cases, on the legislatures of the several States</u>. And the <u>election of the House</u> of Representatives will equally depend on the same authority in the first instance; and will, probably, forever be <u>conducted by the officers</u>, and according to the <u>laws, of the States</u>.

GIVING GOVERNMENT POWER:
Is there anything else that gives power to the federal government?

44:53 **4.** Among the provisions for giving efficacy to the federal powers might be added those which belong to the executive and judiciary departments: but as these are reserved for particular examination in another place, I pass them over in this.

PRESERVING THE UNION:
The powers delegated are critical to preserving the Union. Are there any powers given to the federal government that go too far or don't go far enough?

44:54 We have <u>now reviewed</u>, in detail, all the articles composing the sum or quantity of <u>power delegated by the proposed Constitution</u> to the federal government, and are brought to this undeniable conclusion, that <u>no part of the power is unnecessary or improper</u> for accomplishing the <u>necessary objects</u> of the Union.

POWERS NECESSARY TO PRESERVE GOVERNMENT:
44:55 The question, therefore, whether this amount of power shall be granted or not, resolves itself into another question, <u>whether or not a government commensurate to the exigencies of the Union</u> shall be established; or, in other words, <u>whether the Union itself shall be preserved</u>.

—PUBLIUS

REVIEW QUESTIONS

1. What does Madison intend to talk about in paper No. 44? (44:1)

2. Generally speaking, what activities are the States prohibited from performing? (44:2–18)

3. What would be the consequences if the States could print their own money? (44:8)

4. What happens to law and order if the Constitution is regularly violated to meet the nation's immediate needs? (44:14)

5. Without the power to make all laws necessary and proper, where would that leave the Constitution? (44:21)

6. If that clause ("all laws which shall be necessary and proper") were not included as it is, what are four alternatives whereby the Convention might have given Congress the power to fulfill its duties? (44:24–27)

7. What word creates more questions than it answers? Why? (44:28–30)

8. If a government is authorized to achieve an "end," what must also be authorized for that to happen? (44:37)

9. Without power to pass laws necessary and proper, can the Union itself be preserved? (44:55)

SECTION 6 • PROTECTING THE STATES

Papers 45–48

FEDERALIST NO. 45

FEDERALISM WON'T HARM STATES; THE SIXTH POWER: The powers granted to the federal government don't strip away all the powers left to the States. The States must lose some sovereignty but this is necessary to create a strong Union. This doesn't mean the federal level will become a new monarchy. Examples from history demonstrate that "local sovereignties prevailed" in tests of power with their central governments. This paper discusses one of the main pillars of the Constitution, the compromise between federal and States governments over political authority. See all six federal powers listed in 41:8.

By James Madison—January 26, 1788

FEDERAL POWERS ARE MANAGEABLE:
Will federal powers be too much and too dangerous for the States?

45:1 HAVING shown that <u>no one of the powers</u> transferred to the federal government is <u>unnecessary</u> or <u>improper</u>, the next question to be considered is, whether the <u>whole mass</u> of them will be <u>dangerous to the portion of authority left in the several States</u>.

FEDERAL POWER'S IMPACT ON STATES:
Did the anti-Constitution movement focus on the wrong question?

45:2 The <u>adversaries</u> to the plan of the Convention, <u>instead of considering</u> in the first place what <u>degree of power</u> was absolutely <u>necessary</u> for the purposes of the federal government, have <u>exhausted themselves</u> in a <u>secondary inquiry</u> into the <u>possible consequences</u> of the proposed degree of power to the governments of the particular States.

UNION IS ESSENTIAL, BUT STATES' ROLE NOT DIMINISHED:
Union is critical for safety against both external and internal threats.

45:3 But if the Union, as has been shown, be <u>essential</u> to the <u>security</u> of the people of America against <u>foreign danger</u>; if it be essential to their security against contentions and <u>wars among the different States</u>; if it be essential to guard them against those violent and <u>oppressive factions</u> which embitter the blessings of liberty, and against those military establishments which must gradually poison its very fountain; if, in a word, <u>the Union</u> be <u>essential to</u> the happiness of the people of America, is it not preposterous, to urge as an <u>objection to a government</u>, <u>without</u> which the objects of the <u>Union cannot be attained</u>, that such a government may **derogate**[171] from the importance of the governments of the individual States?

WAR FOUGHT FOR LIBERTY NOT POLITICAL VANITY:
Was the Revolution fought so the States could rule instead of gaining the inherent blessings of forming a more perfect Union?

45:4 Was, then, the American Revolution effected, was the American Confederacy formed, was the precious <u>blood of thousands spilt</u>, and the <u>hard-earned substance of millions lavished</u>, not that the people of America should enjoy peace, liberty, and safety, but that the government of the <u>individual States</u>, that particular municipal establishments, might enjoy a certain extent <u>of power</u>, and be arrayed with certain dignities and attributes of <u>sovereignty</u>?

PEOPLE NOT MADE FOR KINGS:
That old doctrine has no place in a free nation. Will the people willingly submit to a new monarchy or demand new leadership submissive to them?

45:5 We have heard of the impious doctrine in the Old World, that the <u>people</u> were <u>made for kings</u>, <u>not</u> <u>kings for the people</u>. Is the <u>same doctrine</u> to be <u>revived</u> in the New, in another shape that the solid <u>happiness of the people</u> is to be <u>sacrificed</u> to the views of <u>political institutions</u> of a different form?

---

171 *derogate:* To detract or deviate from; to lessen the importance of something that no longer needs to be considered.

PUBLIC WELFARE IS GOVERNMENT'S TOP PRIORITY:

The *form* of government must surrender to *substance*—in other words, to what the people need more than want.

45:6　It is too early for politicians to presume on our forgetting that the public good, the <u>real welfare of the great body of the people</u>, is the <u>supreme object</u> to be <u>pursued</u>; and that <u>no form of government</u> whatever has any other <u>value</u> than as it may be fitted for the attainment of <u>this object</u>.

CONVENTION WAS TRUE TO ITS APPROVED MANDATE:

If any form of new government jeopardizes happiness it should be rejected.

45:7　Were the plan of the Convention adverse to the public happiness, my voice would be, Reject the plan. Were the <u>Union</u> itself <u>inconsistent</u> with the <u>public happiness</u>, it would be, <u>Abolish the Union</u>.

BALANCING STATE SOVEREIGNTY WITH THE PURSUIT OF HAPPINESS:

45:8　In like manner, as far as the <u>sovereignty of the States</u> <u>cannot</u> be <u>reconciled</u> to the <u>happiness of the people</u>, the voice of every good citizen must be, Let the former be <u>sacrificed</u> to the latter. <u>How far</u> the sacrifice is necessary, has been <u>shown</u>. How far the <u>unsacrificed residue</u> will be <u>endangered</u>, is the <u>question</u> before us.

STATES WILL BE MORE INTRUSIVE THAN FEDERAL:

Which is more likely to ruin the Union, the gradual encroachment by the federal government or gradual independence by the States?

45:9　Several important considerations have been touched in the course of these papers, which discountenance the supposition that the operation of the <u>federal government</u> will by degrees prove <u>fatal to the State governments</u>. The more I revolve the subject, the more fully I am persuaded that the balance is much more likely to be disturbed by the <u>preponderancy of the last</u> than of the first scale.

PEOPLE GRANT POLITICAL AUTHORITY:

The general government was to be authorized by the people themselves.

45:10　We have seen, in all the examples of ancient and modern confederacies, the strongest tendency continually betraying itself in the members, to <u>despoil the general government</u> of its authorities, with a very ineffectual capacity in the latter to defend itself against the encroachments. Although, in most of these examples, the system has been so <u>dissimilar</u> from that under consideration as greatly to weaken any inference concerning the latter from the fate of the former, yet, as the <u>States</u> <u>will retain</u>, under the proposed <u>Constitution</u>, a very <u>extensive portion of active sovereignty</u>, the inference ought not to be wholly disregarded.

ANCIENT CONFEDERACIES RUINED BY WEAK LEADERS:

The general governments of the ancient leagues could not prevent dissensions and disunion of their sovereign members.

45:11　In the <u>Achaean league</u> it is probable that the federal head had a degree and species of power, which gave it a considerable likeness to the government framed by the Convention. The <u>Lycian Confederacy</u>, as far as its principles and form are transmitted, must have borne a still greater analogy to it. Yet history does not inform us that either of them ever degenerated, or tended to <u>degenerate, into one consolidated government</u>. On the <u>contrary</u>, we know that the <u>ruin of one</u> of them proceeded from the <u>incapacity of the federal</u> authority to prevent the dissensions, and finally the <u>disunion</u>, of the <u>subordinate authorities</u>.

ANCIENT UNIONS WERE VERY MOTIVATED TO SURVIVE:

45:12　These cases are the more worthy of our attention, as the external causes by which the <u>component parts</u> were <u>pressed together</u> were much more <u>numerous</u> and <u>powerful</u> than in our case; and consequently less powerful ligaments within would be sufficient to bind the members to the head, and to each other.

FEUDAL BARONS OFTEN PREVAILED OVER THE KING:

In a conflict of feudal power, the people usually sided more often with their local baron than the more distant and less-engaged king.

45:13　In the <u>feudal system</u>, we have seen a similar propensity exemplified. Notwithstanding the want of proper sympathy in every instance between the local sovereigns and the people, and the sympathy in some instances between the general sovereign and the latter, it <u>usually happened</u> that the <u>local sovereigns prevailed</u> in the rivalship for encroachments.

EUROPE ALMOST SHATTERED:

If the people had trusted their local leaders more, and if greater threats had arisen, Europe might have become thousands of small kingdoms instead of a few large nations.

45:14　Had no <u>external dangers</u> enforced <u>internal harmony</u> and subordination, and particularly, had the local sovereigns possessed the affections of the people, the great kingdoms in <u>Europe</u> would at this time consist of as <u>many independent</u> princes as there were formerly feudatory barons.

STATE GOVERNMENTS HAVE ADVANTAGE:
When compared side by side, the States retain several advantages over the general government.

45:15 The <u>State governments</u> will have the <u>advantage</u> of the federal government, whether we compare them in <u>respect</u> to the immediate <u>dependence of the one on the other</u>; to the <u>weight of personal</u> influence which each side will possess; to the <u>powers respectively vested</u> in them; to the predilection and probable support of the people; to the disposition and faculty of resisting and frustrating the measures of each other.

FEDERAL DEPENDS ON STATE, NOT VICE VERSA:
Under the new Constitution the federal government depends on the States for its very existence and function.

45:16 The <u>State governments</u> may be regarded as constituent and essential <u>parts of the federal government</u>; whilst the <u>latter is nowise essential to the operation or organization of the former</u>.

LEGISLATURES NECESSARY TO ELECT PRESIDENT:
This intimate tie to the federal process gives constitutional protection to the survival of the State as an entity.

45:17 <u>Without the intervention of the State legislatures, the President of the United States cannot be elected</u> at all. <u>They must in all cases have a great share in his appointment, and will</u>, perhaps, in most cases, <u>of themselves determine it</u>.

Legislatures appoint all the senators.

45:18 The Senate[172] will be <u>elected</u> absolutely and <u>exclusively by the State legislatures</u>.

Legislatures have strong influence on choice for Representatives.

45:19 Even the House of Representatives, though drawn immediately from the people, will be chosen very much under the <u>influence of that class of men</u>, whose influence over the people obtains for themselves an election into the <u>State legislatures</u>. Thus, each of the principal branches of the <u>federal government</u> will owe its existence more or less to the favor of the <u>State governments</u>, and must consequently feel a dependence, which is much more likely to beget a disposition too obsequious than too overbearing towards them.

STATE DOES NOT DEPEND ON FEDERAL GOVERNMENT:
Will any of the State governments likewise be dependent on the federal?

45:20 On the other side, the <u>component parts of the State governments</u> will in <u>no instance</u> be <u>indebted for their appointment</u> to the direct agency of the <u>federal government</u>, and very little, if at all, to the local influence of its members.

STATES MORE INFLUENTIAL:
Which government did the Framers anticipate would be the largest in number, the federal or the State?

45:21 The number of individuals employed under the Constitution of the United States will be much smaller than the number employed under the particular States. There will consequently be less of personal influence on the side of the former than of the latter. The members of the legislative, executive, and judiciary departments of thirteen and more States, the <u>justices of peace</u>, officers of <u>militia</u>, ministerial <u>officers of justice</u>, with all the county, corporation, and town officers, for <u>three millions and more of people</u>, intermixed, and having particular acquaintance with every class and circle of people, <u>must exceed</u>, beyond all proportion, both in number and influence, those of every description who will be employed in the administration of the <u>federal system</u>.

MORE PEOPLE WORK FOR STATES:
The numbers of State officers compared to federal officers in the same positions, including those carrying arms, favors the States in number.

45:22 Compare the members of the three great departments of the thirteen States, excluding from the judiciary department the justices of peace, with the members of the corresponding departments of the single government of the Union; compare the militia officers of three millions of people with the military and marine officers of any establishment which is within the compass of probability, or, I may add, of possibility, and in this view alone, we may pronounce the <u>advantage</u> of the <u>States</u> to be <u>decisive</u>.

BOTH STATE AND FEDERAL LEVELS COLLECT TAXES:
Federal revenue will come mostly from import and export revenue operated at the coastal ports. State collections will be nationwide.

45:23 If the <u>federal</u> government is to have <u>collectors</u> of revenue, the <u>State</u> governments will have <u>theirs</u> also. And as those of the <u>former</u> will be principally on the <u>seacoast</u>, and <u>not very numerous</u>, whilst those of the latter will be spread over the <u>face of the country</u>, and will be very <u>numerous</u>, the advantage in this view also lies on the same side.

---

172 *Editors' Note:* The Seventeenth Amendment destroyed this important link from States to the federal level. No longer do the legislatures have direct representatives on the federal level. Originally they could check the senators' behavior with the power to hire and fire them.

FEDERAL GOVERNMENT'S POWER TO COLLECT REVENUE:

The general government has power to collect taxes but would not turn to that option except to supplement the general needs.

45:24 It is true, that the Confederacy is to possess, and <u>may exercise</u>, the power of collecting <u>internal</u> as well as <u>external taxes</u> throughout the States; but it is <u>probable that</u> this power will <u>not be resorted to</u>, except for <u>supplemental purposes of revenue</u>; that an option will then be given to the States to supply their quotas by previous collections of their own; and that the eventual <u>collection</u>, under the immediate authority of the Union, will generally be made <u>by the officers</u>, and according to the rules, appointed by the <u>several States</u>. Indeed it is extremely probable, that in other instances, particularly in the organization of the <u>judicial power</u>, the <u>officers of the States</u> will be clothed with the correspondent authority of the <u>Union</u>.

FEDERAL TAX COLLECTORS FEWER IN NUMBER:

What does Madison guess would be the ratio of State to federal agents employed to collect revenue?

45:25 Should it happen, however, that separate collectors of internal revenue should be appointed under the federal government, the influence of the whole number would not bear a comparison with that of the multitude of State officers in the opposite scale.

STATE COLLECTORS WOULD OUTNUMBER FEDERAL:

45:26 Within every district to which a <u>federal collector</u> <u>would be allotted</u>, there would not be less than thirty or forty, or even more, officers of different descriptions, and many of them persons of character and weight, whose <u>influence would lie on the side of the State</u>.

FEDERAL RESPONSIBILITIES ARE FEW AND DEFINED:

The federal government is in charge, for the most part, of external affairs and will collect taxes for those.

45:27 <u>The powers delegated by the proposed Constitution to the federal government are few and defined.</u>

STATE RESPONSIBILITIES ARE NUMEROUS:

45:28 <u>Those which are to remain in the State governments are numerous and indefinite.</u>

FEDERAL LEVEL DEALS WITH EXTERNAL AFFAIRS:

45:29 The <u>former</u> will be exercised principally on <u>external objects</u>, as war, peace, negotiation, and foreign commerce;

with which last the power of taxation will, for the most part, be connected.

STATE LEVEL DEALS BETTER WITH INTERNAL AFFAIRS:

The State governments naturally are much closer to the people and therefore more involved in their intimate societies.

45:30 The powers reserved to the several <u>States will extend</u> to <u>all the objects</u> which, in the ordinary course of affairs, <u>concern the lives, liberties, and properties of the people</u>, and the <u>internal</u> order, <u>improvement</u>, and <u>prosperity</u> of the <u>State</u>.

FEDERAL GOVERNMENT HAS ALL WARTIME POWERS:

45:31 The operations of the <u>federal government</u> will be most extensive and important in <u>times of war and danger</u>; those of the <u>State governments</u>, in times of <u>peace and security</u>.

A WELL-PREPARED FEDERAL GOVERNMENT IS SAFER:

45:32 As the former periods will probably bear a small proportion to the latter, the State governments will here enjoy another advantage over the federal government. The <u>more adequate</u>, indeed, the federal powers may be rendered to the <u>national defense</u>, the <u>less frequent</u> will be those scenes of <u>danger</u> which might favor their ascendancy over the governments of the particular States.

INVIGORATING THE ARTICLES' ORIGINAL POWERS:

The new Constitution doesn't add new powers as much as it improves the powers Congress already has under the Articles.

45:33 If the new Constitution be examined with accuracy and candor, it will be found that the change which it proposes consists much less in the addition of <u>NEW POWERS to the Union</u>, than in the <u>invigoration of its ORIGINAL POWERS</u>.

REGULATION OF COMMERCE IS A NEW POWER THAT FEW PEOPLE OPPOSE:

The Articles already give Congress several powers, and the commerce clause simply helps to administer them more effectively.

45:34 The <u>regulation of commerce</u>, it is true, is a <u>new power</u>; but that seems to be an addition which <u>few oppose</u>, and from which no apprehensions are entertained. The <u>powers relating to war and peace</u>, armies and fleets, treaties and finance, with the other more considerable powers, are <u>all vested in the existing Congress</u> by the articles of Confederation. The proposed change does <u>not enlarge</u> these powers; it only substitutes a <u>more effectual mode</u> of administering them.

ARTICLES ALREADY GRANT TAXING AUTHORITY:

This power already exists in the present Congress. Under the new form, it improves the use of existing powers.

45:35 The change relating to taxation may be regarded as the most important; and yet the <u>present Congress</u> have as <u>complete authority</u> to <u>REQUIRE of the States indefinite supplies</u> of money for the common defense and general welfare, as the future Congress will have to require them of individual citizens; and the latter will be no more bound than the States themselves have been, to <u>pay the quotas respectively</u> taxed on them.

IF STATES COULD HAVE WORKED TOGETHER BETTER:

45:36 Had the <u>States complied punctually</u> with the articles of Confederation, or could their compliance have been enforced by as <u>peaceable means</u> as may be used with success towards single persons, our <u>past experience</u> is very far from countenancing [admitting as possible] an opinion, that the <u>State governments</u> would have <u>lost their constitutional powers</u>, and have gradually undergone an entire consolidation. To maintain that such an event would have ensued, <u>would be to say</u> at once, that the existence of the <u>State governments</u> is <u>incompatible</u> with any system whatever that accomplishes the essential <u>purposes of the Union</u>.

—PUBLIUS

REVIEW QUESTIONS

1. Will federal powers as a whole be dangerous to the States? (45:1–3)

2. Was the war fought to sustain the States in their current form, or to establish peace and prosperity for all? (45:5–6)

3. What supreme object the government must pursue? (45:6)

4. Which is more likely, the States intruding to spoil the federal powers or vice versa? (45:9–10)

5. In Madison's famous maxim, "The powers delegated by the proposed Constitution to the federal government are _____ and _____." (45:27)

6. And the second half, "Those which are to remain in the State governments are _____ and _____." (45:28)

7. To what are federal powers to extend? (45:29)

8. To what are the State powers to extend? (45:30)

9. Generally speaking, does the Constitution add new powers or energize the original powers of government? (45:33)

FEDERALIST NO. 46

FEDERAL POWERS ARE FEW, STATE POWERS ARE MANY, CONFLICTS FAVOR THE STATES: The States have inherent advantages over the federal government: The people are closer to State representatives and will trust them more, provided the States don't violate that trust. If the federal level encroached on States' rights, the States would combine together to resist it. If push comes to shove, the State militias and populace are better armed than the federal military. See all six federal powers listed in 41:8.

By James Madison—January 29, 1788

ALL GOVERNMENTS MUST DEPEND ON THE PEOPLE:

The people must be able to trust their governments, State and federal.

46:1 RESUMING the subject of the last paper, I proceed to inquire <u>whether</u> the <u>federal government</u> or the <u>State governments</u> will have the <u>advantage</u> with regard to the predilection and support of the people. Notwithstanding the different modes in which they are appointed, we must consider <u>both</u> of them as substantially <u>dependent</u> on the great body of the <u>citizens</u> of the United States. I assume this position here as it respects the first, reserving the proofs for another place.

GOVERNMENTS ARE TRUSTEES:

The federal and State governments are agents and trustees with different purposes and powers. However, the ultimate political authority resides in the people alone.

46:2 The federal and State governments are in fact but <u>different agents</u> and trustees of the people, constituted with different powers, and designed for <u>different purposes</u>. The adversaries of the Constitution seem to have lost sight of the people altogether in their reasonings on this subject; and to have viewed these different establishments, not only as <u>mutual rivals and enemies</u>, but as uncontrolled by any common superior in their efforts to usurp the authorities of each other.

ULTIMATE POLITICAL AUTHORITY IS THE PEOPLE:

State and federal governments may compete with each other but any expansion of their powers is prohibited without the consent of the people.

46:3 These gentlemen must here be reminded of their error. They must be told that the <u>ultimate authority</u>, wherever the derivative may be found, <u>resides in the people alone</u>, and that it will not depend merely on the comparative ambition or address of the different governments, whether either, or which of them, will be able to <u>enlarge its sphere</u> of jurisdiction at the <u>expense of the other</u>. Truth, no less than decency, requires that the event in every case should be supposed to <u>depend</u> on the <u>sentiments</u> and sanction of their common constituents.[173]

PEOPLE ATTACHED MORE TO THEIR STATE:
The government most trustworthy and closest to the people enjoys the most support.

46:4 Many considerations, besides those suggested on a former occasion, seem to place it beyond doubt that the <u>first and most natural attachment</u> of the people will be to the governments of their <u>respective States</u>.

STATES GOVERN INTIMATELY, FEDERAL GOVERNMENT DOES NOT:
The people will naturally be more intimately connected to State officers, provided these do their job well and remain trustworthy.

46:5 Into the administration of these a greater number of individuals will expect to rise. From the gift of these a greater number of offices and emoluments will flow. By the super intending care of these, all the <u>more domestic and personal interests</u> of the people will be regulated and <u>provided for</u>. With the affairs of these, the people will be more familiarly and minutely conversant. And with the members of these, will a greater proportion of the people have the ties of personal acquaintance and friendship, and of family and party attachments; on the side of these, therefore, the popular bias may well be expected most strongly to incline.

GOVERNMENT HAS VITAL ROLE DESPITE ITS FLAWS:
The federal government proved its importance during the war, but the people still preferred putting their trust in their State government.

46:6 Experience speaks the same language in this case. The federal administration, though hitherto very defective in comparison with what may be hoped under a better system, had, during the war, and particularly whilst the <u>independent fund of paper emissions was in credit</u>, an activity and importance as great as it can well have in any future circumstances whatever.

POSTWAR ENTHUSIASM RETURNED TO STATES:
Early on, Congress was the center of attention during the war but was never as popular as the State governments.

46:7 It was engaged, too, in a course of measures which had for their object the protection of everything that was dear, and the acquisition of everything that could be desirable to the people at large. It was, <u>nevertheless</u>, invariably found, <u>after the transient enthusiasm</u> for the early Congresses <u>was over</u>, that the <u>attention and attachment of the people</u> were turned anew to <u>their own particular governments</u>; that the <u>federal council</u> was at <u>no time</u> the idol of <u>popular favor</u>; and that opposition to proposed enlargements of its powers and importance was the side usually taken by the men who wished to build their political consequence on the **prepossessions**[174] of their fellow-citizens.

FEDERAL POWERS ARE FEWER THAN STATE POWERS:
If the people change and prefer the general government it will be because the federal government is doing a better job meeting their needs.

46:8 <u>If</u>, therefore, as has been elsewhere remarked, the <u>people</u> should in future become <u>more partial</u> to the <u>federal</u> than to the State governments, the change can only result from such manifest and irresistible proofs of a better administration, as will overcome all their antecedent propensities. And in that case, the people ought not surely to be precluded from giving most of <u>their confidence where they may discover it to be most due</u>; but even in that case the State governments could have little to apprehend, because it is <u>only within a certain sphere</u> that the <u>federal power can</u>, in the nature of things, be advantageously administered.

NATURAL CHECK AND BALANCE:
The federal and State governments have resources to check one another's power.

46:9 The remaining points on which I propose to compare the federal and State governments, are the disposition and the faculty they may respectively possess, to <u>resist and frustrate the measures of each other</u>.

CONGRESS DEPENDS ON STATES, NOT VICE VERSA:
The federal government must depend on the States, and both must be beholden to the people.

46:10 It has been already proved that the members of the <u>federal</u> will be more <u>dependent</u> on the members of the <u>State governments</u>, than the latter will be on the former. It has appeared also, that the <u>prepossessions</u> of the people, on whom both will depend, will be more on the side of the State governments,

---

173 John Locke: Legislative authority cannot exceed that of the individual, "The legislative ... is not, nor can possibly be, absolutely arbitrary over the lives and fortunes of the people. For it being but the joint power of every member of the society given up to that person or assembly which is legislator, it can no more than those person had in a state of Nature before they entered into society, and gave it up to the community. For nobody can transfer to another more power than he has in himself, and nobody has an absolute arbitrary power over himself, or over any other, to destroy his own life, or take away the life or property of another." Locke, *Two Treatises of Civil Government*, II, 135.

174 **prepossessions:** Attitudes or impressions formed beforehand, usually more positive than negative as in "prejudice."

than of the federal government. So far as the disposition of each towards the other may be influenced by these causes, the State governments must clearly have the advantage.

STATES RELUCTANT TO FAVOR NATIONAL SPIRIT:

The States will influence Congress but rarely give an advantage to Congress. For the most part, will the States really care about national issues?

46:11 But in a distinct and very important point of view, the advantage will lie on the same side. The prepossessions, which the members themselves will carry into the federal government, will generally be favorable to the States; whilst it will rarely happen, that the members of the State governments will carry into the public councils a bias in favor of the general government. A local spirit will infallibly prevail much more in the members of Congress, than a national spirit will prevail in the legislatures of the particular States.

LEGISLATURES PROTECTIVE OF LOCAL AFFAIRS:

State leaders are biased toward their hometown concerns and neglect the State, just as congressmen are biased toward their State and not the nation.

46:12 Every one knows that a great proportion of the errors committed by the State legislatures proceeds from the disposition of the members to sacrifice the comprehensive and permanent interest of the State, to the particular and separate views of the counties or districts in which they reside. And if they do not sufficiently enlarge their policy to embrace the collective welfare of their particular State, how can it be imagined that they will make the aggregate prosperity of the Union, and the dignity and respectability of its government, the objects of their affections and consultations?

LEADERS UNLIKELY TO STRAY FROM THEIR OWN DOMAINS:

46:13 For the same reason that the members of the State legislatures will be unlikely to attach themselves sufficiently to national objects, the members of the federal legislature will be likely to attach themselves too much to local objects. The States will be to the latter what counties and towns are to the former. Measures will too often be decided according to their probable effect, not on the national prosperity and happiness, but on the prejudices, interests, and pursuits of the governments and people of the individual States.

CURRENT CONGRESS BIASED TOWARD THEIR OWN STATES:

The records show congressmen, under the Articles, are not impartial guardians of the national interests.

46:14 What is the spirit that has in general characterized the proceedings of Congress? A perusal of their journals, as well as the candid acknowledgments of such as have had a seat in that assembly, will inform us, that the members have but too frequently displayed the character, rather of partisans of their respective States, than of impartial guardians of a common interest; that where on one occasion improper sacrifices have been made of local considerations, to the aggrandizement of the federal government, the great interests of the nation have suffered on a hundred, from an undue attention to the local prejudices, interests, and views of the particular States.

NEW CONGRESS NOT INCLINED TO BIAS:

The new government will not be inclined to invade States rights. It will be better balanced and empowered to stay in its proper bounds.

46:15 I mean not by these reflections to insinuate, that the new federal government will not embrace a more enlarged plan of policy than the existing government may have pursued; much less, that its views will be as confined as those of the State legislatures; but only that it will partake sufficiently of the spirit of both, to be disinclined to invade the rights of the individual States, or the prerogatives of their governments. The motives on the part of the State governments, to augment their prerogatives by **defalcations**[175] from the federal government, will be overruled by no reciprocal predispositions in the members.

STATES CAN BLOCK A TRESPASSING CONGRESS:

The States have an advantage over Congress and can resist any attempt to usurp power.

46:16 Were it admitted, however, that the federal government may feel an equal disposition with the State governments to extend its power beyond the due limits, the latter would still have the advantage in the means of defeating such encroachments.

STATES MAY NOT VIOLATE CONSTITUTION:

If a State passes a popular law that is unfriendly to Congress, would Congress seek to force its way on the States?

46:17 If an act of a particular State, though unfriendly to the national government, be generally popular in that State and should not too grossly violate the oaths of the State officers, it is executed immediately and, of course, by means on the spot and depending on the State alone. The opposition of the federal government, or the interposition of federal officers, would but inflame the zeal of all parties on the side of the State, and the evil could not be prevented or repaired, if at all, without the employment of means which must always be resorted to with reluctance and difficulty.

---

175 **defalcation:** Another word for embezzling, when a trusted person in charge of funds misappropriates those funds.

STATES CAN REFUSE AN ENCROACHING CONGRESS:

The ultimate authority of the government derives from the people. If the States felt the federal government had crossed too many lines, would they have the right and obligation to sound the alarm and push back?

46:18　On the other hand, should an <u>unwarrantable measure</u> of the federal government be <u>unpopular</u> in particular States, which would seldom fail to be the case, or even a warrantable measure be so, which may sometimes be the case, the means of opposition to it are powerful and at hand. The <u>disquietude</u> of the <u>people</u>; their <u>repugnance</u> and, perhaps, refusal <u>to co-operate</u> with the officers of the Union; the frowns of the <u>executive magistracy of the State</u>; the <u>embarrassments created by legislative devices</u>, which would often be added on such occasions, would oppose, in any State, difficulties not to be despised; would form, in a large State, very <u>serious impediments</u>; and where the sentiments of <u>several adjoining States</u> happened to be in unison, would present obstructions which the federal government would hardly be willing to encounter.

STATES WILL FIGHT CONGRESSIONAL TAKEOVER:

How would the States respond to an overzealous federal government? Such action would sound a general alarm that would unite all the States in opposition to the federal.

46:19　But <u>ambitious encroachments of the federal government</u>, on the authority of the State governments, <u>would not excite the opposition of a single State</u>, or of a few States only. They would be signals of general alarm. Every government would <u>espouse the common cause</u>. A correspondence would be opened. <u>Plans of resistance</u> would be concerted. One spirit would animate and conduct the whole. The same combinations, in short, would result from an <u>apprehension</u> of the federal, as was produced by the dread of a foreign, yoke; and unless the projected innovations should be voluntarily renounced, the same appeal to a <u>trial of force</u> would be made in the one case as was made in the other. But what degree of madness could ever drive the federal government to such an extremity?

BRITAIN WAGED WAR AGAINST HER OWN CITIZENS AND LOST:

Britain far outnumbered the united colonies but her cause was unjust and unwise.

46:20　In the contest with Great Britain, one part of the empire was employed against the other. The more numerous part invaded the rights of the less numerous part. The attempt was unjust and unwise; but it was not in speculation absolutely chimerical.

CONGRESS FIGHTING CONGRESS?

If Congress waged war against the States, who would they be fighting?

46:21　But what would be the contest in the case we are supposing? Who would be the parties? A few representatives of the people would be opposed to the people themselves; or rather <u>one set of representatives</u> would be contending against <u>thirteen sets</u> of representatives, with the whole body of their common constituents on the side of the latter.

FEDERAL MILITARY ATTACK ON STATES UNTHINKABLE:

The States would not allow the building of an army sufficiently strong to attack and subdue the States.

46:22　The <u>only refuge</u> left for those who prophesy the downfall of the State governments is the <u>visionary supposition</u> that the federal government may previously accumulate a <u>military force</u> for the projects of ambition.

THE PEOPLE WOULD NOT ELECT USURPERS:

46:23　The reasonings contained in these papers must have been employed to little purpose indeed, if it could be necessary now to disprove the reality of this danger. That the people and the States should, for a sufficient period of time, elect an uninterrupted succession of men ready to betray both; that the <u>traitors</u> should, throughout this period, uniformly and systematically pursue some fixed plan for the <u>extension of the military establishment</u>;

THE PEOPLE WOULD NOT STAND BY JUST WATCHING:

46:24　that the governments and the people of the States should silently and patiently behold the gathering storm, and continue to supply the materials, until it should be prepared to burst on their own heads, must appear to every one more like the incoherent dreams of a delirious jealousy, or the misjudged exaggerations of a counterfeit zeal, than like the sober apprehensions of genuine patriotism.

STATE MILITIAS OUTNUMBER FEDERAL TROOPS:

The militia of the States safeguards against federal abuse of power. If the federal government used military force to subdue a State, there are enough armed militias to overthrow such tyranny.

46:25　Extravagant as the supposition is, let it however be made. <u>Let a regular army</u>, fully equal to the resources of the country, <u>be formed; and let it be entirely at the devotion of the federal government</u>; still it would not be going too far to say, that the <u>State governments</u>, with the people on their side, would be <u>able to repel the danger</u>.

HOW LARGE COULD A STANDING ARMY BECOME?

46:26 The <u>highest number</u> to which, according to the best computation, <u>a standing army can be carried in any country,</u> <u>does not exceed one hundredth part of the whole number</u> <u>of souls; or one twenty-fifth part of the number able to bear</u> <u>arms.</u> This proportion would not yield, in the United States, an army of more than twenty-five or thirty thousand men.

HOW LARGE ARE THE STATES' COMBINED MILITIAS?

46:27 To these would be opposed a <u>militia amounting to near</u> <u>half a million of citizens with arms in their hands,</u> officered by men chosen from among themselves, <u>fighting for their com-</u> <u>mon liberties,</u> and united and conducted by governments possessing their <u>affections</u> and <u>confidence.</u>

IN A CONFLICT WHO WOULD WIN, THE STATES OR A FEDERAL ARMY?

46:28 It may well be <u>doubted,</u> whether a <u>militia</u> thus circumstanced <u>could ever be conquered</u> by such a proportion of regular troops. Those who are best acquainted with the last successful resistance of this country against the British arms, will be most inclined to deny the possibility of it.

ARMS AND LOCAL LEADERS PROTECT AGAINST AMBITIONS:

The American people are the best armed citizens in the world. Local political structure also forms a barrier against Congress. Does the right to bear arms sufficiently outweigh a militarized Congress?

46:29 Besides the <u>advantage of being armed, which the</u> <u>Americans possess over the people of almost every other na-</u> <u>tion,</u> the existence of subordinate governments, to which the people are attached, and by which the militia officers are appointed, <u>forms a barrier against the enterprises of ambition,</u> more insurmountable than any which a simple government of any form can admit of.

EUROPEANS CAN'T OWN GUNS:

Even though a government doesn't trust its people with arms, an armed citizenry alone may not be enough to overthrow tyrannical government.

46:30 Notwithstanding the military establishments in the <u>several kingdoms of Europe,</u> which are carried as far as the public resources will bear, the governments are <u>afraid to trust</u> <u>the people with arms.</u> And it is not certain, that with this aid alone they would not be able to shake off their yokes.

LOCAL GOVERNMENTS ENABLE LOCAL LIBERTY:

If Europeans could elect local governments, their local militias could eventually overpower every European throne of tyranny.

46:31 But were the people to possess the <u>additional advan-</u> <u>tages</u> of <u>local governments</u> chosen by themselves, who could collect the national will and <u>direct the national force,</u> and of officers appointed out of the militia, by these governments, and attached both to them and to the militia, it may be affirmed with the greatest assurance, that the <u>throne of every</u> <u>tyranny in Europe</u> would be <u>speedily overturned</u> in spite of the legions which surround it.

AMERICANS ARE WELL EQUIPPED TO DEFEND RIGHTS:

Those in Europe are faced with the uphill battle of winning their rights from tyrannical governments. Americans already won their rights from the recent war and now know what to avoid.

46:32 Let us not <u>insult</u> the free and <u>gallant citizens of America</u> with the suspicion, that they would be less able to defend the rights of which they would be in actual possession, than the debased subjects of arbitrary power would be to rescue theirs from the hands of their oppressors. Let us rather no longer insult them with the supposition that they can ever reduce themselves to the necessity of making the <u>experiment,</u> by a <u>blind</u> and <u>tame submission</u> to the long train of insidious measures which must precede and produce it.

GOVERNMENT TOO DEPENDENT ON PEOPLE:

The government depends too heavily on the people to concoct a scheme to conquer the country. But, will it remain so?

46:33 The argument under the present head may be put into a very concise form, which appears altogether conclusive. Either the mode in which the federal government is to be constructed will <u>render it sufficiently dependent</u> on the people, or it will not. On the first supposition, it will be restrained by that dependence from forming schemes obnoxious to their constituents. On the other supposition, it will not possess the <u>confidence of the people,</u> and its schemes of <u>usurpation</u> will be easily <u>defeated</u> by the <u>State governments,</u> who will be supported by the people.

STATES ARE SAFE FROM FEDERAL POWERS:

Are federal powers sufficiently strong but safe enough to get the job done?

46:34 On summing up the considerations stated in this and the last paper, they seem to amount to the most convincing evidence, that the <u>powers</u> proposed to be lodged in the <u>federal</u>

government are as little formidable to those reserved to the individual States, as they are indispensably necessary to accomplish the purposes of the Union; and that all those alarms which have been sounded, of a meditated and consequential annihilation of the State governments, must, on the most favorable interpretation, be ascribed to the chimerical fears of the authors of them.

—PUBLIUS

REVIEW QUESTIONS

1. Upon whom are both the federal government and the State governments dependent? (46:1)

2. Fill in the blanks: The federal and State governments are different _____ and _____ of the people, with different _____ and designed for different _____. (46:2)

3. To which government are the people typically most attached? (46:4)

4. Did the American people have much respect for the postwar Congress? (46:7)

5. Are the States the focus of political power, or is the federal level? (46:11–17)

6. In the same way State legislators are biased toward their own hometown and county, to what will the federal Congress be biased? (46:11–13)

7. What steps would States take if the federal government overstepped its bounds? (46:19–24)

8. Are the State militias sufficient to repel a regular federal army? (46:25–27)

9. What right of defense do Americans enjoy that Europeans do not? (46:29–30)

10. Generally speaking, will the powers of the federal government under the Constitution be able to violate the powers given to the States? (All of 46)

FEDERALIST NO. 47

SEPARATION OF POWERS IS NOT ABSOLUTE: Political power under the new Constitution is distributed and blended in such a way so it provides checks and balances at most levels (There is no firm check on the judiciary, a serious weakness that Thomas Jefferson lamented). Some overlap is needed for this to work. Allowing all of the political power of the legislative, executive, and judicial branches of government to fall into the same hands is the very definition of tyranny.

By James Madison—January 30, 1788

GOVERNMENT STRUCTURE AND DISTRIBUTION OF POWER:

47:1   HAVING reviewed the general form of the proposed government and the general mass of power allotted to it, I proceed to examine the particular structure of this government, and the distribution of this mass of power among its constituent parts.

THREE BRANCHES ARE NOT TOTALLY SEPARATE:

47:2   One of the principal objections inculcated by the more respectable adversaries to the Constitution, is its supposed violation of the political maxim, that the legislative, executive, and judiciary departments ought to be separate and distinct.

THE BRANCHES MUST OVERLAP TO CHECK EACH OTHER:

This allows the other branches to stop usurpations. For example, the President can veto Congress; Congress can overrule a veto; the President appoints justices, the Senate confirms appointments; courts can rule against legislation; States and Congress must share in the amending process, and so forth.

47:3   In the structure of the federal government, no regard, it is said, seems to have been paid to this essential precaution in favor of liberty. The several departments of power are distributed and blended in such a manner as at once to destroy all symmetry and beauty of form, and to expose some of the essential parts of the edifice to the danger of being crushed by the disproportionate weight of other parts.

47:4   No political truth is certainly of greater intrinsic value, or is stamped with the authority of more enlightened patrons of liberty, than that on which the objection is founded.

DEFINITION OF TYRANNY:

Amassing the political powers together helps one political party become tyrannical over the others.

47:5   The accumulation of all powers, legislative, executive, and judiciary, in the same hands, whether of one, a few, or many, and whether hereditary, self appointed, or elective, may justly be pronounced the very definition of tyranny.

CONSTITUTION IS DESIGNED TO PREVENT TYRANNY. IF IT DOESN'T, REJECT IT:

47:6 Were the federal Constitution, therefore, really chargeable with the accumulation of power, or with a mixture of powers, having a dangerous tendency to such an accumulation, no further arguments would be necessary to inspire a universal reprobation of the system. I persuade myself, however, that it will be made apparent to every one, that the charge cannot be supported, and that the maxim on which it relies has been totally misconceived and misapplied.

THREE BRANCHES SEPARATE AND DISTINCT:

Preserving liberty begins with separating the branches of government.

47:7 In order to form correct ideas on this important subject, it will be proper to investigate the sense in which the preservation of liberty requires that the three great departments of power should be separate and distinct.

MONTESQUIEU AND SEPARATION OF POWERS:

The French political philosopher Baron de Montesquieu (1689–1755) explained how governments could be preserved from corruption by separating the three branches of government.

47:8 The oracle who is always consulted and cited on this subject is the celebrated Montesquieu. If he be not the author of this invaluable precept in the science of politics, he has the merit at least of displaying and recommending it most effectually to the attention of mankind. Let us endeavor, in the first place, to ascertain his meaning on this point.

MONTESQUIEU REVERED THE BRITISH CONSTITUTION:

Not because there is a king, but rather that powers are divided and shared.

47:9 The British Constitution was to Montesquieu what Homer has been to the didactic writers on epic poetry. As the latter have considered the work of the immortal bard as the perfect model from which the principles and rules of the epic art were to be drawn, and by which all similar works were to be judged, so this great political critic appears to have viewed the Constitution of England as the standard, or to use his own expression, as the mirror of political liberty; and to have delivered, in the form of elementary truths, the several characteristic principles of that particular system. That we may be sure, then, not to mistake his meaning in this case, let us **recur**[176] to the source from which the maxim was drawn.

THREE BRITISH BRANCHES NOT TOTALLY SEPARATE:

47:10 On the slightest view of the British Constitution, we must perceive that the legislative, executive, and judiciary departments are by no means totally separate and distinct from each other.

KING'S TIES TO THE LEGISLATURE:

47:11 The executive magistrate forms an integral part of the legislative authority. He alone has the prerogative of making treaties with foreign sovereigns, which, when made, have, under certain limitations, the force of legislative acts.

KING'S TIES TO THE JUDICIARY:

47:12 All the members of the judiciary department are appointed by him, can be removed by him on the address of the two Houses of Parliament, and form, when he pleases to consult them, one of his constitutional councils.

LEGISLATURE'S TIES WITH OTHER BRANCHES:

47:13 One branch of the legislative department forms also a great constitutional council to the executive chief, as, on another hand, it is the sole depositary of judicial power in cases of impeachment, and is invested with the supreme appellate jurisdiction in all other cases.

LEGISLATURE'S TIES WITH THE JUDICIARY:

47:14 The judges, again, are so far connected with the legislative department as often to attend and participate in its deliberations, though not admitted to a legislative vote.

POSSESSING WHOLE POWER IS TYRANNICAL:

47:15 From these facts, by which Montesquieu was guided, it may clearly be inferred that, in saying "There can be no liberty where the legislative and executive powers are united in the same person, or body of magistrates," or, "if the power of judging be not separated from the legislative and executive powers," he did not mean that these departments ought to have no PARTIAL AGENCY in, or no CONTROL over, the acts of each other. His meaning, as his own words import, and still more conclusively as illustrated by the example in his eye, can amount to no more than this, that where the WHOLE power of one department is exercised by the same hands which possess the WHOLE power of another department, the fundamental principles of a free constitution are subverted.

BRITISH CONSTITUTION HAS SOME CHECKS:

47:16 This would have been the case in the constitution examined by him, if the king, who is the sole executive magistrate, had possessed also the complete legislative power, or the supreme administration of justice; or if the entire legislative

---

176 **recur:** Go back to something in thought or speech.

body had possessed the supreme judiciary, or the supreme executive authority. This, however, is not among the vices of that constitution.

CHECKS ON THE KING:

47:17 The magistrate in whom the whole executive power resides cannot of himself make a law, though he can put a negative on every law; nor administer justice in person, though he has the appointment of those who do administer it.

CHECKS ON JUDGES' RELATIONS WITH LEGISLATORS:

47:18 The judges can exercise no executive prerogative, though they are shoots from the executive stock; nor any legislative function, though they may be advised with by the legislative councils. The entire legislature can perform no judiciary act, though by the joint act of two of its branches the judges may be removed from their offices, and though one of its branches is possessed of the judicial power in the last resort.

CHECKS ON LEGISLATURE'S RELATIONS TO KING:

47:19 The entire legislature, again, can exercise no executive prerogative, though one of its branches constitutes the supreme executive magistracy, and another, on the impeachment of a third, can try and condemn all the subordinate officers in the executive department.

MONTESQUIEU'S DEFINITION OF "NO LIBERTY":

47:20 The reasons on which Montesquieu grounds his maxim are a further demonstration of his meaning. "When the legislative and executive powers are united in the same person or body," says he, "there can be no liberty, because apprehensions may arise lest THE SAME monarch or senate should ENACT tyrannical laws to EXECUTE them in a tyrannical manner."

NO LIBERTY IF A JUDGE HAS THE POWERS OF THE LEGISLATURE OR THE EXECUTIVE:

47:21 Again: "Were the power of judging joined with the legislative, the life and liberty of the subject would be exposed to arbitrary control, for THE JUDGE would then be THE LEGISLATOR. Were it joined to the executive power, THE JUDGE might behave with all the violence of AN OPPRESSOR."

THIS IS WHAT MONTESQUIEU REALLY MEANT:

47:22 Some of these reasons are more fully explained in other passages; but briefly stated as they are here, they sufficiently establish the meaning which we have put on this celebrated maxim of this celebrated author.

ALL STATES HAVE BLENDED DEPARTMENTS: The States' branches are legally dependent on each other in various ways.

47:23 If we look into the constitutions of the several States, we find that, notwithstanding the emphatical and, in some instances, the unqualified terms in which this axiom has been laid down, there is not a single instance in which the several departments of power have been kept absolutely separate and distinct.

NEW HAMPSHIRE CONSTITUTION:

47:24 New Hampshire, whose constitution was the last formed, seems to have been fully aware of the impossibility and inexpediency of avoiding any mixture whatever of these departments, and has qualified the doctrine by declaring "that the legislative, executive, and judiciary powers ought to be kept as separate from, and independent of, each other AS THE NATURE OF A FREE GOVERNMENT WILL ADMIT; OR AS IS CONSISTENT WITH THAT CHAIN OF CONNECTION THAT BINDS THE WHOLE FABRIC OF THE CONSTITUTION IN ONE INDISSOLUBLE BOND OF UNITY AND AMITY." Her constitution accordingly mixes these departments in several respects.

New Hampshire's legislative, executive, and judicial branches are mixed.

47:25 The Senate, which is a branch of the legislative department, is also a judicial tribunal for the trial of impeachments. The President, who is the head of the executive department, is the presiding member also of the Senate; and, besides an equal vote in all cases, has a casting vote in case of a tie. The executive head is himself eventually elective every year by the legislative department, and his council is every year chosen by and from the members of the same department.

New Hampshire's departments cross-checked.

47:26 Several of the officers of state are also appointed by the legislature. And the members of the judiciary department are appointed by the executive department.

MASSACHUSETTS CONSTITUTION:

47:27 The constitution of Massachusetts has observed a sufficient though less pointed caution, in expressing this fundamental article of liberty. It declares "that the legislative department shall never exercise the executive and judicial powers, or either of them; the executive shall never exercise the legislative and judicial powers, or either of them; the judicial shall never exercise the legislative and executive powers, or either of them."

Massachusetts' departments forbidden to do the jobs of others.

47:28   This declaration corresponds precisely with the <u>doctrine of Montesquieu</u>, as it has been explained, and is not in a single point violated by the plan of the Convention. <u>It goes no farther than to prohibit any one of the entire departments from exercising the powers of another department</u>.

Massachusetts allows partial mixture.

47:29   In the very Constitution to which it is prefixed, a partial mixture of powers has been admitted. The executive magistrate has <u>a qualified negative on the legislative body</u>, and the <u>Senate, which is a part of the legislature, is a court of impeachment for members both of the executive and judiciary departments</u>. The members of the judiciary department, again, are appointable by the executive department, and removable by the same authority on the address of the two legislative branches.

Massachusetts violated its own general rule of separation.

47:30   Lastly, a number of the officers of government are annually appointed by the legislative department. As the appointment to offices, particularly executive offices, is in its nature an executive function, the compilers of the Constitution have, in this last point at least, violated the rule established by themselves.

RHODE ISLAND AND CONNECTICUT CONSTITUTIONS:

47:31   <u>I pass over the constitutions</u> of <u>Rhode Island</u> and <u>Connecticut</u>, because they were <u>formed prior to the Revolution</u>, and even before the principle under examination had become an object of political attention.

NEW YORK CONSTITUTION:

47:32   The constitution of <u>New York contains no declaration</u> on this subject; but appears very clearly to have been framed with an eye to the danger of improperly blending the different departments. It gives, nevertheless, to the <u>executive</u> magistrate, a <u>partial control</u> over the <u>legislative</u> department; and, what is more, gives a like control to the judiciary department; and even blends the executive and judiciary departments in the exercise of this control.

New York's legislative, executive, and judicial branches are mixed.

47:33   In its council of appointment members of the legislative are associated with the executive authority, in the appointment of officers, both executive and judiciary.

New York's legislature and judicial are partially mixed.

47:34   And its court for the trial of impeachments and correction of errors is to consist of one branch of the legislature and the principal members of the judiciary department.

NEW JERSEY CONSTITUTION:

47:35   The <u>constitution of New Jersey</u> has blended the different powers of government <u>more than any of the preceding</u>. The <u>governor</u>, who is the executive magistrate, is <u>appointed by the legislature</u>; is chancellor and ordinary, or <u>surrogate of the State</u>; is a <u>member of the Supreme Court</u> of Appeals, and president, with a casting vote, of one of the legislative branches. The same legislative branch acts again as executive council of the governor, and with him constitutes the Court of Appeals.

New Jersey's legislative and judicial branches are partially mixed.

47:36   The members of the <u>judiciary</u> department are <u>appointed by the legislative</u> department and removable by one branch of it, on the impeachment of the other.

PENNSYLVANIA CONSTITUTION:

47:37   According to the constitution of <u>Pennsylvania</u>, the president, who is the head of the executive department, is <u>annually elected</u> by a vote in which the legislative department predominates. In conjunction with an executive council, he appoints the members of the judiciary department, and forms a court of impeachment for trial of All officers, judiciary as well as executive.

Pennsylvania's legislative, executive, and judicial branches are mixed.

47:38   The judges of the Supreme Court and justices of the peace seem also to be <u>removable</u> by the <u>legislature</u>; and the executive power of pardoning in certain cases, to be referred to the same department. The members of the executive council are made EX-OFFICIO justices of peace throughout the State.

DELAWARE CONSTITUTION:

47:39   <u>In Delaware</u>, the chief executive magistrate is annually elected by the legislative department. The speakers of the two legislative branches are vice-presidents in the executive department. The executive chief, with six others, appointed, three by each of the legislative branches constitutes the Supreme Court of Appeals; he is joined with the legislative department in the appointment of the other judges.

Delaware's legislative, executive, and judicial branches are mixed.

47:40 Throughout the States, it appears that the members of the legislature may at the same time be justices of the peace; in this State, the members of one branch of it are EX-OFFICIO justices of the peace; as are also the members of the executive council.

Delaware's executive officers are appointed by the legislature.

47:41 The principal officers of the executive department are appointed by the legislative; and one branch of the latter forms a court of impeachments. All officers may be removed on address of the legislature.

MARYLAND CONSTITUTION:

47:42 Maryland has adopted the maxim in the most unqualified terms; declaring that the legislative, executive, and judicial powers of government ought to be forever separate and distinct from each other. Her constitution, notwithstanding, makes the executive magistrate appointable by the legislative department; and the members of the judiciary by the executive department.

VIRGINIA CONSTITUTION:

47:43 The language of Virginia is still more pointed on this subject. Her constitution declares, "that the legislative, executive, and judiciary departments shall be separate and distinct; so that neither exercise the powers properly belonging to the other; nor shall any person exercise the powers of more than one of them at the same time, except that the justices of county courts shall be eligible to either House of Assembly."

Virginia's legislative, executive, and judicial branches are partially mixed.

47:44 Yet we find not only this express exception, with respect to the members of the inferior courts, but that the chief magistrate, with his executive council, are appointable by the legislature; that two members of the latter are triennially displaced at the pleasure of the legislature; and that all the principal offices, both executive and judiciary, are filled by the same department. The executive prerogative of pardon, also, is in one case vested in the legislative department.

NORTH CAROLINA CONSTITUTION:

47:45 The constitution of North Carolina, which declares "that the legislative, executive, and supreme judicial powers of government ought to be forever separate and distinct from each other," refers, at the same time, to the legislative department, the appointment not only of the executive chief, but all the principal officers within both that and the judiciary department.

SOUTH CAROLINA CONSTITUTION:

47:46 In South Carolina, the constitution makes the executive magistracy eligible by the legislative department.

South Carolina's branches of government are partially mixed.

47:47 It gives to the latter, also, the appointment of the members of the judiciary department, including even justices of the peace and sheriffs; and the appointment of officers in the executive department, down to captains in the army and navy of the State.

GEORGIA CONSTITUTION:

47:48 In the constitution of Georgia, where it is declared "that the legislative, executive, and judiciary departments shall be separate and distinct, so that neither exercise the powers properly belonging to the other," we find that the executive department is to be filled by appointments of the legislature; and the executive prerogative of pardon to be finally exercised by the same authority. Even justices of the peace are to be appointed by the legislature.

STATES' SEPARATION OF POWERS IMPERFECT: The thirteen States were obligated by the urgency of the times to establish their forms of government in haste, and from lacking experience to organize things any better.

47:49 In citing these cases, in which the legislative, executive, and judiciary departments have not been kept totally separate and distinct, I wish not to be regarded as an advocate for the particular organizations of the several State governments. I am fully aware that among the many excellent principles which they exemplify, they carry strong marks of the haste, and still stronger of the inexperience, under which they were framed.

Some States allowed too much overlap among their departments.

47:50 It is but too obvious that in some instances the fundamental principle under consideration has been violated by too great a mixture, and even an actual consolidation, of the different powers; and that in no instance has a competent provision been made for maintaining in practice the separation delineated on paper.

NEW CONSTITUTION DOESN'T OVER MIX POWERS:

The claims that the new government will fail to separate the branches and powers of government cannot be supported.

47:51 What I have wished to evince is, that the charge brought against the proposed Constitution, of violating the sacred maxim of free government, is warranted neither by the real meaning annexed to that maxim by its author, nor by the sense in which it has hitherto been <u>understood in America</u>. This interesting subject will be resumed in the ensuing paper.

—PUBLIUS

REVIEW QUESTIONS

1. What is Madison's purpose with paper No. 47? (47:1)

2. In regard to separation of powers, what is the specific concern about the Constitution? (47:2)

3. What is Madison's definition of tyranny? (47:5)

4. What is Montesquieu's definition of "no liberty"? (47:20-21)

5. When did Baron de Montesquieu live? (47:8)

6. What concept in government did Montesquieu promote? (47:7–8)

7. Whose constitution did Montesquieu admire as an excellent example of separation of powers? (47:9)

8. What are some of the overlaps in political power of England's constitution that Montesquieu supported? (47:11–21)

9. Explain what Montesquieu meant that the three branches should have no "whole power" unto themselves. (See heading for 47:3) (47:15, 22)

10. Do the States keep their three branches totally separated? (47:23–48)

FEDERALIST NO. 48

T HE THREE BRANCHES SHOULD OVERLAP: In order for "separation of powers" to work, there must be power in each branch to impose a degree of restraint over the other two branches. The greatest threat to expanding power will come from the federal legislative branch—it, too, must be carefully bounded by checks and balances because it is the branch most likely to abuse power.

By James Madison—February 1, 1788

BRANCHES OF GOVERNMENT SHOULD OVERLAP SLIGHTLY:

Separation of powers is important but without come blending each of the three branches can become too powerful and tyrannical.

48:1 IT WAS shown in the last paper that the <u>political</u> **apothegm**[177] there examined does not require that the <u>legislative</u>, <u>executive</u>, and <u>judiciary</u> departments should be <u>wholly unconnected with each other</u>.

CONSTITUTIONAL CONTROL OVER EACH OTHER IS GOOD:

48:2 I shall undertake, in the next place, to show that <u>unless these departments</u> be so far connected and <u>blended</u> as to give to each a <u>constitutional control over the others</u>, the degree of separation which the maxim requires, as <u>essential</u> to a free government, can <u>never in practice</u> be <u>duly maintained</u>.

BRANCHES CAN'T INFRINGE ON PROPER POWERS:

In those areas where a branch has exclusive power, the other branches may not interfere.

48:3 It is agreed on all sides, that the powers properly belonging to one of the departments ought <u>not to</u> be directly and <u>completely administered</u> by either of the <u>other departments</u>.

BRANCHES MUST CHECK EACH OTHER:

Each branch has its own responsibilities, but keeping those powers within legal limits is also the responsibility of the other two branches.

48:4 It is equally evident, that <u>none</u> of them ought to possess, directly or indirectly, an <u>overruling influence over the others</u>, in the <u>administration</u> of their respective <u>powers</u>. It will not be denied, that <u>power is of</u> an <u>encroaching nature</u>, and that it ought to be effectually <u>restrained</u> from passing the limits assigned to it.

GOVERNMENT BRANCHES ALSO NEED PROTECTION:

Political power is naturally encroaching and must be restrained. This is the most difficult task in writing a Constitution.

48:5 After discriminating, therefore, in theory, the several classes of power, as they may in their nature be legislative, executive, or judiciary, the next and <u>most difficult task</u> is to provide some practical security for each, against the invasion of the others. What this security ought to be, is the great problem to be solved.

PARCHMENT BARRIERS FAIL:

Experience demonstrates that parchment barriers (set up in State constitutions) are not an adequate defense to protect the weak from the strong.

48:6 <u>Will it be sufficient to mark</u>, with <u>precision</u>, the <u>boundaries</u> of these departments, in the constitution of the government, and to <u>trust</u> to these <u>parchment barriers</u> against the en-

---

177 **apothegm:** A terse statement; concise saying or maxim.

croaching spirit of power? This is the security which appears to have been principally <u>relied on</u> by the compilers of most of the <u>American constitutions</u>. But <u>experience assures us</u>, that the efficacy of the provision has been greatly <u>overrated</u>; and that some <u>more adequate defense</u> is indispensably necessary for the <u>more feeble</u>, <u>against</u> the more <u>powerful</u>, members of the government. The legislative department is everywhere <u>extending</u> the sphere of <u>its activity</u>, and <u>drawing all power</u> into its impetuous <u>vortex</u>.

BRANCHES TEND TO USURP EACH OTHER'S POWERS:

Liberty is endangered by assembling all power in the same hands.

48:7 The founders of our republics have so much merit for the wisdom which they have displayed, that no task can be less pleasing than that of pointing out the errors into which they have fallen. A respect for truth, however, obliges us to remark, that they seem <u>never for a moment</u> to have <u>turned their eyes</u> from the <u>danger to liberty</u> from the overgrown and <u>all-grasping prerogative</u> of an <u>hereditary magistrate</u>, supported and fortified by an <u>hereditary branch</u> of the <u>legislative authority</u>. They seem never to have recollected the <u>danger from legislative usurpations</u>, which, by assembling all power in the same hands, must lead to the same <u>tyranny as</u> is threatened by executive usurpations.

MONARCHS BECOME DESPOTIC:

The people are wise to keep a close eye on their executives.

48:8 In a government where numerous and extensive <u>prerogatives</u> are placed in the hands of an <u>hereditary</u> monarch, the executive department is very justly regarded as the source of danger, and watched with all the jealousy which a zeal for liberty ought to inspire.

DEFINITION OF DEMOCRACY:

Democracies vulnerable to usurpers who would use a panic situation to make political gains.

48:9 <u>In a democracy</u>, where a <u>multitude of people</u> exercise in person the <u>legislative functions</u>, and are continually exposed, by their <u>incapacity</u> <u>for regular deliberation</u> and concerted measures, to the ambitious <u>intrigues</u> of their <u>executive magistrates</u>, tyranny may well be apprehended, on some favorable <u>emergency</u>, to start up in the same quarter.

BEWARE OF THE LEGISLATURE IN A REPRESENTATIVE REPUBLIC:

In a representative government the executive is carefully watched, but the body watching him adorns itself with increasingly great powers. This must be watched jealously.

48:10 But in a <u>representative republic</u>, where the executive <u>magistracy</u> is carefully limited; both in the extent and the duration of its power; and where the <u>legislative power</u> is exercised by an assembly, which is inspired, by a supposed influence over the people, with an intrepid confidence in its own strength; which is sufficiently numerous to feel all the passions which actuate a multitude, yet not so numerous as to be incapable of pursuing the objects of its passions, by means which reason prescribes; it is against the enterprising ambition of <u>this department</u> that the people ought to <u>indulge</u> all their <u>jealousy</u> and exhaust all their <u>precautions</u>.

LEGISLATURE CAN HIDE ITS ENCROACHMENTS:

Usurpation by the legislature is less easily detected than that of the executive or judiciary. How can this branch hide its encroachments?

48:11 The <u>legislative</u> department <u>derives</u> a <u>superiority</u> in our governments from other circumstances. Its constitutional <u>powers</u> being at once <u>more extensive</u>, and <u>less susceptible</u> of precise <u>limits</u>, it can, with the greater facility, <u>mask</u>, under complicated and indirect measures, the <u>encroachments</u> which it makes on the co-ordinate departments. It is not unfrequently a question of real nicety in legislative bodies, whether the operation of a particular measure will, or will not, extend beyond the legislative sphere.

EXECUTIVE AND JUDICIAL BRANCHES CAN'T TAKE POWER:

Why is it harder to corrupt the executive and judicial branches?

48:12 On the other side, the <u>executive power</u> being restrained within a <u>narrower compass</u>, and being more <u>simple in its nature</u>, and the <u>judiciary</u> being described by <u>landmarks still less uncertain</u>, projects of usurpation by either of these departments would <u>immediately betray</u> and defeat themselves.

CONTROL OF MONEY PAVES WAY TO USURPATION:

What upper hand does the legislative branch have over the others?

48:13 Nor is this all: as the <u>legislative</u> department alone has <u>access</u> to the <u>pockets of the people</u>, and has in some constitutions full discretion, and in all a prevailing influence, over the pecuniary rewards of those who fill the other departments, a <u>dependence</u> is thus <u>created</u> in the latter, which gives still <u>greater facility</u> to <u>encroachments</u> of the former.

EXAMPLES OF CORRUPTION AND GREED IN EVERY STATE:

Every citizen has experienced firsthand how money corrupts the channels of government. Is there proof in every State's records?

48:14 I have appealed to our own experience for the truth of what I advance on this subject. Were it necessary to verify this experience by particular proofs, they might be multiplied without end. I might find a witness in every citizen who has shared in, or been attentive to, the course of public administrations. I might collect vouchers in abundance from the records and archives of every State in the Union. But as a more concise, and at the same time equally satisfactory, evidence, I will refer to the example of two States, attested by two unexceptionable authorities.

VIRGINIA FORBIDS OVERLAPPING DEPARTMENTS:
Who wrote this restriction into Virginia's constitution?

48:15 The first example is that of Virginia, a State which, as we have seen, has expressly declared in its constitution, that the three great departments ought not to be intermixed. The authority in support of it is Mr. Jefferson, who, besides his other advantages for **remarking**[178] the operation of the government, was himself the chief magistrate of it.

DEFINITION OF DESPOTISM:
Jefferson wrote that when the same hands control the three branches of government, this is despotism. Did Jefferson suggest the entire Virginia legislature could be as despotic as a king?

48:16 In order to convey fully the ideas with which his experience had impressed him on this subject, it will be necessary to quote a passage of some length from his very interesting "Notes on the State of Virginia," p. 195. "All the powers of government, legislative, executive, and judiciary, result to the legislative body. The concentrating these in the same hands, is precisely the definition of despotic government. It will be no alleviation, that these powers will be exercised by a plurality of hands, and not by a single one. One hundred and seventy-three despots would surely be as oppressive as one. [Cont'd]

ELECTIVE DESPOTISM WAS NOT WHAT WE FOUGHT FOR:
Branches of government should be separate— however, some intermingling is needed to achieve balance.

48:17 "Let those who doubt it, turn their eyes on the republic of Venice. As little will it avail us, that they are chosen by ourselves. An ELECTIVE DESPOTISM was not the government we fought for; but one which should not only be founded on free principles, but in which the powers of government should be so divided and balanced among several bodies of magistracy, as that no one could transcend their legal limits, without being effectually checked and restrained by the others." [Cont'd]

BARRIERS MUST BE ERECTED BETWEEN BRANCHES:
Because the legislature was so central to government could it use that power to become despotic?

48:18 "For this reason, that convention which passed the ordinance of government, laid its foundation on this basis, that the legislative, executive, and judiciary departments should be separate and distinct, so that no person should exercise the powers of more than one of them at the same time. BUT NO BARRIER WAS PROVIDED BETWEEN THESE SEVERAL POWERS. The judiciary and the executive members were left dependent on the legislative for their subsistence in office, and some of them for their continuance in it. [Cont'd]

LEGISLATURE CAN'T PASS LAWS TO CONTROL BRANCHES:
If the legislature has all power, it can enact laws that would make the executive and judiciary obedient to it.

48:19 "If, therefore, the legislature assumes executive and judiciary powers, no opposition is likely to be made; nor, if made, can be effectual; because in that case they may put their proceedings into the form of acts of Assembly, which will render them obligatory on the other branches. They have accordingly, IN MANY instances, DECIDED RIGHTS which should have been left to JUDICIARY CONTROVERSY, and THE DIRECTION OF THE EXECUTIVE, DURING THE WHOLE TIME OF THEIR SESSION, IS BECOMING HABITUAL AND FAMILIAR."

PENNSYLVANIA CONSTITUTION VIOLATED:
What did Pennsylvania's "Council of Censors" discover about the behavior of its own State legislature?

48:20 The other State which I shall take for an example is Pennsylvania; and the other authority, the Council of Censors, which assembled in the years 1783 and 1784. A part of the duty of this body, as marked out by the constitution, was "to inquire whether the constitution had been preserved inviolate in every part; and whether the legislative and executive branches of government had performed their duty as guardians of the people, or assumed to themselves, or exercised, other or greater powers than they are entitled to by the constitution."

PENNSYLVANIA LEGISLATURE VIOLATED LAW OFTEN:

48:21 In the execution of this trust, the council were necessarily led to a comparison of both the legislative and executive proceedings, with the constitutional powers of these departments; and from the facts enumerated, and to the truth of most of which both sides in the council subscribed, it appears

---

178 *remarking:* Redesigning.

that the constitution had been flagrantly violated by the legislature in a variety of important instances.

Laws must be printed.

48:22 A great number of laws had been passed, violating, without any apparent necessity, the rule requiring that all bills of a public nature shall be previously printed for the consideration of the people; although this is one of the precautions chiefly relied on by the constitution against improper acts of legislature.

Trial by jury.

48:23 The constitutional trial by jury had been violated, and powers assumed which had not been delegated by the constitution.

Executive powers.

48:24 Executive powers had been usurped.

Salaries of judges.

48:25 The salaries of the judges, which the constitution expressly requires to be fixed, had been occasionally varied; and cases belonging to the judiciary department frequently drawn within legislative cognizance and determination.

See the public records for proof.

48:26 Those who wish to see the several particulars falling under each of these heads, may consult the journals of the council, which are in print. Some of them, it will be found, may be imputable to peculiar circumstances connected with the war; but the greater part of them may be considered as the spontaneous shoots of an ill-constituted government.

Executive department violated law.

48:27 It appears, also, that the executive department had not been innocent of frequent breaches of the constitution. There are three observations, however, which ought to be made on this head:

First: The necessities of the war.

48:28 FIRST, a great proportion of the instances were either immediately produced by the necessities of the war, or recommended by Congress or the commander-in-chief;

Second: Executive branch usually conformed to the legislature's wishes.

48:29 SECONDLY, in most of the other instances, they conformed either to the declared or the known sentiments of the legislative department;

Third: Executive branch is very numerous, similar to legislature.

48:30 THIRDLY, the executive department of Pennsylvania is distinguished from that of the other States by the number of members composing it. In this respect, it has as much affinity to a legislative assembly as to an executive council. And being at once exempt from the restraint of an individual responsibility for the acts of the body, and deriving confidence from mutual example and joint influence, unauthorized measures would, of course, be more freely hazarded, than where the executive department is administered by a single hand, or by a few hands.

WRITTEN LAW NOT ENOUGH:

48:31 The conclusion which I am warranted in drawing from these observations is, that a mere demarcation on parchment of the constitutional limits of the several departments, is not a sufficient guard against those encroachments which lead to a tyrannical concentration of all the powers of government in the same hands.

—PUBLIUS

REVIEW QUESTIONS

1. Can the three branches of government do their jobs if they are not blended together at some level? (48:2)

2. Fill in the blanks: Seeking balance among the three branches, any branch must retain power over its own proper responsibilities and should not be _____ and _____ administered by the others. (48:3)

3. Are parchment barriers strong enough to stop the branches from encroaching on each other? Which branch is most prone to taking over the others? (48:6–7)

4. In a democracy, how do those in charge expand their power? (48:9)

5. Does Congress's control of the money pave the way to corruption and usurpation? (48:13)

6. Why is it easier for Congress to hide its corruption? (48:11)

7. Why is it harder for the President and the courts to infringe on Congress? (48:12)

8. How does Thomas Jefferson define despotism? (48:16)

9. Fill in the blanks: In the government America needs, the powers should be so _____ and _____ among_____ bodies of magistracy, as that no one could _____ their legal limits without being checked and _____ by the others. (48:17)

SECTION 7 • CHECKS AND BALANCES

Papers 49–51

FEDERALIST NO. 49

FREQUENT REVIEWS OF GOVERNMENT COULD UNDERMINE CONSTITUTION: Jefferson's idea of calling constitutional conventions to look at government's adherence to the Constitution is dangerous for several reasons: The people can't stop two branches from combining against the third; frequent experimentation can destroy credibility; and Congress would nearly always win a mud-slinging contest between the three branches, even if Congress itself was the guilty party.

By James Madison—February 2, 1788

APPEALING TO THE PEOPLE DIRECTLY:
Madison admires Jefferson's constitution drafted for Virginia, and offers for discussion one of Jefferson's ideas.

49:1 THE author of the "Notes on the State of Virginia" [by Thomas Jefferson], quoted in the last paper, has subjoined to that valuable work the draught of a constitution, which had been prepared in order to be laid before a convention, expected to be called in 1783, by the legislature, for the establishment of a constitution for that commonwealth.

JEFFERSON'S PLAN IS WORTHY OF EXAMINATION:

49:2 The plan, like every thing from the same pen, marks a turn of thinking, original, comprehensive, and accurate; and is the more worthy of attention as it equally displays a fervent attachment to republican government and an enlightened view of the dangerous propensities against which it ought to be guarded.

A CAUTION REGARDING WEAK POWERS:
Is there a way to protect smaller departments from larger?

49:3 One of the precautions which he proposes, and on which he appears ultimately to rely as a palladium to the weaker departments of power against the invasions of the stronger, is

perhaps altogether his own, and as it immediately relates to the subject of our present inquiry, ought not to be overlooked.

JEFFERSON SUPPORTS FREQUENT "CORRECTING" CONVENTIONS:
What is Jefferson's proposal about amendments?

49:4 His proposition is, "that whenever any two of the three branches of government shall concur in opinion, each by the voices of two thirds of their whole number, that a convention is necessary for altering the constitution, or CORRECTING BREACHES OF IT, a convention *shall* be called for the purpose.

PEOPLE MUST BE ABLE TO CALL A CONVENTION:
Jefferson's idea suggests a convention be called to correct the government whenever it strays from its boundaries.

49:5 As the people are the only legitimate fountain of power, and it is from them that the constitutional charter, under which the several branches of government hold their power, is derived, it seems strictly consonant to the republican theory, to recur to the same original authority, not only whenever it may be necessary to enlarge, diminish, or new-model the powers of the government, but also whenever any one of the departments may commit encroachments on the chartered authorities of the others.

ALWAYS REFER BACK TO ORIGINAL CONSTITUTION:
When encroachments are made, look back to the "rock" on which the government is founded ("rock," see Isaiah 51:1).

49:6 The several departments being perfectly co-ordinate by the terms of their common commission, none of them, it is evident, can pretend to an exclusive or superior right of settling the boundaries between their respective powers; and how are the encroachments of the stronger to be prevented, or the wrongs of the weaker to be redressed, without an appeal to the people themselves, who, as the grantors of the commissions, can alone declare its true meaning, and enforce its observance?

CONSTITUTIONAL ROAD TO AMENDING MUST BE KEPT OPEN:

This refers to an Article V Constitutional Convention of the people.

49:7   There is certainly great force in this reasoning, and it must be allowed to prove that a <u>constitutional road to the decision of the people ought to be marked out and kept open</u>, for certain great and extraordinary occasions. But there appear to be **insuperable**[179] <u>objections</u> against the proposed recurrence to the people, as a provision in all cases for keeping the several departments of power <u>within their constitutional limits</u>.

FREQUENT CONVENTIONS IS A RISKY AND DAMAGING IDEA:

Madison warns about problems from frequent conventions, suggesting that amendments are better solutions.

49:8   In the first place, the provision does not reach the case of a <u>combination of two of the departments</u> against the <u>third</u>. If the legislative authority, which possesses so many means of operating on the motives of the other departments, should be able to gain to its interest either of the others, or even one third of its members, the <u>remaining department</u> could derive <u>no advantage</u> from its remedial provision. I do not dwell, however, on this objection, because it may be thought to be rather against the modification of the principle, than against the principle itself.

FREQUENT REWRITING DIMINISHES LEGITIMACY:

Constant change in the supreme law destabilizes its legitimacy and the people begin to distrust it as a stable, reliable law.

49:9   In the next place, it may be considered as an objection inherent in the principle, that as every appeal to the people would carry an implication of some defect in the government, <u>frequent appeals</u> would, in a great measure, <u>deprive</u> the <u>government</u> of that **veneration**[180] which time bestows on every thing, and without which perhaps the wisest and freest governments would not possess the requisite <u>stability</u>.[181]

OPINION IS POWER:

A nation tends to support leaders whose opinion the people value. Ancient opinions are revered even more.

49:10   If it be true that all governments rest on opinion, it is no less true that the <u>strength of opinion</u> in each individual, and its practical influence on his conduct, <u>depend</u> much on the <u>number</u> which he supposes to have entertained the same opinion. The <u>reason of man</u>, like man himself, is <u>timid</u> and cautious when left <u>alone</u>, and acquires firmness and confidence in proportion to the number with which it is associated. When the examples which fortify opinion are ANCIENT as well as NUMEROUS, they are known to have a double effect.

A NATION OF PHILOSOPHERS IS BEST, BUT SUCH A NATION IS IMPOSSIBLE:

Such a nation is as impossible as Plato's idea of a race of kings.

49:11   In a <u>nation of philosophers</u>, this consideration ought to be disregarded. A reverence for the laws would be sufficiently inculcated by the voice of an <u>enlightened reason</u>. <u>But a nation of philosophers is as little to be expected as the philosophical race of kings wished for by Plato</u>.

POPULAR PREJUDICES HELP THOSE IN POWER:
But they can also be seriously damaging to liberty.

49:12   And in every other nation, the most rational government will not find it a superfluous <u>advantage</u> to have the prejudices of the <u>community on its side</u>.

FREQUENT MEDDLING DIMINISHES STABILITY:
If amending the Constitution was made easy, American society would suffer from "trying on" every experiment introduced. Amendments should not be attempted too often.

49:13   The danger of <u>disturbing the public tranquility</u> by interesting too strongly the public passions, is a still more <u>serious objection</u> against a frequent reference of constitutional questions to the <u>decision of the whole society</u>.

EXPERIMENTS THUS FAR HAVE BEEN RISKY:

49:14   Notwithstanding the success which has attended the revisions of our established forms of government, and which does so much honor to the virtue and intelligence of the people of America, it must be confessed that the <u>experiments</u> are of <u>too ticklish</u> a nature to be <u>unnecessarily multiplied</u>.

---

179   ***Insuperable:*** Impossible to overcome, insurmountable or overwhelming.

180   *veneration:* Great respect or reverence.

181   Daniel Webster said amendments have the power to destroy the Constitution: "Our form of government is superior to all others, inasmuch as it provides, in a fair and honorable manner for its own amendment. But it requires no gift of prophecy to foresee that this privilege may be seized on by demagogues, to introduce wild and destructive innovations. Under the gentle name of amendments changes may be proposed which, if unresisted, will undermine the national compact, mar its fairest features, and reduce it finally to a dead letter. It abates nothing of the danger to say that alterations may be trifling and inconsiderable. If the Constitution be picked away by piecemeal, it is gone—and gone as effectually as if some military despot had grasped it at once, trampled it beneath his feet, and scattered its loose leaves in the wild winds." C. H. Van Tyne, *The Letters of Daniel Webster* (McClure, Phillips & Co., New York, 1902), p. 12.

UNIVERSAL CRISIS INVITES UNIVERSAL ACCORD:

People generally rush to unite behind trusted leaders to support them against common enemies.

49:15 We are to recollect that all the existing constitutions were formed in the midst of a danger which repressed the passions most unfriendly to order and concord; of an enthusiastic confidence of the people in their patriotic leaders, which stifled the ordinary diversity of opinions on great national questions; of a universal ardor for new and opposite forms, produced by a universal resentment and indignation against the ancient government; and whilst no spirit of party connected with the changes to be made, or the abuses to be reformed, could mingle its leaven in the operation. The future situations in which we must expect to be usually placed, do not present any equivalent security against the danger which is apprehended.

REPUBLICAN FORM TENDS TO ELEVATE THE LEGISLATURE:

The same men who might be elected at the conventions would most likely also be behind any scheme to usurp the government.

49:16 But the greatest objection of all is, that the decisions which would probably result from such appeals would not answer the purpose of maintaining the constitutional equilibrium of the government. We have seen that the tendency of republican governments is to an aggrandizement of the legislative at the expense of the other departments. The appeals to the people, therefore, would usually be made by the executive and judiciary departments. But whether made by one side or the other, would each side enjoy equal advantages on the trial? Let us view their different situations.

EXECUTIVE AND JUDICIARY VIEWED DISTANTLY:

The smaller branches of government suffer from their appointments and distance from the people.

49:17 The members of the executive and judiciary departments are few in number, and can be personally known to a small part only of the people. The latter, by the mode of their appointment, as well as by the nature and permanency of it, are too far removed from the people to share much in their prepossessions. The former are generally the objects of jealousy, and their administration is always liable to be discolored and rendered unpopular.

LEGISLATIVE BRANCH CLOSEST TO THE PEOPLE:

The people's representatives enjoy support for many reasons.

49:18 The members of the legislative department, on the other hand, are numerous. They are distributed and dwell among the people at large. Their connections of blood, of friendship, and of acquaintance embrace a great proportion of the most influential part of the society.

LEGISLATIVE BRANCH IS GUARDIAN OF LIBERTY:

Why is the legislature more trusted than the other branches?

49:19 The nature of their public trust implies a personal influence among the people, and that they are more immediately the confidential guardians of the rights and liberties of the people. With these advantages, it can hardly be supposed that the adverse party would have an equal chance for a favorable issue.

49:20 But the legislative party would not only be able to plead their cause most successfully with the people. They would probably be constituted themselves the judges.

POLITICIANS WOULD WIN OR INFLUENCE SEATS AT A CONSTITUTIONAL CONVENTION:

The same persuasive influence some politicians have for winning office would allow those same people to bring their prejudices as delegates to a constitutional convention.

49:21 The same influence which had gained them an election into the legislature, would gain them a seat in the convention. If this should not be the case with all, it would probably be the case with many, and pretty certainly with those leading characters, on whom every thing depends in such bodies. The convention, in short, would be composed chiefly of men who had been, who actually were, or who expected to be, members of the department whose conduct was arraigned. They would consequently be parties to the very question to be decided by them.

POPULAR PASSIONS CAN SWAY POLITICAL POWER:

In a contest among the branches, partisan passions will usually override reason.

49:22 It might, however, sometimes happen, that appeals would be made under circumstances less adverse to the executive and judiciary departments. The usurpations of the legislature might be so flagrant and so sudden, as to admit of no specious coloring. A strong party among themselves might take side with the other branches. The executive power might be in the hands of a peculiar favorite of the people. In such a posture of things, the public decision might be less swayed by prepossessions in favor of the legislative party. But still it could never be expected to turn on the true merits of the question. It would inevitably be connected with the <u>spirit of pre-existing parties</u>, or of parties springing out of the question itself.

OPPOSITION LED BY POLITICAL OPPONENTS: If influential leaders were allowed to participate in the conventions they could change the outcome.

49:23 It would be connected with persons of distinguished character and extensive influence in the community. It would be <u>pronounced by the very men</u> who had been <u>agents in</u>, or <u>opponents of, the measures</u> to which the decision would relate.

PASSION NOT REASON SITS IN JUDGMENT: Unfortunately, when those popular voices enter into a convention they stir party loyalty (passion) to lead instead of what's best (reason).

49:24 The <u>PASSIONS</u>, therefore, not the <u>REASON</u>, of the public would sit in <u>judgment</u>. But it is the reason, alone, of the public, that ought to control and regulate the government.

How would government control the passions?

49:25 The passions ought to be controlled and <u>regulated by the government</u>.

MERE PAPER RESTRICTIONS NOT SUFFICIENT: Frequent appeals to the people in convention is not the best solution.

49:26 We found in the last paper, that <u>mere declarations in the written constitution are not sufficient to restrain the several departments</u> within their legal rights. It appears in this, that occasional <u>appeals to the people would be neither a proper nor an effectual provision for that purpose.</u> How far the provisions of a different nature contained in the plan above quoted might be adequate, I do not examine. Some of them are unquestionably founded on sound political principles, and All of them are framed with singular ingenuity and precision.

—PUBLIUS

REVIEW QUESTIONS

1. What did Jefferson include in his "Notes on the State of Virginia" that caught Madison's attention? (49:1–2)

2. What does Jefferson propose about conventions that has Madison concerned? (49:3–4)

3. What is Jefferson's idea about correcting constitutional abuses? (49:5)

4. Are frequent conventions a good or bad idea? Why? (49:8–9, 13–14)

5. Which leads and guides the best, opinion by leaders, or

truth? Why? (49:10–12)

6. Is a nation of philosophers as impossible as Plato's nation of philosopher kings? (49:11–12)

7. Although America successfully rebuilt its government, can too much experimenting with other ideas for government be dangerous? (49:13–14)

8. What can quickly unite a people otherwise removed from national causes? (49:15)

9. Under the influence of persuasive speakers, what might ultimately end up controlling Jefferson's corrective conventions? (49:24)

10. If a written law is not enough to prevent the branches from encroaching on each other, would occasional conventions be a good corrective solution? Why? (49:26)

FEDERALIST NO. 50

PENNSYLVANIA PROVES THAT REVIEWS OF GOVERNMENT ARE INEFFECTIVE: Subjecting the government to regular scrutiny by a Council of Censors for breaches in its adherence to the Constitution has several serious problems. These Council members would be subject to the inflamed passions, bias, and prejudices that could be sweeping the nation at any given time. While such reviews are very republican in nature, the disruptions they could create would be bad for the overall good of the nation. The built-in checks and balances with the ballot box are the best form of review.

By James Madison—February 5, 1788

REFERENDUMS CAN BE DANGEROUS: Should the Constitution regularly be opened for the public to review and revise how things are going?

50:1 IT MAY be contended, perhaps, that instead of <u>OCCASIONAL</u> appeals to the people, which are liable to the objections urged against them, <u>PERIODICAL</u> appeals are the proper and adequate means of <u>PREVENTING AND CORRECTING INFRACTIONS</u> OF THE CONSTITUTION.[182]

---

182 This is the role of a ***referendum***, a direct and universal vote by citizens who may vote for or against an act brought before the legislature before it becomes law.

RETURNING TO EXISTING AMENDING PROCESS IS BETTER THAN REVIEWS:

Regular conventions for Constitutional review are no better than as-needed conventions. Frequent rewriting fails to fix problem.

50:2 It will be attended to, that in the examination of these expedients, I confine myself to their aptitude for ENFORCING the Constitution, by keeping the several departments of power within their due bounds, without particularly considering them as provisions for ALTERING the Constitution itself. In the first view, appeals to the people at fixed periods appear to be nearly as ineligible as appeals on particular occasions as they emerge.

EITHER DELAYED OR SPEEDY REVIEWS OF GOVERNMENT ACTIONS MUST FAIL:

If reviews came too quickly the people's passions will distort the search for truth. If a review waits too long, the need for serious and legitimate repair might be ignored.

50:3 If the periods be separated by short intervals, the measures to be reviewed and rectified will have been of recent date, and will be connected with all the circumstances which tend to vitiate and pervert the result of occasional revisions. If the periods be distant from each other, the same remark will be applicable to all recent measures; and in proportion as the remoteness of the others may favor a dispassionate review of them, this advantage is inseparable from inconveniences which seem to counterbalance it.

DELAYED EXPOSURE WON'T DETER BRASH ACTIONS:

People bent on a cause won't worry about public rebuke if that action is delayed for years to come.

50:4 In the first place, a distant prospect of public censure would be a very feeble restraint on power from those excesses to which it might be urged by the force of present motives. Is it to be imagined that a legislative assembly, consisting of a hundred or two hundred members, eagerly bent on some favorite object, and breaking through the restraints of the Constitution in pursuit of it, would be arrested in their career, by considerations drawn from a censorial revision of their conduct at the future distance of ten, fifteen, or twenty years?

DAMAGE DONE BEFORE CORRECTIONS MADE:

50:5 In the next place, the abuses would often have completed their mischievous effects before the remedial provision would be applied.

LONG-STANDING ACTS NOT EASILY UPROOTED:

50:6 And in the last place, where this might not be the case, they would be of long standing, would have taken deep root, and would not easily be extirpated.

PENNSYLVANIA LOOKED FOR ENCROACHMENTS:

A council was set up to look for breaches.

50:7 The scheme of revising the constitution, in order to correct recent breaches of it, as well as for other purposes, has been actually tried in one of the States. One of the objects of the Council of Censors which met in Pennsylvania in 1783 and 1784, was, as we have seen, to inquire, "whether the constitution had been violated, and whether the legislative and executive departments had encroached upon each other."

THEIR EXPERIMENT HELPS PROVE A POINT:

50:8 This important and novel experiment in politics merits, in several points of view, very particular attention. In some of them it may, perhaps, as a single experiment, made under circumstances somewhat peculiar, be thought to be not absolutely conclusive. But as applied to the case under consideration, it involves some facts, which I venture to remark, as a complete and satisfactory illustration of the reasoning which I have employed.

COUNCIL MEMBERS BIASED TOWARD STATUS QUO:

Some of the most senior members of the Council of Censors had been in public office for many years. Was Pennsylvania's Council of Censors an unbiased body?

50:9 First. It appears, from the names of the gentlemen who composed the council, that some, at least, of its most active members had also been active and leading characters in the parties which pre-existed in the State.

COUNCILMEN WERE PARTIES TO ENCROACHMENTS:

Members of the very council called to investigate violations of the constitution had precipitated the violations.

50:10 Second. It appears that the same active and leading members of the council had been active and influential members of the legislative and executive branches, within the period to be reviewed; and even patrons or opponents of the very measures to be thus brought to the test of the constitution.

Bias was built in.

50:11 Two of the members had been vice-presidents of the State, and several other members of the executive council, within the seven preceding years. One of them had been speaker, and a number of others distinguished members, of the legislative assembly within the same period.

COUNCIL DEBATES WERE RULED BY PASSION NOT REASON:

The records show the investigation into breaches were dominated by violent feelings and arguments instead of thoughtful reason.

50:12 Third. Every page of their proceedings witnesses the effect of all these circumstances on the temper of their deliberations. Throughout the continuance of the council, it was split into two fixed and violent parties. The fact is acknowledged and lamented by themselves. Had this not been the case, the face of their proceedings exhibits a proof equally satisfactory. In all questions, however unimportant in themselves, or unconnected with each other, the same names stand invariably contrasted on the opposite columns. Every unbiased observer may infer, without danger of mistake, and at the same time without meaning to reflect on either party, or any individuals of either party, that, unfortunately, PASSION, not REASON, must have presided over their decisions.

COMMON PASSION LEADS TO COMMON OPINIONS:

50:13 When men exercise their reason coolly and freely on a variety of distinct questions, they inevitably fall into different opinions on some of them. When they are governed by a common passion, their opinions, if they are so to be called, will be the same.

PENNSYLVANIA'S CONSTITUTION MISINTERPRETED FOR GAIN:

Instead of applying the constitution as a boundary, they ignored parts.

50:14 Fourth. It is at least problematical, whether the decisions of this body do not, in several instances, misconstrue the limits prescribed for the legislative and executive departments, instead of reducing and limiting them within their constitutional places.

COUNCIL FAILED TO REIN IN LEGISLATURE:

The council's efforts made no correction. The legislature was left stronger.

50:15 Fifth. I have never understood that the decisions of the council on constitutional questions, whether rightly or erroneously formed, have had any effect in varying the practice founded on legislative constructions. It even appears, if I mistake not, that in one instance the contemporary legislature denied the constructions of the council, and actually prevailed in the contest.

COUNCIL OF CENSORS FAILED IN ITS MISSION:

This failure is to be blamed on the council alone, it can't be blamed on some major crisis in the State or rabid party quarreling.

50:16 This censorial body, therefore, proves at the same time, by its researches, the existence of the disease, and by its example, the inefficacy of the remedy.

PARTIES IN CONFLICT WILL ALWAYS EXIST:

The States won't be free from parties and crises in the future, and if parties are extinguished, that means a State's real problems are much greater than cracks in its constitution.

50:17 This conclusion cannot be invalidated by alleging that the State in which the experiment was made was at that crisis, and had been for a long time before, violently heated and distracted by the rage of party. Is it to be presumed, that at any future septennial epoch the same State will be free from parties? Is it to be presumed that any other State, at the same or any other given period, will be exempt from them? Such an event ought to be neither presumed nor desired; because an extinction of parties necessarily implies either a universal alarm for the public safety, or an absolute extinction of liberty.

EXCLUDING POLITICIANS WON'T SOLVE BASIC ISSUE:

What if the Council of Censors was reorganized somehow with non-politicians, would that solve the council's problems?

50:18 Were the precaution taken of excluding from the assemblies elected by the people, to revise the preceding administration of the government, all persons who should have been concerned with the government within the given period, the difficulties would not be obviated. The important task would probably devolve on men, who, with inferior capacities, would in other respects be little better qualified. Although they might not have been personally concerned in the administration, and therefore not immediately agents in the measures to be examined, they would probably have been involved in the parties connected with these measures, and have been elected under their auspices.

—PUBLIUS

REVIEW QUESTIONS

1. What topic does Madison continue discussing here? (50:1–2)

2. Why would the prospect of some future performance review not restrain determined people from violating the Constitution? (50:4)

3. Would constitutional review conventions take action to

prevent more damage to the Constitution, or just react to harm already done? Why would time delay further complicate an effort to correct the violation? (50:5–6)

4. What are the lessons learned from Pennsylvania's Council of Censors? (50:7–16)

5. Would preventing politicians from being on the council keep it more pure? (50:18)

FEDERALIST NO. 51

STRUCTURE OF GOVERNMENT MUST FURNISH PROPER CHECKS AND BALANCES: The structure of government under the new Constitution is what makes liberty possible. The people are empowered to select their leaders but an election for every office is not practical in many cases. For example, electors who are wise and studious are better prepared to examine each candidate and elect one for President—not by popular vote of the whole national population which is always prone to passionate distraction. The legislators who are experienced in real issues, law, debate, and bills should elect from their own numbers two Senators of similar background—not by the whole State population that is always prone to passionate distraction. In this way the very best will select the very best without popular passions and party campaigns masking weaknesses that could be detrimental. Members of the three branches must be subject to some control by the other branches but only within reason. "If men were angels, no government would be necessary," Madison writes. The government must have the means to control the people, but also it must be forced to control itself. The large numbers of groups in America help protect liberty. The "have nots" will always be attacking the "haves," it is a normal class struggle in any society. The Constitution grants those freedoms of class conflict but guards "one part of the society against the injustice of the other." Madison says that to reduce tyranny by a majority or tyranny by a minority, the government must be divided and arranged "in such a manner as that each may be a check on each other." Preserving State sovereignty was key to this division and arrangement.

By James Madison—February 6, 1788

INTERNAL CHECKS AND BALANCES NEEDED:
If the people can't control the expansion of government, let territorial jealousies work to naturally control the tendency.

51:1 TO WHAT expedient, then, shall we finally resort, for maintaining in practice the necessary partition of power among the several departments, as laid down in the Constitution? The only answer that can be given is, that as all these exterior provisions are found to be inadequate, the defect must be supplied, by so contriving the interior structure of the government as that its several constituent parts may, by their mutual relations, be the means of keeping each other in their proper places. Without presuming to undertake a full development of this important idea, I will hazard a few general observations, which may perhaps place it in a clearer light, and enable us to form a more correct judgment of the principles and structure of the government planned by the Convention.

PEOPLE APPOINT ALL POLITICAL OFFICERS:
The various departments should not have power to appoint members of other departments.

51:2 In order to lay a due foundation for that separate and distinct exercise of the different powers of government, which to a certain extent is admitted on all hands to be essential to the preservation of liberty, it is evident that each department should have a will of its own; and consequently should be so constituted that the members of each should have as little agency as possible in the appointment of the members of the others.

JUDGES ARE AN EXCEPTION:
Because high qualifications must be measured for judges, the people would do better to establish how they are selected instead of who is selected.

51:3 Were this principle rigorously adhered to, it would require that all the appointments for the supreme executive, legislative, and judiciary magistracies should be drawn from the same fountain of authority, the people, through channels having no communication whatever with one another. Perhaps such a plan of constructing the several departments would be less difficult in practice than it may in contemplation appear. Some difficulties, however, and some additional expense would attend the execution of it. Some deviations, therefore, from the principle must be admitted. In the constitution of the judiciary department in particular, it might be inexpedient to insist rigorously on the principle: first, because peculiar qualifications being essential in the members, the primary consideration ought to be to select that mode of choice which best secures these qualifications; secondly, because the permanent tenure by which the appointments are held in that department, must soon destroy all sense of dependence on the authority conferring them.

BRANCHES MUST NOT CONTROL EACH OTHER:
The three branches must not have power to compel, blackmail, or other wise pressure the other branches to certain actions.

51:4 It is equally evident, that the members of each department should be as little dependent as possible on those of the others, for the emoluments annexed to their offices. Were the executive magistrate, or the judges, not independent of the legislature in this particular, their independence in every other would be merely nominal.

EMPOWER OFFICERS TO RESIST ENCROACHMENTS:
The Constitution must grant leaders sufficient power to retain their place and control, but not allow it to expand.

51:5 But the great security against a gradual concentration of the several powers in the same department, consists in giving to those who administer each department the necessary constitutional means and personal motives to resist encroachments of the others. The provision for defense must in this, as in all other cases, be made commensurate to the danger of attack.

IF MEN WERE ANGELS, NO NEED FOR GOVERNMENT:
Government is a reflection of human nature. Where weakness could gain strength, the government imposes barriers. What ultimate foe must the government be obliged to control?

51:6 Ambition must be made to counteract ambition. The interest of the man must be connected with the constitutional rights of the place. It may be a reflection on human nature, that such devices should be necessary to control the abuses of government. But what is government itself, but the greatest of all reflections on human nature? If men were angels, no government would be necessary. If angels were to govern men, neither external nor internal controls on government would be necessary. In framing a government which is to be administered by men over men, the great difficulty lies in this: you must first enable the government to control the governed; and in the next place oblige it to control itself.

CAN PEOPLE ALONE CONTROL GOVERNMENT?
What additional aid is needed to help the people control its leaders?

51:7 A dependence on the people is, no doubt, the primary control on the government; but experience has taught mankind the necessity of auxiliary precautions.

PRIVATE INTEREST IS THE BEST SENTINEL:
Arranging political power is best done by giving individuals well-bounded rights that they will always defend from usurpation.

51:8 This policy of supplying, by opposite and rival interests, the defect of better motives, might be traced through the whole system of human affairs, private as well as public. We see it particularly displayed in all the subordinate distributions of power, where the constant aim is to divide and arrange the several offices in such a manner as that each may be a check on the other that the private interest of every individual may be a sentinel over the public rights. These inventions of prudence cannot be less requisite in the distribution of the supreme powers of the State.

CONTROL LEGISLATURE BY DIVIDING IT:
How does the Constitution put a check on the powerful Legislative Branch?

51:9 But it is not possible to give to each department an equal power of self-defense. In republican government, the legislative authority necessarily predominates. The remedy for this inconveniency is to divide the legislature into different branches; and to render them, by different modes of election and different principles of action, as little connected with each other as the nature of their common functions and their common dependence on the society will admit.

FORTIFY THE EXECUTIVE TO HAVE SOME CONTROL OVER CONGRESS:
What role can the executive branch play as a check and balance?

51:10 It may even be necessary to guard against dangerous encroachments by still further precautions. As the weight of the legislative authority requires that it should be thus divided, the weakness of the executive may require, on the other hand, that it should be fortified. An absolute negative on the legislature appears, at first view, to be the natural defense with which the executive magistrate should be armed. But perhaps it would be neither altogether safe nor alone sufficient. On ordinary occasions it might not be exerted with the requisite firmness, and on extraordinary occasions it might be perfidiously abused. May not this defect of an absolute negative be supplied by some qualified connection between this weaker department and the weaker branch of the stronger department, by which the latter may be led to support the constitutional rights of the former, without being too much detached from the rights of its own department?

TRUE PRINCIPLES OF BALANCED POWER WILL WORK WELL FOR BOTH STATE AND FEDERAL:
If checks and balances don't work from the Constitution's organization of power, could checks and balances work in the States?

51:11 If the principles on which these observations are founded be just, as I persuade myself they are, and they be applied as a criterion to the several State constitutions, and to the federal Constitution it will be found that if the latter does not perfectly correspond with them, the former are infinitely less able to bear such a test.

51:12 There are, moreover, <u>two considerations</u> particularly applicable to the <u>federal system of America</u>, which place that system in a very interesting point of view.

COMPOUND REPUBLIC DEFINED:

The people's power is divided between the State and federal governments. This gives the people a double security against usurpation by either government. Will the States and federal levels control each other?

51:13 First. In a single republic, all the power surrendered by the people is submitted to the administration of a single government; and the usurpations are guarded against by a <u>division</u> of the government into <u>distinct</u> and separate <u>departments</u>. In the <u>compound republic of America</u>, the power surrendered by the people is first divided between two distinct governments, and then the portion allotted to each subdivided among distinct and <u>separate departments</u>. Hence a double security arises to the rights of the people. The <u>different governments will control each other, at the same time that each will be controlled by itself</u>.

UNBRIDLED MAJORITY RULE MAKES MINORITY RIGHTS UNSAFE:

How does a government of representatives serve to be a check on factions and the tyranny of the majority?

51:14 Second. It is of great importance in a republic not only to <u>guard</u> the <u>society against</u> the oppression of its <u>rulers</u>, but to <u>guard one</u> part of the society against the <u>injustice</u> of the other part. Different interests necessarily exist in different classes of citizens. If a majority be united by a common interest, the rights of the <u>minority</u> will be <u>insecure</u>.

TWO METHODS TO PROTECT ALL RIGHTS:

Forcing people to think alike is impossible in liberty but that level of "group think" is the goal of every monarchy. Such a power is destructive to everyone.

51:15 There are but two methods of providing against this evil: the one by <u>creating a will</u> in the community <u>independent</u> of the majority that is, of the <u>society itself</u>; the other, by comprehending in the <u>society</u> so many <u>separate</u> <u>descriptions</u> of <u>citizens</u> as will render an unjust <u>combination</u> of a majority of the whole very <u>improbable</u>, if not impracticable. The first method prevails in all governments possessing an hereditary or self-appointed authority. This, at best, is but a precarious security; because a <u>power</u> <u>independent</u> of the <u>society</u> may as well espouse the <u>unjust</u> views of the major, as the rightful interests of the minor party, and may possibly be turned against both parties.

ALL AUTHORITY DIVIDED IN MANY SMALL PARTS:

The second method is to break up all of society into as many parts possible. This will protect minority rights.

51:16 The <u>second method</u> will be exemplified in the federal republic of the <u>United States</u>. Whilst all authority in it will be derived from and dependent on the society, the <u>society</u> itself will be broken into so <u>many parts</u>, interests, and classes of citizens, that the <u>rights of individuals</u>, or of the minority, will be in <u>little danger</u> from interested combinations of the majority.

RELIGIOUS AND CIVIL RIGHTS MUST BE HONORED TO SAME DEGREE:

51:17 In a free government the security for <u>civil rights</u> must be the <u>same as that</u> for <u>religious rights</u>. It consists in the one case in the <u>multiplicity of interests</u>, and in the other in the <u>multiplicity of sects</u>. The degree of security in both cases will depend on the number of interests and sects; and this may be presumed to depend on the extent of country and number of people comprehended under the same government.

CONFEDERACY DIMINISHES RIGHTS OF ALL CLASSES:

A confederacy will not have these layers of protection and will ultimately oppress and destroy rights.

51:18 This view of the subject must particularly recommend a proper federal system to all the sincere and considerate friends of republican government, since it shows that in exact proportion as the territory of the Union may be formed into more circumscribed Confederacies, or States oppressive combinations of a majority will be facilitated: the <u>best security</u>, under the republican forms, for the <u>rights of every class of citizens, will be diminished</u>: and consequently the stability and independence of some member of the government, the only other security, must be proportionately increased.

JUSTICE IS THE END OF GOVERNMENT:

51:19 <u>Justice is the end of government</u>. It is the <u>end of civil society</u>. It ever has been and ever will be <u>pursued</u> until it be <u>obtained</u>, or until liberty be lost in the pursuit.

ALL CONSTITUTIONS MUST PROTECT THE WEAKER PARTS:

Even if a faction is stronger than everyone else, would it not be to its advantage to have a government that protected both its rights and that of the weak?

51:20 In a society under the forms of which the <u>stronger faction</u> can readily <u>unite and oppress the weaker</u>, <u>anarchy</u> may as truly be said to reign as in a <u>state of nature</u>, where the <u>weaker individual is not secured against the violence</u> of the stronger; and as, in the latter state, even the stronger individuals are <u>prompted</u>, by the <u>uncertainty</u> of their condition, to submit to a government which may <u>protect the weak</u> as well as themselves; so, in the former state, will the <u>more powerful factions or parties be gradually induced</u>, by a like motive, to wish for a government which will <u>protect</u> all parties, the <u>weaker</u> as well as the more <u>powerful</u>.

RHODE ISLAND WOULD SEEK OUTSIDE HELP IF LEFT OUT OF UNION:

51:21 It can be little doubted that if the <u>State of Rhode Island</u> was <u>separated</u> from the Confederacy and <u>left to itself</u>, the insecurity of rights under the popular form of government within such narrow limits would be displayed by such reiterated <u>oppressions of factious majorities</u> that some power altogether independent of the <u>people would soon be called for by the voice of the very factions whose misrule had proved the necessity of it</u>.

JUSTICE FOR ALL IS THE BASIS OF A REPUBLIC:
United sovereign States in a republic works only if it is founded on justice for all. In this manner are the rights of the majority and the minority protected.

51:22 In the extended republic of the United States, and among the great variety of interests, parties, and sects which it embraces, a <u>coalition of a majority of the whole society could seldom take place on any other principles than those of justice and the general good</u>; whilst there being thus less danger to a minor from the will of a major party, there must be less pretext, also, to provide for the security of the former, by <u>introducing</u> into the <u>government</u> a <u>will</u> <u>not dependent</u> on the <u>latter</u>, or, in other words, a <u>will independent of the society itself</u>.

REPUBLICAN FORM WORKS BETTER WITH LARGE NATIONS:
The federal system lends itself to self-government over large sectors. A very large number of people complicates the government's temptation to control private matters.

51:23 It is no less certain than it is important, notwithstanding the contrary opinions which have been entertained, that the <u>larger the society</u>, provided it lie within a practical sphere, the <u>more duly capable it will be of self-government</u>. And happily for the REPUBLICAN CAUSE, the practicable sphere may be carried to a very great extent, by a <u>judicious modification</u> and mixture of the <u>FEDERAL PRINCIPLE</u>.

—PUBLIUS

REVIEW QUESTIONS

1. Fill in the blanks: Referring to his prior papers, Madison says the only way to truly secure a government's proper role is by designing the interior _____ so that its several parts, by their mutual _____, will keep each other in their _____ _____. (51:1)

2. It is ideal for the people to select their leaders but in what branch of government would the people be under qualified to make good choices? (51:3)

3. Should the incentives of office depend on the other branches? Why? (51:4)

4. What's the best defense against ambitious men? (51:6)

5. Fill in the blanks: If men were _____, no government would be needed. If _____ were to govern men, no controls on government would be necessary. What does that mean? (51:7)

6. Is depending upon people's good faith and oath enough to control government? (51:7)

7. What remarkable outcome can be created by carefully dividing and arranging powers so they are opposed and rivals to each other? (51:8)

8. Is this check on each other equal for all departments? In which department is that check most difficult? (51:9)

9. Fill in the blanks: Controlling the legislature is done by _____ it into _____ branches, and disconnect the modes of _____ and principles of _____ or responsibilities. (51:9)

10. Why is the power of total veto, or "absolute negative," so dangerous in the hands of the President as a means to exert control over the legislature? (51:10)

11. What is the difference between a single republic and a "compound republic"? (51:13)

12. What two forces of tyranny can exist in a republic if not properly controlled? (51:14)

13. What are the two options to prevent such oppressions listed in 51:14? (51:15–16)

14. Are religious rights just as secure as civil rights in a free government? (51:17)

15. What is the main purpose of government? (51:19–21)

16. Do these principles work best in small or large societies? What does Madison call this principle in general? (51:23)

PART II

THE THREE BRANCHES

SECTION 8 • HOUSE OF REPRESENTATIVES

Papers 52–61

FEDERALIST NO. 52

HOUSE OF REPRESENTATIVES—QUALIFICATIONS AND FREQUENCY OF ELECTIONS: There is safety in electing representatives every two years instead of every one year. Examples of this can be found in European and American history. And if Britain can secure its liberties with elections every three years, the American system of two years is even better. Biennial elections give representatives just enough incentive to stay beholden to the needs of the nation.

By James Madison—February 8, 1788

THE HOUSE OF REPRESENTATIVES:
Qualifications, elections, and terms that are safe to liberty.

52:1 FROM the more general inquiries pursued in the four last papers, I pass on to a more particular examination of the several parts of the government. I shall begin with the House of Representatives.

QUALIFICATIONS OF ELECTORS AND THE ELECTED:

52:2 The first view to be taken of this part of the government relates to the qualifications of the electors and the elected. Those of the former are to be the same with those of the electors of the most numerous branch of the State legislatures.

SUFFRAGE IS A CORE REPUBLICAN PRINCIPLE:
Congress and the States may not regulate this basic right to vote. The right to vote is the essence of representative government.

52:3 The definition of the right of suffrage is very justly regarded as a fundamental article of republican government. It was incumbent on the Convention, therefore, to define and establish this right in the Constitution. To have left it open for the occasional regulation of the Congress, would have been improper for the reason just mentioned. To have submitted it to the legislative discretion of the States, would have been

improper for the same reason; and for the additional reason that it would have rendered too dependent on the State governments that branch of the federal government which ought to be dependent on the people alone.

THE CONVENTION SET A UNIFORM RULE TO VOTE:

52:4 To have reduced the different qualifications in the different States to one uniform rule, would probably have been as dissatisfactory to some of the States as it would have been difficult to the Convention. The provision made by the Convention appears, therefore, to be the best that lay within their option.

STATES CAN'T DIMINISH VOTING RIGHTS:

52:5 It must be satisfactory to every State, because it is conformable to the standard already established, or which may be established, by the State itself. It will be safe to the United States, because, being fixed by the State constitutions, it is not alterable by the State governments, and it cannot be feared that the people of the States will alter this part of their constitutions in such a manner as to abridge the rights secured to them by the federal Constitution.

QUALIFICATION OF A REPRESENTATIVE:
The person must be twenty-five years old, a citizen for seven years, and must not hold another federal office.

52:6 The qualifications of the elected, being less carefully and properly defined by the State constitutions, and being at the same time more susceptible of uniformity, have been very properly considered and regulated by the Convention. A representative of the United States must be of the age of twenty-five years; must have been seven years a citizen of the United States; must, at the time of his election, be an inhabitant of the State he is to represent; and, during the time of his service, must be in no office under the United States.

ALMOST ANYONE CAN BE A REPRESENTATIVE:
The door is open to almost anyone to serve in the lower House.

52:7 Under these reasonable limitations, the door of this part of the federal government is open to merit of every description, whether native or adoptive, whether young or old, and without regard to poverty or wealth, or to any particular profession of religious faith.

TWO-YEAR TERMS ARE SAFE AND NECESSARY:
What two questions arise regarding the term of a representative?

52:8 The term for which the representatives are to be elected falls under a second view which may be taken of this branch. In order to decide on the propriety of this article, two questions must be considered: first, whether biennial elections will, in this case, be safe; secondly, whether they be necessary or useful.

GOVERNMENT MUST BE DEPENDENT ON PEOPLE:
Liberty survives when the federal level is close to the people. Frequent elections help serve this purpose.

52:9 First. As it is essential to liberty that the government in general should have a common interest with the people, so it is particularly essential that the branch of it under consideration should have an immediate dependence on, and an intimate sympathy with, the people. Frequent elections are unquestionably the only policy by which this dependence and sympathy can be effectually secured. But what particular degree of frequency may be absolutely necessary for the purpose, does not appear to be susceptible of any precise calculation, and must depend on a variety of circumstances with which it may be connected. Let us consult experience, the guide that ought always to be followed whenever it can be found.

REPRESENTATIVES ARE SUBSTITUTES FOR CITIZENS:
What impractical mass movement does representation help avoid?

52:10 The scheme of representation, as a substitute for a meeting of the citizens in person, being at most but very imperfectly known to ancient polity, it is in more modern times only that we are to expect instructive examples. And even here, in order to avoid a research too vague and diffusive, it will be proper to confine ourselves to the few examples which are best known, and which bear the greatest analogy to our particular case.

BRITAIN'S HOUSE OF COMMONS:
How often was Parliament supposed to sit in session? What's the longest recess allowed between parliamentary sessions?

52:11 The first to which this character ought to be applied, is the House of Commons in Great Britain. The history of this branch of the English Constitution, anterior to the date of **Magna Charta**,[183] is too obscure to yield instruction. The very existence of it has been made a question among political antiquaries. The earliest records of subsequent date prove that parliaments were to SIT only every year; not that they were to be ELECTED every year. And even these annual sessions were left so much at the discretion of the monarch, that, under various pretexts, very long and dangerous intermissions were often contrived by royal ambition. To remedy this grievance, it was provided by a statute in the reign of Charles II, that the intermissions should not be protracted beyond a period of three years.

PARLIAMENT SHOULD ASSEMBLE IN SESSION FREQUENTLY:
The term "frequently" was later defined to be how long?

52:12 On the accession of William III, when a revolution took place in the government, the subject was still more seriously resumed, and it was declared to be among the fundamental rights of the people that parliaments ought to be held FREQUENTLY. By another statute, which passed a few years later in the same reign, the term "frequently," which had alluded to the triennial period settled in the time of Charles II, is reduced to a precise meaning, it being expressly enacted that a new parliament shall be called within three years after the termination of the former. The last change, from three to seven years, is well known to have been introduced pretty early in the present century, under an alarm for the Hanoverian succession.

REPRESENTATIVES' TERMS ARE TWO YEARS:
Britain's three-year terms have served to protect liberty. Does that make two years even more safe?

52:13 From these facts it appears that the greatest frequency of elections which has been deemed necessary in that kingdom, for binding the representatives to their constituents, does not exceed a triennial return of them. And if we may argue from the degree of liberty retained even under septennial elections, and all the other vicious ingredients in the parliamentary constitution, we cannot doubt that a reduction of the period from seven to three years, with the other necessary reforms, would so far extend the influence of the people over their representatives as to satisfy us that biennial elections, under the federal system, cannot possibly be dangerous to the requisite dependence of the House of Representatives on their constituents.

---

183 **Magna Charta:** Latin, "great charter." The great charter obtained by English barons from King John, AD 1215. "Charta" is pronounced with a hard "k" sound. At the end of the 18th century, English speakers were mispronouncing Charta with a "ch" sound. The spelling began changing to drop the "h" to "Carta" to encourage correct pronunciation. Both spellings are correctly pronounced with a hard "K" sound: KAHR-tuh.

IRELAND'S PARLIAMENT SELDOM ELECTED:
Once appointed, an Irish parliamentarian could stay in office for decades. What's the only time that representatives were dependent on the people?

52:14 Elections in Ireland, till of late, were regulated entirely by the discretion of the crown, and were seldom repeated, except on the accession of a new prince, or some other contingent event. The parliament which commenced with George II. was continued throughout his whole reign, a period of about thirty-five years. The only dependence of the representatives on the people consisted in the right of the latter to supply occasional vacancies by the election of new members, and in the chance of some event which might produce a general new election.

IRELAND'S PARLIAMENT PUT ON EIGHT-YEAR CYCLES:
Ireland's protections of the people's rights were limited by the monarchy. If their system protected liberties with eight-year terms, would America's be as safe with only two-year terms?

52:15 The ability also of the Irish parliament to maintain the rights of their constituents, so far as the disposition might exist, was extremely shackled by the control of the crown over the subjects of their deliberation. Of late these shackles, if I mistake not, have been broken; and octennial parliaments have besides been established. What effect may be produced by this partial reform, must be left to further experience. The example of Ireland, from this view of it, can throw but little light on the subject. As far as we can draw any conclusion from it, it must be that if the people of that country have been able under all these disadvantages to retain any liberty whatever, the advantage of biennial elections would secure to them every degree of liberty, which might depend on a due connection between their representatives and themselves.

PRE-REVOLUTION CONGRESS WASN'T DANGEROUS:
The colonial States had varied terms in their legislatures and these were never deemed dangerous to the people's liberties.

52:16 Let us bring our inquiries nearer home. The example of these States, when British colonies, claims particular attention, at the same time that it is so well known as to require little to be said on it. The principle of representation, in one branch of the legislature at least, was established in All of them. But the periods of election were different. They varied from one to seven years. Have we any reason to infer, from the spirit and conduct of the representatives of the people, prior to the Revolution, that biennial elections would have been dangerous to the public liberties?

SPIRIT OF LIBERTY WAS STRONG BEFORE THE WAR:
Length of a congressman's term had no impact on the colonists being united in liberty.

52:17 The spirit which everywhere displayed itself at the commencement of the struggle, and which vanquished the obstacles to independence, is the best of proofs that a sufficient portion of liberty had been everywhere enjoyed to inspire both a sense of its worth and a zeal for its proper enlargement. This remark holds good, as well with regard to the then colonies whose elections were least frequent, as to those whose elections were most frequent Virginia was the colony which stood first in resisting the parliamentary usurpations of Great Britain; it was the first also in espousing, by public act, the resolution of independence.

VIRGINIA PROVES BIENNIAL ELECTIONS ARE SAFE:

52:18 In Virginia, nevertheless, if I have not been misinformed, elections under the former government were septennial. This particular example is brought into view, not as a proof of any peculiar merit, for the priority in those instances was probably accidental; and still less of any advantage in SEPTENNIAL elections, for when compared with a greater frequency they are inadmissible; but merely as a proof, and I conceive it to be a very substantial proof, that the liberties of the people can be in no danger from BIENNIAL elections.

GREAT POWER IS SAFER WITH SHORTER TERMS:
What term of office should the smaller powers be given?

52:19 The conclusion resulting from these examples will be not a little strengthened by recollecting three circumstances. The first is, that the federal legislature will possess a part only of that supreme legislative authority which is vested completely in the British Parliament; and which, with a few exceptions, was exercised by the colonial assemblies and the Irish legislature. It is a received and well-founded maxim, that where no other circumstances affect the case, the greater the power is, the shorter ought to be its duration; and, conversely, the smaller the power, the more safely may its duration be protracted.

CONGRESS WATCHED BY BOTH GOVERNMENT AND PEOPLE:
Checks and balances by the judicial and executive branches (the collateral legislatures), along with the people, keep Congress in check.

52:20 In the second place, it has, on another occasion, been shown that the federal legislature will not only be restrained by its dependence on its people, as other legislative bodies are, but that it will be, moreover, watched and controlled by the several collateral legislatures, which other legislative bodies are not.

LESS POWER EQUALS LESS TEMPTATION TO ABUSE:

Did the Framers anticipate powerful political parties, gerrymandering, or political action groups distorting election results?

52:21   And in the third place, no comparison can be made between the means that will be possessed by the more permanent branches of the federal government for seducing, if they should be disposed to seduce, the House of Representatives from their duty to the people, and the means of influence over the popular branch possessed by the other branches of the government above cited. With less power, therefore, to abuse, the federal representatives can be less tempted on one side, and will be doubly watched on the other.

—PUBLIUS

REVIEW QUESTIONS

1. What does Madison explain in this paper? (52:1)

2. Why is Congress allowed to make or alter the times and places of elections that are established by the States? (52:3–4)

3. What are the restrictions to be a member of the House of Representatives? (52:6)

4. Are two-year terms safe for the people and their liberties? (52:8)

5. Should offices bearing great political power enjoy a long term or short? (52:19)

6. Do shorter terms and less power result in less temptation and less opportunity to abuse power? (52:21)

FEDERALIST NO. 53

REPRESENTATIVES—ANNUAL ELECTIONS ARE HARMFUL: Congressional terms of one year are not long enough for a representative to come up to speed on the many complex issues they must face. And, one year is too short of a time to root out possible corruption. Two-year terms are also made safe because liberty has additional protections—the amending process, by constitutional limits placed on Congress, and by other checks and balances. While one-year terms might be a good virtue of republican government, they are not practical or efficient.

By James Madison—February 9, 1788

THE MYTH OF ANNUAL ELECTIONS BEING A GUARD AGAINST TYRANNY:

53:1   I SHALL here, perhaps, be reminded of a current observation, "that where annual elections end, tyranny begins." If it be true, as has often been remarked, that sayings which become proverbial are generally founded in reason, it is not less true, that when once established, they are often applied to cases to which the reason of them does not extend. I need not look for a proof beyond the case before us. What is the reason on which this proverbial observation is founded?

LIBERTY IS NOT CONFINED TO A SINGLE POINT IN TIME:

Liberty is at the balanced center between chaos and tyranny.

53:2   No man will subject himself to the ridicule of pretending that any natural connection subsists between the sun or the seasons, and the period within which human virtue can bear the temptations of power. Happily for mankind, liberty is not, in this respect, confined to any single point of time; but lies within extremes, which afford sufficient latitude for all the variations which may be required by the various situations and circumstances of civil society.

LENGTH OF TERMS IS SET LOCALLY:

53:3   The election of magistrates might be, if it were found expedient, as in some instances it actually has been, daily, weekly, or monthly, as well as annual; and if circumstances may require a deviation from the rule on one side, why not also on the other side?

VARIETY OF TERMS AMONG STATE LEGISLATURES:

The States are not uniform in duration of terms for their representatives and State officers. Does length of term prove which State is best governed?

53:4   Turning our attention to the periods established among ourselves, for the election of the most numerous branches of the State legislatures, we find them by no means coinciding any more in this instance, than in the elections of other civil magistrates. In Connecticut and Rhode Island, the periods are half-yearly. In the other States, South Carolina excepted, they are annual. In South Carolina they are biennial as is proposed in the federal government. Here is a difference, as four to one, between the longest and shortest periods; and yet it would be not easy to show, that Connecticut or Rhode Island is better governed, or enjoys a greater share of rational liberty, than South Carolina; or that either the one or the other of these

States is distinguished in these respects, and by these causes, from the States whose <u>elections</u> are <u>different</u> from both.

CONGRESS CAN'T ARBITRARILY CHANGE CONSTITUTION:

Congress can, however establish laws and later go back and alter them.

53:5 In searching for the grounds of this doctrine, I can discover but one, and that is wholly inapplicable to our case. The important distinction so well understood in America, between a <u>Constitution established by the people</u> and <u>unalterable by the government</u>, and a <u>law established by the government</u> and <u>alterable by the government</u>, seems to have been little understood and less observed in any other country.

FOREIGN LEGISLATURES CAN CHANGE THEIR OWN FORM:

Britain's Parliament can change the form of government, the period of elections, and even keep themselves in office longer than elected.

53:6 Wherever the supreme <u>power of legislation</u> has resided, has been supposed to reside also a full power to <u>change the form of the government</u>. Even in <u>Great Britain</u>, where the principles of political and civil liberty have been most discussed, and where we hear most of the rights of the Constitution, it is maintained that the <u>authority of the Parliament</u> is <u>transcendent</u> and uncontrollable, as well with regard to the <u>Constitution</u>, as the ordinary objects of legislative provision. They have accordingly, in <u>several instances</u>, actually <u>changed, by legislative acts</u>, some of the most fundamental articles of the government. They have in particular, on several occasions, <u>changed the period of election</u>; and, on the last occasion, not only introduced <u>septennial</u> in place of <u>triennial elections</u>, but by the same act, continued themselves in place <u>four years beyond the term for which they were elected</u> by the people.

MANY NATIONS RELY ON TERM LIMITS FOR SAFETY:

Without a constitution, the people's best recourse to protect their liberties is to establish time limits on their elected officers.

53:7 An attention to these dangerous practices has produced a very natural alarm in the votaries of free government, of which frequency of elections is the corner-stone; and has led them to seek for some security to liberty, against the danger to which it is exposed. Where <u>no Constitution</u>, paramount to the government, either existed or could be obtained, no constitutional security, similar to that established in the <u>United States</u>, was to be <u>attempted</u>. Some other security, therefore, was to be sought for; and what better security would the case admit, than that of selecting and appealing to some simple and familiar <u>portion of time</u>, as a standard for measuring the

danger of innovations, for fixing the national sentiment, and for uniting the patriotic exertions?

TERM LIMIT OF ONE YEAR IS AN ARBITRARY BOUNDARY:

Elections every year is a popular standard, but has no reason in fact. Deviations are perfectly safe.

53:8 The most simple and familiar portion of time, applicable to the subject was that of <u>a year</u>; and hence the doctrine has been inculcated by a laudable zeal, to erect some barrier against the gradual innovations of an unlimited government, that the <u>advance towards tyranny</u> was to be calculated by the <u>distance of departure</u> from the fixed point of <u>annual elections</u>.

Can America's congressional election cycle be easily changed?

53:9 But what necessity can there be of applying this expedient to a government limited, as the federal government will be, by the authority of a paramount Constitution? Or who will pretend that the liberties of the people of America will not be more secure under <u>biennial</u> elections, unalterably <u>fixed</u> by such a <u>Constitution</u>, than those of any other nation would be, where elections were annual, or even more frequent, but <u>subject to alterations</u> by the ordinary power of the government?

ARE BIENNIAL ELECTIONS NECESSARY?

53:10 The second question stated is, <u>whether biennial elections</u> be necessary or useful. The propriety of answering this question in the <u>affirmative</u> will appear from several very obvious considerations.

EXPERIENCE AND KNOWLEDGE FOR OFFICE HOLDERS:

How long should a person be allowed to stay in office to become knowledgeable and effective?

53:11 No man can be a competent legislator who does not add to an <u>upright</u> <u>intention</u> and a <u>sound judgment</u> a certain degree of <u>knowledge</u> of the subjects on which he is to <u>legislate</u>. A part of this knowledge may be acquired by means of information which lie within the compass of men in private as well as public stations. Another <u>part can only be attained</u>, or at least thoroughly attained, by <u>actual experience in the station</u> which requires the use of it. The <u>period</u> of service, ought, therefore, in all such cases, to bear <u>some proportion</u> to the extent of <u>practical knowledge requisite</u> to the due performance of the service.

TWO YEARS BETTER THAN ONE:

53:12 The <u>period of legislative service established</u> in most of the States for the more numerous branch is, as we have seen, <u>one year</u>. The question then may be put into this simple form: does the period of <u>two years bear no greater</u> proportion to the knowledge requisite for federal legislation than <u>one year</u> does to the knowledge requisite for State legislation? The very statement of the question, in this form, suggests the answer that ought to be given to it.

HAVING A BASIC LEVEL OF LOCAL KNOWLEDGE IS GOOD:

What kinds of State-level knowledge should representatives have acquired before serving on the national level?

53:13 In a <u>single State</u>, the <u>requisite knowledge</u> relates to the existing laws which are uniform throughout the State, and with which all the citizens are more or less conversant; and to the general affairs of the State, which lie within a <u>small compass</u>, are not very diversified, and occupy much of the attention and conversation of every class of people.

NATIONAL KNOWLEDGE TAKES TIME:

Since national affairs are so complex, it is reasonable to expect elected officials to come in "cold" and require training, skills, and experience.

53:14 The great theatre of the <u>United States</u> presents a very <u>different</u> scene. The laws are so far from being uniform, that they vary in every State; whilst the <u>public affairs</u> of the Union are spread throughout a very <u>extensive region</u>, and are <u>extremely diversified</u> by the local affairs connected with them, and can with difficulty be correctly learnt in any other place than in the central councils to which a knowledge of them will be brought by the representatives of every part of the empire.

KNOWLEDGE REQUIRED OF REPRESENTATIVES:

How can congressmen conduct business without a degree of understanding about commerce, taxes, the militia, and so forth?

53:15 Yet <u>some knowledge of</u> the affairs, and <u>even of the</u> <u>laws</u>, of <u>all the States</u>, ought to be <u>possessed by the members</u> <u>from each of the States</u>. How can foreign trade be properly regulated by uniform laws, without some acquaintance with the <u>commerce</u>, the <u>ports</u>, the <u>usages</u>, and the regulations of the different States? How can the trade between the <u>different</u> States be duly regulated, without some knowledge of their <u>relative situations</u> in these and other respects? <u>How can taxes be</u> <u>judiciously imposed</u> and effectually collected, if they be not accommodated to the different laws and <u>local circumstances</u> relating to these objects in the different States? How can uniform <u>regulations</u> for the <u>militia</u> be duly provided, without a similar knowledge of many internal circumstances by which the States are distinguished from each other? These are the principal <u>objects of federal legislation</u>, and suggest most forcibly the <u>extensive information</u> which the <u>representatives ought</u> <u>to acquire</u>. The other interior objects will require a proportional degree of information with regard to them.

GOVERNMENT EVENTUALLY WILL BE EMBRACED:

As the new system of government is worked out, justification for longer terms of service will become clear.

53:16 It is true that all these difficulties will, by degrees, be very much diminished. The most <u>laborious task</u> will be the <u>proper inauguration</u> of the <u>government</u> and the primeval formation of a federal code. Improvements on the first draughts will every year become both easier and fewer. Past transactions of the government will be a ready and accurate source of information to new members. The affairs of the Union will become more and more objects of curiosity and conversation among the citizens at large. And the increased intercourse among those of <u>different States</u> will contribute not a little to diffuse a <u>mutual knowledge of their affairs</u>, as this again will contribute to a general <u>assimilation of their manners and laws</u>. But with all these abatements, the business of federal legislation must continue so far to exceed, both in novelty and difficulty, the legislative business of a single State, as to justify the longer period of service assigned to those who are to transact it.

KNOWLEDGE OF FOREIGN AFFAIRS IS IMPORTANT:

For issues related to foreign affairs and trade, should elected officials have some prior knowledge, or can they learn on the job?

53:17 A branch of knowledge which belongs to the acquirements of a federal representative, and which has not been mentioned is that of <u>foreign affairs</u>. In regulating our own commerce he ought to be not only acquainted with the <u>treaties</u> between the United States and <u>other nations</u>, but also with the <u>commercial policy</u> and <u>laws of other nations</u>. He ought not to be altogether ignorant of the <u>law of nations</u>; for that, as far as it is a proper object of municipal legislation, is submitted to the federal government.

INDIVIDUALS WILL LEARN THE MOST ON THE JOB:

Elected officers will bring their own knowledge into their new positions, but will gain the most from serving in office.

53:18 And although the House of Representatives is not immediately to participate in foreign negotiations and arrangements, yet from the necessary connection between the several branches of public affairs, those particular branches will frequently deserve attention in the ordinary course of legislation, and will <u>sometimes demand particular legislative sanction and</u> <u>co-operation</u>. Some portion of this knowledge may, no doubt, be acquired in a man's closet; but some of it also can only be derived from the public sources of information; and All of it will be acquired to best effect by a attention to the subject during the period of actual service in the legislature.

ONE-YEAR TERM FURTHER COMPLICATED:
One year is not enough time considering travel and housing needs.

53:19   There are other considerations, of less importance, perhaps, but which are not unworthy of notice. The <u>distance</u> which <u>many</u> of the <u>representatives</u> will be <u>obliged to travel</u>, and the arrangements rendered necessary by that circumstance, might be much more serious objections with fit men to this service, if <u>limited to a single year</u>, than if <u>extended to two</u> years. No argument can be drawn on this subject, from the case of the delegates to the <u>existing Congress</u>. They are <u>elected annually</u>, it is true; but their <u>re-election is considered</u> by the legislative assemblies almost as a <u>matter of course</u>. The election of the representatives by the people would <u>not be</u> governed by the <u>same principle</u>.

LACK OF EXPERIENCE ALLOWS ABUSE BY SENIORS:
Representatives with superior talents will frequently be re-elected. But the rest will be new, ill-informed, and vulnerable to manipulation by more senior members, and by the Senate.

53:20   <u>A few of the members</u>, as happens in all such assemblies, will possess <u>superior talents</u>; will, by <u>frequent reelections</u>, become members of long <u>standing</u>; will be <u>thoroughly</u> masters of the public business, and perhaps not unwilling to avail themselves of those advantages. The <u>greater the proportion</u> of <u>new members</u>, and <u>the less the information</u> of the bulk of the members the more apt will they be to <u>fall into the snares</u> that may be laid for them. This remark is no less applicable to the relation which will subsist between the <u>House</u> of Representatives and the <u>Senate</u>.

FREQUENT ELECTIONS INHIBIT UNCOVERING FRAUD:
In larger States, investigating election fraud would take much too long if one-year terms were adopted. Do longer terms give enough time to root out dishonest elections?

53:21   It is an inconvenience mingled with the advantages of our frequent elections even in single States, where they are large, and hold but one legislative session in a year, that <u>spurious elections cannot be investigated and annulled in time</u> for the decision to have its due effect. If a return can be obtained, no matter by what unlawful means, the irregular member, who takes his seat of course, is sure of holding it a sufficient time to answer his purposes. Hence, a <u>very pernicious encouragement</u> is given to the use of unlawful means, for obtaining irregular returns. Were elections for the federal legislature to

be annual, this practice might become a very serious abuse, particularly in the more distant States.

Fraud could take a year to uncover.

53:22   <u>Each house</u> is, as it necessarily must be, the <u>judge of the elections</u>, <u>qualifications</u>, and <u>returns</u> of its members; and whatever improvements may be suggested by experience, for <u>simplifying and accelerating</u> the process in <u>disputed cases</u>, so great a portion of a year would unavoidably elapse, before an illegitimate member could be dispossessed of his seat, that the prospect of such an event would be little check to unfair and illicit means of obtaining a seat.

BIENNIAL ELECTIONS ARE SAFE AND USEFUL:
53:23   All these considerations taken together warrant us in affirming, that <u>biennial elections</u> will be as <u>useful to the</u> affairs of the public as we have seen that they will be <u>safe to the liberty of the people</u>.

—PUBLIUS

REVIEW QUESTIONS

1. Is the idea of annual elections, versus biennial or any other cycle, founded on true principles? (53:1, 8)

2. Is liberty confined to a single point of time, such as one defined by the sun or seasons? (53:2)

3. What limitation is on Congress that makes the length of their terms less risky? (53:5)

4. Why is a longer time in office more valuable than a shorter time? (53:11–18)

5. Opinion: Madison says two-year terms for the House are sufficient for on-the-job training and experience. And two years is short enough for the electorate to test their representatives and vote out the poor performers before they can do too much damage. Why, then, is it safer for senators to serve for six years?

FEDERALIST NO. 54

THE THREE-FIFTHS COMPROMISE OVER SLAVERY, TAXES, AND REPRESENTATION: Should slaves be taxed as well as represented in the House of Representatives? Counting the slave population as three-fifths is one of the three compromises made at the Constitutional Convention (see Art. I, Sec. 2, Clause 3). It was negotiated to keep the slave States from breaking from the Union and forming their own confederacy. This anti-slavery compromise helps keep the States honest when it comes to doing a census for representation. A slave State would not be tempted to inflate its population numbers to win more seats in the House because that would also increase its required tax payment. There were 60,000 free blacks in America when the three-fifths clause was ratified. Those free blacks who could vote were not suddenly deprived of their full voting privilege by this clause. In other words, the three-fifths clause was not aimed at the black race but at slavery as an institution. As for individual voting rights, the States took on the responsibility to set voter qualifications. These were different in each State, varying from allowing only white male property owners to vote, to allowing anyone of age to vote. The land-owning policy was a temporary requirement to give those whose land it was the power over its use and regulation. It is the same arguments used regarding representatives in the House. The larger States with more wealth didn't want the smaller States telling them how to use that wealth, and demanded representation based on population. The Constitution left voter qualifications up to the individual State legislatures to define.

By James Madison—February 12, 1788

TAX RULES APPLIED TO SYSTEM OF REPRESENTATION:

By what rule are representatives to be appointed to Congress?

54:1 THE next view which I shall take of the House of Representatives relates to the appointment [apportionment] of its members to the several States which is to be determined by the same rule with that of direct taxes.

TWO DIFFERENT PRINCIPLES AT WORK:
Upon what rule does proportional representation rest?

54:2 It is not contended that the number of people in each State ought not to be the standard for regulating the proportion of those who are to represent the people of each State. The establishment of the same rule for the appointment of taxes, will probably be as little contested; though the rule itself in this case, is by no means founded on the same principle. In the former case, the rule is understood to refer to the personal rights of the people, with which it has a natural and universal connection.

PROPORTION OF WEALTH IS A POOR MEASUREMENT:
A flat tax as the least of all evils was accepted by the Convention.

54:3 In the latter, it has reference to the proportion of wealth, of which it is in no case a precise measure, and in ordinary cases a very unfit one. But notwithstanding the imperfection of the rule as applied to the relative wealth and contributions of the States, it is evidently the least objectionable among the practicable rules, and had too recently obtained the general sanction of America, not to have found a ready preference with the Convention.

NORTH SAYS SLAVES CAN'T BE COUNTED FOR REPRESENTATION.

A State could have one congressman for every 30,000 inhabitants.[184] Slave States wanted to count their slaves in order to qualify for additional pro slavery congressmen.

54:4 All this is admitted, it will perhaps be said; but does it follow, from an admission of numbers for the measure of representation, or of slaves combined with free citizens as a ratio of taxation, that slaves ought to be included in the numerical rule of representation? Slaves are considered as property, not as persons. They ought therefore to be comprehended in estimates of taxation which are founded on property, and to be excluded from representation which is regulated by a census of persons. This is the objection, as I understand it, stated in its full force. I shall be equally candid in stating the reasoning which may be offered on the opposite side.

SOUTH SAYS SLAVES CAN'T BE TAXED.

The slave States didn't want slaves counted as people because the "owners" would have to pay taxes for each individual. Madison addresses those issues from the South's perspective.

54:5 [*Madison now assumes the voice of his "Southern brethren" (up through paragraph 23).*]

"We subscribe to the doctrine," might one of our Southern brethren observe, "that representation relates more immediately to persons, and taxation more immediately to property, and we join in the application of this distinction to the case of our slaves. But we must deny the fact, that slaves are considered merely as property, and in no respect whatever as persons. The true state of the case is, that they partake of both these qualities: being considered by our laws, in some respects, as persons, and in other respects as property. In being compelled to labor, not for himself, but for a master; in being **vendible**[185] by one master to another master; and in being subject at all times to be restrained in his liberty and chastised in his body, by the capricious will of another, the slave may appear to be degraded from the human rank, and classed with those irrational animals which fall under the legal denomination of property.

---

184 *Editors' Note:* While a State may have one representative for every 30,000 people, counting the slaves as three fifths means that a State would need 50,000 slaves to get an additional representative, a number harder to reach. It also meant slaves would be taxed at only three fifths the regular rate. This anti-slavery compromise was agreed to by the Northern and Southern States.

185 *vendible:* Capable of being sold or traded; marketable.

SLAVES REGARDED AS MORAL PERSON, NOT PROPERTY:

54:6 "In being protected, on the other hand, in his life and in his limbs, against the violence of all others, even the master of his labor and his liberty; and in being punishable himself for all violence committed against others, the slave is no less evidently regarded by the law as a member of the society, not as a part of the irrational creation; as a moral person, not as a mere article of property.

LAW MAKES SLAVES BOTH PERSONS AND PROPERTY:

54:7 "The federal Constitution, therefore, decides with great propriety on the case of our slaves, when it views them in the mixed character of persons and of property. This is in fact their true character. It is the character bestowed on them by the laws under which they live; and it will not be denied, that these are the proper criterion; because it is only under the pretext that the laws have transformed the negroes into subjects of property, that a place is disputed them in the computation of numbers; and it is admitted, that if the laws were to restore the rights which have been taken away, the negroes could no longer be refused an equal share of representation with the other inhabitants.

THE CONVENTION HAD TO CONSIDER BOTH REPRESENTATION AND TAXATION:

Rejecting slaves as inhabitants but counting them for tax purposes is not being impartial.

54:8 "This question may be placed in another light. It is agreed on all sides, that numbers are the best scale of wealth and taxation, as they are the only proper scale of representation. Would the Convention have been impartial or consistent, if they had rejected the slaves from the list of inhabitants, when the shares of representation were to be calculated, and inserted them on the lists when the tariff of contributions was to be adjusted?

CAN'T HAVE IT BOTH WAYS:

It's not reasonable to consider slaves humans for representation but not humans for tax purposes.

54:9 "Could it be reasonably expected, that the Southern States would concur in a system, which considered their slaves in some degree as men, when burdens were to be imposed, but refused to consider them in the same light, when advantages were to be conferred? Might not some surprise also be expressed, that those who reproach the Southern States with the barbarous policy of considering as property a part of their human brethren, should themselves contend, that the government to which all the States are to be parties, ought to consider this unfortunate race more completely in the unnatural light of property, than the very laws of which they complain?

CONSTITUTION CAN EXCLUDE SLAVES:

54:10 "It may be replied, perhaps, that slaves are not included in the estimate of representatives in any of the States possessing them. They neither vote themselves nor increase the votes of their masters. Upon what principle, then, ought they to be taken into the federal estimate of representation? In rejecting them altogether, the Constitution would, in this respect, have followed the very laws which have been appealed to as the proper guide.

NUMBER OF VOTERS AND REPRESENTATIVES:

Constitution sets the number of representatives based on the total population of the State. But the States are allowed to decide its own rules of suffrage.

54:11 "This objection is repelled by a single observation. It is a fundamental principle of the proposed Constitution, that as the aggregate number of representatives allotted to the several States is to be determined by a federal rule, founded on the aggregate number of inhabitants, so the right of choosing this allotted number in each State is to be exercised by such part of the inhabitants as the State itself may designate. The qualifications on which the right of suffrage depend are not, perhaps, the same in any two States. In some of the States the difference is very material.

ALL STATES DEPRIVE SOME CITIZENS OF SUFFRAGE:

54:12 "In every State, a certain proportion of inhabitants are deprived of this right by the constitution of the State, who will be included in the census by which the federal Constitution apportions the representatives.

CONSTITUTION DOESN'T REQUIRE CONSISTENCY:

States might argue that suffrage need not be the same in every State.

54:13 "In this point of view the Southern States might retort the complaint, by insisting that the principle laid down by the Convention required that no regard should be had to the policy of particular States towards their own inhabitants; and consequently, that the slaves, as inhabitants, should have been admitted into the census according to their full number, in like manner with other inhabitants, who, by the policy of other States, are not admitted to all the rights of citizens.

SLAVE STATES WILLING TO COMPROMISE:

54:14 "A rigorous adherence, however, to this principle, is waived by those who would be gainers by it. All that they ask is that equal moderation be shown on the other side. Let the case of the slaves be considered, as it is in truth, a peculiar one. Let the compromising expedient of the Constitution be mutually adopted, which regards them as inhabitants, but as debased by servitude below the equal level of free inhabitants, which regards the SLAVE as divested of two fifths of the MAN.

DOES REPRESENTATION RELATE TO PEOPLE, NOT PROPERTY?

54:15 "After all, may not another ground be taken on which this article of the Constitution will admit of a still more ready defense? We have hitherto proceeded on the idea that representation related to persons only, and not at all to property. But is it a just idea?

GOVERNMENT PROTECTS PEOPLE AND PROPERTY:

54:16 "Government is instituted no less for protection of the property, than of the persons, of individuals. The one as well as the other, therefore, may be considered as represented by those who are charged with the government.

NEW YORK DIVIDES THIS ROLE:
The elected representatives deal with issues of property.

54:17 "Upon this principle it is, that in several of the States, and particularly in the State of New York, one branch of the government is intended more especially to be the guardian of property, and is accordingly elected by that part of the society which is most interested in this object of government.

PROPERTY RIGHTS AND PERSONAL (CIVIL) RIGHTS ARE CONSIDERED THE SAME:

54:18 "In the federal Constitution, this policy does not prevail. The rights of property are committed into the same hands with the personal rights. Some attention ought, therefore, to be paid to property in the choice of those hands.

MORE WEALTHY STATES PROBABLY MORE POPULOUS:

54:19 "For another reason, the votes allowed in the federal legislature to the people of each State, ought to bear some proportion to the comparative wealth of the States.

STATES CAN'T COMPEL OTHER STATES:
Wealthy citizens might indirectly have an advantage by their influence on other voters, but that doesn't increase the number of votes.

54:20 "States have not, like individuals, an influence over each other, arising from superior advantages of fortune. If the law allows an opulent citizen but a single vote in the choice of his representative, the respect and consequence which he derives from his fortunate situation very frequently guide the votes of others to the objects of his choice; and through this imperceptible channel the rights of property are conveyed into the public representation.

ONLY ADVANTAGE OF WEALTHY STATES IS NUMBERS:
All voters have the same weight regardless of wealth. The wealthier States have greater populations and more representatives. That would be their only advantage over other States.

54:21 "A State possesses no such influence over other States. It is not probable that the richest State in the Confederacy will ever influence the choice of a single representative in any other State. Nor will the representatives of the larger and richer States possess any other advantage in the federal legislature, over the representatives of other States, than what may result from their superior number alone. As far, therefore, as their superior wealth and weight may justly entitle them to any advantage, it ought to be secured to them by a superior share of representation.

POWER OF STATES TO CONTROL POLICY:
In the Articles as well as in places like the Netherlands, where states are the voting members, each may hold out a vote until concessions are met.

54:22 "The new Constitution is, in this respect, materially different from the existing Confederation, as well as from that of the United Netherlands, and other similar confederacies. In each of the latter, the efficacy of the federal resolutions depends on the subsequent and voluntary resolutions of the states composing the union. Hence the states, though possessing an equal vote in the public councils, have an unequal influence, corresponding with the unequal importance of these subsequent and voluntary resolutions.

CONSTITUTION PREVENTS STATE PREEMPTION:
A State may not "hold out for concessions" because under the new Constitution all federal acts take effect regardless.

54:23 "Under the proposed Constitution, the federal acts will take effect without the necessary intervention of the individual States. They will depend merely on the majority of votes in the federal legislature, and consequently each vote, whether proceeding from a larger or smaller State, or a State more or less wealthy or powerful, will have an equal weight and efficacy: in the same manner as the votes individually given in a State legislature, by the representatives of unequal counties or other districts, have each a precise equality of value and effect; or if there be any difference in the case, it proceeds from the difference in the personal character of the individual representative, rather than from any regard to the extent of the district from which he comes." [*End of Madison's reasoning as a Southern advocate*]

THE THREE-FIFTHS RULE—IMPERFECT BUT NECESSARY:[186]

The compromise was sufficient to retain the Southern States in the Union, and deal with the complexities of slaves as property.

54:24 Such is the reasoning which an advocate for the Southern interests might employ on this subject; and although it may appear to be a little strained in some points, yet, on the whole, I must confess that it <u>fully reconciles</u> me to the <u>scale of representation</u> which the Convention have established.

IMPORTANT TO MINIMIZE BIAS IN CENSUS:

54:25 In one respect, the establishment of a <u>common measure for representation and taxation</u> will have a very salutary effect. As the accuracy of the census to be obtained by the Congress will necessarily depend, in a considerable degree on the disposition, if not on the co-operation, of the States, it is of great importance that the <u>States should feel as little bias as possible</u>, to swell or to reduce the amount of their numbers.

STATES TEMPTED TO INFLATE THEIR CENSUS:
Without a tax burden on the slaves, the States would want to inflate their populations to gain more seats in Congress.

54:26 Were their share of <u>representation</u> alone to be governed by this rule, they would <u>have an interest in exaggerating</u> their inhabitants. Were the rule to decide their share of taxation alone, a <u>contrary temptation</u> would prevail. By extending the rule to both objects, the States will have <u>opposite interests</u>, which will control and balance each other, and produce the requisite impartiality.

—Publius

REVIEW QUESTIONS

1. What does Madison address in this paper? (54:1)

2. What complications did slavery introduce regarding the use of population for representation? (54:4–24)

3. In the South, were slaves considered persons or property? (54:4)

4. What proof is there that the slave States considered slaves as more than just property? (54:6)

5. Could a slave master be punished for physical violence against a slave? (54:6)

6. Did the Constitution establish that slaves were only three fifths of a person? (54:4 and footnote; 54:14; 54:24 and footnote)

7. What voice does Madison assume to conduct an uncomfortable conversation about slavery? (54:5–23)

8. Explain the incentives for States to stay honest when counting populations for the census. (54:25)

FEDERALIST NO. 55

ADDRESSING OBJECTION #1, TOO FEW IN HOUSE OF REPRESENTATIVES: First, how many should be in the House? Madison argues the House is large enough to guard against cabals but small enough to be efficient and orderly. Ultimately, a government built on the consent of the people depends on their virtue. Without virtue only a tyrant could "restrain them from destroying and devouring one another." See the list of all four objections at 55:3–6.

By James Madison—February 13, 1788

HOW MANY MEMBERS SHOULD BE IN CONGRESS?

55:1 THE number of which the House of Representatives is to consist, forms another and a very interesting point of view, under which this branch of the federal legislature may be contemplated.

55:2 Scarce any article, indeed, in the whole Constitution seems to be rendered more worthy of attention, by the weight of character and the apparent force of argument with which it has been assailed.

THE CHALLENGES LISTED:
What's the problem with too few representatives? What's the problem as the population grows?

55:3 The <u>charges</u> exhibited against it are, first, that <u>so small a number</u> of representatives will be an unsafe depositary of the public interests;

Lacking local knowledge

55:4 secondly, that they will <u>not possess a proper knowledge</u> of the <u>local circumstances</u> of their numerous constituents;

---

186 *Editors' note:* Compromise means each side surrenders something critical to achieve an important end goal. Without the three-fifth compromise the slave States threatened to not join the Union. They would have formed their own confederacy and eventually would have invited Spain or France to help strengthen their new international border with the anti-slavery States. That action sadly would introduce European-style conflict into the American continent. The three-fifths compromise is not a moral flaw that stains the Constitution but is instead a brilliant anti-slavery strategy that worked to undo the deeply entrenched presence of British-imposed slavery. The alternative (breaking the Union) was fully denounced in Nos. 1–14. The Framers did a masterful job of winding their way through that minefield and forcing an end to importation of slaves in twenty years. The failings that followed were the fault of Congress, not of the Convention or the Constitution.

Biased toward local priorities

55:5 thirdly, that they will be <u>taken from that class</u> of citizens which will <u>sympathize least</u> with the feelings of the mass of <u>the people</u>, and be most likely to aim at a <u>permanent elevation</u> of the <u>few</u> on the depression of the <u>many</u>;

Problems of population growth

55:6 fourthly, that defective as the number will be in the first instance, it will be more and more <u>disproportionate</u>, by the <u>increase</u> of the <u>people</u>, and the obstacles which will prevent a correspondent increase of the representatives.

NO PRECISE SOLUTION POSSIBLE:
Do the States give us a logical template for choosing the number of representatives?

55:7 In general it may be remarked on this subject, that no <u>political problem</u> is less susceptible of a precise solution than that which relates to the <u>number</u> most convenient for a <u>representative legislature</u>; nor is there any point on which the policy of the several <u>States</u> is more <u>at variance</u>, whether we compare their legislative assemblies directly with each other, or consider the proportions which they respectively bear to the number of their constituents.

DISPARITY AMONG FORMULAS USED BY STATES:
Do any of the States use a formula that is consistent with others? Consider Delaware and Massachusetts.

55:8 Passing over the difference between the smallest and largest States, as <u>Delaware</u>, whose most numerous branch consists of <u>twenty-one representatives</u>, and <u>Massachusetts</u>, where it amounts to <u>between three and four hundred</u>, a very considerable <u>difference</u> is observable among States nearly <u>equal in population</u>.

Pennsylvania, New York, South Carolina

55:9 The number of representatives in <u>Pennsylvania</u> is not more than <u>one fifth</u> of that in the State last mentioned. <u>New York</u>, whose population is to that of South Carolina as six to five, has little more than one third of the number of representatives.

Georgia, Delaware, Rhode Island, Pennsylvania

55:10 As great a disparity prevails between the States of Georgia and Delaware or Rhode Island. In Pennsylvania, the representatives do not bear a greater proportion to their constituents than of <u>one for every four or five thousand</u>.

Rhode Island, Georgia

55:11 In <u>Rhode Island</u>, they bear a proportion of at least <u>one for every thousand</u>. And according to the constitution of <u>Georgia</u>, the proportion may be carried to <u>one to every ten</u> electors; and must unavoidably far exceed the proportion in any of the other States.

PROPORTIONS WON'T WORK:
The differences in populations would eventually inflate the number of representatives into the thousands.

55:12 Another general remark to be made is that the ratio between the representatives and the people ought not to be the same where the latter are very numerous as where they are very few. Were the representatives <u>in Virginia</u> to be regulated by the <u>standard in Rhode Island</u>, they would, at this time, amount to between <u>four and five hundred</u>; and twenty or thirty years hence, to a <u>thousand</u>. On the other hand, the <u>ratio of Pennsylvania</u>, if applied to the State of <u>Delaware</u>, would reduce the representative assembly of the latter to <u>seven or eight members</u>.

ARITHMETIC PRINCIPLES WON'T WORK:
Common sense needs to guide the limits set for the number of representatives.

55:13 Nothing can be more <u>fallacious</u> than to found our political calculations on <u>arithmetical principles</u>. <u>Sixty or seventy men may be more properly trusted with a given degree of power than six or seven</u>. But it does not follow that <u>six or seven hundred would be proportionably a better depositary</u>. And if we carry on the supposition to six or seven thousand, the whole reasoning ought to be reversed.

NUMBER SHOULD BE KEPT WITHIN BOUNDARIES:
Regardless of how many representatives are agreed upon, that number should be limited to avoid confusion of a multitude.

55:14 The truth is, that in all cases a <u>certain number</u> at least seems to be <u>necessary to secure</u> the benefits of free consultation and discussion, and to guard against too easy a combination for improper purposes; as, on the other hand, <u>the number</u> ought at most to be <u>kept within a certain limit</u>, in order to <u>avoid the confusion</u> and <u>intemperance</u> of a <u>multitude</u>. In all very numerous assemblies, of whatever character composed, passion never fails to wrest the sceptre from reason.

SIZE OF HOUSE IS NO GUARANTEE OF QUALITY:
The quality of the House doesn't necessarily improve in proportion to size.

55:15 Had every Athenian <u>citizen</u> been a <u>Socrates</u>, every Athenian assembly would <u>still have been a mob</u>.

SMALLER NUMBERS CAN BE EFFECTIVE:
Are smaller groups more productive and active?

55:16 It is necessary also to recollect here the observations which were applied to the case of biennial elections. For the same reason that the limited powers of the Congress, and the control of the State legislatures, justify less frequent elections than the public safely might otherwise require, the members of the Congress need be less numerous than if they possessed the whole power of legislation, and were under no other than the ordinary restraints of other legislative bodies.

TOO FEW MEMBERS CAN'T BE TRUSTED WITH SUCH POWER:

Who is least trustworthy with power, a great number or small number?

55:17   With these general ideas in our minds, let us weigh the objections which have been stated against the number of members proposed for the House of Representatives. It is said, in the first place, that so small a number cannot be safely trusted with so much power.

START WITH SIXTY-FIVE, EXPAND SIZE AFTER THE NEXT CENSUS:

At Washington's request, the number of representatives was dropped from 1 in 40,000 to 1 in 30,000. How many representatives are proposed at the outset?

55:18   The number of which this branch of the legislature is to consist, at the outset of the government, will be sixty five. Within three years a census is to be taken, when the number may be augmented to one for every thirty thousand[187] inhabitants; and within every successive period of ten years the census is to be renewed, and augmentations may continue to be made under the above limitation.

US POPULATION WILL SOON GROW TO THREE MILLION:

55:19   It will not be thought an extravagant conjecture that the first census will, at the rate of one for every thirty thousand, raise the number of representatives to at least one hundred. Estimating the negroes in the proportion of three fifths, it can scarcely be doubted that the population of the United States will by that time, if it does not already, amount to three millions.

HOUSE WILL GROW TO FOUR HUNDRED IN FIFTY YEARS:

55:20   At the expiration of twenty-five years, according to the computed rate of increase, the number of representatives will amount to two hundred, and of fifty years, to four hundred.

FIRST CONGRESS IS LARGE ENOUGH TO BE SAFE:

Will the number of representatives continue to grow or will Congress augment it?

55:21   This is a number which, I presume, will put an end to all fears arising from the smallness of the body. I take for granted here what I shall, in answering the fourth objection, hereafter show, that the number of representatives will be augmented from time to time in the manner provided by the Constitution. On a contrary supposition, I should admit the objection to have very great weight indeed.

THE STARTING NUMBER OF SIXTY-FIVE IS NOT DANGEROUS:

Can the country get along with so few representatives for a few years?

55:22   The true question to be decided then is, whether the smallness of the number, as a temporary regulation, be dangerous to the public liberty? Whether sixty-five members for a few years, and a hundred or two hundred for a few more, be a safe depositary for a limited and well-guarded power of legislating for the United States?

THE PEOPLE CAN BE TRUSTED TO PLACE LIMITS:

Is there safety over this topic in the virtue of the people?

55:23   I must own that I could not give a negative answer to this question, without first obliterating every impression which I have received with regard to the present genius of the people of America, the spirit which actuates the State legislatures, and the principles which are incorporated with the political character of every class of citizens

TWO-YEAR TERM TEMPERS THE POWER-HUNGRY:

Would Americans be so lazy as to reelect corrupt leaders?

55:24   I am unable to conceive that the people of America, in their present temper, or under any circumstances which can speedily happen, will choose, and every second year repeat the choice of, sixty-five or a hundred men who would be disposed to form and pursue a scheme of tyranny or treachery.

STATES CAN DETECT AND REPAIR A CONSPIRACY:

Are America's liberties safe with the State legislatures and their federal representatives keeping an eye on things?

55:25   I am unable to conceive that the State legislatures, which must feel so many motives to watch, and which pos-

---

187   On September 17, 1787, just moments before the delegates to the Constitutional Convention rose to affix their signatures to the newly engrossed Constitution, Nathaniel Gorham of Massachusetts proposed one last hotly debated point be taken off the table by changing the ratio of representatives from 1:40,000 to 1:30,000. George Washington then stood and made his only recorded assertion during the Convention, stating he, too, was concerned, saying "It would give much satisfaction to see it adopted." The change was adopted unanimously. See James Madison, *Notes of Debates in the Federal Convention of 1787*, Session of Monday, September 17, 1787.

sess so many means of counteracting, the federal legislature, would fail either to detect or to <u>defeat a conspiracy</u> of the latter against the liberties of their common constituents. I am equally unable to conceive that there are at this time, or can be in any short time, in the United States, any sixty-five or a hundred men capable of recommending themselves to the choice of the people at large, who would either desire or <u>dare</u>, within the short space of two years, to <u>betray the solemn trust committed</u> to them.

AMERICA IS SAFE WITH THE FORMULA IN CONSTITUTION:

See the formula in Art. I, Sec. 2, Clause 4.

55:26 What change of circumstances, time, and a fuller population of our country may produce, requires a prophetic spirit to declare, which makes no part of my pretensions. But judging from the circumstances now before us, and from the probable state of them within a moderate period of time, I must pronounce that the <u>liberties of America</u> <u>cannot be unsafe</u> in the <u>number</u> of hands proposed by the federal <u>Constitution</u>.

FOREIGN CORRUPTION HAS NOT APPEARED:

55:27 From what quarter can the danger proceed? Are we afraid of foreign gold? If <u>foreign gold</u> could so easily <u>corrupt our federal rulers</u> and enable them to ensnare and betray their constituents, how <u>has it happened</u> that we are at this time a free and <u>independent</u> nation?

WAR-ERA CONGRESS LESS NUMEROUS THAN FUTURE:

Second Continental Congress averaged sixty delegates, much smaller than what is anticipated under the new Constitution.

55:28 The <u>Congress</u> which conducted us <u>through</u> the <u>Revolution</u> was a <u>less numerous</u> body than their successors will be; they were not chosen by, nor responsible to, their fellow citizens at large; though appointed from year to year, and recallable at pleasure, they were generally continued for three years, and prior to the ratification of the federal articles, for a still longer term.

EVEN WITH SECRECY CONGRESS WAS TRUSTWORTHY:

Did the Continental Congress betray the public trust during the war?

55:29 They held their <u>consultations always</u> under the <u>veil of secrecy</u>; they had the sole transaction of our affairs with foreign nations; through the <u>whole course of the war</u> they had the fate of their country more in their hands than it is to be hoped will ever be the case with our future representatives; and from the greatness of the prize at stake, and the eagerness

of the party which lost it, it may well be supposed that the use of other means than force would not have been scrupled. Yet we know by happy experience that the <u>public trust was not betrayed</u>; nor has the purity of our public councils in this particular ever suffered, even from the whispers of calumny.

PUBLIC TRUST WAS NOT BETRAYED:

55:30 Is the danger apprehended from the other branches of the federal government?

OTHER BRANCHES WON'T CORRUPT CONGRESS:

Could the executive or Senate corrupt those in the House?

55:31 But where are the means to be found by the President, or the Senate, or both? Their emoluments of office, it is to be presumed, will not, and without a previous corruption of the House of Representatives cannot, more than suffice for very different purposes; their private fortunes, as they must all be American citizens, cannot possibly be sources of danger.

EXECUTIVE APPOINTMENTS CAN'T CORRUPT:

Could a conspiracy from presidential appointments stand strong enough to topple our government?

55:32 The <u>only means</u>, then, which they can possess, will be in the dispensation of <u>appointments</u>. Is it here that suspicion rests her charge? Sometimes we are told that this fund of corruption is to be exhausted by the President in <u>subduing the virtue of the Senate</u>. Now, the fidelity of the other House is to be the victim.

GENERAL FORM MAKES CONSPIRACY IMPROBABLE:

55:33 The improbability of such a mercenary and perfidious combination of the several members of government, standing on as different foundations as republican principles will well admit, and at the same time <u>accountable</u> to the society over which they are placed, ought alone to <u>quiet this apprehension</u>.

CONGRESS MEMBERS CAN'T HOLD OTHER JOBS:

Officers in the government are forbidden to hold any other office or benefit from a salary increase during a term.

55:34 But, fortunately, the Constitution has provided a still <u>further safeguard</u>. The <u>members of the Congress</u> are rendered ineligible to any civil offices that may be created, or of which the emoluments may be increased, during the term of their election.

TRUE SERVANTS OF THE PEOPLE STAY CIRCUMSPECT:

55:35 No offices therefore can be dealt out to the existing members but such as may become vacant by ordinary casualties: and to suppose that these would be sufficient to purchase the guardians of the people, selected by the people themselves, is to renounce every rule by which events ought to be calculated, and to substitute an indiscriminate and unbounded jealousy, with which all reasoning must be vain. The sincere friends of liberty, who give themselves up to the extravagancies of this passion, are not aware of the injury they do their own cause.

PEOPLE EXHIBIT BOTH SUNSHINE AND SHADOW:

Republican government better invokes from the people their basic human virtues than any other system. Such government fundamentally depends on the people's virtue, and Americans are sufficiently virtuous to choose self-government over despotism.

55:36 As there is a degree of depravity in mankind which requires a certain degree of circumspection and distrust, so there are other qualities in human nature which justify a certain portion of esteem and confidence. Republican government presupposes the existence of these qualities in a higher degree than any other form. Were the pictures which have been drawn by the political jealousy of some among us faithful likenesses of the human character, the inference would be, that there is not sufficient virtue among men for self-government; and that nothing less than the chains of despotism can restrain them from destroying and devouring one another.

—PUBLIUS

REVIEW QUESTIONS

1. What does Madison discuss in this paper? (55:1)

2. What do critics say the Constitution doesn't handle very well? (55:3–6)

3. How many people are required for every representative? (55:18)

4. When the first census is held, how many people does Madison expect will be in the United States? (55:19)

5. Was the war-era Congress trustworthy? Was it smaller than what is being proposed in the new Constitution? (55:28–30)

6. Does self-government truly rest, at its core, on the virtue of the people? Without virtue, what will be needed to protect the people from destroying each other? (55:36)

FEDERALIST NO. 56

ADDRESSING OBJECTION #2, REPRESENTATIVES WILL BE ILL-EQUIPPED: Representatives will gain adequate on-the-job understanding. Will the House be too small and underrepresented to manage the interests of all the people? Madison says the representatives need adequate local knowledge on commerce, taxation, and the militia, but over time the needs of all the States will become familiar to them. See the list of all four objections at 55:3–6.

By James Madison—February 16, 1788

SECOND CONCERN: TOO LITTLE KNOWLEDGE? Would the House be too small to manage the issues of so large a nation?

56:1 THE SECOND charge against the House of Representatives is, that it will be too small to possess a due knowledge of the interests of its constituents.

NATIONAL CONGRESS LESS EQUIPPED THAN LOCAL: Could the national Congress ever understand local circumstances as well as a State's legislature?

56:2 As this objection evidently proceeds from a comparison of the proposed number of representatives with the great extent of the United States, the number of their inhabitants, and the diversity of their interests, without taking into view at the same time the circumstances which will distinguish the Congress from other legislative bodies, the best answer that can be given to it will be a brief explanation of these peculiarities.

NATIONAL CONGRESS HAS DIFFERENT DUTIES: While representatives should be familiar with their districts, with what aspects should they be most familiar?

56:3 It is a sound and important principle that the representative ought to be acquainted with the interests and circumstances of his constituents. But this principle can extend no further than to those circumstances and interests to which the authority and care of the representative relate. An ignorance of a variety of minute and particular objects, which do not lie within the compass of legislation, is consistent with every attribute necessary to a due performance of the legislative trust. In determining the extent of information required in the exercise of a particular authority, recourse then must be had to the objects within the purview of that authority.

CONGRESS'S THREE DUTIES: COMMERCE, TAXES, MILITIA:

56:4 What are to be the <u>objects of federal legislation</u>? Those which are of most importance, and which seem most to require local knowledge, are <u>commerce</u>, <u>taxation</u>, and the <u>militia</u>.

PROPER REGULATION OF COMMERCE:

Very few representatives are needed to track issues of commerce.

56:5 A proper regulation of commerce requires much information, as has been elsewhere remarked; but as far as this information relates to the laws and local situation of each individual State, a very <u>few representatives</u> would be very sufficient vehicles of it to the federal councils.

PROPER REGULATION OF TAXES:

The collection of duties requires very few representatives.

56:6 <u>Taxation</u> will consist, in a great measure, of <u>duties</u> which will be involved in the <u>regulation of commerce</u>. So far the preceding remark is applicable to this object. As far as it may consist of <u>internal collections</u>, a <u>more</u> diffusive <u>knowledge</u> of the circumstances of the State may be <u>necessary</u>. But will not this also be possessed in sufficient degree by a very <u>few intelligent men</u>, diffusively elected within the State?

DELEGATING IMPROVES GATHERING OF KNOWLEDGE:

Creating districts helps the States perform critical duties they would best perform, freeing Congress to focus on larger issues.

56:7 <u>Divide the largest State</u> into ten or twelve <u>districts</u>, and it will be found that there will be no peculiar local interests in either, which will not be within the knowledge of the representative of the district. Besides this source of information, the <u>laws of the State</u>, <u>framed by representatives from every part</u> of it, will be almost of themselves a <u>sufficient guide</u>. In every State there have been made, and must continue to be made, regulations on this subject which will, in many cases, leave little more to be done by the <u>federal legislature</u>, than to <u>review</u> the different laws, and reduce them in <u>one general act</u>.

LOCAL KNOWLEDGE HELPS FORM NATIONAL POLICY:

How would representatives save a lot of effort assessing internal taxes?

56:8 A skillful <u>individual in his closet</u> with all the local codes before him, might compile a law on some subjects of taxation for the whole union, <u>without any aid</u> from oral information,

and it may be expected that whenever <u>internal taxes</u> may be necessary, and particularly in cases requiring <u>uniformity throughout the States</u>, the more <u>simple objects</u> will be <u>preferred</u>.

A SUBDIVIDED STATE:

Representatives of each part of a State would have intimate local knowledge.

56:9 To be fully sensible of the facility which will be given to this branch of federal legislation by the assistance of the State codes, we need only suppose for a moment that this or any other <u>State were divided into a number of parts</u>, each having and exercising within itself a <u>power of local legislation</u>. Is it not evident that a degree of local <u>information</u> and preparatory labor would be found in the several <u>volumes of their proceedings</u>, which would very much shorten the labors of the general legislature, and render a much <u>smaller number</u> of members <u>sufficient</u> for it?

SENATORS APPOINTED BY STATE LEGISLATURES:

Senators bring considerable knowledge from their duty in the legislature.

56:10 The federal councils will derive great advantage from another circumstance. The <u>representatives of each State</u> will not only bring with them a considerable <u>knowledge of its laws</u>, and a local knowledge of their respective districts, but will probably in all cases have been members, and may even at the very time be <u>members, of the State legislature</u>, where all the local information and interests of the State are assembled, and from whence they may easily be <u>conveyed by a very few hands</u> into the <u>legislature</u> of the <u>United States</u>.

STATES' RULES FOR MILITIA VARY:

Do militia rules vary among the States?

56:11 With regard to the regulation of the militia, there are scarcely any circumstances in reference to which local knowledge can be said to be necessary. The general face of the country, whether mountainous or level, most of it for the operations of infantry or calvary, is almost the only consideration of this nature that can occur. The art of war teaches general principles of organization, movement, and discipline, which apply universally.[188]

CREATING UNIFORM NATIONAL LAW IS DIFFICULT:

Will it take many or few people to fairly represent a single State?

---

188 *Editors' note:* This paragraph is rewritten in other editions of *The Federalist* as "The observations made on the subject of taxation apply with greater force to the case of the militia. For however different the rules of discipline may be in different States, they are the same throughout each particular State; and depend on circumstances which can differ but little in different parts of the same State."

56:12 The attentive reader will discern that the reasoning here used, to prove the sufficiency of a moderate number of representatives, does not in any respect contradict what was urged on another occasion with regard to the extensive <u>information</u> which the representatives ought to possess, and the <u>time</u> that might be necessary for acquiring it.

CONGRESS IS CHALLENGED TO KNOW ALL THE STATES:

56:13 This information, so far as it may relate to <u>local objects</u>, is rendered necessary and difficult, not by a difference of laws and local circumstances within a single State, but of those among different States.

FEW MEN NEEDED TO KNOW THEIR OWN STATE:

56:14 Taking each State by itself, its <u>laws are the same</u>, and its interests but little diversified. A <u>few men</u>, therefore, will possess all the knowledge requisite for a <u>proper representation</u> of them.

NATIONAL KNOWLEDGE ELUSIVE FOR CONGRESS:

Is knowledge about one's own State going to be enough to perform the role of an effective federal representative?

56:15 Were the interests and affairs of each individual State perfectly simple and uniform, a knowledge of them in one part would involve a knowledge of them in every other, and the whole State might be <u>competently represented</u> by a <u>single member</u> taken from any part of it.

CONGRESS WILL NEED TIME TO LEARN:

Each representative will know enough about his own State, but learning enough about the others to legislate will take time and experience.

56:16 On a comparison of the different States together, we find a great dissimilarity in their laws, and in many other circumstances connected with the objects of federal legislation, with All of which the <u>federal representatives ought to have some acquaintance</u>. Whilst a few representatives, therefore, from each State, may bring with them a due knowledge of their own State, <u>every representative</u> will have <u>much information to acquire</u> concerning all the <u>other States</u>.

CONSTITUTION ACCOMMODATES GROWTH:

Over time the States' general concerns and issues will become similar while internal issues become complex.

56:17 The changes of time, as was formerly remarked, on the comparative situation of the different States, will have an <u>assimilating</u> effect. The effect of time on the <u>internal</u> affairs of the States, taken singly, will be just the <u>contrary</u>.

GROWING STATES WON'T BE LEFT UNDER-REPRESENTED:

Where farm areas in a particular State have not yet enjoyed other commercial activities, the potential for growth still remains, thanks to the Constitution.

56:18 At present <u>some of the States</u> are little more than a <u>society of husbandmen</u>. Few of them have made much progress in those branches of industry which give a variety and complexity to the affairs of a nation. These, however, will in All of them be the fruits of a more advanced population, and will require, on the part of each State, a fuller representation. The foresight of the Convention has accordingly taken care that the progress of population may be accompanied with a <u>proper increase</u> of the <u>representative branch</u> of the government.

BRITAIN EXEMPLIFIES BASIC PRINCIPLES DISCUSSED:

How many representatives for the eight million in Great Britain?

56:19 The <u>experience of Great Britain</u>, which presents to mankind so many political lessons, both of the monitory and exemplary kind, and which has been frequently consulted in the course of these inquiries, corroborates the result of the reflections which we have just made. The <u>number of inhabitants</u> in the two kingdoms of <u>England</u> and <u>Scotland</u> cannot be stated at less than <u>eight millions</u>. The representatives of these eight millions in the House of Commons amount to <u>five hundred and fifty-eight</u>.

Forms of proportional representation.

56:20 Of this number, <u>one ninth</u> are <u>elected</u> by <u>three hundred and sixty-four persons</u>, and <u>one half</u>, by <u>five thousand seven hundred and twenty-three persons</u>.[189]

BRITAIN'S SYSTEM CORRUPTED BY MONARCH:

Even though Britain has the right structure in place, implementing those positives isn't correctly executed. Whose interests are really being safeguarded by the representatives in Great Britain?

56:21 It cannot be supposed that the <u>half thus elected</u>, and who do <u>not even reside among the people at large</u>, can add any thing either to the security of the people against the government, or to the knowledge of their circumstances and interests in the legislative councils. On the contrary, it is notorious, that they are <u>more frequently</u> the representatives and <u>instruments</u> of the <u>executive magistrate</u>, than the <u>guardians</u> and advocates of the <u>popular rights</u>. They might therefore, with great propriety, be considered as something more than a mere deduction from the real representatives of the nation. We will, however, consider them in this light alone, and will

---

189 *Publius:* Burgh's "Political Disquisitions"

not extend the deduction to a considerable number of others, who <u>do not reside</u> among their <u>constituents</u>, are very faintly connected with them, and have <u>very little</u> particular <u>knowledge</u> of their <u>affairs</u>.

BRITAIN'S CORRUPTED SYSTEM STILL HELPS:
Despite imbalances and some obvious flaws, the representation in Britain's system does preserve some freedoms in that country.

56:22 With all these concessions, <u>two hundred and seventy-nine persons only will be the depository of the safety, interest, and happiness of eight millions</u> that is to say, there will be one representative only to maintain the rights and explain the situation OF <u>TWENTY-EIGHT THOUSAND SIX HUNDRED AND SEVENTY</u> constituents, in an assembly exposed to the whole force of executive influence, and extending its authority to every object of legislation within a nation whose affairs are in the highest degree diversified and complicated.

56:23 Yet it is very certain, not only that a <u>valuable portion</u> of <u>freedom has been preserved</u> under all these circumstances, but that the defects in the British code are chargeable, in a very small proportion, on the ignorance of the legislature concerning the circumstances of the people.

ONE REPRESENTATIVE FOR 30,000 IS REASONABLE:
Given all the experiences from other nations and States, is 30,000 as good of a starting place as any?

56:24 Allowing to this case the weight which is due to it, and comparing it with that of the House of Representatives as above explained it seems to give the fullest assurance, that a representative for every <u>THIRTY THOUSAND INHABITANTS</u> will render the latter both a <u>safe</u> and <u>competent</u> guardian of the interests which will be confided to it.

—PUBLIUS

REVIEW QUESTIONS

1. What main issue does Madison discuss in paper No. 56? (56:1)

2. Do the representatives need to know everything about the country to do their job? (56:3)

3. What are the three objects of federal legislation? (56:4)

4. Why will congressmen need to gain knowledge of other States? (56:16)

5. As the country develops over time, will the interests of each State become similar? How will their internal affairs develop? (56:17)

6. Which country does Madison refer to that gives a good example of how representation works? (56:19–20)

7. What corrupting influence damages the role of Britain's representatives? (56:21)

8. Because of Britain's monarchy corrupting their Parliament, whose interests are the representatives actually protecting and promoting? (56:21)

9. Given this corruption in Britain, has their freedom nevertheless been preserved? (56:22–23)

10. By comparison how will the House of Representatives serve America? (56:24)

FEDERALIST NO. 57

ADDRESSING OBJECTION #3, REPRESENTATIVES WILL BE ELITISTS: Representatives will come from the body of the people regardless of status or wealth. The "American Spirit" will demand of them maximum integrity and fairness. Will the members of the House have little sympathy for the masses and sacrifice the many to glorify the few? This paper addresses the third of four objections by the Anti-Federalists who feared that the House would become an oligarchy—the many ruled by a few. Madison uses examples to show there exist sufficient safeguards against tyranny. And the great American spirit "which is vigilant and manly" and "nourishes freedom" will stand against any attempt to rule the many by the few. The Representatives will be motivated to keep the voters' support by proper behavior if they want to be reelected. See the list of all four objections at 55:3–6.

By James Madison—February 19, 1788

THIRD CONCERN: THE ELITE WILL TAKE OVER.
57:1 THE THIRD charge against the House of Representatives is, that it will be <u>taken</u> from that <u>class of citizens</u> which will have least sympathy with the <u>mass of the people</u>, and be most likely to aim at an ambitious sacrifice of the many to the aggrandizement of the few.

AN ELITE TAKEOVER IS A VAIN IMAGINATION:
Is this worry even feasible given the nature of a republican government?

57:2 Of all the objections which have been framed against the federal Constitution, this is perhaps the <u>most extraordinary</u>.

THE CHARACTERISTICS OF THE REPUBLICAN FORM:

Electing virtuous leaders is the defining attribute of republican government. Keeping them virtuous is complex.

57:3 Whilst the objection itself is leveled against a pretended oligarchy, the principle of it strikes at the very root of republican government. The aim of every political constitution is, or ought to be, first to obtain for rulers men who possess most wisdom to discern, and most **virtue**[190] to pursue, the common good of the society; and in the next place, to take the most effectual precautions for keeping them virtuous whilst they continue to hold their public trust. The elective mode of obtaining rulers is the characteristic policy of republican government.

SHORTER TERMS IN OFFICE HELP PROTECT LIBERTY:

What is the strongest tool to prevent corruption in government?

57:4 The means relied on in this form of government for preventing their degeneracy are numerous and various. The most effectual one, is such a limitation of the term of appointments as will maintain a proper responsibility to the people.

NO PART OF CONSTITUTION IS ANTI-REPUBLICAN:

Are there any lapses in the Constitution that would allow corruption?

57:5 Let me now ask what circumstance there is in the constitution of the House of Representatives that violates the principles of republican government, or favors the elevation of the few on the ruins of the many? Let me ask whether every circumstance is not, on the contrary, strictly conformable to these principles, and scrupulously impartial to the rights and pretensions of every class and description of citizens?

NO BIAS IN WHO MAY VOTE FOR REPRESENTATIVES:

Who are the electors who choose the representatives?

57:6 Who are to be the electors of the federal representatives? Not the rich, more than the poor; not the learned, more than the ignorant; not the haughty heirs of distinguished names, more than the humble sons of obscurity and unpropitious fortune. The electors are to be the great body of the people of the United States. They are to be the same who exercise the right in every State of electing the corresponding branch of the legislature of the State.

EASY REQUIREMENTS TO RUN FOR OFFICE:

What qualifications are generally dismissed to win public office in America?

57:7 Who are to be the objects of popular choice? Every citizen whose merit may recommend him to the esteem and confidence of his country. No qualification of wealth, of birth, of religious faith, or of civil profession is permitted to fetter the judgment or disappoint the inclination of the people.

ELECTION PROCESS HAS SAFETY BUILT IN:

Does America's political system help ensure integrity and safety?

57:8 If we consider the situation of the men on whom the free suffrages of their fellow-citizens may confer the representative trust, we shall find it involving every security which can be devised or desired for their fidelity to their constituents.

CANDIDATES MUST EXEMPLIFY GOOD TRAITS:

57:9 In the first place, as they will have been distinguished by the preference of their fellow-citizens, we are to presume that in general they will be somewhat distinguished also by those qualities which entitle them to it, and which promise a sincere and scrupulous regard to the nature of their engagements.

VOTERS APPRECIATE HONOR AND INTEGRITY:

Does our current political system acknowledge integrity?

57:10 In the second place, they will enter into the public service under circumstances which cannot fail to produce a temporary affection at least to their constituents. There is in every breast a sensibility to marks of honor, of favor, of esteem, and of confidence, which, apart from all considerations of interest, is some pledge for grateful and benevolent returns.

THE ELECTED PERFORM WELL TO SHOW GRATITUDE:

57:11 Ingratitude is a common topic of declamation against human nature; and it must be confessed that instances of it are but too frequent and flagrant, both in public and in private life. But the universal and extreme indignation which it inspires is itself a proof of the energy and prevalence of the contrary sentiment.

PRIDE PROMOTES BEST EFFORTS:

57:12 In the third place, those ties which bind the representative to his constituents are strengthened by motives of a more selfish nature. His pride and vanity attach him to a form of government which favors his pretensions and gives him a share in its honors and distinctions. Whatever hopes or projects might be entertained by a few aspiring characters, it must generally happen that a great proportion of the men deriving their advancement from their influence with the people, would have more to hope from a preservation of the favor, than from innovations in the government subversive of the authority of the people.

---

190 **_virtue:_** The word _virtue_ here means the strength and determination to stand up for what is right and defend it.

FREQUENT ELECTIONS ENCOURAGE FAITHFULNESS:

How do frequent elections help keep the elected faithful?

57:13 All these securities, however, would be found very insufficient without the restraint of <u>frequent elections</u>. Hence, in the <u>fourth place</u>, the House of Representatives is so constituted as to support in the members an habitual recollection of their dependence on the people. Before the sentiments impressed on their minds by the mode of their elevation can be effaced by the exercise of power, they will be <u>compelled</u> to <u>anticipate</u> the moment when their <u>power is to cease</u>, when their exercise of it is to be <u>reviewed</u>, and when they must <u>descend</u> to the <u>level</u> from which they were <u>raised</u>; there forever to remain unless a <u>faithful discharge</u> of <u>their trust</u> shall have established their title to a renewal of it.

CONGRESS MUST ABIDE BY LAWS IT PASSES:

Congress cannot pass a law that does not apply to them, although this has been violated numerous times.

57:14 I will add, as a <u>fifth</u> circumstance in the situation of the House of Representatives, restraining them from oppressive measures, that they can make <u>no law which</u> will not have its <u>full operation on themselves</u> and their friends, as well as on the great mass of the society. This has always been deemed one of the strongest bonds by which human policy can connect the rulers and the people together. It creates between them that <u>communion</u> of <u>interests</u> and sympathy of sentiments, of which few governments have furnished examples; but without which every government degenerates into tyranny.

THE PEOPLE WON'T TOLERATE DESPOTISM:

Both the Constitution and the spirit of the people look down on self-serving kingdom building in Congress. Can Congress make legal discriminations in favor of themselves?

57:15 If it be asked, what is to restrain the House of Representatives from making <u>legal discriminations in favor of themselves</u> and a particular class of the society? I answer: the <u>genius of the whole system</u>; the nature of just and constitutional laws; and above all, the <u>vigilant and</u> <u>manly spirit</u> which actuates the <u>people</u> of America, a spirit which <u>nourishes freedom</u>, and in return is nourished by it.

PEOPLE WON'T TOLERATE SELF-SERVING LAW:

Congress must never have leeway to pass laws that apply to some and not all, especially to Congress. If that level of arrogance is ever tolerated by the people, then liberty is lost.

57:16 <u>If this spirit</u> shall ever be so far <u>debased</u> as to tolerate a law not <u>obligatory on the legislature</u>, as well as on the people, the people will be prepared to tolerate any thing but <u>liberty</u>.

FOUR ATTRIBUTES:

What are the four attributes of republicanism that bind the representative's faithfulness to the citizens?

57:17 Such will be the relation between the House of Representatives and their constituents. <u>Duty</u>, <u>gratitude</u>, <u>interest</u>, <u>ambition</u> itself, are the chords by which they will be bound to fidelity and sympathy with the great mass of the people.

PROCESS IS NOT PERFECT BUT IS BEST AVAILABLE:

Is there any other conceivable way to elect honest people than this? Can people calling for liberty, at the same time be calling for tyranny?

57:18 It is possible that these <u>may all be insufficient</u> to control the caprice and <u>wickedness</u> of man. But are they not all that government will admit, and that human <u>prudence can devise</u>? Are they not the genuine and the characteristic means by which republican government provides for the liberty and happiness of the people? Are they not the identical means on which every State government in the Union relies for the attainment of these important ends?

ELECTED MUST PROVE THEMSELVES WORTHY:

People given power often work to grow their power by eliminating the checks placed upon them.

57:19 What then are we to understand by the objection which this paper has combated? What are we to <u>say to the men</u> who profess the <u>most flaming zeal</u> for <u>republican government</u>, yet boldly <u>impeach</u> the <u>fundamental principle</u> of it; who pretend to be champions for the right and the capacity of the people to choose their own rulers, yet maintain that they will prefer those only who will immediately and infallibly betray the trust committed to them?

CONSTITUTION ENSURES GREATEST PROTECTIONS:

If someone hasn't read the Constitution, how might he view the means whereby a person gained political power?

57:20 <u>Were the objection</u> to be <u>read</u> by <u>one who</u> had <u>not seen</u> the mode prescribed by the <u>Constitution</u> for the choice of representatives, he could <u>suppose</u> nothing less than that some <u>unreasonable qualification of property</u> was annexed to the <u>right of suffrage</u>; or that the <u>right of eligibility</u> was limited to persons of <u>particular families or fortunes</u>; or at least that the mode prescribed by the <u>State constitutions</u> was in some respect or other, very grossly departed from. We have seen how far such a supposition would err, as to the two first points. Nor would it, in fact, be less erroneous as to the last.

CONGRESS IS PROTECTED:
The people at large elect the representatives (the House), and the State legislatures elect theirs (the Senate). Both processes reduce the chances for corruption.

57:21 The only difference discoverable between the two cases is, that each representative of the United States will be elected by five or six thousand citizens; whilst in the individual States, the election of a representative is left to about as many hundreds. Will it be pretended that this difference is sufficient to justify an attachment to the State governments, and an abhorrence to the federal government? If this be the point on which the objection turns, it deserves to be examined.

GREAT NUMBERS OF CHOICES ALWAYS SAFER:
Is it reasonable to believe that six thousand citizens are less likely to find a fit candidate for office than six hundred?

57:22 Is it supported by REASON? This cannot be said, without maintaining that five or six thousand citizens are less capable of choosing a fit representative, or more liable to be corrupted by an unfit one, than five or six hundred. Reason, on the contrary, assures us, that as in so great a number a fit representative would be most likely to be found, so the choice would be less likely to be diverted from him by the intrigues of the ambitious or the ambitious or the bribes of the rich.

FIXING NUMBERS OF ELECTORS DOESN'T HELP:
Specifying the number of electors is reckless. What happens when the ratio of electors needed is less than five or six hundred?

57:23 Is the CONSEQUENCE from this doctrine admissible? If we say that five or six hundred citizens are as many as can jointly exercise their right of suffrage, must we not deprive the people of the immediate choice of their public servants, in every instance where the administration of the government does not require as many of them as will amount to one for that number of citizens?

WHAT ARE SOME REQUIREMENTS TO HOLD OFFICE IN ENGLAND?
57:24 Is the doctrine warranted by FACTS? It was shown in the last paper, that the real representation in the British House of Commons very little exceeds the proportion of one for every thirty thousand inhabitants.

BRITISH REPRESENTATIVES MUST PROVE WEALTH:
Even though a certain degree of property and security is required to hold office, it does not admit to elevating a few over the ruins of others. Candidates and voters are required to possess so much real estate to run or vote.

57:25 Besides a variety of powerful causes not existing here, and which favor in that country the pretensions of rank and wealth, no person is eligible as a representative of a county, unless he possess real estate of the clear value of six hundred pounds sterling per year; nor of a city or borough, unless he possess a like estate of half that annual value. To this qualification on the part of the county representatives is added another on the part of the county electors, which restrains the right of suffrage to persons having a freehold estate of the annual value of more than twenty pounds sterling, according to the present rate of money.

DESPITE BRITISH SYSTEM, MANY FIT CANDIDATES FOUND:
57:26 Notwithstanding these unfavorable circumstances, and notwithstanding some very unequal laws in the British code, it cannot be said that the representatives of the nation have elevated the few on the ruins of the many.

VOTING DISTRICTS IN AMERICA ARE ALREADY LARGE ENOUGH:
Which three States already have districts large enough to safely elect representatives?

57:27 But we need not resort to foreign experience on this subject. Our own is explicit and decisive. The districts in New Hampshire in which the senators are chosen immediately by the people, are nearly as large as will be necessary for her representatives in the Congress. Those of Massachusetts are larger than will be necessary for that purpose; and those of New York still more so.

NEW YORK DISTRICTS ALREADY FUNCTIONING:
If voters today are qualified to elect four or five representatives, are they incapable of electing just one? States get one representative for every 30,000 inhabitants.

57:28 In the last State the members of Assembly for the cities and counties of New York and Albany are elected by very nearly as many voters as will be entitled to a representative in the Congress, calculating on the number of sixty-five representatives only. It makes no difference that in these senatorial districts and counties a number of representatives are voted for by each elector at the same time. If the same electors at the same time are capable of choosing four or five representatives, they cannot be incapable of choosing one.

PENNSYLVANIA DISTRICTS ALREADY FUNCTIONING:

Madison anticipated the eventual need for congressional districts. How many representatives would Philadelphia have?

57:29 Pennsylvania is an additional example. Some of her counties, which elect her State representatives, are almost as large as her districts will be by which her federal representatives will be elected. The city of Philadelphia is supposed to contain between fifty and sixty thousand souls. It will therefore form nearly two districts for the choice of federal representatives. It forms, however, but one county, in which every elector votes for each of its representatives in the State legislature. And what may appear to be still more directly to our purpose, the whole city actually elects a SINGLE MEMBER for the executive council. This is the case in all the other counties of the State.

REPRESENTATIVE SYSTEMS ALREADY SUCCESSFUL:

Has there been evidence of the liberties of the many being sacrificed for the benefit of the few?

57:30 Are not these facts the most satisfactory proofs of the fallacy which has been employed against the branch of the federal government under consideration? Has it appeared on trial that the senators of New Hampshire, Massachusetts, and New York, or the executive council of Pennsylvania, or the members of the Assembly in the two last States, have betrayed any peculiar disposition to sacrifice the many to the few, or are in any respect less worthy of their places than the representatives and magistrates appointed in other States by very small divisions of the people?

CURRENT PROCESSES DON'T ELEVATE TRAITORS:

Do any of the experiments in representative government give any evidence whatsoever that traitors are put into high office?

57:31 But there are cases of a stronger complexion than any which I have yet quoted. One branch of the legislature of Connecticut is so constituted that each member of it is elected by the whole State. So is the governor of that State, of Massachusetts, and of this State, and the president of New Hampshire. I leave every man to decide whether the result of any one of these experiments can be said to countenance a suspicion, that a diffusive mode of choosing representatives of the people tends to elevate traitors and to undermine the public liberty.

—PUBLIUS

REVIEW QUESTIONS

1. What is the third concern that Madison addresses in this paper? (57:1-3)

2. What word does Madison use to characterize this attack on the Constitution, the claim that it allows for elitists to rule? (57:2)

3. What are some of the traits that rulers in a republican form of government must possess to become elected and perform their duties with integrity and wisdom? (57:3)

4. What does "virtue" mean? (57:3 footnote)

5. Would an elite class of voters have any more advantage at the polls than all the rest? (57:6)

6. What three components of American culture will prevent the House of Representatives from becoming despotic? (57:15)

7. What are the four attributes that bind representatives to the great mass of the people? (57:17)

FEDERALIST NO. 58

ADDRESSING OBJECTION #4, NUMBER IN THE HOUSE WON'T ADJUST AS POPULATION GROWS: Should the number of representatives be allowed to grow as the population increases? The people were far more attached to their own State than the nation, and were suspicious of anything that would give one State power over another. The large States feared that any restriction put on the growth of the House would weaken and dilute their control. They didn't want the small States telling them how to use their greater wealth. And likewise, the small States didn't want to be forever subservient to the large States. The Senate gives equality to all States large and small, but the House of Representatives was a focal point of concern. This paper addresses the fourth of four objections by the Anti-Federalists regarding the House of Representatives as formulated in the new Constitution. See the list of all four objections at 55:3–6.

By James Madison—February 20, 1788

HOUSE OF REPRESENTATIVES DESIGNED TO GROW:

58:1 THE remaining charge against the House of Representatives, which I am to examine, is grounded on a supposition that the number of members will not be augmented from time to time, as the progress of population may demand.

CRITICISMS OF THESE CONSTITUTIONAL PROVISIONS ARE DECEPTIVE:

From what typical flaw do most anti-Constitution arguments arise?

58:2 It has been admitted, that this objection, if well supported, would have great weight. The following observations will show that, like most other objections against the Constitution, it can only proceed from a <u>partial view</u> of the subject, or from a <u>jealousy</u> which discolors and disfigures every object which is beheld.

CONSTITUTION'S STARTING PLACE IS TEMPORARY:

The number of representatives in each State is temporary just to get things started. How long before this allotment is revised?

58:3 **1.** Those who urge the objection seem not to have recollected that the federal Constitution will not suffer by a comparison with the State constitutions, in the security provided for a <u>gradual augmentation</u> of the <u>number of representatives</u>. The <u>number</u> which is to prevail in the first instance is declared to be <u>temporary</u>. Its duration is limited to the short term of <u>three years</u>.

CENSUS HAS TWO MAIN OBJECTIVES:

(1) Reapportion the representatives from time to time and (2) augment the number so long that it doesn't exceed one for every 30,000 individuals.

58:4 Within every successive term of <u>ten years</u> a <u>census</u> of inhabitants is to be repeated. The unequivocal objects of these regulations are, first, to readjust, from time to time, the <u>apportionment of representatives</u> to the number of inhabitants, under the single exception that each State shall have <u>one representative at least</u>; secondly, to augment the number of representatives at the same periods, under the sole limitation that the whole number shall not <u>exceed one for every thirty thousand inhabitants</u>. If we review the constitutions of the <u>several States</u>, we shall find that <u>some of them contain no determinate regulations</u> on this subject, that others correspond pretty much on this point with the federal Constitution, and that the most effectual security in any of them is resolvable into a mere directory provision.

STATES ALLOW INCREASE IN NUMBER OF REPRESENTATIVES AS POPULATION GROWS:

State constitutions allow for more legislators to match their increasing populations.

58:5 **2.** As far as experience has taken place on this subject, a gradual <u>increase of representatives</u> under the <u>State constitutions</u> has at least kept pace with that of the constituents, and it appears that the former have been as ready to concur in such measures as the latter have been to call for them.

SENATE AND HOUSE TO PROTECT SMALLER STATES:

All States have equal representation in the Senate. Which part of Congress most benefits the smaller States?

58:6 **3.** There is a peculiarity in the federal Constitution which insures a watchful attention in a <u>majority</u> both of the people and of their representatives to a constitutional augmentation of the latter. The peculiarity lies in this, that <u>one branch of the legislature is a representation of citizens</u>, the <u>other of the States</u>: in the former, consequently, the larger States will have most weight; in the latter, the advantage will be in <u>favor of the smaller States</u>.

LARGER STATES PUSH TO ENLARGE THE HOUSE:

The large States will work to increase weight and advantage of the House of Representatives. How many already have the majority?

58:7 From this circumstance it may with certainty be inferred that the larger States will be strenuous advocates for increasing the number and weight of that part of the legislature in which their influence predominates. And it so happens that <u>four only of the largest</u> will have a <u>majority</u> of the <u>whole</u> votes in the <u>House of Representatives</u>.

SMALLER STATES CAN OVERRIDE LARGE STATES:

By design a coalition of small states, of which there are more, can unite to shift the balance of power in their direction.

58:8 Should the representatives or people, therefore, of the smaller States oppose at any time a reasonable addition of members, a coalition of a very <u>few States will be sufficient to overrule the opposition</u>; a coalition which, notwithstanding the rivalship and local prejudices which might prevent it on ordinary occasions, would not fail to take place, when not merely prompted by common interest, but justified by equity and the principles of the Constitution.

CAN THE SENATE BLOCK THE HOUSE?

Does the Senate really have powers and advantages over the House, or does it just look that way?

58:9 It may be alleged, perhaps, that the Senate would be prompted by like motives to an <u>adverse coalition</u>; and as their concurrence would be indispensable, the just and constitutional views of the other branch might be defeated. This is the difficulty which has probably created the <u>most serious apprehensions</u> in the jealous friends of a numerous representation. Fortunately it is among the difficulties which, <u>existing only</u>

in appearance, vanish on a close and accurate inspection. The following reflections will, if I mistake not, be admitted to be conclusive and satisfactory on this point.

HOUSE HAS SUPERIOR AUTHORITY OVER SENATE:
Is the House designed to have advantages over the Senate?

58:10 Notwithstanding the equal authority which will subsist between the two houses on all legislative subjects, except the originating of money bills, it <u>cannot be doubted</u> that the <u>House</u>, composed of the greater number of members, when <u>supported by the more powerful States</u>, and speaking the known and determined sense of a majority of the people, will have <u>no small advantage</u> in a question depending on the comparative firmness of the two houses.

HOUSE POSITION SUPPORTED BY CONSTITUTION:
The advantages of the House rest on its rights and on reason.

58:11 This advantage must be increased by the consciousness, felt by the same side of being supported in its demands by <u>right</u>, <u>by reason</u>, and by the <u>Constitution</u>; and the consciousness, on the opposite side, of contending against the force of all these solemn considerations.

UNLIKELY THE SENATE WOULD OVERRIDE HOUSE:
There would be natural support in both Houses to agree to increasing the numbers of representatives.

58:12 It is farther to be considered, that in the gradation between the smallest and largest States, there are several, which, though most likely in general to arrange themselves among the former are too little removed in extent and population from the latter, to second an opposition to their just and legitimate pretensions. Hence it is by <u>no means certain</u> that a <u>majority of votes</u>, even in the Senate, would be <u>unfriendly</u> to proper augmentations in the number of representatives.

ADDING AND ADJUSTING THE NUMBER OF REPRESENTATIVES AMONG THE STATES:
Both the Senate and House will be looking for frequent readjustments in numbers of representatives and adjusting who gets the most based on population growth.

58:13 It will not be looking too far to add, that the <u>senators</u> from all the <u>new States may</u> be gained over to the just views of the <u>House</u> of Representatives, by an expedient too obvious to be overlooked. As these States will, for a great length of time, <u>advance in population</u> with <u>peculiar rapidity</u>, they will be interested in <u>frequent reapportionments</u> of the representatives to the number of inhabitants. The <u>large States</u>, therefore, who will prevail in the House of Representatives, will have nothing to do but to <u>make reapportionments</u> and augmentations mutually conditions of each other; and the senators from all the <u>most growing States</u> will be bound to contend for the latter, by the interest which their States will feel in the former.

LARGE STATES CAN OVERRULE SMALL STATES IN THE HOUSE, IF NEEDED:
If the small States in the Senate combine against the large, what does the House have as a last resort to prevent abuse?

58:14 These considerations seem to afford ample security on this subject, and ought alone to satisfy all the doubts and fears which have been indulged with regard to it. Admitting, however, that they should all be insufficient to subdue the unjust <u>policy of the smaller States</u>, or their predominant influence in the councils of the Senate, a constitutional and infallible <u>resource</u> still remains with the <u>larger States</u>, by which they will be able at all times to accomplish their just purposes.

POWER OF THE PURSE:
Control is held by both withholding money and proposing how it's spent.

58:15 The <u>House</u> of Representatives cannot only refuse, but they alone can propose, the supplies requisite for the <u>support</u> of government. They, in a word, <u>hold the purse</u> that powerful instrument by which we behold, in the history of the British Constitution, an infant and humble representation of the people gradually enlarging the sphere of its activity and importance, and finally <u>reducing</u>, as far as it seems to have wished, all the <u>overgrown prerogatives</u> of the <u>other branches</u> of the government.

POWER OF THE PURSE PREVENTS ABUSE:
Controlling the money is how the House can reduce the overflowing expenses of the other branches.

58:16 This <u>power over the purse may</u>, in fact, be regarded as the most <u>complete and effectual weapon</u> with which any constitution can arm the immediate representatives of the people, for obtaining a redress of every <u>grievance</u>, and for carrying into effect every just and <u>salutary measure</u>.

HOUSE WON'T SURRENDER TO SENATE:
If the Senate ventures where it shouldn't, would the House follow?

58:17 But will not the <u>House</u> of Representatives be as much interested as the <u>Senate</u> in maintaining the government in its <u>proper functions</u>, and will they not therefore be unwilling to stake its existence or its reputation on the **pliancy**[191] of the Senate? Or, if such a trial of firmness between the two branches were hazarded, would not the one be as likely first to yield as the other?

---

191 *pliancy:* The state of being easily persuaded.

HOUSE AND SENATE DRIVEN BY NATIONAL DUTIES:

Smaller, select groups more likely to sustain good government.

58:18 These questions will create no difficulty with those who reflect that in all cases the smaller the number, and the more permanent and conspicuous the station, of men in power, the stronger must be the interest which they will individually feel in whatever concerns the government. Those who represent the dignity of their country in the eyes of other nations, will be particularly sensible to every prospect of public danger, or of dishonorable stagnation in public affairs.

BRITAIN'S HOUSE SUCCESSFULLY HOLDS LINE:

Using Britain as an example, which part of its government tends to overpower the others when stability is threatened?

58:19 To those causes we are to ascribe the continual triumph of the British House of Commons over the other branches of the government, whenever the engine of a money bill has been employed. An absolute inflexibility on the side of the latter, although it could not have failed to involve every department of the state in the general confusion, has neither been apprehended nor experienced. The utmost degree of firmness that can be displayed by the federal Senate or President, will not be more than equal to a resistance in which they will be supported by constitutional and patriotic principles.

EXPENSE PLAYS A ROLE IN NUMBER OF PEOPLE:

The cost of a large body of leaders can impact the decisions about the numbers of representatives.

58:20 In this review of the Constitution of the House of Representatives, I have passed over the circumstances of economy, which, in the present state of affairs, might have had some effect in lessening the temporary number of representatives, and a disregard of which would probably have been as rich a theme of declamation against the Constitution as has been shown by the smallness of the number proposed.

58:21 I omit also any remarks on the difficulty which might be found, under present circumstances, in engaging in the federal service a large number of such characters as the people will probably elect.

THE GREATER THE NUMBER THE FEWER TO ACTUALLY DIRECT THE PROCEEDINGS:

An oversized legislature becomes an arena for passion to overtake reason.

58:22 One observation, however, I must be permitted to add on this subject as claiming, in my judgment, a very serious attention. It is, that in all legislative assemblies the greater the number composing them may be, the fewer will be the men who will in fact direct their proceedings.

LARGE ASSEMBLIES VULNERABLE TO THE RULE OF PASSION OVER REASON:

58:23 In the first place, the more numerous an assembly may be, of whatever characters composed, the greater is known to be the ascendency of passion over reason.

GREAT NUMBERS LESS KNOWLEDGEABLE:

Selecting only a few leaders raises the standard and expectation for excellence. Those standards drop when the numbers grow too large.

58:24 In the next place, the larger the number, the greater will be the proportion of members of limited information and of weak capacities. Now, it is precisely on characters of this description that the eloquence and address of the few are known to act with all their force.

GREAT NUMBERS VULNERABLE TO SINGLE ORATORS:

Manipulating large groups is much easier than smaller groups who generally feel more free to be outspoken.

58:25 In the ancient republics, where the whole body of the people assembled in person, a single orator, or an artful statesman, was generally seen to rule with as complete a sway as if a scepter had been placed in his single hand. On the same principle, the more multitudinous a representative assembly may be rendered, the more it will partake of the infirmities incident to collective meetings of the people.

MANY REPRESENTATIVES DOESN'T MEAN BETTER OUTCOME:

Great numbers look more democratic when in reality these degenerate into an oligarchy. Is it possible to have too many representatives?

58:26 Ignorance will be the dupe of cunning, and passion the slave of sophistry and **declamation**.[192] The people can never err more than in supposing that by multiplying their representatives beyond a certain limit, they strengthen the barrier against the government of a few. Experience will forever admonish them that, on the contrary, AFTER SECURING A SUFFICIENT NUMBER FOR THE PURPOSES OF SAFETY, OF LOCAL INFORMATION, AND OF DIFFUSIVE SYMPATHY WITH THE WHOLE SOCIETY, they will counteract their own views by every addition to their representatives. The countenance of the government may become more democratic, but the soul that animates it will be more **oligarchic**.[193] The machine will be enlarged, but the

---

192 *declamation:* Passionate, emotional speech.
193 *oligarchic, oligarchy:* Small group of people having control of a country; rule by factions.

fewer, and often the more secret, will be the springs by which its motions are directed.

SUPER MAJORITY IS NOT THE BEST:

58:27　As connected with the objection against the number of representatives, may properly be here noticed, that which has been suggested against the number made competent for legislative business. It has been said that more than a majority ought to have been required for a quorum; and in particular cases, if not in all, more than a majority of a quorum for a decision. That some advantages might have resulted from such a precaution, cannot be denied. It might have been an additional shield to some particular interests, and another obstacle generally to hasty and partial measures.

SUPER MAJORITY IS VULNERABLE TO EXTORTION:

With a super majority required (two thirds or three fourths) to pass any bill, the minority can more easily abuse the tight margins and use a single vote to extort an outcome. Such extortion is harder when only fifty-one percent is needed for passage.

58:28　But these considerations are outweighed by the inconveniences in the opposite scale. In all cases where justice or the general good might require new laws to be passed, or active measures to be pursued, the fundamental principle of free government would be reversed. It would be no longer the majority that would rule: the power would be transferred to the minority. Were the defensive privilege limited to particular cases, an interested minority might take advantage of it to screen themselves from equitable sacrifices to the general weal, or, in particular emergencies, to extort unreasonable indulgences.

MINORITY CONTROL LEADS TO RUIN:

When special interests can manipulate the outcome desired by the majority, the people have responded by formally withdrawing from the group.

58:29　Lastly, it would facilitate and foster the baneful practice of secessions; a practice which has shown itself even in States where a majority only is required; a practice subversive of all the principles of order and regular government; a practice which leads more directly to public convulsions, and the ruin of popular governments, than any other which has yet been displayed among us.

—Publius

Review Questions

1. What topic is Madison handling in essay No. 58? (58:1)

2. Is the number of representatives in the first Congress a permanent number or temporary? When will it next change? (58:3)

3. What example proves that a gradual increase in the number of representatives can be managed? (58:5)

4. What are some disadvantages to letting the House grow too numerous? (58:22–26)

5. Why is "more than a majority" (a super majority) for a quorum or for passing laws a bad idea? (58:27–28)

FEDERALIST NO. 59

CONGRESS SHOULD REGULATE ELECTION OF ITS MEMBERS: Stability in the central government is possible only if the central government can regulate how and when representatives flow into that body. If the States were allowed too much control, they could delay or prevent federal representatives from attending to national business in a timely fashion and shut down the federal government. This carefully balanced process shows how the federal government and the States are interdependent with one another as a means of protecting personal liberties and State sovereignty while maintaining a strong Union.

By Alexander Hamilton—February 22, 1788

REGULATING ELECTIONS OF CONGRESS:

59:1　THE natural order of the subject leads us to consider, in this place, that provision of the Constitution which authorizes the national legislature to regulate, in the last resort, the election of its own members.

CONGRESS CAN REGULATE ELECTIONS OF ITSELF:

Do the States decide when and where to hold elections, or does Congress?

59:2　It is in these words: "The TIMES, PLACES, and MANNER of holding elections for senators and representatives shall be prescribed in each State by the legislature thereof; but the Congress may, at any time, by law, make or alter SUCH REGULATIONS, except as to the PLACES of choosing senators."[194]

THIS ELECTION PROVISION IS WIDELY CRITICIZED:

59:3　This provision has not only been declaimed against by those who condemn the Constitution in the gross, but it has been censured by those who have objected with less latitude

---

194　*Publius:* 1st clause, 4th section, of the I.ist article. [Art. I, Sec. 4, Clause 1]

and greater moderation; and, in one instance it has been thought exceptionable by a gentleman who has declared himself the advocate of every other part of the system.

GOVERNMENT HAS POWER TO PRESERVE ITSELF:
What could happen if it didn't have this power, or lost it? See Art. I Sec. 4.

59:4 I am greatly mistaken, notwithstanding, if there be any article in the whole plan more completely defensible than this. Its propriety rests upon the evidence of this plain proposition, that <u>EVERY GOVERNMENT OUGHT TO CONTAIN IN ITSELF THE MEANS OF ITS OWN PRESERVATION</u>.

ANY DEVIATION FROM THE PROVISION WILL FAIL:
Altering this balance in the least way will one day upset it all.

59:5 Every just reasoner will, at first sight, approve an adherence to this rule, in the work of the Convention; and will disapprove every deviation from it which may not appear to have been dictated by the necessity of incorporating into the work some particular ingredient, with which a rigid conformity to the rule was incompatible. Even in this case, though he may acquiesce in the necessity, yet he will not cease to regard and to regret a <u>departure</u> from so fundamental a principle, as a portion of imperfection in the system which may prove the <u>seed of future weakness</u>, and perhaps <u>anarchy</u>.

THREE OPTIONS TO MANAGE ELECTIONS:
No election law in the Constitution could predict every contingency.

59:6 It will not be alleged, that an election law could have been framed and <u>inserted in the Constitution</u>, which would have been always applicable to <u>every</u> probable <u>change</u> in the situation of the country; and it will therefore not be denied, that a <u>discretionary</u> power over elections ought to exist somewhere.

Only three ways to manage election laws in the Constitution.

59:7 It will, I presume, be as readily conceded, that there were only <u>three ways</u> in which this power could have been reasonably modified and disposed: [1] that it must either have been lodged wholly in the <u>national</u> legislature, or [2] wholly in the <u>State</u> legislatures, or [3] <u>primarily in the latter and ultimately in the former</u>.

PROPER MANAGEMENT OF ELECTIONS IS CRUCIAL:
Congress must allow the States to determine their own election processes, but States must agree to federal controls to preserve the process.

59:8 The last mode has, with reason, been preferred by the Convention. They have submitted the regulation of elections for the federal government, in the first instance, to the local administrations; which, in ordinary cases, and when no improper views prevail, may be both more convenient and more satisfactory; but they have reserved to the <u>national authority</u> a <u>right to interpose</u>, whenever extraordinary circumstances might render that interposition <u>necessary</u> to its safety.

STATE CONTROL COULD END GOVERNMENT:
Is it safer to keep the power of regulating elections on the federal level or the State level? If State level, could that be dangerous?

59:9 Nothing can be more evident, than that an <u>exclusive power</u> of regulating elections for the national government, in the hands of the <u>State legislatures</u>, would leave the existence of the Union entirely at their mercy. They could at any moment <u>annihilate it</u>, by neglecting to provide for the choice of persons to administer its affairs.

THIS PRECAUTION IS WARRANTED:
The election abuses feared from the federal government also apply to the States.

59:10 It is to little purpose to say, that a neglect or omission of this kind would <u>not be likely</u> to take place. The constitutional possibility of the thing, without an equivalent for the risk, is an unanswerable objection. Nor has any satisfactory reason been yet assigned for incurring that risk. The extravagant surmises of a distempered jealousy can never be dignified with that character. If we are in a humor to <u>presume abuses</u> of power, it is as fair to presume them on the part of the State governments as on the part of the general government.

CONTROLLING ELECTIONS IS SAFEST IN FEDERAL HANDS:
Survival of the federal government is best left in its own hands.

59:11 And as it is more consonant to the rules of a just theory, to trust the Union with the care of its own existence, than to transfer that care to any other hands, if abuses of power are to be hazarded on the one side or on the other, it is <u>more rational to hazard</u> them where the power would <u>naturally</u> be <u>placed</u>, than where it would unnaturally be placed.

STATE ELECTIONS ARE BEST LEFT TO THE STATES:

States would view federal meddling in their election process as excessive power bent on destroying State sovereignty.

59:12 Suppose an article had been introduced into the Constitution, empowering the United States to regulate the elections for the particular States, would any man have hesitated to <u>condemn</u> it, both as an unwarrantable <u>transposition of power</u>, and as a premeditated engine for the destruction of the State governments?

BOTH THE STATE AND FEDERAL GOVERNMENT MUST BE RESPONSIBLE:

The two governments must have tools to preserve themselves.

59:13 The violation of principle, in this case, would have required no comment; and, to an unbiased observer, it will not be less apparent in the project of <u>subjecting</u> the existence of the <u>national</u> government, in a similar respect, to the <u>pleasure of the State</u> governments. An impartial view of the matter cannot fail to result in a conviction, that <u>each</u>, as far as possible, <u>ought to depend on itself for its own preservation.</u>

STATES' PARTICIPATION IN FEDERAL ELECTIONS:

59:14 As an objection to this position, it may be remarked that the constitution of the national Senate would involve, in its full extent, the danger which it is suggested might flow from an exclusive power in the State legislatures to regulate the federal elections.

STATES COULD REFUSE TO SEND THEIR SENATORS:

59:15 It may be alleged, that by <u>declining the appointment of Senators, they might at any time give a fatal blow to the Union</u>; and from this it may be inferred, that as its existence would be thus rendered dependent upon them in so essential a point, there can be no objection to intrusting them with it in the particular case under consideration.

STATES SEND SENATORS TO WATCH FOR ABUSE:

59:16 The <u>interest</u> of each <u>State</u>, it may be added, to <u>maintain its representation</u> in the national councils, would be a complete <u>security against an abuse</u> of the trust.

STATES AGREED TO A SENATE:

If the States were not allowed to decide on their own elections, would this destroy their trust in being able to impact the national government to which they agreed to be subservient?

59:17 This argument, though specious, will not, upon examination, be found solid. It is certainly true that the State legislatures, by <u>forbearing</u> the appointment of <u>senators</u>, may destroy the national government. But it will not follow that, because they have a power to do this in one instance, they ought to have it in every other. There are cases in which the pernicious tendency of such a power may be far more decisive, without any motive equally cogent with that which must have regulated the conduct of the Convention in respect to the formation of the Senate, to recommend their admission into the system.

STATES HAD TO HAVE POWER OVER SENATE ELECTIONS:

If the States did not have the power to withhold senators, those constitutional restrictions would deny the States a safeguard against the power and usurpations by the central government.

59:18 So far as that construction may expose the Union to the possibility of injury from the State legislatures, it is an evil; but it is an <u>evil</u> which could <u>not</u> have been <u>avoided</u> without <u>excluding the States, in their political capacities, wholly from a place in the organization of the national government.</u>[195]

STATES MUST BE PART OF FEDERAL GOVERNMENT:

59:19 If this had been done, it would doubtless have been interpreted into an entire dereliction of the federal principle; and would certainly have <u>deprived the State governments of that absolute safeguard which they will enjoy under this provision.</u>

GRANTING POWER TO STATES IS NECESSARY:

Allowing the States to appoint senators, even though that could be used to thwart government action, was a necessary trust.

59:20 But however wise it may have been to have submitted in this instance to an inconvenience, for the attainment of a necessary advantage or a greater good, no inference can be drawn from thence to favor an accumulation of the evil, where no necessity urges, nor any greater good invites.

STATES MANAGING THE ELECTIONS OF THEIR REPRESENTATIVES WOULD BE HARMFUL:

If the State legislatures could meddle in the elections of representatives in the way they do their senators, that too could disrupt the whole government.

59:21 It may be easily discerned also that the national government would run a much <u>greater risk</u> from a power in the <u>State legislatures</u> over the elections of its <u>House of Representatives</u>,

---

195 *Editors' Note:* Removing the State legislatures' power to choose senators (Seventeenth Amendment), the States' direct participation in the national government is broken, diluting State sovereignty and a direct link from the people to the federal government.

than from their power of appointing the members of its Senate. The senators are to be chosen for the period of six years; there is to be a rotation, by which the seats of a third part of them are to be vacated and replenished every two years; and no State is to be entitled to more than two senators; a quorum of the body is to consist of sixteen members.

CONSPIRACIES WOULD BE SHORT LIVED:
If a few States tried to overturn the government, the weight of the nation would hold it intact.

59:22 The joint result of these circumstances would be, that a temporary combination of a few States to intermit the appointment of senators, could neither annul the existence nor impair the activity of the body; and it is not from a general and permanent combination of the States that we can have any thing to fear.

THE PEOPLE WILL REJECT A GOVERNMENT CORRUPTED BY INEPTITUDE:
If the whole nation rejected the federal government, it would be because it failed to do its primary job.

59:23 The first might proceed from sinister designs in the leading members of a few of the State legislatures; the last would suppose a fixed and rooted disaffection in the great body of the people, which will either never exist at all, or will, in all probability, proceed from an experience of the inaptitude of the general government to the advancement of their happiness in which event no good citizen could desire its continuance.

STATES CONTROLLING THE HOUSE ELECTIONS WON'T WORK:
If State legislatures could meddle in the election cycles of representatives, the House would be in a constant state of turmoil.

59:24 But with regard to the federal House of Representatives, there is intended to be a general election of members once in two years. If the State legislatures were to be invested with an exclusive power of regulating these elections, every period of making them would be a delicate crisis in the national situation, which might issue in a dissolution of the Union, if the leaders of a few of the most important States should have entered into a previous conspiracy to prevent an election.

STATES WILL DEFEND THEIR REPRESENTATION:
The States' desires to hold influence in Congress will serve to detect and eliminate conspiracies by others to gain unfair advantage.

59:25 I shall not deny that there is a degree of weight in the observation, that the interests of each State, to be represented in the federal councils, will be a security against the abuse of a power over its elections in the hands of the State legislatures. But the security will not be considered as complete, by those who attend to the force of an obvious distinction between the interest of the people in the public felicity, and the interest of their local rulers in the power and consequence of their offices.

THE UNION WILL CREATE ITS OWN COHESION:
The States will be jealous of their positions regarding other States, and will watch closely for encroachments.

59:26 The people of America may be warmly attached to the government of the Union, at times when the particular rulers of particular States, stimulated by the natural rivalship of power, and by the hopes of personal aggrandizement, and supported by a strong faction in each of those States, may be in a very opposite temper. This diversity of sentiment between a majority of the people, and the individuals who have the greatest credit in their councils, is exemplified in some of the States at the present moment, on the present question.

THE POWER-HUNGRY WILL SEEK PERSONAL GAIN:
The idea of breaking away, seceding from the whole, will always be a luring temptation whereby usurpers will seek political power.

59:27 The scheme of separate confederacies, which will always multiply the chances of ambition, will be a never failing bait to all such influential characters in the State administrations as are capable of preferring their own emolument and advancement to the public weal.

TYRANNY ADVANCES IN TIMES OF CRISIS:
This is how a nation loses its liberty. The usurpers use popular dissatisfactions or crises or concerns to rashly enact laws that limit the people's liberties. The Constitution can only go so far to protect the people. There must be patriots in charge who desire liberty more than power.

59:28 With so effectual a weapon in their hands as the exclusive power of regulating elections for the national government, a combination of a few such men, in a few of the most considerable States, where the temptation will always be the strongest, might accomplish the destruction of the Union, by seizing the opportunity of some casual dissatisfaction among the people (and which perhaps they may themselves have excited), to discontinue the choice of members for the federal House of Representatives.

A STRONG UNION BEST RESISTS FOREIGN INFLUENCE:
Would foreign powers be tempted to involve themselves if States abused the regulation of elections?

59:29 It ought never to be forgotten, that a firm union of this country, under an efficient government, will probably be an <u>increasing object of jealousy</u> to <u>more than one nation of Europe</u>; and that <u>enterprises to subvert it will sometimes originate in the intrigues of foreign powers, and will seldom fail to be patronized and abetted by some of them</u>. Its preservation, therefore ought in no case that can be avoided, to be committed to the guardianship of any but those whose situation will uniformly beget an immediate interest in the faithful and vigilant performance of the trust.

—PUBLIUS

REVIEW QUESTIONS

1. Where in the Constitution is Congress given power to regulate the election of its members, in both the House and the Senate? (59:2 footnote)

2. What exception is there to Congress's power to regulate elections? (59:2)

3. What should every government retain in regard to holding its place of authority? (59:4)

4. Why would it be bad to let the States regulate elections for national offices? (59:9–11)

5. Regarding the appointment of senators, how do the State legislatures stand as a check and balance against federal abuse? (59:14–20)

6. Could the State legislatures use their appointment power over Senators to shut down the Senate? (59:21–22)

7. If a quorum is a simple majority, as stated in the Constitution (Art. I, Sec. 5, Clause 1), did Hamilton make a mistake in 59:21 when he said a Senate quorum is sixteen members? (59:21)

8. Why would it be unwise to let the State legislatures regulate elections to the House of Representatives? (59:24)

FEDERALIST NO. 60

CONGRESS'S REGULATION OF ELECTIONS IS SAFE: Congressional control over the times, places and manner of electing representatives will not deprive people of their property or elevate the wealthy over the poor. Separation of the branches of government and their sharing the power makes it more difficult for the federal government to conspire against the States using their election-process powers. This helps illustrate the complex nature of federalism, the relation of the Union to the States.

By Alexander Hamilton— February 23, 1788

DANGER OF FEDERAL GOVERNMENT REGULATING ELECTIONS:

Could the Union's control over its own elections ever be used to exclude a State from the elections?

60:1 <u>WE HAVE seen</u>, that an uncontrollable power over the elections to the federal government could not, without hazard, be committed to the State legislatures. Let us now see, what would be the <u>danger</u> on the <u>other side</u>; that is, from confiding the ultimate right of regulating its own elections to the Union itself. It is not pretended, that this right would ever be used for the exclusion of any State from its share in the representation. The interest of all would, in this respect at least, be the security of all.

UNION MUST NOT BE BIASED IN THE ELECTION PROCESS:

If such a tyrannical spirit rose up to abuse the election process, would not we see evidence of that before things got that far?

60:2 But it is alleged, that it might be employed in such a manner as to promote the <u>election</u> of some <u>favorite class</u> of men in exclusion of others, by <u>confining</u> the places of election to particular <u>districts</u>, and <u>rendering it impracticable</u> to the citizens at large to partake in the choice. Of all chimerical suppositions, this seems to be the most chimerical.

FEDERAL BIAS IS IMPROBABLE BUT WILL QUICKLY BE MADE EVIDENT:

60:3 On the one hand, no rational calculation of probabilities would lead us to imagine that the disposition which a conduct so violent and extraordinary would imply, could ever find its way into the national councils; and on the other, it may be concluded with certainty, that <u>if so improper a spirit</u> should ever <u>gain admittance</u> into them, it would <u>display</u> itself in a form <u>altogether different</u> and far more decisive.

STATES WILL QUICKLY REVOLT AGAINST FEDERAL BIAS:

Who would resist this federal bias, and who would head up the resistance?

60:4 The improbability of the attempt may be satisfactorily inferred from this single reflection, that it <u>could never be made</u> without causing an <u>immediate revolt</u> of the great body of the people, <u>headed</u> and directed by the <u>State governments</u>. It is not difficult to conceive that this characteristic right of freedom may, in certain turbulent and factious seasons, be violated, in respect to a particular class of citizens, by a victorious and overbearing majority; but that so fundamental a privilege, in a country so situated and enlightened, should be invaded to the prejudice of the great mass of the people, by the deliberate policy of the government, without occasioning a popular revolution, is altogether inconceivable and incredible.

FEDERAL DIVERSITY HELPS PREVENT BIAS:
Jealousies and political powers put in opposition make the rise of a corrupted government difficult.

60:5 In addition to this general reflection, there are considerations of a more precise nature, which forbid all apprehension on the subject. The dissimilarity in the ingredients which will compose the national government, and in still more in the manner in which they will be brought into action in its various branches, must form a powerful obstacle to a concert of views in any partial scheme of elections.

GENIUS, MANNERS AND HABITS CREATE DIVERSE VIEWS:

60:6 There is sufficient diversity in the state of property, in the genius, manners, and habits of the people of the different parts of the Union, to occasion a material diversity of disposition in their representatives towards the different ranks and conditions in society.

USURPATION PLOT NOT LIKELY IN THE THREE BRANCHES:
There is little chance for collusion considering Reps are elected directly by the people, Senators by the legislatures, and the President by electors.

60:7 And though an intimate intercourse under the same government will promote a gradual assimilation in some of these respects, yet there are causes, as well physical as moral, which may, in a greater or less degree, permanently nourish different propensities and inclinations in this respect. But the circumstance which will be likely to have the greatest influence in the matter, will be the dissimilar modes of constituting the several component parts of the government. The House of Representatives being to be elected immediately by the people, the Senate by the State legislatures, the President by electors chosen for that purpose by the people, there would be little probability of a common interest to cement these different branches in a predilection for any particular class of electors.

STATE LEGISLATURES IMMUNE FROM INFLUENCE:
The general government cannot coerce or influence the selection of the senators.

60:8 As to the Senate, it is impossible that any regulation of "time and manner," which is all that is proposed to be submitted to the national government in respect to that body, can affect the spirit which will direct the choice of its members.

The collective sense of the State legislatures can never be influenced by extraneous circumstances of that sort; a consideration which alone ought to satisfy us that the discrimination apprehended would never be attempted.

SENATE CAN'T CONCUR TO AN ACT THAT EXCLUDES IT:
A conspiracy against the Senate would also pollute the House.

60:9 For what inducement could the Senate have to concur in a preference in which itself would not be included? Or to what purpose would it be established, in reference to one branch of the legislature, if it could not be extended to the other? The composition of the one would in this case counteract that of the other.

STATES MUST CONSPIRE TO CORRUPT SENATE:
The State legislatures would have to conspire to send delegates with ulterior missions. If that ever took place would it be immaterial who had the political power?

60:10 And we can never suppose that it would embrace the appointments to the Senate, unless we can at the same time suppose the voluntary co-operation of the State legislatures. If we make the latter supposition, it then becomes immaterial where the power in question is placed whether in their hands or in those of the Union.

WHAT INTERESTS OR CLASSES WOULD THE FEDERAL LEVEL COVET OVER ALL OTHERS?
What social interests might the federal powers choose to favor?

60:11 But what is to be the object of this capricious partiality in the national councils? Is it to be exercised in a discrimination between the different departments of industry, or between the different kinds of property, or between the different degrees of property? Will it lean in favor of the landed interest, or the moneyed interest, or the mercantile interest, or the manufacturing interest? Or, to speak in the fashionable language of the adversaries to the Constitution, will it court the elevation of "the wealthy and the well-born," to the exclusion and debasement of all the rest of the society?

PARTIALITY BETWEEN LANDOWNERS AND MERCHANTS:
Bias would be strongest in the State legislatures and local governments.

60:12 If this partiality is to be exerted in favor of those who are concerned in any particular description of industry or property, I presume it will readily be admitted, that the competition for it will lie between landed men and merchants. And I scruple not to affirm, that it is infinitely less likely that either of them should gain an ascendant in the national councils, than that the one or the other of them should predominate in all the <u>local councils</u>. The inference will be, that a conduct tending to give an undue preference to either is much less to be dreaded from the former than from the latter.

STATE INTERESTS ARE EVIDENT IN FEDERAL COUNCILS:
Given the variety and plurality of American interests, any single interest could not unite sufficient support to overthrow other interests and their fair representation.

60:13 The several <u>States</u> are in various degrees <u>addicted</u> to <u>agriculture</u> and <u>commerce</u>. In most, if not All of them, agriculture is predominant. In a few of them, however, <u>commerce</u> nearly divides its empire, and in most of them has a <u>considerable</u> share of <u>influence</u>. In proportion as either prevails, it will be conveyed into the national representation; and for the very reason, that this will be an <u>emanation</u> from a greater <u>variety of interests</u>, and in much more various proportions, than are to be found in any single State, it will be <u>much less apt</u> to <u>espouse either</u> of them with a decided partiality, <u>than the representation of any single State</u>.

AGRICULTURAL INTERESTS WILL DOMINATE:
Because agriculture dominates America's economy, external influence toward other interests would not have very much success.

60:14 In a <u>country consisting chiefly of the cultivators of land</u>, where the rules of an equal representation obtain, the <u>landed interest</u> must, upon the whole, <u>preponderate</u> in the government. As long as this interest prevails in most of the State legislatures, so long it must maintain a correspondent superiority in the national Senate, which will generally be a <u>faithful copy</u> of the <u>majorities of those assemblies</u>. It <u>cannot</u> therefore be <u>presumed</u>, that a <u>sacrifice</u> of the <u>landed</u> to the mercantile class will ever be a favorite object of this branch of the federal legislature.

FEDERAL AND STATE BIAS UNLIKELY:
The States' legislatures would resist improper influence at every level.

60:15 In applying thus particularly to the Senate a general observation suggested by the situation of the country, I am governed by the consideration, that the credulous votaries of <u>State power cannot</u>, upon their own principles, suspect, that the State legislatures would be <u>warped from their duty</u> by any <u>external influence</u>. But in reality the <u>same</u> situation must have the same effect, in the primitive composition at least of the federal <u>House</u> of Representatives: an improper bias towards the mercantile class is as little to be expected from this quarter as from the other.

NO DANGER OF AN OPPOSITE BIAS TOWARD LANDED CLASS:
60:16 In order, perhaps, to give countenance to the objection at any rate, it may be asked, is there not <u>danger</u> of an <u>opposite bias</u> in the national government, which may dispose it to endeavor to secure a monopoly of the federal administration <u>to the landed class</u>? As there is little likelihood that the supposition of such a bias will have any terrors for those who would be immediately injured by it, a labored answer to this question will be dispensed with.

THREE REASONS:
What are the reasons why the landed class would not be elevated above others?

1. It is less likely.

60:17 It will be sufficient to remark, first, that for the reasons elsewhere assigned, it is <u>less likely</u> that any decided <u>partiality</u> should prevail in the councils of the <u>Union</u> than in those of any of its <u>members</u>.

2. Congress is not empowered to pick winners; the winners will pick themselves.

60:18 Secondly, that there would be <u>no temptation to violate the Constitution</u> in favor of the landed class, because that class would, in the natural course of things, <u>enjoy</u> as great a <u>preponderancy</u> as itself could desire.

3. Commerce is too important for national prosperity to manipulate.

60:19 And thirdly, that men accustomed to investigate the sources of public prosperity upon a large scale, must be too well convinced of the utility of commerce, to be <u>inclined to inflict</u> upon it so deep a <u>wound</u> as would result from the entire <u>exclusion</u> of those who would <u>best understand</u> its interest from a share in the management of them. The importance of commerce, in the view of revenue alone, must effectually guard it against the enmity of a body which would be continually importuned in its favor, by the urgent calls of public necessity.

WILL WEALTHY AND WELL-BORN TAKE OVER?
60:20 I rather consult brevity in discussing the probability of a preference founded upon a discrimination between the different kinds of industry and property, because, as far as I understand the <u>meaning of the objectors</u>, they contemplate a discrimination of another kind. They appear to have in view, as the objects of the preference with which they endeavor to alarm us, those whom they designate by the description of "<u>the wealthy and the well-born</u>."

TWO THEORETICAL ROUTES FOR ELITE TO TAKE OVER:

60:21 These, it seems, are to be exalted to an odious pre-eminence over the rest of their fellow-citizens. At one time, however, their <u>elevation</u> is to be a necessary <u>consequence</u> of the <u>smallness of the representative body</u>; at another time it is to be effected by <u>depriving the people</u> at large of the opportunity of exercising their right of <u>suffrage</u> in the choice of <u>that body</u>.

NO PATH EXISTS FOR ELITE TO UNIFORMLY RISE:

The Constitution leaves no room for the rich to manipulate things so they alone can win elections and political power.

60:22 But upon <u>what principle</u> is the discrimination of the places of election to be made, in order to answer the purpose of the meditated preference? Are "the <u>wealthy and the well-born</u>," as they are called, <u>confined to particular spots</u> in the several States? Have they, by some <u>miraculous instinct</u> or foresight, set apart in each of them a <u>common place of residence</u>? Are they only to be met with in the towns or cities? <u>Or</u> are they, on the contrary, <u>scattered</u> over the face of the country as avarice or chance may have happened to cast their own lot or that of their predecessors? If the latter is the case, (as every intelligent man knows it to be)[196] is it not evident that the policy of <u>confining the places of election</u> to particular districts <u>would be as subversive of its own aim</u> as it would be exceptionable on every other account?

PROPERTY OWNERSHIP IS NOT A QUALIFICATION FOR PUBLIC OFFICE:

The only means to give the elite an advantage is to require property ownership as a condition for holding office. This condition was rejected by the Convention. Congress cannot alter that.

60:23 The truth is, that there is no method of securing to the rich the preference apprehended, but by prescribing qualifications of property either for those who may elect or be elected. But <u>this forms no part of the power</u> to be conferred upon the national government. Its authority would be expressly restricted to the regulation of the <u>TIMES, the PLACES, the MANNER</u> of elections. The <u>qualifications</u> of the persons who may choose or be chosen, as has been remarked upon other occasions, are <u>defined and fixed</u> in the Constitution, and are <u>unalterable by the legislature</u>.

ONLY MILITARY FORCE WILL SUSTAIN DESPOTISM:

The American people will revolt if their liberties are usurped. Military force would be required to compel them.

60:24 Let it, however, be admitted, <u>for argument sake</u>, that the expedient suggested <u>might be successful</u>; and let it at the same time be equally taken for granted that all the scruples which a sense of duty or an apprehension of the danger of the experiment might inspire, were overcome in the breasts of the national rulers, still I imagine it will hardly be pretended that they <u>could ever hope</u> to carry such an enterprise into execution <u>without the aid of a military force sufficient to subdue</u> the resistance of the great body of the people.

IF MILITARY WERE USED, TO WHAT END WOULD THAT LEAD?

60:25 The improbability of the existence of a force equal to that object has been discussed and demonstrated in different parts of these papers; but that the futility of the objection under consideration may appear in the strongest light, it shall be conceded for a moment that such a force might exist, and the national government shall be supposed to be in the actual possession of it. <u>What will be the conclusion</u>?

ELITIST ACTION WOULD BE MET WITH UPRISING:

A takeover by the elites would probably not involve the slower and cumbersome act of fabricating elections laws.

60:26 With a disposition to invade the essential rights of the community, and with the means of gratifying that disposition, is it presumable that the persons who were actuated by it would amuse themselves in the ridiculous task of <u>fabricating election laws for securing a preference to a favorite class of men</u>?

A single, decisive act would seem more successful, but would the people stand for it?

60:27 Would they not be likely to <u>prefer a conduct better adapted</u> to their own immediate aggrandizement? Would they not rather boldly resolve to perpetuate themselves in office by one decisive act of usurpation, than to trust to precarious expedients which, in spite of all the precautions that might accompany them, might terminate in the dismission, disgrace, and ruin of their authors?

The elites would fear the voters' discovering their evil intentions and react by voting them out.

60:28 Would they not <u>fear</u> that <u>citizens</u>, not less tenacious than conscious of their rights, would flock from the remote extremes of their respective States to the places of election, to <u>overthrow</u> their <u>tyrants</u>, and to <u>substitute men</u> who would be disposed to <u>avenge the violated majesty</u> of the people?

—PUBLIUS

---

196 *Publius:* Particularly in the Southern States and in this State [New York].

REVIEW QUESTIONS

1. What danger regarding federal regulation of elections does Hamilton address in this paper? (60:1–3)

2. If such a power grab was attempted, how would the States respond? (60:4)

3. Fill in the blanks: A conspiracy would be difficult to organize because each branch is elected by different populations, the House by the _____; the Senate by the _____ _____, and the President by _____ chosen by the _____. (60:7)

4. Can the federal government influence who the State legislatures choose as their senators? (60:8)

5. What are the reasons why the landed class would not be elevated above the others? (60:16–19)

6. Fill in the blanks: Hamilton mocks the fear that "the wealthy and the well-born" could control elections or offices, asking if they are _____ to particular spots, or by some _____ _____ located to a _____ place of residence, or in the _____ or _____, and not out on the farms. (60:22)

7. If the federal government did become so corrupted that it could elevate any class of rich or connected class into higher office, would the people stand for that? (60:24–28)

8. What would the federal government turn to as the tool of enforcing their usurpation of the election process? (60:24)

9. To what end would a takeover attempt lead? (60:28)

FEDERALIST NO. 61

DATES AND PLACES FOR ELECTIONS: In many States the location of elections is not specified in their constitutions, and no harm has come from this. Allowing Congress to set the date ensures regular cycling in and out of office holders in a predictable pattern, helping to break any conspiracies of faction from perpetuating themselves. This issue is not important enough to prevent passage of the Constitution, and objecting to it is actually a delaying tactic deployed by its critics.

By Alexander Hamilton—February 26, 1788

VOTING PLACES SET BY CONGRESS NOT NEEDED:

Is specifying where elections are held really necessary? Is it of such severe importance that this should be put into the Constitution?

61:1 THE more candid opposers of the provision respecting elections, contained in the plan of the Convention, when pressed in argument, will sometimes concede the propriety of that provision; with this qualification, however, that it ought to have been accompanied with a declaration, that all elections should be had in the counties where the electors resided. This, say they, was a necessary precaution against an abuse of the power.

CONGRESS CHOOSING VOTING PLACES ADDS NO ADDITIONAL SECURITY:

61:2 A declaration of this nature would certainly have been harmless; so far as it would have had the effect of quieting apprehensions, it might not have been undesirable. But it would, in fact, have afforded little or no additional security against the danger apprehended; and the want of it will never be considered, by an impartial and judicious examiner, as a serious, still less as an insuperable, objection to the plan.

CONSTITUTION CAN'T BE BLAMED FOR USURPATIONS:

61:3 The different views taken of the subject in the two preceding papers [Nos. 59 and 60] must be sufficient to satisfy all dispassionate and discerning men, that if the public liberty should ever be the victim of the ambition of the national rulers, the power under examination, at least, will be guiltless of the sacrifice.

COMPARE FEDERAL CONTROLS TO STATE CONTROLS:

Do the States exercise tighter control over elections than would Congress?

61:4 If those who are inclined to consult their jealousy only, would exercise it in a careful inspection of the several State constitutions, they would find little less room for disquietude and alarm, from the latitude which most of them allow in respect to elections, than from the latitude which is proposed to be allowed to the national government in the same respect.

The States' constitutions already protect elections, but reviewing them would take too long. To illustrate, let's look at New York.

61:5 A review of their situation, in this particular, would tend greatly to remove any ill impressions which may remain in regard to this matter. But as that view would lead into long and tedious details, I shall content myself with the single example of the State in which I write.

EXAMPLE OF NEW YORK'S ELECTION PROCESS:
The State has power to control elections by making the distance to vote too far away. Should Congress be granted this power?

61:6 The constitution of New York makes no other provision for LOCALITY of elections, than that the members of the Assembly shall be elected in the COUNTIES;

The New York Senate

61:7 those of the Senate, in the great districts into which the State is or may be divided: these at present are four in number, and comprehend each from two to six counties. It may readily be perceived that it would not be more difficult to the legislature of New York to defeat the suffrages of the citizens of New York, by confining elections to particular places, than for the legislature of the United States to defeat the suffrages of the citizens of the Union, by the like expedient.

EXAMPLE OF ALBANY:
Do the challenges of managing elections on the State level differ from the challenges on the federal level?

61:8 Suppose, for instance, the city of Albany was to be appointed the sole place of election for the county and district of which it is a part, would not the inhabitants of that city speedily become the only electors of the members both of the Senate and Assembly for that county and district? Can we imagine that the electors who reside in the remote subdivisions of the counties of Albany, Saratoga, Cambridge, etc., or in any part of the county of Montgomery, would take the trouble to come to the city of Albany, to give their votes for members of the Assembly or Senate, sooner than they would repair to the city of New York, to participate in the choice of the members of the federal House of Representatives? The alarming indifference discoverable in the exercise of so invaluable a privilege under the existing laws, which afford every facility to it, furnishes a ready answer to this question.

INCONVENIENCE ALWAYS GIVES SAME END RESULT:
If the State or Congress puts the ballot box 20 miles or 20,000 miles distance doesn't matter. The effect is the same.

61:9 And, abstracted from any experience on the subject, we can be at no loss to determine, that when the place of election is at an INCONVENIENT DISTANCE from the elector, the effect upon his conduct will be the same whether that distance be twenty miles or twenty thousand miles.

NOTHING GAINED BY GIVING CONGRESS THIS POWER:

61:10 Hence it must appear, that objections to the particular modification of the federal power of regulating elections will, in substance, apply with equal force to the modification of the like power in the constitution of this State; and for this reason it will be impossible to acquit the one, and to condemn the other. A similar comparison would lead to the same conclusion in respect to the constitutions of most of the other States.

STATE CONSTITUTIONS ARE IMPERFECT AS IS THE CONSTITUTION, BUT BOTH WILL WORK:
The States don't neglect liberty. Yet the same alleged flaws in the Constitution must apply also to the States. If the imperfect States can manage things, shouldn't the same allowance be afforded to the Constitution?

61:11 If it should be said that defects in the State constitutions furnish no apology for those which are to be found in the plan proposed, I answer, that as the former have never been thought chargeable with inattention to the security of liberty, where the imputations thrown on the latter can be shown to be applicable to them also, the presumption is that they are rather the **cavilling**[197] refinements of a predetermined opposition, than the well-founded inferences of a candid research after truth.

STATE AND FEDERAL REPS ARE THE SAME:
There is no reason to believe that representatives on the State level are somehow more righteous than on the federal level.

61:12 To those who are disposed to consider, as innocent omissions in the State constitutions, what they regard as unpardonable blemishes in the plan of the Convention, nothing can be said; or at most, they can only be asked to assign some substantial reason why the representatives of the people in a single State should be more impregnable to the lust of power, or other sinister motives, than the representatives of the people of the United States?

MORE DIFFICULT TO SUBVERT A NATION THAN A STATE:
If subverting liberties is difficult on the State level, can the Anti-Federalists prove why it would be easier on the national level?

61:13 If they cannot do this, they ought at least to prove to us that it is easier to subvert the liberties of three millions of people, with the advantage of local governments to head their opposition, than of two hundred thousand people who are destitute of that advantage.

---

197 *cavilling:* To argue or find fault over trivial matters.

NATIONAL CONSPIRACY MORE DIFFICULT:

The Anti-Federalists cannot prove that a conspiracy to control power is easier done nationally than in a single State.

61:14 And in relation to the point immediately under consideration, they ought to convince us that it is less probable that a predominant faction in a single State should, in order to maintain its superiority, incline to a preference of a particular class of electors, than that a similar spirit should take possession of the representatives of thirteen States, spread over a vast region, and in several respects distinguishable from each other by a diversity of local circumstances, prejudices, and interests.

POSITIVE ADVANTAGES OF UNIFORM VOTING:

61:15 Hitherto my observations have only aimed at a vindication of the provision in question, on the ground of theoretic propriety, on that of the danger of placing the power elsewhere, and on that of the safety of placing it in the manner proposed. But there remains to be mentioned a <u>positive advantage</u> which will result from this disposition, and which could not as well have been obtained from any other:

UNIFORM HOUSE ELECTIONS MAKE IT MORE SECURE:

61:16 I allude to the circumstance of <u>uniformity</u> in the <u>time of elections</u> for the federal House of Representatives. It is more than possible that this uniformity may be found by experience to be of great importance to the public welfare, both as a <u>security</u> against the <u>perpetuation</u> of the <u>same spirit</u> in the body, and as a <u>cure</u> for the diseases of <u>faction</u>.

NO UNIFORMITY FOR START DATE MEANS NO ABILITY TO START FRESH EVERY TWO YEARS:

If the States could schedule elections haphazardly there would be no chance to clean house if needed.

61:17 If each State may choose its own time of election, it is possible there may be at least <u>as many different periods</u> as there are <u>months</u> in the year. The times of election in the several States, as they are now established for local purposes, vary between extremes as wide as March and November. The consequence of this diversity would be that there could never happen a <u>total dissolution</u> <u>or</u> <u>renovation</u> of the body <u>at one time</u>.

IMPROPER SPIRIT IS TOO EASILY PERPETUATED:

Without a fresh start reckless ideas will transmit to new members and continue a blight that uniform elections can help root out.

61:18 If an improper spirit of any kind should happen to prevail in it, that <u>spirit</u> would be apt to <u>infuse</u> itself into the <u>new members</u>, as they come forward in succession. The <u>mass</u> would be likely to <u>remain nearly the same</u>, assimilating constantly to itself its gradual accretions. There is a contagion in example which few men have sufficient force of mind to resist.

ELECTION PATTERN FOR SENATE AND HOUSE IS SAFER:

Replacing the Senate a third (treble) at a time and making a total House replacement every time, is more secure and less alarming.

61:19 I am inclined to think that treble the duration in office, with the condition of a <u>total dissolution</u> of the body at the <u>same time</u>, might be <u>less formidable</u> to liberty than one third of that duration subject to <u>gradual</u> and successive <u>alterations</u>.

SENATE PATTERN GOOD FOR STATES:

State legislatures across the nation will meet at the same time to appoint senators.

61:20 <u>Uniformity</u> in the time of elections seems <u>not less requisite</u> for executing the idea of a regular rotation in the <u>Senate</u>, and for conveniently assembling the legislature at a stated period in each year.

TIME FOR ELECTIONS BEST LEFT TO CONGRESS:

New York's doesn't set a time for elections so why should new constitution?

61:21 It may be asked, <u>Why</u>, then, could <u>not a time</u> have been fixed in the <u>Constitution</u>? As the most zealous adversaries of the plan of the Convention in this State are, in general, not less zealous admirers of the constitution of the State, the question may be retorted, and it may be asked, <u>Why</u> was <u>not a time</u> for the like purpose fixed in the constitution of <u>this State</u>?

CONGRESS AND STATES WILL EXPERIMENT:

Leaving national elections up to Congress avoids the sticky problem of choosing a particular date that might fall on a bad time.

61:22 No better answer can be given than that it was a matter which might safely be <u>intrusted</u> to <u>legislative discretion</u>; and that if a time had been appointed, it might, upon <u>experiment</u>, have been found <u>less convenient</u> than some other time. The same answer may be given to the question put on the other side. And it may be added that the supposed danger of a gradual change being merely speculative, it would have been hardly advisable upon that speculation to establish, as a fundamental point, what would <u>deprive several States of the convenience</u> of having the elections for their own governments and for the national government at the same epochs.

—PUBLIUS

Review Questions

1. Would holding elections in the counties where the electors reside be an added safety against federal meddling in the States? (61:1–2)

2. Do any of the existing State constitutions require that elections be held where voters reside? (61:4–5)

3. Does it make any difference where elections are held when it comes to how the voters cast their votes? (61:7–9)

4. What is the pleasant outcome of uniform elections? (61:16)

5. What are some advantages to the House having a fresh start every two years? (61:16, 18)

6. Does New York's constitution set a date for elections? Who decides? (61:20–21)

7. If the States don't need specific dates for elections in their constitutions, should there be one in the federal constitution? (61:22)

SECTION 9 • THE SENATE

Papers 62–66

FEDERALIST NO. 62

THE SENATE'S ROLE AND ITS MEMBERSHIP DESCRIBED: The Senate helps stabilize the flightiness of the House. Five important points are discussed about the Senate as established by the new Constitution: Individual qualifications, how to select Senators, equal representation in the Senate, and the number of Senators and their six-year term. Powers of the Senate are also examined. The Anti-Federalists feared the Senate system because the senators were not subject to mandatory recall (as in the Articles), fearing they could serve for life. While members in the House of Representatives come and go, sometimes passions can grow that result in the passage of bad law. The Senate's longer duration in office can help prevent this.

By James Madison—February 27, 1788

EXAMINATION OF THE SENATE:

62:1 HAVING examined the constitution of the House of Representatives, and answered such of the objections against it as seemed to merit notice, I enter next on the <u>examination of the Senate</u>.

FIVE TOPICS:

62:2 The heads into which this member of the government may be considered are: I. The qualification of senators; II. The appointment of them by the State legislatures; III. The equality of representation in the Senate; IV. The number of senators, and the term for which they are to be elected; V. The powers vested in the Senate.

I. QUALIFICATIONS FOR SENATOR:

Why is it important to possess longer experience compared to a representative?

62:3 I. The <u>qualifications</u> proposed for senators, as distinguished from those of representatives, consist in a more <u>advanced age</u> and a <u>longer period of citizenship</u>.

Age and citizenship distinctions.

62:4 A senator must be <u>thirty years</u> of age at least; as a representative must be twenty-five. And the former must have been a <u>citizen nine years</u>; as seven years are required for the latter.

More experience preferred.

62:5 The propriety of these distinctions is <u>explained by</u> the nature of the <u>senatorial trust</u>, which, requiring greater extent of information and stability of character, requires at the same time that the senator should have reached a period of life most likely to supply these advantages;

Must prove allegiance to the United States, with no foreign preference.

62:6 and which, participating immediately in transactions with foreign nations, ought to be exercised by <u>none</u> who are <u>not thoroughly weaned</u> from the prepossessions and habits incident to <u>foreign birth</u> and education.

Qualifications: Why nine years as a citizen?

62:7 The term of nine years appears to be a prudent mediocrity between a total exclusion of adopted citizens, whose merits and talents may claim a share in the public confidence, and an indiscriminate and hasty admission of them, which <u>might create a channel</u> for <u>foreign influence</u> on the national councils.

II. LEGISLATIVE APPOINTMENT:

Having the State legislatures appoint their senators instead of the population electing them gives the States a role in forming the federal government.

62:8 II. It is equally unnecessary to **dilate**[198] on the <u>appointment</u> of senators <u>by the State legislatures</u>. Among the various modes which might have been devised for constituting this branch of the government, that which has been proposed by the Convention is probably the <u>most congenial</u> with the public <u>opinion</u>.[199] It is recommended by the <u>double advantage</u> of favoring a select appointment, and of <u>giving to the State</u>

---

198 *dilate:* To relate at large, to tell copiously or diffusely (Noah Webster, *American Dictionary of the English Language*, 1828.)

199 *Editors' Note:* The Senate is the people's best link to the federal level. The people elect the State legislature, the legislators appoint their representatives, the two senators. Having served as legislators, the senators had intimate knowledge of a State's priorities. The Seventeenth Amendment destroyed that linkage. Today, senators are not beholden to the legislatures who before had the power to hire and fire them, thereby losing an important check on the senator's loyalty

governments such an agency in the formation of the federal government as must secure the authority of the former, and may form a convenient link between the two systems.

III. EQUALITY OF REPRESENTATION:
The Senate establishes equality between the States for voting purposes, and affirms State sovereignty.

62:9 III. The equality of representation in the Senate is another point, which, being evidently the result of compromise between the opposite pretensions of the large and the small States, does not call for much discussion.

COMPOUND REPUBLIC DEFINED:
A compound republic is a mixture of proportional differences (national) and equality (federal) characteristics.

62:10 If indeed it be right, that among a people thoroughly incorporated into one nation, every district ought to have a PROPORTIONAL share in the government, and that among independent and sovereign States, bound together by a simple league, the parties, however unequal in size, ought to have an EQUAL share in the common councils, it does not appear to be without some reason that in a compound republic, partaking both of the national and federal character, the government ought to be founded on a mixture of the principles of proportional and equal representation.

SENATE COMPROMISE ALSO FOUNDED ON THEORY:
The claim that the Senate is the result of compromise is not totally accurate. There is positive political science behind the idea of equal suffrage in Congress.

62:11 But it is superfluous to try, by the standard of theory, a part of the Constitution which is allowed on all hands to be the result, not of theory, but "of a spirit of amity, and that mutual deference and concession which the peculiarity of our political situation rendered indispensable."

SENATE COMPROMISE IS LESSER OF TWO EVILS:
Whether evil or not depends on the size of the State.

62:12 A common government, with powers equal to its objects, is called for by the voice, and still more loudly by the political situation, of America. A government founded on principles more consonant to the wishes of the larger States, is not likely to be obtained from the smaller States. The only option, then, for the former, lies between the proposed government and a government still more objectionable. Under this alternative, the advice of prudence must be to embrace

the lesser evil; and, instead of indulging a fruitless anticipation of the possible mischiefs which may ensue, to contemplate rather the advantageous consequences which may qualify the sacrifice.

DEFINITION OF SIMPLE REPUBLIC:
Equality of votes in the Senate is a constitutional protection of the States as an entity. Without this all the people would merge into one massive body called a "simple republic," having lost State sovereignty.

62:13 In this spirit it may be remarked, that the equal vote allowed to each State is at once a constitutional recognition of the portion of sovereignty remaining in the individual States, and an instrument for preserving that residuary sovereignty. So far the equality ought to be no less acceptable to the large than to the small States; since they are not less solicitous to guard, by every possible expedient, against an improper consolidation of the States into one simple republic.

NEW LAWS DEPENDENT ON BOTH STATES AND PEOPLE:
Evidence of the "compound republic" is seen with a majority of the people (the House) and a majority of the States (the Senate) required to pass laws.

62:14 Another advantage[200] accruing from this ingredient in the constitution of the Senate is, the additional impediment it must prove against improper acts of legislation. No law or resolution can now be passed without the concurrence, first, of a majority of the people [the House], and then, of a majority of the States [the Senate].

COMPLICATED CHECK ON THE LEGISLATURE:
While the process may appear complicated on paper, in practice it works.

62:15 It must be acknowledged that this complicated check on legislation may in some instances be injurious as well as beneficial; and that the peculiar defense which it involves in favor of the smaller States, would be more rational, if any interests common to them, and distinct from those of the other States, would otherwise be exposed to peculiar danger. But as the larger States will always be able, by their power over the supplies [the purse], to defeat unreasonable exertions of this prerogative of the lesser States, and as the faculty and excess of law-making seem to be the diseases to which our governments are most liable, it is not impossible that this part of the Constitution may be more convenient in practice than it appears to many in contemplation.

---

to the States' priorities.

200 *Editors' Note:* Benjamin Franklin observed (at the Constitutional Convention) that the larger States didn't want to surrender control over their wealth to the smaller States, so those larger States were allowed a majority in the House, a means to protect their wealth. But the smaller States hated inequality so they demanded an equal vote in the Senate. This dividing of federalization was one of the three major compromises (slavery and interstate commerce being the other two).

IV. NUMBER OF SENATORS AND LENGTH OF TERM:

62:16 IV. The <u>number of senators</u>, and the <u>duration</u> of their appointment, come next to be considered. In order to form an accurate judgment on both of these points, it will be proper to inquire into the purposes which are to be answered by a senate; and in order to ascertain these, it will be necessary to <u>review the inconveniences</u> which a republic must <u>suffer</u> from the want of such an institution.

SENATE IS PREVENTATIVE CHECK ON HOUSE:
How does the Senate "double the security" against bad law?

62:17 <u>First</u>. It is a <u>misfortune incident to republican government</u>, though in a less degree than to other governments, that <u>those who administer</u> it may <u>forget</u> their obligations to their constituents, and prove <u>unfaithful</u> to their important trust. In this point of view, a senate, as a <u>second branch</u> of the legislative assembly, distinct from, and dividing the power with, a first, must be in all cases a <u>salutary check</u> on the government. It doubles the security to the people, by <u>requiring</u> the <u>concurrence</u> of two distinct bodies in <u>schemes of usurpation</u> or perfidy, where the ambition or corruption of one would otherwise be sufficient.

UNITY OF MISSION OF HOUSE AND SENATE SECURES SAFETY:

62:18 This is a precaution founded on such clear principles, and now so well understood in the United States, that it would be more than superfluous to enlarge on it. I will barely remark, that as the improbability of sinister combinations will be in proportion to the dissimilarity in the genius of the two bodies, it must be politic to distinguish them from each other by every circumstance which will consist with a due harmony in all proper measures, and with the genuine principles of republican government.

CAUTION: LARGE ASSEMBLIES OFTEN BECOME SUBJECT TO FACTIOUS LEADERS.
Do charismatic leaders and passionate causes steer large bodies into emotional upheavals that pass rash and foolish laws?

62:19 <u>Second</u>. The necessity of a senate is not less indicated by the propensity of all single and numerous assemblies to <u>yield</u> to the <u>impulse</u> of sudden and <u>violent passions</u>, and to be <u>seduced</u> by <u>factious leaders</u> into intemperate and pernicious resolutions.

SENATE'S JOB IS TO CALM PERIODIC RAMPAGES:
Is the Senate subject to similar rashness as feared from the House?

62:20 Examples on this subject might be cited without number; and from proceedings within the United States, as well as from the history of other nations. But a position that will not be contradicted, need not be proved. All that need be remarked is, that <u>a body which is to correct this infirmity ought itself to be free from it, and consequently ought to be less numerous</u>. It ought, moreover, to possess great firmness, and consequently ought to hold its authority by a <u>tenure</u> of <u>considerable duration</u>.

SENATE TENURE BRINGS STABILITY TO CONGRESS:
The representative's shorter term in office, lack of experience and knowledge leads to governmental blunders.

62:21 <u>Third</u>. Another defect to be supplied by a senate lies in a want of due <u>acquaintance with the objects</u> and principles of <u>legislation</u>.

TWO-YEAR TERMS RESULTS IN MORE RISK TO ERROR:

62:22 It is not possible that an assembly of <u>men called</u> for the most part from pursuits of a private nature, continued in appointment for a <u>short time</u>, and led by no permanent motive to devote the intervals of public occupation to a study of the laws, the affairs, and the comprehensive interests of their country, should, if left wholly to themselves, <u>escape</u> a variety of important <u>errors</u> in the exercise of their legislative trust.

VOLUMES OF LAWS TESTIFY TO THE NEED FOR A SENATE:
Would there be so many corrective laws on the books if a Senate had been around to urge caution and correction?

62:23 It may be affirmed, on the best grounds, that no small share of the present embarrassments of America is to be charged on the <u>blunders of our governments</u>; and that these have proceeded from the heads rather than the hearts of most of the authors of them.

ARTICLES ALSO FAILED FOR WANT OF A SENATE:

62:24 What indeed are all the <u>repealing</u>, <u>explaining</u>, and <u>amending laws</u>, which fill and disgrace our voluminous codes, but so many <u>monuments of deficient wisdom</u>; so many impeachments exhibited by each succeeding against each preceding session; so many admonitions to the people, of the value of those aids which may be expected from a <u>well-constituted senate</u>?

GOOD GOVERNMENT POSSESSES TWO QUALITIES:
What are the two qualities of good government? In which quality is America deficient?

62:25 A good government implies two things: first, fidelity to the object of government, which is the happiness of the people; secondly, a knowledge of the means by which that object can be best attained.

Constitution provides the means to bring about the first object, the happiness in the people.

62:26 Some governments are deficient in both these qualities; most governments are deficient in the first. I scruple not to assert, that in American governments too little attention has been paid to the last. The federal Constitution avoids this error; and what merits particular notice, it provides for the last in a mode which increases the security for the first.

CONTINUOUS CHANGE IS DESTABILIZING:
If the enemy of national success is constant change in its councils, isn't the stability from the Senate its truest friend?

62:27 Fourth. The **mutability**[201] in the public councils arising from a rapid succession of new members, however qualified they may be, points out, in the strongest manner, the necessity of some stable institution in the government. Every new election in the States is found to change one half of the representatives. From this change of men must proceed a change of opinions; and from a change of opinions, a change of measures. But a continual change even of good measures is inconsistent with every rule of prudence and every prospect of success. The remark is verified in private life, and becomes more just, as well as more important, in national transactions.

FREQUENT CHANGE IS ALWAYS HARMFUL TO THE WHOLE:

62:28 To trace the mischievous effects of a mutable government would fill a volume. I will hint a few only, each of which will be perceived to be a source of innumerable others.

MUTABILITY DESTROYS RESPECT AND CONFIDENCE:
How are relations between individuals the same as with nations?

62:29 In the first place, it forfeits the respect and confidence of other nations, and all the advantages connected with national character.

Tendency to continually change makes a person untrustworthy.

62:30 An individual who is observed to be inconstant to his plans, or perhaps to carry on his affairs without any plan at all, is marked at once, by all prudent people, as a speedy victim to his own unsteadiness and folly. His more friendly neighbors may pity him, but all will decline to connect their fortunes with his; and not a few will seize the opportunity of making their fortunes out of his.

Nation to nation is similar to individual to individual.

62:31 One nation is to another what one individual is to another; with this melancholy distinction perhaps, that the former, with fewer of the benevolent emotions than the latter, are under fewer restraints also from taking undue advantage from the indiscretions of each other.

AN UNSTABLE AMERICA IS NOT RESPECTED GLOBALLY:
Does the ever-changing nature of government under the Articles of Confederation damage foreign affairs?

62:32 Every nation, consequently, whose affairs betray a want of wisdom and stability, may calculate on every loss which can be sustained from the more systematic policy of their wiser neighbors.

America is a victim of her own making; she is not trusted.

62:33 But the best instruction on this subject is unhappily conveyed to America by the example of her own situation. She finds that she is held in no respect by her friends; that she is the derision of her enemies; and that she is a prey to every nation which has an interest in speculating on her fluctuating councils and embarrassed affairs.

INSTABILITY AND FLUID LAW DESTROYS LIBERTY:

62:34 The internal effects of a mutable policy are still more calamitous. It poisons the blessing of liberty itself.

LONG, COMPLICATED LAW SERVES NO GOOD:
The Constitution was written to be easily understood by all people.

62:35 It will be of little avail to the people, that the laws are made by men of their own choice, if the laws be so voluminous that they cannot be read, or so incoherent that they cannot be understood; if they be repealed or revised before they are promulgated, or undergo such incessant changes that no man, who knows what the law is to-day, can guess what it will be to-morrow.

CAN AN ILL-DESCRIBED LAW ACTUALLY BE A LAW?

62:36 Law is defined to be a rule of action; but how can that be a rule, which is little known, and less fixed?

MANIPULATORS PROFIT FROM IGNORANCE:
Without the Senate, could dishonest manipulators more easily profit from the industrious and uniformed masses?

---

201 *mutability:* Changeableness; inconsistency; capability to change; variability.

62:37 Another effect of public instability is the <u>unreasonable advantage</u> it gives to the <u>sagacious</u>, the <u>enterprising</u>, and the <u>moneyed few over</u> the industrious and <u>uniformed mass</u> of the people.

SOME LAWS HELP THE FEW BUT NOT THE MANY:

62:38 <u>Every new regulation</u> concerning commerce or revenue, or in any way affecting the value of the different species of property, <u>presents a new harvest</u> to those who watch the change, and can trace its consequences; a harvest, reared not by themselves, but by the toils and cares of the great body of their fellow-citizens. This is a state of things in which it may be said with some truth that <u>laws</u> are <u>made</u> for the <u>FEW</u>, not for the MANY.

UNSTABLE GOVERNMENT IS DAMAGING IN MANY WAYS:

62:39 In another point of view, great injury results from an unstable government. The want of confidence in the public councils damps every useful undertaking, the success and profit of which may depend on a continuance of existing arrangements.

STRONG COMMERCE IS HURT BY INSTABILITY:
Without a Senate to calm the volatile House, why should merchants, farmers, or manufacturers ever risk growing their businesses?

62:40 What <u>prudent merchant will hazard his fortunes</u> in any new branch of commerce when he knows not but that his <u>plans</u> may be <u>rendered unlawful before they can be executed</u>? What <u>farmer</u> or <u>manufacturer</u> will lay himself out for the encouragement given to any particular cultivation or establishment, when he can have no assurance that his preparatory labors and advances will not <u>render him a victim</u> to an inconstant government?

STABLE GOVERNMENT REQUIRED FOR PROGRESS:
When government is unstable, the people tend to harbor a wait-and-see attitude before embarking on risky and great projects.

62:41 In a word, no great improvement or laudable enterprise can go forward which requires the auspices of a steady system of national policy.

TO BE RESPECTED ONE MUST FIRST BE RESPECTABLE:
Without a Senate to help bring order and stability would the government eventually lose respect and disappoint everyone?

62:42 But the <u>most deplorable</u> effect of all is that diminution of attachment and reverence which <u>steals</u> into the <u>hearts</u> of the people, towards a political system which <u>betrays</u> so many marks of infirmity, and <u>disappoints</u> so many of their flattering hopes. <u>No government</u>, any more than an individual, will long be <u>respected without being truly respectable</u>; nor be <u>truly respectable, without possessing a certain portion of order and stability</u>.

—PUBLIUS

REVIEW QUESTIONS

1. What are the five topics Madison discusses in paper No. 62? (62:2)

2. What is the advantage gained by setting a high standard of qualifications for the Senate? (62:3–7)

3. How are States protected from becoming abolished as entities and the parts consolidated into one giant republic? (62:13)

4. How does the Senate prevent unwise acts of legislation from passing? (62:14–17)

5. Are large assemblies vulnerable to the impulse of sudden and violent passions? Can they be seduced by factious leaders into intemperate and pernicious resolutions? (62:19)

6. If the Senate is to have a calming, corrective influence on actions by the House, what then must it, too, be free of? How is this done? (62:20)

7. Where can the proof be seen that the Articles of Confederation failed by not having a senate? (62:24)

8. What did Madison call the disgraceful and voluminous codes that were amassed under the Articles? (62:24)

9. What are the two qualities of good government? (62:25)

10. Why does constant change destroy government? (62:27–33)

11. Fill in the blanks: Without a senate to stabilize the government under the Articles, America has become a _____ to every _____ which has an interest in _____ on her _____ councils and embarrassed affairs. (62:33)

12. Fill in the blanks: In 62:35, Madison says the mass of ill-conceived laws that emerged from the Articles are useless because such laws are so _____ that they cannot be _____, or so _____ that they cannot be _____; if they are _____ or _____ before they are promulgated, or undergo such incessant _____ that __ _____ who knows what the law is today can guess what it ____ ___ tomorrow. (62:35)

13. What is the law? (62:36)

14. Can a law be obeyed if it is little understood, little known, and changeable? (62:36)

15. How does a government and its individual members become respected? (62:42)

FEDERALIST NO. 63

SENATE PREVENTS BAD LAW, STABILIZES INTERNATIONAL PRESENCE: This paper was written in response to critics who feared the Senate would be elitist, aristocratic, and too powerful. Corruption of the Senate is made extremely difficulty. Such a conspiracy would require the Senate to corrupt itself, and the State legislatures, the House of Representatives, and the people at large. A good example of such stability can be found in Maryland and Britain's House of Lords. As to its job internationally, the Senate helps establish America's international reputation and character by offering to the world a "due sense of national character." It is designed to stand as a solemn, seasoned body of deliberators who stay in office sufficiently long to ripen into wisdom—yet not so long of a time as to create a new aristocracy. The Senate also serves to protect the people from their own bad ideas, bad laws, and prejudices that will erupt on occasion from the House.

By James Madison—March 1, 1788

Cont'd: V. SENATE IS CRUCIAL FOR AMERICA'S INTERNATIONAL REPUTATION:

63:1 A FIFTH desideratum, illustrating the utility of a senate, is the want of a due sense of national character. Without a select and stable member of the government, the esteem of foreign powers will not only be forfeited by an unenlightened and variable policy, proceeding from the causes already mentioned, but the national councils will not possess that sensibility to the opinion of the world, which is perhaps not less necessary in order to merit, than it is to obtain, its respect and confidence.

WHAT POSITIVE EFFECT DOES STABILITY HAVE ON NATIONS?

63:2 An attention to the judgment of other nations is important to every government for two reasons:

Must appear trustworthy.

63:3 the one is, that, independently of the merits of any particular plan or measure, it is desirable, on various accounts, that it should appear to other nations as the offspring of a wise and honorable policy;

International norms can help guide.

63:4 the second is, that in doubtful cases, particularly where the national councils may be warped by some strong passion or momentary interest, the presumed or known opinion of the impartial world may be the best guide that can be followed.

Many national blunders could have been avoided.

63:5 What has not America lost by her want of character with foreign nations; and how many errors and follies would she not have avoided, if the justice and propriety of her measures had, in every instance, been previously tried by the light in which they would probably appear to the unbiased part of mankind?

RESPECT AND HONOR IN OFFICE IS A DRIVING FACTOR:

The smaller the legislative body, the greater the spotlight shines on responsibility.

63:6 Yet however requisite a sense of national character may be, it is evident that it can never be sufficiently possessed by a numerous and changeable body. It can only be found in a number so small that a sensible degree of the praise and blame of public measures may be the portion of each individual; or in an assembly so durably invested with public trust, that the pride and consequence of its members may be sensibly incorporated with the reputation and prosperity of the community.

WHAT IF RHODE ISLAND HAD A SENATE TO CALM ITS ACTIONS?

If Rhode Island had a more stable governing body to review its lower house, it would have avoided its present problems.

63:7 The half-yearly representatives of Rhode Island would probably have been little affected in their deliberations on the iniquitous measures of that State, by arguments drawn from the light in which such measures would be viewed by foreign nations, or even by the sister States; whilst it can scarcely be doubted that if the concurrence of a select and stable body had been necessary, a regard to national character alone would have prevented the calamities under which that misguided people is now laboring.

VI. TOO-FREQUENT ELECTIONS CAN CAUSE PROBLEMS:

63:8 I add, as a <u>SIXTH defect</u> the want, in some important cases, of a due **responsibility**[202] in the government to the people, arising from that frequency of elections which in other cases produces this responsibility. <u>This remark</u> will, perhaps, appear not only new, but <u>paradoxical</u>. It must nevertheless be acknowledged, when explained, to be as undeniable as it is important.

RESPONSIBILITY WORKS ONLY WITHIN BOUNDS:

Can a government be responsible for things over which it has no power?

63:9 <u>Responsibility</u>, in order to be reasonable, must be <u>limited</u> to objects <u>within the power</u> of the responsible party,

63:10 and in order to be <u>effectual</u>, must relate to operations of that <u>power</u>, of which a ready and proper judgment can be formed by the constituents.

TWO MAIN PURPOSES OF GOVERNMENT:

63:11 The <u>objects of government</u> may be divided into <u>two general classes</u>: [1] the one depending on measures which have singly an immediate and <u>sensible operation</u>; [2] the other depending on a succession of well-chosen and <u>well-connected measures</u>, which have a gradual and perhaps unobserved operation.

LONG-TERM IMPACT OF LAWS HARD TO MEASURE:

A representative assembly with short election terms cannot be held totally responsible for all the actions that came before or after.

63:12 The importance of the latter description to the collective and permanent <u>welfare</u> of every country, needs no explanation. And yet it is evident that an <u>assembly elected for so short a term</u> as to be unable to provide more than <u>one or two links</u> in a chain of measures, on which the general welfare may essentially depend, ought not to be answerable for the final result, any more than a steward or tenant, engaged for one year, could be justly made to answer for places or improvements which could not be accomplished in less than half a dozen years.

HARD TO ESTIMATE CONGRESS'S SHARE OF INFLUENCE:

63:13 Nor is it possible for the people to <u>estimate</u> the SHARE of <u>influence</u> which their annual assemblies may respectively have on events resulting from the mixed transactions of <u>several years</u>.

PERSONAL RESPONSIBILITY:

63:14 It is sufficiently <u>difficult</u> to preserve a personal <u>responsibility</u> in the members of a <u>NUMEROUS body</u>, for such acts of the body as have an immediate, detached, and palpable operation on its constituents.

SENATE HELPS SECURE LONG-TERM OBJECTIVES:

How would the Senate help prevent legislative risks and errors?

63:15 The proper <u>remedy</u> for this defect must be an <u>additional body</u> in the legislative department, which, having sufficient permanency to provide for such objects as require a <u>continued attention</u>, and a <u>train of measures</u>, may be justly and effectually answerable for the attainment of those objects.

A well-constructed Senate is necessary to achieve these ends.

63:16 Thus far I have considered the circumstances which point out the necessity of a well-constructed Senate only as they relate to the representatives of the people.

COOL AND DELIBERATE REVIEW HELPS PREVENT BAD LAW:

When rash, impulsive and ultimately damaging law is passed in the House, it falls to the Senate to stop such folly.

63:17 To a people as little blinded by prejudice or corrupted by flattery as those whom I address, I shall not scruple to add, that such an institution may be <u>sometimes necessary</u> as a defense to the people against their own <u>temporary errors and delusions</u>. As the <u>cool</u> and <u>deliberate</u> sense of the community ought, in all governments, and actually will, in all free governments, <u>ultimately prevail</u> over the views of its rulers;

SENATE CALMS HEATED AND MISGUIDED MEASURES:

In the heat of the moment, laws are enacted that are later regretted.

63:18 so there are particular moments in public affairs when the people, stimulated by some <u>irregular passion</u>, or some illicit advantage, or misled by the artful misrepresentations of

---

202 ***Responsibility*** (63:8): This word was coined by James Madison, appearing for the first time in No. 63:8. For more than a century it was wrongly believed Hamilton wrote No. 63, but research since then accurately attributes it to Madison. Before this clarification, *A New English Dictionary on Historical Principles*, published in 1914, mis-attributed the invention of the word to Hamilton writing in Federalist No. 63, and then mistakenly attributed a direct quote from 63:9. This is the misleading quote: "1787 Hamilton Federalist No. 63 II. 193, Responsibility in order to be reasonable must be limited to objects within the power of the responsible party."

interested men, <u>may call for measures</u> which they themselves will <u>afterwards</u> be the most ready to <u>lament</u> and condemn.

SENATE INTERVENES UNTIL REASON AND TRUTH CAN PREVAIL:

63:19   In these critical moments, how salutary will be the interference of some <u>temperate and respectable body</u> of citizens, in order to check the misguided career, and to <u>suspend the blow</u> meditated by the people against themselves, <u>until reason, justice, and truth</u> can regain their authority over the public mind?

ATHENS COULD HAVE BENEFITED FROM A SENATE:

How did Athens suffer under rash decisions?

63:20   What bitter anguish would not the people of <u>Athens</u> have often escaped if their government had contained so provident a <u>safeguard</u> against the <u>tyranny of their own passions</u>? Popular liberty might then have escaped the indelible reproach of <u>decreeing to the same citizens the hemlock on one day and statues on the next</u>.

PRECAUTIONS FOR WIDESPREAD REPUBLICS ARE IMPORTANT:

Is a nation spread over so large an area more susceptible to rash decisions, or is a spirit of thoughtfulness built in?

63:21   It may be suggested, that a <u>people spread over an extensive</u> region <u>cannot</u>, like the crowded inhabitants of a small district, <u>be subject</u> to the infection of <u>violent passions</u>, or to the danger of combining in pursuit of unjust measures. I am far from denying that this is a distinction of peculiar importance. I have, on the contrary, endeavored in a former paper to show, that it is one of the principal recommendations of a confederated republic.

LONG-TERM EVILS MUST BE PREVENTED AND REMOVED:

63:22   At the same time, this advantage ought not to be considered as superseding the use of <u>auxiliary precautions</u>. It may even be remarked, that the same extended situation, which will exempt the people of America from some of the dangers incident to lesser republics, will <u>expose</u> them to the <u>inconveniency</u> of remaining for a longer time under the influence of those misrepresentations which the combined industry of interested men may succeed in distributing among them.

LONGEST-LIVED REPUBLICS HAD A SENATE:

Does history give examples of a stable, thoughtful senate that has calmed the rush of the People's House?

63:23   It adds no small weight to all these considerations, to recollect that history informs us of no long-lived republic which had not a senate. <u>Sparta</u>, <u>Rome</u>, and <u>Carthage</u> are, in fact, the only states to whom that character can be applied.

Ancient senators acted as society's anchors and served for life.

63:24   In each of the <u>two first</u> there was a <u>senate for life</u>. The constitution of the senate in the <u>last</u> is less known. Circumstantial evidence makes it probable that it was <u>not different</u> in this particular from the two others. It is at least certain, that it had some quality or other which rendered it an anchor against popular fluctuations; and that a smaller council, drawn out of the senate, was appointed not only for life, but filled up vacancies itself.

ANCIENT REPUBLICS OFFER LESSONS TO BE LEARNED:

Many similarities between then and now illustrate the need of a deliberative body such as the Senate.

63:25   These examples, though as unfit for the imitation, as they are repugnant to the genius, of America, are, notwithstanding, when compared with the fugitive and turbulent existence of other ancient republics, very <u>instructive proofs</u> of the <u>necessity</u> of some institution that will <u>blend stability with liberty</u>.

America's Senate is unique, but its role is similar to that of the ancients.

63:26   I am not unaware of the circumstances which distinguish the American from other popular governments, as well ancient as modern; and which render extreme circumspection necessary, in reasoning from the one case to the other. But after allowing due weight to this consideration, it may still be maintained, that there are many points of similitude which render these examples not unworthy of our attention.

ANCIENT REPUBLICS SUFFERED WITHOUT A SENATE:

63:27   Many of the <u>defects</u>, as we have seen, which can only be supplied by a senatorial institution, are <u>common</u> to a numerous assembly <u>frequently elected</u> by the people, and to the people themselves. <u>There are others</u> peculiar to the former, <u>which require the control</u> of such an institution.

REPRESENTATIVE BODIES HAVE BETRAYED THE PEOPLE:

Will a people betray their own best interests? Would their representatives? Is this not proof a second legislative body is good?

63:28   The <u>people can never willfully betray their own interests</u>; but they may possibly <u>be betrayed</u> by the <u>representatives</u> of the people; and the danger will be evidently greater where the <u>whole legislative trust</u> is lodged in the <u>hands of one body</u>

of men, than where the <u>concurrence</u> of <u>separate</u> and <u>dissimilar</u> bodies is <u>required</u> in every public act.

ANCIENT REPUBLICS EXAMINED:

Is America's two-tiered form of representation unique in the world?

63:29 The <u>difference</u> most relied on, between the <u>American and other republics</u>, consists in the principle of <u>representation</u>; which is the pivot on which the former move, and which is supposed to have been unknown to the latter, or at least to the ancient part of them.

HOUSE AND SENATE EXISTED IN DIFFERENT FORMS:

63:30 The use which has been made of this difference, in reasonings contained in former papers, will have shown that I am disposed neither to deny its existence nor to undervalue its importance. I feel the less restraint, therefore, in observing, that the position concerning the ignorance of the ancient governments on the subject of representation, is by no means precisely true in the latitude commonly given to it. Without entering into a disquisition which here would be misplaced, I will refer to a few known facts, in support of what I advance.

GREECE:

In the ancient democracy of Greece, who performed some executive functions instead of the people themselves?

63:31 In the most pure democracies of <u>Greece</u>, many of the <u>executive functions</u> were performed, not by the people themselves, but by <u>officers</u> elected by the people, and <u>REPRESENTING</u> the people in their EXECUTIVE capacity.

ATHENS, CARTHAGE, AND OTHERS:

Did ancient Athens have a senate? Where?

63:32 Prior to the reform of <u>Solon</u>, Athens was governed by nine **Archons**,[203] annually <u>ELECTED BY THE PEOPLE AT LARGE</u>. The degree of power delegated to them seems to be left in great obscurity.

Six hundred representatives elected annually.

63:33 Subsequent to that period, we find an <u>assembly</u>, first of four, and afterwards of <u>six hundred</u> members, <u>annually ELECTED</u> BY THE PEOPLE; and PARTIALLY representing them in their <u>LEGISLATIVE</u> capacity, since they were not only associated with the people in the function of making laws, but had the <u>exclusive right</u> of <u>originating legislative</u> propositions to the people.

Carthage and others republics had elected senators.

63:34 The <u>senate</u> of <u>Carthage</u>, also, whatever might be its power, or the duration of its appointment, appears to have been ELECTIVE by the suffrages of the people. <u>Similar instances</u> might be traced in most, if not all the <u>popular governments of antiquity</u>.

SPARTA AND CRETE:

Were these countries ruled, at least to some extent, by elected representatives?

63:35 Lastly, in <u>Sparta</u> we meet with the <u>Ephori</u>, and in <u>Rome</u> with the <u>Tribunes</u>; <u>two bodies</u>, small indeed in numbers, but <u>annually ELECTED</u> BY THE WHOLE BODY OF THE PEOPLE, and considered as the REPRESENTATIVES of the people, almost in their **PLENIPOTENTIARY**[204] capacity.

In Crete the senators were elected by the elite members of society.

63:36 The Cosmi of Crete were also annually ELECTED BY THE PEOPLE, and have been considered by some authors as an institution analogous to those of Sparta and Rome, with this difference only, that in the election of that representative body the right of <u>suffrage</u> was communicated to <u>a part only</u> of the people.

PRINCIPLE OF REPRESENTATION IS ANCIENT:

Has the idea of representative government been around a long time? How was the ancients' form lacking compared to America's form?

63:37 <u>From these facts</u>, to which many others might be added, <u>it is clear</u> that the <u>principle of representation was neither unknown to the ancients nor wholly overlooked</u> in their political constitutions. The <u>true distinction</u> between these and the American governments, lies IN THE <u>TOTAL EXCLUSION OF THE PEOPLE, IN THEIR COLLECTIVE CAPACITY</u>, from any share in the LATTER, and not in the TOTAL EXCLUSION OF THE REPRESENTATIVES OF THE PEOPLE from the administration of the FORMER.

AMERICAN ADVANTAGES OF PEOPLE AND TERRITORY:

Unlike other republics, Americans enjoy an intimate connection and control over their government. And it has a very large territory over which true representation is tested.

63:38 The distinction, however, thus qualified, must be admitted to leave a most advantageous <u>superiority in favor of the United States</u>. But to insure to this advantage its full effect, we must be careful not to separate it from the other advantage, of an extensive territory. For it <u>cannot</u> be believed, that any form

---

203 *Archon:* A chief magistrate in ancient Athens.
204 *plenipotentiary:* Person with full power of independent action on behalf of their government.

of representative government could have succeeded within the narrow limits occupied by the democracies of Greece.

SENATE APPOINTED BY STATES IS SECURE:
It is said that because the Senate is not elected by the people, it will eventually grow into an aristocracy. Who actually appoints the Senate?

63:39   In answer to all these arguments, suggested by reason, illustrated by examples, and enforced by our own experience, the jealous adversary of the Constitution will probably content himself with repeating, that a senate appointed not immediately by the people, and for the term of six years, must gradually acquire a dangerous pre-eminence in the government, and finally transform it into a tyrannical aristocracy.

ABUSE OF POWER AND ABUSE OF LIBERTY:
Is there such a thing as too much liberty?

63:40   To this general answer, the general reply ought to be sufficient, that liberty may be endangered by the abuses of liberty as well as by the abuses of power; that there are numerous instances of the former as well as of the latter; and that the former, rather than the latter, are apparently most to be apprehended by the United States. But a more particular reply may be given.

CORRUPTING THE SENATE IS COMPLICATED:
To overthrow the government, who would the Senate need as allies?

63:41   Before such a revolution can be effected, the Senate, it is to be observed, must in the first place corrupt itself; must next corrupt the State legislatures;

A corrupted Senate would also need support of the House and the people.

63:42   must then corrupt the House of Representatives; and must finally corrupt the people at large. It is evident that the Senate must be first corrupted before it can attempt an establishment of tyranny.

The State legislatures would have to be corrupted because they're the body that appoints senators.

63:43   Without corrupting the State legislatures, it cannot prosecute the attempt, because the periodical change of members would otherwise regenerate the whole body.

This multi-layered protection both prevents corruption and restores to normalcy a government rotted out by corruption.

63:44   Without exerting the means of corruption with equal success on the House of Representatives, the opposition of that coequal branch of the government would inevitably defeat the attempt; and without corrupting the people themselves, a succession of new representatives would speedily restore all things to their pristine order.

The Senate could not behave so recklessly given all of the obstructions put in the way.

63:45   Is there any man who can seriously persuade himself that the proposed Senate can, by any possible means within the compass of human address, arrive at the object of a lawless ambition, through all these obstructions?

MARYLAND'S SENATE IS GOOD EXAMPLE OF FEDERAL SENATE:
Maryland's senate offers an excellent example of how the federal Senate will be selected, seated, and controlled without danger to liberty.

63:46   If reason condemns the suspicion, the same sentence is pronounced by experience. The constitution of Maryland furnishes the most apposite example. The Senate of that State is elected, as the federal Senate will be, indirectly by the people, and for a term less by one year only than the federal Senate. It is distinguished, also, by the remarkable prerogative of filling up its own vacancies within the term of its appointment, and, at the same time, is not under the control of any such rotation as is provided for the federal Senate.

MARYLAND SENATE SHOWS NO SYMPTOMS OF DEFICIENCY:
If dangers were built in, as feared, they would have shown by now.

63:47   There are some other lesser distinctions, which would expose the former to colorable objections, that do not lie against the latter. If the federal Senate, therefore, really contained the danger which has been so loudly proclaimed, some symptoms at least of a like danger ought by this time to have been betrayed by the Senate of Maryland, but no such symptoms have appeared. On the contrary, the jealousies at first entertained by men of the same description with those who view with terror the correspondent part of the federal Constitution, have been gradually extinguished by the progress of the experiment; and the Maryland constitution is daily deriving, from the salutary operation of this part of it, a reputation in which it will probably not be rivalled by that of any State in the Union.

THE BRITISH EXAMPLE:
Did the much more abusive senate in Britain show dangers of taking over the government?

63:48   But if any thing could silence the jealousies on this subject, it ought to be the British example.

British Senate consists of hereditary nobles.

63:49   The Senate [House of Lords] there instead of being elected for a term of six years, and of being unconfined to particular families or fortunes, is an hereditary assembly of opulent nobles.

British House elected for seven years.

63:50   The House of Representatives [House of Commons], instead of being elected for two years, and by the whole body of the people, is elected for seven years, and, in very great proportion, by a very small proportion of the people.

ARISTOCRATIC ASSEMBLY CRUSHED BY POPULAR BRANCH:

Instead of the elite taking over, the popular branch reigned supreme.

63:51   Here, unquestionably, ought to be seen in full display the aristocratic usurpations and tyranny which are at some future period to be exemplified in the United States. Unfortunately, however, for the anti-federal argument, the British history informs us that this hereditary assembly has not been able to defend itself against the continual encroachments of the House of Representatives; and that it no sooner lost the support of the monarch, than it was actually crushed by the weight of the popular branch.

ANCIENT SENATES SUFFERED SAME DEMISE:

Did the ancient senates, in whatever form, ever pose a danger?

63:52   As far as antiquity can instruct us on this subject, its examples support the reasoning which we have employed.

Sparta:

63:53   In Sparta, the Ephori, the annual representatives of the people, were found an overmatch for the senate for life, continually gained on its authority and finally drew all power into their own hands.

Rome:

63:54   The Tribunes of Rome, who were the representatives of the people, prevailed, it is well known, in almost every contest with the senate for life, and in the end gained the most complete triumph over it. The fact is the more remarkable, as unanimity was required in every act of the Tribunes, even after their number was augmented to ten. It proves the irresistible force possessed by that branch of a free government, which has the people on its side.

Carthage:

63:55   To these examples might be added that of Carthage, whose senate, according to the testimony of Polybius, instead of drawing all power into its vortex, had, at the commencement of the second Punic War, lost almost the whole of its original portion.

THE HOUSE WILL SERVE TO REIN IN A CORRUPTED SENATE:

Who is entrusted to keep the Senate under control?

63:56   Besides the conclusive evidence resulting from this assemblage of facts, that the federal Senate will never be able to transform itself, by gradual usurpations, into an independent and aristocratic body, we are warranted in believing, that if such a revolution should ever happen from causes which the foresight of man cannot guard against, the House of Representatives, with the people on their side, will at all times be able to bring back the Constitution to its primitive form and principles. Against the force of the immediate representatives of the people, nothing will be able to maintain even the constitutional authority of the Senate, but such a display of enlightened policy, and attachment to the public good, as will divide with that branch of the legislature the affections and support of the entire body of the people themselves.

—Publius

Review Questions

1. What is the problem that an unstable government has in the eyes of foreign nations? (63:1)

2. What are two reasons why attention to international reputation is important? (63:2–5)

3. Why is the House of Representatives the wrong instrument to set national character? Why is Rhode Island an example of this? (63:6–7)

4. Who coined the word *responsibility*? (63:8 footnote)

5. Responsibility can't be reasonable unless it is limited to what? (63:9–10)

6. What are the two general purposes of government? (63:11)

7. What is the "proper remedy" for unwise laws passed by the House? (63:15–16)

8. What are three reasons the House would call for measures that they would later regret? (63:18)

9. Fill in the blanks: By interfering in the House business, the Senate can effect a necessary delay until _____, _____, and _____ can regain their authority in the public mind. (63:19)

10. Fill in the blanks: Even though Americans are spread over a large land the Senate can still protect them from the _____ of _____ _____. (63:21)

11. Which of the long-lived republics in ancient times had a senate? (63:23)

12. Because the Senate is not elected directly by the people, could it eventually become aristocratic and elitist? (63:39–40)

13. What steps must the Senate take to become aristocratic and elitist? (63:41–42)

14. If the Senate did manage to corrupt itself, who would rein it "back to the Constitution and its primitive form and principles"? (63:56)

FEDERALIST NO. 64

TREATIES BY PRESIDENT AND SENATE: The need for stability in foreign affairs is important for making treaties. Requiring that treaties be approved by both the President and Senate will always involve the country's most able and mature thinkers. The House doesn't have the long-term wisdom and perspective as does the Senate. This process established by the new Constitution prevents any changes being made haphazardly by the House to ratified treaties by simple legislative acts.

By John Jay—March 5, 1788

ANTI-FEDERALISTS TARGET POINTLESS ISSUES:
Critics without a firm argument against issues worthy of blame or criticism often turn to attacking innocuous points.

64:1   IT IS a just and not a new observation, that <u>enemies</u> to particular persons, and opponents to particular measures, <u>seldom confine their censures</u> to such things only in either as are worthy of blame. Unless on this principle, it is difficult to explain the motives of their conduct, who condemn the proposed Constitution in the aggregate, and treat with severity some of the most unexceptionable articles in it.

SENATE MUST RATIFY TREATIES:
Can the President make treaties without the Senate's approval?

64:2   The second section gives power to the President, "BY AND WITH THE <u>ADVICE AND CONSENT OF THE SENATE</u>, TO MAKE TREATIES, PROVIDED TWO THIRDS OF THE SENATORS PRESENT CONCUR."

TREATY MAKING RESERVED TO THE BEST QUALIFIED PEOPLE:

64:3   The power of making treaties is an important one, especially as it relates to <u>war</u>, <u>peace</u>, and <u>commerce</u>; and it should not be delegated but in such a mode, and with such precautions, as will afford the <u>highest security</u> that it will be exercised by men the <u>best qualified</u> for the purpose, and in the manner <u>most conducive</u> to the public good.

INDIRECT ELECTION OF PRESIDENT AND SENATE:
Using indirect processes to elect these leaders is wise. The best minds consider who would make the best leaders.

64:4   <u>The Convention</u> appears to have been attentive to both these points: <u>they have directed the President to be chosen by select bodies of electors, to be deputed by the people for that express purpose</u>; and they have <u>committed</u> the appointment of <u>senators</u> to the State <u>legislatures</u>.

LEGISLATIVE APPOINTMENT MORE SECURE:
Direct election of senators is fraught with party zeal and ignorance.

64:5   This mode has, in such cases, vastly the advantage of elections by the people in their collective capacity, where the <u>activity of party zeal</u>, <u>taking the advantage</u> of the **supineness**,[205] the <u>ignorance</u>, and the hopes and fears of the unwary and interested, often <u>places men in office</u> by the votes of a small proportion of the electors.

MOST QUALIFIED CITIZENS CHOOSE LEADERS:
The electoral college[206] and State legislatures will in general be the most enlightened and respectable citizens.

64:6   As the select assemblies for choosing the President, as well as the State legislatures who appoint the senators, will in general be composed of the <u>most enlightened and respectable citizens</u>, there is reason to presume that <u>their attention</u> and their votes will be directed to those men only who have become the most distinguished by their abilities and virtue, and in whom the people perceive just grounds for confidence.

SELECT ELECTORS ARE KNOWN AND TESTED:
Those who are known among the people as being wise and knowledgeable about politics are less likely to be deceived by manipulators.

64:7   <u>The Constitution</u> manifests very particular attention to this object. By excluding men under thirty-five from the first office, and those under thirty from the second, <u>it confines the electors to men of whom the people have had time to form a</u>

---

205   **supineness:** Negligence, inattentiveness, heedlessness.

206   **electoral college:** The Framers didn't use the term "Electoral College." *College* was used in those days to mean groups of people with a common purpose or duty, but was not attributed to the American election process until decades later. A State choose a number of electors equal to its representatives in the House and Senate. These electors studied the candidates and cast their votes for President. This indirect process was meant to prevent bullying by the large States and avoid the tendency of the mass of voters to vote according to passion instead of reason.

judgment, and with respect to whom they will not be liable to be deceived by those brilliant appearances of genius and patriotism, which, like transient meteors, sometimes mislead as well as dazzle.

ELECTORS AND LEADERS ARE KNOWLEDGEABLE:

Does the system of election and appointment create in the President and the senators leaders of outstanding character and quality?

64:8 If the observation be well founded, that wise kings will always be served by able ministers, it is fair to argue, that as an assembly of select electors possess, in a greater degree than kings, the means of extensive and accurate information relative to men and characters, so will their appointments bear at least equal marks of discretion and discernment.

THE GOAL IS LEADERS WITH GREAT UNDERSTANDING:

64:9 The inference which naturally results from these considerations is this, that the President and senators so chosen will always be of the number of those who best understand our national interests, whether considered in relation to the several States or to foreign nations, who are best able to promote those interests, and whose reputation for integrity inspires and merits confidence. With such men the power of making treaties may be safely lodged.

SENATORS TO BE AMERICA'S MOST SEASONED STATESMEN:

Senators are bound to knowledge and study, unlike the House Representatives, where violent passions can result in misguided and dangerous law.

64:10 Although the absolute necessity of system, in the conduct of any business, is universally known and acknowledged, yet the high importance of it in national affairs has not yet become sufficiently impressed on the public mind. They who wish to commit the power under consideration to a popular assembly, composed of members constantly coming and going in quick succession, seem not to recollect that such a body must necessarily be inadequate to the attainment of those great objects, which require to be steadily contemplated in all their relations and circumstances, and which can only be approached and achieved by measures which not only talents, but also exact information, and often much time, are necessary to concert and to execute.

IMPORTANCE OF SIX-YEAR TERM:

It takes times and experienced to acquire the traits of a good statesman.

64:11 It was wise, therefore, in the Convention to provide, not only that the power of making treaties should be committed to able and honest men, but also that they should continue in place a sufficient time to become perfectly acquainted with our national concerns, and to form and introduce a system for the management of them. The duration prescribed is such as will give them an opportunity of greatly extending their political information, and of rendering their accumulating experience more and more beneficial to their country.

IMPORTANCE OF ROTATING ELECTIONS:

Electing a third of the Senators at each election cycle creates security.

64:12 Nor has the Convention discovered less prudence in providing for the frequent elections of senators in such a way as to obviate the inconvenience of periodically transferring those great affairs entirely to new men; for by leaving a considerable residue of the old ones in place, uniformity and order, as well as a constant succession of official information will be preserved.

SENATE ENSURES CONFORMITY IN TRADE POLICY:

Are the affairs of trade, navigation, treaties, and laws best assigned to the House or to the Senate?

64:13 There are a few who will not admit that the affairs of trade and navigation should be regulated by a system cautiously formed and steadily pursued; and that both our treaties and our laws should correspond with and be made to promote it. It is of much consequence that this correspondence and **conformity**[207] be carefully maintained; and they who assent to the truth of this position will see and confess that it is well provided for by making concurrence of the Senate necessary both to treaties and to laws.

THE PROBLEM OF SECRECY:

Even though the Senate must agree on treaties the President still has the power to negotiate treaties in secret.

64:14 It seldom happens in the negotiation of treaties, of whatever nature, but that perfect SECRECY and immediate DESPATCH are sometimes requisite. These are cases where the most useful intelligence may be obtained, if the persons possessing it can be relieved from apprehensions of discovery. Those apprehensions will operate on those persons whether they are actuated by mercenary or friendly motives; and there doubtless are many of both descriptions, who would rely on the secrecy of the President, but who would not confide in that of the Senate, and still less in that of a large popular Assembly.

---

207 **conformity:** Compliance with standards, laws, and rules.

The constitutional process is a good balance for managing matters of national security while preserving liberty.

64:15   The Convention have done well, therefore, in so disposing of the power of making <u>treaties</u>, that although the <u>President must, in forming them, act by the advice and consent of the Senate</u>, yet he will be able to <u>manage</u> the business of intelligence in such a manner as <u>prudence</u> may suggest.

DEALING WITH FLUCTUATING POLITICAL CLIMATE:

64:16   They who have turned their attention to the affairs of men, must have perceived that there are <u>tides</u> in them; tides very <u>irregular</u> in their duration, strength, and direction, and seldom found to run twice exactly in the same manner or measure.

PRESIDENT MUST BE ABLE TO RESPOND QUICKLY:

In instances where timing is critical, the President can respond in the best interests of America.

64:17   To discern and to profit by these tides in national affairs is the business of those who preside over them; and they who have had much experience on this head inform us, that there frequently are occasions when days, nay, even when hours, are precious. The <u>loss of a battle</u>, the <u>death</u> of a prince, the <u>removal</u> of a minister, or <u>other circumstances</u> intervening to <u>change the present posture</u> and aspect of affairs, may turn the most favorable tide into a course opposite to our wishes.

When crisis demands it, flexibility needs to be present.

64:18   As in the field, so in the cabinet, there are <u>moments to be seized</u> as they pass, and they who <u>preside</u> in either should be <u>left in capacity to improve them</u>.

CONSTITUTION PROVIDES FOR EMERGENCIES:
What about secrecy, things only the President can know?

64:19   So often and so essentially have we heretofore suffered from the want of secrecy and despatch, that the Constitution would have been inexcusably defective, if no attention had been paid to those objects. Those matters which in negotiations usually require the <u>most secrecy</u> and the most <u>despatch</u>, are those preparatory and auxiliary measures which are not otherwise important in a national view, than as they tend to <u>facilitate</u> the attainment of the <u>objects</u> of the negotiation. For these, the President will find no difficulty to provide; and should any circumstance occur which requires the advice and consent of the Senate, he may at any time convene them.

CONSTITUTION PROVIDES ALL ADVANTAGES FOR TREATIES:

64:20   Thus we see that the <u>Constitution provides that our negotiations for treaties shall have every advantage</u> which can be derived from <u>talents, information, integrity, and deliberate investigations, on the one hand</u>, and from <u>secrecy and despatch on the other</u>.

OBJECTIONS TO THIS SYSTEM ARE CONTRIVED:

64:21   But to this plan, as to most others that have ever appeared, objections are contrived and urged.

TREATIES HAVE FORCE OF LAW AS DO JUDGMENTS OF COURTS:

64:22   Some are <u>displeased</u> with it, not on account of any errors or defects in it, but because, as the <u>treaties</u>, when made, are to have the <u>force of laws</u>, they should be <u>made only by men invested with legislative authority</u>. These gentlemen seem not to consider that the <u>judgments</u> of our <u>courts</u>, and the <u>commissions</u> constitutionally given by our <u>governor</u>, are as valid and as <u>binding</u> on all persons whom they concern, as the laws passed by our legislature.

CONGRESS HAS NO SOVEREIGNTY BEYOND WHAT CONSTITUTION GRANTS:
Treaties can't be casually amended like other laws.

64:23   <u>All constitutional acts of power</u>, whether in the executive or in the judicial department, <u>have as much legal validity</u> and obligation as if they proceeded from the legislature; and therefore, whatever name be given to the power of making treaties, or however obligatory they may be when made, certain it is, that the <u>people may</u>, with much propriety, <u>commit the power</u> to a distinct body from the <u>legislature</u>, the <u>executive</u>, <u>or</u> the <u>judicial</u>. It surely <u>does not follow</u>, that because they have given the power of making laws to the <u>legislature</u>, that therefore they should likewise give them the <u>power to do every other act of sovereignty</u> by which the citizens are to be bound and affected.

TREATIES ARE CONTRACTS:
No nations would make contracts with America if these could be easily repealed or amended.

64:24   <u>Others</u>, though <u>content that treaties</u> should be made in the mode proposed, are <u>averse</u> to their being the SUPREME <u>laws</u> of the land. They insist, and profess to believe, that treaties like acts of assembly, should be repealable at pleasure. This idea seems to be new and peculiar to this country, but new errors, as well as new truths, often appear. These gentlemen would do well to reflect that a <u>treaty is only another name for a bargain</u>, and that it would be impossible to find a nation who would make any bargain with us, which should be <u>binding on them</u> ABSOLUTELY, <u>but on us only so long</u> and so far as we may think proper to be bound by it. They who make laws may, without doubt, amend or repeal them; and it will not be disputed that they who make treaties may alter or cancel them; but still let us not forget that treaties are made, not by only one of the contracting parties, but by both; and consequently, that as the consent of both was essential to their formation at first, so must it ever afterwards be to alter or cancel them.

TREATIES ARE SAFE FROM ANY CHANGES ATTEMPTED BY LEGISLATIVE ACTS:

64:25 The proposed Constitution, therefore, has not in the least extended the obligation of treaties. They are just as binding, and just as far beyond the lawful reach of legislative acts now, as they will be at any future period, or under any form of government.

FAVORITISM IN TREATIES IS A FALSE CRITICISM:

There is unfounded fear that treaties could harm some States.

64:26 However useful jealousy may be in republics, yet when like bile in the natural, it abounds too much in the body politic, the eyes of both become very liable to be deceived by the delusive appearances which that malady casts on surrounding objects.

CAN TREATIES BENEFIT SOME PEOPLE BUT NOT OTHERS?

64:27 From this cause, probably, proceed the fears and apprehensions of some, that the President and Senate may make treaties without an equal eye to the interests of all the States. Others suspect that two thirds will oppress the remaining third, and ask whether those gentlemen are made sufficiently responsible for their conduct; whether, if they act corruptly, they can be punished; and if they make disadvantageous treaties, how are we to get rid of those treaties?

TREATIES ARE EQUALLY BINDING ON ALL THE STATES:

The good of the whole depends on advancing the good of the parts.

64:28 As all the States are equally represented in the Senate, and by men the most able and the most willing to promote the interests of their constituents, they will all have an equal degree of influence in that body, especially while they continue to be careful in appointing proper persons, and to insist on their punctual attendance. In proportion as the United States assume a national form and a national character, so will the good of the whole be more and more an object of attention, and the government must be a weak one indeed, if it should forget that the good of the whole can only be promoted by advancing the good of each of the parts or members which compose the whole.

TREATIES IMPACT ELITE AND COMMON PEOPLE THE SAME:

64:29 It will not be in the power of the President and Senate to make any treaties by which they and their families and estates will not be equally bound and affected with the rest of the community; and, having no private interests distinct from that of the nation, they will be under no temptations to neglect the latter.

THE LAW OF NATIONS WILL VOID CORRUPT TREATIES:

If a corrupt treaty did manage to be passed, what would be the remedy?

64:30 As to corruption, the case is not supposable. He must either have been very unfortunate in his intercourse with the world, or possess a heart very susceptible of such impressions, who can think it probable that the President and two thirds of the Senate will ever be capable of such unworthy conduct. The idea is too gross and too invidious to be entertained. But in such a case, if it should ever happen, the treaty so obtained from us would, like all other fraudulent contracts, be null and void by the law of nations.

GOOD CHARACTER ENSURES GOOD TREATIES:

The reason for the careful selection process for the President and senators is to prevent corruption. If that fails, what is the remedy?

64:31 With respect to their responsibility, it is difficult to conceive how it could be increased. Every consideration that can influence the human mind, such as honor, oaths, reputations, conscience, the love of country, and family affections and attachments, afford security for their fidelity. In short, as the Constitution has taken the utmost care that they shall be men of talents and integrity, we have reason to be persuaded that the treaties they make will be as advantageous as, all circumstances considered, could be made; and so far as the fear of punishment and disgrace can operate, that motive to good behavior is amply afforded by the article on the subject of impeachments.

—PUBLIUS

REVIEW QUESTIONS

1. What topic does Jay discuss in No. 64? (64:2)

2. What three crucial qualifications for making treaties must be maintained? (64:3)

3. What caliber of persons does the Constitution direct to select the President, the State legislatures, and the senators? (64:6)

4. Why would treaty making be poorly managed and

executed by the House of Representatives? (64:10)

5. What do longer terms provide to the senators that shorter House terms do not provide the representatives? (64:11)

6. Why is the Senate more stable as an institution than the House? (64:12)

7. Who will best deal with emergencies, a representative body of fluid opinions and positions, or a leader focused on the nation's best interests, supported by seasoned knowledgeable senators? (64:16–18)

8. Are treaties meant to be like regular law that can be changed or rejected by Congress? (64:22–23, 24–25)

9. What are some of the moral influences on the people who make treaties for America? (64:31)

10. Fill in the blanks: Is it reasonable to expect that under the new Constitution that men of _____ and _____ should make treaties for America, that the resulting treaties will be as _____ as possible? (64:31)

FEDERALIST NO. 65

SENATE IS BEST VENUE TO PUT IMPEACHMENTS ON TRIAL: A political institution trying an impeachment is risky, but the Senate is the best and safest venue. It being a political body, however, leaves open the possibility of politically motivated trials and verdicts. While this process is imperfect, it is still necessary, and far better than the provisions outlined in the Articles of Confederation.

By Alexander Hamilton—March 7, 1788

THE JUDICIAL CHARACTER OF THE SENATE:
What power could be called the "judicial character" of the Senate?

65:1 THE remaining powers which the plan of the Convention allots to the Senate, in a distinct capacity, are comprised in their participation with the executive in the appointment to offices, and in their judicial character as a court for the trial of impeachments. As in the business of appointments the executive will be the principal agent, the provisions relating to it will most properly be discussed in the examination of that department. We will, therefore, conclude this head with a view of the judicial character of the Senate.

IMPEACHMENTS ARE VERY DIFFICULT BUT IMPORTANT:
Why are impeachments needed in a wholly-elected government?

65:2 A well-constituted court for the trial of impeachments is an object not more to be desired than difficult to be obtained in a government wholly elective.

IMPEACHMENTS ARE DIVISIVE:
Impeachments are political and partisan events meant to address injury done to the whole country.

65:3 The subjects of its jurisdiction are those offenses which proceed from the misconduct of public men, or, in other words, from the abuse or violation of some public trust. They are of a nature which may with peculiar propriety be denominated POLITICAL, as they relate chiefly to injuries done immediately to the society itself. The prosecution of them, for this reason, will seldom fail to agitate the passions of the whole community, and to divide it into parties more or less friendly or inimical to the accused.

IMPEACHMENT TRIALS ARE SUBJECT TO FACTIONS MORE THAN TRUTH:
The outcome of an impeachment trial is decided more by whichever party is the strongest instead of by actual truth.

65:4 In many cases it will connect itself with the pre-existing factions, and will enlist all their animosities, partialities, influence, and interest on one side or on the other; and in such cases there will always be the greatest danger that the decision will be regulated more by the comparative strength of parties, than by the real demonstrations of innocence or guilt.

LEADERSHIP DEPENDS ON PERSONAL INTEGRITY:
Upon what does America's government rest?

65:5 The delicacy and magnitude of a trust which so deeply concerns the political reputation and existence of every man engaged in the administration of public affairs, speak for themselves.

PURE NEUTRALITY IS IMPOSSIBLE:
65:6 The difficulty of placing it rightly, in a government resting entirely on the basis of periodical elections, will as readily be perceived, when it is considered that the most conspicuous characters in it will, from that circumstance, be too often the leaders or the tools of the most cunning or the most numerous faction, and on this account, can hardly be expected to possess the requisite neutrality towards those whose conduct may be the subject of scrutiny.

SENATE BEST EQUIPPED TO BE METHODICAL:
Which House is least hasty and more inclined to look at the facts?

65:7 The Convention, it appears, thought the Senate the most fit depositary of this important trust. Those who can <u>best discern</u> the intrinsic difficulty of the thing, will be <u>least hasty in condemning</u> that opinion, and will be most inclined to <u>allow due weight</u> to the arguments which may be supposed to have produced it.

THE HOUSE IMPEACHES:

65:8 What, it may be asked, is the true spirit of the institution itself? Is it not designed as a method of <u>NATIONAL INQUEST</u> into the conduct of public men? If this be the design of it, <u>who can so properly be the inquisitors</u> for the nation as the representatives of the nation themselves? It is not disputed that the <u>power of originating</u> the inquiry, or, in other words, of preferring the impeachment, ought to be <u>lodged in the hands of one branch</u> of the legislative body.

THE SENATE TRIES THE IMPEACHMENT:
Whose model did the Framers borrow regarding impeachments?

65:9 Will not the reasons which indicate the propriety of this arrangement strongly plead for an admission of the <u>other branch</u> of that body to a <u>share</u> of the inquiry? The <u>model</u> from which the idea of this institution has been borrowed, pointed out that course to the Convention. In <u>Great Britain</u> it is the province of the <u>House of Commons</u> to prefer the <u>impeachment</u>, and of the <u>House of Lords to decide</u> upon it.

STATES FOLLOW THE SAME IMPEACHMENT PATTERN:

65:10 Several of the <u>State constitutions</u> have <u>followed</u> the example. As well the latter, as the former, seem to have regarded the practice of impeachments as a bridle in the hands of the legislative body upon the executive servants of the government. Is not this the true light in which it ought to be regarded?

SENATE IS BEST JUDGE AND JURY:
What attributes render the Senate the best choice for a more equitable impeachment trial?

65:11 Where else than in the <u>Senate</u> could have been found a tribunal sufficiently <u>dignified</u>, or sufficiently <u>independent</u>? What other body would be likely to feel CONFIDENCE ENOUGH IN ITS OWN SITUATION, to preserve, unawed and uninfluenced, the necessary <u>impartiality</u> between an INDIVIDUAL accused, and the <u>REPRESENTATIVES OF THE PEOPLE, HIS ACCUSERS</u>?

SUPREME COURT NOT SUITED TO TRY IMPEACHMENTS:
What two qualifiers are lacking in the Supreme Court for such a trial?

65:12 Could the <u>Supreme Court</u> have been <u>relied upon</u> as answering this description? It is much to be <u>doubted</u>, whether the members of that tribunal would at all times be <u>endowed</u> with so eminent a portion of **fortitude**,[208] as would be called for in the execution of so difficult a task; and it is still more to be <u>doubted</u>, whether they would possess the <u>degree of credit and authority</u>, which might, on certain occasions, be indispensable towards reconciling the people to a decision that should happen to clash with an accusation brought by their immediate representatives.

SOME REASONS WHY SUPREME COURT IS NOT A GOOD OPTION:

65:13 A deficiency in the first [fortitude], would be fatal to the accused; in the last [credibility], dangerous to the public tranquility. The <u>hazard</u> in both these respects, could only be <u>avoided</u>, if at all, <u>by rendering</u> that tribunal <u>more numerous</u> than would consist with a reasonable attention to economy.

IMPEACHMENT TRIALS ARE DANGEROUS AND COMPLEX:
Impeachment is a political process not a moral process. The Supreme Court would have to be very large to handle an impeachment without bias.

65:14 <u>The necessity of a numerous court</u> for the trial of impeachments, is equally dictated by the nature of the proceeding. This can never be tied down by such strict rules, either in the delineation of the offense by the prosecutors, or in the construction of it by the judges, as in common cases serve to limit the discretion of courts in favor of personal security. There will be <u>no jury</u> to stand between the judges who are to pronounce the sentence of the law, and the party who is to receive or suffer it. <u>The awful discretion</u> which a court of impeachments must necessarily have, <u>to doom to honor or to infamy</u> the most confidential and the most distinguished characters of the community, <u>forbids the commitment of the trust to a small number of persons</u>.

COURT NOT A GOOD SUBSTITUTE FOR SENATE:
65:15 These considerations seem alone sufficient to authorize a conclusion, that the <u>Supreme Court</u> would have been an <u>improper substitute for the Senate</u>, as a court of impeachments.

---

208 **fortitude:** Strength or firmness of mind or soul which enables a person to encounter danger with coolness and courage." Noah Webster, *An American Dictionary of the English Language*, 1828.

THE PROBLEM OF BIASED JUDGES HEARING AN APPEAL:

Supreme Court should not be involved because the impeached person could be charged with other offenses that could be appealed all the way to the Supreme Court.

65:16 There remains a further consideration, which will not a little strengthen this conclusion. It is this: The punishment which may be the consequence of conviction upon impeachment, is not to terminate the chastisement of the offender. After having been sentenced to a perpetual ostracism from the esteem and confidence, and honors and emoluments of his country, he will still be liable to prosecution and punishment in the ordinary course of law.

SAME IMPEACHMENT JUDGES COULD BE IN BOTH A POLITICAL AND A CIVIL TRIAL:

65:17 Would it be proper that the persons who had disposed of his fame, and his most valuable rights as a citizen in one trial, should, in another trial, for the same offense, be also the disposers of his life and his fortune? Would there not be the greatest reason to apprehend, that error, in the first sentence, would be the parent of error in the second sentence? That the strong bias of one decision would be apt to overrule the influence of any new lights which might be brought to vary the complexion of another decision?

DON'T DEPRIVE DEFENDANT OF A FAIR HEARING:

65:18 Those who know anything of human nature, will not hesitate to answer these questions in the affirmative; and will be at no loss to perceive, that by making the same persons judges in both cases, those who might happen to be the objects of prosecution would, in a great measure, be deprived of the double security intended them by a double trial.

65:19 The loss of life and estate would often be virtually included in a sentence which, in its terms, imported nothing more than dismission from a present, and disqualification for a future, office.

A JURY IS EASILY SWAYED BY THE OPINIONS OF JUDGES:

65:20 It may be said, that the intervention of a jury, in the second instance, would obviate the danger. But juries are frequently influenced by the opinions of judges. They are sometimes induced to find special verdicts, which refer the main question to the decision of the court. Who would be willing to stake his life and his estate upon the verdict of a jury acting under the auspices of judges who had predetermined his guilt?

WHAT ABOUT SENATE AND SUPREME COURT TEMPORARILY JOINED AS ONE?

Such a union has the same problem: the accused would be subject to future judgments by the same judges.

65:21 Would it have been an improvement of the plan, to have united the Supreme Court with the Senate, in the formation of the court of impeachments? This union would certainly have been attended with several advantages; but would they not have been overbalanced by the signal disadvantage, already stated, arising from the agency of the same judges in the double prosecution to which the offender would be liable?

COMPROMISE:

Let chief justice preside in Senate hearings.

65:22 To a certain extent, the benefits of that union will be obtained from making the chief justice of the Supreme Court the president of the court of impeachments, as is proposed to be done in the plan of the Convention; while the inconveniences of an entire incorporation of the former into the latter will be substantially avoided. This was perhaps the prudent mean.

65:23 I forbear to remark upon the additional pretext for clamor against the judiciary, which so considerable an augmentation of its authority would have afforded.

A COURT OF OUTSIDERS OR PRIVATE CITIZENS ALSO FAILS:

Why would a court of private or State individuals never work?

65:24 Would it have been desirable to have composed the court for the trial of impeachments, of persons wholly distinct from the other departments of the government? There are weighty arguments, as well against, as in favor of, such a plan. To some minds it will not appear a trivial objection, that it could tend to increase the complexity of the political machine, and to add a new spring to the government, the utility of which would at best be questionable.

OUTSIDERS WOULD BE TOO EXPENSIVE AND RISKY:

Such a body would be an undesired new agency in government.

65:25 But an objection which will not be thought by any unworthy of attention, is this: a court formed upon such a plan, would either be attended with a heavy expense, or might in practice be subject to a variety of casualties and inconveniences. It must either consist of permanent officers, stationary at the seat of government, and of course entitled to fixed and regular stipends, or of certain officers of the State governments to be called upon whenever an impeachment was actually depending.

NO OTHER MODE FOR JUDGING IS FEASIBLE: An enlarged Supreme Court would be rejected by the people.

65:26 It will not be easy to imagine any third mode materially different, which could rationally be proposed. As the court, for reasons already given, ought to be numerous, the first scheme will be **reprobated**[209] by every man who can compare the extent of the public wants with the means of supplying them.

USING OUTSIDERS IS FRAUGHT WITH DANGER: Time delays, corruption, intrigue all work to frustrate justice.

65:27 The second will be espoused with caution by those who will seriously consider the difficulty of collecting men dispersed over the whole Union; the injury to the innocent, from the procrastinated determination of the charges which might be brought against them; the advantage to the guilty, from the opportunities which delay would afford to intrigue and corruption; and in some cases the detriment to the State, from the prolonged inaction of men whose firm and faithful execution of their duty might have exposed them to the persecution of an intemperate or designing majority in the House of Representatives.

FACTIONS CAN CORRUPT ANY POLITICAL PROCESS:

65:28 Though this latter supposition may seem harsh, and might not be likely often to be verified, yet it ought not to be forgotten that the demon of faction will, at certain seasons, extend his sceptre over all numerous bodies of men.

CONSTITUTION IS NOT PERFECT, BUT IT'S VERY CLOSE:

Even if another system for impeachments is found more suitable, this singular point of debate is not enough reason to reject the Constitution.

65:29 But though one or the other of the substitutes which have been examined, or some other that might be devised, should be thought preferable to the plan in this respect, reported by the Convention, it will not follow that the Constitution ought for this reason to be rejected.

PERFECT GOVERNMENT WILL NEVER BE POSSIBLE:

65:30 If mankind were to resolve to agree in no institution of government, until every part of it had been adjusted to the most exact standard of perfection, society would soon become

a general scene of anarchy, and the world a desert. Where is the standard of perfection to be found? Who will undertake to unite the discordant opinions of a whole community, in the same judgment of it; and to prevail upon one conceited projector to renounce his INFALLIBLE criterion for the FALLIBLE criterion of his more CONCEITED NEIGHBOR?

ANTI-FEDERALISTS MUST PROVE CONSTITUTION'S FLAWS:

65:31 To answer the purpose of the adversaries of the Constitution, they ought to prove, not merely that particular provisions in it are not the best which might have been imagined, but that the plan upon the whole is bad and pernicious.

—Publius

Review Questions

1. What are the two examples of the Senate stepping outside of its legislative branch to participate in duties normally reserved to the executive and judicial branches? (65:1)

2. Why are impeachments political in nature, even though there could be criminal or civil violations involved? (65:3)

3. Will impeachments be decided by truth, or by the passions of whichever party is the strongest? (65:4)

4. Why is the Supreme Court the wrong group to stand in judgment of an impeachment trial? (65:12–18)

5. What are some of the alternatives to the Senate being the final judge of an impeachment? (65:20–26)

6. If governments were rejected until every part of it had been adjusted to every contingency, society would soon become a scene of _____ and the world a _____. (65:30)

FEDERALIST NO. 66

SENATE'S ROLE IN IMPEACHMENTS, CONTINUED: This paper addresses four objections by the Anti-Federalists to the Senate's constitutional role in impeachments. First, they allege that the legislative and judicial branches are illegally combined in impeachment proceedings. Second, the Senate has too much power already. Third, the Senate couldn't be impartial to impeached people they earlier had confirmed. Fourth, the senators couldn't judge themselves for impeachable acts they committed.

---

209 *reprobated:* To express or feel disapproval of.

By Alexander Hamilton—March 8, 1788

ADDITIONAL OBJECTIONS TO IMPEACHMENT RULES:

66:1 A REVIEW of the principal objections that have appeared against the proposed court for the trial of impeachments, will not improbably eradicate the remains of any unfavorable impressions which may still exist in regard to this matter.

GIVES JUDICIAL POWERS TO LEGISLATURE:
What is the main objection some people have to the Senate serving as a court over impeachments?

66:2 The FIRST of these objections is, that the provision in question confounds legislative and judiciary authorities in the same body, in violation of that important and well established maxim which requires a separation between the different departments of power.

SHARING A DUTY IS OKAY FOR SPECIAL REASONS:
Separate branches of the government are necessary but some partial mixture is acceptable.

66:3 The true meaning of this maxim has been discussed and ascertained in another place, and has been shown to be entirely compatible with a partial intermixture of those departments for special purposes, preserving them, in the main, distinct and unconnected.

SHARING DUTIES CAN ALSO BE QUITE NECESSARY AT TIMES:

66:4 This partial intermixture is even, in some cases, not only proper but necessary to the mutual defense of the several members of the government against each other. An absolute or qualified negative in the executive upon the acts of the legislative body, is admitted, by the ablest adepts in political science, to be an indispensable barrier against the encroachments of the latter upon the former. And it may, perhaps, with no less reason be contended, that the powers relating to impeachments are, as before intimated, an essential check in the hands of that body upon the encroachments of the executive.

INTERMIXING PREVENTS FACTIOUS SPIRIT:
Giving the Senate some judiciary duties avoids the same people acting as both accusers and judges.

66:5 The division of them between the two branches of the legislature, assigning to one the right of accusing, to the other the right of judging, avoids the inconvenience of making the same persons both accusers and judges; and guards against the danger of persecution, from the prevalency of a factious spirit in either of those branches. As the concurrence of two thirds of the Senate will be requisite to a condemnation, the security to innocence, from this additional circumstance, will be as complete as itself can desire.

NEW YORK ALREADY MIXES GOVERNMENT DUTIES
The mixture of Senate and judicial duties in impeachments already exists in New York but to a much stronger degree.

66:6 It is curious to observe, with what vehemence this part of the plan is assailed, on the principle here taken notice of, by men who profess to admire, without exception, the constitution of this State; while that constitution makes the Senate, together with the chancellor and judges of the Supreme Court, not only a court of impeachments, but the highest judicatory in the State, in all causes, civil and criminal. The proportion, in point of numbers, of the chancellor and judges to the senators, is so inconsiderable, that the judiciary authority of New York, in the last resort, may, with truth, be said to reside in its Senate.

IF THE CONVENTION WAS WRONG THEN SO IS NEW YORK:
Critics who oppose the Constitution but revere their State constitution must look again:

66:7 If the plan of the Convention be, in this respect, chargeable with a departure from the celebrated maxim which has been so often mentioned, and seems to be so little understood, how much more culpable must be the constitution of New York?[210]

DOES MIXING WITH JUDICIAL MAKE SENATE TOO POWERFUL?
Granting the Senate power to try impeachments does not make it too powerful.

66:8 A SECOND objection to the Senate, as a court of impeachments, is, that it contributes to an undue accumulation of power in that body, tending to give to the government a countenance too aristocratic. The Senate, it is observed, is to have concurrent authority with the Executive in the formation of treaties and in the appointment to offices: if, say the objectors, to these prerogatives is added that of deciding in all cases of impeachment, it will give a decided predominancy to senatorial influence. To an objection so little precise in itself, it is not easy to find a very precise answer.

HOW DO WE MEASURE "TOO POWERFUL"?
Such vagueness is better weighed by what powers already exist.

---

210 *Publius:* In that of New Jersey, also, the final judiciary authority is in a branch of the legislature. In New Hampshire, Massachusetts, Pennsylvania, and South Carolina, one branch of the legislature is the court for the trial of impeachments.

66:9 Where is the measure or criterion to which we can appeal, for determining what will give the Senate too much, too little, or barely the proper degree of influence? Will it not be more safe, as well as more simple, to dismiss such vague and uncertain calculations, to examine each power by itself, and to decide, on general principles, where it may be deposited with most advantage and least inconvenience?

SENATE AND EXECUTIVE SHARE DUTIES REGARDING TREATIES:

What two assignments are deemed acceptable for which the Senate and the executive may team up together?

66:10 If we take this course, it will lead to a more intelligible, if not to a more certain result. The disposition of the power of making treaties, which has obtained in the plan of the Convention, will, then, if I mistake not, appear to be fully justified by the considerations stated in a former number, and by others which will occur under the next head of our inquiries.

SENATE AND EXECUTIVE SHARE DUTIES IN APPOINTMENTS:

66:11 The expediency of the junction of the Senate with the Executive, in the power of appointing to offices, will, I trust, be placed in a light not less satisfactory, in the disquisitions under the same head.

THE HOUSE IS BEST FOR IMPEACHING:

Therefore, the Senate really plays a lesser role in that process.

66:12 And I flatter myself the observations in my last paper must have gone no inconsiderable way towards proving that it was not easy, if practicable, to find a more fit receptacle for the power of determining impeachments, than that which has been chosen. If this be truly the case, the hypothetical dread of the too great weight of the Senate ought to be discarded from our reasonings.

THE HOUSE IS THE STRONGEST BODY IN GOVERNMENT:

Which part of Congress is already strong enough?

66:13 But this hypothesis, such as it is, has already been refuted in the remarks applied to the duration in office prescribed for the senators. It was by them shown, as well on the credit of historical examples, as from the reason of the thing, that the most POPULAR branch of every government, partaking of the republican genius, by being generally the favorite of the people, will be as generally a full match, if not an overmatch, for every other member of the Government.

HOUSE DUTIES OUTWEIGH SENATE DUTIES:

What three important tasks are assigned to the House?

66:14 But independent of this most active and operative principle, to secure the equilibrium of the national House of Representatives, the plan of the Convention has provided in its favor several important counterpoises to the additional authorities to be conferred upon the Senate.

Money bills.

66:15 The exclusive privilege of originating money bills will belong to the House of Representatives.

Impeachments.

66:16 The same house will possess the sole right of instituting impeachments: is not this a complete counterbalance to that of determining them?

Elections.

66:17 The same house will be the umpire in all elections of the President, which do not unite the suffrages of a majority of the whole number of electors; a case which it cannot be doubted will sometimes, if not frequently, happen. The constant possibility of the thing must be a fruitful source of influence to that body. The more it is contemplated, the more important will appear this ultimate though contingent power, of deciding the competitions of the most illustrious citizens of the Union, for the first office in it. It would not perhaps be rash to predict, that as a mean of influence it will be found to outweigh all the peculiar attributes of the Senate.

CRITICS WARN THAT SENATE WOULD BE LENIENT:

Would the Senate go easy on a person it had previously approved for high office?

66:18 A THIRD objection to the Senate as a court of impeachments, is drawn from the agency they are to have in the appointments to office. It is imagined that they would be too indulgent judges of the conduct of men, in whose official creation they had participated. The principle of this objection would condemn a practice, which is to be seen in all the State governments, if not in all the governments with which we are acquainted: I mean that of rendering those who hold offices during pleasure, dependent on the pleasure of those who appoint them. With equal plausibility might it be alleged in this case, that the favoritism of the latter would always be an asylum for the misbehavior of the former.

SENATE REMAINS JEALOUS OF ITS OFFICIAL DUTIES:

Appointees are trusted to fulfill their oaths and are watched for any violations of that trust. Expeditious removal would be fair.

66:19 But that practice, in contradiction to this principle, proceeds upon the presumption, that the responsibility of those who appoint, for the fitness and competency of the persons on whom they bestow their choice, and the interest they will have in the respectable and prosperous administration of affairs, will inspire a sufficient disposition to dismiss from a share in it all such who, by their conduct, shall have proved themselves unworthy of the confidence reposed in them.

SENATE WON'T IGNORE A PERSON'S GUILT:

The Senate would not allow a person who attracted the impeachment attention of the House to get by without a closer look.

66:20 Though facts may not always correspond with this presumption, yet if it be, in the main, just, it must destroy the supposition that the Senate, who will merely sanction the choice of the Executive, should feel a bias, towards the objects of that choice, strong enough to blind them to the evidences of guilt so extraordinary, as to have induced the representatives of the nation to become its accusers.

SENATE'S ROLE IN APPOINTMENTS:

66:21 If any further arguments were necessary to evince the improbability of such a bias, it might be found in the nature of the agency of the Senate in the business of appointments.

SENATE CAN'T APPOINT, ONLY RATIFY:

When it comes to presidential nominations to office, may the Senate make or demand their own choice? What is the most they can do?

66:22 It will be the office of the President to NOMINATE, and, with the advice and consent of the Senate, to APPOINT. There will, of course, be no exertion of CHOICE on the part of the Senate. They may defeat one choice of the Executive, and oblige him to make another; but they cannot themselves CHOOSE, they can only ratify or reject the choice of the President.

SENATE TRYING TO IMPOSE THEIR PREFERENCE IS RISKY:

If the Senate voted a nominee down to promote their own choice they could never be sure their preferred person would be appointed.

66:23 They might even entertain a preference to some other person, at the very moment they were assenting to the one proposed, because there might be no positive ground of opposition to him; and they could not be sure, if they withheld their assent, that the subsequent nomination would fall upon their own favorite, or upon any other person in their estimation more meritorious than the one rejected.

SENATE IS RESIGNED TO HAVING LITTLE INFLUENCE:

66:24 Thus it could hardly happen, that the majority of the Senate would feel any other complacency towards the object of an appointment than such as the appearances of merit might inspire, and the proofs of the want of it destroy.

MAKING CORRUPT TREATIES:

If the Senate passed a corrupt treaty and they were caught, is there a chance they would be their own judges in an impeachment trial?

66:25 A FOURTH objection to the Senate in the capacity of a court of impeachments, is derived from its union with the Executive in the power of making treaties. This, it has been said, would constitute the senators their own judges, in every case of a corrupt or perfidious execution of that trust. After having combined with the Executive in betraying the interests of the nation in a ruinous treaty, what prospect, it is asked, would there be of their being made to suffer the punishment they would deserve, when they were themselves to decide upon the accusation brought against them for the treachery of which they have been guilty?

SENATE JUDGING ITS OWN CORRUPTION:

Critics claiming an impeachable Senate could be in a position to judge itself builds the accusation on a false foundation.

66:26 This objection has been circulated with more earnestness and with greater show of reason than any other which has appeared against this part of the plan; and yet I am deceived if it does not rest upon an erroneous foundation.

STATE LEGISLATURES ARE GUARDIANS:

What is the built-in protection against corruption in treaties and appointments to office? (Note: The Seventeenth Amendment removed this check.)

66:27 The security essentially intended by the Constitution against corruption and treachery in the formation of treaties, is to be sought for in the numbers and characters of those who are to make them. The JOINT AGENCY of the Chief Magistrate of the Union, and of two thirds of the members of a body selected by the collective wisdom of the legislatures of the several States, is designed to be the pledge for the fidelity of the national councils in this particular.

HOW COULD A CORRUPT CONGRESS IMPEACH ITSELF?

66:28 The Convention might with propriety have meditated the punishment of the Executive, for a deviation from the instructions of the Senate, or a want of integrity in the conduct of the negotiations committed to him; they might also have had in view the punishment of a few leading individuals in the Senate, who should have prostituted their influence in that body as the mercenary instruments of foreign corruption: but they could not, with more or with equal propriety, have contemplated the impeachment and punishment of two thirds of the Senate, consenting to an improper treaty, than of a majority of that or of the other branch of the national legislature, consenting to a pernicious or unconstitutional law, a principle which, I believe, has never been admitted into any government. How, in fact, could a majority in the House of Representatives impeach themselves?

CORRUPTION IS GUARDED AGAINST:

Chances of two thirds of Senate acting illegally is as unlikely as two thirds of the House acting illegally and impeaching themselves.

66:29 Not better, it is evident, than two thirds of the Senate might try themselves. And yet what reason is there, that a majority of the House of Representatives, sacrificing the interests of the society by an unjust and tyrannical act of legislation, should escape with impunity, more than two thirds of the Senate, sacrificing the same interests in an injurious treaty with a foreign power?

CONFIDING TRUST TO PROPER HANDS IS IMPORTANT:

Whose job is it to ensure only the best are elected to these important places of judgment?

66:30 The truth is, that in all such cases it is essential to the freedom and to the necessary independence of the deliberations of the body, that the members of it should be exempt from punishment for acts done in a collective capacity; and the security to the society must depend on the care which is taken to confide the trust to proper hands, to make it their interest to execute it with fidelity, and to make it as difficult as possible for them to combine in any interest opposite to that of the public good.

HUMAN NATURE WILL INFLAME SENATE'S PRIDE:

The executive cannot casually contravene the Senate.

66:31 So far as might concern the misbehavior of the Executive in perverting the instructions or contravening the views of the Senate, we need not be apprehensive of the want of a disposition in that body to punish the abuse of their confidence or to vindicate their own authority. We may thus far count upon their pride, if not upon their virtue.

SENATE WILL PUT BLAME WHERE IT IS DESERVED:

66:32 And so far even as might concern the corruption of leading members, by whose arts and influence the majority may have been inveigled into measures odious to the commu-

nity, if the proofs of that corruption should be satisfactory, the usual propensity of human nature will warrant us in concluding that there would be commonly no defect of inclination in the body to divert the public resentment from themselves by a ready sacrifice of the authors of their mismanagement and disgrace.

—PUBLIUS

REVIEW QUESTIONS

1. When the Senate convenes to sit in judgment of an impeachment, what great maxim do critics say it violates? (66:2)

2. Is partial intermixing of the three branches of government proper and permissible in certain situations, such as impeachments? (66:3)

3. What are the two places where the Senate and the President must work together? (66:10–11)

4. What are the three main duties of the House of Representatives? (66:14–17)

5. Despite the Senate's connection to the Executive, will it ignore a person's guilt? (66:20)

6. If the President misbehaves, the people can still count on the Senate's _____, if not its _____ to take action. (66:31)

SECTION 10 • EXECUTIVE BRANCH

Papers 67–77

FEDERALIST NO. 67

PRESIDENT'S POWER TO FILL SENATE VACANCIES: The President does not have power to fill vacancies in the Senate or exercise kingly powers to build the executive branch. The Anti-Federalists published extraordinary deceptions to play on the fears of the people who worried that a new king might rise through the unguarded labyrinth of the Constitution.

By Alexander Hamilton—March 11, 1788

WEAK ARGUMENTS AGAINST THE EXECUTIVE:

67:1 THE constitution of the executive department of the proposed government, claims next our attention.

The office of President was heavily examined by the Convention.

67:2 There is hardly any part of the system which could have been attended with greater difficulty in the arrangement of it than this; and there is, perhaps, none which has been inveighed against with less candor or criticised with less judgment.

CRITICS INFLATE OFFICE OF THE PRESIDENT INTO A NEW MONARCHY:

67:3 Here the writers against the Constitution seem to have taken pains to signalize their talent of misrepresentation. Calculating upon the aversion of the people to monarchy, they have endeavored to enlist all their jealousies and apprehensions in opposition to the intended President of the United States; not merely as the embryo, but as the full-grown progeny, of that detested parent. To establish the pretended affinity, they have not scrupled to draw resources even from the regions of fiction.

What does Hamilton accuse the skeptical New Yorkers of permitting while putting on airs of shock over the office of a President?

67:4 The authorities of a magistrate, in few instances greater, in some instances less, than those of a governor of New York, have been magnified into more than royal prerogatives. He has been decorated with attributes superior in dignity and splendor to those of a king of Great Britain. He has been shown to us with the diadem sparkling on his brow and the imperial purple flowing[211] in his train. He has been seated on a throne surrounded with minions and mistresses, giving audience to the envoys of foreign potentates, in all the supercilious pomp of majesty. The images of Asiatic despotism and voluptuousness have scarcely been wanting to crown the exaggerated scene. We have been taught to tremble at the terrific visages of murdering **janizaries**,[212] and to blush at the unveiled mysteries of a future **seraglio**.

ANTI-FEDERALISTS USE EXTREME DECEPTIONS:

According to Hamilton, what needs to be unmasked?

67:5 Attempts so extravagant as these to disfigure or, it might rather be said, to metamorphose the object, render it necessary to take an accurate view of its real nature and form: in order as well to ascertain its true aspect and genuine appearance, as to unmask the disingenuity and expose the fallacy of the counterfeit resemblances which have been so insidiously, as well as industriously, propagated.

HARD TO TAKE EXTREME CRITICISMS SERIOUSLY:

67:6 In the execution of this task, there is no man who would not find it an arduous effort either to behold with moderation, or to treat with seriousness, the devices, not less weak than wicked, which have been contrived to pervert the public opinion in relation to the subject.

---

211 *Editors' Note:* Hamilton saves some of his sharpest mockery for the New York governor.
212 **Janizaries** were the Sultan's personal guard in medieval Turkey. A **seraglio** was the place where the wives and concubines resided in a harem.

Even those who typically support the critics are indignant.

67:7   They so far exceed the usual though unjustifiable licenses of party artifice, that even in a disposition the most candid and tolerant, they must force the sentiments which favor an indulgent construction of the conduct of political adversaries to give place to a voluntary and unreserved indignation.

What do detractors labor over to make a negative comparison?

67:8   It is impossible not to bestow the imputation of deliberate imposture and deception upon the gross pretense of a similitude between a king of Great Britain and a magistrate of the character marked out for that of the President of the United States. It is still more impossible to withhold that imputation from the rash and barefaced expedients which have been employed to give success to the attempted imposition.

PRESIDENT CANNOT FILL SENATE VACANCIES:
What Executive power do the critics condemn, yet the same power also exists in their very own State?

67:9   In one instance, which I cite as a sample of the general spirit, the **temerity**[213] has proceeded so far as to ascribe to the President of the United States a power which by the instrument reported is EXPRESSLY allotted to the Executives of the individual States. I mean the power of filling casual vacancies in the Senate.

FALSE PREMISE TO JUSTIFY FALSE CONCLUSION:
What does Hamilton now challenge the critics to do?

67:10   This bold experiment upon the discernment of his countrymen has been hazarded by a writer[214] who (whatever may be his real merit) has had no inconsiderable share in the applauses of his party; and who, upon this false and unfounded suggestion, has built a series of observations equally false and unfounded. Let him now be confronted with the evidence of the fact, and let him, if he be able, justify or extenuate the shameful outrage he has offered to the dictates of truth and to the rules of fair dealing.

PRESIDENT APPOINTS ALL OFFICERS NOT SPECIFIED:

67:11   The second clause of the second section of the second article empowers the President of the United States "to nominate, and by and with the advice and consent of the Senate, to appoint ambassadors, other public ministers and consuls, judges of the Supreme Court, and all other OFFICERS of United States whose appointments are NOT in the Constitution OTHERWISE PROVIDED FOR, and WHICH SHALL BE ESTABLISHED BY LAW" [Art. II, Sec. 2, Clause 2].

PRESIDENT FILLS VACANCIES IN SENATE RECESS:
Does this include vacancies in the Senate?

67:12   Immediately after this clause follows another in these words: "The President shall have power to fill up all VACANCIES that may happen DURING THE RECESS OF THE SENATE, by granting commissions which shall EXPIRE AT THE END OF THEIR NEXT SESSION" [Art. II, Sec. 2, Clause 3]. It is from this last provision that the pretended power of the President to fill vacancies in the Senate has been deduced. A slight attention to the connection of the clauses, and to the obvious meaning of the terms, will satisfy us that the deduction is not even **colorable**.[215]

PRESIDENT AND NON-CONSTITUTIONAL OFFICERS:
What class of federal officers may the President appoint?

67:13   The first of these two clauses, it is clear, only provides a mode for appointing such officers, "whose appointments are NOT OTHERWISE PROVIDED FOR in the Constitution, and which SHALL BE ESTABLISHED BY LAW"; of course it cannot extend to the appointments of senators, whose appointments are OTHERWISE PROVIDED FOR in the Constitution,[216] and who are ESTABLISHED BY THE CONSTITUTION, and will not require a future establishment by law. This position will hardly be contested.

PRESIDENT CAN'T APPOINT SENATORS:
Four reasons listed (see 67:15-19).

67:14   The last of these two clauses, it is equally clear, cannot be understood to comprehend the power of filling vacancies in the Senate, for the following reasons:

PRESIDENT AND SENATE ACT JOINTLY:
If the Senate and President must act jointly, how could the President "act jointly" if the Senate is in recess?

67:15   First. The relation in which that clause stands to the other, which declares the general mode of appointing officers of the United States, denotes it to be nothing more than a supplement to the other, for the purpose of establishing an auxiliary method of appointment, in cases to which the general method was inadequate. The ordinary power of appointment is confined to the President and Senate JOINTLY, and can therefore only be exercised during the session of the Senate;

---

213   *temerity:* Audacity, excessive confidence or boldness.
214   *Publius:* See CATO, No. V [an Anti-Federalist, probably New York Governor George Clinton].
215   *colorable:* Plausible; giving the appearance of being right.
216   *Publius:* Article I, section 3, clause I.

but as it would have been <u>improper</u> to oblige this body <u>to be continually in session</u> for the appointment of officers and as vacancies might happen IN THEIR RECESS, which it might be necessary for the public service to fill without delay, the succeeding clause is evidently intended to authorize the President, SINGLY, to make <u>temporary appointments</u> "during the recess of the Senate, by granting commissions which shall expire at the end of their next session."

SENATORS ARE NOT OFFICERS:

The word *vacancies* must be construed according to the prior clause. That construction excludes senators.

67:16   <u>Secondly</u>. If this clause is to be considered as supplementary to the one which precedes, the <u>VACANCIES</u> of which it speaks must be <u>construed</u> to relate to the "<u>officers</u>" described in the preceding one; and this, we have seen, <u>excludes</u> from its description the members of the <u>Senate</u>.

FEDERAL SESSION NOT SAME AS STATE SESSION:

If appointments last until the end of the next session, how could the President appoint a senator without stipulating a State legislature's session? They are all different. Does "recess of the Senate" and "end of the next session" refer to the States or federal Senate?

67:17   <u>Thirdly</u>. The time within which the power is to operate, "<u>during the recess of the Senate</u>," and the duration of the appointments, "to the <u>end of the next session</u>" of that body, conspire to elucidate the sense of the provision, which, if it had been intended to comprehend senators, would naturally have <u>referred</u> the temporary power of filling vacancies to the <u>recess of the State legislatures</u>, who are to make the permanent appointments, and <u>not</u> to the recess of the <u>national Senate</u>, who are to have no concern in those appointments; and would have <u>extended</u> the duration in office of the temporary senators to the <u>next session</u> of the <u>legislature of the State</u>, in whose representation the vacancies had happened, instead of making it to expire at the end of the ensuing session of the national Senate. The circumstances of the <u>body authorized</u> to make the permanent appointments would, of course, have <u>governed the modification</u> of a power which related to the temporary appointments; and as the national Senate is the body, whose situation is alone contemplated in the clause upon which the suggestion under examination has been founded, the <u>vacancies</u> to which it <u>alludes</u> can only be deemed to respect those officers in whose appointment <u>that body</u> has a <u>concurrent agency with the President</u>.

STATE LEGISLATURE FILLS VACANCIES IN SENATE:

If the State legislature is in recess, the duty to fill a vacancy in that State's pair of senators falls to the governor of that State.

67:18   <u>But lastly</u>, the first and second clauses of the third section of the first article, not only obviate all possibility of doubt, but destroy the pretext of misconception. The former provides, that "the Senate of the United States shall be <u>composed of two Senators</u> from each State, <u>chosen BY THE LEGISLATURE THEREOF for six years</u>"; and the latter directs, that, "if vacancies in that body should happen by resignation or otherwise, DURING THE <u>RECESS</u> OF THE <u>LEGISLATURE</u> OF ANY <u>STATE</u>, the <u>Executive THEREOF</u> may make temporary appointments until the NEXT MEETING OF THE LEGISLATURE, which shall then fill such vacancies." [See Const. Art. I, Sec. 3]

State executives have the clear and unambiguous power to make temporary appointments.

67:19   Here is an <u>express power given</u>, in clear and unambiguous terms, to the <u>State Executives</u>, to <u>fill casual vacancies in the Senate</u>, by temporary appointments; which not only <u>invalidates</u> the supposition, that the clause before considered could have been intended to confer that <u>power</u> upon the <u>President</u> of the United States, but proves that this supposition, destitute as it is even of the merit of plausibility, must have <u>originated in an intention to deceive the people</u>, too palpable to be obscured by sophistry, too atrocious to be palliated by hypocrisy.

ANTI-FEDERALISTS ARE UNDERHANDED, DECEITFUL:

For what reason does Hamilton want to use this example of lies and distortion regarding filling vacancies?

67:20   I have taken the <u>pains</u> to select this instance of <u>misrepresentation</u>, and to place it in a clear and strong light, as an unequivocal proof of the <u>unwarrantable arts</u> which are practiced to <u>prevent</u> a <u>fair</u> and <u>impartial judgment</u> of the real merits of the <u>Constitution</u> submitted to the consideration of the people. Nor have I scrupled, in so flagrant a case, to allow myself a severity of **animadversion**[217] little congenial with the general spirit of these papers. I hesitate not to submit it to the decision of any candid and honest adversary of the proposed government, whether <u>language can furnish epithets</u> of too much asperity, <u>for so shameless</u> and so prostitute an <u>attempt to impose</u> on the citizens of America.

—PUBLIUS

---

217   ***animadversion:*** A comment or remark that criticizes or places blame.

REVIEW QUESTIONS

1. At the beginning of No. 67, what does Hamilton accuse the Anti-Federalists of doing to distort the role of the executive? (67:1–4)

2. After so much colorful vitriol leveled against the Anti-Federalists' deep dive into blatant lies, what is the lie that Hamilton highlights here? (67:9)

3. Does the President have to power to appoint officers in the federal government? (67:13; Art. II, Sec. 2, Clause 2)

4. Whose consent must the President have to appoint ambassadors, public ministers, consuls, Supreme Court justices, and so forth? (67:11)

5. If the Senate is in recess and a vacancy occurs that must be filled, can the President fill those vacancies? (67:12)

6. Can the President fill a vacancy if there already exists another means in the Constitution for the vacancy to be filled? (67:13)

7. From which phrase in the Constitution do the critics allege the President is given power to fill a vacancy in the Senate during a recess? Explain. (67:12)

8. Who appoints the Senators in the first place? (67:18)

9. If the State legislature is in recess, who has the constitutional power to fill a vacancy in the Senate? 67:18)

10. In conclusion, if the Senate's consent is required to make an appointment and the Senate is in recess, and there exists the means to fill that senate vacancy, could the President in any way, shape or form ever be in a position of appointing a senator? (67:18-19)

FEDERALIST NO. 68

T HE ELECTORAL SYSTEM IS SUPERIOR TO DIRECT ELECTIONS: The genius of the system for electing the President protects America from mob rule. In a democracy where the popular vote always prevails, the majority decides everything, the minority is always defeated. Such mob rule could put into office an incompetent or conspiring man whose interests could be to silence all opposition and undermine the Constitution. This system worked for its intended fairness until some of the States started to compel electoral voters to abide by the outcome of popular State vote.

By Alexander Hamilton—March 12, 1788

218 *Publius:* Vide FEDERAL FARMER

APPOINTING PRESIDENT IS BALANCED AND SECURE:
Has the Electoral College been subjected to deep criticism?

68:1 THE mode of appointment of the Chief Magistrate of the United States is almost the only part of the system, of any consequence, which has escaped without severe censure, or which has received the slightest mark of approbation from its opponents. The most plausible of these, who has appeared in print, has even deigned to admit that the election of the President is pretty well guarded.[218] I venture somewhat further, and hesitate not to affirm, that if the manner of it be not perfect, it is at least excellent. It unites in an eminent degree all the advantages, the union of which was to be wished for.

PEOPLE HAVE RIGHT TO CHOOSE ELECTORS:
Are electors tasked with carrying forward a sacred trust? How are they different from other elected officers?

68:2 It was desirable that the sense of the people should operate in the choice of the person to whom so important a trust was to be confided. This end will be answered by committing the right of making it, not to any preestablished body, but to men chosen by the people for the special purpose, and at the particular conjuncture.

ELECTORS SHOULD BE GOOD INVESTIGATORS:
As the people's direct representatives, what good attributes should the electors exhibit to properly and fairly fulfill their assignment?

68:3 It was equally desirable, that the immediate election should be made by men most capable of analyzing the qualities adapted to the station, and acting under circumstances favorable to deliberation, and to a judicious combination of all the reasons and inducements which were proper to govern their choice. A small number of persons, selected by their fellow-citizens from the general mass, will be most likely to possess the information and discernment requisite to such complicated investigations.

SEVERAL ELECTORS BETTER THAN ONE:
With many possible electors to select from in each State, and then casting their votes at their home State, the partisan tumult and disorder of a single gathering is avoided.

68:4 It was also peculiarly desirable to afford as little opportunity as possible to tumult and disorder. This evil was not least to be dreaded in the election of a magistrate, who was to have so important an agency in the administration of the government as the President of the United States. But the precautions which have been so happily concerted in the system under consideration, promise an effectual security against this mischief. The choice of SEVERAL, to form an intermediate body of electors, will be much less apt to convulse the community with any extraordinary or violent movements, than the choice of ONE who was himself to be the final object of the public wishes. And as the electors, chosen in each State, are to assemble and vote in the State in which they are chosen, this detached and divided situation will expose them much less to heats and ferments, which might be communicated from them to the people, than if they were all to be convened at one time, in one place.

FOREIGN INFLUENCE IS POSSIBLE IN THE REPUBLIC:

What are the three deadly adversaries of republic government?

68:5 Nothing was more to be desired than that every practicable obstacle should be opposed to [1.] cabal, [2.] intrigue, and [3.] corruption. These most deadly adversaries of republican government might naturally have been expected to make their approaches from more than one quarter, but chiefly from the desire in foreign powers to gain an improper ascendant in our councils. How could they better gratify this, than by raising a creature of their own to the chief magistracy of the Union?

ELECTORAL SYSTEM THWARTS FOREIGN INFLUENCE:

Preexisting bodies of elected officers are susceptible to foreign influence. Making the President appointed by the people's electors is more secure.

68:6   But the Convention have guarded against all danger of this sort, with the most provident and judicious attention. They have not made the appointment of the President to depend on any preexisting bodies of men, who might be tampered with beforehand to prostitute their votes; but they have referred it in the first instance to an immediate act of the people of America, to be exerted in the choice of persons for the temporary and sole purpose of making the appointment.

REQUIREMENTS TO BE AN ELECTOR:

What is the advantage of not allowing an elected office holder to be an elector?

68:7   And they have excluded from eligibility to this trust, all those who from situation might be suspected of too great devotion to the President in office. No senator, representative, or other person holding a place of trust or profit under the United States, can be of the numbers of the electors. Thus without corrupting the body of the people, the immediate agents in the election will at least enter upon the task free from any sinister bias. Their transient existence, and their detached situation, already taken notice of, afford a satisfactory prospect of their continuing so, to the conclusion of it. The

business of corruption, when it is to embrace so considerable a number of men, requires time as well as means.

CONSPIRACIES MORE DIFFICULT IN A LARGE NATION:

68:8   Nor would it be found easy suddenly to embark them, dispersed as they would be over thirteen States, in any combinations founded upon motives, which though they could not properly be denominated corrupt, might yet be of a nature to mislead them from their duty.

PRESIDENT IS INDEPENDENT FROM ALL BUT THE PEOPLE:

Why is it good for the President's reelection to be separated from a popular vote by the people? Might it otherwise become a popularity contest?

68:9   Another and no less important desideratum was, that the Executive should be independent for his continuance in office on all but the people themselves. He might otherwise be tempted to sacrifice his duty to his complaisance for those whose favor was necessary to the duration of his official consequence. This advantage will also be secured, by making his re-election to depend on a special body of representatives, deputed by the society for the single purpose of making the important choice.

ELECTORAL PROCESS EXPLAINED:

68:10   All these advantages will happily combine in the plan devised by the Convention; which is, that the people of each State shall choose a number of persons as electors, equal to the number of senators and representatives of such State in the national government, who shall assemble within the State, and vote for some fit person as President. Their votes, thus given, are to be transmitted to the seat of the national government, and the person who may happen to have a majority of the whole number of votes will be the President.

If the leading candidate doesn't have a majority who decides the winner?

68:11   But as a majority of the votes might not always happen to centre in one man, and as it might be unsafe to permit less than a majority to be conclusive, it is provided that, in such a contingency, the House of Representatives shall select out of the candidates who shall have the five highest number of votes, the man who in their opinion may be best qualified for the office.

PRESIDENT MUST APPEAL TO MAJORITY:

What positive traits in a President does this new electoral system promote? What is the test of good government?

68:12   This process of election affords a moral certainty, that the office of President will never fall to the lot of any man who is not in an eminent degree endowed with the requisite qualifications.

Qualifications that carry a popular man into winning local office won't mean as much when trying to win national support.

68:13   Talents for low intrigue, and the little arts of popularity, may alone suffice to elevate a man to the first honors in a single State; but it will require other talents, and a different kind of merit, to establish him in the esteem and confidence of the whole Union, or of so considerable a portion of it as would be necessary to make him a successful candidate for the distinguished office of President of the United States. It will not be too strong to say, that there will be a constant probability of seeing the station filled by characters pre-eminent for ability and virtue.

This solution should convince people who worry a new monarch is being created, that the Constitution's solution is elegant.

68:14   And this will be thought no inconsiderable recommendation of the Constitution, by those who are able to estimate the share which the executive in every government must necessarily have in its good or ill administration.

WHAT IS A TEST OF GOOD GOVERNMENT?

68:15   Though we cannot acquiesce in the political heresy of the poet who says:

"For forms of government let fools contest
That which is best administered is best,"

yet we may safely pronounce, that the true test of a good government is its aptitude and tendency to produce a good administration.

CONCERNING THE VICE PRESIDENT:

The issues discussed by Hamilton in this part of his paper were resolved by the Twelfth Amendment, ratified in 1804.

68:16   The Vice-President is to be chosen in the same manner with the President; with this difference, that the Senate is to do, in respect to the former, what is to be done by the House of Representatives, in respect to the latter.

SENATE APPOINTMENT OF VICE PRESIDENT:

It was suggested the Senate choose from among its body a person to be Vice President. This is a bad idea for two reasons.

68:17   The appointment of an extraordinary person, as Vice-President, has been objected to as superfluous, if not mischievous. It has been alleged, that it would have been preferable to have authorized the Senate to elect out of their own body an officer answering that description. But two consid-

erations seem to justify the ideas of the Convention in this respect.

ROLE OF VICE PRESIDENT IN THE SENATE:

The Vice President acts as president of the Senate with only one purpose, to cast a tie-breaking vote should a tie occur. To put a senator in this position as president of the Senate would ensure that his tie-breaking vote would always be biased in favor of his State.

68:18   One is, that to secure at all times the possibility of a definite resolution of the body, it is necessary that the President should have only a casting vote. And to take the senator of any State from his seat as senator, to place him in that of President of the Senate, would be to exchange, in regard to the State from which he came, a constant for a contingent vote.

VICE PRESIDENT MIGHT SUBSTITUTE AS PRESIDENT:

Because the Vice President could serve as President all of the same precautions to select the best person should be used, rather than leave it up to the senators to make the choice.

68:19   The other consideration is, that as the Vice-President may occasionally become a substitute for the President, in the supreme executive magistracy, all the reasons which recommend the mode of election prescribed for the one, apply with great if not with equal force to the manner of appointing the other.

New York critics can't complain about this process because it already exists in New York's constitution.

68:20   It is remarkable that in this, as in most other instances, the objection which is made would lie against the constitution of this State. We have a Lieutenant-Governor, chosen by the people at large, who presides in the Senate, and is the constitutional substitute for the Governor, in casualties similar to those which would authorize the Vice-President to exercise the authorities and discharge the duties of the President.

—PUBLIUS

REVIEW QUESTIONS

1.   What topic does Hamilton address in paper No. 68? (68:1)

2.   What are some attributes of members of the electoral college? (68:2–3)

3.   Why is it important for electors to cast their votes in their home States? (68:4)

4.   Why are politicians not allowed to be electors? (68:5–7)

5.   How does this electoral college process eliminate presiden-

tial candidates of weak qualifications? (68:13)

6. Which amendment resolves the processes and potential difficulties discussed in paragraphs 68:16–20? (68:16)

FEDERALIST NO. 69

THE EXECUTIVE BRANCH IS NOT A MONARCHY: Comparing the office of the President to Britain's king or New York's governor demonstrates how the President can be energetic, effective and sufficiently powerful by being dependent on others in government and under control of the people. This can be seen in his veto power that Congress can reverse, his reliance on the Senate for treaties and appointments, in his position as commander in chief, and in regards to commerce and currency. In short, the President has fewer powers than the Governor of New York.

By Alexander Hamilton—March 14, 1788

COMPARING AMERICA'S EXECUTIVE TO BRITAIN'S:

69:1 I PROCEED now to trace the real characters of the proposed Executive, as they are marked out in the plan of the Convention. This will serve to place in a strong light the unfairness of the representations which have been made in regard to it.

PRESIDENT COMPARED TO KINGS:
Beyond the fact that it's one person, the President doesn't resemble kings at all.

69:2 The first thing which strikes our attention is, that the executive authority, with few exceptions, is to be vested in a single magistrate. This will scarcely, however, be considered as a point upon which any comparison can be grounded; for if, in this particular, there be a resemblance to the king of Great Britain, there is not less a resemblance to the Grand Seignior, to the khan of Tartary, to the Man of the Seven Mountains, or to the governor of New York.

DURATION OF PRESIDENTIAL TERM IS ANOTHER SECURITY:
How long is the President's term? How long for the British king?

69:3 That magistrate is to be elected for FOUR years; and is to be re-eligible as often as the people of the United States shall think him worthy of their confidence. In these circumstances there is a total dissimilitude between HIM and a king of Great Britain, who is an HEREDITARY monarch, possessing the crown as a patrimony descendible to his heirs forever; but there is a close analogy between HIM and a governor of New York, who is elected for THREE years, and is re-eligible without limitation or intermission. If we consider how much less time would be requisite for establishing a dangerous influence in a single State, than for establishing a like influence throughout the United States, we must conclude that a duration of FOUR years for the Chief Magistrate of the Union is a degree of permanency far less to be dreaded in that office, than a duration of THREE years for a corresponding office in a single State.

AMERICAN IMPEACHMENT PROCESS:
May the President be removed from office? What about punishment outside of office? Does Britain's king suffer under similar checks?

69:4 The President of the United States would be liable to be impeached, tried, and, upon conviction of treason, bribery, or other high crimes or misdemeanors, removed from office; and would afterwards be liable to prosecution and punishment in the ordinary course of law. The person of the king of Great Britain is sacred and inviolable; there is no constitutional tribunal to which he is amenable; no punishment to which he can be subjected without involving the crisis of a national revolution. In this delicate and important circumstance of personal responsibility, the President of Confederated America would stand upon no better ground than a governor of New York, and upon worse ground than the governors of Maryland and Delaware.

VETO POWER OF THE PRESIDENT:
Does the President have total power to reject a bill? Can Congress override the President?

69:5 The President of the United States is to have power to return a bill, which shall have passed the two branches of the legislature, for reconsideration; and the bill so returned is to become a law, if, upon that reconsideration, it be approved by two thirds of both houses. The king of Great Britain, on his part, has an absolute negative upon the acts of the two houses of Parliament. The disuse of that power for a considerable time past does not affect the reality of its existence; and is to be ascribed wholly to the crown's having found the means of substituting influence to authority, or the art of gaining a majority in one or the other of the two houses, to the necessity of exerting a prerogative which could seldom be exerted without hazarding some degree of national agitation.

AMERICAN VETO DIFFERENT FROM BRITISH:
Is Britain's king restricted in this fashion?

68:6 The qualified negative of the President differs widely from this absolute negative of the British sovereign; and tallies exactly with the revisionary authority of the council of revision of this State, of which the governor is a constituent part. In this respect the power of the President would exceed that of the governor of New York, because the former would possess, singly, what the latter shares with the chancellor and judges; but it would be precisely the same with that of the governor of Massachusetts, whose constitution, as to this article, seems to have been the original from which the Convention have copied.

PRESIDENTIAL DUTIES LISTED IN CONSTITUTION, ARTICLE II:

What are some similarities in duties between the President and Britain's king?

69:7 The President is to be the "commander-in-chief of the army and navy of the United States, and of the militia of the several States, when called into the actual service of the United States."

Grant reprieves and pardons.

69:8 He is to have "power to grant reprieves and pardons for offenses against the United States, EXCEPT IN CASES OF IMPEACHMENT";

Bring important matters to the attention of Congress.

69:9 to recommend to the consideration of Congress "such measures as he shall judge necessary and expedient";

Emergency convening of Congress.

69:10 to convene, on extraordinary occasions, both houses of the legislature, "or either of them, and, in case of disagreement between them WITH RESPECT TO THE TIME OF ADJOURNMENT," to "adjourn them to such time as he shall think proper";

Execute the laws.

69:11 to "take care that the laws be faithfully executed";

Commission military officers.

69:12 and to "commission All officers of the United States."

President's powers resemble New York's governor and Britain's king.

69:13 In most of these particulars, the power of the President will resemble equally that of the king of Great Britain and of the governor of New York.

PRIMARY DIFFERENCES BETWEEN PRESIDENT AND KING:

69:14 The most material points of difference are these:

1. MILITIA:
When is the President in command of the militia?

69:15 First. The President will have only the occasional command of such part of the militia of the nation as by legislative provision may be called into the actual service of the Union. The king of Great Britain and the governor of New York have at all times the entire command of all the militia within their several jurisdictions. In this article, therefore, the power of the President would be inferior to that of either the monarch or the governor.

2. DECLARING WAR AND COMMANDING THE MILITARY:
Can the President declare war? Can Britain's king?

69:16 Secondly. The President is to be commander-in-chief of the army and navy of the United States. In this respect his authority would be nominally the same with that of the king of Great Britain, but in substance much inferior to it. It would amount to nothing more than the supreme command and direction of the military and naval forces, as first General and admiral of the Confederacy; while that of the British king extends to the DECLARING of war and to the RAISING and REGULATING of fleets and armies, all which, by the Constitution under consideration, would appertain to the legislature.[219]

GOVERNOR AS COMMANDER-IN-CHIEF:
69:17 The governor of New York, on the other hand, is by the constitution of the State vested only with the command of its militia and navy. But the constitutions of several of the States expressly declare their governors to be commanders-in-chief, as well of the army as navy; and it may well be a question, whether those of New Hampshire and Massachusetts, in particular, do not, in this instance, confer larger powers upon their respective governors, than could be claimed by a President of the United States.

3. POWER OF PARDONS:
Can an impeached President pardon himself? Can he protect others who are impeached? Can the governor of New York do likewise?

69:18 Thirdly. The power of the President, in respect to pardons, would extend to all cases, EXCEPT THOSE OF IM-

---

219 *Publius:* A writer in a Pennsylvania paper, under the signature of TAMONY, has asserted that the king of Great Britain owes his prerogative as commander-in-chief to an annual mutiny bill. The truth is, on the contrary, that his prerogative, in this respect, is immemorial, and was only disputed, "contrary to all reason and precedent," as Blackstone vol. i, page 262, expresses it, by the Long Parliament of Charles I but by the statute the 13th of Charles II, chap. 6, it was declared to be in the king alone, for that the sole supreme government and command of the militia within his Majesty's realms and dominions, and of all forces by sea and land, and of all forts and places of strength, EVER WAS AND IS the undoubted right of his Majesty and his royal predecessors, kings and queens of England, and that both or either house of Parliament cannot nor ought to pretend to the same.

PEACHMENT. The governor of New York may pardon in all cases, even in those of impeachment, except for treason and murder.

New York's governor can pardon criminals except for murder and treason.

69:19   Is not the power of the governor, in this article, on a calculation of political consequences, greater than that of the President? All conspiracies and plots against the government, which have not been matured into actual treason, may be screened from punishment of every kind, by the interposition of the prerogative of pardoning. If a governor of New York, therefore, should be at the head of any such conspiracy, until the design had been ripened into actual hostility he could insure his accomplices and adherents an entire impunity.

PRESIDENT CAN'T STOP IMPEACHMENT:

69:20   A President of the Union, on the other hand, though he may even pardon treason, when prosecuted in the ordinary course of law, could shelter no offender, in any degree, from the effects of impeachment and conviction.

Criminals and conspirators would feel more free to act if they knew the President could pardon even their worst criminal behavior.

69:21   Would not the prospect of a total indemnity for all the preliminary steps be a greater temptation to undertake and persevere in an enterprise against the public liberty, than the mere prospect of an exemption from death and confiscation, if the final execution of the design, upon an actual appeal to arms, should miscarry?

PRESIDENT'S ROLE INFLUENCES EXPECTATIONS:

69:22   Would this last expectation have any influence at all, when the probability was computed, that the person who was to afford that exemption might himself be involved in the consequences of the measure, and might be incapacitated by his agency in it from affording the desired impunity?

TREASON:
How does the Constitution define treason?

69:23   The better to judge of this matter, it will be necessary to recollect, that, by the proposed Constitution, the offense of treason is limited "to levying war upon the United States, and adhering to their enemies, giving them aid and comfort"; and that by the laws of New York it is confined within similar bounds.

4. ADJOURNING CONGRESS:
Can the President force Congress to adjourn? For what reason? Can he dissolve Congress? Can Britain's king dissolve Parliament?

69:24   Fourthly. The President can only adjourn the national legislature in the single case of disagreement about the time of adjournment. The British monarch may **prorogue**[220] or even dissolve the Parliament. The governor of New York may also prorogue the legislature of this State for a limited time; a power which, in certain situations, may be employed to very important purposes.

MAKING TREATIES:
How much of the Senate is required to pass a President's treaty?

69:25   The President is to have power, with the advice and consent of the Senate, to make treaties, provided two thirds of the senators present concur.

BRITISH KING CONTROLS ALL FOREIGN RELATIONS:
Is the king restricted in foreign relations?

69:26   The king of Great Britain is the sole and absolute representative of the nation in all foreign transactions. He can of his own accord make treaties of peace, commerce, alliance, and of every other description. It has been insinuated, that his authority in this respect is not conclusive, and that his conventions with foreign powers are subject to the revision, and stand in need of the ratification, of Parliament. But I believe this doctrine was never heard of, until it was broached upon the present occasion.

BRITISH CROWN CONTROLS TREATIES:

69:27   Every jurist[221] of that kingdom, and every other man acquainted with its Constitution, knows, as an established fact, that the prerogative of making treaties exists in the crown in its utmost plentitude; and that the compacts entered into by the royal authority have the most complete legal validity and perfection, independent of any other sanction.

PARLIAMENT'S ROLE IN TREATIES:

69:28   The Parliament, it is true, is sometimes seen employing itself in altering the existing laws to conform them to the stipulations in a new treaty; and this may have possibly given birth to the imagination, that its co-operation was necessary to the obligatory efficacy of the treaty. But this parliamentary interposition proceeds from a different cause: from the necessity of adjusting a most artificial and intricate system of revenue and commercial laws, to the changes made in them by the operation of the treaty; and of adapting new provisions

---

220 **prorogue:** Put off, delay, or end a legislative session, but *not* dissolve the assembly.
221 *Publius:* Vide Blackstone's "Commentaries," vol i., p. 257.

and precautions to the new state of things, to keep the machine from running into disorder.

PRESIDENT'S HANDS ARE TIED ON PURPOSE:

69:29   In this respect, therefore, there is no comparison between the intended power of the President and the actual power of the British sovereign. The one can perform alone what the other can do only with the concurrence of a branch of the legislature.

PRESIDENT HAS MORE POWER THAN GOVERNORS:

Who has the power to make treaties?

69:30   It must be admitted, that, in this instance, the power of the federal Executive would exceed that of any State Executive. But this arises naturally from the sovereign power which relates to treaties. If the Confederacy were to be dissolved, it would become a question, whether the Executives of the several States were not solely invested with that delicate and important prerogative.

RECEIVING AMBASSADORS AND MINISTERS:

Does it matter that the President receives ambassadors? What big inconvenience does that "matter of dignity" avoid for Congress?

69:31   The President is also to be authorized to receive ambassadors and other public ministers. This, though it has been a rich theme of declamation, is more a matter of dignity than of authority. It is a circumstance which will be without consequence in the administration of the government; and it was far more convenient that it should be arranged in this manner, than that there should be a necessity of convening the legislature, or one of its branches, upon every arrival of a foreign minister, though it were merely to take the place of a departed predecessor.

SENATE APPROVES TREATIES:

Can the President appoint officers without the consent of the Senate?

69:32   The President is to nominate, and, WITH THE ADVICE AND CONSENT OF THE SENATE, to appoint ambassadors and other public ministers, judges of the Supreme Court, and in general All officers of the United States established by law, and whose appointments are not otherwise provided for by the Constitution.

BRITAIN'S KING CONTROLS FOREIGN AFFAIRS:

How does the President's powers over foreign affairs compare to those of Britain's king?

69:33   The king of Great Britain is emphatically and truly styled the fountain of honor. He not only appoints to All offices, but can create offices. He can confer titles of nobility at pleasure; and has the disposal of an immense number of church preferments. There is evidently a great inferiority in the power of the President, in this particular, to that of the British king; nor is it equal to that of the governor of New York, if we are to interpret the meaning of the constitution of the State by the practice which has obtained under it.

NOMINATING POWER IN NEW YORK:

Comparing the President to NY's governor, what power does the governor have superior to the President's?

69:34   The power of appointment is with us lodged in a council, composed of the governor and four members of the Senate, chosen by the Assembly. The governor CLAIMS, and has frequently EXERCISED, the right of nomination, and is ENTITLED to a casting vote in the appointment. If he really has the right of nominating, his authority is in this respect equal to that of the President, and exceeds it in the article of the casting vote. In the national government, if the Senate should be divided, no appointment could be made; in the government of New York, if the council should be divided, the governor can turn the scale, and confirm his own nomination.[222]

GOVERNOR MORE INFLUENTIAL:

Comparing their stations in politics, is the governor more able to influence his council than the President able to influence the entire Senate?

69:35   If we compare the publicity which must necessarily attend the mode of appointment by the President and an entire branch of the national legislature, with the privacy in the mode of appointment by the governor of New York, closeted in a secret apartment with at most four, and frequently with only two persons; and if we at the same time consider how much more easy it must be to influence the small number of which a council of appointment consists, than the considerable number of which the national Senate would consist, we cannot hesitate to pronounce that the power of the chief magistrate of this State, in the disposition of offices, must, in practice, be greatly superior to that of the Chief Magistrate of the Union.

PRESIDENT HAS LESS POWER THAN A KING:

Does the President also have more power than New York's governor?

---

222   *Publius:* Candor, however, demands an acknowledgment that I do not think the claim of the governor to a right of nomination well founded. Yet it is always justifiable to reason from the practice of a government, till its propriety has been constitutionally questioned. And independent of this claim, when we take into view the other considerations, and pursue them through all their consequences, we shall be inclined to draw much the same conclusion.

69:36 Hence it appears that, <u>except as to the concurrent authority</u> of the President in the article of <u>treaties</u>, it would be <u>difficult to determine</u> whether that <u>magistrate</u> would, in the aggregate, possess <u>more or less power</u> than the <u>Governor</u> of New York. And it appears yet more unequivocally, that there is no pretense for the <u>parallel</u> which has been attempted between him and the <u>king</u> of Great Britain. But to render the contrast in this respect still more striking, it may be of use to throw the principal circumstances of dissimilitude into a closer group.

COMPARING PRESIDENT'S POWERS TO A KING'S POWERS:

What are some of the differences between the President and Britain's king?

69:37 The <u>President</u> of the United States would be an <u>officer elected</u> by the people for <u>FOUR years</u>; the <u>king</u> of Great Britain is a <u>perpetual</u> and <u>HEREDITARY</u> prince.

Impeachment.

69:38 The one would be amenable to <u>personal punishment</u> and disgrace; the person of the other is <u>sacred and inviolable</u>.

Veto Power.

69:39 The one would have a <u>QUALIFIED</u> negative upon the acts of the legislative body; the other has an <u>ABSOLUTE negative</u>.

Military Leader.

69:40 The one would have a right to <u>command</u> the military and naval forces of the nation; the other, in addition to this right, possesses that of <u>DECLARING</u> war, and of RAISING and REGULATING fleets and armies by his own authority.

Treaties.

69:41 The one would have a concurrent power with a branch of the legislature in the formation of <u>treaties</u>; the other is the SOLE POSSESSOR of the power of making treaties.

Political Appointments.

69:42 The one would have a like concurrent authority in <u>appointing</u> to offices; the other is the <u>sole author</u> of all appointments. The one can <u>confer no privileges</u> whatever; the other can make <u>denizens of aliens, noblemen of commoners</u>; can erect corporations with all the rights incident to corporate bodies.

Commerce.

69:43 The one can prescribe no rules concerning the <u>commerce or currency</u> of the nation; the other is in several respects the arbiter of commerce, and in this capacity can establish <u>markets</u> and fairs, can regulate <u>weights and measures</u>, can lay embargoes for a limited time, can <u>coin money</u>, can authorize or prohibit the circulation of foreign coin.

Religion.

69:44 The one has <u>no particle of spiritual jurisdiction</u>; the other is the supreme head and <u>governor of the national church</u>! <u>What answer shall we give to those who would persuade us that things so unlike resemble each other?</u>

PRESIDENT IS FAR REMOVED FROM KINGLY POWER:

Given these controls and restrictions there is no reason to fear that the President could become king in America.

69:45 The same that ought to be given to those who tell us that a government, the whole power of which would be in the hands of the elective and periodical servants of the people, is an aristocracy, a monarchy, and a despotism.

—PUBLIUS

REVIEW QUESTIONS

1. What unfair representation of the President is Hamilton addressing in paper No. 69? (69:1–2)

2. What is the primary difference between the President's term of office and the term of the king of Great Britain? (69:3)

3. How can the President be removed from office? How about the king of Britain? (69:4)

4. How is the President's power of veto different than for Britain's king? (69:5–6)

5. Can the President declare war? Can Britain's king declare war? (69:15–17)

6. Can the President pardon treason? (69:20)

7. How does the Constitution define treason? (69:23)

8. In what areas of political operations is the President's powers much more controlled and restrained than the king of Great Britain? (69:37–44)

FEDERALIST NO. 70

A SINGLE PRESIDENT BRINGS ENERGY AND SAFETY: A strong President properly constrained from becoming a monarch is essential to good republican government. Anything more than one president, or an executive council, leads to debate, delay, and conflict at the highest level of government. Unity, power and the management of secrets are necessary attributes to expeditiously execute the laws passed by Congress. The executive must be openly liable and impeachable for his actions as a means of checking executive power from misuse.

By Alexander Hamilton—March 15, 1788

ENERGY IN THE PRESIDENCY IS ESSENTIAL:

What are some reasons why an actively involved President is crucial to a republic?

70:1 THERE is an idea, which is not without its advocates, that a vigorous Executive is inconsistent with the genius of republican government. The enlightened well-wishers to this species of government must at least hope that the supposition is destitute of foundation; since they can never admit its truth, without at the same time admitting the condemnation of their own principles. Energy in the Executive is a leading character in the definition of good government.

ONE HEAD IN AN EMERGENCY IS BETTER THAN MANY:

For what four responsibilities is "energy" essential? A committee often takes too long when responsiveness is crucial.

70:2 It is essential to the protection of the community against[1.] foreign attacks; [2.] it is not less essential to the steady administration of the laws; [3.] to the protection of property against those irregular and high-handed combinations which sometimes interrupt the ordinary course of justice; [4.] to the security of liberty against the enterprises and assaults of ambition, of faction, and of anarchy.

IN WAR ONE LEADER IS BEST:

A single leader is crucial in an attack, but such power must be constrained lest it grow.

70:3 Every man the least conversant in Roman history, knows how often that republic was obliged to take refuge in the absolute power of a single man, under the formidable title of Dictator, as well against the intrigues of ambitious individuals who aspired to the tyranny, and the seditions of whole classes of the community whose conduct threatened the existence of all government, as against the invasions of external enemies who menaced the conquest and destruction of Rome.

FEEBLE EXECUTIVE IS VERY HARMFUL TO NATION:

What does a feeble executive ultimately create?

70:4 There can be no need, however, to multiply arguments or examples on this head. A feeble Executive implies a feeble execution of the government. A feeble execution is but another phrase for a bad execution; and a government ill executed, whatever it may be in theory, must be, in practice, a bad government.

INGREDIENTS FOR ENERGY:

What does Hamilton describe as ingredients for having "energy" in the President?

70:5 Taking it for granted, therefore, that all men of sense will agree in the necessity of an energetic Executive, it will only remain to inquire, what are the ingredients which constitute this energy? How far can they be combined with those other ingredients which constitute safety in the republican sense? And how far does this combination characterize the plan which has been reported by the Convention?

70:6 The ingredients which constitute energy in the Executive are, first, unity;[223] secondly, duration; thirdly, an adequate provision for its support; fourthly, competent powers.

What are the ingredients in national political safety?

70:7 The ingredients which constitute safety in the republican sense are, first, a due dependence on the people, secondly, a due responsibility.

ONE EXECUTIVE, MANY LEGISLATORS:

If the President is to have power and resources to address problems and move America forward, what role is Congress supposed to play?

70:8 Those politicians and statesmen who have been the most celebrated for the soundness of their principles and for the justice of their views, have declared in favor of a single Executive and a numerous legislature. They have with great propriety, considered energy as the most necessary qualification of the former, and have regarded this as most applicable to power in a single hand, while they have, with equal propriety, considered the latter as best adapted to deliberation and wisdom, and best calculated to conciliate the confidence of the people and to secure their privileges and interests.

ENERGY AND UNITY IN ONE EXECUTIVE WORKS BEST:

If the executive's "energy" is spread out among too many others, what happens in the event of a quick response in an emergency?

70:9 That unity is conducive to energy will not be disputed. Decision, activity, secrecy, and dispatch will generally characterize the proceedings of one man in a much more eminent degree than the proceedings of any greater number; and in proportion as the number is increased, these qualities will be diminished.

TWO WAYS TO DESTROY UNITY:

The executive loses its advantages if there are too many or if he is too controlled by others.

223 *Editors' Note:* By "unity" Hamilton means oneness—just one President, not several, with certain powers not diluted among others at the executive level.

70:10   This <u>unity</u> may be <u>destroyed</u> in two ways: either by vesting the power in two or more magistrates of equal dignity and authority; or by vesting it ostensibly <u>in one man</u>, <u>subject</u>, <u>in whole</u> or in part, to the <u>control</u> and <u>co-operation of others</u>, in the capacity of counselors to him.

EXAMPLES OF MULTIPLE EXECUTIVES:
Rome had two consuls. Many of the States have executive committees who control the governor.

70:11   Of the first, the two Consuls of <u>Rome</u> may serve as an example; of the last, we shall find examples in the constitutions of several of the States. <u>New York</u> and <u>New Jersey</u>, if I recollect right, are the only States which have intrusted the executive authority wholly to single men.[224]

DESTROYING UNITY IN THE EXECUTIVE HAS SUPPORTERS:
The form of an executive council has popular support, but both are subject to weaknesses.

70:12   Both these methods of destroying the unity of the Executive have their <u>partisans</u>; but the votaries of an executive council are the most numerous. They are <u>both liable, if not to equal</u>, to similar <u>objections</u>, and may in most lights be examined in conjunction.

PLURAL EXECUTIVES ARE DESTRUCTIVE:
What do the lessons of history teach about the problems of more than one executive?

70:13   The experience of <u>other nations</u> will afford <u>little instruction</u> on this head. As far, however, as it teaches any thing, it teaches us not to be **enamoured**[225] of plurality in the Executive.

ROMAN INFIGHTING ILLUSTRATES THE PROBLEM:

70:14   We have seen that the <u>Achaeans</u>, on an experiment of two <u>Praetors</u>, were induced to <u>abolish one</u>. The <u>Roman</u> history records many instances of mischiefs to the republic from the dissensions between the <u>Consuls</u>, and between the military <u>Tribunes</u>, who were at times substituted for the Consuls.

NO HISTORICAL BENEFIT:
There were power struggles among the classes but no advantages shown in plural executives.

70:15   But it gives us no specimens of any peculiar advantages derived to the state from the circumstance of the plurality of those magistrates. That the <u>dissensions</u> between them were <u>not more frequent or more fatal</u>, is a matter of astonishment, until we advert to the singular position in which the republic was almost continually placed, and to the prudent policy pointed out by the circumstances of the state, and pursued by the Consuls, of making a <u>division</u> of the government <u>between them</u>. The <u>patricians</u> engaged in a perpetual struggle with the <u>plebeians</u> for the preservation of their ancient authorities and dignities; the Consuls, who were generally chosen out of the former body, were commonly united by the personal interest they had in the defense of the privileges of their order.

ROME TOOK STEPS TO DILUTE EXECUTIVE POWER:
How did Rome avoid power struggles among its top leaders?

70:16   In addition to this motive of union, after the arms of the republic had considerably expanded the bounds of its empire, it became an established custom with the <u>Consuls to divide the administration</u> between themselves by lot one of them <u>remaining at Rome to govern</u> the city and its environs, the other taking the <u>command in the more distant provinces</u>. This expedient must, no doubt, have had great influence in <u>preventing</u> those collisions and <u>rivalships</u> which might otherwise have embroiled the peace of the republic.

SHARING TOP LEADERSHIP HAS NEVER BEEN SUCCESSFUL:
Doesn't common sense conclude that sharing top leadership is bad?

70:17   But <u>quitting</u> the dim light of <u>historical</u> research, attaching ourselves purely to the <u>dictates of reason and good sense</u>, we shall discover much <u>greater cause to reject</u> than to approve the idea of plurality in the Executive, under any modification whatever.

COMPETING POWERS OF DECISION ARE BAD IN A CRISIS:
What possible tragedy could hit if leaders charged with national defense were locked in argument?

70:18   <u>Wherever two or more persons are engaged in any common enterprise or pursuit, there is always danger of difference of opinion. If it be a public trust or office</u>, in which they are clothed with equal dignity and authority, there is peculiar danger of personal emulation and even animosity. From either, and especially from all these causes, the most bitter dissensions are apt to spring. Whenever these happen, they lessen the respectability, weaken the authority, and distract the plans and operation of those whom they divide.

---

224 *Publius:* New York has no council except for the single purpose of appointing to offices; New Jersey has a council whom the governor may consult. But I think, from the terms of the constitution, their resolutions do not bind him.

225 **enamoured:** British form of enamored; filled with a strong feeling of love.

MULTIPLE LEADERS SLOW DOWN IMPORTANT DECISIONS:

Indecision because of too many heads of state could lead to disaster in an emergency, or worse, split the nation with civil bickering.

70:19   If they should unfortunately assail the supreme executive magistracy of a country, consisting of a plurality of persons, they might impede or frustrate the most important measures of the government, in the most critical emergencies of the state. And what is still worse, they might split the community into the most violent and irreconcilable factions, adhering differently to the different individuals who composed the magistracy.

WHEN PERSONAL PRIDE CORRUPTS THE SYSTEM:

Why do politicians often fight for political power instead of tending to the nation's best interests? By what actions can true patriotic leaders be recognized?

70:20   Men often oppose a thing, merely because they have had no agency in planning it, or because it may have been planned by those whom they dislike. But if they have been consulted, and have happened to disapprove, opposition then becomes, in their estimation, an indispensable duty of self-love. They seem to think themselves bound in honor, and by all the motives of personal infallibility, to defeat the success of what has been resolved upon contrary to their sentiments.

POLITICIANS NEGLECT WHAT'S GOOD FOR COUNTRY FOR PERSONAL VANITY:

What secrets are blatantly exposed in politicians who sacrifice what's best for America just to attack a successful political rival?

70:21   Men of upright, benevolent tempers have too many opportunities of remarking, with horror, to what desperate lengths this disposition is sometimes carried, and how often the great interests of society are sacrificed to the vanity, to the conceit, and to the obstinacy of individuals, who have credit enough to make their passions and their caprices interesting to mankind.

Proof of the damage from human vices can be witnessed right now.

70:22   Perhaps the question now before the public may, in its consequences, afford melancholy proofs of the effects of this despicable frailty, or rather detestable vice, in the human character.

UNWISE TO DILUTE ENERGY OF EXECUTIVE:

Deliberately injecting dissension into the executive by adding more leaders would prove itself a fatal mistake.

70:23   Upon the principles of a free government, inconveniences from the source just mentioned must necessarily be submitted to in the formation of the legislature; but it is unnecessary, and therefore unwise, to introduce them into the constitution of the Executive. It is here too that they may be most pernicious.

SLOW DELIBERATION IS GOOD IN LEGISLATIVE PROCESSES:

Longer consideration helps avoid rash and ill-conceived laws.

70:24   In the legislature, promptitude of decision is oftener an evil than a benefit. The differences of opinion, and the jarrings of parties in that department of the government, though they may sometimes obstruct salutary plans, yet often promote deliberation and circumspection, and serve to check excesses in the majority. When a resolution too is once taken, the opposition must be at an end. That resolution is a law, and resistance to it punishable.

SLOW DELIBERATION IN EXECUTIVE IS DANGEROUS:

When national best interests need immediate attention, a slow executive process does more damage than good.

70:25   But no favorable circumstances palliate or atone for the disadvantages of dissension in the executive department. Here, they are pure and unmixed. There is no point at which they cease to operate. They serve to embarrass and weaken the execution of the plan or measure to which they relate, from the first step to the final conclusion of it. They constantly counteract those qualities in the Executive which are the most necessary ingredients in its composition, vigor and expedition, and this without any counterbalancing good.

ONE EXECUTIVE CRITICAL IN TIMES OF WAR:

70:26   In the conduct of war, in which the energy of the Executive is the bulwark of the national security, every thing would be to be apprehended from its plurality.

PLURALITY OF EXECUTIVES IS PROVEN DANGEROUS:

70:27   It must be confessed that these observations apply with principal weight to the first case supposed that is, to a plurality of magistrates of equal dignity and authority a scheme, the advocates for which are not likely to form a numerous sect;

SINGLE EXECUTIVE UNDER A COUNCIL IS PERILOUS:

If a council of advisors opposed the President and also could legally restrain him, would this not be damaging to the people's best interests?

70:28 but they apply, though not with equal, yet with considerable weight to the project of a <u>council</u>, whose concurrence is made constitutionally necessary to the operations of the ostensible Executive.

DIFFERING OPINIONS OF EQUAL AUTHORITY ARE RUINOUS:

70:29 An <u>artful cabal</u> in that <u>council</u> would be able to <u>distract</u> and to enervate the whole system of administration. If no such cabal should exist, <u>the mere diversity of views</u> and opinions <u>would alone be sufficient</u> to tincture the exercise of the executive authority with a spirit of <u>habitual feebleness</u> and dilatoriness.

EASIER TO HIDE FAULTS AND DESTROY RESPONSIBILITY:

What is the deep-rooted damage inflicted by multiple executive leaders?

70:30 <u>But one of the weightiest objections to a plurality in the Executive, and which lies as much against the last as the first plan, is, that it tends to conceal faults and destroy responsibility.</u>

TWO TYPES OF POLITICAL RESPONSIBILITY:

Would multiple leaders better conceal their faults and destroy their responsibility than a single leader acting alone?

70:31 <u>Responsibility</u> is of two kinds—to <u>censure</u> and to <u>punishment</u>. The first is the more important of the two, especially in an elective office. Man, in public trust, will much <u>oftener act</u> in such a manner as to render him <u>unworthy</u> of being any longer <u>trusted</u>, than in such a manner as to make him obnoxious to legal punishment.

PLURAL EXECUTIVES CONFUSES MORAL COMPASS:

With no single executive to take responsibility, could multiple presidents get away with being sloppy or with criminal behavior?

70:32 <u>But the multiplication of the Executive adds to the difficulty of detection in either case. It often becomes impossible, amidst mutual accusations, to determine on whom the blame or the punishment of a pernicious measure, or series of pernicious measures, ought really to fall. It is shifted from one to another with so much dexterity, and under such plausible appearances, that the public opinion is left in suspense about the real author.</u>

MISMANAGEMENT MUST BE DISCOVERABLE:

Can leadership failures be corrected if they can't be directly blamed?

70:33 The circumstances which may have led to any national miscarriage or misfortune are sometimes so complicated that, where there are a number of actors who may have had different degrees and kinds of agency, though we may clearly see upon the whole that there has been mismanagement, yet it may be impracticable to pronounce to whose account the evil which may have been incurred is truly chargeable.

THE PEOPLE MUST BE ABLE TO POINT BLAME ACCURATELY:

If a President had to concede to the rule of his council, would the truth about who made a bad decision ever be discovered?

70:34 "<u>I was overruled by my council. The council were so divided in their opinions that it was impossible to obtain any better resolution on the point.</u>" These and similar pretexts are constantly at hand, whether true or false. And <u>who</u> is there that will either take the trouble or incur the odium, of a <u>strict scrutiny</u> into the secret springs of the transaction? Should there be found a citizen zealous enough to undertake the unpromising task, if there happen to be collusion between the parties concerned, <u>how easy it is to clothe the circumstances with so much ambiguity</u>, as to render it uncertain what was the precise conduct of any of those parties?

NEW YORK'S EXAMPLE:

The governor made bad appointments to a council that were improper and resulted in damaging consequences. Was it easy for the people to place the blame?

70:35 In the single instance in which the <u>governor</u> of this State is coupled with a council—that is, in the appointment to offices, we have seen the mischiefs of it in the view now under consideration. <u>Scandalous appointments</u> to important offices have been made. Some cases, indeed, have been so flagrant that <u>ALL PARTIES</u> have agreed in the <u>impropriety</u> of the thing.

Governor could put blame on his council, and council could deflect it, leaving the people confused about where to demand change.

70:36 When inquiry has been made, the <u>blame has been laid by the governor on the members of the council</u>, who, on their part, have charged it upon his nomination; while the people remain altogether at a loss to determine, by whose influence their <u>interests</u> have been <u>committed</u> to hands so <u>unqualified</u> and so manifestly improper. In tenderness to individuals, I forbear to descend to particulars.

TWO GREAT SECURITIES WITH ONE EXECUTIVE:

What are the two great securities that would be lost with no single president in charge to take responsibility?

70:37 It is evident from these considerations, that the <u>plurality of the Executive</u> tends to <u>deprive</u> the people of the <u>two greatest securities</u> they can have for the faithful exercise of any delegated power,

Public reproach.

70:38 first, the <u>restraints</u> of public opinion, which lose their efficacy, as well on account of the division of the censure attendant on bad measures among a number, as on account of the uncertainty on whom it ought to fall;

Finding the culprit.

70:39 and, <u>secondly</u>, the opportunity of <u>discovering</u> with facility and clearness the <u>misconduct</u> of the persons they trust, in order either to their removal from office or to their actual punishment in cases which admit of it.

BRITAIN'S KING IS UNACCOUNTABLE:
Would an executive council make Britain's king more responsible?

70:40 In <u>England</u>, the <u>king</u> is a perpetual magistrate; and it is a maxim which has obtained for the sake of the public peace, that he is <u>unaccountable</u> for his administration, and his person sacred. Nothing, therefore, can be <u>wiser</u> in that kingdom, than to <u>annex to the king a constitutional council</u>, who may be responsible to the nation for the advice they give. <u>Without</u> this, there would be <u>no responsibility whatever</u> in the executive department an idea inadmissible in a free government.

King is not subordinate to his council of advisors.

70:41 But even there the <u>king is not bound</u> by the resolutions of his council, though they are answerable for the advice they give. He is the absolute master of his own conduct in the exercise of his office, and may <u>observe or disregard the counsel</u> given to him at his sole discretion.

COUNCIL BECOMES THE PROXY TO RECEIVE THE BLAME INSTEAD OF THE INDIVIDUAL:
In America are the top leaders personally responsible? How would a constitutionally endowed council destroy that responsibility?

70:42 <u>But in a republic</u>, where every magistrate ought to be <u>personally responsible</u> for his behavior in office the reason which in the British Constitution dictates the propriety of a <u>council</u>, not only ceases to apply, but turns against the institution.

In Britain an executive council takes the brunt of the king's action.

70:43 In the monarchy of Great Britain, it furnishes a substitute for the prohibited responsibility of the chief magistrate, which serves in some degree as a hostage to the national justice for his good behavior.

In America an executive council would undermine the president.

70:44 In the American republic, it would serve to destroy, or would <u>greatly diminish</u>, the intended and necessary responsibility of the Chief Magistrate himself.

EXECUTIVE SAFER AS ONE INSTEAD OF MANY:
If power is safer in the hands of many, does the Constitution help contain that power in the President?

70:45 <u>The idea of a council to the Executive, which has so generally obtained in the State constitutions, has been derived from that maxim of republican jealousy which considers power as safer in the hands of a number of men than of a single man.</u> If the maxim should be admitted to be applicable to the case, I should contend that the advantage on that side would not counterbalance the numerous disadvantages on the opposite side.

EASIER TO CONTAIN POWER WHEN CONFINED TO ONE:

70:46 But I do not think the rule at all applicable to the executive power. <u>I clearly concur</u> in opinion, in this particular, with a writer[226] whom the celebrated Junius pronounces to be "deep, solid, and ingenious," that "<u>the executive power is more easily confined when it is ONE</u>";[227] that it is <u>far more safe there should be a single object for the jealousy and watchfulness of the people</u>; and, in a word, that <u>all multiplication of the Executive is rather dangerous than friendly to liberty</u>.

SINGLE LEADER EASIER TO SCRUTINIZE:
Is power most easily corrupted in a small number of men, a large number, or a single magistrate?

70:47 A little consideration will satisfy us, that the species of security sought for in the multiplication of the Executive, is attainable. <u>Numbers must be so great as to render combination difficult</u>, or they are rather a source of danger than of security. The united credit and influence of several individuals must be more formidable to liberty, than the credit and influence of either of them separately.

---

226 *Editors' Note:* Jean Louis De Lolme (1740–1806), *The Constitution of England*, Book II, Chapter 2, London 1796.
227 *Publius:* De Lolme

STANDING ALONE UNDER SCRUTINY IS SAFER:
Power spread among many makes it difficult to pinpoint
blame and instigator. But when carefully measured out to
one person, responsibility is easier placed and enforced.

70:48   When power, therefore, is placed in the hands of so small a number of men, as to admit of their interests and views being easily combined in a common enterprise, by an artful leader, it becomes more liable to abuse, and more dangerous when abused, than if it be lodged in the hands of one man; who, from the very circumstance of his being alone, will be more narrowly watched and more readily suspected, and who cannot unite so great a mass of influence as when he is associated with others.

TEN ROMAN LAWMAKERS WERE MORE DANGEROUS THAN ANY SINGLE MEMBER:

70:49   The **Decemvirs**[228] of Rome, whose name denotes their number,[229] were more to be dreaded in their usurpation than any ONE of them would have been.

TOO MANY EXECUTIVES COULD BECOME A CABAL:

70:50   No person would think of proposing an Executive much more numerous than that body; from six to a dozen have been suggested for the number of the council. The extreme of these numbers, is not too great for an easy combination; and from such a combination America would have more to fear, than from the ambition of any single individual.

COUNCILS USUALLY BECOME CO-CONSPIRATORS:

70:51   A council to a magistrate, who is himself responsible for what he does, are generally nothing better than a clog upon his good intentions, are often the instruments and accomplices of his bad and are almost always a cloak to his faults.

PLURALITY OF EXECUTIVES IS EXPENSIVE:
Before the Constitution, what did people say was the best
feature of New York's constitution?

70:52   I forbear to dwell upon the subject of expense; though it be evident that if the council should be numerous enough to answer the principal end aimed at by the institution, the salaries of the members, who must be drawn from their homes to reside at the seat of government, would form an item in the catalogue of public expenditures too serious to be incurred for an object of equivocal utility.

SINGLE EXECUTIVE IS BEST FEATURE OF ALL:

70:53   I will only add that, prior to the appearance of the Constitution, I rarely met with an intelligent man from any of the States, who did not admit, as the result of experience, that the UNITY of the executive of this State was one of the best of the distinguishing features of our constitution.

—PUBLIUS

REVIEW QUESTIONS

1. How is a strong and vigorous president compatible with a republic and good government? (70:1–2)

2. In light of the President's duties, why is protecting property so important? (70:2)

3. If one energetic executive is good, why not have several? (70:8–10)

4. What are some of the problems that emerge with more than one executive? (70:10–19)

5. Human Nature: Why do people often stand in opposition to something regardless of the benefit or goodness to be achieved? (70:20–22)

6. Why is conflicting opinion in the legislature a good thing? (70:24)

7. Why is slow deliberation in the executive dangerous for the country? (70:25–26)

8. Why is laying blame more difficult with multiple executives? (70:32–34)

9. What two great securities come with a single executive? (70:38–39)

10. Does an executive council make the leader more personally responsible? (70:40–44)

11. Why is it easier to contain power when it is confined to one person? (70:46–48)

12. Why is an executive council so dangerous? (70:50–51)

FEDERALIST NO. 71

THE PRESIDENT'S FOUR-YEAR TERM: Is four years in office enough time for the President to enact his plans and to pursue his vision for America? The President needs enough independence to put forward the policies that got him elected. He shouldn't be compelled to respond to "every sudden breeze of passion" racing through the public. Alexis De Tocqueville's warning about dictatorship by the majority can be checked every four years with a new presidential election cycle.

---

228 **Decemvirs:** Ten men in ancient Rome who prepared 10 tables of law to settle differences between the rich landed class and the small farmers in 451 BC.
229 *Editors' Note:* Ten.

By Alexander Hamilton—March 15, 1788

DURATION IN OFFICE:

People tend to invest more energy into an effort when they know it is theirs for a sufficient time.

71:1 <u>DURATION</u> in office has been mentioned as the second requisite to the energy of the Executive authority. This has relation to <u>two objects</u>: to the <u>personal firmness</u> of the executive magistrate, in the employment of his constitutional powers; and to the <u>stability of the system</u> of administration which may have been adopted under his auspices.

More time in office translates to more effort by President.

71:2 With regard to the first, it must be evident, that the <u>longer the duration</u> in office, the greater will be the probability of obtaining so important an <u>advantage</u>.

SENSE OF STEWARDSHIP IN OFFICE GROWS WITH TIME:

Human nature is to prize the long term over short term.

71:3 It is a <u>general principle of human nature, that a man will be interested in whatever he possesses, in proportion to the firmness or precariousness of the tenure by which he holds it</u>; will be less attached to what he holds by a momentary or uncertain title, than to what he enjoys by a durable or certain title; and, of course, will be willing to risk more for the sake of the one, than for the sake of the other. This remark is not less <u>applicable</u> to a <u>political privilege</u>, or honor, or trust, than to any article of ordinary property.

LIMITED OPPORTUNITY BREEDS AMBIVALENCE:

If a President knows his term soon ends, is he more likely to exert hazardous risks or play things safe?

71:4 The inference from it is, that a man acting in the capacity of chief magistrate, under a consciousness that in a <u>very short time he MUST lay down his office</u>, will be apt to feel himself too <u>little interested</u> in it to <u>hazard</u> any material <u>censure</u> or perplexity, from the independent exertion of his powers, or from encountering the ill-humors, however transient, which may happen to prevail, either in a considerable part of the society itself, or even in a predominant <u>faction</u> in the legislative body.

A President fearing the end of power might behave extravagantly.

71:5 If the case should only be, that he <u>MIGHT lay it down</u>, unless continued by a new choice, and if he should be desirous of being continued, <u>his wishes</u>, conspiring with his fears, would tend still more powerfully to <u>corrupt</u> his <u>integrity</u>, or debase his fortitude.

The end of power is a part of the job.

71:6 In either case, feebleness and irresolution must be the characteristics of the station.

PRESIDENT MUST KEEP LARGER PERSPECTIVE:

Do the people expect their President to focus on the most important issues or respond to every passion and impulse that comes along?

71:7 There are some who would be inclined to regard the servile pliancy of the Executive to a <u>prevailing current</u>, either in the community or in the legislature, as its best recommendation. But such men entertain very <u>crude notions</u>, as well of the purposes for which government was instituted, as of the true means by which the public happiness may be promoted.

POPULAR PASSION DOESN'T MERIT POLICY CHANGES:

President must keep the entire nation's interests at heart regardless of sudden swells of passions over this issue or that.

71:8 The <u>republican principle demands</u> that the <u>deliberate sense</u> of the community should <u>govern</u> the conduct of those to whom they intrust the management of their affairs; but it does <u>not require</u> an unqualified complaisance to every <u>sudden breeze</u> of <u>passion</u>, or to every transient <u>impulse</u> which the people may receive from the arts of men, who flatter their prejudices to betray their interests.

PEOPLE INTEND WELL BUT DON'T ALWAYS REASON RIGHT:

71:9 It is a just observation, that the <u>people commonly INTEND the PUBLIC GOOD</u>. This often applies to their very errors. But their good sense would despise the adulator who should pretend that they always REASON RIGHT about the <u>MEANS of promoting it</u>.

FACTIONS CREATE DISORDER AND DISTRUST:

Even though the people know they are stirred up to imperfection, are not their intentions usually for the good?

71:10 They <u>know</u> from experience that they <u>sometimes err</u>; and the wonder is that they so <u>seldom err as they do</u>, beset, as they continually are, by the wiles of parasites and sycophants, by the snares of the ambitious, the avaricious, the desperate, by the artifices of men who possess their confidence more than they deserve it, and of those who seek to possess rather than to deserve it.

PRESIDENT MUST RESIST EMOTIONAL UPHEAVALS:

When people are tempted to sacrifice what's most important for a passing passion, what should be the government's role?

71:11 When occasions present themselves, in which the interests of the people are at variance with their inclinations, it is the duty of the persons whom they have appointed to be the guardians of those interests, to withstand the temporary delusion, in order to give them time and opportunity for more cool and sedate reflection.

LEADERS EXPECTED TO STAY THE COURSE:
Great leaders hold to principles even when popular pressure is otherwise.

71:12 Instances might be cited in which a conduct of this kind has saved the people from very fatal consequences of their own mistakes, and has procured lasting monuments of their gratitude to the men who had courage and magnanimity enough to serve them at the peril of their displeasure.

PRESIDENT MUST REMAIN INDEPENDENT:
Should the President be empowered to act on his own best judgment regardless of what the people may want?

71:13 But however inclined we might be to insist upon an unbounded complaisance in the Executive to the inclinations of the people, we can with no propriety contend for a like complaisance to the humors of the legislature. The latter may sometimes stand in opposition to the former, and at other times the people may be entirely neutral. In either supposition, it is certainly desirable that the Executive should be in a situation to dare to act his own opinion with vigor and decision.

AVOIDING LEGISLATIVE DOMINANCE:
If the President and the Supreme Court were beholden to every wish of the legislature, where would that always lead?

71:14 The same rule which teaches the propriety of a partition between the various branches of power, teaches us likewise that this partition ought to be so contrived as to render the one independent of the other. To what purpose separate the executive or the judiciary from the legislative, if both the executive and the judiciary are so constituted as to be at the absolute devotion of the legislative? Such a separation must be merely nominal, and incapable of producing the ends for which it was established.

Great leaders constantly work to be obedient to the Constitution.

71:15 It is one thing to be subordinate to the laws, and another to be dependent on the legislative body. The first comports with, the last violates, the fundamental principles of good government; and, whatever may be the forms of the Constitution, unites all power in the same hands.

CONGRESS FORGETS ITS TRUE SOURCE OF POWER:
Congress often acts as if it is the whole people themselves. Does it tend to take over the whole government?

71:16 The tendency of the legislative authority to absorb every other, has been fully displayed and illustrated by examples in some preceding numbers. In governments purely republican, this tendency is almost irresistible. The representatives of the people, in a popular assembly, seem sometimes to fancy that they are the people themselves, and betray strong symptoms of impatience and disgust at the least sign of opposition from any other quarter; as if the exercise of its rights, by either the executive or judiciary, were a breach of their privilege and an outrage to their dignity.

CONGRESS ENTICES PEOPLE'S SUPPORT:
With the people on its side Congress gains momentum toward imperial control.

71:17 They often appear disposed to exert an imperious control over the other departments; and as they commonly have the people on their side, they always act with such momentum as to make it very difficult for the other members of the government to maintain the balance of the Constitution.

SHORTNESS OF TERM REDUCES INDEPENDENCE:
What are the two reasons why the President's short term makes him hesitant to demand too much from Congress?

71:18 It may perhaps be asked, how the shortness of the duration in office can affect the independence of the Executive on the legislature, unless the one were possessed of the power of appointing or displacing the other.

Little interest to risk much because of a short term.

71:19 One answer to this inquiry may be drawn from the principle already remarked that is, from the slender interest a man is apt to take in a short-lived advantage, and the little inducement it affords him to expose himself, on account of it, to any considerable inconvenience or hazard.

Recognizes Congress's ability to prevent second term.

71:20 Another answer, perhaps more obvious, though not more conclusive, will result from the consideration of the influence of the legislative body over the people; which might be employed to prevent the re-election of a man who, by an upright resistance to any sinister project of that body, should have made himself obnoxious to its resentment.

SHORTER TERM IS BETTER THAN LONGER TERM:

If shorter terms protect America from presidential ambitions, are four years enough to encourage good performance?

71:21 It may be asked also, whether a duration of four years would answer the end proposed; and if it would not, whether a less period, which would at least be recommended by greater security against ambitious designs, would not, for that reason, be preferable to a longer period, which was, at the same time, too short for the purpose of inspiring the desired firmness and independence of the magistrate.

FOUR YEARS SEEMS THE BEST BALANCE:

While four years is still somewhat an arbitrary term, does it still achieve the desired goals of energetic, limited, and controlled government?

71:22 It cannot be affirmed, that a duration of four years, or any other limited duration, would completely answer the end proposed; but it would contribute towards it in a degree which would have a material influence upon the spirit and character of the government. Between the commencement and termination of such a period, there would always be a considerable interval, in which the prospect of annihilation would be sufficiently remote, not to have an improper effect upon the conduct of a man indued with a tolerable portion of fortitude; and in which he might reasonably promise himself, that there would be time enough before it arrived, to make the community sensible of the propriety of the measures he might incline to pursue.

FOUR YEARS IS ENOUGH TO EARN RE-ELECTION BID:

Is four years long enough for the President to enact a plan yet short enough to prevent him from causing serious harm? How does the hope of reelection impact his behavior?

71:23 Though it be probable that, as he approached the moment when the public were, by a new election, to signify their sense of his conduct, his confidence, and with it his firmness, would decline; yet both the one and the other would derive support from the opportunities which his previous continuance in the station had afforded him, of establishing himself in the esteem and good-will of his constituents. He might, then, hazard with safety, in proportion to the proofs he had given of his wisdom and integrity, and to the title he had acquired to the respect and attachment of his fellow-citizens.

Four years seems about right to establish an agenda but still be accountable.

71:24 As, on the one hand, a duration of four years will contribute to the firmness of the Executive in a sufficient degree to render it a very valuable ingredient in the composition; so, on the other, it is not enough to justify any alarm for the public liberty.

BRITISH REINED IN CROWN AND CHURCH:

If the British system evolved to hold power over the king, is not the President that much more restrained given all of the constitutional barriers surrounding him?

71:25 If a British House of Commons, from the most feeble beginnings, FROM THE MERE POWER OF ASSENTING OR DISAGREEING TO THE IMPOSITION OF A NEW TAX, have, by rapid strides, reduced the prerogatives of the crown and the privileges of the nobility within the limits they conceived to be compatible with the principles of a free government, while they raised themselves to the rank and consequence of a coequal branch of the legislature; if they have been able, in one instance, to abolish both the royalty and the aristocracy, and to overturn all the ancient establishments, as well in the Church as State;

PRESIDENT'S POWER IS CONTROLLED:

If the British people can make the king tremble with worry that his power might be curtailed, how much more is the President controlled under much tighter boundaries?

71:26 if they have been able, on a recent occasion, to make the monarch tremble at the prospect of an innovation[230] attempted by them, what would be to be feared from an elective magistrate of four years' duration, with the confined authorities of a President of the United States? What, but that he might be unequal to the task which the Constitution assigns him?

71:27 I shall only add, that if his duration be such as to leave a doubt of his firmness, that doubt is inconsistent with a jealousy of his encroachments.

—PUBLIUS

REVIEW QUESTIONS

1. Human Nature: What helps a person to embrace a political job with great vigor, enthusiasm, and responsibility? (71:4–5)

2. Why should the executive resist micromanaging America? (71:7–11)

3. Why should the President be empowered to stand up

---

230 *Publius:* This was the case with respect to Mr. Fox's India bill, which was carried in the House of Commons, and rejected in the House of Lords, to the entire satisfaction, as it is said, of the people.

against the legislature? (71:12–14)

4. Fill in the blanks: "It is one thing to be _____ to the laws, and another to be _____ on the legislative body. The first _____ with, the last violates" the Constitution. (71:15)

5. Human nature: Why is a four-year term long enough for a President to embrace the office and get some things accomplished? (71: 21–24)

FEDERALIST NO. 72

LET PERFORMANCE DECIDE REELECTION OF PRESIDENT: Limiting the President to one term is a misguided idea for many critical reasons including on-the-job experience, disruption in the executive branch, and the removal of incentives to remain worthy of reelection by doing a good job.

By Alexander Hamilton—March 19, 1788

PRESIDENT HAS SEVERAL SPECIFIC DUTIES:

While the President must consider every aspect of federal government, what are his general areas of responsibility? May he have separate managers over these various departments?

72:1 THE administration of government, in its largest sense, comprehends all the operations of the body politic, whether legislative, executive, or judiciary; but in its most usual, and perhaps its most precise signification, it is limited to executive details, and falls peculiarly within the province of the executive department.

Executive duties listed.

72:2 The actual conduct of foreign negotiations, the preparatory plans of finance, the application and disbursement of the public moneys in conformity to the general appropriations of the legislature, the arrangement of the army and navy, the directions of the operations of war, these, and other matters of a like nature, constitute what seems to be most properly understood by the administration of government.

Those aiding the President should be of his own choosing.

72:3 The persons, therefore, to whose immediate management these different matters are committed, ought to be considered as the assistants or deputies of the chief magistrate, and on this account, they ought to derive their offices from his appointment, at least from his nomination, and ought to be subject to his superintendence.

NEW ADMINISTRATION SHOULD ALLOW FOR NEW OFFICERS AND APPOINTEES:

Should these managers stay or go according to who sits as President? Does such an upheaval hurt stability or help by correcting a predecessor's flaws?

72:4 This view of the subject will at once suggest to us the intimate connection between the duration of the executive magistrate in office and the stability of the system of administration. To reverse and undo what has been done by a predecessor, is very often considered by a successor as the best proof he can give of his own capacity and desert; and in addition to this propensity, where the alteration has been the result of public choice, the person substituted is warranted in supposing that the dismission of his predecessor has proceeded from a dislike to his measures; and that the less he resembles him, the more he will recommend himself to the favor of his constituents.

A President sensing he was elected for his "agenda" will feel encouraged to change out all of the positions.

72:5 These considerations, and the influence of personal confidences and attachments, would be likely to induce every new President to promote a change of men to fill the subordinate stations; and these causes together could not fail to occasion a disgraceful and ruinous mutability in the administration of the government.

REELECTION MOTIVATES GOOD PERFORMANCE:

What are the two main purposes of the four-year term for the President? Does the country benefit from experienced executives?

72:6 With a positive duration of considerable extent, I connect the circumstance of re-eligibility.

Incentive to do well.

72:7 The first is necessary to give to the officer himself the inclination and the resolution to act his part well, and to the community time and leisure to observe the tendency of his measures, and thence to form an experimental estimate of their merits.

Reward good conduct.

72:8 The last is necessary to enable the people, when they see reason to approve of his conduct, to continue him in his station, in order to prolong the utility of his talents and virtues, and to secure to the government the advantage of permanency in a wise system of administration.

TERM LIMITS IS A BAD IDEA:
Could the President do his job if he had only one term, or had to wait a period of time before running for a second term?

72:9 Nothing appears more plausible at first sight, nor more ill-founded upon close inspection, than a <u>scheme</u> which in relation to the present point has had some respectable advocates, I mean that of <u>continuing</u> the chief magistrate <u>in office</u> for a certain time, <u>and then excluding him</u> from it, either for a limited period or forever after. This <u>exclusion</u>, whether <u>temporary</u> or <u>perpetual</u>, would have nearly the <u>same effects</u>, and these effects would be for the most part rather pernicious than salutary.

REELECTION ENCOURAGES BEST BEHAVIOR:
Would the President do his job as well if he knew he had only one term? Would he do better if he knew he could win additional terms in office because of his excellent performance?

72:10 One ill effect of the exclusion would be a <u>diminution</u> of the <u>inducements</u> to <u>good behavior</u>. There are few men who would not feel <u>much less zeal</u> in the discharge of a duty when they were conscious that the advantages of the station with which it was connected <u>must be relinquished</u> at a determinate period, than when they were permitted to entertain a hope of <u>OBTAINING</u>, by <u>MERITING</u>, a continuance of them.

STRONGEST HUMAN INCENTIVE:
Everyone wants a reward.

72:11 This position will not be disputed so long as it is admitted that the <u>desire of reward is one of the strongest incentives of human conduct</u>; or that the best security for the fidelity of mankind is to make their interests coincide with their duty.

POSSIBLE REELECTION IMPACTS BEHAVIOR:
A President is motivated to do well if additional terms are possible.

72:12 Even the <u>love of fame</u>, the <u>ruling passion of the noblest minds</u>, which would prompt a man to plan and undertake extensive and arduous enterprises for the public benefit, requiring considerable time to mature and perfect them, if he could flatter himself with the prospect of being <u>allowed to finish what he had begun</u>, would, on the contrary, <u>deter him</u> from the undertaking, when he <u>foresaw</u> that he must <u>quit the scene before he could accomplish the work</u>, and must <u>commit that</u>, together with his own reputation, <u>to hands</u> which might be <u>unequal or unfriendly to the task</u>. The most to be expected from the generality of men, in such a situation, is the <u>negative merit of not doing harm</u>, instead of the <u>positive merit of doing good</u>.

MOTIVATED TO BE SELFISH?
What are some temptations a one-term President might pursue to benefit himself while doing harm to America?

72:13 <u>Another ill effect</u> of the exclusion would be the <u>temptation to sordid views</u>, to peculation, and, in some instances, to <u>usurpation</u>. An avaricious man, who might happen to fill the office, looking forward to a time when he must at all events yield up the emoluments he enjoyed, would feel a propensity, not easy to be resisted by such a man, to make the <u>best use of the opportunity</u> he enjoyed while it lasted, and might not scruple to have recourse to the most corrupt expedients to <u>make the harvest as abundant as it was transitory</u>;

SAME MAN MIGHT CHOOSE GOOD:
The reward of another term would discourage bad behavior and conspiracy.

72:14 though the same man, probably, with a different prospect before him, might content himself with the regular perquisites of his situation, and might even be <u>unwilling to risk the consequences of an abuse of his opportunities</u>. His **avarice**[231] might be a guard upon his avarice.

One term could induce presidents to recklessly enact all they could, regardless of the good or harm it might do the country.

72:15 Add to this that the same man might be <u>vain or ambitious</u>, as well as avaricious. And if he could expect to <u>prolong his honors by his good conduct</u>, he might hesitate to sacrifice his appetite for them to his appetite for gain. But with the prospect before him of approaching an inevitable annihilation, <u>his avarice would be likely to get the victory over his caution, his vanity, or his ambition</u>.

ONLY ONE TERM CREATES AMBITIOUS TEMPTATIONS:
Would one term also tempt a President to seek ways to extend his power? To behave with reckless abandon instead of doing his duties?

72:16 An <u>ambitious man</u>, too, when he found himself seated on the summit of his country's honors, when he <u>looked forward</u>[232] to the time at which he <u>must descend</u> from the exalted eminence for ever, and reflected that no exertion of merit on his part could save him from the unwelcome reverse; such a man, in such a situation, would be much more violently <u>tempted</u> to embrace a favorable conjuncture for <u>attempting the prolongation of his power</u>, at every personal hazard, than if he had the probability of answering the same end by doing his duty.

---

231 **avarice:** Covetousness or insatiable desire for gain; **greed** is the selfish desire for more than is needed. The difference is *to have* versus *to have more*.

232 *Editors' Note:* An example of this are the pardons Presidents tend to grant during their last days of office, oftentimes very unpopular pardons.

DISCONTENTED EX-PRESIDENTS MIGHT BEHAVE AS ACTIVISTS:
Their voice would carry far after leaving office, and could stir antagonism toward the new President's labors.

72:17 Would it promote the peace of the community, or the stability of the government to have half a dozen men who had had credit enough to be raised to the seat of the supreme magistracy, wandering among the people like discontented ghosts, and sighing for a place which they were destined never more to possess?

ONE-TERM LIMIT PREVENTS THE ADVANTAGES OF EXPERIENCE:
What precious perspective is the nation deprived of because of a single term limitation?

72:18 A third ill effect of the exclusion would be, the depriving the community of the advantage of the experience gained by the chief magistrate in the exercise of his office.

PRESIDENTIAL EXPERIENCE IS THE PARENT OF WISDOM:
72:19 That experience is the parent of wisdom, is an adage the truth of which is recognized by the wisest as well as the simplest of mankind. What more desirable or more essential than this quality in the governors of nations? Where more desirable or more essential than in the first magistrate of a nation? Can it be wise to put this desirable and essential quality under the ban of the Constitution, and to declare that the moment it is acquired, its possessor shall be compelled to abandon the station in which it was acquired, and to which it is adapted?

Term limits disqualify the seasoned leader.

72:20 This, nevertheless, is the precise import of all those regulations which exclude men from serving their country, by the choice of their fellow citizens, after they have by a course of service fitted themselves for doing it with a greater degree of utility.

TERM LIMITS DANGEROUS IN TIMES OF WAR:
Could single terms endanger the country in the face of war or crisis?

72:21 A fourth ill effect of the exclusion would be the banishing men from stations in which, in certain emergencies of the state, their presence might be of the greatest moment to the public interest or safety. There is no nation which has not, at one period or another, experienced an absolute necessity of the services of particular men in particular situations; perhaps it would not be too strong to say, to the preservation of its political existence. How unwise, therefore, must be every such self-denying ordinance as serves to prohibit a nation from making use of its own citizens in the manner best suited to its exigencies and circumstances!

Changing leadership during war could be disastrous.

72:22 Without supposing the personal essentiality of the man, it is evident that a change of the chief magistrate, at the breaking out of a war, or at any similar crisis, for another, even of equal merit, would at all times be detrimental to the community, inasmuch as it would substitute inexperience to experience, and would tend to unhinge and set afloat the already settled train of the administration.

CONSISTENCY IMPORTANT FOR STABILITY:
Is a single term foolish when stability of the government is the end goal?

72:23 A fifth ill effect of the exclusion would be, that it would operate as a constitutional interdiction of stability in the administration. By NECESSITATING a change of men, in the first office of the nation, it would necessitate a mutability of measures. It is not generally to be expected, that men will vary and measures remain uniform. The contrary is the usual course of things. And we need not be apprehensive that there will be too much stability, while there is even the option of changing;

LET THE PEOPLE REELECT WHOMEVER THEY WISH:
72:24 nor need we desire to prohibit the people from continuing their confidence where they think it may be safely placed, and where, by constancy on their part, they may obviate the fatal inconveniences of fluctuating councils and a variable policy.

DELAYED TERMS ARE AS HARMFUL AS PARTIAL EXCLUSION:
Would a delay between terms be as bad as no additional term at all?

72:25 These are some of the disadvantages which would flow from the principle of exclusion. They apply most forcibly to the scheme of a perpetual exclusion; but when we consider that even a partial exclusion would always render the readmission of the person a remote and precarious object, the observations which have been made will apply nearly as fully to one case as to the other.

SOME ADVANTAGES OF TERM LIMITS:
Do term limits remove the concern about being judged and leave the President more independence to act?

72:26 What are the advantages promised to counterbalance these disadvantages? They are represented to be: 1st, greater independence in the magistrate; 2d, greater security to the people.

REDUCES TEMPTATION TO LEAVE ON BAD NOTE:

72:27 Unless the exclusion be perpetual, there will be no pretense to infer the first advantage. But even in that case, may he have no object beyond his present station, to which he may sacrifice his independence? May he have no connections, no friends, for whom he may sacrifice it? May he not be <u>less willing</u> by a firm conduct, <u>to make personal enemies</u>, when he acts under the impression that a time is fast approaching, on the arrival of which he not only MAY, but MUST, be <u>exposed</u> to their <u>resentments</u>, upon an equal, perhaps <u>upon an inferior, footing</u>?

Hard to know if term limits help or hurt independent action.

72:28 It is not an easy point to determine whether his independence would be most <u>promoted or impaired</u> by such an arrangement.

SECURITY STILL AT RISK WITH TERM LIMITS:

Do term limits really bring greater security to America? Would a power-hungry, one-term President not conspire to gain power using his office as the tool?

72:29 <u>As to the second supposed advantage</u>, there is still greater reason to entertain doubts concerning it.

72:30 If the exclusion were to be perpetual, a man of irregular ambition, of whom alone there could be reason in any case to entertain apprehension, would, with infinite reluctance, yield to the necessity of taking his leave forever of a post in which his <u>passion for power</u> and pre-eminence had acquired the force of habit.

A popular leader might lead a movement to overthrow the one-term limit.

72:31 And if he had been fortunate or adroit enough to conciliate the good-will of the people, he might induce them to <u>consider</u> as a very <u>odious</u> and unjustifiable <u>restraint</u> upon themselves, a provision which was calculated to debar them of the right of giving a fresh proof of their attachment to a favorite.

The people stirred to passion might seek amending away the one-term limit.

72:32 There may be conceived circumstances in which this disgust of the people, seconding the thwarted ambition of such a favorite, <u>might occasion greater danger to liberty</u>, than could ever reasonably be dreaded from the possibility of a perpetuation in office, by the voluntary suffrages of the community, exercising a constitutional privilege.

LET THE PEOPLE DECIDE TERM LIMITS BY VOTING, NOT BY EDICT:

Do the advantages of many terms outweigh the disadvantages of one term?

72:33 There is an excess of refinement in the idea of <u>disabling the people</u> to <u>continue in office men</u> who had entitled themselves, in their opinion, to approbation and confidence; the advantages of which are at best speculative and equivocal, and are overbalanced by <u>disadvantages</u> <u>far more certain</u> and decisive.

—Publius

Review Questions

1. Why should the President be allowed to pick his own staff and leaders for the executive branch? (72:3–5)

2. What are some reasons why term limits are bad for the executive? (72:10–17)

3. What on-the-job experience in office is lost with one term? (72:18–19)

4. How could the loss of experience and wisdom play a role should war suddenly erupt? (72:21–22)

5. If a one-term limit on the office of President was unpopular would that stir the people's passions to overthrow it? Doesn't it make more sense to simply let voters decide who stays or goes? (72:31–33)

FEDERALIST NO. 73

Salary and veto power for president: This paper highlights the principle of checks and balances. It shows how Congress is prevented from influencing the President by controlling his salary. Likewise, the President may directly veto legislation harmful to the nation, but he can be overridden by Congress if it has a super majority of votes (two thirds of both houses). The Framers intentionally created conflict and jealousies in the Constitution as additional means to secure the people's liberties.

By Alexander Hamilton—March 21, 1788

CONTROL OF SALARY IS CONTROL OF PRESIDENT:

Why is the President's salary an important part of maintaining the separation of powers?

73:1 THE third ingredient towards constituting the vigor of the executive authority, is an adequate provision for its support. It is evident that, without proper attention to this article, the separation of the executive from the legislative department would be merely nominal and nugatory.

CONGRESS COULD COERCE BY FAMINE OR TEMPT BY LARGESS:

Congress could force or bribe using salary as the weapon. Which modern-day Presidents removed such doubt by donating their salaries?

73:2 The legislature, with a discretionary power over the salary and emoluments of the Chief Magistrate, could render him as obsequious to their will as they might think proper to make him. They might, in most cases, either reduce him by famine, or tempt him by largesses, to surrender at discretion his judgment to their inclinations. These expressions, taken in all the latitude of the terms, would no doubt convey more than is intended.

MEN OF INTEGRITY CAN'T BE BOUGHT, BUT OTHERS ARE:

73:3 There are men who could neither be distressed nor won into a sacrifice of their duty; but this stern virtue is the growth of few soils; and in the main it will be found that a power over a man's support is a power over his will.

Plenty of examples exist to prove this truth.

73:4 If it were necessary to confirm so plain a truth by facts, examples would not be wanting, even in this country, of the intimidation or seduction of the Executive by the terrors or allurements of the pecuniary arrangements of the legislative body.

CONSTITUTION PROTECTS THE PRESIDENT AND HIS SALARY:

What does the Constitution say about a President's salary during a term?

73:5 It is not easy, therefore, to commend too highly the judicious attention which has been paid to this subject in the proposed Constitution. It is there provided that "The President of the United States shall, at stated times, receive for his services a compensation WHICH SHALL NEITHER BE INCREASED NOR DIMINISHED DURING THE PERIOD FOR WHICH HE SHALL HAVE BEEN ELECTED; and he SHALL NOT RECEIVE WITHIN THAT PERIOD ANY OTHER EMOLUMENT from the United States, or any of them."

73:6 It is impossible to imagine any provision which would have been more eligible than this. The legislature, on the appointment of a President, is once for all to declare what shall be the compensation for his services during the time for which he shall have been elected.

CONSTITUTION REMOVES THREATS AND TEMPTATIONS:

What two influences would Congress have on the President if they did indeed have power to alter salary?

73:7 This done, they will have no power to alter it, either by increase or diminution, till a new period of service by a new election commences. They can neither weaken his fortitude by operating on his necessities, nor corrupt his integrity by appealing to his avarice. Neither the Union, nor any of its members, will be at liberty to give, nor will he be at liberty to receive, any other emolument than that which may have been determined by the first act. He can, of course, have no pecuniary inducement to renounce or desert the independence intended for him by the Constitution.

WHAT POWERS ARE GIVEN TO THE PRESIDENT?

73:8 The last of the requisites to energy, which have been enumerated, are competent powers. Let us proceed to consider those which are proposed to be vested in the President of the United States.

VETO:

The Framers used the word "negative" to mean veto. How many votes in each house of Congress are needed to override a veto?

73:9 The first thing that offers itself to our observation, is the qualified negative of the President upon the acts or resolutions of the two houses of the legislature; or, in other words, his power of returning all bills with objections, to have the effect of preventing their becoming laws, unless they should afterwards be ratified by two thirds of each of the component members of the legislative body.

EACH BRANCH NEEDS ITS OWN PROTECTION:

The means for each branch to protect itself are built into the Constitution. But paper boundaries are not necessarily sufficient.

73:10 The propensity of the legislative department to intrude upon the rights, and to absorb the powers, of the other departments, has been already suggested and repeated; the insufficiency of a mere parchment delineation of the boundaries of each, has also been remarked upon; and the necessity of furnishing each with constitutional arms for its own defense, has been inferred and proved.

WITHOUT VETO POWER, PRESIDENT IS VULNERABLE:

Congress would strip the President of all authority.

73:11 From these clear and indubitable principles results the propriety of a negative, either absolute or qualified, in the Executive, upon the acts of the legislative branches. Without the one or the other, the former would be absolutely unable to defend himself against the depredations of the latter. He might gradually be stripped of his authorities by successive resolutions, or annihilated by a single vote. And in the one mode or the other, the legislative and executive powers might speedily come to be blended in the same hands.

EXECUTIVE SHOULDN'T BE AT MERCY OF CONGRESS:
The separation of powers must be preserved from legislative takeover.

73:12 If even no propensity had ever discovered itself in the legislative body to invade the rights of the Executive, the rules of just reasoning and theoretic propriety would of themselves teach us, that the one ought not to be left to the mercy of the other, but ought to possess a constitutional and effectual power of self defense.

VETO IS A DEFENSE AGAINST MISGUIDED LAW:
Should a faction sway a majority in Congress toward improper laws, the President serves as a check to protect the nation.

73:13 But the power in question has a further use. It not only serves as a shield to the Executive, but it furnishes an additional security against the enaction of improper laws. It establishes a salutary check upon the legislative body, calculated to guard the community against the effects of faction, precipitancy, or of any impulse unfriendly to the public good, which may happen to influence a majority of that body.

PRESIDENT CAN'T OVERRIDE NATIONAL WILL:
Is giving one man power over Congress too much like a king?

73:14 The propriety of a negative has, upon some occasions, been combated by an observation, that it was not to be presumed a single man would possess more virtue and wisdom than a number of men; and that unless this presumption should be entertained, it would be improper to give the executive magistrate any species of control over the legislative body.

VETO INTENDED TO PREVENT RASH OR MISGUIDED LAW:
The President's power of veto validates the belief that Congress won't be perfect.

73:15 But this observation, when examined, will appear rather specious than solid. The propriety of the thing does not turn upon the supposition of superior wisdom or virtue in the Executive, but upon the supposition that the legislature will not be infallible;

The veto also stands guard against corruption.

73:16 that the love of power may sometimes betray it into a disposition to encroach upon the rights of other members of the government; that a spirit of faction may sometimes pervert its deliberations; that impressions of the moment may sometimes hurry it into measures which itself, on maturer reflection, would condemn.

MAIN PURPOSE OF VETO IS TO PROTECT THE PRESIDENT:
Does that power encourage more thoughtful consideration of laws being written and debated by Congress?

73:17 The primary inducement to conferring the power in question upon the Executive is, to enable him to defend himself;

President's veto power also gives Congress incentive to be cautious.

73:18 the secondary one is to increase the chances in favor of the community against the passing of bad laws, through haste, inadvertence, or design. The oftener the measure is brought under examination, the greater the diversity in the situations of those who are to examine it, the less must be the danger of those errors which flow from want of due deliberation, or of those missteps which proceed from the contagion of some common passion or interest. It is far less probable, that culpable views of any kind should infect all the parts of the government at the same moment and in relation to the same object, than that they should by turns govern and mislead every one of them.

CAN A VETO BE USED AGAINST GOOD LAWS?
While the veto can defeat good laws this would run contrary to the entire government process. Should this be of concern?

73:19 It may perhaps be said that the power of preventing bad laws includes that of preventing good ones; and may be used to the one purpose as well as to the other. But this objection will have little weight with those who can properly estimate the mischiefs of that inconstancy and mutability in the laws, which form the greatest blemish in the character and genius of our governments. They will consider every institution calculated to restrain the excess of law-making, and to keep things in the same state in which they happen to be at any given period, as much more likely to do good than harm; because it is favorable to greater stability in the system of legislation.

AVERTING BAD LAWS IS PREFERABLE TO DEFEATING A FEW GOOD LAWS:

73:20 The injury which may possibly be done by defeating a few good laws, will be amply compensated by the advantage of preventing a number of bad ones.

VETO WILL BE RARELY USED AGAINST PEOPLE'S WILL:

Can the veto be casually used or does it stir up a huge hornet's nest?

73:21 Nor is this all. The superior weight and influence of the legislative body in a free government, and the hazard to the Executive in a trial of strength with that body, afford a satisfactory security that the negative would generally be employed with great caution; and there would oftener be room for a charge of timidity than of rashness in the exercise of it.

THE KING WOULD HESITATE GOING AGAINST PARLIAMENT :

73:22 A king of Great Britain, with all his train of sovereign attributes, and with all the influence he draws from a thousand sources, would, at this day, hesitate to put a negative upon the joint resolutions of the two houses of Parliament. He would not fail to exert the utmost resources of that influence to strangle a measure disagreeable to him, in its progress to the throne, to avoid being reduced to the dilemma of permitting it to take effect, or of risking the displeasure of the nation by an opposition to the sense of the legislative body.

KING HAS NOT VETOED PARLIAMENT FOR A LONG TIME:

73:23 Nor is it probable, that he would ultimately venture to exert his prerogatives, but in a case of manifest propriety, or extreme necessity. All well-informed men in that kingdom will accede to the justness of this remark. A very considerable period has elapsed since the negative of the crown has been exercised.

VETO MORE RISKY FOR PRESIDENT THAN KING:

If an all-powerful British king has difficulty using the veto, the President have even greater difficulty.

73:24 If a magistrate so powerful and so well fortified as a British monarch, would have scruples about the exercise of the power under consideration, how much greater caution may be reasonably expected in a President of the United States, clothed for the short period of four years with the executive authority of a government wholly and purely republican?

NOT USING VETO OUT OF FEAR IS A CONCERN:

A President might not exercise his veto power out of fear of political fallout. Which is worse, using the veto too much or too little?

73:25 It is evident that there would be greater danger of his not using his power when necessary, than of his using it too often, or too much. An argument, indeed, against its expediency, has been drawn from this very source. It has been represented, on this account, as a power odious in appearance, useless in practice. But it will not follow, that because it might be rarely exercised, it would never be exercised.

TWO REASONS TO USE VETO:

73:26 In the case for which it is chiefly designed, that of [1.] an immediate attack upon the constitutional rights of the Executive, or [2.] in a case in which the public good was evidently and palpably sacrificed, a man of tolerable firmness would avail himself of his constitutional means of defense, and would listen to the admonitions of duty and responsibility. In the former supposition, his fortitude would be stimulated by his immediate interest in the power of his office; in the latter, by the probability of the sanction of his constituents, who, though they would naturally incline to the legislative body in a doubtful case, would hardly suffer their partiality to delude them in a very plain case.

LEADERS WITH INTEGRITY DO THEIR DUTY REGARDLESS:

73:27 I speak now with an eye to a magistrate possessing only a common share of firmness. There are men who, under any circumstances, will have the courage to do their duty at every hazard.

THE COMPROMISE MADE OVER VETO POWER WAS THAT IT WOULD NOT BE ABSOLUTE:

The President may send a law back for reconsideration instead of totally preventing its passage. What does a "qualified negative" mean?

73:28 But the Convention have pursued a mean in this business, which will both facilitate the exercise of the power vested in this respect in the executive magistrate, and make its efficacy to depend on the sense of a considerable part of the legislative body. Instead of an absolute negative, it is proposed to give the Executive the qualified negative already described. This is a power which would be much more readily exercised than the other. A man who might be afraid to defeat a law by his single VETO, might not scruple to return it for reconsideration; subject to being finally rejected only in the event of more than one third of each house concurring in the sufficiency of his objections. He would be encouraged by the reflection, that if his opposition should prevail, it would embark in it a very respectable proportion of the legislative body, whose influence would be united with his in supporting the propriety of his conduct in the public opinion.

VETO IS INTENDED TO GENERATE RECONSIDERATION OF A LAW OR ACT:
President should not have power to override a super majority of Congress's will.

73:29   A direct and <u>categorical negative</u> has something in the appearance of it more harsh, and <u>more apt to irritate</u>, than the mere suggestion of argumentative objections to be approved or disapproved by those to whom they are addressed. In proportion as it would be less apt to offend, it would be more apt to be exercised; and for this very reason, it may in practice be found more effectual.

HOPEFULLY CONGRESS WILL AVOID RASH BEHAVIOR:
If the President properly vetoes a dangerous bill, hopefully Congress will take proper note and reexamine it.

73:30   It is to be hoped that it will not often happen that <u>improper views</u> will govern so large a proportion as <u>two thirds of both branches</u> of the legislature at the same time; and this, too, in spite of the counterposing weight of the Executive. It is at any rate far less probable that this should be the case, than that such views should <u>taint the resolutions and conduct of a bare majority</u>.

CONGRESS WILL EXERCISE CAUTION IN VIEW OF VETO:
The mere presence of a possible veto will dampen rash behavior.

73:31   A power of this nature in the Executive, will often have a <u>silent</u> and unperceived, though forcible, <u>operation</u>. When men, engaged in unjustifiable pursuits, are <u>aware that obstructions</u> may come from a quarter which they cannot control, they will often be <u>restrained</u> by the bare apprehension of opposition, from doing what they would with <u>eagerness rush</u> into, if no such external impediments were to be feared.

NEW YORK'S USE OF THE VETO:
Have these same executive tools worked for New York?

73:32   <u>This qualified negative</u>, as has been elsewhere remarked, is in <u>this State</u> vested in a council, consisting of the <u>governor</u>, with the chancellor and judges of the Supreme Court, or any two of them. It has been <u>freely employed</u> upon a variety of occasions, and frequently with success. And its utility has become so apparent, that persons who, in compiling the Constitution, were <u>violent opposers</u> of it, have from experience become its <u>declared admirers</u>.[233]

Massachusetts plan improves on this by removing the judges.

73:33   I have in another place remarked, that the <u>Convention</u>, in the formation of this part of their plan, had <u>departed</u> from the model of the constitution of this State, in favor of that of <u>Massachusetts</u>.

Judges might be biased.

73:34   Two strong reasons may be imagined for this preference. One is that the <u>judges</u>, who are to be the <u>interpreters</u> of the law, might receive an improper <u>bias</u>, from having given a <u>previous opinion</u> in their <u>revisionary capacities</u>;

Judges might show favoritism toward executive.

73:35   the <u>other</u> is that by being often <u>associated with the Executive</u>, they might be induced to embark too far in the political views of that magistrate, and thus a dangerous combination might by <u>degrees be cemented between the executive and judiciary departments</u>.

Impossible to insulate judges from corruption or influence.

73:36   It is impossible to keep the judges too distinct from every other avocation than that of <u>expounding the laws</u>. It is peculiarly dangerous to place them in a situation to be either corrupted or influenced by the Executive.

—PUBLIUS

REVIEW QUESTIONS

1. How could Congress control the President's political power? (73:1–2)

2. Fill in the blanks: Power over a man's _____ is a power over his _____. (73:3)

3. How does the Constitution protect the President from congressional manipulation? (73:5)

4. If the President finds a congressional law dangerous and vetoes it, how much of each House is needed to override the veto? (73:9)

5. Without the veto, what might Congress do to the executive? (73:11–12)

6. What kind of negatives is the veto intended to prevent? (73:15–16)

7. How does the power to veto encourage good law? (73:18, 28, 31)

8. What are the two main reasons for using the veto? (73:26, 31)

---

233 *Publius*: Mr. Abraham Yates, a warm opponent of the plan of the convention is of this number.

FEDERALIST NO. 74

THE PRESIDENT AS COMMANDER IN CHIEF AND THE POWER TO PARDON: Putting power over the military into one supreme leader is critically important during an attack when instant action is necessary. Leaving that authority spread around among various supreme leaders could be disastrous in an emergency when instant action is required. Also, the power to grant reprieves and pardons is best left in the President who can act quickly when the needs and opportunities best present themselves. Over the years this controversial power to pardon has been used for political profit or payback instead of serving justice or showing mercy.

By Alexander Hamilton—March 25, 1788

THE PRESIDENT COMMANDS THE MILITARY:
Who is commander in chief? Is he the same who controls the direction of war? What act must first take place before the President can also be commander of the militia?

74:1 THE President of the United States is to be "commander-in-chief of the army and navy of the United States, and of the militia of the several States WHEN CALLED INTO THE ACTUAL SERVICE of the United States." The propriety of this provision is so evident in itself, and it is, at the same time, so consonant to the precedents of the State constitutions in general, that little need be said to explain or enforce it. Even those of them which have, in other respects, coupled the chief magistrate with a council, have for the most part concentrated the military authority in him alone.

SINGLE HAND BEST FOR DIRECTING WAR:
Directing war can bog down if decisions are made by committee. Does the President have advisers and the military to inform him?

74:2 Of all the cares or concerns of government, the direction of war most peculiarly demands those qualities which distinguish the exercise of power by a single hand. The direction of war implies the direction of the common strength; and the power of directing and employing the common strength, forms a usual and essential part in the definition of the executive authority.

PRESIDENT CAN SOLICIT INPUT:
Regarding defense or other national issues, from where can the President draw additional input and opinion for his decisions?

74:3 "The President may require the opinion, in writing, of the principal officer in each of the executive departments, upon any subject relating to the duties of their respective officers." This I consider as a mere redundancy in the plan, as the right for which it provides would result of itself from the office.

REPRIEVES AND PARDONS:
What is the one crime for which the President cannot issue a reprieve or pardon?

74:4 He is also to be authorized to grant "reprieves and pardons for offenses against the United States, EXCEPT IN CASES OF IMPEACHMENT." Humanity and good policy conspire to dictate, that the benign prerogative of pardoning should be as little as possible fettered or embarrassed. The criminal code of every country partakes so much of necessary severity, that without an easy access to exceptions in favor of unfortunate guilt, justice would wear a countenance too sanguinary and cruel. As the sense of responsibility is always strongest, in proportion as it is undivided, it may be inferred that a single man would be most ready to attend to the force of those motives which might plead for a mitigation of the rigor of the law, and least apt to yield to considerations which were calculated to shelter a fit object of its vengeance.

PRESIDENT BEST FOR SHOWING MERCY BY PARDONING:
Should mercy (reprieves and pardons) reside in one hand? What do groups assembled for such purposes tend to do that discourages mercy?

74:5 The reflection that the fate of a fellow-creature depended on his sole fiat, would naturally inspire scrupulousness and caution; the dread of being accused of weakness or connivance, would beget equal circumspection, though of a different kind. On the other hand, as men generally derive confidence from their numbers, they might often encourage each other in an act of **obduracy**,[234] and might be less sensible to the apprehension of suspicion or censure for an injudicious or affected clemency. On these accounts, one man appears to be a more eligible dispenser of the mercy of government, than a body of men.

TREASON IS PARDONABLE:
74:6 The expediency of vesting the power of pardoning in the President has, if I mistake not, been only contested in relation to the crime of treason. This, it has been urged, ought to have depended upon the assent of one, or both, of the branches of the legislative body. I shall not deny that there are strong reasons to be assigned for requiring in this particular the concurrence of that body, or of a part of it. As treason is a crime leveled at the immediate being of the society, when the laws

---

234 *obduracy:* State of being unmoved by persuasion or pity, hardened against good. The opposite is tenderness, flexibility, and amenability.

have once ascertained the guilt of the offender, there seems a fitness in referring the expediency of an <u>act of mercy</u> towards him to the <u>judgment of the legislature</u>. And this ought the rather to be the case, as the supposition of the connivance of the Chief Magistrate ought not to be entirely excluded.

SINGLE MAN OF PRUDENCE BETTER THAN CONGRESS:

Would pardons become political decisions rather than moral and merciful decisions if left in the hands of Congress?

74:7 But there are also strong objections to such a plan. It is not to be doubted, that a <u>single man of prudence</u> and good sense is <u>better fitted</u>, <u>in delicate conjunctures</u>, to <u>balance the motives</u> which may plead for and against the remission of the punishment, <u>than any numerous body</u> whatever.

CONGRESS CAN BECOME BIASED AGAINST ACCUSED:

A problem with Congress having power to pardon is that Congress itself might be implicated in the offense.

74:8 It deserves particular attention, that treason will often be connected with <u>seditions which embrace a large proportion of the community</u>; as lately happened in Massachusetts. In every such case, we might expect to see the representation of the people tainted with the same spirit which had given birth to the offense. And when <u>parties</u> were pretty equally matched, the secret sympathy of the friends and <u>favorers of the condemned</u> person, availing itself of the good-nature and weakness of others, might frequently <u>bestow impunity where</u> the terror of an <u>example was necessary</u>.

CONGRESS COULD ALSO BE BIASED IN FAVOR:

74:9 On the other hand, when the sedition had proceeded from causes which had inflamed the resentments of the major party, they might often be found obstinate and inexorable, when <u>policy demanded</u> a conduct of forbearance and <u>clemency</u>.

A WELL-TIMED PARDON CAN RESTORE PEACE:

Under what unique circumstances would the power to pardon treason best rest in the President?

74:10 But the principal argument for reposing the power of pardoning in this case to the Chief Magistrate is this: in <u>seasons of insurrection or rebellion</u>, there are often <u>critical moments</u>, when a well-timed offer of <u>pardon to the insurgents or rebels may restore the tranquility</u> of the commonwealth;

and which, if suffered to pass unimproved, it may never be possible afterwards to recall. The **dilatory**[235] process of <u>convening the legislature</u>, or one of its branches, for the purpose of obtaining its sanction to the measure, would frequently be the occasion of <u>letting slip the golden opportunity</u>. The <u>loss of a week, a day, an hour</u>, may sometimes be <u>fatal</u>.[236]

WOULD CONGRESS SURRENDER PARDON POWER?

If the President did not have power to pardon, would Congress turn that duty over to him, especially if it believed the person guilty, and the President leaning toward pardoning?

74:11 If it should be observed, that a discretionary power, with a view to such contingencies, might be occasionally conferred upon the President, it may be answered in the first place, that it is questionable, whether, in a limited Constitution, that power could be delegated by law; and in the second place, that it would generally be impolitic beforehand to take any step which might hold out the prospect of impunity. A proceeding of this kind, out of the usual course, would be likely to be construed into an argument of timidity or of weakness, and would have a tendency to embolden guilt.

—Publius

Review Questions

1. What two presidential powers does Hamilton defend in paper No. 74? (74:1, 4)

2. Is a single man or a group of men best suited to possess all power to pardon? Why? (74:5–8)

3. Can the President pardon treason? (74:6, 8)

4. Can the power to pardon help restore peace? (74:10 and footnote)

FEDERALIST NO. 75

PRESIDENT'S POWER TO MAKE TREATIES IS SHARED: This power is best shared between the President and the Senate. If concentrated in the President he might make treaties beneficial to himself after leaving office. If left to Congress a treaty might be unnecessarily delayed by intrigues, fac-

---

235 *dilatory:* Slow to act, drawing out or extending the time; deferring action.

236 *Editors' Note:* In reference to 74:10, the 1794 "Whiskey Rebellion" tax protest proved the principle of allowing the President to pardon treason. President Washington sent troops to end an insurrection, but then restored peace by pardoning those convicted of treason. Washington later told Congress, "The misled have abandoned their errors. For though I shall always think it a sacred duty to exercise with firmness and energy the constitutional powers with which I am vested, yet it appears to me no less consistent with the public good than it is with my personal feelings to mingle in the operations of Government every degree of moderation and tenderness which the national justice, dignity, and safety may permit." John C. Fitzpatrick, *The Writings of George Washington from the Original Manuscript Sources 1745-1799 Volume 34 October 11, 1794–March 29, 1796.* [Washington DC: US Government Printing Office, 1931].

tions, and inefficiencies, thereby weakening America's negotiating position. The Senate is the best partner in treaties, but only by a majority of senators present, not the total, lest a single senator have power to prevent a treaty by sheer obstinacy or absence.

By Alexander Hamilton—March 26, 1788

PRESIDENT AND SENATE MAKE TREATIES:
75:1 THE President is to have power, "by and with the advice and consent of the Senate, to make <u>treaties</u>, provided two thirds of the senators present concur."

TWO OBJECTIONS BY ANTI-FEDERALISTS:
What are the two main objections to presidential treaty-making powers?
75:2 Though this provision has been assailed, on different grounds, with no small degree of vehemence, I scruple not to declare my firm persuasion, that it is one of the <u>best digested</u> and <u>most unexceptionable parts</u> of the plan.

(1) Intermixing powers.
75:3 One ground of objection is the trite topic of the <u>intermixture</u> of powers; some contending that the <u>President ought alone</u> to possess the power of making treaties; others, that it ought to have been <u>exclusively</u> deposited in the <u>Senate</u>.

(2) Too few persons.
75:4 Another source of objection is derived from the <u>small number of persons</u> by whom a treaty may be made. Of those who espouse this objection, a part are of opinion that the <u>House of Representatives ought to have been associated</u> in the business, while another part seem to think that nothing more was necessary than to have substituted two thirds of <u>ALL</u> the members of the Senate, to two thirds of the members <u>PRESENT</u>.

75:5 As I flatter myself the observations made in a preceding number upon this part of the plan must have sufficed to place it, to a discerning eye, in a very favorable light, I shall here content myself with offering only some supplementary remarks, principally with a view to the objections which have been just stated.

SEPARATION OF POWERS:
Does the power of making treaties violate the rule of separation of the executive branch from the legislative branch?
75:6 With regard to the <u>intermixture</u> of powers, I shall rely upon the explanations already given in other places, of the true sense of the rule upon which that objection is founded; and shall take it for granted, as an inference from them, that the <u>union</u> of the <u>Executive</u> with the <u>Senate</u>, in the article of

treaties, is <u>no infringement</u> of that rule. I venture to add, that the particular nature of the power of making treaties <u>indicates a peculiar propriety in that union</u>.

MAKING TREATIES IS ACT OF EXECUTIVE AND LEGISLATIVE:
75:7 Though several writers on the subject of government place that power in the class of executive authorities, yet this is evidently an arbitrary disposition; for if we attend carefully to its operation, it will be found to <u>partake more of the legislative than of the executive character</u>, though it does not seem strictly to fall within the definition of either of them.

MAIN DUTIES:
What is the main duty of Congress? What is the main duty of the President? Does a treaty fall into one or the other category?
75:8 The essence of the <u>legislative authority</u> is to <u>enact laws</u>, or, in other words, to prescribe rules for the regulation of the society; while the <u>execution</u> of the laws, and the employment of the common strength, either for this purpose or for the common defense, seem to comprise all the functions of the <u>executive</u> magistrate.

POWER OF MAKING TREATIES:
75:9 The <u>power of making treaties is, plainly, neither the one nor the other</u>. It relates <u>neither</u> to the <u>execution</u> of the subsisting laws, nor to the <u>enaction</u> of new ones; and still less to an exertion of the common strength.

TREATY IS A CONTRACT:
Treaties have the force of law dependent on good faith from all parties involved.
75:10 Its objects are <u>CONTRACTS with foreign nations</u>, which have the <u>force of law</u>, but derive it from the <u>obligations</u> of good <u>faith</u>. They are not rules prescribed by the sovereign to the subject, but <u>agreements</u> between <u>sovereign and sovereign</u>. The power in question seems therefore to form a distinct department, and to belong, properly, neither to the legislative nor to the executive.

TREATIES ARE BOTH LAWS AND NEGOTIATIONS:
75:11 The qualities elsewhere detailed as indispensable in the management of <u>foreign negotiations</u>, point out the <u>Executive</u> as the most fit agent in those transactions; while the vast importance of the trust, and the operation of <u>treaties as laws</u>, plead strongly for the participation of the whole or a portion of the <u>legislative</u> body in the office of making them.

TREATY MAKING IS NOT SAFE IN PRESIDENT ALONE:

75:12 <u>However proper</u> or safe it may be in governments where the executive magistrate is an hereditary <u>monarch</u>, to commit to him the <u>entire power</u> of making treaties, it would be <u>utterly unsafe</u> and improper to intrust that power to an <u>elective magistrate of four years' duration</u>.

King needs to retain support of his own government.

75:13 It has been remarked, upon another occasion, and the remark is unquestionably just, that an <u>hereditary monarch</u>, though often the oppressor of his people, has personally too much stake in the government to be in any material danger of being corrupted by foreign powers.

Compared to the reign of Britain's king the presidency is a short-term office.

75:14 But a <u>man raised</u> from the station of a private citizen to the <u>rank of chief magistrate</u>, possessed of a moderate or slender fortune, and looking forward to a period not very remote when he may probably be obliged to return to the station from which he was taken, might sometimes be <u>under temptations to sacrifice his duty</u> to his interest, which it would require superlative virtue to withstand.

HISTORY SHOWS IT'S BEST TO SHARE TREATY-MAKING POWER:

Does human history show that great national powers in the hands of one leader leads to creating personal fortunes?

75:15 An <u>avaricious man</u> might be tempted to <u>betray</u> the interests of the state to the acquisition of wealth. An <u>ambitious man</u> might make his own <u>aggrandizement</u>, by the aid of a <u>foreign power</u>, the price of his treachery to his constituents. The <u>history of human conduct</u> does not warrant that exalted opinion of human virtue which would make it wise in a nation to <u>commit interests</u> of so delicate and momentous a kind, as those which concern its intercourse with the rest of the world, to the <u>sole disposal</u> of a magistrate created and circumstanced as would be a <u>President</u> of the United States.

SENATE WOULD UNDO BENEFITS OF ONE NEGOTIATOR:

Would giving the Senate sole power over treaties dilute or emasculate the President's powers to negotiate face to face with other leaders?

75:16 To have intrusted the power of making treaties to the <u>Senate alone</u>, would have been to <u>relinquish</u> the benefits of the constitutional agency of the <u>President in the conduct of foreign negotiations</u>. It is true that the Senate would, in that case, have the <u>option of employing him</u> in this capacity, but they would also have the option of letting it alone, and pique or cabal might induce the latter rather than the former.

Sovereigns want face-to-face negotiations with sovereigns, not a body of men.

75:17 Besides this, the <u>ministerial servant</u> of the Senate could <u>not</u> be expected to enjoy the confidence and <u>respect</u> of foreign powers in the same degree with the constitutional representatives of the nation, and, of course, would <u>not be able to act</u> with an equal degree of weight or <u>efficacy</u>.

PRESIDENT ADDS TO THE SECURITY OF TREATIES:

What advantages does the President bring to the treaty-making process? Is a joint power with the Senate safer than either alone?

75:18 While the Union would, from this cause, lose a considerable advantage in the management of its external concerns, the <u>people</u> would <u>lose</u> the additional security which would result from the co-operation of the Executive. Though it would be imprudent to confide in him solely so important a trust, yet it cannot be doubted that his participation would <u>materially add to the safety</u> of the society.

PRESIDENT ADDS INTEGRITY TO TREATIES:

75:19 It must indeed be clear to a demonstration that the <u>joint possession</u> of the power in question, by the President and Senate, would afford a <u>greater</u> prospect of <u>security</u>, than the separate possession of it by either of them. And whoever has maturely weighed the circumstances which must concur in the appointment of a President, will be satisfied that the <u>office</u> will always bid fair to be <u>filled by men of such characters</u> as to render their concurrence in the <u>formation of treaties peculiarly desirable</u>, as well on the score of wisdom, as on that of integrity.

HOUSE IS TOO FLUID TO CARRY THIS TRUST:

Why is it a risky idea to include the House of Representatives in treaty making?

75:20 The remarks made in a former number, which have been alluded to in another part of this paper, will apply with conclusive force <u>against</u> the admission of the <u>House</u> of Representatives to a <u>share</u> in the formation of treaties. The <u>fluctuating</u> and, taking its future increase into the account, the <u>multitudinous composition</u> of that body, forbid us to expect in it those qualities which are essential to the proper execution of such a trust.

What are some reasons why the House would be such a drag on progress and a betrayer of the nuances needed in treaty making?

75:21 Accurate and <u>comprehensive knowledge of foreign politics</u>; a steady and systematic adherence to the <u>same views</u>; a nice and <u>uniform sensibility</u> to national character; <u>decision</u>, SECRECY, and <u>dispatch</u>, are incompatible with the genius of a body so variable and so numerous. The very complication of the business, by introducing a necessity of the concurrence of so many different bodies, would of itself afford a solid objection. The greater frequency of the calls upon the House of Representatives, and the greater length of time which it would often be necessary to keep them together when convened, to obtain their sanction in the progressive stages of a treaty, would be a source of so great inconvenience and expense as alone ought to condemn the project.

CALCULATING A MAJORITY:
Which works best, two thirds of all senators or two thirds of those present?

75:22   The only objection which remains to be canvassed, is that which would substitute the proportion of two thirds of all the members composing the senatorial body, to that of two thirds of the members PRESENT. It has been shown, under the second head of our inquiries, that all provisions which require more than the majority of any body to its resolutions, have a direct tendency to embarrass the operations of the government, and an indirect one to subject the sense of the majority to that of the minority.

TWO THIRDS OF *TOTAL* SENATE IS HARMFUL FOR TREATIES:
Requiring too large of a majority for routine congressional activities always bogs down progress.

75:23   This consideration seems sufficient to determine our opinion, that the Convention have gone as far in the endeavor to secure the advantage of numbers in the formation of treaties as could have been reconciled either with the activity of the public councils or with a reasonable regard to the major sense of the community.

MAJORITY OF SENATORS *PRESENT* IS A BETTER RULE:
A permanent number has been proven a stubborn failure from experience with the Articles of Confederation, and in history.

75:24   If two thirds of the whole number of members had been required, it would, in many cases, from the non-attendance of a part, amount in practice to a necessity of unanimity. And the history of every political establishment in which this principle has prevailed, is a history of impotence, perplexity, and disorder. Proofs of this position might be adduced from the examples of the Roman Tribuneship, the Polish Diet, and the States-General of the Netherlands, did not an example at home render foreign precedents unnecessary.

A FIXED NUMBER IS NO ADVANTAGE:
Would it help or hurt to put in law a solid number of senators required to be present to pass on a treaty?

75:25   To require a fixed proportion of the whole body would not, in all probability, contribute to the advantages of a numerous agency, better then merely to require a proportion of the attending members.

Punctual attendance minimized.
75:26   The former, by making a determinate number at all times requisite to a resolution, diminishes the motives to punctual attendance.

A single senator's absence could frustrate the whole body.
75:27   The latter, by making the capacity of the body to depend on a PROPORTION which may be varied by the absence or presence of a single member, has the contrary effect.

Promoting punctuality reduces chances of delay.
75:28   And as, by promoting punctuality, it tends to keep the body complete, there is great likelihood that its resolutions would generally be dictated by as great a number in this case as in the other; while there would be much fewer occasions of delay.

NEW PROCESS AS EFFECTIVE AS CURRENT PROCESS:
Allowing senators to vote individually instead of as States improves participation.

75:29   It ought not to be forgotten that, under the existing Confederation, two members MAY, and usually DO, represent a State; whence it happens that Congress, who now are solely invested with ALL THE POWERS of the Union, rarely consist of a greater number of persons than would compose the intended Senate. If we add to this, that as the members vote by States, and that where there is only a single member present from a State, his vote is lost, it will justify a supposition that the active voices in the Senate, where the members are to vote individually, would rarely fall short in number of the active voices in the existing Congress.

PARTICIPATION OF PRESIDENT ENSURES SAFER TREATIES:
75:30   When, in addition to these considerations, we take into view the co-operation of the President, we shall not hesitate to infer that the people of America would have greater security against an improper use of the power of making treaties, under the new Constitution, than they now enjoy under the Confederation. And when we proceed still one step further, and look forward to the probable augmentation of the Senate, by the erection of new States, we shall not only perceive ample ground of confidence in the sufficiency of the members to whose agency that power will be intrusted, but we shall probably be led to conclude that a body more numerous than the

Senate would be likely to become, would be very little fit for the proper discharge of the trust.

—PUBLIUS

REVIEW QUESTIONS

1. Does the act of making a treaty fall cleanly into the legislative or executive branch? Why? (75:8–9)

2. Do treaties have the force of law? What is their power of enforcement? (75:10)

3. Why is there danger in giving treaty-making power to the President alone? (75:12–15)

4. Why is treaty making in the hands of the Senate alone a bad idea? (75:16–19)

5. Which is better to ratify a treaty, two thirds of the whole senate or two thirds of senators present? Why? (75:22–24)

6. Does the Constitution grant senators one vote per State or one vote per senator? (See Constitution Art. I, Sec. 3, Clause 1) Why should this matter? (75:29; see Articles of Confederation Article V, Clauses 2 and 4)

FEDERALIST NO. 76

PRESIDENT'S POWER TO APPOINT IS SHARED: There are three options to appointments—by the President only, by a select assembly, or by a combination of the two. The first two are liable to corruption, favoritism, and factions. Because there are defects in the presidency and the senators, sharing this power between them is safest to liberty. While the President could pressure the Senate to support him, there will always be some virtue among the senators so that the President's pressure tactics can't succeed.

By Alexander Hamilton—April 1, 1788

PRESIDENTIAL POWERS TO APPOINT:
What does the Constitution say about the President's appointment powers?

76:1 THE President is "to <u>NOMINATE</u>, and, by and with the advice and consent of the Senate, to <u>appoint</u> ambassadors, other public ministers and consuls, judges of the Supreme Court, and all other officers of the United States whose appointments are not otherwise provided for in the Constitution. But the <u>Congress may by law vest the appointment of such inferior officers as they think proper</u>, in the President alone, or in the courts of law, or in the heads of departments.

The President shall have power to fill up <u>ALL VACANCIES</u> which may happen <u>DURING THE RECESS OF THE SENATE</u>, by granting commissions which shall <u>EXPIRE</u> at the end of their next session."

WHAT IS THE TEST OF GOOD GOVERNMENT?

76:2 It has been observed in a former paper, that "the true <u>test of a good government</u> is its aptitude and tendency to produce a <u>good administration</u>." If the justness of this observation be admitted, the mode of appointing the officers of the United States contained in the foregoing clauses, must, when examined, be allowed to be entitled to particular commendation. It is <u>not easy to conceive a plan better calculated than this</u> to promote a judicious choice of men for filling the offices of the Union; and it will not need proof, that on this point must essentially depend the character of its administration.

THREE OPTIONS TO MAKE APPOINTMENTS:
Why would having the people at large approve appointments be harmful?

76:3 It will be agreed on all hands, that the power of appointment, in ordinary cases, ought to be modified in one of <u>three ways</u>. It ought either to be vested in a <u>single man</u>, or in a SELECT <u>assembly</u> of a moderate number; or in a <u>single man, with the concurrence of such an assembly</u>. The exercise of it by the people at large will be readily admitted to be impracticable; as waiving every other consideration, it would leave them <u>little time to do anything else</u>.

SPIRIT OF CABAL AND INTRIGUE CAN CORRUPT THE PEOPLE'S ASSEMBLIES:
For this discussion, a body of men means a select body as already described.

76:4 When, therefore, mention is made in the subsequent reasonings of an assembly or body of men, what is said must be understood to relate to a select body or assembly, of the description already given. The <u>people collectively</u>, from their number and from their dispersed situation, <u>cannot be regulated</u> in their movements by that systematic spirit of cabal and intrigue, which will be urged as the chief objections to reposing the power in question in a body of men.

ONE MAN IS A BETTER JUDGE OF CHARACTER THAN MANY:

76:5 Those who have themselves reflected upon the subject, or who have attended to the observations made in other parts of these papers, in relation to the appointment of the President, will, I presume, agree to the position, that there would always be <u>great probability</u> of having the place <u>supplied by a man of abilities</u>, at least respectable. Premising this, I proceed to lay it down as a rule, that <u>one man of discernment is better fitted</u> to analyze and estimate the peculiar qualities adapted to particular offices, than a body of men of equal or perhaps even of superior discernment.

GROUPS ARE MORE DIFFICULT FOR APPOINTING THAN SINGLE EXECUTIVE:
What are some reasons why a group is so much more difficult to be fair in the selection processes?

76:6 The sole and undivided responsibility of one man will naturally beget a livelier sense of duty and a more exact regard to reputation. He will, on this account, feel himself under stronger obligations, and more interested to investigate with care the qualities requisite to the stations to be filled, and to prefer with impartiality the persons who may have the fairest pretensions to them.

President has fewer entangling alliances than a large council.

76:7 He will have FEWER personal attachments to gratify, than a body of men who may each be supposed to have an equal number; and will be so much the less liable to be misled by the sentiments of friendship and of affection. A single well-directed man, by a single understanding, cannot be distracted and warped by that diversity of views, feelings, and interests, which frequently distract and warp the resolutions of a collective body.

A multitude of biases will render the process impossible.

76:8 There is nothing so apt to agitate the passions of mankind as personal considerations whether they relate to ourselves or to others, who are to be the objects of our choice or preference.

PARTISAN BICKERING OVER APPOINTMENTS:
When groups appoint officers, does the process usually erupt in partisan bickering and deal making?

76:9 Hence, in every exercise of the power of appointing to offices, by an assembly of men, we must expect to see a full display of all the private and party likings and dislikes, partialities and antipathies, attachments and animosities, which are felt by those who compose the assembly. The choice which may at any time happen to be made under such circumstances, will of course be the result either of a victory gained by one party over the other, or of a compromise between the parties.

INTRINSIC MERITS OVERLOOKED:
The power to appoint is destined to become a quest for partisan political power.

76:10 In either case, the intrinsic merit of the candidate will be too often out of sight. In the first, the qualifications best adapted to uniting the suffrages of the party, will be more considered than those which fit the person for the station. In the last, the coalition will commonly turn upon some interested

equivalent: "Give us the man we wish for this office, and you shall have the one you wish for that." This will be the usual condition of the bargain. And it will rarely happen that the advancement of the public service will be the primary object either of party victories or of party negotiations.

CRITICS ARGUE THAT THE PRESIDENT ALONE SHOULD APPOINT:
Some insist the President should have sole power to appoint officers in federal government.

76:11 The truth of the principles here advanced seems to have been felt by the most intelligent of those who have found fault with the provision made, in this respect, by the Convention. They contend that the President ought solely to have been authorized to make the appointments under the federal government.

PRESIDENT MAY NOMINATE:
Giving the President absolute power to appoint can be dangerous and should be avoided.

76:12 But it is easy to show, that every advantage to be expected from such an arrangement would, in substance, be derived from the power of NOMINATION, which is proposed to be conferred upon him; while several disadvantages which might attend the absolute power of appointment in the hands of that officer would be avoided.

President evaluates and then points out qualified candidates.

76:13 In the act of nomination, his judgment alone would be exercised; and as it would be his sole duty to point out the man who, with the approbation of the Senate, should fill an office, his responsibility would be as complete as if he were to make the final appointment.

Nominations and appointments are not very different.

76:14 There can, in this view, be no difference between nominating and appointing. The same motives which would influence a proper discharge of his duty in one case, would exist in the other. And as no man could be appointed but on his previous nomination, every man who might be appointed would be, in fact, his choice.

SENATE COULD OVERRULE:
Despite Senate rejection, every candidate nominated by the President would be his preferred person.

76:15 But might not his nomination be overruled? I grant it might, yet this could only be to make place for another nomination by himself. The person ultimately appointed must be the object of his preference, though perhaps not in the first degree. It is also not very probable that his nomination would often be overruled.

DIFFICULT FOR SENATE TO MANIPULATE THE PROCESS:
There is no guarantee a Senate preference would be nominated.

76:16   The <u>Senate could not be tempted</u>, by the preference they might feel to another, to <u>reject</u> the one proposed; because they <u>could not assure</u> themselves, that the <u>person</u> they might wish would be brought forward by a second or by any subsequent nomination. They could <u>not even be certain</u>, that a <u>future nomination</u> would present a candidate in any degree <u>more acceptable</u> to them; and as their <u>dissent</u> might cast a kind of <u>stigma</u> upon the individual <u>rejected</u>, and might have the appearance of a reflection upon the judgment of the chief magistrate, it is not likely that their sanction would often be refused, where there were not special and strong reasons for the refusal.

SENATE INFLUENCES PRESIDENT'S DECISION:
How does Senate participation help the President stay true to the primary goal of building a stable government?

76:17   <u>To what purpose</u> then require the co-operation of the <u>Senate</u>? I answer, that the necessity of their concurrence would have a <u>powerful</u>, though, in general, a <u>silent operation</u>. It would be an excellent <u>check</u> upon a spirit of <u>favoritism in the President</u>, and would tend greatly to prevent the appointment of <u>unfit</u> characters from <u>State prejudice</u>, from <u>family connection</u>, from personal <u>attachment</u>, or from a view to <u>popularity</u>. In addition to this, it would be an efficacious <u>source of stability</u> in the administration.

SOLE DISCRETION INVITES RISK AND FOLLY:
What evils and selfish motives are prevented if the President knows he must include the Senate in his filling of offices?

76:18   It will readily be comprehended, that a <u>man</u> who had himself the <u>sole disposition of offices</u>, would be <u>governed</u> much more by his <u>private</u> inclinations and <u>interests</u>, than when he was bound to <u>submit</u> the propriety of his choice to the discussion and determination of a different and independent body, and that body <u>an entire branch</u> of the legislature. The possibility of <u>rejection</u> would be a <u>strong motive</u> to care in proposing. The <u>danger</u> to his own <u>reputation</u>, and, in the case of an elective magistrate, to his <u>political</u> existence, from <u>betraying a spirit of favoritism</u>, or an unbecoming pursuit of popularity, to the observation of a body whose opinion would have great weight in forming that of the public, could not fail to operate as a barrier to the one and to the other. He would be both <u>ashamed and afraid</u> to bring forward, for the most distinguished or lucrative stations, candidates who had <u>no other merit</u> than that of coming from the <u>same State</u> to which he particularly belonged, or of being in some way or other <u>personally allied</u> to him, or of possessing the necessary insignificance and pliancy to render them the obsequious instruments of his pleasure.

PRESIDENT'S INFLUENCE ON SENATE:
The Senate may have weaknesses, but it also has strengths to resist.

76:19   To this reasoning it has been objected that the President, by the influence of the power of nomination, may secure the complaisance of the Senate to his views. This supposition of <u>universal **venality**</u>[237] in human nature is <u>little less an error</u> in political reasoning, than the supposition of <u>universal rectitude</u>.

DELEGATED POWERS REQUIRE THE HIGHEST INTEGRITY:
The fact that a republican form puts power in the hands of leaders implies there is virtue and honor in mankind.

76:20   The institution of <u>delegated power implies</u>, that there is a portion of virtue and honor among mankind, which may be a reasonable foundation of confidence; and experience justifies the theory. It has been <u>found</u> to exist in the most corrupt periods of the <u>most corrupt governments</u>.

BRITISH SYSTEM CORRUPTED BUT IT WORKS:
Even in Britain where the people's leadership is corrupted, there remains enough virtue to overcome unrealistic demands of their king.

76:21   The <u>venality</u> of the <u>British House of Commons</u> has been long a topic of accusation against that body, in the country to which they belong as well as in this; and it cannot be doubted that the charge is, to a considerable extent, well founded. But it is as little to be doubted, that there is always a <u>large proportion</u> of the body, which consists of <u>independent and public-spirited men</u>, who have an influential weight in the councils of the nation. Hence it is (the present reign not excepted) that the sense of <u>that body</u> is often seen to <u>control</u> the inclinations of the <u>monarch</u>, both with regard to men and to measures.

PRESIDENT COULDN'T COMPROMISE THE ENTIRE SENATE:

76:22   Though it might therefore be <u>allowable to suppose</u> that the <u>Executive</u> might occasionally <u>influence</u> some individuals in the <u>Senate</u>, yet the supposition, that he could in <u>general purchase the integrity of the whole body</u>, would be forced and <u>improbable</u>.

---

237   **venality:** Ability to be bribed; being influenced by money; corruptibility.

HUMAN NATURE IS RESTRAINED IN THIS PROCESS:

Is it clear, then, that the Senate is a sufficient restraint on the President?

76:23 A man disposed to view human nature as it is, without either flattering its virtues or exaggerating its vices, will see sufficient ground of confidence in the probity of the Senate, to rest satisfied, not only that it will be impracticable to the Executive to corrupt or seduce a majority of its members, but that the necessity of its co-operation, in the business of appointments, will be a considerable and salutary restraint upon the conduct of that magistrate. Nor is the integrity of the Senate the only reliance.

ADDITIONAL PROTECTIONS:

May officers in the federal government hold additional offices? May their salaries be changed while serving?

76:24 The Constitution has provided some important guards against the danger of executive influence upon the legislative body: it declares that "No senator or representative shall during the time FOR WHICH HE WAS ELECTED, be appointed to any civil office under the United States, which shall have been created, or the emoluments whereof shall have been increased, during such time; and no person, holding any office under the United States, shall be a member of either house during his continuance in office."

—Publius

Review Questions

1. With the job of the President being to keep the government going, what power is he given when it comes to appointing officers and vacancies? Can he do this alone? (76:1)

2. Why is it a bad idea to let Congress or a panel of many decide who should fill federal positions? (76:4–10)

3. Could the President influence or coerce the Senate to go along with his choices? (76:19–23)

4. What additional protection exists from improper bribing or influencing by the President to win Senate support for his nominations? (76:24)

FEDERALIST NO. 77

SENATE'S ROLE IN PRESIDENTIAL APPOINTMENTS: Giving the Senate a role in the President's power to appoint helps keep that process stable, safer, and subject to public scrutiny. Leaving total appointment power to small groups opens them to corruption and favoritism. With the Senate involved, the President remains accountable but "energetic"—that is, he has enough power to do the job while liberties are preserved.

By Alexander Hamilton—April 2, 1788

SENATE HELPS STABILIZE GOVERNMENT:

The Senate's involvement in appointments plays a supportive role each time a new President takes office.

77:1 IT HAS been mentioned as one of the advantages to be expected from the cooperation of the Senate, in the business of appointments, that it would contribute to the stability of the administration. The consent of that body would be necessary to displace [remove] as well as to appoint. A change of the Chief Magistrate, therefore, would not occasion so violent or so general a revolution in the officers of the government as might be expected, if he were the sole disposer of offices. Where a man in any station had given satisfactory evidence of his fitness for it, a new President would be restrained from attempting a change in favor of a person more agreeable to him, by the apprehension that a discountenance of the Senate might frustrate the attempt, and bring some degree of discredit upon himself.

SENATE HAS GREATER PERMANENCY:

With the Senate's longer terms and slower turnover, its impact helps keep the government stable, even as Presidents change from time to time.

77:2 Those who can best estimate the value of a steady administration, will be most disposed to prize a provision which connects the official existence of public men with the approbation or disapprobation of that body which, from the greater permanency of its own composition, will in all probability be less subject to inconstancy than any other member of the government.

GOOD BALANCE IS ACHIEVED FOR PRESIDENTIAL APPOINTMENTS:

Is there validity to the claim that the President can influence Congress?

77:3 To this union of the Senate with the President, in the article of appointments, it has in some cases been suggested that it would serve to give the President an undue influence over the Senate, and in others that it would have an opposite tendency, a strong proof that neither suggestion is true.

PRESIDENT HAS NO IMPROPER INFLUENCE:

Are fears of overreach justified when the Senate can restrain the President?

77:4 To state the first in its proper form, is to refute it. It amounts to this: the President would have an improper IN-

FLUENCE OVER the Senate, because the Senate would have the power of RESTRAINING him. This is an absurdity in terms. It cannot admit of a doubt that the entire power of appointment would enable him much more effectually to establish a dangerous empire over that body, than a mere power of nomination subject to their control.

SENATE HAS NO IMPROPER INFLUENCE:

77:5 Let us take a view of the converse of the proposition: "the Senate would influence the Executive."

How might the Senate influence the President?

77:6 As I have had occasion to remark in several other instances, the indistinctness of the objection forbids a precise answer. In what manner is this influence to be exerted? In relation to what objects?

INFLUENCE ON PRESIDENT IS DEFINED:

Are there many political times where the Senate could bribe the President?

77:7 The power of influencing a person, in the sense in which it is here used, must imply a power of conferring a benefit upon him. How could the Senate confer a benefit upon the President by the manner of employing their right of negative upon his nominations? If it be said they might sometimes gratify him by an acquiescence in a favorite choice, when public motives might dictate a different conduct, I answer, that the instances in which the President could be personally interested in the result, would be too few to admit of his being materially affected by the compliances of the Senate.

THE POWER TO DISTRIBUTE REWARDS IS ALWAYS MORE ALLURING:

77:8 The POWER which can ORIGINATE the disposition of honors and emoluments, is more likely to attract than to be attracted by the POWER which can merely obstruct their course.

SOURCE OF RESTRAINT DOES GOOD, AVOIDS EVIL:

77:9 If by influencing the President be meant RESTRAINING him, this is precisely what must have been intended. And it has been shown that the restraint would be salutary, at the same time that it would not be such as to destroy a single advantage to be looked for from the uncontrolled agency of that Magistrate. The right of nomination would produce all the good of that of appointment, and would in a great measure avoid its evils.

COMPARING NEW YORK TO THE FEDERAL GOVERNMENT:

Whose system of appointing is better?

77:10 Upon a comparison of the plan for the appointment of the officers of the proposed government with that which is established by the constitution of this State, a decided preference must be given to the former. In that plan the power of nomination is unequivocally vested in the Executive.

NOMINATIONS BECOME PUBLICLY KNOWN:

Blame is more easily placed when parties are known.

77:11 And as there would be a necessity for submitting each nomination to the judgment of an entire branch of the legislature, the circumstances attending an appointment, from the mode of conducting it, would naturally become matters of notoriety; and the public would be at no loss to determine what part had been performed by the different actors.

PLENTY OF BLAME TO SHARE:

President takes the blame for a bad nomination. The Senate takes the blame for rejecting a good one.

77:12 The blame of a bad nomination would fall upon the President singly and absolutely. The censure of rejecting a good one would lie entirely at the door of the Senate; aggravated by the consideration of their having counteracted the good intentions of the Executive. If an ill appointment should be made, the Executive for nominating, and the Senate for approving, would participate, though in different degrees, in the opprobrium and disgrace.

NEW YORK'S COUNCIL OF APPOINTMENT:

What are some flaws in New York's Council of Appointment process?

77:13 The reverse of all this characterizes the manner of appointment in this State. The council of appointment consists of from three to five persons, of whom the governor is always one. This small body, shut up in a private apartment, impenetrable to the public eye, proceed to the execution of the trust committed to them.

GOVERNOR'S NOMINATION POWER IS NOT WELL DEFINED:

77:14 It is known that the governor claims the right of nomination, upon the strength of some ambiguous expressions in the constitution; but it is not known to what extent, or in what manner he exercises it; nor upon what occasions he is contradicted or opposed.

NEW YORK'S SYSTEM IS CLOAKED IN SECRECY:

There is room for conspiracy and corruption, start to finish.

77:15 The censure of a bad appointment, on account of the uncertainty of its author, and for want of a determinate object, has neither poignancy nor duration. And while an unbounded field for cabal and intrigue lies open, all idea of responsibility is lost. The most that the public can know, is that the governor claims the right of nomination; that TWO out of the inconsiderable number of FOUR men can too often be managed without much difficulty; that if some of the members of a particular council should happen to be of an uncomplying character, it is frequently not impossible to get rid of their opposition by regulating the times of meeting in such a manner as to render their attendance inconvenient; and that from whatever cause it may proceed, a great number of very improper appointments are from time to time made.

IMPORTANT QUESTIONS IN NY ARE NOT OPEN TO PUBLIC SCRUTINY:

New York's governor is able to manipulate the State system.

77:16   Whether a governor of this State avails himself of the ascendant he must necessarily have, in this delicate and important part of the administration, to prefer to offices men who are best qualified for them, or whether he prostitutes that advantage to the advancement of persons whose chief merit is their implicit devotion to his will, and to the support of a despicable and dangerous system of personal influence, are questions which, unfortunately for the community, can only be the subjects of speculation and conjecture.

PROPOSED COUNCIL OF APPOINTMENT IS A BAD IDEA:

Why is a council of appointment destructive to all parties involved?

77:17   Every mere council of appointment, however constituted, will be a conclave, in which cabal and intrigue will have their full scope. Their number, without an unwarrantable increase of expense, cannot be large enough to preclude a facility of combination.

Scandalous bartering erodes the process.

77:18   And as each member will have his friends and connections to provide for, the desire of mutual gratification will beget a scandalous bartering of votes and bargaining for places. The private attachments of one man might easily be satisfied; but to satisfy the private attachments of a dozen, or of twenty men, would occasion a monopoly of all the principal employments of the government in a few families, and would lead more directly to an aristocracy or an oligarchy than any measure that could be contrived.

NY's council of appointment is not independent or subject to public scrutiny:

77:19   If, to avoid an accumulation of offices, there was to be a frequent change in the persons who were to compose the council, this would involve the mischiefs of a mutable administration in their full extent. Such a council would also be more liable to executive influence than the Senate, because they would be fewer in number, and would act less immediately under the public inspection.

A council of appointment adds more cost to government.

77:20   Such a council, in fine, as a substitute for the plan of the Convention, would be productive of an increase of expense, a multiplication of the evils which spring from favoritism and intrigue in the distribution of public honors, a decrease of stability in the administration of the government, and a diminution of the security against an undue influence of the Executive.

Some wish a council would be added by constitutional amendment.

77:21   And yet such a council has been warmly contended for as an essential amendment in the proposed Constitution.

HOUSE HAS NO ROLE IN MAKING APPOINTMENTS:

Why is it better to leave the House of Representatives out of the appointment-making process?

77:22   I could not with propriety conclude my observations on the subject of appointments without taking notice of a scheme for which there have appeared some, though but few advocates; I mean that of uniting the House of Representatives in the power of making them. I shall, however, do little more than mention it, as I cannot imagine that it is likely to gain the countenance of any considerable part of the community. A body so fluctuating and at the same time so numerous, can never be deemed proper for the exercise of that power. Its unfitness will appear manifest to all, when it is recollected that in half a century it may consist of three or four hundred persons. All the advantages of the stability, both of the Executive and of the Senate, would be defeated by this union, and infinite delays and embarrassments would be occasioned. The example of most of the States in their local constitutions encourages us to reprobate the idea.

REMAINING EXECUTIVE POWERS:

What are the remaining powers of the President?

77:23   The only remaining powers of the Executive are comprehended in giving information to Congress of the state of the Union; in recommending to their consideration such measures as he shall judge expedient; in convening them, or either branch, upon extraordinary occasions; in adjourning them when they cannot themselves agree upon the time of adjournment; in receiving ambassadors and other public ministers; in faithfully executing the laws; and in commissioning all the officers of the United States.

POWER TO CONVENE CONGRESS:
What is a good reason why the President should have the power to convene the Senate? Does such a reason exist for convening the House?

77:24   Except some **cavils**[238] about the power of convening EITHER house of the legislature, and that of receiving ambassadors, no objection has been made to this class of authorities; nor could they possibly admit of any. It required, indeed, an insatiable avidity for censure to invent exceptions to the parts which have been excepted to.

Convening the Senate is appropriate, convening the House is not.

77:25   In regard to the power of convening either house of the legislature, I shall barely remark, that in respect to the Senate at least, we can readily discover a good reason for it. As this body has a concurrent power with the Executive in the article of treaties, it might often be necessary to call it together with a view to this object, when it would be unnecessary and improper to convene the House of Representatives.

Receiving ambassadors.

77:26   As to the reception of ambassadors, what I have said in a former paper will furnish a sufficient answer.

BUILT-IN SAFETY MEASURES IN THE OFFICE OF PRESIDENT:
What are some precautions to restrain the President?

77:27   We have now completed a survey of the structure and powers of the executive department, which, I have endeavored to show, combines, as far as republican principles will admit, all the requisites to energy.

The remaining question.

77:28   The remaining inquiry is: Does it also combine the requisites to safety, in a republican sense, a due dependence on the people, a due responsibility?

Basic protections are in place to protect the people from a king.

77:29   The answer to this question has been anticipated in the investigation of its other characteristics, and is satisfactorily deducible from these circumstances; from the election of the President once in four years by persons immediately chosen by the people for that purpose; and from his being at all times liable to impeachment, trial, dismission from office, incapacity to serve in any other, and to forfeiture of life and estate by subsequent prosecution in the common course of law.

Crucial presidential responsibilities are checked by Congress.

77:30   But these precautions, great as they are, are not the only ones which the plan of the Convention has provided in favor of the public security. In the only instances in which the abuse of the executive authority was materially to be feared, the Chief Magistrate of the United States would, by that plan, be subjected to the control of a branch of the legislative body. What more could be desired by an enlightened and reasonable people?

—PUBLIUS

REVIEW QUESTIONS

1. How does the Senate help the government in regard to major political changes such as presidential appointments and other formal activities? (77:1)

2. How does Hamilton define "having the power to influence"? (77:7)

3. Is there a way for the Senate to bribe or extort the President to make certain appointments? If they found a way, would it be an event that would happen all the time? (77:7)

4. Why do councils of appointments in any form never work? (77:17–20)

5. Did councils of appointments work for New York? (77:10–16)

6. Why is involvement by the House in appointments a bad idea? (77:22)

7. What are some of the ways that the office of President remains bound and dependent on the people? (77:29)

8. Do the constitutional provisions spoken of so far give the President all of the "requisites to energy" needed without violating republican principles? (77:27)

---

238   *cavil:* An objection that is petty or unnecessary; carping or grumbling.

SECTION 11 • JUDICIARY BRANCH

Papers 78–83

FEDERALIST NO. 78

INDEPENDENT JUDICIARY AND JUDICIAL REVIEW ARE NECESSARY: The court must be both neutral and protected so it can fairly judge the other branches and test their actions against the Constitution. The court is the weakest of the three branches, having no power to enforce or compel obedience to its decisions. The importance of tenure in judges both ensures their independence and helps build needed experience and knowledge to become wise judges.

By Alexander Hamilton—June 14, 1788

EXAMINING THE NEW JUDICIARY

78:1 WE PROCEED now to an examination of the judiciary department of the proposed government.

NEED FOR FEDERAL JUDICIARY NOT QUESTIONED:

There was no judiciary under the Articles. What questions remain to be answered about a Supreme Court under the new Constitution?

78:2 In unfolding the defects of the existing Confederation, the utility and necessity of a federal judicature have been clearly pointed out. It is the less necessary to recapitulate the considerations there urged, as the propriety of the institution in the abstract is not disputed; the only questions which have been raised being relative to the manner of constituting it, and to its extent. To these points, therefore, our observations shall be confined.

78:3 The manner of constituting it seems to embrace these several objects:

78:4 1st. The mode of appointing the judges.

78:5 2d. The tenure by which they are to hold their places.

78:6 3d. The partition of the judiciary authority between different courts, and their relations to each other.

1ST—APPOINTING JUDGES:

78:7 First. As to the mode of appointing the judges; this is the same with that of appointing the officers of the Union in general, and has been so fully discussed in the two last numbers, that nothing can be said here which would not be useless repetition.

2ND—TENURE OF JUDGES:

What are the three primary elements when considering tenure?

78:8 Second. As to the tenure by which the judges are to hold their places; this chiefly concerns their duration in office; the provisions for their support; the precautions for their responsibility.

JUDGES HOLD OFFICE DURING GOOD BEHAVIOR:

What two barriers does the provision of "during good behavior" put in place? Do State governments also support this provision?

78:9 According to the plan of the Convention, all judges who may be appointed by the United States are to hold their offices DURING GOOD BEHAVIOR; which is conformable to the most approved of the State constitutions and among the rest, to that of this State.

Standards of good behavior are important to establish.

78:10 Its propriety having been drawn into question by the adversaries of that plan, is no light symptom of the rage for objection, which disorders their imaginations and judgments. The standard of good behavior for the continuance in office of the judicial magistracy, is certainly one of the most valuable of the modern improvements in the practice of government.

Behavior is an excellent protection in monarchies and republics.

78:11 In a monarchy it is an excellent barrier to the despotism of the prince; in a republic it is a no less excellent barrier to the encroachments and oppressions of the representative body. And it is the best expedient which can be devised in any government, to secure a steady, upright, and impartial administration of the laws.

COURTS MUST OBEY CONSTITUTION:
Why is the judiciary considered the least dangerous branch?

78:12 Whoever attentively considers the different departments of power must perceive, that, in a government in which they are separated from each other, the judiciary, from the nature of its functions, will always be the least dangerous to the political rights of the Constitution; because it will be least in a capacity to annoy or injure them.

Role of the executive.

78:13 The Executive not only dispenses the honors, but holds the sword of the community.

Role of the legislature.

78:14 The legislature not only commands the purse, but prescribes the rules by which the duties and rights of every citizen are to be regulated.

Role of the judiciary.

78:15 The judiciary, on the contrary, has no influence over either the sword or the purse; no direction either of the strength or of the wealth of the society; and can take no active resolution whatever.

NO FORCE OR WILL:
Judiciary should be judges only.

78:16 It may truly be said to have neither FORCE nor WILL, but merely judgment; and must ultimately depend upon the aid of the executive arm even for the efficacy of its judgments.

JUDICIARY SHOULD BE WEAKEST BRANCH:
The court cannot attack the other two branches. How could the judiciary gain strength that it shouldn't have?

78:17 This simple view of the matter suggests several important consequences. It proves incontestably, that the judiciary is beyond comparison the weakest of the three departments of power;[239] that it can never attack with success either of the other two; and that all possible care is requisite to enable it to defend itself against their attacks.

JUDICIARY CAN'T THREATEN LIBERTY UNLESS—
Unless the Courts try to make new law or cause enforcement of law.

78:18 It equally proves, that though individual oppression may now and then proceed from the courts of justice, the general liberty of the people can never be endangered from that quarter; I mean so long as the judiciary remains truly distinct from both the legislature and the Executive. For I agree, that "there is no liberty, if the power of judging be not separated from the legislative and executive powers."[240]

LIBERTY AT RISK IF JUDICIARY JOINS OTHER BRANCHES:

78:19 And it proves, in the last place, that as liberty can have nothing to fear from the judiciary alone, but would have every thing to fear from its union with either of the other departments; that as all the effects of such a union must ensue from a dependence of the former on the latter, notwithstanding a nominal and apparent separation;

INDEPENDENCE ENSURED BY PERMANENCY:
Judges can remain independent because they can't be fired or have their salaries changed as a bribe or as a punishment.

78:20 that as, from the natural feebleness of the judiciary, it is in continual jeopardy of being overpowered, awed, or influenced by its co-ordinate branches; and that as nothing can contribute so much to its firmness and independence as permanency in office, this quality may therefore be justly regarded as an indispensable ingredient in its constitution, and, in a great measure, as the citadel of the public justice and the public security.

INDEPENDENCE OF THE COURT IS DEPENDENT ON A LIMITED CONSTITUTION:
What are some of the limitations placed on the legislature?

78:21 The complete independence of the courts of justice is peculiarly essential in a limited Constitution. By a limited Constitution, I understand one which contains certain specified exceptions to the legislative authority;

Bills of attainder, ex-post-facto laws.

78:22 such, for instance, as that it shall pass no bills of attainder, no ex-post-facto laws, and the like. Limitations of this kind can be preserved in practice no other way than through the medium of courts of justice, whose duty it must be to declare all acts contrary to the manifest tenor of the Constitution void. Without this, all the reservations of particular rights or privileges would amount to nothing.

IS JUDICIARY SUPERIOR TO CONGRESS?
Does the judiciary have the right to void a law from the legislative?

---

239 *Publius:* The celebrated Montesquieu, speaking of them, says: "Of the three powers above mentioned, the judiciary is next to nothing," "Spirit of Laws." vol. i., page 186.

240 *Publius:* Idem, page 181.

78:23   Some perplexity respecting the rights of the courts to pronounce legislative acts void, because contrary to the Constitution, has arisen from an imagination that the doctrine would imply a superiority of the judiciary to the legislative power. It is urged that the authority which can declare the acts of another void, must necessarily be superior to the one whose acts may be declared void.

78:24   As this doctrine is of great importance in all the American constitutions, a brief discussion of the ground on which it rests cannot be unacceptable.

CONGRESS AND COURT CAN'T PUT THEIR WILL ABOVE CONSTITUTION:

Congress cannot substitute its will for the Constitution. Since the Constitution was ratified, has this ever happened?

78:25   There is no position which depends on clearer principles, than that every act of a delegated authority, contrary to the tenor of the commission under which it is exercised, is void. No legislative act, therefore, contrary to the Constitution, can be valid.

The court must not act superior to the Constitution. Ever.

78:26   To deny this, would be to affirm, that the deputy is greater than his principal; that the servant is above his master; that the representatives of the people are superior to the people themselves; that men acting by virtue of powers, may do not only what their powers do not authorize, but what they forbid.

JUDICIAL REVIEW OF THE OTHER BRANCHES:

This is the act of the judiciary branch reviewing the actions of the other two branches to ensure they're inside the letter and law of the Constitution. Congress can't declare its own bills as constitutional; that is the job of the court.

78:27   If it be said that the legislative body are themselves the constitutional judges of their own powers, and that the construction they put upon them is conclusive upon the other departments, it may be answered, that this cannot be the natural presumption, where it is not to be collected from any particular provisions in the Constitution.

CONGRESS CAN'T VIOLATE OR CHANGE THE CONSTITUTION:

78:28   It is not otherwise to be supposed, that the Constitution could intend to enable the representatives of the people to substitute their WILL to that of their constituents. It is far more rational to suppose, that the courts were designed to be an intermediate body between the people and the legislature, in order, among other things, to keep the latter within the limits assigned to their authority.

CONSTITUTION IS FUNDAMENTAL LAW:

Therefore, judicial review is necessary to preserve the Constitution and liberty.

78:29   The interpretation of the laws is the proper and peculiar province of the courts. A constitution is, in fact, and must be regarded by the judges, as a fundamental law. It therefore belongs to them to ascertain its meaning, as well as the meaning of any particular act proceeding from the legislative body. If there should happen to be an irreconcilable variance between the two, that which has the superior obligation and validity ought, of course, to be preferred;

CONSTITUTION IS SUPREME, NOT THE STATUES:

78:30   or, in other words, the Constitution ought to be preferred to the statute, the intention of the people to the intention of their agents.

JUDGES MUST BE GOVERNED BY CONSTITUTION

If the court violates the Constitution can it be said it is also violating the will of the people?

78:31   Nor does this conclusion by any means suppose a superiority of the judicial to the legislative power. It only supposes that the power of the people is superior to both;

WHAT IS "THE WILL" OF THE PEOPLE? :

78:32   and that where the will of the legislature, declared in its statutes, stands in opposition to that of the people, declared in the Constitution, the judges ought to be governed by the latter rather than the former. They ought to regulate their decisions by the fundamental laws, rather than by those which are not fundamental.

COURTS OBLIGATED TO DECIDE VALID PRINCIPLES:

When two laws clash, what two options does the court have to resolve the matter?

78:33   This exercise of judicial discretion, in determining between two contradictory laws, is exemplified in a familiar instance. It not uncommonly happens, that there are two statutes existing at one time, clashing in whole or in part with each other, and neither of them containing any repealing clause or expression. In such a case, it is the province of the courts to liquidate and fix their meaning and operation.

PROBLEM OF LEGAL IMPASSE:

If two equal but contradictory laws are at play, the court is obligated to choose one.

78:34   So far as they can, by any fair construction, be reconciled to each other, reason and law conspire to dictate that this should be done; where this is impracticable, it becomes a matter of necessity to give effect to one, in <u>exclusion of the other</u>.

WHEN IN DOUBT, FAVOR MOST RECENT:
When determining the first of two equals, choose the most recent.

78:35 The rule which has obtained in the courts for determining their relative validity is, that <u>the last in order of time shall be preferred to the first</u>. But this is a mere rule of construction, not derived from any positive law, but from the nature and reason of the thing. It is a rule not enjoined upon the courts by legislative provision, but adopted by themselves, as consonant to truth and propriety, for the direction of their conduct as interpreters of the law. They thought it reasonable, that between the interfering acts of an EQUAL authority, <u>that which was the last indication of its will should have the preference</u>.

HIGHEST COURT PREVAILS:
If two laws from a higher and lower court clash, to which is preference given? If they clash with the Constitution, which receives preference?

78:36 But in regard to the interfering acts of a superior and subordinate authority, of an original and derivative power, the nature and reason of the thing indicate the <u>converse of that rule</u> as proper to be followed. They teach us that the <u>prior act of a superior ought</u> to be preferred to the subsequent act of an inferior and subordinate authority;

LAWS VIOLATING CONSTITUTION MUST BE REJECTED:
78:37 and that accordingly, <u>whenever a particular statute contravenes the Constitution, it will be the duty of the judicial tribunals to adhere to the latter and disregard the former</u>.

COURT MUST FOLLOW THE CONSTITUTION:
The Constitution is not "living." It embodies eternal principles and should resist arbitrary change.

78:38 <u>It can be of no weight to say that the courts, on the pretense of a repugnancy, may substitute their own pleasure to the constitutional intentions of the legislature.</u> This might as well happen in the case of two contradictory statutes; or it might as well happen in every adjudication upon any single statute.

COURT MUST EXERCISE JUDGMENT NOT WILL:
The court must never become activist, submitting rulings based on personal agendas instead of the Constitution.

78:39 <u>The courts must declare the sense of the law</u>; and if they should be disposed to exercise <u>WILL</u> instead of <u>JUDG-

<u>MENT</u>, the consequence would equally be the substitution of <u>their pleasure to that of the legislative body</u>. The observation, if it prove any thing, would prove that there ought to be no judges distinct from that body.

PERMANENT TENURE CRITICAL FOR INDEPENDENCE:
If the court is to be the defender of the will of the people, what best protects them from the negative influence of the other branches?

78:40 If, then, the <u>courts of justice are to be considered as the bulwarks of a limited Constitution against legislative encroachments</u>, this consideration will afford a strong argument for the permanent tenure of judicial offices, since nothing will contribute so much as this to that independent spirit in the judges which must be essential to the faithful performance of so arduous a duty.

BIASED COURT CAN OPPRESS INDIVIDUAL RIGHTS:
What danger must be avoided so federal judges adhere to letter and spirit of Constitution? Have some justices shown political bias?

78:41 This independence of the judges is equally requisite to guard the Constitution and the rights of individuals from the effects of those ill humors, which the <u>arts of designing men</u>, or the <u>influence</u> of particular <u>conjunctures</u>, sometimes disseminate among the people themselves, and which, though they speedily give place to better information, and more deliberate reflection, have a tendency, in the meantime, to <u>occasion dangerous innovations</u> in the government, and serious <u>oppressions</u> of the minor party in the community.

CAN'T USURP CONSTITUTIONAL PROTECTIONS:
Neither Congress nor a convention of the States, called under the authority of the Constitution, can turn against and abolish the Constitution.

78:42 Though I trust the friends of the proposed Constitution will never concur with its enemies,[241] in questioning that fundamental principle of republican government, which <u>admits the right</u> of the people to <u>alter</u> or <u>abolish</u> the established <u>Constitution</u>, whenever they find it <u>inconsistent</u> with their <u>happiness</u>, yet it is not to be inferred from this principle, that the representatives of the people, whenever a <u>momentary inclination</u> happens to lay hold of a <u>majority</u> of their constituents, <u>incompatible</u> with the provisions in the existing <u>Constitution</u>, would, on that account, be justifiable in a violation of those provisions; or that the <u>courts would be under a greater obligation to **connive**[242] at infractions</u> in this shape, than

---

241 *Publius:* Vide "Protest of the Minority of the Convention of Pennsylvania," Martin's Speech, etc.
242 **connive:** Conspire to do something considered wrong, immoral, or illegal.

when they had proceeded wholly from the cabals of the representative body. Until the people have, by some solemn and authoritative act, annulled or changed the established form, it is binding upon themselves collectively, as well as individually; and no presumption, or even knowledge, of their sentiments, can warrant their representatives in a departure from it, prior to such an act.[243]

JUDGES ARE GUARDIANS OF THE CONSTITUTION:

78:43 But it is easy to see, that it would require an uncommon portion of fortitude in the judges to do their duty as faithful guardians of the Constitution, where legislative invasions of it had been instigated by the major voice of the community.

COURT ADDRESSES BAD LAWS:

What else should the courts safeguard besides the Constitution?

78:44 But it is not with a view to infractions of the Constitution only, that the independence of the judges may be an essential safeguard against the effects of occasional ill humors in the society. These sometimes extend no farther than to the injury of the private rights of particular classes of citizens, by unjust and partial laws.

COURT ALSO ACTS AS A CHECK ON CONGRESS:

78:45 Here also the firmness of the judicial magistracy is of vast importance in mitigating the severity and confining the operation of such laws. It not only serves to moderate the immediate mischiefs of those which may have been passed, but it operates as a check upon the legislative body in passing them; who, perceiving that obstacles to the success of iniquitous intention are to be expected from the scruples of the courts, are in a manner compelled, by the very motives of the injustice they meditate, to qualify their attempts. This is a circumstance calculated to have more influence upon the character of our governments, than but few may be aware of.

HONEST COURTS ALREADY BENEFITING STATES:

78:46 The benefits of the integrity and moderation of the judiciary have already been felt in more States than one; and though they may have displeased those whose sinister expectations they may have disappointed, they must have commanded the esteem and applause of all the virtuous and disinterested.

ALWAYS CONSIDER HOW COURTS MIGHT SEE YOU:

Because injustice can quickly befall anyone, the people should support the independence of the courts as their safe-guarded system of true justice.

78:47 Considerate men of every description ought to prize whatever will tend to beget or fortify that temper in the courts: as no man can be sure that he may not be tomorrow the victim of a spirit of injustice, by which he may be a gainer today. And every man must now feel, that the inevitable tendency of such a spirit is to sap the foundations of public and private confidence, and to introduce in its stead universal distrust and distress.

JUDGES BOUND BY ALLEGIANCE TO CONSTITUTION:

Can judges be trusted who might be feel they owe a favor to the person who appointed them?

78:48 That inflexible and uniform adherence to the rights of the Constitution, and of individuals, which we perceive to be indispensable in the courts of justice, can certainly not be expected from judges who hold their offices by a temporary commission.

TEMPORARY TERM HURTS INDEPENDENCE:

An appointed judge would feel obligations toward whatever branch appointed them to office, and his judgment be tainted.

78:49 Periodical appointments, however regulated, or by whomsoever made, would, in some way or other, be fatal to their necessary independence. If the power of making them was committed either to the Executive or legislature, there would be danger of an improper complaisance to the branch which possessed it;

Tainted judges would look to what's politically popular, instead.

78:50 if to both, there would be an unwillingness to hazard the displeasure of either; if to the people, or to persons chosen by them for the special purpose, there would be too great a disposition to consult popularity, to justify a reliance that nothing would be consulted but the Constitution and the laws.

---

243 *Editors' Note:* See George Washington, *Farewell Address*, September 19, 1796: "If, in the opinion of the people, the distribution or modification of the constitutional powers be in any particular wrong, let it be corrected by an amendment in the way which the Constitution designates. But let there be no change by usurpation; for though this, in one instance, may be the instrument of good, it is the customary weapon by which free governments are destroyed. The precedent must always greatly overbalance in permanent evil any partial or transient benefit, which the use can at any time yield" (underlining added by editors).

Could temporary judges honestly absorb enough of the voluminous code of laws to be of value before their commissions ended?

78:51 There is yet a further and a weightier reason for the permanency of the judicial offices, which is deducible from the nature of the qualifications they require.

KNOWLEDGE AND EXPERIENCE IN LAW IS RARE:

If reliable, seasoned justices are rare, is that another reason to make their terms for life, to allow maximum learning opportunities?

78:52 It has been frequently remarked, with great propriety, that a voluminous code of laws is one of the inconveniences necessarily connected with the advantages of a free government. To avoid an arbitrary discretion in the courts, it is indispensable that they should be bound down by strict rules and precedents, which serve to define and point out their duty in every particular case that comes before them; and it will readily be conceived from the variety of controversies which grow out of the folly and wickedness of mankind, that the records of those precedents must unavoidably swell to a very considerable bulk, and must demand long and laborious study to acquire a competent knowledge of them.

ONLY FEW PEOPLE HAVE SUFFICIENT SKILL:
Does any legally-minded person qualify for a seat on the top court?

78:53 Hence it is, that there can be but few men in the society who will have sufficient skill in the laws to qualify them for the stations of judges. And making the proper deductions for the ordinary depravity of human nature, the number must be still smaller of those who unite the requisite integrity with the requisite knowledge.

THERE ARE LIMITED CHOICES:
Would lawyers doing well in private practice surrender that income and steady business for a temporary federal job?

78:54 These considerations apprise us, that the government can have no great option between fit character; and that a temporary duration in office, which would naturally discourage such characters from quitting a lucrative line of practice to accept a seat on the bench, would have a tendency to throw the administration of justice into hands less able, and less well qualified, to conduct it with utility and dignity.

TEMPORARY TENURE MORE DANGEROUS THAN PERMANENT:

78:55 In the present circumstances of this country, and in those in which it is likely to be for a long time to come, the disadvantages on this score would be greater than they may at first sight appear; but it must be confessed, that they are far inferior to those which present themselves under the other aspects of the subject.

LIFE-TIME TENURE AND GOOD BEHAVIOR IS WISE:

Was it wise that the Framers adopted the life-time tenure for justices? What two sources are highlighted as good examples that were followed?

78:56 Upon the whole, there can be no room to doubt that the Convention acted wisely in copying from the models of those constitutions which have established GOOD BEHAVIOR as the tenure of their judicial offices, in point of duration;

78:57 and that so far from being blamable on this account, their plan would have been inexcusably defective, if it had wanted this important feature of good government. The experience of Great Britain affords an illustrious comment on the excellence of the institution.

—PUBLIUS

REVIEW QUESTIONS

1. Having a judicial branch in government is important, but what two questions need to be answered about such a branch? (78:2–6)

2. Why is the judiciary considered the least dangerous to political rights in the Constitution? Over what two things has it no influence? (78:12–15)

3. When Hamilton says the judiciary must remain separate from the legislature, what is he suggesting the judiciary might do to harm liberty? (78:18)

4. Is any bill passed out of Congress valid if it is contrary to the Constitution? (78:25)

5. Who decides if a bill passed by Congress is contrary to the Constitution? (78:27)

6. Why do the courts stand between Congress and the Constitution? Does this mean the Constitution is superior to the laws of Congress? (78:28)

7. Who interprets the laws passed by Congress? (78:29)

8. What is the "will of the people" that Congress may not violate? (78:32)

9. In cases where two laws are in conflict, or the truth is difficult to discern, what must the court do in all such cases? (78:37)

10. What must the court never exercise in its role of declaring the sense of the law? (78:39)

11. What avenue must the people take to correct a provision

in the Constitution? May the judicial branch simply pronounce a new law to fix a problem? (78:42–43, see footnote)

12. What should judicial activists be wary of if they stray from constitutional principles? (78:47)

13. Of what value is lifetime tenure for a judge compared to temporary terms? (78:49–52)

14. Are there many people in society with sufficient knowledge and skill who could really qualify for the complex job of sitting on the Supreme Court or any federal court? (78:53)

FEDERALIST NO. 79

JUDGES' INDEPENDENT SALARY AND REMOVAL FROM OFFICE: Power over a man's income is power over his mind. The judiciary, therefore, should be independently secure in their income. Also, a judge's ability and age cannot be reasons for removing a judge.

By Alexander Hamilton—June 18, 1788

USING SALARY TO CONTROL JUDGES:

79:1 NEXT to permanency in office, nothing can contribute more to the independence of the judges than a fixed provision for their support. The remark made in relation to the President is equally applicable here. In the general course of human nature, A POWER OVER A MAN'S SUBSISTENCE AMOUNTS TO A POWER OVER HIS WILL.

Separation of branches only possible if financially separated as well.

79:2 And we can never hope to see realized in practice, the complete separation of the judicial from the legislative power, in any system which leaves the former dependent for pecuniary resources on the occasional grants of the latter.

INDEPENDENCE AND CONTROL OVER SALARY:
Are judges to be paid? Is a permanent salary a good formula? If salaries change may they be diminished?

79:3 The enlightened friends to good government in every State, have seen cause to lament the want of precise and explicit precautions in the State constitutions on this head. Some of these indeed have declared that PERMANENT[244] salaries should be established for the judges; but the experiment has in some instances shown that such expressions are not sufficiently definite to preclude legislative evasions. Some-

thing still more positive and unequivocal has been evinced to be requisite. The plan of the Convention accordingly has provided that the judges of the United States "shall at STATED TIMES receive for their services a compensation which shall not be DIMINISHED during their continuance in office."

SALARIES CAN'T BE REDUCED:
Salaries may be adjusted but not to the disadvantage of a judge. Does the value of money remain the same? Who may increase a judicial officer's salary?

79:4 This, all circumstances considered, is the most eligible provision that could have been devised. It will readily be understood that the fluctuations in the value of money and in the state of society rendered a fixed rate of compensation in the Constitution inadmissible. What might be extravagant to-day, might in half a century become penurious and inadequate. It was therefore necessary to leave it to the discretion of the legislature to vary its provisions in conformity to the variations in circumstances, yet under such restrictions as to put it out of the power of that body to change the condition of the individual for the worse. A man may then be sure of the ground upon which he stands, and can never be deterred from his duty by the apprehension of being placed in a less eligible situation.

SALARY OF JUDGES MAY NOT BE REDUCED DURING TENURE:

79:5 The clause which has been quoted combines both advantages. The salaries of judicial officers may from time to time be altered, as occasion shall require, yet so as never to lessen the allowance with which any particular judge comes into office, in respect to him.

COST OF LIVING INCREASES FOR LIFETIME JOBS:
Why is the compensation for the President frozen from being raised or lowered, but for the judges it can only be raised?

79:6 It will be observed that a difference has been made by the Convention between the compensation of the President and of the judges. That of the former can neither be increased nor diminished; that of the latter can only not be diminished. This probably arose from the difference in the duration of the respective offices. As the President is to be elected for no more than four years, it can rarely happen that an adequate salary, fixed at the commencement of that period, will not continue to be such to its end.

Judges' salary must grow with the passage of time.

79:7 But with regard to the judges, who, if they behave properly, will be secured in their places for life, it may well happen,

---

244 *Publius:* Vide "Constitution of Massachusetts," chapter 2, section I, article 13.

especially in the early stages of the government, that a stipend, which would be very sufficient at their first appointment, would become <u>too small in the progress</u> of their service.

What does the constitutional provisions of lifetime tenure and no decrease in salary do for the independence of the judges?

79:8 This provision for the support of the judges bears every mark of prudence and efficacy; and it may be safely affirmed that, together with the permanent tenure of their offices, it <u>affords a better prospect of their independence</u> than is discoverable in the constitutions of any of the <u>States</u> in regard to their own judges.

IMPEACHING A JUDGE:

What tool does Congress have to guard against a court that behaves badly in terms of sustaining and defending the Constitution?

79:9 The <u>precautions for their responsibility</u> are comprised in the article respecting impeachments. They are liable to be <u>impeached for malconduct</u> by the House of Representatives, and tried by the Senate; and, if convicted, may be dismissed from office, and disqualified for holding any other. This is the <u>only provision</u> on the point which is consistent with the necessary independence of the judicial character, and is the only one which we find in our own Constitution in respect to our own judges.

Mental ability.

79:10 The want of a <u>provision for removing</u> the judges on account of <u>inability</u> has been a subject of complaint. But all considerate men will be sensible that such a provision would either not be practiced upon or would be more liable to abuse than calculated to answer any good purpose.

Is there a way to accurately measure the *ability* of a judge? Should judges be liable for removal based on ability?

79:11 The **mensuration**[245] of the <u>faculties of the mind</u> has, I believe, no place in the catalogue of known arts. An attempt to fix the boundary between the regions of <u>ability</u> and <u>inability</u>, would much oftener give scope to personal and party attachments and enmities than advance the interests of justice or the public good. The result, except in the case of <u>insanity</u>, must for the most part be <u>arbitrary</u>; and insanity, without any formal or express provision, may be safely pronounced to be a virtual <u>disqualification</u>.

Is a set age a legitimate measure by which to dismiss a judge? What age did New York decide was the ending of a judge's ability to judge?

79:12 The constitution of New York, to avoid investigations that must forever be vague and dangerous, has taken a particular <u>age</u> as the criterion of inability. <u>No man can be a judge beyond sixty</u>. I believe there are few at present who do not disapprove of this provision. There is no station, in relation to which it is less proper than to that of a judge. The deliberating and comparing faculties generally preserve their strength much beyond that period in men who survive it; and when, in addition to this circumstance, we consider <u>how few there are who outlive the season of intellectual vigor</u>, and how improbable it is that any considerable portion of the bench, whether more or less numerous, should be in such a situation at the same time, we shall be ready to conclude that <u>limitations of this sort have little to recommend them</u>.

RETIREMENT NOT FORCED:

79:13 In a republic, where fortunes are not affluent, and pensions not expedient, the dismission of men from stations in which they have <u>served their country long and usefully</u>, on which they <u>depend for subsistence</u>, and from which it will be <u>too late to resort to any other occupation for a livelihood</u>, ought to have some better apology to humanity than is to be found in the imaginary danger of a **superannuated**[246] bench.

—Publius

REVIEW QUESTIONS

1. How does one person gain power over another man's will? (79:1)

2. Can the salary of judges ever be decreased? Why? (79:3–5)

3. Can a judge be removed from office? How? (79:9)

4. Can assessing mental ability be used fairly to retire a judge? Can age be used fairly to retire a judge? (79:10–12)

FEDERALIST NO. 80

FEDERAL COURTS' FIVE JURISDICTIONS: Discussed here are the five specific areas where the federal courts should have the final say, and the Constitution provides for that. Also discussed is the importance of equity courts. These are cases where no specific law applies or where strict application would create injustice. In those cases the court uses its discretion to find solutions that result in maximum fairness.

---

245 **mensuration:** The act of measuring the dimensions.
246 **superannuated:** Deemed obsolete because of age.

By Alexander Hamilton—June 21, 1788

PROPER ROLE OF THE JUDICIARY:

80:1 To JUDGE with accuracy of the proper extent of the federal judicature, it will be necessary to consider, in the first place, what are its proper objects.

FIVE CASES HEARD IN FEDERAL COURT:

What are the five areas of cases the federal judges should have authority to examine?

80:2 It seems scarcely to admit of controversy, that the judiciary authority of the Union ought to extend to these several descriptions of cases:

Constitutional laws.

80:3 1st, to all those which arise out of the laws of the United States, passed in pursuance of their just and constitutional powers of legislation;

Enforcement.

80:4 2d, to all those which concern the execution of the provisions expressly contained in the articles of Union;

United States.

80:5 3d, to all those in which the United States are a party;

Peace.

80:6 4th, to all those which involve the PEACE of the CONFEDERACY, whether they relate to the intercourse between the United States and foreign nations, or to that between the States themselves;

High seas.

80:7 5th, to all those which originate on the high seas, and are of admiralty or maritime jurisdiction;

In general, all cases prone to bias.

80:8 and, lastly, to all those in which the State tribunals cannot be supposed to be impartial and unbiased.

1. ENFORCING CONSTITUTIONAL PROVISIONS:

If the federal court is to have power to rule on national laws, what enforcement power is needed to see that they are obeyed?

80:9 The first point depends upon this obvious consideration, that there ought always to be a constitutional method of **giving efficacy**[247] to constitutional provisions. What, for instance, would avail restrictions on the authority of the State legislatures, without some constitutional mode of enforcing the observance of them?

STATES PROHIBITED FROM FEDERAL DUTIES:

80:10 The States, by the plan of the Convention, are prohibited from doing a variety of things, some of which are incompatible with the interests of the Union, and others with the principles of good government. The imposition of duties on imported articles, and the emission of paper money, are specimens of each kind.

FEDERAL POWER TO CORRECT STATE INFRACTIONS:

80:11 No man of sense will believe, that such prohibitions would be scrupulously regarded, without some effectual power in the government to restrain or correct the infractions of them. This power must either be a direct negative on the State laws, or an authority in the federal courts to overrule such as might be in manifest contravention of the articles of Union. There is no third course that I can imagine. The latter appears to have been thought by the Convention preferable to the former, and, I presume, will be most agreeable to the States.

2. NATIONAL LAWS INTERPRETED THE SAME:

Without one all-powerful court to decide national matters, what would be the obvious result?

80:12 As to the second point, it is impossible, by any argument or comment, to make it clearer than it is in itself. If there are such things as political axioms, the propriety of the judicial power of a government being coextensive with its legislative, may be ranked among the number.

Thirteen State courts, thirteen different interpretations.

80:13 The mere necessity of uniformity in the interpretation of the national laws, decides the question. Thirteen independent courts of final jurisdiction over the same causes, arising upon the same laws, is a hydra in government, from which nothing but contradiction and confusion can proceed.

3. UNITED STATES VS PEOPLE OR VS THE STATES:

80:14 Still less need be said in regard to the third point. Controversies between the nation and its members or citizens, can only be properly referred to the national tribunals. Any other plan would be contrary to reason, to precedent, and to decorum.

4. STATES CAN'T SPEAK FOR AMERICA IN FOREIGN AFFAIRS:

To prevent international misunderstanding should the federal courts deal with legal cases involving foreigners inside US boundaries?

80:15 The fourth point rests on this plain proposition, that the peace of the WHOLE ought not to be left at the disposal

---

247 ***giving efficacy:*** Producing the desired result.

of a PART. The Union will undoubtedly be answerable to foreign powers for the conduct of its members. And the responsibility for an injury ought ever to be accompanied with the faculty of preventing it.

JUST CAUSES OF WAR INVOLVE THE FEDERAL COURT:

80:16   As the denial or perversion of justice by the sentences of courts, as well as in any other manner, is with reason classed among the just causes of war, it will follow that the federal judiciary ought to have cognizance of all causes in which the citizens of other countries are concerned. This is not less essential to the preservation of the public faith, than to the security of the public tranquility.

TREATIES SEPARATE FROM LOCAL LAW AND FOREIGNERS:

Foreigners transgressing State laws could also be violating a treaty.

80:17   A distinction may perhaps be imagined between cases arising upon treaties and the laws of nations and those which may stand merely on the footing of the municipal law. The former kind may be supposed proper for the federal jurisdiction, the latter for that of the States. But it is at least problematical, whether an unjust sentence against a foreigner, where the subject of controversy was wholly relative to the **lex loci**,[248] would not, if unredressed, be an aggression upon his sovereign, as well as one which violated the stipulations of a treaty or the general law of nations.

COURTS PRESIDE OVER CASES WITH NATIONAL QUESTIONS

80:18   And a still greater objection to the distinction would result from the immense difficulty, if not impossibility, of a practical discrimination between the cases of one complexion and those of the other. So great a proportion of the cases in which foreigners are parties, involve national questions, that it is by far most safe and most expedient to refer all those in which they are concerned to the national tribunals.

CASES BETWEEN STATES AND CITIZENS:

80:19   The power of determining causes between two States, between one State and the citizens of another, and between the citizens of different States, is perhaps not less essential to the peace of the Union than that which has been just examined.

What impact did Germany's national courts have on their internal discords?

80:20   History gives us a horrid picture of the dissensions and private wars which distracted and desolated Germany prior to the institution of the **Imperial Chamber**[249] by Maximilian, towards the close of the fifteenth century; and informs us, at the same time, of the vast influence of that institution in appeasing the disorders and establishing the tranquillity of the empire. This was a court invested with authority to decide finally all differences among the members of the Germanic body.

TERRITORIAL DISPUTES:

What is the criterion for choosing what area of jurisdiction is proper?

80:21   A method of terminating territorial disputes between the States, under the authority of the federal head, was not unattended to, even in the imperfect system by which they have been hitherto held together. But there are many other sources, besides interfering claims of boundary, from which bickerings and animosities may spring up among the members of the Union.

SOME DISPUTES WILL REOCCUR:

Even though some acts of bickering and dispute will be prevented in the new government, the causes of them will no doubt reappear in other forms.

80:22   To some of these we have been witnesses in the course of our past experience. It will readily be conjectured that I allude to the fraudulent laws which have been passed in too many of the States. And though the proposed Constitution establishes particular guards against the repetition of those instances which have heretofore made their appearance, yet it is warrantable to apprehend that the spirit which produced them will assume new shapes, that could not be foreseen nor specifically provided against.

JUDICIAL OVERSIGHT OF INTERSTATE ISSUES:

80:23   Whatever practices may have a tendency to disturb the harmony between the States, are proper objects of federal superintendence and control.

NATIONAL JUDICIARY NECESSARY:

A court that has no local ties to prejudice its rulings is best suited for resolving conflict between the States and their citizens.

80:24   It may be esteemed the basis of the Union, that "the citizens of each State shall be entitled to all the privileges and immunities of citizens of the several States." And if it be a just

---

248   ***lex loci:*** Latin for the "law of the place." The law of the nation, state, county, or place where a crime is committed.
249   The ***Imperial Chamber Court*** was founded by Maximilian I in 1495 as the Holy Roman Empire's permanent high court. The court helped calm regional quarrellings in imperial Germany.

principle that every government OUGHT TO POSSESS THE MEANS OF EXECUTING ITS OWN PROVISIONS BY ITS OWN AUTHORITY, it will follow, that in order to the inviolable maintenance of that equality of privileges and immunities to which the citizens of the Union will be entitled, the national judiciary ought to preside in all cases in which one State or its citizens are opposed to another State or its citizens.

IMPARTIAL TRIBUNAL HELPFUL AND NEEDED:
80:25 To secure the full effect of so fundamental a provision against all evasion and subterfuge, it is necessary that its construction should be committed to that tribunal which, having no local attachments, will be likely to be impartial between the different States and their citizens, and which, owing its official existence to the Union, will never be likely to feel any bias inauspicious to the principles on which it is founded.

5. FEDERAL MARITIME JURISDICTION:
80:26 The fifth point will demand little **animadversion**.[250] The most bigoted idolizers of State authority have not thus far shown a disposition to deny the national judiciary the cognizances of maritime causes. These so generally depend on the laws of nations, and so commonly affect the rights of foreigners, that they fall within the considerations which are relative to the public peace. The most important part of them are, by the present Confederation, submitted to federal jurisdiction.

FEDERAL COURTS ARE PROPER WHERE STATES ARE BIASED:
80:27 The reasonableness of the agency of the national courts in cases in which the State tribunals cannot be supposed to be impartial, speaks for itself.

No one can be a fair judge in his own cause.
80:28 No man ought certainly to be a judge in his own cause, or in any cause in respect to which he has the least interest or bias. This principle has no inconsiderable weight in designating the federal courts as the proper tribunals for the determination of controversies between different States and their citizens. And it ought to have the same operation in regard to some cases between citizens of the same State.

STATES WITH LAND DISPUTES WILL BE BIASED:
A State judiciary or legislature cannot be fair if a dispute falls within its own boundaries. A neutral party is needed.
80:29 Claims to land under grants of different States, founded upon adverse pretensions of boundary, are of this description. The courts of neither of the granting States could be expected to be unbiased. The laws may have even prejudged the question, and tied the courts down to decisions in favor

of the grants of the State to which they belonged. And even where this had not been done, it would be natural that the judges, as men, should feel a strong predilection to the claims of their own government.

TESTING THE PRINCIPLES THAT REGULATE THE JUDICIARY:
What are the main areas over which the Courts will judge?
80:30 Having thus laid down and discussed the principles which ought to regulate the constitution of the federal judiciary, we will proceed to test, by these principles, the particular powers of which, according to the plan of the Convention, it is to be composed.

All constitutional cases, and equity cases.
80:31 It is to comprehend "all cases in law and equity arising under the Constitution, the laws of the United States,

Treaties.
80:32 "and treaties made, or which shall be made, under their authority;

Ambassadors.
80:33 "to all cases affecting ambassadors, other public ministers, and consuls;

Maritime.
80:34 "to all cases of admiralty and maritime jurisdiction;

Federal level controversies.
80:35 "to controversies to which the United States shall be a party;

Between States and citizens.
80:36 "to controversies between two or more States; between a State and citizens of another State; between citizens of different States;

Interstate controversies.
80:37 "between citizens of the same State claiming lands and grants of different States;

Involving foreign controversies.
80:38 "and between a State or the citizens thereof and foreign states, citizens, and subjects." This constitutes the entire mass of the judicial authority of the Union.

CONSTITUTIONAL AND FEDERAL DISPUTES:
What's the difference between cases "under the Constitution" and cases arising "under the laws"?
80:39 Let us now review it in detail. It is, then, to extend:

---

250 ***animadversion:*** A comment or remark that criticizes or places blame.

80:40 First. To all cases in law and equity, <u>ARISING UN-DER THE CONSTITUTION</u> and <u>THE LAWS OF THE UNITED STATES</u>. This corresponds with the <u>two first classes</u> of causes, which have been enumerated, as proper for the jurisdiction of the United States.

80:41 It has been asked, what is meant by "cases arising <u>under the Constitution</u>," in contradiction from those "<u>arising under the laws</u> of the United States"?

RESTRICTIONS ON EMITTING PAPER MONEY:
The restriction on States from emitting paper money is an example of the difference between constitutional law and federal law.

80:42 The difference has been already explained. All the <u>restrictions upon the authority of the State legislatures</u> furnish examples of it. They are not, for instance, to emit paper money; but the interdiction results from the Constitution, and will have no connection with any law of the United States. Should paper money, notwithstanding, be emitted, the controversies concerning it would be cases arising under the Constitution and not the laws of the United States, in the ordinary signification of the terms. This may <u>serve as a sample</u> of the whole.

DESCRIBING EQUITABLE JURISDICTION:
What is equitable jurisdiction? How is that different from legal jurisdiction?

80:43 It has also been asked, what need of the word "<u>equity</u>?" What equitable causes can grow out of the Constitution and laws of the United States?

Cases where a loss has been suffered and restitution is wanted would go to courts of equity to make things balanced again.

80:44 There is hardly a subject of litigation between individuals, which may not involve those ingredients of <u>FRAUD</u>, <u>ACCIDENT</u>, <u>TRUST</u>, or <u>HARDSHIP</u>, which would render the matter an object of <u>equitable rather than of legal</u> jurisdiction, as the distinction is known and established in several of the States.

HARD BARGAIN CONTRACTS:
Some issues need resolution but the specifics don't rise to the levels appropriate in any single legal jurisdiction.

80:45 It is the peculiar province, for instance, of a court of equity to relieve against what are called <u>hard bargains</u>: these are <u>contracts</u> in which, though there may have been <u>no direct fraud or deceit</u>, sufficient to invalidate them in a court of law, yet there may have been some undue and <u>unconscionable advantage</u> taken of the <u>necessities</u> or <u>misfortunes</u> of one of the parties, which a court of equity would not tolerate. In such cases, where <u>foreigners</u> were concerned on either side, it

would be impossible for the federal judicatories to do justice without an equitable as well as a legal jurisdiction.

State land disputes are examples of equity law.

80:46 Agreements to <u>convey lands</u> claimed under the grants of different States, may afford another example of the necessity of an equitable jurisdiction in the federal courts. This reasoning may not be so palpable in those States where the formal and technical distinction between <u>LAW and EQUITY</u> is not maintained, as in this State, where it is exemplified by every day's practice.

TO WHAT DOES THE JUDICIAL AUTHORITY EXTEND?

80:47 The judiciary authority of the Union is to extend:

Treaties and Ambassadors.

80:48 Second. To <u>treaties</u> made, or which shall be made, under the authority of the United States, and to all cases affecting <u>ambassadors</u>, other public ministers, and consuls. These belong to the fourth class of the enumerated cases, as they have an evident connection with the preservation of the national peace.

Admiralty and maritime.

80:49 Third. To cases of <u>admiralty</u> and <u>maritime</u> jurisdiction. These form, altogether, the fifth of the enumerated classes of causes proper for the cognizance of the national courts.

When the United States is a party.

80:50 Fourth. To controversies to which the United States shall be a party. These constitute the third of those classes.

Between the States and citizens.

80:51 Fifth. To controversies between <u>two or more States</u>; between a State and <u>citizens</u> of another State; between citizens of different States. These belong to the fourth of those classes, and partake, in some measure, of the nature of the last.

Land claims between citizens of the same or different State.

80:52 Sixth. To cases between the citizens of the same State, CLAIMING <u>LANDS UNDER GRANTS OF DIFFERENT STATES</u>. These fall within the last class, and ARE THE <u>ONLY INSTANCES</u> IN WHICH THE PROPOSED CONSTITUTION DIRECTLY CONTEMPLATES THE COGNIZANCE OF DISPUTES BETWEEN THE <u>CITIZENS OF THE SAME STATE</u>.

Foreign affairs involving States or citizens.

80:53 Seventh. To cases between a State and the citizens thereof, and <u>foreign States</u>, <u>citizens</u>, or <u>subjects</u>. These have been already explained to belong to the fourth of the enumerated classes, and have been shown to be, in a peculiar manner, the proper subjects of the national judicature.

JUDICIARY CONFORMS TO APPLICABLE PRINCIPLES:

80:54 From this review of the particular powers of the federal judiciary, as marked out in the Constitution, it appears that they are all conformable to the principles which ought to have governed the structure of that department, and which were necessary to the perfection of the system.

CONGRESS CAN MAKE A FEW EXCEPTIONS:

If some complications arise beyond the general powers of the judiciary, who can make the proper exceptions to resolve the matter?

80:55 If some partial inconveniences should appear to be connected with the incorporation of any of them into the plan, it ought to be recollected that the national legislature will have ample authority to make such EXCEPTIONS, and to prescribe such regulations as will be calculated to obviate or remove these inconveniences. The possibility of particular mischiefs can never be viewed, by a well-informed mind, as a solid objection to a general principle, which is calculated to avoid general mischiefs and to obtain general advantages.

—PUBLIUS

REVIEW QUESTIONS

1. What are the five areas of jurisdiction to which judicial authority has rights to review? (80:3–7)

2. Would federal laws be obeyed if the government had no power to enforce them? (80:9–11)

3. Without one all-powerful court to decide national matters what would be the result? (80:12–13)

4. Why should the federal court rule on issues relating to possible war? (80:15–16)

5. What positive impact did a central court have in Germany in the late 1400s? (80:20)

6. Can a State be impartial and fair in a case to which it is a main party? In what example given does this prove true? (80:28-29)

7. What are "equitable" cases? (80:43–44)

8. What are some instances where the supreme court would have reason to review equity cases? (80:45–46)

9. What is the only instance where the Supreme Court would expect to be involved in a case between citizens of the same State? (80:52)

10. What relief is available if a condition arises where the Supreme Court's involvement is unknown? (80:54–55)

FEDERALIST NO. 81

FEDERAL COURTS MUST ABIDE BY THE CONSTITUTION: People who make the law (Congress) cannot be trusted to apply it impartially. A separate court will do that. Could the Supreme Court rewrite the Constitution using its power to make legally binding decisions? Yes. Misgivings about an uncontrollable court were urgently expressed by both Anti-Federalists and Thomas Jefferson, among others. Those fears were proven prophetic as significant changes to the Constitution have been made by the court abusing its authorities of interpretation. Hamilton uses an abundance of legal language to assure everyone that such judicial tyranny could never develop, although it has.

By Alexander Hamilton—June 25, 1788

AUTHORITY OF THE VARIOUS COURTS:

81:1 LET US now return to the partition of the judiciary authority between different courts, and their relations to each other,

Quoting the Constitution, Article 3 Section 1.

81:2 "The judicial power of the United States is" (by the plan of the Convention) "to be vested in one Supreme Court, and in such inferior courts as the Congress may, from time to time, ordain and establish."

ONE SUPREME COURT:

What question remains about the independence of the Court?

81:3 That there ought to be one court of supreme and final jurisdiction, is a proposition which is not likely to be contested. The reasons for it have been assigned in another place, and are too obvious to need repetition.

MAKE THE COURT A BRANCH OF CONGRESS?

If it were aligned with Congress it would not be free of persuasion or coercion.

81:4 The only question that seems to have been raised concerning it, is, whether it ought to be a distinct body or a branch of the legislature. The same contradiction is observable in regard to this matter which has been remarked in several other cases.

CRITICS OF THE CONSTITUTION ARE NOT CONSISTENT IN THEIR OBJECTIONS.

81:5 The very men who object to the Senate as a court of impeachments, on the ground of an improper intermixture of powers, advocate, by implication at least, the propriety of <u>vesting the ultimate decision</u> of all causes, in the whole or in a part of the <u>legislative body</u>.

WARNINGS ABOUT AN UNCONTROLLABLE COURT:

What did the Anti-Federalists fear the Supreme Court would eventually become? Did their fears eventually come to pass?

81:6 The arguments, or rather suggestions, upon which this charge is founded, are to this effect:

Veto power by the legislature, or parliament, over the courts.

81:7 "The authority of the proposed Supreme Court of the United States, which is to be a separate and independent body, <u>will be superior</u> to that of the legislature. The power of **construing**[251] the laws according to the SPIRIT of the Constitution, will enable that court to <u>mould them</u> into whatever shape it may think proper; especially as its <u>decisions</u> will not be in any manner <u>subject to the revision or correction</u> of the legislative body. This is as unprecedented as it is dangerous. <u>In Britain, the judicial power, in the last resort, resides in the House of Lords</u>, which is a branch of the legislature; and this part of the British government has been imitated in the State constitutions in general. The Parliament of Great Britain, and the legislatures of the several States, can at any time rectify, by law, the exceptionable decisions of their respective courts. But the errors and usurpations of the Supreme Court of the United States will be uncontrollable and remediless." This, upon examination, will be found to be made up altogether of <u>false reasoning</u> upon <u>misconceived fact</u>.[252]

NO CHECK ON THE COURT:

The Supreme Court can't rule according to the "spirit of the Constitution," or infer or read into it things not explicitly stated (meaning, to construe the law). It is not policed with enough checks to trust its rulings in all cases.

81:8 In the first place, there is <u>not a syllable in the plan</u> under consideration which <u>DIRECTLY</u> empowers the <u>national courts to construe the laws</u> according to the <u>spirit</u> of the Constitution, or which gives them any greater latitude in this respect than may be claimed by the courts of every State.[253]

CONSTITUTION'S UNIVERSAL SUPREMACY:

If any law contradicts the Constitution, the Constitution must take precedence. The States already acknowledge this.

81:9 <u>I admit, however</u>, that the <u>Constitution ought to be the standard of construction for the laws</u>, and that wherever there is an evident opposition, the <u>laws ought to give place to the Constitution</u>. But this doctrine is not deducible from any circumstance peculiar to the plan of the Convention, but from the general theory of a limited Constitution; and as far as it is true, is <u>equally applicable</u> to most, if not to all the <u>State</u> governments.

Supremacy of the federal Constitution is as accepted and expected as supremacy of the States' constitutions.

81:10 There can be no objection, therefore, on this account, to the federal judicature which will not lie against the local judicatures in general, and which will not serve to condemn every constitution that attempts to set bounds to legislative discretion.

DIFFERENT SKILLS FOR COURT COMPARED TO SKILLS FOR CONGRESS:

Can Congress be trusted to interpret its own laws without bias?

81:11 But perhaps the force of the <u>objection</u> may be thought to consist in the <u>particular organization</u> of the Supreme Court; in its being composed of a <u>distinct body</u> of magistrates, instead of being <u>one of the branches</u> of the legislature, as in the government of Great Britain and that of the State.

CONGRESS OVER-RULING THE COURT VIOLATES SEPARATION OF POWERS:

Critics who want the judiciary to be subservient to Congress do not believe in the importance of the separation of powers.

81:12 To insist upon this point, the authors of the objection must renounce the meaning they have labored to annex to the celebrated maxim, requiring a separation of the depart-

---

251 **construe:** To interpret a word in a particular way to give meaning that might not have been intended.

252 *Editors' Note:* Thomas Jefferson also feared an uncontrollable court. He wrote in 1821, "It has long however been my opinion, and I have never shrunk from its expression ... that the <u>germ of dissolution</u> of our federal government is in the constitution of the federal judiciary; an <u>irresponsible</u> body, (for impeachment is scarcely a scare-crow) <u>working like gravity by night and by day, gaining a little to-day & a little tomorrow, and advancing its noiseless step like a thief, over the field of jurisdiction, until all shall be usurped from the states, & the government of all be consolidated into one</u>. To this I am opposed; because whenever all government, domestic and foreign, in little as in great things, shall be drawn to Washington as the center of all power, it will <u>render powerless the checks</u> provided of one government on another, and will become as <u>venal and oppressive</u> as the government from which we <u>separated</u>" (underlining added by editors). Jefferson to C. Hammond, August 18, 1821. See Albert Ellery Bergh, ed., *The Writings of Thomas Jefferson*, 20 vols. (Washington, DC: Thomas Jefferson Memorial Association, 1907), vol. 15, pp. 330–332.

253 *Editors' Note:* Thomas Jefferson considered this lack of a check on the Court to be one of the Convention's biggest mistakes. "I deem it indispensable to the continuance of this government that they [the opinions of the Supreme Court] should be submitted to some <u>practical and impartial control</u>; and this, to be impartial, must be compounded of a mixture of state and federal authorities....I do not charge the judges with willful and ill-intentioned error; but honest error must be arrested where its toleration leads to public ruin" (underlining added by editors). Bergh, *Writings*, vol. 1, p. 120.

ments of power. It shall, nevertheless, be conceded to them, agreeably to the interpretation given to that maxim in the course of these papers, that it is not violated by vesting the ultimate power of judging in a <u>PART</u> of the legislative body. But though this be not an absolute violation of that excellent rule, yet it verges so nearly upon it, as on this account alone to be less eligible than the mode preferred by the Convention.

IF NOT RESTRAINED, CONGRESS WOULD NEARLY ALWAYS OVERRULE THE COURT:
Congress has proven it can pass unwise laws. If the Court declared them unconstitutional, Congress would always oppose those judgments.

81:13 <u>From a body which had even a partial agency in passing bad laws</u>, we could <u>rarely expect</u> a disposition to temper and <u>moderate</u> them in the application. The <u>same spirit</u> which had operated in making them, would be too apt in <u>interpreting them</u>; still less could it be expected that <u>men who had infringed</u> the Constitution in the character of legislators, would be <u>disposed to repair</u> the breach in the character of judges.

THE TEMPORARY CONGRESS SHOULD NOT CONTROL THE PERMANENT COURT:
The court is a lifetime appointment and should not be subjected to the ebbs and flows of members in Congress.

81:14 Nor is this all. Every reason which recommends the tenure of <u>good behavior</u> for judicial offices, <u>militates against placing</u> the judiciary power, in the last resort, <u>in a body composed of men chosen for a limited period</u>.

ABSURD TO SUBJECT JUSTICES TO POLITICIANS:
81:15 There is an absurdity in referring the determination of causes, in the first instance, to judges of permanent standing; in the last, to those of a temporary and mutable constitution. And there is a still greater <u>absurdity</u> in subjecting the <u>decisions of men</u>, selected for their knowledge of the laws, acquired by long and <u>laborious study</u>, to the revision and <u>control of men</u> who, for want of the same advantage, cannot but be <u>deficient</u> in that knowledge.

PARTISANSHIP IN JUDICIARY:
Politicians are not skilled attorneys and are subject to party loyalty more than equity.

81:16 The members of the legislature will rarely be chosen with a view to those <u>qualifications</u> which fit men for the stations of <u>judges</u>; and as, on this account, there will be great reason to apprehend all the ill consequences of defective information, so, on account of the natural propensity of such bodies to party divisions, there will be no less reason to fear that the pestilential breath of <u>faction</u> may <u>poison the fountains of justice</u>. The habit of being continually marshalled on opposite sides will be too apt to stifle the voice both of law and of equity.

IT IS WISE OF THE STATES TO KEEP JUDICIARY INDEPENDENT:
81:17 These considerations teach us to <u>applaud the wisdom</u> of those States who have committed the <u>judicial</u> power, in the last resort, <u>not to a part</u> of the <u>legislature</u>, but to distinct and <u>independent bodies</u> of men.

SEPARATE COURT SYSTEM IS NOT A NEW OR UNIQUE IDEA:
The judiciary as an independent body is already working well among the States.

81:18 Contrary to the supposition of those who have represented the plan of the Convention, in this respect, as novel and unprecedented, it is but a copy of the constitutions of New Hampshire, Massachusetts, Pennsylvania, Delaware, Maryland, Virginia, North Carolina, South Carolina, and Georgia; and the preference which has been given to those models is highly to be commended.

CONGRESS CAN'T CHANGE LEGAL RULINGS:
81:19 It is <u>not true</u>, in the second place, that the Parliament of Great Britain, or the legislatures of the particular States, can rectify the exceptionable decisions of their respective courts, in any other sense than might be done by a future legislature of the United States. The theory, neither of the British, nor the State constitutions, <u>authorizes the revisal of a judicial sentence</u> by a legislative act. Nor is there any thing in the proposed Constitution, more than in either of them, by which it is forbidden. In the former, as well as in the latter, the impropriety of the thing, on the general principles of law and reason, is the sole obstacle.

CONGRESS CAN SET NEW RULES OR LAWS, BUT CAN'T REVERSE A COURT RULING:
State and national legislatures cannot change what the courts decide, but they can pass new laws to cover future circumstances.

81:20 A <u>legislature</u>, without exceeding its province, <u>cannot reverse a determination</u> once made in a particular case; <u>though it may prescribe a new rule for future cases</u>. This is the principle, and it <u>applies</u> in all its consequences, exactly in the same manner and extent, to the <u>State</u> governments, as to the <u>national</u> government now under consideration. Not the least difference can be pointed out in any view of the subject.

JUDICIARY WON'T INTERFERE WITH LEGISLATURE:
81:21 It may in the last place be observed that the <u>supposed danger</u> of <u>judiciary encroachments</u> on the legislative authority,

which has been upon many occasions reiterated, is in reality a phantom. Particular misconstructions and contraventions of the will of the legislature may now and then happen; but they can never be so extensive as to amount to an inconvenience, or in any sensible degree to affect the order of the political system.

JUDICIARY CAN'T ENFORCE JUDGMENTS:

81:22 This may be inferred with certainty, from the general nature of the judicial power, from the objects to which it relates, from the manner in which it is exercised, from its comparative weakness, and from its total incapacity to support its usurpations by force.

CONGRESS CAN IMPEACH MEMBERS OF JUDICIARY:

81:23 And the inference is greatly fortified by the consideration of the important constitutional check which the power of instituting impeachments in one part of the legislative body, and of determining upon them in the other, would give to that body upon the members of the judicial department.

IMPEACHMENT POWER IS SUFFICIENT SECURITY:

81:24 This is alone a complete security. There never can be danger that the judges, by a series of deliberate usurpations on the authority of the legislature, would hazard the united resentment of the body intrusted with it, while this body was possessed of the means of punishing their presumption, by degrading them from their stations.

SENATE CONFIRMS JUDGES AND TRIES IMPEACHMENTS:

81:25 While this ought to remove all apprehensions on the subject, it affords, at the same time, a cogent argument for constituting the Senate a court for the trial of impeachments.

ORGANIZING INFERIOR COURTS:

Aside from the Supreme Court, what other courts may Congress organize?

81:26 Having now examined, and, I trust, removed the objections to the distinct and independent organization of the Supreme Court, I proceed to consider the propriety of the power of constituting inferior courts,[254] and the relations which will subsist between these and the former.

SHARING THE CASE LOAD AMONG INFERIOR COURTS:

What is the purpose of State or district federal courts?

81:27 The power of constituting inferior courts is evidently calculated to obviate the necessity of having recourse to the Supreme Court in every case of federal cognizance. It is intended to enable the national government to institute or AUTHORIZE, in each State or district of the United States, a tribunal competent to the determination of matters of national jurisdiction within its limits.

WHY CREATE INFERIOR COURTS?

81:28 But why, it is asked, might not the same purpose have been accomplished by the instrumentality of the State courts? This admits of different answers.

COULD STATE COURTS TAKE ON THE ROLE OF "INFERIOR COURTS"?

81:29 Though the fitness and competency of those courts should be allowed in the utmost latitude, yet the substance of the power in question may still be regarded as a necessary part of the plan, if it were only to empower the national legislature to commit to them the cognizance of causes arising out of the national Constitution. To confer the power of determining such causes upon the existing courts of the several States, would perhaps be as much "to constitute tribunals," as to create new courts with the like power.

LOCAL BIAS IN STATE COURTS NULLIFIES ITS OBJECTIVITY TO TRY NATIONAL CAUSES:

81:30 But ought not a more direct and explicit provision to have been made in favor of the State courts? There are, in my opinion, substantial reasons against such a provision: the most discerning cannot foresee how far the prevalency of a local spirit may be found to disqualify the local tribunals for the jurisdiction of national causes; whilst every man may discover, that courts constituted like those of some of the States would be improper channels of the judicial authority of the Union.

ELECTED JUDGES NOT AS INDEPENDENT:

State judges would be tempted to always rule in favor of their States to win votes and keep their jobs.

81:31 State judges, holding their offices during pleasure, or from year to year, will be too little independent to be relied upon for an inflexible execution of the national laws. And if there was a necessity for confiding the original cognizance of causes arising under those laws to them there would be a correspondent necessity for leaving the door of appeal as wide as possible. In proportion to the grounds of confidence in, or distrust of, the subordinate tribunals, ought to be the facility or difficulty of appeals. And well satisfied as I am of the propriety of the appellate jurisdiction, in the several classes of

---

254 *Publius:* This power has been absurdly represented as intended to abolish all the county courts in the several States, which are commonly called inferior courts. But the expressions of the Constitution are, to constitute "tribunals INFERIOR TO THE SUPREME COURT"; and the evident design of the provision is to enable the institution of local courts, subordinate to the Supreme, either in States or larger districts. It is ridiculous to imagine that county courts were in contemplation.

causes to which it is extended by the plan of the Convention. I should consider every thing calculated to give, in practice, an UNRESTRAINED COURSE to appeals, as a source of public and private inconvenience.

HAMILTON FORESEES NATIONAL DISTRICT COURTS:

Why would district courts be better than a federal court in each State? Would this help ensure neutrality in those courts?

81:32   I am not sure, but that it will be found highly expedient and useful, to divide the United States into four or five or half a dozen districts; and to institute a federal court in each district, in lieu of one in every State. The judges of these courts, with the aid of the State judges, may hold circuits for the trial of causes in the several parts of the respective districts. Justice through them may be administered with ease and despatch; and appeals may be safely circumscribed within a narrow compass.

INFERIOR COURTS SHOULD BE ESTABLISHED:

81:33   This plan appears to me at present the most eligible of any that could be adopted; and in order to it, it is necessary that the power of constituting inferior courts should exist in the full extent in which it is to be found in the proposed Constitution.

EXCLUDING THE POWER TO CREATE INFERIOR COURTS WOULD HAVE BEEN WRONG:

Hamilton says keeping from Congress the power to set up inferior courts would be a defect.

81:34   These reasons seem sufficient to satisfy a candid mind, that the want of such a power would have been a great defect in the plan. Let us now examine in what manner the judicial authority is to be distributed between the supreme and the inferior courts of the Union.

SOME CASES MAY BE BROUGHT DIRECTLY TO SUPREME COURT:

81:35   The Supreme Court is to be invested with original jurisdiction only "in cases affecting ambassadors, other public ministers, and consuls, and those in which A STATE shall be a party."[255]

PUBLIC MINISTERS REPRESENTING THEIR OWN SOVEREIGNTIES:

81:36   Public ministers of every class are the immediate representatives of their sovereigns. All questions in which they are concerned are so directly connected with the public peace, that, as well for the preservation of this, as out of respect to the sovereignties they represent, it is both expedient and proper

that such questions should be submitted in the first instance to the highest judicatory of the nation.

RESPECT FOR FOREIGN DIGNITARIES:

Dealing with foreign consuls at highest level shows respect to their nations.

81:37   Though consuls have not in strictness a diplomatic character, yet as they are the public agents of the nations to which they belong, the same observation is in a great measure applicable to them.

STATES DESERVE RESPECT:

81:38   In cases in which a State might happen to be a party, it would ill suit its dignity to be turned over to an inferior tribunal.

81:39   Though it may rather be a digression from the immediate subject of this paper, I shall take occasion to mention here a supposition which has excited some alarm upon very mistaken grounds.

MAY STATES BE SUED IN FEDERAL COURT?

81:40   It has been suggested that an assignment of the public securities of one State to the citizens of another, would enable them to prosecute that State in the federal courts for the amount of those securities; a suggestion which the following considerations prove to be without foundation.

SOVEREIGN CAN'T BE SUED WITHOUT CONSENT:

If a State is to be free and independent may it be dragged to court without its permission?

81:41   It is inherent in the nature of sovereignty not to be amenable to the suit of an individual WITHOUT ITS CONSENT. This is the general sense, and the general practice of mankind; and the exemption, as one of the attributes of sovereignty, is now enjoyed by the government of every State in the Union.

STATES STILL OBLIGATED TO PAY THEIR OWN DEBTS IN THEIR OWN WAY:

81:42   Unless, therefore, there is a surrender of this immunity in the plan of the Convention, it will remain with the States, and the danger intimated must be merely ideal. The circumstances which are necessary to produce an alienation of State sovereignty were discussed in considering the article of taxation, and need not be repeated here. A recurrence to the principles there established will satisfy us, that there is no color to pretend that the State governments would, by the adoption of that plan, be divested of the privilege of paying

---

255 **appellate court:** Also called an "appeals court" that can review the trial record sent up by a lower court to judge if the law was correctly applied.

their own debts in their own way, free from every constraint but that which flows from the obligations of good faith.

STATES CAN'T BE SUED:
Contracts between a nation and individuals are only binding on their good faith.

81:43 <u>The contracts between a nation and individuals are only binding on the conscience of the sovereign, and have no pretensions to a compulsive force</u>. They confer no right of action, independent of the sovereign will.

How can the repayment of war debts be enforced without waging war?

81:44 To what purpose would it be to authorize suits against States for the debts they owe? How could recoveries be enforced? It is evident, it could not be done without waging war against the contracting State; and to ascribe to the federal courts, by mere implication, and in destruction of a pre-existing right of the State governments, a power which would involve such a consequence, would be altogether forced and unwarrantable.

SUPREME COURT USED FOR TWO GENERAL CLASSES OF CAUSES:

81:45 Let us resume the train of our observations. We have seen that the original jurisdiction of the Supreme Court would be confined to two classes of causes, and those of a nature rarely to occur.

PROTECT SUPREME COURT FROM CASES HAVING NO NATIONAL BEARING:
The intent of exceptions and regulations by Congress was to protect the Court from becoming buried in a mountain of frivolous cases. Also, to save litigants from financial ruin with perpetual appeals.

81:46 In all other cases of federal cognizance, <u>the original jurisdiction would appertain to the inferior tribunals; and the Supreme Court would have nothing more than an appellate jurisdiction</u>, "with such EXCEPTIONS and under such REGULATIONS as the Congress shall make."

SOME WORRY OVER ISSUE OF FACTS, NOT LAW:
81:47 The propriety of this appellate jurisdiction has been scarcely called in question in regard to **matters of law**;[256] but the clamors have been loud against it as applied to **matters of fact**.[257]

THREAT TO JURY SYSTEM?
Does the Supreme Court's role as the court of last appeal end up destroying the important guarantee of trial by jury? Does the word "appellate" mean the same to everyone?

81:48 Some well-intentioned men in this State, deriving their notions from the language and forms which obtain in our courts, have been induced to consider it as an implied <u>supersedure of the trial by jury</u>, in favor of the civil-law mode of trial, which prevails in our courts of admiralty, probate, and chancery. A technical sense has been affixed to the term "appellate," which, in our law parlance, is commonly used in reference to appeals in the course of the civil law.

APPELLATE: ITS MEANING VARIES.
81:49 But if I am not misinformed, the <u>same meaning would not be given to it in any part of New England</u>. There an appeal from one jury to another, is familiar both in language and practice, and is even a matter of course, until there have been two verdicts on one side.

APPELLATE IS NOT UNIFORMLY UNDERSTOOD:
81:50 The word "appellate," therefore, will not be understood in the same sense in New England as in New York, which shows the impropriety of a technical interpretation derived from the jurisprudence of any particular State.

ONE TRIBUNAL REVIEWING ANOTHER:
Looking at the facts or at the law is the role of the Supreme Court.

81:51 The expression, taken in the abstract, <u>denotes nothing more than the power of one tribunal to review the proceedings of another</u>, either as to the <u>law or fact</u>, or both. The mode of doing it may depend on ancient custom or legislative provision (in a new government it must depend on the latter), and may be <u>with or without the aid of a jury</u>, as may be judged advisable.

IF THE FIRST ROUND IS BY JURY, SO IS THE APPEAL BY JURY:
81:52 If, therefore, the re-examination of a fact once determined by a jury, should in any case be admitted under the proposed Constitution, it may be so regulated as to be done by a second jury, either by remanding the cause to the court below for a second <u>trial of the fact</u>, or by directing an issue immediately out of the Supreme Court.

THE FACTS IN A CASE CAN'T BE TRIED AGAIN:
Can the Supreme Court retry a fact that a jury has already examined?

81:53 But it does not follow that the <u>re-examination</u> of a fact once ascertained by a jury, will be permitted in the Supreme Court.

---

256 ***matters of law:*** How the law applies, the definition of a law.
257 ***matters of fact:*** The existence of facts or occurrence of events.

Court may consider facts when looking at laws.

81:54 Why may not it be said, with the strictest propriety, when a writ of error is brought from an inferior to a superior court of law in this State, that the latter has jurisdiction of the fact as well as the law? It is true it <u>cannot institute a new inquiry concerning the fact</u>, but it takes cognizance of it <u>as it appears upon the record</u>, and <u>pronounces</u> the <u>law</u> arising upon it.[258]

Juries try the facts and the laws. These can't be separated.

81:55 This is jurisdiction of <u>both fact and law</u>; nor is it even possible to separate them. Though the common-law courts of this State ascertain disputed facts by a jury, yet they unquestionably have jurisdiction of both fact and law; and accordingly when the former is agreed in the pleadings, they have no recourse to a jury, but proceed at once to judgment.

SUPREME COURT DOESN'T RETRY FACTS:

81:56 I contend, therefore, on this ground, that the expressions, "appellate jurisdiction, both as to law and fact," <u>do not necessarily imply a re-examination</u> in the Supreme Court of facts decided by juries in the inferior courts.

81:57 The following train of ideas may well be imagined to have influenced the Convention, in relation to this particular provision.

TOP COURT CONSIDERS COMMON LAW AND FACTS:

Common law is based on social custom and validated in courts of law. Civil law concerns regulating ordinary private matters where juries are to rule based on the facts.

81:58 The <u>appellate jurisdiction</u> of the Supreme Court (it may have been argued) <u>will extend to causes</u> determinable in different modes, some in the course of the <u>COMMON LAW</u>, others in the course of the <u>CIVIL LAW</u>. In the former, the revision of the law only will be, generally speaking, the proper province of the Supreme Court; in the latter, the re-examination of the fact is agreeable to usage, and in some cases, of which **prize causes**[259] are an example, might be essential to the preservation of the public peace. It is therefore necessary that the appellate jurisdiction should, in certain cases, extend in the broadest sense to matters of fact.

It's dangerous to make exceptions about juries because in some States all cases are tried by jury. Also, only a jury may reexamine the facts.

81:59 It will not answer to make an express exception of cases which shall have been originally tried by a jury, because in the courts of some of the States <u>ALL CAUSES are tried in this mode</u>;[260] and such an exception would preclude the revision of matters of fact, as well where it might be proper, as where it might be improper.

It is better to be safe than sorry and allow the Supreme Court to examine both law and fact.

81:60 To avoid all inconveniences, it will be <u>safest to declare generally</u>, that the <u>Supreme Court shall possess appellate jurisdiction both as to law and FACT</u>, and that this jurisdiction shall be subject to such <u>EXCEPTIONS</u> and regulations as the <u>national legislature may prescribe</u>. This will enable the government to modify it in such a manner as will best answer the ends of public justice and security.

THERE IS NO SCHEME TO ABOLISH TRIAL BY JURY:

Congress may limit the Supreme Court's ability to re-examine facts, if it wishes. In those cases Congress should restrict the power to civil cases only.

81:61 This view of the matter, at any rate, <u>puts it out of all doubt</u> that the supposed <u>ABOLITION</u> of the <u>trial by jury</u>, by the operation of this provision, is fallacious and untrue. The legislature of the United States would certainly have full power to provide, that in appeals to the Supreme Court there should be <u>no re-examination of facts</u> where they had been tried in the original causes by juries. This would certainly be an authorized exception; but if, for the reason already intimated, it should be thought too extensive, it might be qualified with a limitation to such causes only as are determinable at common law in that mode of trial.

FEDERAL COURTS RESTRICTED TO CERTAIN CASES:

Only those cases obviously concerning the national well-being are to be considered by the Supreme Court. What are the five points Hamilton makes about the Supreme Court?

81:62 The amount of the observations hitherto made on the authority of the judicial department is this:

Supreme Court is restricted regarding direct appeals.

81:63 that it has been <u>carefully restricted</u> to those causes which are manifestly proper for the cognizance of the national judicature;

---

258 *Publius:* This word is composed of JUS and DICTIO, juris dictio or a speaking and pronouncing of the law.

259 **prize causes:** Ships and cargo that are taken from an enemy in war, seized by force as spoil or plunder.

260 *Publius:* I hold that the States will have concurrent jurisdiction with the subordinate federal judicatories, in many cases of federal cognizance, as will be explained in my next paper.

Most cases go to the lower courts.

81:64 that in the partition of this authority <u>a very small portion of original jurisdiction</u> has been preserved to the Supreme Court, and the rest consigned to the subordinate tribunals;

Appeals regarding both law and fact may go to Supreme Court.

81:65 that the Supreme Court will possess an appellate jurisdiction, both as to <u>law and fact</u>, in all the cases referred to them, both subject to any EXCEPTIONS and REGULATIONS which may be thought advisable;

Trial by jury is not abolished.

81:66 that this appellate jurisdiction does, <u>in no case, ABOLISH the trial by jury</u>;

Appointing good judges will prevent bad rulings.

81:67 and that an ordinary degree of <u>prudence and integrity</u> in the national councils will insure us solid advantages from the establishment of the proposed judiciary, without exposing us to any of the inconveniences which have been predicted from that source.

—Publius

Review Questions

1. What is the question Hamilton will deal with in No. 81? (81:4)

2. Fill in the blanks: Anti-Federalists claim the court as now defined will have "The power of _____ the laws according to the _____ of the Constitution will enable that court to _____ them into whatever shape it may think proper" (81:7)

3. What other famous founding father worried about the same uncontrollable power in the Supreme Court? What did he say would happen? (81:7–8 footnotes)

4. Does the Constitution grant the Supreme Court leeway to rule according to the spirit of the Constitution? Why? (81:8)

5. May the Supreme Court change the Constitution by issuing legal rulings? Why? (80:8-10)

6. Is the Supreme Court held to the same standards of constitutional fidelity as the State courts? (81:8-9)

7. Could Congress with its record of errors be trusted to fill the job of interpreting laws impartially? (81:13)

8. Can Congress overrule the court? What can it do after a ruling? (81:20)

9. What protection is there to ensure the Supreme Court is the weakest of the three branches? (81:22–23)

10. Why shouldn't federal cases be shared with State courts? (81:27–31)

11. What is a "matter of law"? (81:47 footnote)

12. What is a "matter of fact?" (81:47 footnote)

13. Does the Supreme Court ultimately abolish the jury system by retaining the power to retry facts? Why? (81:61)

FEDERALIST NO. 82

STATE AND FEDERAL COURTS SHARE DUTIES: The Anti-Federalists worried the State judiciary systems would become obsolete in the face of the overpowering federal judiciary. That is not the case. States will have jurisdiction over most issues, the federal over a few. This detailed debate shows how the choices and reasoning of politicians in the 1700s was just as animated and energetic about this issue as today.

By Alexander Hamilton—July 2, 1788

CONSTITUTION AN IMPERFECT WORK IN PROGRESS:

Was the Constitution born whole, complete, and perfect? What is needed for all the parts to fully develop?

82:1 THE <u>erection of a new government</u>, whatever care or wisdom may distinguish the work, cannot fail to originate <u>questions of intricacy</u> and nicety; and these may, in a particular manner, be expected to flow from the establishment of a constitution founded upon the total or partial incorporation of a number of <u>distinct sovereignties</u>. 'Tis <u>time only</u> that can mature and perfect so compound a system, can liquidate the meaning of all the parts, and can <u>adjust them to each other</u> in a harmonious and consistent WHOLE.

HOW STATE AND FEDERAL COURTS WORK TOGETHER:

Two questions to answer: Whose ruling stands supreme, the State's or the federal's? Or both at the same time?

82:2 Such questions, accordingly, have arisen upon the plan proposed by the Convention, and particularly concerning the judiciary department. The principal of these respect the situation of the <u>State courts in regard to those causes which are to be submitted to federal jurisdiction</u>.

CONCURRENT JURISDICTION:

82:3 Is this to be <u>exclusive</u>, or are those courts to possess a **concurrent jurisdiction**?[261] If the latter, in what relation will they stand to the national tribunals? These are inquiries which

---

261 ***concurrent jurisdiction:*** Two or more courts may hear the same case. A bank robber can be tried and convicted in State court for robbery, and then tried

we meet with in the mouths of men of sense, and which are certainly entitled to attention.

STATES RETAIN AUTHORITIES:
The States will retain the jurisdictions they have unless delegated by what conditions?

82:4 The principles established in a former paper [No. 31] teach us that the States will retain all PRE-EXISTING authorities which may not be exclusively delegated to the federal head; and that this exclusive delegation can only exist in one of three cases:

Exclusive authority.

82:5 where an exclusive authority is, in express terms, granted to the Union;

Particular authority.

82:6 or where a particular authority is granted to the Union, and the exercise of a like authority is prohibited to the States;

Conflicts in authority.

82:7 or where an authority is granted to the Union, with which a similar authority in the States would be utterly incompatible.

Sovereign authorities remain in States unless delegated away.

82:8 Though these principles may not apply with the same force to the judiciary as to the legislative power, yet I am inclined to think that they are, in the main, just with respect to the former, as well as the latter. And under this impression, I shall lay it down as a rule, that the State courts will RETAIN the jurisdiction they now have, unless it appears to be taken away in one of the enumerated modes.

EXCLUSIVE JUDICIAL POWER IS MISUNDERSTOOD:
A passage in the Constitution is being misunderstood.

82:9 The only thing in the proposed Constitution, which wears the appearance of confining the causes of federal cognizance to the federal courts, is contained in this passage: "The JUDICIAL POWER of the United States SHALL BE VESTED in one Supreme Court, and in SUCH inferior courts as the Congress shall from time to time ordain and establish."

Passage might imply all federal courts have national judiciary power as one body making up a Supreme Court.

82:10 This might either be construed to signify, [1] that the supreme and subordinate courts of the Union should alone have the power of deciding those causes to which their authority is to extend; or simply to denote, that the organs of the national judiciary should be one Supreme Court, and as many subordinate courts as Congress should think proper to appoint;

OR, MORE SIMPLY, THAT CONGRESS MAY APPOINT INFERIOR COURTS:

82:11 [2] or in other words, that the United States should exercise the judicial power with which they are to be invested, through one supreme tribunal, and a certain number of inferior ones, to be instituted by them.

THE FIRST (SUPERIOR) EXCLUDES, AND THE LAST ADMITS (INFERIOR):

82:12 The first excludes, the last admits, the concurrent jurisdiction of the State tribunals; and as the first would amount to an alienation of State power by implication, the last appears to me the most natural and the most defensible construction.

CONCURRENT JURISDICTION IS LIMITED:
In what cases do State courts have concurrent jurisdiction?

82:13 But this doctrine of concurrent jurisdiction is only clearly applicable to those descriptions of causes of which the State courts have previous cognizance. It is not equally evident in relation to cases which may grow out of, and be PECULIAR to, the Constitution to be established; for not to allow the State courts a right of jurisdiction in such cases, can hardly be considered as the abridgment of a pre-existing authority.

CONGRESS MAY DIRECT CASES TO FEDERAL LEVEL:
At the same time the States will not lose any rights either.

82:14 I mean not therefore to contend that the United States, in the course of legislation upon the objects intrusted to their direction, may not commit the decision of causes arising upon a particular regulation to the federal courts solely, if such a measure should be deemed expedient; but I hold that the State courts will be divested of no part of their primitive jurisdiction, further than may relate to an appeal;

Except for specifically designated federal cases, the States remain involved in cases resulting from Congress's actions.

82:15 and I am even of opinion that in every case in which they were not expressly excluded by the future acts of the national legislature, they will of course take cognizance of the causes to which those acts may give birth.

JUDICIARIES LOOK FAR AND WIDE FOR RESOLUTIONS:

82:16 This I infer from the nature of judiciary power, and from the general genius of the system. The judiciary power

---

and convicted in federal court for robbing a federally-charted bank.

of every government looks beyond its own local or municipal laws, and in civil cases lays hold of all subjects of litigation between parties within its jurisdiction, though the causes of dispute are relative to the laws of the most distant part of the globe. Those of Japan, not less than of New York, may furnish the objects of legal discussion to our courts.

STATES RETAIN A VOICE IN CASES:
The States are excluded only in those cases that are specifically set aside as federal.

82:17 When in addition to this we consider the State governments and the national governments, as they truly are, in the light of kindred systems, and as parts of ONE WHOLE, the inference seems to be conclusive, that the State courts would have a concurrent jurisdiction in all cases arising under the laws of the Union, where it was not expressly prohibited.

HOW WILL FEDERAL AND STATE COURTS INTERACT?
Can any court decision made on the State level (that impacts federal rights and authorities) be appealed to the federal level?

82:18 Here another question occurs: What relation would subsist between the national and State courts in these instances of concurrent jurisdiction?

STATE-LEVEL APPEALS CAN GO TO SUPREME COURT:
The Supreme Court is the court of last resort in every case with federal significance.

82:19 I answer, that an appeal would certainly lie from the latter, to the Supreme Court of the United States. The Constitution in direct terms gives an appellate jurisdiction to the Supreme Court in all the enumerated cases of federal cognizance in which it is not to have an original one, without a single expression to confine its operation to the inferior federal courts.

OBJECT OF THE APPEAL IS MORE IMPORTANT THAN COURT:
Appeals to higher courts are based on the case itself, not the court in which it first appeared.

82:20 The objects of appeal, not the tribunals from which it is to be made, are alone contemplated. From this circumstance, and from the reason of the thing, it ought to be construed to extend to the State tribunals.

If local cases can't be appealed to the Supreme Court, the local courts can set national precedent, letting people defy federal authority and elude the Supreme Court.

82:21 Either this must be the case, or the local courts must be excluded from a concurrent jurisdiction in matters of national concern, else the judiciary authority of the Union may be eluded at the pleasure of every plaintiff or prosecutor.

Eluding the Supreme Court defeats its entire purpose for existing.

82:22 Neither of these consequences ought, without evident necessity, to be involved; the latter would be entirely inadmissible, as it would defeat some of the most important and avowed purposes of the proposed government, and would essentially embarrass its measures. Nor do I perceive any foundation for such a supposition.

Federal and State systems should be regarded a parts of one whole system.

82:23 Agreeably to the remark already made, the national and State systems are to be regarded as ONE WHOLE. The courts of the latter will of course be natural auxiliaries to the execution of the laws of the Union, and an appeal from them will as naturally lie to that tribunal which is destined to unite and assimilate the principles of national justice and the rules of national decisions.

The Constitution's goal is to bring all cases that have national significance to be heard first or last in the federal courts.

82:24 The evident aim of the plan of the Convention is, that all the causes of the specified classes shall, for weighty public reasons, receive their original or final determination in the courts of the Union. To confine, therefore, the general expressions giving appellate jurisdiction to the Supreme Court, to appeals from the subordinate federal courts, instead of allowing their extension to the State courts, would be to abridge the latitude of the terms, in subversion of the intent, contrary to every sound rule of interpretation.

STATES CAN APPEAL TO LOWER FEDERAL COURTS:
Can a State appeal a decision to one of inferior federal courts?

82:25 But could an appeal be made to lie from the State courts to the subordinate federal judicatories? This is another of the questions which have been raised, and of greater difficulty than the former. The following considerations countenance the affirmative.

Congress can establish inferior courts.

82:26 The plan of the Convention, in the first place, authorizes the national legislature "to constitute tribunals inferior to the Supreme Court."[262] It declares, in the next place, that "the JUDICIAL POWER of the United States SHALL BE

---

262 *Publius:* See Sec. 8, Art. 1

VESTED in one Supreme Court, and in such inferior courts as Congress shall ordain and establish";

Congress decides which cases go to the federal courts.

82:27   and it then proceeds to enumerate the cases to which this judicial power shall extend.

Congress divides the court into its proper roles.

82:28   It afterwards divides the jurisdiction of the Supreme Court into original and appellate, but gives no definition of that of the subordinate courts. The only outlines described for them, are that they shall be "inferior to the Supreme Court," and that they shall not exceed the specified limits of the federal judiciary.

Congress may decide the role the various courts are to play.

82:29   Whether their authority shall be original or appellate, or both, is not declared. All this seems to be left to the discretion of the legislature.

TWO ADVANTAGES FOR STATES TO APPEAL:

What are two of the advantages to allowing States to appeal to the federal courts?

82:30   And this being the case, I perceive at present no impediment to the establishment of an appeal from the State courts to the subordinate national tribunals; and many advantages attending the power of doing it may be imagined.

Reduces the desire to create of more inferior federal courts.

82:31   [1] It would diminish the motives to the multiplication of federal courts, and would admit of arrangements calculated to contract the appellate jurisdiction of the Supreme Court. The State tribunals may then be left with a more entire charge of federal causes;

Allows most cases to be resolved in the lower courts.

82:32   [2] and appeals, in most cases in which they may be deemed proper, instead of being carried to the Supreme Court, may be made to lie from the State courts to district courts of the Union.

—PUBLIUS

REVIEW QUESTIONS

1. Will the States retain all of their pre-existing judicial powers and authorities when the Constitution is adopted? What are the exceptions? (82:4–8)

2. What is concurrent jurisdiction? (82:3 footnote)

3. Does concurrent jurisdiction apply to new situations that will arise from the new Constitution? Why? (82:13)

4. Fill in the blanks: In expressing the plan to create a system of uniform enforcement of laws all across America, Hamilton says the State and federal court systems are part of ___ _____. (82:17)

5. Do the States enjoy concurrent jurisdiction in all cases in the Union? Why? (82:17)

6. What is the only power the federal courts have over cases tried in the States? Explain. (82:18–23)

7. May court cases decided on the State level be appealed to the federal level? Why is this important? (82:20–24)

8. What are some advantages to having the States try cases in the "inferior courts"? (82:30–32)

FEDERALIST NO. 83

TRIAL BY JURY: While the Constitution requires a jury for criminal trials it does not for civil trials. Calling juries for civil infractions should be decided on a case-by-case basis, but most important and key to this discussion is that juries for civil cases are not forbidden by the Constitution as alleged by the Anti-Federalists. When this paper first appeared in a bound volume on May 28, 1778, the Constitution was three weeks away from being ratified (June 21, 1788). It appears that Hamilton wrote this essay, the longest paper of all (5,707 words), as more of an argument for the proper use of juries than an attempt to push New York toward ratification.

By Alexander Hamilton—July 5, 1788

IS TRIAL BY JURY IN CIVIL CASES ABOLISHED IN CONSTITUTION?

That juries for civil cases is not mentioned does not mean it is abolished. That is a false argument by the Anti-Federalists.

83:1   THE objection to the plan of the Convention, which has met with most success in this State, and perhaps in several of the other States, is THAT RELATIVE TO THE WANT OF A CONSTITUTIONAL PROVISION for the trial by jury in **civil cases**.[263] The disingenuous form in which this objection is usually stated has been repeatedly adverted to and exposed, but continues to be pursued in all the conversations and writings of the opponents of the plan.

---

263   ***civil and criminal cases:*** A civil case is a legal dispute between two or more people. A criminal case is a legal examination of a person's conduct in relation to the laws of the land.

CRITICS APPLY THIS MYTH TO CIVIL AND CRIMINAL CASES:

Civil law resolves disputes between *individuals* and their legal responsibilities (negligence, breach of contract, libel). Criminal law resolves crimes against *society* (murder, assault, theft).

83:2 The mere silence of the Constitution in regard to CIVIL CAUSES, is represented as an abolition of the trial by jury, and the declamations to which it has afforded a pretext are artfully calculated to induce a persuasion that this pretended abolition is complete and universal, extending not only to every species of civil, but even to CRIMINAL CAUSES.

IT IS POINTLESS TO ARGUE THAT CIVIL JURIES ARE BANNED:

83:3 To argue with respect to the latter would, however, be as vain and fruitless as to attempt the serious proof of the EXISTENCE of MATTER, or to demonstrate any of those propositions which, by their own internal evidence, force conviction, when expressed in language adapted to convey their meaning.

SILENCE ABOUT JURIES DOES NOT MEAN THEY ARE ABOLISHED:

83:4 With regard to civil causes, subtleties almost too contemptible for refutation have been employed to countenance the surmise that a thing which is only NOT PROVIDED FOR, is entirely ABOLISHED.

Any reasonable person understands silence.

83:5 Every man of discernment must at once perceive the wide difference between SILENCE and ABOLITION. But as the inventors of this fallacy have attempted to support it by certain LEGAL MAXIMS of interpretation, which they have perverted from their true meaning, it may not be wholly useless to explore the ground they have taken.

CRITICS BUILD ARGUMENT ON FALSE MAXIMS:

Upon what maxims do the Anti-Federalists lay their claims about juries being abolished?

83:6 The maxims on which they rely are of this nature: [1] "A specification of particulars is an exclusion of generals"; or, [2] "The expression of one thing is the exclusion of another."

STATING "CRIMINAL JURY" BUT NOT "CIVIL JURY" IS NO RESTRICTION:

83:7 Hence, say they, as the Constitution has established the trial by jury in criminal cases, and is silent in respect to civil, this silence is an implied prohibition of trial by jury in regard to the latter.

LEGAL RULES ARE BUILT ON COMMON SENSE:

83:8 The rules of legal interpretation are rules of COMMONSENSE, adopted by the courts in the construction of the laws. The true test, therefore, of a just application of them is its conformity to the source from which they are derived.

DOES COMMON SENSE APPLY?

83:9 This being the case, let me ask if it is consistent with common-sense to suppose that a provision obliging the legislative power to commit the trial of criminal causes to juries, is a privation of its right to authorize or permit that mode of trial in other cases?

CRITICS' ARGUMENT IS NOT RATIONAL:

Logically speaking, allowing trial by jury in one instance means it is allowed in the other.

83:10 Is it natural to suppose, that a command to do one thing is a prohibition to the doing of another, which there was a previous power to do, and which is not incompatible with the thing commanded to be done? If such a supposition would be unnatural and unreasonable, it cannot be rational to maintain that an injunction of the trial by jury in certain cases is an interdiction of it in others.

POWER TO FORM COURTS IS POWER OVER JURIES:

If the Constitution made no mention of juries at all, what part of government would be at liberty to require juries?

83:11 A power to constitute courts is a power to prescribe the mode of trial; and consequently, if nothing was said in the Constitution on the subject of juries, the legislature would be at liberty either to adopt that institution or to let it alone.

CONGRESS DECIDES ABOUT JURIES IN CIVIL COURTS:

83:12 This discretion, in regard to criminal causes, is abridged by the express injunction of trial by jury in all such cases; but it is, of course, left at large in relation to civil causes, there being a total silence on this head.

POWER TO DECIDE FOR CIVIL CASES IS PRESERVED:

While trial by jury is mandated for criminal cases, leaving that to the discretion of the legislature for civil cases is preserved.

83:13 The specification of an obligation to try all criminal causes in a particular mode, excludes indeed the obligation or necessity of employing the same mode in civil causes, but does not abridge THE POWER of the legislature to exercise that mode if it should be thought proper. The pretense, therefore, that the national legislature would not be at full liberty to submit all the civil causes of federal cognizance to the determination of juries, is a pretense destitute of all just foundation.

TRIAL BY JURY IN CIVIL CASES IS PROTECTED:
By this reasoning, what two conclusions must be reached?

83:14 From these observations this <u>conclusion</u> results: that the trial by <u>jury</u> in civil cases would <u>not be abolished</u>; and that the use attempted to be made of the <u>maxims</u> which have been quoted, is contrary to reason and common-sense, and therefore <u>not admissible</u>.

CRITICS' MISUSE OF THEIR MAXIMS (SEE 83:6):

83:15 Even if these maxims had a precise technical sense, corresponding with the idea of those who employ them upon the present occasion, which, however, is not the case, they would still be inapplicable to a constitution of government. In relation to such a subject, the natural and obvious sense of its provisions, apart from any technical rules, is the true criterion of construction.

EXAMPLES:

83:16 Having now seen that the maxims relied upon will not bear the use made of them, let us endeavor to <u>ascertain their proper use</u> and true meaning. This will be best done by <u>examples</u>.

CONGRESS'S AUTHORITY IS RESTRICTED:
It is pointless to make a list of Congress's powers if its powers are unlimited. Therefore, the list (see Art. I, Sec. 8) is indeed meant as a permission to tax and spend for those items *only*.

83:17 The plan of the Convention declares that the <u>power of Congress</u>, or, in other words, of the NATIONAL LEGISLATURE, shall extend to <u>certain enumerated cases</u>. This specification of particulars evidently excludes all pretension to a general legislative authority, because an <u>affirmative grant of special powers would be absurd, as well as useless, if a general authority was intended</u>.

COURT'S JURISDICTION ALSO LIMITED:
Similarly, can the federal judiciary try cases beyond its specific boundaries?

83:18 <u>In like manner</u> the <u>judicial</u> authority of the federal judicatures is declared by the Constitution to <u>comprehend certain cases particularly specified</u>. The expression of those cases marks the precise <u>limits</u>, beyond which the federal courts <u>cannot extend</u> their jurisdiction, because the objects of their cognizance being <u>enumerated</u>, the specification would be nugatory if it did not exclude all ideas of more extensive authority.

EXAMPLES SHOW IMPROPER USE OF MAXIMS:
These examples show weaknesses and flaws in the critics' arguments.

83:19 These examples are sufficient to elucidate the <u>maxims</u> which have been mentioned, and to designate the manner in which they should be used. But that there may be no misapprehensions upon this subject, <u>I shall add one case more</u>, to demonstrate the proper use of these maxims, and the abuse which has been made of them.

PROPER USE OF MAXIMS:
In another example, if the legislature passes a law to help a married woman dispose of property, may contrary requirements also be made to apply?

83:20 Let us suppose that by the laws of this State a <u>married woman</u> was incapable of <u>conveying her estate</u>, and that the <u>legislature</u>, considering this as an evil, should <u>enact</u> that she might dispose of her property by deed executed in the presence of a magistrate. In such a case there can be no doubt but the <u>specification</u> would amount to an <u>exclusion</u> of any other mode of conveyance, because the woman having no previous power to alienate her property, the specification determines the particular mode which she is, for that purpose, to avail herself of.

THE EXAMPLE IS TAKEN A STEP FURTHER:

83:21 But let us <u>further suppose</u> that in a subsequent part of the same act it should be <u>declared</u> that no woman should dispose of any estate of a determinate value without the <u>consent</u> of <u>three of her nearest relations</u>, signified by their signing the deed; could it be inferred from this regulation that a married woman might not procure the approbation of her relations to a deed for conveying property of inferior value? The position is too <u>absurd</u> to merit a refutation, and yet this is precisely the position which those must establish who contend that the trial by <u>juries in civil cases is abolished, because it is expressly provided for in cases of a criminal nature</u>.

EXAMPLES PROVE JURIES ARE NOT ABOLISHED BY CONSTITUTION:
In cases where the general populace has a great interest, trial by juries will continue in those States where their State constitutions require it.

83:22 From these observations it must appear <u>unquestionably true</u>, that trial by <u>jury</u> is in <u>no case abolished</u> by the proposed Constitution, and it is equally true, that in those controversies between individuals in which the great body of the people are likely to be interested, that institution will remain precisely in the same situation in which it is placed by the <u>State constitutions</u>, and will be in <u>no degree altered</u> or influenced by the adoption of the plan under consideration.

In cases where the federal courts have no jurisdiction anyway, the issue of trial by jury doesn't apply. Cases will be tried by State courts only, according to their constitutions.

83:23 The foundation of this assertion is, that the national judiciary will have no cognizance of them, and of course they will remain determinable as heretofore by the State courts only, and in the manner which the State constitutions and laws prescribe.

CASES BOUND TO STATES ARE TRIED IN THE STATES:

83:24 All land causes, except where claims under the grants of different States come into question, and all other controversies between the citizens of the same State, unless where they depend upon positive violations of the articles of union, by acts of the State legislatures, will belong exclusively to the jurisdiction of the State tribunals.

JURIES NOT NEEDED IN EQUITY AND ADMIRALTY CASES:

It is clear that Hamilton wants to dig down deeply into some of these obscure points to outline issues he thinks need discussion.

83:25 Add to this, that admiralty causes, and almost all those which are of equity jurisdiction, are determinable under our own government without the intervention of a jury,

NEW CONSTITUTION WON'T CHANGE JURY PROCESS:

83:26 and the inference from the whole will be, that this institution, as it exists with us at present, cannot possibly be affected to any great extent by the proposed alteration in our system of government.

ALL AGREE TRIAL BY JURY IS A NECESSARY SAFEGUARD:

83:27 The friends and adversaries of the plan of the Convention, if they agree in nothing else, concur at least in the value they set upon the trial by jury; or if there is any difference between them it consists in this: the former regard it as a valuable safeguard to liberty; the latter represent it as the very palladium of free government.

Jury guards against tyrannical magistrates.

83:28 For my own part, the more the operation of the institution has fallen under my observation, the more reason I have discovered for holding it in high estimation; and it would be altogether superfluous to examine to what extent it deserves to be esteemed useful or essential in a representative republic,

or how much more merit it may be entitled to, as a defense against the oppressions of an hereditary monarch, than as a barrier to the tyranny of popular magistrates in a popular government. Discussions of this kind would be more curious than beneficial, as all are satisfied of the utility of the institution, and of its friendly aspect to liberty.

Disputes between individuals are not as vulnerable to judicial despotism as are accusations of crimes against society.

83:29 But I must acknowledge that I cannot readily discern the inseparable connection between the existence of liberty, and the trial by jury in civil cases.

JUDICIAL DESPOTISM IS A SERIOUS THREAT TO LIBERTY:

What are the four arbitrary judicial actions that constitute corruption in the judiciary?

83:30 [1.] Arbitrary impeachments, [2.] arbitrary methods of prosecuting pretended offenses, [3.] and arbitrary punishments upon [4.] arbitrary convictions, have ever appeared to me to be the great engines of **judicial despotism**;[264] and these have all relation to criminal proceedings. The trial by jury in criminal cases, aided by the **habeas corpus**[265] act, seems therefore to be alone concerned in the question. And both of these are provided for, in the most ample manner, in the plan of the Convention.

JURY TRIALS AND POWER OF TAXATION:

How does a jury protect people from judicial despotism in taxation?

83:31 It has been observed, that trial by jury is a safeguard against an oppressive exercise of the power of taxation. This observation deserves to be canvassed.

Areas where trial by jury cannot exert influence.

83:32 It is evident that it can have no influence upon the legislature, in regard to the AMOUNT of taxes to be laid, to the OBJECTS upon which they are to be imposed, or to the RULE by which they are to be apportioned.

Areas where trial by jury can indeed exert influence.

83:33 If it can have any influence, therefore, it must be upon the mode of collection, and the conduct of the officers intrusted with the execution of the revenue laws.

NEW YORK'S STANDARD OF REVENUE COLLECTION:

83:34 As to the mode of collection in this State, under our own Constitution, the trial by jury is in most cases out of use.

---

264 *judicial despotism:* When the judiciary rules with absolute power.
265 *habeas corpus:* A legal order demanding a detained person be brought into court, and that the government show cause for the imprisonment.

The taxes are usually levied by the more summary proceeding of distress and sale, as in cases of rent. And it is acknowledged on all hands, that this is essential to the efficacy of the revenue laws.

The cost to recover back taxes could be higher than the tax debts due.

83:35   The dilatory course of a trial at law to <u>recover the taxes</u> imposed on individuals, would neither suit the exigencies of the public nor promote the convenience of the citizens. It would often occasion an <u>accumulation of costs</u>, <u>more burdensome</u> than the <u>original sum</u> of the tax to be levied.

ABUSE OF AUTHORITY BY TAX COLLECTORS IS A FELONY:
Trial by jury protect taxpayers from tax collectors who violate their human rights to collect taxes.

83:36   And as to the <u>conduct of the officers</u> of the revenue, the provision in favor of trial by jury in criminal cases, will afford the security aimed at. Willful <u>abuses</u> of a public authority, to the oppression of the subject, and every species of official extortion, are <u>offenses</u> against the government, for which the persons who commit them may be indicted and <u>punished</u> according to the circumstances of the case.

ARE JUDGES MORE CORRUPTIBLE THAN JURIES?
Is it easier to corrupt a permanent body of judges or a quickly assembled and temporary jury?

83:37   The excellence of the trial by jury in civil cases appears to depend on circumstances foreign to the preservation of liberty. The strongest argument in its favor is, that it is a <u>security against corruption</u>.

It appears that long-standing bodies are easier to corrupt. Does this assumption hold up to scrutiny?

83:38   As there is always more time and better opportunity to tamper with a standing body of magistrates than with a jury summoned for the occasion, there is room to suppose that a corrupt influence would more easily find its way to the former than to the latter. The force of this consideration is, however, diminished by others.

Where is corruption more likely to happen?

83:39   The <u>sheriff</u>, who is the summoner of ordinary juries, and the <u>clerks</u> of courts, who have the nomination of special juries, are themselves standing officers, and, acting individually, may be supposed more accessible to the touch of corruption than the judges, who are a collective body.

Juries can be corrupted.

83:40   It is not difficult to see, that it would be in the <u>power of those officers to select jurors</u> who would serve the purpose of the party as well as a <u>corrupted bench</u>. In the next place, it may fairly be supposed, that there would be less difficulty in gaining some of the jurors promiscuously taken from the public mass, than in gaining men who had been chosen by the government for their probity and good character.

Regardless of the vulnerabilities, a trial by jury is still valuable.

83:41   But making every deduction for these considerations, the <u>trial by jury must still be a valuable check upon corruption</u>. It greatly multiplies the impediments to its success.

DOUBLE SECURITY:
What two bodies help secure the integrity of a court case, as well as protect individual liberties?

83:42   As matters now stand, it would be necessary to <u>corrupt both court and jury</u>; for where the <u>jury</u> have gone evidently <u>wrong</u>, the court will generally <u>grant a new trial</u>, and it would be in most cases of little use to practice upon the jury, unless the court could be likewise gained.

REDUCING CORRUPTION:
Increasing the challenges to succeed in a trial also helps discourage any efforts to corrupt the process.

83:43   Here then is a <u>double security</u>; and it will readily be perceived that this complicated agency tends to preserve the purity of both institutions. By increasing the obstacles to success, it <u>discourages attempts to seduce</u> the integrity of either. The temptations to prostitution which the judges might have to surmount, must certainly be much fewer, while the co-operation of a jury is necessary, than they might be, if they had themselves the exclusive determination of all causes.

MUST JURIES FOR PROPERTY CASES BE EXPLICITLY STATED IN THE CONSTITUTION?
Considering the many variables involved in civil disputes, would inserting limits to these into the Constitution even be possible?

83:44   Notwithstanding, therefore, the doubts I have expressed, as to the essentiality of trial by jury in civil cases to liberty, I admit that it is in most cases, under proper regulations, an excellent method of determining <u>questions of property</u>; and that on this account alone it would be entitled to a <u>constitutional provision in its favor if it were possible to fix the limits within which it ought to be comprehended</u>.

TOO MANY VARIABLES FOR CONSTITUTIONAL LAW:
Disputes over property would be a good place to set constitutional boundaries, but it's impossible to include all civil disputes.

83:45 There is, however, in all cases, great difficulty in this; and men not blinded by enthusiasm must be sensible that in a federal government, which is a composition of societies whose ideas and institutions in relation to the matter materially vary from each other, that difficulty must be not a little augmented. For my own part, at every new view I take of the subject, I become more convinced of the reality of the obstacles which, we are authoritatively informed, <u>prevented the insertion</u> of a provision on this head in the plan of the Convention.

TRIAL BY JURY DIFFERS AMONG THE STATES:
Before complaining about leaving out more specifics on trial by jury in the Constitution, understanding the States' use of juries will help.

83:46 The great <u>difference</u> between the limits of the jury trial in different <u>States</u> is not generally understood; and as it must have considerable influence on the sentence we ought to pass upon the omission complained of in regard to this point, an explanation of it is necessary.

Courts in New York similar to Britain.

83:47 In this <u>State</u>, our judicial establishments <u>resemble</u>, more nearly than in any other, those of <u>Great Britain</u>. We have courts of common law, courts of probates (analogous in certain matters to the spiritual courts in England), a court of admiralty and a court of chancery. In the courts of common law only, the trial by jury prevails, and this with some exceptions. In all the others a <u>single judge presides</u>, and proceeds in general either according to the course of the canon or civil law, without the aid of a jury.[266]

Courts in New Jersey.

83:48 In <u>New Jersey</u>, there is a court of chancery which proceeds like ours, but neither courts of admiralty nor of probates, in the sense in which these last are established with us. In that State the courts of common law have the cognizance of those causes which with us are determinable in the courts of admiralty and of probates, and of course the jury trial is more extensive in New Jersey than in New York.

Courts in Pennsylvania.

83:49 In <u>Pennsylvania</u>, this is perhaps still more the case, for there is no court of chancery in that State, and its common-law courts have equity jurisdiction. It has a court of admiralty, but none of probates, at least on the plan of ours.

Courts in Delaware, Maryland, Virgina, North Carolina, South Carolina.

83:50 <u>Delaware</u> has in these respects imitated Pennsylvania. <u>Maryland</u> approaches more nearly to New York, as does also <u>Virginia</u>, except that the latter has a plurality of chancellors. <u>North Carolina</u> bears most affinity to Pennsylvania; <u>South Carolina</u> to Virginia. I believe, however, that in some of those States which have distinct <u>courts of admiralty</u>, the causes depending in them are triable by <u>juries</u>.

Courts in Georgia.

83:51 In <u>Georgia</u> there are none but common-law courts, and an appeal of course lies from the verdict of one jury to another, which is called a special jury, and for which a particular mode of appointment is marked out.

Courts in Connecticut.

83:52 In <u>Connecticut</u>, they have no distinct courts either of chancery or of admiralty, and their courts of probates have no jurisdiction of causes. Their common-law courts have admiralty and, to a certain extent, equity jurisdiction. In cases of importance, their General Assembly is the only court of chancery. In Connecticut, therefore, the trial by jury extends in PRACTICE further than in any other State yet mentioned.

Courts in Rhode Island, Massachusetts, and New Hampshire.

83:53 <u>Rhode Island</u> is, I believe, in this particular, pretty much in the situation of Connecticut. Massachusetts and <u>New Hampshire</u>, in regard to the blending of law, equity, and admiralty jurisdictions, are in a similar predicament. In the four Eastern States, the trial by jury not only stands upon a broader foundation than in the other States, but it is attended with a peculiarity unknown, in its full extent, to any of them. There is an appeal OF COURSE from one jury to another, till there have been two verdicts out of three on one side.

SURVEY OF STATES SHOWS BROAD DIFFERENCES:
The Convention couldn't invent a standard use of trials by jury.

83:54 From this sketch it appears that there is a <u>material diversity</u>, as well in the modification as in the extent of the institution of <u>trial by jury in civil cases</u>, in the several States; and from this fact these obvious reflections flow:

---

266 *Publius:* It has been erroneously insinuated, with regard to the court of chancery, that this court generally tries disputed facts by a jury. The truth is, that references to a jury in that court rarely happen, and are in no case necessary but where the validity of a devise of land comes into question. [*Editors' note:* Canon law is ecclesiastical law developed within Christianity, and includes laws of the Roman Catholic Church.]

No standard would apply to all States.

83:55 <u>first</u>, that no general rule could have been fixed upon by the Convention which would have corresponded with the circumstances of all the States;

Applying one State's example would create unneeded problems.

83:56 and <u>secondly</u>, that more or at least as much might have been hazarded by taking the system of any one State for a standard, as by omitting a provision altogether and leaving the matter, as has been done, to <u>legislative regulation</u>.

ISSUES RAISED THUS FAR PROVE HOW DIFFICULT JURY RULES CAN BECOME:

Suggested amendments also fail to achieve the right balance.

83:57 The propositions which have been made for supplying the omission have rather served to illustrate than to obviate the difficulty of the thing.

Pennsylvania's proposed amendment.

83:58 The minority of <u>Pennsylvania</u> have proposed this mode of expression for the purpose "Trial by jury shall be as heretofore" and this I maintain would be senseless and nugatory.

Federal government has no power where trial by jury is used. Why does the term "heretofore" fail?

83:59 The <u>United States</u>, in their united or collective capacity, are the <u>OBJECT</u> to which all general provisions in the Constitution must necessarily be construed to refer. Now it is evident that though trial by jury, with various limitations, is <u>known in each State individually</u>, yet in the United States, AS SUCH, it is at this time <u>altogether unknown</u>, because the present federal government has no judiciary power whatever; and consequently there is <u>no proper antecedent or previous establishment</u> to which the term HERETOFORE could relate. It would therefore be <u>destitute of a precise meaning</u>, and inoperative from its uncertainty.

PROMOTERS OF AMENDMENTS WILL NEVER BE SATISFIED:

Even if such words were added to the Constitution, could it achieve the desired result?

83:60 As, on the one hand, the <u>form of the provision</u> would not fulfil the intent of its proposers, so, on the other, if I apprehend that intent rightly, it would be in itself inexpedient.

The States where a federal court sits would have differing rules.

83:61 I presume it to be, that causes in the federal courts should be tried by jury, if, in the State where the courts sat, that mode of trial would obtain in a similar case in the State

courts; that is to say, admiralty causes should be tried in Connecticut by a jury, in New York without one.

Choice of trial by jury or no jury would depend on pure chance.

83:62 The capricious operation of so dissimilar a method of trial in the same cases, under the same government, is of itself sufficient to indispose every well regulated judgment towards it. <u>Whether the cause should be tried with or without a jury, would depend, in a great number of cases, on the accidental situation of the court and parties</u>.

TRIAL BY JURY NOT APPROPRIATE IN SOME CASES:

What are some instances where trial by jury should not be used?

83:63 But this is not, in my estimation, the greatest objection. I feel a deep and deliberate conviction that there are <u>many cases in which the trial by jury is an ineligible one</u>. I think it so particularly in cases which concern the <u>public peace with foreign nations</u> that is, in most cases where the question turns wholly on the laws of nations.

JURIES ARE NOT COMPETENT IN INTERNATIONAL LAW:

83:64 Of this nature, among others, are all prize causes. <u>Juries cannot be supposed competent to investigations</u> that require a thorough knowledge of the <u>laws and usages of nations</u>; and they will sometimes be under the influence of impressions which will not suffer them to pay sufficient regard to those considerations of <u>public policy</u> which ought to guide their inquiries. There would of course be always danger that the <u>rights of other nations</u> might be infringed by their decisions, so as to afford occasions of reprisal and war.

While juries try facts, there are legal consequences regarding laws between nations that are far too complex to leave to a jury of unskilled, untrained, and inexperienced members.

83:65 Though the proper province of juries be to determine matters of fact, yet in most cases legal consequences are complicated with fact in such a manner as to render a separation impracticable.

TREATIES AND PRIZE CASES ARE ALSO COMPLEX:

Would trial by jury be wise or workable for foreign affairs?

83:66 It will add great weight to this remark, in relation to <u>prize causes</u>, to mention that the method of determining them has been thought worthy of particular regulation in <u>various treaties</u> between different <u>powers of Europe</u>, and that, pursuant to such treaties, they are determinable in <u>Great Britain</u>, in the last resort, <u>before the king himself</u>, in his privy council, where the fact, as well as the law, undergoes a re-examination.

STATE JURY SYSTEM NOT A GOOD FEDERAL FORUM:

The federal government's duty is to represent the nation as a whole. Would encumbering it to one State's jury form help or hinder?

83:67　<u>This alone</u> demonstrates the impolicy of inserting a fundamental provision in the Constitution which would make the State systems a standard for the national government in the article under consideration, and the <u>danger of encumbering</u> the government with any constitutional provisions the propriety of which is not indisputable.

EQUITY COURTS SEEK REMEDIES, NOT DAMAGES:

These courts look at remedies other than monetary, such as injunctions to stop violating someone's copyright. They seek fairness. A court of law hears criminal cases involving monetary damages. Why should equity cases[267] be tried by a judge and not a jury?

83:68　My convictions are equally strong that great advantages result from the separation of the <u>equity</u> from the law jurisdiction, and that the causes which belong to the former would be <u>improperly committed to juries</u>.

EQUITY COURTS EXAMINE EXCEPTIONS TO LAWS:

Keeping equity cases separate from criminal law allows fairness to lead the way instead of the lure of a large money settlement.

83:69　The great and primary use of a court of equity is to <u>give relief IN EXTRAORDINARY CASES</u>, which are <u>EXCEPTIONS</u>[268] to general rules. To unite the jurisdiction of such cases with the ordinary jurisdiction, must have a tendency to unsettle the general rules, and to subject every case that arises to a SPECIAL determination; while a separation of the one from the other has the contrary effect of rendering one a sentinel over the other, and of keeping each within the expedient limits.

EQUITY CASES INVOLVE COMPLEX LEGAL ISSUES:

Equity cases are often filled with complex legal explorations not suitable for juries not trained or exposed to such intricacies.

83:70　Besides this, the circumstances that constitute cases proper for courts of equity are in many instances so nice and intricate, that they are <u>incompatible</u> with the <u>genius of trials by jury</u>. They require often such long, deliberate, and critical investigation as would be <u>impracticable to men called from their occupations</u>, and obliged to decide before they were permitted to return to them.

JURIES BEST FOR SIMPLE OBVIOUS POINTS:

Juries work best trying a single obvious point. Such clarity is rarely at work in complex, deeply involved equity cases.

83:71　The simplicity and expedition which form the distinguishing characters of this mode of trial require that the matter to be decided should be reduced to some single and obvious point; while the litigations usual in chancery frequently comprehend a long train of minute and independent particulars.

CASES OF EQUITY AND CRIME CAN'T EASILY COMBINE:

Is it easy for a court of equity to consider legal matters if necessary? How about courts of law, can they easily address matters of equity?

83:72　It is true that the <u>separation of the equity</u> from the legal jurisdiction is peculiar to the English system of jurisprudence: which is the <u>model</u> that has been followed in several of the <u>States</u>.

83:73　But it is equally true that the trial by jury has been unknown in every case in which they have been united. And the separation is essential to the preservation of that institution in its pristine purity.

Courts of equity can consider legal matters, but the reverse is not true.

83:74　The nature of a <u>court of equity</u> will readily permit the <u>extension</u> of its jurisdiction to <u>matters of law</u>; but it is not a little to be suspected, that the attempt to <u>extend</u> the jurisdiction of the <u>courts of law</u> to <u>matters of equity</u> will not only be unproductive of the advantages which may be derived from courts of chancery, on the plan upon which they are established in this State, but will tend <u>gradually to change the nature of the courts of law</u>, and to undermine the trial by jury, by <u>introducing questions too complicated</u> for a decision in that mode.

GOOD REASON TO AVOID ADOPTING STATES' FORMS:

With such complexities should the federal government use the States' examples for forming the nation's courts?

83:75　These appeared to be conclusive <u>reasons against incorporating</u> the systems of <u>all</u> the <u>States</u>, in the formation of the

---

267　*equity:* A <u>court of law</u> must follow laws on the books, good or bad. A *court of equity* considers the issues of fair and equal. Stealing bread is a crime in the King's court of law, but a court of equity would consider the fact the king had already taken *all* of the man's bread.

268　*Publius:* It is true that the principles by which that relief is governed are now reduced to a regular system; but it is not the less true that they are in the main applicable to SPECIAL circumstances, which form exceptions to general rules.

national judiciary, according to what may be conjectured to have been the attempt of the Pennsylvania minority.

83:76 Let us now examine how far the proposition of Massachusetts is calculated to remedy the supposed defect.

MASSACHUSETTS' PLAN CALLS FOR THE TRYING OF FACTS:

83:77 It is in this form: "In civil actions between citizens of different States, every issue of fact, arising in ACTIONS AT COMMON LAW, may be tried by a jury if the parties, or either of them request it."

Their plan calls for Trials of Fact *only* on federal level.

83:78 This, at best, is a proposition confined to one description of causes; and the inference is fair, either that the Massachusetts convention considered that as the only class of federal causes, in which the trial by jury would be proper; or that if desirous of a more extensive provision, they found it impracticable to devise one which would properly answer the end.

Massachusetts plan proves the difficulty of putting an equity trial by jury standard into the Constitution.

83:79 If the first, the omission of a regulation respecting so partial an object can never be considered as a material imperfection in the system. If the last, it affords a strong corroboration of the extreme difficulty of the thing.

TRIAL BY JURY IS POORLY DEFINED IN STATES:
Are the States' rules for using a jury well defined and uniform?

83:80 But this is not all: if we advert to the observations already made respecting the courts that subsist in the several States of the Union, and the different powers exercised by them, it will appear that there are no expressions more vague and indeterminate than those which have been employed to characterize THAT species of causes which it is intended shall be entitled to a trial by jury.

New York jurisdiction boundaries similar to British system.

83:81 In this State, the boundaries between actions at common law and actions of equitable jurisdiction, are ascertained in conformity to the rules which prevail in England upon that subject. In many of the other States the boundaries are less precise.

In some States, every case goes to trial by jury.

83:82 In some of them every cause is to be tried in a court of common law, and upon that foundation every action may be considered as an action at common law, to be determined by a jury, if the parties, or either of them, choose it. Hence the same irregularity and confusion would be introduced by a compliance with this proposition, that I have already noticed as resulting from the regulation proposed by the Pennsylvania minority.

IDENTICAL CASES TRIED DIFFERENTLY:
Because the States are not uniform, the very same kind of case would get a jury in one but no jury in the other.

83:83 In one State a cause would receive its determination from a jury, if the parties, or either of them, requested it; but in another State, a cause exactly similar to the other, must be decided without the intervention of a jury, because the State judicatories varied as to common-law jurisdiction.

MASSACHUSETTS PLAN WON'T WORK, EITHER:
What must the States decide on before any particular plan could work? Is such an effort even feasible and realistic?

83:84 It is obvious, therefore, that the Massachusetts proposition, upon this subject cannot operate as a general regulation, until some uniform plan, with respect to the limits of common-law and equitable jurisdictions, shall be adopted by the different States. To devise a plan of that kind is a task arduous in itself, and which it would require much time and reflection to mature. It would be extremely difficult, if not impossible, to suggest any general regulation that would be acceptable to all the States in the Union, or that would perfectly **quadrate**[269] with the several State institutions.

WHY NOT ADOPT NEW YORK'S SYSTEM?
Would the Convention delegates be willing to adopt any particular State's jury plan over that with which they are already familiar?

83:85 It may be asked, Why could not a reference have been made to the constitution of this State, taking that, which is allowed by me to be a good one, as a standard for the United States?

Other States already prefer their own forms.

83:86 I answer that it is not very probable the other States would entertain the same opinion of our institutions as we do ourselves. It is natural to suppose that they are hitherto more attached to their own, and that each would struggle for the preference.

If one State's system for deciding jurisdictions of common-law and equity had been sought at the Convention, the delegates would have squabbled and fought, promoting their own form.

83:87 If the plan of taking one State as a model for the whole had been thought of in the Convention, it is to be presumed

---

269 *quadrate:* To conform with other elements, or cause to conform—"a values system that would quadrate with his morality."

that the adoption of it in that body would have been rendered difficult by the predilection of each representation in favor of its own government; and it must be uncertain which of the States would have been taken as the model. It has been shown that many of them would be improper ones.

CHAOS WOULD ERUPT IF NY'S OR ANOTHER STATE'S FORM WAS FORMALLY ADOPTED:
Favoritism to one State jury system would create firestorm of complaints.

83:88   And I leave it to conjecture, whether, under all circumstances, it is most likely that New York, or some other State, would have been preferred. But admit that a judicious selection could have been effected in the Convention, still there would have been great danger of jealousy and disgust in the other States, at the partiality which had been shown to the institutions of one. The enemies of the plan would have been furnished with a fine pretext for raising a host of local prejudices against it, which perhaps might have hazarded, in no inconsiderable degree, its final establishment.

TRYING ALL CASES BY JURY IS A BIG MISTAKE:
A simple statement about all cases tried by jury would be easy to add.

83:89   To avoid the embarrassments of a definition of the cases which the trial by jury ought to embrace, it is sometimes suggested by men of enthusiastic tempers, that a provision might have been inserted for establishing it in all cases whatsoever.

Making all trials by jury would have been an unpardonable error.

83:90   For this I believe, no precedent is to be found in any member of the Union; and the considerations which have been stated in discussing the proposition of the minority of Pennsylvania, must satisfy every sober mind that the establishment of the trial by jury in ALL cases would have been an unpardonable error in the plan.

EVEN THE ATTEMPT IS OBVIOUSLY ARDUOUS:
If jury rules had been included in the Constitution might this have opened up more problems than it solved?

83:91   In short, the more it is considered the more arduous will appear the task of fashioning a provision in such a form as not to express too little to answer the purpose, or too much to be advisable; or which might not have opened other sources of opposition to the great and essential object of introducing a firm national government.

EXISTING POLICY ON JURY TRIALS IS WELL BALANCED:
This discussion concludes the concerns by pointing out three important conclusions.

83:92   I cannot but persuade myself, on the other hand, that the different lights in which the subject has been placed in the course of these observations, will go far towards removing in candid minds the apprehensions they may have entertained on the point.

(1) Liberty is most jeopardized in criminal cases; therefore a trial by jury is well justified.

83:93   They have tended to show that the security of liberty is materially concerned only in the trial by jury in criminal cases, which is provided for in the most ample manner in the plan of the Convention;

(2) States will individually govern how civil cases are best handled.

83:94   that even in far the greatest proportion of civil cases, and those in which the great body of the community is interested, that mode of trial will remain in its full force, as established in the State constitutions, untouched and unaffected by the plan of the Convention;

(3) The Constitution does not abolish trial by jury.

83:95   that it is in no case abolished[270] by that plan; and that there are great if not insurmountable difficulties in the way of making any precise and proper provision for it in a Constitution for the United States.

JURY TRIALS CAN BE RISKY FOR SOME CIVIL CASES:
As the nation grows is it reasonable to expect other solutions to legal cases will also evolve and develop?

83:96   The best judges of the matter will be the least anxious for a constitutional establishment of the trial by jury in civil cases, and will be the most ready to admit that the changes which are continually happening in the affairs of society may render a different mode of determining questions of property preferable in many cases in which that mode of trial now prevails.

NEW YORK'S FORM SHOULD BE CHANGEABLE:
83:97   For my part, I acknowledge myself to be convinced that even in this State it might be advantageously extended to some cases to which it does not at present apply, and might as advantageously be abridged in others.

---

270   *Publius:* Vide No. 81, in which the supposition of its being abolished by the appellate jurisdiction in matters of fact being vested in the Supreme Court, is examined and refuted.

CAN TRIAL BY JURY BE OVERUSED?

83:98   It is conceded by all reasonable men that it <u>ought not to obtain in all cases</u>. The examples of innovations which contract its ancient limits, as well in these States as in <u>Great Britain</u>, afford a strong presumption that its former extent has been found inconvenient, and give room to suppose that <u>future experience</u> may discover the propriety and utility of other <u>exceptions</u>. I suspect it to be impossible in the nature of the thing to fix the salutary point at which the operation of the institution ought to stop, and this is with me a strong argument for <u>leaving the matter to the discretion of the legislature</u>.

NEW YORK ENCROACHES ON TRIAL BY JURY:

83:99   This is now clearly understood to be the case in Great Britain, and it is equally so in the State of Connecticut; and yet it may be safely affirmed that more numerous <u>encroachments</u> have been made upon the <u>trial by jury in this State</u> since the Revolution, though <u>provided</u> for by a positive article of our <u>constitution</u>, than has happened in the same time either in <u>Connecticut or Great Britain</u>.

Promoters of that encroachment is by men who say one thing and do another regarding liberty and security of rights.

83:100   It may be added that these encroachments have generally originated with the men who endeavor to persuade the people they are the warmest defenders of popular liberty, but who have rarely suffered constitutional obstacles to arrest them in a favorite career.

GENERAL IDEA OF GOVERNMENT:

The genius of the balances in the Constitution stand above its particulars. Should the overall good be thrown out because the Constitution lacks perfect provisions for each and every specific case?

83:101   The truth is that the <u>general GENIUS</u> of a government is all that can be substantially relied upon for permanent effects. Particular provisions, though not altogether useless, have far less virtue and efficacy than are commonly ascribed to them; and the want of them will never be, with men of sound discernment, a decisive objection to any plan which exhibits the <u>leading characters of a good government</u>.

ABSURD TO CLAIM CONSTITUTION FAILS:

It is outrageous to hold to the claim that the Constitution fails just because it establishes juries for criminal trials but leaves that option open for civil trials.

83:102   It certainly sounds not a little harsh and extraordinary to affirm that there is <u>no security for liberty in a Constitution which expressly establishes the trial by jury in criminal cases, because it does not do it in civil also</u>; while it is a notorious fact that <u>Connecticut</u>, which has been always regarded as the most popular State in the Union, can boast of no constitutional provision for either.

—Publius

Review Questions

1. How many words are in this, the longest of all papers in the Federalist? What general topic does Hamilton address? (See introductory paragraph; 83:1–3)

2. Does the fact the Constitution only mentions jury trials for criminal cases and not for civil cases mean that juries for civil cases are banned and abolished? (83:4–5)

3. What are the two maxims on which the critics base their allegation of "no civil jury allowed" in the Constitution? (83:6)

4. Does lack of mention of juries in civil cases mean juries are barred? What outlet is provided to determine the need for juries in civil cases? (83:12–13)

5. When a State constitution demands juries for civil issues, does the Constitution strip away that power? (83:22–24)

6. Why is trial by jury in criminal cases important? (83:27–30)

7. Why is trial by jury in taxation issues important? (83:31–35)

8. Why would specific permission for jury trials in civil land disputes be helpful? (83:44–45)

9. Are there instances of civil dispute where juries would not be helpful or appropriate? Explain. (83:63–67)

10. Why is an equity court usually the wrong place to use a jury? (83:68–70)

11. Why was adopting any of the forms of trials and juries and equity now used in the States wisely rejected by the Convention? (83:85–88)

12. (A) Which of the States also has no constitutional directive regarding juries? (B) Is that State famously popular across the nation? (C) Does this help prove the point that the Constitution is innocent of the pointless and hypocritical allegations made against it, of leaving civil juries up to the discretion of others? (83:102)

SECTION 12 • BILL OF RIGHTS, CONCLUDING REMARKS

Papers 84–85

FEDERALIST NO. 84

BILL OF RIGHTS NOT NEEDED: In Federalist No. 84, Publius says a Bill of Rights is not necessary for two reasons: (1) it's redundant because the Constitution already reserves all rights to the people except those specifically granted to the federal government by the Constitution, and (2) an actual list of rights will almost certainly be incomplete, risk misinterpretation, and—worst of all—somehow grant powers to the federal government that the Constitution did not intend. Madison had originally opposed a separate Bill of Rights, arguing that the Constitution granted only limited powers to the federal government, leaving all other rights with their source, the People. In his view, specifically listing the rights reserved to the People would be redundant and inelegant. Others feared that the new American government would refuse to recognize their rights and, therefore, supported an actual list of some basic rights. This approach is understandable under a monarchy, where the king is the source of all rights, rights that he can arbitrarily create, change, or destroy. It is for these reasons that, in 1215, King John was forced to list rights retained by the English people in the Magna Carta. Publius' fears have, in some ways, been realized today. Every word, every punctuation in the Bill of Rights is scrutinized in great detail. And what about rights that are not listed? Take the issue of abortion, for example. It is easy to understand that the federal government has no authority to regulate this issue since it is not listed in the Bill of Rights. Therefore that issue is obviously left to the people and the States to resolve. But when the Bill of Rights specifically lists a right to be protected, it creates a false assumption, according to Publius, that the federal government can regulate that right. For example, gun rights are specifically listed in the Second Amendment, but does that mean the federal government has the power to regulate them but not abolish, or is that right retained by the People, or maybe even the States? Even when rights are rightly recognized by the federal government, listing those rights can imply that the federal government has power to regulate those rights—something that Publius was warning about in Federalist No. 84. In 1789, Madison was forced to compromise on a bill of rights when Rhode Island and North Carolina refused to ratify the Constitution without one. However he was able to help craft the Bill of Rights as he reconciled the various proposals from the

States. In 1791, Virginia became the last state to ratify the Bill of Rights. –JPS

By Alexander Hamilton—July 16, 1788

OTHER OBJECTIONS TO CONSTITUTION:

84:1 IN THE course of the foregoing review of the Constitution, I have taken notice of, and endeavored to <u>answer</u> most of the <u>objections</u> which have appeared against it. There, however, <u>remain a few</u> which either did not fall naturally under any particular head or were forgotten in their proper places. These shall now be discussed; but as the subject has been drawn into great length, I shall so far consult <u>brevity</u> as to comprise all my observations on these miscellaneous points in a single paper.

NO BILL OF RIGHTS:

Does the Constitution protect human rights even though they are not specifically mentioned?

84:2 The most considerable of the remaining objections is that the plan of the Convention contains <u>no bill of rights</u>. Among other answers given to this, it has been upon different occasions remarked that the constitutions of several of the States are in a similar predicament.

NEW YORK HAS NO BILL OF RIGHTS.

84:3 I add that New York is of the number. And yet the opposers of the new system, in this State, who profess an unlimited admiration for its constitution, are among the most intemperate partisans of a bill of rights. To justify their zeal in this matter, they allege two things:

NEW YORK HAS RIGHTS IN ITS CONSTITUTION.

84:4 one is that, though the <u>constitution of New York</u> has no bill of rights prefixed to it, yet it <u>contains</u>, in the body of it, various provisions in favor of particular <u>privileges and rights</u>, which, in substance amount to the same thing;

Laws of Britain secure all rights not mentioned.

84:5 the other is, that the <u>Constitution adopts, in their full extent, the common and statute law of Great Britain, by which many other rights, not expressed in it, are equally secured</u>.

The new Constitution does protect human rights.

84:6 To the first I answer, that the Constitution proposed by the Convention contains, as well as the constitution of this State, a number of such provisions.

EXAMPLES OF RIGHTS UNDER REPUBLICANISM:
What are some of the rights already guaranteed in the Constitution?

84:7 Independent of those which relate to the structure of the government, we find the following: Article I, section 3, clause 7 "Judgment in cases of impeachment shall not extend further than to removal from office, and disqualification to hold and enjoy any office of honor, trust, or profit under the United States; but the party convicted shall, nevertheless, be liable and subject to indictment, trial, judgment, and punishment according to law."

Writ of habeas corpus.

84:8 Section 9, of the same article, clause 2 "The privilege of the writ of habeas corpus shall not be suspended, unless when in cases of rebellion or invasion the public safety may require it."

Attainder and ex-post-facto law.

84:9 Clause 3 "No bill of attainder or ex-post-facto law shall be passed."

Nobility and foreign emoluments.

84:10 Clause 7 "No title of nobility shall be granted by the United States; and no person holding any office of profit or trust under them, shall, without the consent of the Congress, accept of any present, emolument, office, or title of any kind whatever, from any king, prince, or foreign state."

Trials by jury.

84:11 Article 3, section 2, clause 3 "The trial of all crimes, except in cases of impeachment, shall be by jury; and such trial shall be held in the State where the said crimes shall have been committed; but when not committed within any State, the trial shall be at such place or places as the Congress may by law have directed."

Treason and its definition.

84:12 Section 3, of the same article "Treason against the United States shall consist only in levying war against them, or in adhering to their enemies, giving them aid and comfort. No person shall be convicted of treason, unless on the testimony of two witnesses to the same overt act, or on confession in open court."

Punishment of treason.

84:13 And clause 3, of the same section "The Congress shall have power to declare the punishment of treason; but no attainder of treason shall work corruption of blood, or forfeiture, except during the life of the person attainted."

NEW YORK FALLS SHORT IN COMPARISON:

84:14 It may well be a question, whether these are not, upon the whole, of equal importance with any which are to be found in the constitution of this State.

What are the three rights in the US Constitution that New York's constitution does not contain?

84:15 The establishment of the writ of habeas corpus, the prohibition of ex-post-facto laws, and of TITLES OF NOBILITY, TO WHICH WE HAVE NO CORRESPONDING PROVISION IN OUR [State] CONSTITUTION, are perhaps greater securities to liberty and republicanism than any it contains.

TOOLS OF TYRANNY:
Ex post facto laws and arbitrary imprisonment are among the worst.

84:16 The creation of crimes after the commission of the fact, or, in other words, the subjecting of men to punishment for things which, when they were done, were breaches of no law, and the practice of arbitrary imprisonments, have been, in all ages, the favorite and most formidable instruments of tyranny.

SIR WILLIAM BLACKSTONE (1723–1780):
What rights does Blackstone consider the backbone of British law?

84:17 The observations of the judicious Blackstone,[271] in reference to the latter, are well worthy of recital: "To bereave a man of life, [says he,] or by violence to confiscate his estate, without accusation or trial, would be so gross and notorious an act of despotism, as must at once convey the alarm of tyranny throughout the whole nation; but confinement of the person, by secretly hurrying him to jail, where his sufferings are unknown or forgotten, is a less public, a less striking, and therefore A MORE DANGEROUS ENGINE of arbitrary government."

84:18 And as a remedy for this fatal evil he is everywhere peculiarly emphatical in his **encomiums**[272] on the habeas-cor-

---

271 *Publius:* Vide Blackstone's "Commentaries," vol. 1., p. 136.
272 **encomiums:** A speech or writing that praises something or someone.

pus act, which in one place he calls "the **BULWARK**[273] of the British Constitution."[274]

NO TITLES OF NOBILITY:
Can titles of nobility and government recognition of "special classes" of people destroy America?

84:19 Nothing need be said to illustrate the importance of the prohibition of titles of nobility. This may truly be denominated the corner-stone of republican government; for so long as they are excluded, there can never be serious danger that the government will be any other than that of the people.

QUOTING FROM NEW YORK'S CONSTITUTION:
New York's State legislature can change its bill of rights and common law at will.

84:20 To the second that is, to the pretended establishment of the common and state law by the Constitution, I answer, that they are expressly made subject "to such alterations and provisions as the legislature shall from time to time make concerning the same." They are therefore at any moment liable to repeal by the ordinary legislative power, and of course have no constitutional sanction.

ESTABLISHING LAWS AFTER THE REVOLUTION:
84:21 The only use of the declaration [*Editor:* from New York's constitution] was to recognize the ancient law and to remove doubts which might have been occasioned by the Revolution. This consequently can be considered as no part of a declaration of rights, which under our constitutions must be intended as limitations of the power of the government itself.

PEOPLE RETAIN ALL RIGHTS AND POWER:
A bill of rights must list rights kept by the people, leaving others to the king. Without a king, a list isn't needed.

84:22 It has been several times truly remarked that bills of rights are, in their origin, stipulations between kings and their subjects, abridgments of prerogative in favor of privilege, reservations of rights not surrendered to the prince.

EARLY BILLS OF RIGHTS:
Listed here are some instances where bills of rights were created between kings their subjects.

84:23 Such was MAGNA CHARTA, obtained by the barons, sword in hand, from King John. Such were the subsequent confirmations of that charter by succeeding princes. Such was the PETITION OF RIGHT assented to by Charles the First

in the beginning of his reign. Such, also, was the Declaration of Right presented by the Lords and Commons to the Prince of Orange in 1688, and afterwards thrown into the form of an act of parliament called the Bill of Rights.

BILL OF RIGHTS FLIPS CONSTITUTION:
Hamilton opposed a Bill of Rights because the new Constitution did not give the government any power over those rights.[275] Saying "No" implies powers not granted.

84:24 It is evident, therefore, that, according to their primitive signification, they have no application to constitutions professedly founded upon the power of the people, and executed by their immediate representatives and servants. Here, in strictness, the people surrender nothing; and as they retain every thing they have no need of particular reservations.

CONSTITUTION GIVES NO POWER OVER RIGHTS:
84:25 "WE, THE PEOPLE of the United States, to secure the blessings of liberty to ourselves and our posterity, do ORDAIN and ESTABLISH this Constitution for the United States of America."

Create a treatise of ethics that is separate from the Constitution.

84:26 Here is a better recognition of popular rights, than volumes of those aphorisms which make the principal figure in several of our State bills of rights, and which would sound much better in a treatise of ethics than in a constitution of government.

CONSTITUTION REGULATES GENERAL INTERESTS, NOT PRIVATE RIGHTS:
The new Constitution is to divide, balance, and limit the general political interests of the nation, and does not need to list out a bill of rights for personal and private concerns.

84:27 But a minute detail of particular rights is certainly far less applicable to a Constitution like that under consideration, which is merely intended to regulate the general political interests of the nation, than to a constitution which has the regulation of every species of personal and private concerns. If, therefore, the loud clamors against the plan of the Convention, on this score, are well founded, no epithets of reprobation will be too strong for the constitution of this State. But the truth is, that both of them contain all which, in relation to their objects, is reasonably to be desired.

---

273 **bulwark:** A strong means of defense, support, or protection.

274 *Publius:* Vide Blackstone's "Commentaries," vol. iv., p. 438.

275 *Editors' Note:* Using Hamilton's reasoning (84:24-31), the 1791 Bill of Rights flipped the Constitution from a document of permissions to a document of restrictions. The original 20 permissions listed in Art. I, Sec. 8 were intended to keep the federal divided, balanced and limited. If an action by Congress didn't conform to that list, it was automatically unconstitutional and the government couldn't do it. The Bill of Rights and the 1936 Butler case (see 41:49 footnote) flipped that on its head. Today, if the list doesn't *restrict* an action, the government acts like it is free to do it. Since that change the federal government has involved itself in just about everything. A return to the Framers' original intent was demonstrated in 2022 when the Supreme Court returned management of abortion to the States. The Framers warned against granting the government any new powers whatsoever (84:28), but if it did, it *must* be done by amendment.

WHY NO BILL OF RIGHTS?

A specific list of rights implies the government has power over those rights—which it doesn't—and will expand its powers beyond the specific restriction.

84:28 I go further, and affirm that bills of rights, in the sense and to the extent in which they are contended for, are not only unnecessary in the proposed Constitution, but would even be dangerous. They would contain various exceptions to powers not granted; and, on this very account, would afford a colorable pretext to claim more than were granted. For why declare that things shall not be done which there is no power to do?

Why declare liberty of the press when no federal power is granted to restrict anything, including the press?

84:29 Why, for instance, should it be said that the liberty of the press shall not be restrained, when no power is given by which restrictions may be imposed? I will not contend that such a provision would confer a regulating power; but it is evident that it would furnish, to men disposed to usurp, a plausible pretense for claiming that power.

ACKNOWLEDGING POWER BY IMPLICATION:

Restricting a power implies that that very same power already exists. By this measure, other intentions may arise.

84:30 They might urge with a semblance of reason, that the Constitution ought not to be charged with the absurdity of providing against the abuse of an authority which was not given, and that the provision against restraining the liberty of the press afforded a clear implication, that a power to prescribe proper regulations concerning it was intended to be vested in the national government.

84:31 This may serve as a specimen of the numerous handles which would be given to the doctrine of constructive powers, by the indulgence of an injudicious zeal for bills of rights.

LIBERTY OF THE PRESS:

84:32 On the subject of the liberty of the press, as much as has been said, I cannot forbear adding a remark or two:

Not mentioned in New York's constitution.

84:33 in the first place, I observe, that there is not a syllable concerning it in the constitution of this State;

Is there even a definition of "liberty of the press"?

84:34 in the next, I contend, that whatever has been said about it in that of any other State, amounts to nothing. What signifies a declaration, that "the liberty of the press shall be inviolably preserved"? What is the liberty of the press? Who can give it any definition which would not leave the utmost latitude for evasion?

Opinion of the people is what ultimately defines liberty of the press.

84:35 I hold it to be impracticable; and from this I infer, that its security, whatever fine declarations may be inserted in any constitution respecting it, must altogether depend on public opinion, and on the general spirit of the people and of the government.[276] And here, after all, as is intimated upon another occasion, must we seek for the only solid basis of all our rights.

CONSTITUTION ALREADY *IS* A NATIONAL BILL OF RIGHTS:

84:36 There remains but one other view of this matter to conclude the point. The truth is, after all the declamations we have heard, that the Constitution is itself, in every rational sense, and to every useful purpose, A BILL OF RIGHTS.

All constitutions are bills of rights.

84:37 The several bills of rights in Great Britain form its Constitution, and conversely the constitution of each State is its bill of rights. And the proposed Constitution, if adopted, will be the bill of rights of the Union.

Constitution declares the political privileges of the citizens.

84:38 Is it one object of a bill of rights to declare and specify the political privileges of the citizens in the structure and administration of the government? This is done in the most ample and precise manner in the plan of the Convention; comprehending various precautions for the public security, which are not to be found in any of the State constitutions.

Constitution defines immunities and modes of proceeding.

84:39 Is another object of a bill of rights to define certain immunities and modes of proceeding, which are relative to personal and private concerns? This we have seen has also been attended to, in a variety of cases, in the same plan.

---

276 *Publius:* To show that there is a power in the Constitution by which the liberty of the press may be affected, recourse has been had to the power of taxation. It is said that duties may be laid upon the publications so high as to amount to a prohibition. I know not by what logic it could be maintained, that the declarations in the State constitutions, in favor of the freedom of the press, would be a constitutional impediment to the imposition of duties upon publications by the State legislatures. It cannot certainly be pretended that any degree of duties, however low, would be an abridgment of the liberty of the press. We know that newspapers are taxed in Great Britain, and yet it is notorious that the press nowhere enjoys greater liberty than in that country. And if duties of any kind may be laid without a violation of that liberty, it is evident that the extent must depend on legislative discretion, respecting the liberty of the press, will give it no greater security than it will have without them. The same invasions of it may be effected under the State constitutions which contain those declarations through the means of taxation, as under the proposed Constitution, which has nothing of the kind. It would be quite as significant to declare that government ought to be free, that taxes ought not to be excessive, etc., as that the liberty of the press ought not to be restrained (underlining added by editors).

The meaning of a bill of rights proves it is in the Constitution.

84:40 Adverting therefore to the substantial meaning of a bill of rights, it is absurd to allege that it is not to be found in the work of the Convention. It may be said that it <u>does not go far enough</u>, though it will not be easy to make this appear; but it can with no propriety be contended that there is no such thing. It certainly must be immaterial <u>what mode is observed as to the order of declaring the rights of the citizens</u>, if they are to be found in any part of the instrument which establishes the government. And hence it must be apparent, that much of what has been said on this subject rests merely on verbal and nominal distinctions, entirely foreign from the substance of the thing.

OBJECTION: WASHINGTON, D.C., IS TOO FAR FROM THE STATES:

Is distance from the seat of government (and therefore hard to keep an eye on it) a valid reason for rejecting a general government?

84:41 <u>Another objection</u> which has been made, and which, from the frequency of its repetition, it is to be presumed is relied on, is of this nature: "It is <u>improper</u> [say the objectors] to <u>confer such large powers</u>, as are proposed, upon the <u>national government</u>, because the seat of that government must of necessity be <u>too remote</u> from many of the States to admit of a proper knowledge on the part of the constituent, of the conduct of the representative body."

If that were the biggest problem, then there should be no federal government at all.

84:42 <u>This argument, if it proves any thing, proves that there ought to be no general government whatever.</u> For the powers which, it seems to be agreed on all hands, ought to be vested in the Union, <u>cannot be safely intrusted</u> to <u>a body which is not under every requisite control</u>.

Problems of distance are really imaginary and ill-founded.

84:43 But there are satisfactory reasons to show that the objection is in reality not well founded. There is in most of the arguments which relate to distance a palpable illusion of the imagination.

HOW DO CITIZENS MONITOR THEIR LEGISLATURES?

Most citizens are already too far from their State governments to keep close watch. How, then, can distance be a valid criticism against Washington, D.C.?

84:44 What are the sources of information by which the people in Montgomery County must <u>regulate</u> their judgment of the <u>conduct</u> of their representatives in the State legislature? Of personal observation they can have no benefit. This is confined to the <u>citizens on the spot</u>. They must therefore <u>depend</u> on the <u>information</u> of intelligent men, in whom they confide; and how must these men obtain their information? Evidently from the <u>complexion of public measures</u>, from the public <u>prints</u>, from <u>correspondences</u> with their representatives, and with other persons who reside at the place of their deliberations.

Montgomery County's example applies to all the States.

84:45 This does not <u>apply</u> to Montgomery County only, but to all the <u>counties at any considerable distance from the seat of government</u>.

The same resources apply to watching the conduct of the people's representatives in the federal government.

84:46 It is equally evident that the same sources of information would be open to the people in relation to the conduct of their representatives in the general government, and the impediments to a prompt communication which distance may be supposed to create, will be overbalanced by the effects of the vigilance of the State governments.

STATES' LEADERSHIP WATCHES FOR FEDERAL ABUSE:

84:47 <u>The executive and legislative bodies of each State will be so many sentinels over the persons employed in every department of the national administration; and as it will be in their power to adopt and pursue a regular and effectual system of intelligence, they can never be at a loss to know the behavior of those who represent their constituents in the national councils, and can readily communicate the same knowledge to the people.</u> Their disposition to apprise the community of whatever may prejudice its interests from another quarter, may be relied upon, if it were only from the <u>rivalship of power</u>.

MORE EYES ON FEDERAL THAN ON STATES:

84:48 And we may conclude with the fullest assurance that <u>the people</u>, through that channel, <u>will be better informed</u> of the conduct of their national representatives, than they can be by any means they now possess of that of their State representatives.

LOCAL CITIZENS NEAR THE CAPITAL WILL SOUND AN ALARM:

Are the interests of those closest to the seat of government action the same interests as those who are distant?

84:49 It ought also to be remembered that the <u>citizens</u> who inhabit the country at and <u>near</u> the seat of government will, in all questions that affect the general liberty and prosperity, have the <u>same interest with those who are at a distance</u>, and that they will stand ready to sound the <u>alarm</u> when necessary, and to point out the actors in any pernicious project.

Important role of official government publications and an unbiased media.

84:50   The <u>public papers</u> will be expeditious messengers of intelligence to the most remote inhabitants of the Union.

ARE DEBTS OWED TO THE US NOT COVERED?

84:51   Among the many <u>curious objections</u> which have appeared against the proposed Constitution, the most extraordinary and the least colorable is derived from the want of some provision respecting the <u>debts due TO the United States</u>.

Critics claim the new government will not collect on outstanding debts, either domestic or foreign.

84:52   This has been represented as a tacit relinquishment of those debts, and as a <u>wicked contrivance</u> to <u>screen public defaulters</u>. The <u>newspapers</u> have teemed with the most inflammatory railings on this head; yet there is nothing clearer than that the suggestion is entirely void of foundation, the offspring of extreme ignorance or extreme dishonesty. In addition to the remarks I have made upon the subject in another place, I shall only observe that as it is a plain dictate of common-sense, so it is also an established doctrine of political law, that "STATES NEITHER LOSE ANY OF THEIR RIGHTS, <u>NOR ARE DISCHARGED</u> FROM ANY OF THEIR OBLIGATIONS, BY A CHANGE IN THE FORM OF THEIR CIVIL GOVERNMENT."

WHAT ABOUT THE COST OF THE NEW GOVERNMENT?

Will the new government create a lot of new expenses?

84:53   The <u>last objection</u> of any consequence, which I at present recollect, turns upon the article of <u>expense</u>. If it were even true, that the adoption of the proposed government would occasion a considerable increase of expense, it would be an objection that ought to have no weight against the plan.

UNION CAN'T BE PRESERVED UNDER THE ARTICLES:

A single government under Congress is unsafe. The power must be divided in a different organization of three separate branches.

84:54   The great bulk of the citizens of America are with reason convinced, that <u>Union is the basis of their political happiness</u>. Men of sense of all parties now, with few exceptions, agree that it <u>cannot be preserved</u> under the <u>present system</u>, nor without radical alterations; that new and <u>extensive powers</u> ought to be granted to the national head, and that these require a <u>different organization</u> of the federal government a single body being an unsafe depositary of such ample authorities.

COST IS NOT A VALID REASON TO REJECT CONSTITUTION:

Will the number of members in Congress and associated costs always grow?

84:55   In conceding all this, the question of expense must be given up; for it is <u>impossible</u>, with any degree of safety, to <u>narrow the foundation</u> upon which the system is to stand. The <u>two branches</u> of the legislature are, in the first instance, to consist of only sixty-five persons, which is the same number of which Congress, under the <u>existing Confederation</u>, may be composed. It is <u>true that this number is intended to be increased</u>; but this is to <u>keep pace</u> with the progress of the <u>population</u> and resources of the country.

Fewer congressmen would be cheaper but not safer.

84:56   It is evident that a less number would, even in the first instance, have been unsafe, and that a continuance of the present number would, in a more advanced stage of population, be a very inadequate representation of the people.

NEW OFFICES ADD TO NECESSARY EXPENSE:

Will greater expense arise from the creation of new offices?

84:57   Whence is the dreaded augmentation of expense to spring? One source indicated, is the <u>multiplication of offices</u> under the new government. Let us examine this a little.

PRINCIPAL DEPARTMENTS REMAIN THE SAME AS UNDER THE ARTICLES:

84:58   It is evident that the principal departments of the administration under the present government, are the same which will be required under the new.

Secretaries of War, Foreign and Domestic Affairs, and Treasury.

84:59   There are now a Secretary of <u>War</u>, a Secretary of <u>Foreign Affairs</u>, a Secretary for <u>Domestic Affairs</u>, a Board of <u>Treasury</u>, consisting of three persons, a Treasurer, assistants, clerks, etc. These officers are indispensable under any system, and will suffice under the new as well as the old.

Ambassadors and ministers.

84:60   As to <u>ambassadors</u> and other <u>ministers</u> and agents in foreign countries, the proposed Constitution can make no other difference than to render their characters, where they reside, more respectable, and their services more useful.

Tax collectors.

84:61   As to persons to be employed in the <u>collection of the revenues</u>, it is unquestionably true that these will form a very considerable addition to the number of federal officers; but it will not follow that this will occasion an increase of public expense. It will be in most cases nothing more than an exchange of State for national officers.

Collectors of customs duties and the States.

84:62 In the collection of all duties, for instance, the persons employed will be wholly of the latter description. The States individually will stand in no need of any for this purpose. What difference can it make in point of expense to pay officers of the customs appointed by the State or by the United States? There is no good reason to suppose that either the number or the salaries of the latter will be greater than those of the former.

NEW COSTS NOT TOO DIFFERENT THAN OLD COSTS:
It's difficult to pinpoint extra costs, as critics claim there will be.

84:63 Where then are we to seek for those additional articles of expense which are to swell the account to the enormous size that has been represented to us?

FEDERAL JUDGES WILL ADD MORE EXPENSE:
84:64 The chief item which occurs to me respects the support of the judges of the United States.

Cost of President already included in Articles.

84:65 I do not add the President, because there is now a president of Congress, whose expenses may not be far, if any thing, short of those which will be incurred on account of the President of the United States.

Support of judges will be an extra, though insignificant, expense.

84:66 The support of the judges will clearly be an extra expense, but to what extent will depend on the particular plan which may be adopted in regard to this matter. But upon no reasonable plan can it amount to a sum which will be an object of material consequence.

CONGRESS WILL BE LESS COSTLY:
84:67 Let us now see what there is to counterbalance any extra expense that may attend the establishment of the proposed government.

Will the transfer of responsibilities to the President save money?

84:68 The first thing which presents itself is that a great part of the business which now keeps Congress sitting through the year will be transacted by the President. Even the management of foreign negotiations will naturally devolve upon him, according to general principles concerted with the Senate, and subject to their final concurrence. Hence it is evident that a portion of the year will suffice for the session of both the Senate and the House of Representatives; we may suppose about a fourth for the latter and a third, or perhaps half, for the former. The extra business of treaties and appointments may give this extra occupation to the Senate.

Duration of congressional sessions will be shorter and less costly.

84:69 From this circumstance we may infer that, until the House of Representatives shall be increased greatly beyond its present number, there will be a considerable saving of expense from the difference between the constant session of the present and the temporary session of the future Congress.

STATE LEGISLATURES WILL BE LESS COSTLY:
More than half the States' time has been used for national issues. Under the new Constitution, that labor will be largely lifted.

84:70 But there is another circumstance of great importance in the view of economy. The business of the United States has hitherto occupied the State legislatures, as well as Congress. The latter has made requisitions which the former have had to provide for. Hence it has happened that the sessions of the State legislatures have been protracted greatly beyond what was necessary for the execution of the mere local business of the States. More than half their time has been frequently employed in matters which related to the United States.

NUMBER OF STATE EMPLOYEES GREATLY REDUCED:
84:71 Now the members who compose the legislatures of the several States amount to two thousand and upwards, which number has hitherto performed what under the new system will be done in the first instance by sixty-five persons, and probably at no future period by above a fourth or fifth of that number.

STATES RELIEVED OF MANY FEDERAL BURDENS:
84:72 The Congress under the proposed government will do all the business of the United States themselves, without the intervention of the State legislatures, who thenceforth will have only to attend to the affairs of their particular States, and will not have to sit in any proportion as long as they have heretofore done. This difference in the time of the sessions of the State legislatures will be clear gain, and will alone form an article of saving, which may be regarded as an equivalent for any additional objects of expense that may be occasioned by the adoption of the new system.

NEW EXPENSES OFFSET BY SAVINGS:

84:73 The result from these observations is that the <u>sources of additional expense</u> from the establishment of the proposed Constitution are <u>much fewer</u> than may have been imagined; that they are <u>counterbalanced</u> by considerable objects of <u>saving</u>; and that while it is questionable on which side the scale will preponderate, it is certain that a government less expensive would be incompetent to the purposes of the Union.

—PUBLIUS

REVIEW QUESTIONS

1. Are there additional objections to the Constitution not yet addressed in the Federalist papers? What specific objection is discussed in paper No. 84? (84:1–2)

2. Why doesn't New York's constitution have a bill of rights? (84:4–5)

3. What are some of the rights already written into the Constitution? (84:7–13)

4. Why is a bill of rights not needed in the Constitution? (84:25–26)

5. Regarding a bill of rights, what does Hamilton mean by "They would contain various exceptions to powers not granted," and "why declare that things shall not be done which there is no power to do?" (84:28–29; see 41:49 footnote)

6. Is the Constitution itself a bill of rights? Why? (84:36–40)

7. Will the government under the new Constitution cost more than the current government under the Articles? Does that even matter? (84:53–56)

8. How will the Constitution save the States time and money? (84:70–72)

FEDERALIST NO. 85

CONCLUDING REMARKS: The Constitution needs first to be ratified before we can refine it. We're too close to the end to distract our national effort. Two final issues that need attention are the Constitution's relation to the constitution of New York, and how a strong republican government in a single Union will secure all the promises we wish with our new government and our new United States.

By Alexander Hamilton—August 13, 1788

TWO REMAINING POINTS TO DISCUSS:

85:1 ACCORDING to the formal division of the subject of these papers, announced in my first number, there would appear still to remain for discussion <u>two points</u>: "the analogy of the <u>proposed government</u> to your own <u>State constitution</u>," and "the <u>additional security</u> which its adoption will afford to republican government, to liberty, and to property."

85:2 But these heads have been so fully anticipated and exhausted in the progress of the work, that it would now scarcely be possible to do any thing more than <u>repeat</u>, in a more dilated form, what has been heretofore said, which the advanced stage of the question, and the time already spent upon it, conspire to forbid.

CONSTITUTION RESEMBLES NEW YORK'S:
What alleged defects does the new Constitution have in common with New York's constitution?

85:3 It is remarkable, that the <u>resemblance</u> of the plan of the Convention to the act which organizes the government of <u>this State</u> holds, not less with regard to many of the supposed defects, than to the real excellences of the former.

Four pretended defects.

85:4 Among the pretended <u>defects</u> are the <u>re-eligibility</u> of the <u>Executive</u>, the want of a <u>council</u>, the omission of a formal <u>bill of rights</u>, the omission of a provision respecting the liberty of the <u>press</u>.

Same defects in New York's constitution.

85:5 These and several others which have been noted in the course of our inquiries are as much chargeable on the existing constitution of this State, as on the one proposed for the Union; and a man must have slender pretensions to consistency, who can <u>rail at the latter</u> for imperfections which he finds no difficulty in <u>excusing in the former</u>.

CRITICS AGAINST THE NEW CONSTITUTION ARE HYPOCRITES:

85:6 Nor indeed can there be a better proof of the insincerity and affectation of some of the zealous adversaries of the plan of the Convention among us, who profess to be the devoted admirers of the government under which they live, than the fury with which they have attacked that plan, for matters in regard to which our own constitution is equally or perhaps more vulnerable.

CONSTITUTION ESTABLISHES NEW SECURITIES TO PROTECT RIGHTS AND LIBERTY:
Restraints are added to better manage factions and ambitious people.

85:7 The <u>additional securities</u> to republican government, to liberty and to property, to be derived from the adoption of the plan under consideration, consist chiefly in the <u>restraints</u> which the preservation of the Union will impose on local <u>factions and insurrections</u>, and on the ambition of <u>powerful individuals</u> in single States, who may acquire credit and influence enough, from leaders and favorites, to become the <u>despots</u> of the people;

Prevents foreign encroachment by strengthening the union.

85:8   in the diminution of the opportunities to <u>foreign</u> intrigue, which the dissolution of the <u>Confederacy would invite</u> and facilitate;

Prevents massive war preparations by preserving the Union.

85:9   in the prevention of extensive <u>military</u> establishments, which could not fail to grow out of wars between the States in a disunited situation;

Requires republican government for each State; no nobilities.

85:10 in the express guaranty of a <u>republican form</u> of government to each; in the absolute and universal exclusion of <u>titles</u> of nobility;

Establishes uniform standards.

85:11   and in the precautions against the repetition of those practices on the part of the State governments which have undermined the foundations of <u>property and credit</u>, have planted mutual distrust in the breasts of all <u>classes</u> of citizens, and have occasioned an almost universal prostration of morals.

HAMILTON PRESENTED HIS BEST ARGUMENTS:
85:12 Thus have I, fellow-citizens, executed the task I had assigned to myself; with what success, your conduct must determine. I trust at least you will admit that I have not failed in the assurance I gave you respecting the spirit with which my endeavors should be conducted.

HAMILTON WAS RATIONAL WITHOUT BEING HARSH:
85:13 I have addressed myself purely to your judgments, and have <u>studiously avoided those asperities</u> which are too apt to disgrace political disputants of all parties, and which have been not a little provoked by the language and conduct of the opponents of the Constitution.

ANTI-FEDERALISTS MISLED PEOPLE AND MISREPRESENTED TRUTH:
85:14 The <u>charge</u> of a <u>conspiracy</u> against the liberties of the people, which has been indiscriminately brought against the

advocates of the plan, has something in it too wanton and too malignant, not to excite the indignation of every man who feels in his own bosom a refutation of the calumny. The perpetual changes which have been rung upon the wealthy, the well-born, and the great, have been such as to inspire the disgust of all sensible men. And the <u>unwarrantable concealments and misrepresentations</u> which have been in various ways practiced to <u>keep the truth from the public eye</u>, have been of a nature to demand the reprobation of all honest men.

HAMILTON ADMITS LOSING HIS TEMPER A FEW TIMES:
85:15 It is not impossible that these circumstances may have occasionally betrayed me into intemperances of expression which I did not intend; it is certain that I have frequently felt a struggle between sensibility and moderation; and if the former has in some instances prevailed, it must be my excuse that it has been neither often nor much.

CONSTITUTION WAS WELL DEFENDED:
Hamilton next calls on New York to consider honestly and without prejudice the new Constitution as a duty affecting the existence of what?

85:16   Let us now pause and ask ourselves whether, in the course of these papers, the proposed Constitution has not been <u>satisfactorily vindicated</u> from the aspersions thrown upon it; and whether it has not been shown to be worthy of the public approbation, and necessary to the public safety and prosperity.

LET EVERY MAN NOW CONSIDER:
85:17 Every man is bound to answer these questions to himself, according to the best of his conscience and understanding, and to act <u>agreeably</u> to the genuine and sober dictates of his <u>judgment</u>. This is a duty from which nothing can give him a dispensation. This is one that he is called upon, nay, constrained by all the obligations that form the bands of society, to discharge sincerely and <u>honestly</u>. No partial motive, no particular interest, no pride of opinion, no temporary passion or <u>prejudice</u>, will justify to himself, to his country, or to his posterity, an improper election of the part he is to act.

CONSTITUTION IS TECHNICALLY RATIFIED:
Let each man avoid stubborn, blind party affiliation and consider casting a personal vote in support of its merits.

85:18 Let him <u>beware</u> of an <u>obstinate adherence to party</u>; let him reflect that the object upon which he is to decide is not a particular interest of the community, but the <u>very existence of the nation</u>; and let him remember that a <u>majority</u> of America has already <u>given its sanction</u> to the plan which he is to approve or reject.

CONSTITUTION IS THE BEST SOLUTION:
How does Hamilton rate the new Constitution?

85:19 I shall not dissemble that I feel an entire confidence in the arguments which recommend the proposed system to your adoption, and that I am unable to discern any real force in those by which it has been opposed. I am persuaded that it is the best which our political situation, habits, and opinions will admit, and superior to any the revolution has produced.

CONSTITUTION IS NOT PERFECT:
Is the Constitution perfect? What reason does Hamilton give for not amending it before it is fully ratified?

85:20 Concessions on the part of the friends of the plan, that it has not a claim to absolute perfection, have afforded matter of no small triumph to its enemies. "Why," say they, "should we adopt an imperfect thing? Why not amend it and make it perfect before it is irrevocably established?"

CONSTITUTION NOT RADICALLY DEFECTIVE:
The Constitution provides all the securities the people want. It is, on the whole, the best we can do.

85:21 This may be plausible enough, but it is only plausible. In the first place I remark, that the extent of these concessions has been greatly exaggerated. They have been stated as amounting to an admission that the plan is radically defective, and that without material alterations the rights and the interests of the community cannot be safely confided to it. This, as far as I have understood the meaning of those who make the concessions, is an entire perversion of their sense. No advocate of the measure can be found, who will not declare as his sentiment, that the system, though it may not be perfect in every part, is, upon the whole, a good one; is the best that the present views and circumstances of the country will permit; and is such an one as promises every species of security which a reasonable people can desire.

PERFECTION IN A LARGE GROUP IS NOT POSSIBLE:
Why is it important to ratify the Constitution now?

85:22 I answer in the next place, that I should esteem it the extreme of imprudence to prolong the precarious state of our national affairs, and to expose the Union to the jeopardy of successive experiments, in the chimerical pursuit of a perfect plan.

Can imperfect man create a perfect government?

85:23 I never expect to see a perfect work from imperfect man. The result of the deliberations of all collective bodies must necessarily be a compound, as well of the errors and prejudices, as of the good sense and wisdom, of the individuals of whom they are composed. The compacts which are to embrace thirteen distinct States in a common bond of amity and union, must as necessarily be a compromise of as many dissimilar interests and inclinations. How can perfection spring from such materials?

THIS CONVENTION CAN'T BE DUPLICATED:
Another convention could never match the favorable circumstances of this one.

85:24 The reasons assigned in an excellent little pamphlet[277] lately published in this city, are unanswerable to show the utter improbability of assembling a new convention, under circumstances in any degree so favorable to a happy issue, as those in which the late Convention met, deliberated, and concluded. I will not repeat the arguments there used, as I presume the production itself has had an extensive circulation. It is certainly well worthy the perusal of every friend to his country.

A REMAINING POINT ABOUT AMENDMENTS:

85:25 There is, however, one point of light in which the subject of amendments still remains to be considered, and in which it has not yet been exhibited to public view. I cannot resolve to conclude without first taking a survey of it in this aspect.

CHANGING CONSTITUTION NOW IS HARMFUL:

85:26 It appears to me susceptible of absolute demonstration, that it will be far more easy to obtain subsequent than previous amendments to the Constitution. The moment an alteration is made in the present plan, it becomes, to the purpose of adoption, a new one, and must undergo a new decision of each State. To its complete establishment throughout the Union, it will therefore require the concurrence of thirteen States.

NINE STATES CAN AMEND AT ANY TIME:

85:27 If, on the contrary, the Constitution proposed should once be ratified by all the States as it stands, alterations in it may at any time be effected by nine[278] States. Here, then, the chances are as thirteen to nine in favor of subsequent amendment, rather than of the original adoption of an entire system.

ACCOMMODATING THIRTEEN STATES IS IMMENSELY DIFFICULT:
Given all of the different wants and desires in the Constitution, could rehashing the many variables ever result in something all States would accept?

85:28 This is not all. Every Constitution for the United States must inevitably consist of a great variety of particulars, in

---

277 *Publius:* Entitled "An Address to the People of the State of New York." [Editors' note: By John Jay, first published 1788]
278 *Publius:* It may rather be said TEN, for though two thirds may set on foot the measure, three fourths must ratify.

which <u>thirteen independent States</u> are to be <u>accommodated</u> in their interests or opinions of interest. We may of course expect to see, in any body of men charged with its original formation, very different combinations of the parts upon different points. <u>Many of those who form a majority on one question, may become the minority on a second</u>, and an association dissimilar to either may constitute the majority on a third.

COLLECTIVE ASSENT IS IMMENSELY DIFFICULT:
Satisfying all the States was an almost impossible task.

85:29 Hence the necessity of <u>moulding and arranging all the particulars</u> which are to compose the whole, in such a manner as to <u>satisfy all the parties</u> to the compact; and hence, also, an immense multiplication of difficulties and casualties in obtaining the collective assent to a final act. The degree of that multiplication must evidently be in a ratio to the number of particulars and the number of parties.

AMENDMENTS SHOULD ADDRESS SINGLE ISSUES:
How many issues should an amendment contain?

85:30 <u>But every amendment to the Constitution, if once established, would be a single proposition</u>, and might be <u>brought forward singly</u>. There would then be no necessity for management or <u>compromise</u>, in relation to any other point no giving nor taking. The will of the requisite number would at once bring the matter to a decisive issue. And consequently, whenever <u>nine, or rather ten States</u>, were united in the desire of a <u>particular amendment</u>, <u>that amendment must infallibly take place</u>.

ARTICLE V CONVENTION MUCH DIFFERENT:
Conventions to amend the Constitution are vastly different than a convention to create the Constitution.

85:31 There can, therefore, be <u>no comparison</u> between the facility of <u>affecting an amendment</u>, and that of establishing in the first instance a <u>complete Constitution</u>.

RULERS MUST ALLOW AMENDMENTS:

85:32 In opposition to the probability of subsequent amendments, it has been urged that the <u>persons</u> delegated to the administration of the national government will always be <u>disinclined to yield up</u> any portion of the <u>authority</u> of which they were once possessed.

AMENDMENTS ARE TO IMPROVE EFFICIENCY:
Amendments should never grant additional powers to the government, only refine its structure.

85:33 For my own part I acknowledge a thorough conviction that any amendments which may, upon mature consideration, be thought useful, will be <u>applicable to the organization</u> of <u>the government, not to the mass of its powers</u>; and on this account alone, I think there is no weight in the observation just stated.

FEDERAL LEADERS SHOULD BE ACCOMMODATING TO THE PEOPLE:

85:34 I also think there is little weight in it on another account. The intrinsic difficulty of governing THIRTEEN STATES at any rate, independent of calculations upon an ordinary degree of public spirit and integrity, will, in my opinion constantly impose on the national rulers the necessity of a <u>spirit of accommodation</u> to the reasonable expectations of their constituents.

CONGRESS MUST ALLOW A CONVENTION OF STATES:
Article V allows the states to meet in convention and propose amendments. This lets them protect themselves against encroachments by the national government.

85:35 But there is yet a further consideration, which proves beyond the possibility of a doubt, that the observation is futile. It is this: that the <u>national rulers</u>, <u>whenever nine States concur</u>, will have <u>no option</u> upon the <u>subject</u>. By the <u>fifth article</u> of the plan, the Congress will be *obliged* "on the application of the legislatures of <u>two thirds</u> of the States (which at present amount to nine), to call a convention for <u>proposing amendments</u>, which *shall be valid*, to all intents and purposes, as part of the <u>Constitution</u>, when <u>ratified</u> by the <u>legislatures of three fourths of the States</u>, <u>or</u> by <u>conventions</u> in three fourths thereof."

"SHALL" MEANS CONGRESS MUST CALL A CONVENTION:

85:36 The <u>words</u> of this article are <u>peremptory</u>. The <u>Congress</u> "*shall* call a convention." <u>Nothing in this particular is left to the discretion of that body</u>.

NO RUNAWAY CONVENTION IS POSSIBLE:
Fear of a "runaway" convention that rewrites the Constitution is alleviated because States will erect barriers beyond which their delegates may not act. Can an Article V Convention of the States end up drastically altering or rewriting the Constitution?

85:37 And of consequence, all the declamation about the disinclination to a change vanishes in air. Nor however difficult it may be supposed to unite two thirds or three fourths of the State legislatures, in amendments which may affect local interests, can there be any room to apprehend any such difficulty in a union on points which are merely <u>RELATIVE to the GENERAL LIBERTY OR SECURITY</u> of the people. <u>We may safely rely on the disposition of the State legislatures</u>

to erect barriers against the encroachments of the national authority.

RATIFICATION IS THE BEST PATH TO AMENDING:

85:38 If the foregoing argument is a fallacy, certain it is that I am myself deceived by it, for it is, in my conception, one of those rare instances in which a political truth can be brought to the test of a mathematical demonstration. Those who see the matter in the same light with me, however zealous they may be for amendments, must agree in the propriety of a previous adoption, as the most direct road to their own object.

Quoting Hume, Hamilton highlights the enormity of the task to unite the nation. What are the four elements present in that task that no single human could undertake or well manage?

85:39 The zeal for attempts to amend, prior to the establishment of the Constitution, must abate in every man who is ready to accede to the truth of the following observations of a writer equally solid and ingenious:

85:40 "To balance a large state or society (says he), whether monarchical or republican, on general laws, is a work of so great difficulty, that no human genius, however comprehensive, is able, by the mere dint of reason and reflection, to effect it. The judgments of many must unite in the work; EXPERIENCE must guide their labor; TIME must bring it to perfection, and the FEELING of inconveniences must correct the mistakes which they INEVITABLY fall into in their first trials and experiments."[279]

ARTICLES HAVE FAILED AMERICA, CONSTITUTION WILL SUCCEED:

Does dragging out ratification any longer risk those disasters?

85:41 These judicious reflections contain a lesson of moderation to all the sincere lovers of the Union, and ought to put them upon their guard against hazarding anarchy, civil war, a perpetual alienation of the States from each other, and perhaps the military despotism of a victorious demagoguery, in the pursuit of what they are not likely to obtain, but from TIME and EXPERIENCE. It may be in me a defect of political fortitude, but I acknowledge that I cannot entertain an equal tranquility with those who affect to treat the dangers of a longer continuance in our present situation as imaginary.

ENEMIES AWAIT OUR FAILURE—RATIFY NOW:

What does Hamilton fear if the nation fails to act now?

85:42 A NATION, without a NATIONAL GOVERNMENT, is, in my view, an awful spectacle. The establishment of a Constitution, in time of profound peace, by the voluntary consent of a whole people, is a PRODIGY,[280] to the completion of which I look forward with trembling anxiety. I can reconcile it to no rules of prudence to let go the hold we now have, in so arduous an enterprise, upon seven out of the thirteen States, and after having passed over so considerable a part of the ground, to recommence the course. I dread the more the consequences of new attempts, because I know that POWERFUL INDIVIDUALS, in this and in other States, are enemies to a general national government in every possible shape.

—PUBLIUS

REVIEW QUESTIONS

1. At the publication of paper No. 85, was the new Constitution already ratified? Explain.

2. To draw out the hypocrisy of the Anti-Federalists in New York, what are the four defects they list against the new Constitution that also existed in their own New York constitution that they love and admire? (85:4–6)

3. What are the new securities established by the Constitution that the Articles of Confederation lacked? (85:11)

4. How does Hamilton rate the new Constitution? (85:19)

5. Is the Constitution perfect? (85:20)

6. What was one of the basic challenges of creating a Constitution that would be acceptable to all thirteen States? (85:28)

7. Why not amend the imperfections before it becomes law? (85:30–31)

8. Should amendments grant new powers to the government or deal with its organization and efficiency? (85:33)

9. What additional safety measure exists for the States as written in Article V? (85:35–37)

10. The fear of a Convention of the States is a modern phenomenon based on the concern that such a convention would give opportunity to rewrite the Constitution. What does Hamilton say that will make destroying the Constitution in such a convention virtually impossible? (85:37)

11. What is the best path to amending the Constitution at this late stage? (85:38)

12. What single word does Hamilton use to describe the new Constitution? (85:42)

---

279 *Publius:* Hume's "Essays," vol. i., page 128: "The Rise of Arts and Sciences." *Editors' Note:* David Hume (1711-1776) was a Scottish philosopher, historian and economist whose many essays on nature and human understanding were highly influential and admired throughout the world.

280 ***prodigy:*** Something so extraordinary as to excite wonder or astonishment (from Noah Webster's American Dictionary of the English Language, 1828).

APPENDIX

THE DECLARATION OF INDEPENDENCE

IN CONGRESS JULY 4, 1776

THE UNANIMOUS DECLARATION OF

THE THIRTEEN UNITED STATES OF AMERICA

When in the Course of human events, it becomes necessary for one people to dissolve the political bands which have connected them with another, and to assume among the powers of the earth, the separate and equal station to which the Laws of Nature and of Nature's God entitle them, a decent respect to the opinions of mankind requires that they should declare the causes which impel them to the separation.

We hold these truths to be self-evident, that all men are created equal, that they are endowed by their Creator with certain unalienable Rights, that among these are Life, Liberty and the pursuit of Happiness.—That to secure these rights, Governments are instituted among Men, deriving their just powers from the consent of the governed, —That whenever any Form of Government becomes destructive of these ends, it is the Right of the People to alter or to abolish it, and to institute new Government, laying its foundation on such principles and organizing its powers in such form, as to them shall seem most likely to effect their Safety and Happiness. Prudence, indeed, will dictate that Governments long established should not be changed for light and transient causes; and accordingly all experience hath shewn, that mankind are more disposed to suffer, while evils are sufferable, than to right themselves by abolishing the forms to which they are accustomed. But when a long train of abuses and usurpations, pursuing invariably the same Object evinces a design to reduce them under absolute Despotism, it is their right, it is their duty, to throw off such Government, and to provide new Guards for their future security.—Such has been the patient sufferance of these Colonies; and such is now the necessity which constrains them to alter their former Systems of Government. The history of the present King of Great Britain is a history of repeated injuries and usurpations, all having in direct object the establishment of an absolute Tyranny over these States. To prove this, let Facts be submitted to a candid world.

[1.][281] He has refused his Assent to Laws, the most wholesome and necessary for the public good.

[2.] He has forbidden his Governors to pass Laws of immediate and pressing importance, unless suspended in their operation till his Assent should be obtained; and when so suspended, he has utterly neglected to attend to them.

[3.] He has refused to pass other Laws for the accommodation of large districts of people, unless those people would relinquish the right of Representation in the Legislature, a right inestimable to them and formidable to tyrants only.

[4.] He has called together legislative bodies at places unusual, uncomfortable, and distant from the depository of their public Records, for the sole purpose of fatiguing them into compliance with his measures.

[5.] He has dissolved Representative Houses repeatedly, for opposing with manly firmness his invasions on the rights of the people.

[6.] He has refused for a long time, after such dissolutions, to cause others to be elected; whereby the Legislative powers, incapable of Annihilation, have returned to the People at large for their exercise; the State remaining in the mean time exposed to all the dangers of invasion from without, and convulsions within.

[7.] He has endeavoured to prevent the population of these States; for that purpose obstructing the Laws for Naturalization of Foreigners; refusing to pass others to encourage their migrations hither, and raising the conditions of new Appropriations of Lands.

---

281 *Editors' Note:* The numbers in brackets are added as a reference tool to each indictment or crime, and are not part of the original *Declaration*.

[8.] He has obstructed the Administration of Justice, by refusing his Assent to Laws for establishing Judiciary powers.

[9.] He has made Judges dependent on his Will alone, for the tenure of their offices, and the amount and payment of their salaries.

[10.] He has erected a multitude of New Offices, and sent hither swarms of Officers to harass our people, and eat out their substance.

[11.] He has kept among us, in times of peace, Standing Armies without the Consent of our legislatures.

[12.] He has affected to render the Military independent of and superior to the Civil power.

[13.] He has combined with others to subject us to a jurisdiction foreign to our constitution, and unacknowledged by our laws; giving his Assent to their Acts of pretended Legislation:

[14.] For Quartering large bodies of armed troops among us:

[15.] For protecting them, by a mock Trial, from punishment for any Murders which they should commit on the Inhabitants of these States:

[16.] For cutting off our Trade with all parts of the world:

[17.] For imposing Taxes on us without our Consent:

[18.] For depriving us in many cases, of the benefits of Trial by Jury:

[19.] For transporting us beyond Seas to be tried for pretended offences

[20.] For abolishing the free System of English Laws in a neighbouring Province, establishing therein an Arbitrary government, and enlarging its Boundaries so as to render it at once an example and fit instrument for introducing the same absolute rule into these Colonies:

[21.] For taking away our Charters, abolishing our most valuable Laws, and altering fundamentally the Forms of our Governments:

[22.] For suspending our own Legislatures, and declaring themselves invested with power to legislate for us in all cases whatsoever.

[23.] He has abdicated Government here, by declaring us out of his Protection and waging War against us.

[24.] He has plundered our seas, ravaged our Coasts, burnt our towns, and destroyed the lives of our people.

[25.] He is at this time transporting large Armies of foreign Mercenaries to compleat the works of death, desolation and tyranny, already begun with circumstances of Cruelty & perfidy scarcely paralleled in the most barbarous ages, and totally unworthy the Head of a civilized nation.

[26.] He has constrained our fellow Citizens taken Captive on the high Seas to bear Arms against their Country, to become the executioners of their friends and Brethren, or to fall themselves by their Hands.

[27.] He has excited domestic insurrections amongst us, and has endeavoured to bring on the inhabitants of our frontiers, the merciless Indian Savages, whose known rule of warfare, is an undistinguished destruction of all ages, sexes and conditions.

In every stage of these Oppressions We have Petitioned for Redress in the most humble terms: Our repeated Petitions have been answered only by repeated injury. A Prince whose character is thus marked by every act which may define a Tyrant, is unfit to be the ruler of a free people.

Nor have We been wanting in attentions to our British brethren. We have warned them from time to time of attempts by their legislature to extend an unwarrantable jurisdiction over us. We have reminded them of the circumstances of our emigration and settlement here. We have appealed to their native justice and magnanimity, and we have conjured them by the ties of our common kindred to disavow these usurpations, which, would inevitably interrupt our connections and correspondence. They too have been deaf to the voice of justice and of consanguinity. We must, therefore, acquiesce in the necessity, which denounces our Separation, and hold them, as we hold the rest of mankind, Enemies in War, in Peace Friends.

We, therefore, the Representatives of the united States of America, in General Congress, Assembled, appealing to the Supreme Judge of the world for the rectitude of our intentions, do, in the Name, and by Authority of the good People of these Colonies, solemnly publish and declare, That these United Colonies are, and of Right ought to be Free and Independent States; that they are Absolved from all Allegiance to the British Crown, and that all political connection between them and the State of Great Britain, is and ought to be totally dissolved; and that as Free and Independent States, they have full Power to levy War, conclude Peace, contract Alliances, establish Commerce, and to do all other Acts and Things which Independent States may of right do. And for the support of this Declaration, with a firm reliance on the protection of divine Providence, we mutually pledge to each other our Lives, our Fortunes and our sacred Honor.

THE ARTICLES OF CONFEDERATION

ARTICLES OF CONFEDERATION AND PERPETUAL UNION between the States of New Hampshire, Massachusetts-bay, Rhode-island and Providence Plantations, Connecticut, New York, New Jersey, Pennsylvania, Delaware, Maryland, Virginia, North-Carolina, South-Carolina, And Georgia.

In Congress November 15, 1777

[*Editor's note*: A few underlines have been added by the editors for emphasis and to show several of the listed rights that were retained in the new Constitution. Also, the **bold numbers in brackets** are added for clarity and as a reference tool and are not part of the original text.]

ARTICLE I

The Stile of this confederacy shall be, "The United States of America."

ARTICLE II

Each state retains its sovereignty, freedom and independence, and every Power, Jurisdiction and right, which is not by this confederation expressly delegated to the United States, in Congress assembled.

ARTICLE III

The said states hereby severally enter into a firm league of friendship with each other, for their common defence, the security of their Liberties, and their mutual and general welfare, binding themselves to assist each other, against all force offered to, or attacks made upon them, or any of them, on account of religion, sovereignty, trade, or any other pretence whatever.

ARTICLE IV

[1.] The better to secure and perpetuate mutual friendship and intercourse among the people of the different states in this union, the free inhabitants of each of these states, paupers, vagabonds and fugitives from Justice excepted, shall be entitled to all privileges and immunities of free citizens in the several states; and the people of each state shall have free ingress and regress to and from any other state, and shall enjoy therein all the privileges of trade and commerce, subject to the same duties, impositions and restrictions as the inhabitants thereof respectively, provided that such restrictions shall not extend so far as to prevent the removal of property imported into any state, to any other State of which the Owner is an inhabitant; provided also that no imposition, duties or restriction shall be laid by any state, on the property of the united states, or either of them.

[2.] If any Person guilty of, or charged with, treason, felony, or other high misdemeanor in any state, shall flee from Justice, and be found in any of the united states, he shall upon demand of the Governor or executive power of the state from which he fled, be delivered up, and removed to the state having jurisdiction of his offence.

[3.] Full faith and credit shall be given in each of these states to the records, acts and judicial proceedings of the courts and magistrates of every other state.

ARTICLE V

[1.] For the more convenient management of the general interests of the united states, delegates shall be annually appointed in such manner as the legislature of each state shall direct, to meet in Congress on the first Monday in November, in every year, with a power reserved to each state to recall its delegates, or any of them, at any time within the year, and to send others in their stead, for the remainder of the Year.

[2.] No State shall be represented in Congress by less than two, nor by more than seven Members; and no person shall be capable of being delegate for more than three years, in any term of six years; nor shall any person, being a delegate, be capable of holding any office under the united states, for which he, or another for his benefit receives any salary, fees or emolument of any kind.

[3.] <u>Each State</u> shall maintain its own <u>delegates</u> in a meeting of the states, and while they act as members of the committee of the states.

[4.] In determining questions in the united states, in Congress assembled, each <u>state</u> shall have <u>one vote</u>.

[5.] <u>Freedom of speech</u> and debate in Congress shall not be impeached or questioned in any Court, or place out of Congress, and the <u>members of congress shall be protected in their persons from arrests</u> and imprisonments, during the time of their going to and from, and attendance on congress, except for treason, felony, or breach of the peace.

ARTICLE VI

[1.] <u>No State</u>, without the Consent of the united States, in congress assembled, <u>shall send any embassy to, or receive any embassy from</u>, or enter into any conferrence, agreement, alliance, or treaty, with any <u>King prince or state</u>; nor shall any person holding any office of profit or trust under the united states, or any of them, accept of any present, emolument, office, or title of any kind whatever, from any king, prince, or foreign state; nor shall the united states, in congress assembled, or any of them, grant any title of nobility.

[2.] <u>No two or more states</u> shall enter into any <u>treaty</u>, confederation, or alliance whatever between them, without the consent of the united states, in congress assembled, specifying accurately the purposes for which the same is to be entered into, and how long it shall continue.

[3.] <u>No State</u> shall lay any <u>imposts or duties</u>, which may interfere with any stipulations in treaties, entered into by the united States in congress assembled, with any king, prince, or State, in pursuance of any treaties already proposed by congress, to the courts of France and Spain.

[4.] <u>No vessels of war</u> shall be kept up in <u>time of peace</u>, by any state, except such number only, as shall be deemed necessary by the united states, in congress assembled, for the defence of such state, or its trade; <u>nor shall any body of forces</u> be kept up, by any state, in time of peace, except such number only as, in the judgment of the united states, in congress assembled, shall be deemed requisite to garrison the forts necessary for the defence of such state; but <u>every state shall</u> always keep up a well regulated and disciplined <u>militia</u>, sufficiently armed and accounted, and shall provide and constantly have ready for use, in public stores, a due number of field pieces and tents, and a proper quantity of arms, ammunition, and camp equipage.

[5.] <u>No State</u> shall engage in any <u>war</u> without the consent of the united States in congress assembled, un-

less such State be actually invaded by enemies, or shall have received certain advice of a resolution being formed by some nation of Indians to invade such State, and the danger is so imminent as not to admit of a delay till the united states in congress assembled, can be consulted: nor shall any state grant commissions to any ships or vessels of war, nor letters of marque or reprisal, except it be after a declaration of war by the united states in congress assembled, and then only against the kingdom or State, and the subjects thereof, against which war has been so declared, and under such regulations as shall be established by the united states in congress assembled, unless such state be infested by pirates, in which case vessels of war may be fitted out for that occasion, and kept so long as the danger shall continue, or until the united states in congress assembled shall determine otherwise.

ARTICLE VII

When <u>land forces</u> are raised by any state, for the common defence, <u>all officers</u> of or under the rank of colonel, shall be <u>appointed by the legislature</u> of each state respectively by whom such forces shall be raised, or in such manner as such state shall direct, and all vacancies shall be filled up by the state which first made appointment.

ARTICLE VIII

<u>All charges of war</u>, and all other expenses that shall be incurred for the common defence or general welfare, and allowed by the united states in congress assembled, shall be <u>defrayed out of a common treasury</u>, which shall be supplied by the several states, in <u>proportion</u> to the <u>value of all land</u> within each state, granted to or surveyed for any Person, as such land and the buildings and improvements thereon shall be estimated, according to such mode as the united states, in congress assembled, shall, from time to time, direct and appoint. The <u>taxes for paying</u> that proportion shall be laid and levied by the <u>authority</u> and direction of the <u>legislatures</u> of the several states within the time agreed upon by the united states in congress assembled.

ARTICLE IX

[1.] The <u>united states, in congress assembled</u>, shall have the <u>sole and exclusive right</u> and power of determining on <u>peace and war</u>, except in the cases mentioned in the sixth article—of sending and receiving ambassadors—entering into treaties and alliances, provided that no treaty of commerce shall be made, whereby the legislative power of the <u>respective states shall be restrained</u>

from imposing such imposts and duties on foreigners, as their own people are subjected to, or from prohibiting the exportation or importation of any species of goods or commodities whatsoever—of establishing rules for deciding, in all cases, what captures on land or water shall be legal, and in what manner prizes taken by land or naval forces in the service of the united Sates, shall be divided or appropriated—of granting letters of marque and reprisal in times of peace—appointing courts for the trial of piracies and felonies committed on the high seas; and establishing courts; for receiving and determining finally appeals in all cases of captures; provided that no member of congress shall be appointed a judge of any of the said courts.

[2.] The united states, in congress assembled, shall also be the last resort on appeal, in all disputes and differences now subsisting, or that hereafter may arise between two or more states concerning boundary, jurisdiction, or any other cause whatever; which authority shall always be exercised in the manner following. Whenever the legislative or executive authority, or lawful agent of any state in controversy with another, shall present a petition to congress, stating the matter in question, and praying for a hearing, notice thereof shall be given, by order of congress, to the legislative or executive authority of the other state in controversy, and a day assigned for the appearance of the parties by their lawful agents, who shall then be directed to appoint, by joint consent, commissioners or judges to constitute a court for hearing and determining the matter in question: but if they cannot agree, congress shall name three persons out of each of the united states, and from the list of such persons each party shall alternately strike out one, the petitioners beginning, until the number shall be reduced to thirteen; and from that number not less than seven, nor more than nine names, as congress shall direct, shall, in the presence of congress, be drawn out by lot, and the persons whose names shall be so drawn, or any five of them, shall be commissioners or judges, to hear and finally determine the controversy, so always as a major part of the judges, who shall hear the cause, shall agree in the determination: and if either party shall neglect to attend at the day appointed, without showing reasons which congress shall judge sufficient, or being present, shall refuse to strike, the congress shall proceed to nominate three persons out of each State, and the secretary of congress shall strike in behalf of such party absent or refusing; and the judgment and sentence of the court, to be appointed in the manner before prescribed, shall be final and conclusive; and if any of the parties shall refuse to submit to the authority of such court, or

to appear or defend their claim or cause, the court shall nevertheless proceed to pronounce sentence, or judgment, which shall in like manner be final and decisive; the judgment or sentence and other proceedings being in either case transmitted to congress, and lodged among the acts of congress, for the security of the parties concerned: provided that every commissioner, before he sits in judgment, shall take an oath to be administered by one of the judges of the supreme or superior court of the State where the cause shall be tried, "well and truly to hear and determine the matter in question, according to the best of his judgment, without favour, affection, or hope of reward: "provided, also, that no State shall be deprived of territory for the benefit of the united states.

[3.] All controversies concerning the private right of soil claimed under different grants of two or more states, whose jurisdictions as they may respect such lands, and the states which passed such grants are adjusted, the said grants or either of them being at the same time claimed to have originated antecedent to such settlement of jurisdiction, shall, on the petition of either party to the congress of the united states, be finally determined, as near as may be, in the same manner as is before prescribed for deciding disputes respecting territorial jurisdiction between different states.

[4.] The united states, in congress assembled, shall also have the sole and exclusive right and power of regulating the alloy and value of coin struck by their own authority, or by that of the respective states—fixing the standard of weights and measures throughout the united states—regulating the trade and managing all affairs with the Indians, not members of any of the states; provided that the legislative right of any state, within its own limits, be not infringed or violated—establishing and regulating post-offices from one state to another, throughout all the united states, and exacting such postage on the papers passing through the same, as may be requisite to defray the expenses of the said office—appointing all officers of the land forces in the service of the united States, excepting regimental officers—appointing all the officers of the naval forces, and commissioning all officers whatever in the service of the united states; making rules for the government and regulation of the said land and naval forces, and directing their operations.

[5.] The united States, in congress assembled, shall have authority to appoint a committee, to sit in the recess of congress, to be denominated, "A Committee of the States," and to consist of one delegate from each State; and to appoint such other committees and civil officers as may be necessary for managing the general affairs of the united states under their direction—to appoint one of their number to preside; provided that no person be allowed to serve in the office of president more than one year in any term of three years; to <u>ascertain</u> the necessary <u>sums of money</u> to be raised for the service of the united states, and to appropriate and apply the same for <u>defraying the public expenses</u>; to borrow money or emit bills on the credit of the united states, transmitting every half year to the respective states an account of the sums of money so borrowed or emitted,—to build and equip a navy—to agree upon the number of land forces, and to <u>make requisitions from each state for its quota, in proportion to the number of white inhabitants</u> in such state, which requisition shall be binding; and thereupon the legislature of <u>each state shall appoint the regimental officers</u>, raise the men, and clothe, arm, and equip them, in a soldier-like manner, at the expense of the united states; and the officers and men so clothed, armed, and equipped, shall march to the place appointed, and within the time agreed on by the united states, in congress assembled; but if the united states, in congress assembled, shall, on consideration of circumstances, judge proper that any state should not raise men, or should raise a smaller number than its quota, and that any other state should raise a greater number of men than the quota thereof, such extra number shall be raised, officered, clothed, armed, and equipped in the same manner as the quota of such state, unless the legislature of such state shall judge that such extra number cannot be safely spared out of the same, in which case they shall raise, officer, clothe, arm, and equip, as many of such extra number as they judge can be safely spared. And the officers and men so clothed, armed, and equipped, shall march to the place appointed, and within the time agreed on by the united states in congress assembled.

[6.] <u>The united states, in congress assembled, shall never</u> engage in a <u>war</u>, nor grant letters of marque and reprisal in time of peace, nor enter into any <u>treaties</u> or alliances, nor coin <u>money</u>, nor regulate the value thereof nor ascertain the sums and expenses necessary for the <u>defence</u> and welfare of the united states, or any of them, nor emit bills, nor borrow money on the credit of the united states, nor appropriate money, nor agree upon the number of vessels of war to be built or purchased, or the number of land or sea forces to be raised, nor appoint a commander in chief of the army or navy, <u>unless nine states assent to the same</u>, nor shall a question on any other point, except for adjourning from day to day, be determined, unless by the votes of a majority of the united states in congress assembled.

[7.] The congress of the united states shall have <u>power to adjourn</u> to any time within the year, and to any place within the united states, so that no period of adjournment be for a longer duration than the space of six Months, and shall publish the Journal of their proceedings monthly, except such parts thereof relating to treaties, alliances, or military operations, as in their judgment require secrecy; and the <u>yeas and nays of the delegates</u> of each State, on any question, shall be entered on the <u>Journal</u>, when it is desired by any delegate; and the delegates of a State, or any of them, at his or their request, shall be furnished with a transcript of the said Journal, except such parts as are above excepted, to lay before the legislatures of the several states.

ARTICLE X.

The committee of the states, or any <u>nine of them</u>, shall be authorized to <u>execute, in the recess of congress</u>, such of the <u>powers of congress</u> as the united states, in congress assembled, by the consent of nine states, shall, from time to time, think expedient to vest them with; provided that no power be delegated to the said committee, for the exercise of which, by the articles of confederation, the voice of nine states, in the congress of the united states assembled, is requisite.

ARTICLE XI

<u>Canada</u> acceding to this confederation, and joining in the measures of the united states, <u>shall be admitted</u> into, and <u>entitled to all the advantages</u> of this union: but <u>no other colony</u> shall be admitted into the same, unless such admission be agreed to by <u>nine states</u>.

ARTICLE XII

<u>All bills of credit</u> emitted, monies borrowed, and debts contracted by or under the authority of congress, before the assembling of the united states, in pursuance of the present confederation, <u>shall be deemed and considered as a charge against the united States</u>, for payment and satisfaction whereof the said united states and the public faith are hereby solemnly pledged.

ARTICLE XIII

[1.] <u>Every State shall abide</u> by the determinations of the united states, in congress assembled, on all questions which by this confederation are submitted to them. And the Articles of this confederation shall be inviolably observed by every state, and the union shall be perpetual; <u>nor shall any alteration at any time hereafter be made in any of them, unless such alteration be agreed to in a congress of the united states, and be afterwards confirmed by the legislatures of every state</u>.

[2.] And Whereas it hath pleased the Great Governor of the World to incline the hearts of the legislatures we respectively represent in congress, to approve of, and to authorize us to ratify the said articles of confederation and perpetual union, Know Ye, that we, the undersigned delegates, by virtue of the power and authority to us given for that purpose, do, by these presents, in the name and in behalf of our respective constituents, fully and entirely ratify and confirm each and every of the said articles of confederation and perpetual union, and all and singular the matters and things therein contained. And we do further solemnly plight and engage the faith of our respective constituents, that they shall abide by the determinations of the united states in congress assembled, on all questions, which by the said confederation are submitted to them. And that the articles thereof shall be inviolably observed by the states we respectively represent, and that the union shall be perpetual. In Witness whereof, we have hereunto set our hands, in Congress. Done at Philadelphia, in the State of Pennsylvania, the ninth Day of July, in the Year of our Lord one Thousand seven Hundred and Seventy eight, and in the third year of the Independence of America.

THE CONSTITUTION OF
THE UNITED STATES OF AMERICA

AS AGREED UPON BY THE CONVENTION
SEPTEMBER 17, 1787

We the People of the United States, in Order to form a more perfect Union, establish Justice, ensure domestic Tranquility, provide for the common defense, promote the general Welfare, and secure the Blessings of Liberty to ourselves and our Posterity, do ordain and establish this Constitution for the United States of America.

ARTICLE I.

SECTION 1. All legislative Powers herein granted shall be vested in a Congress of the United States, which shall consist of a Senate and House of Representatives.

SECTION 2. The House of Representatives shall be composed of Members chosen every second Year by the People of the several States, and the Electors in each State shall have the Qualifications requisite for Electors of the most numerous Branch of the State Legislature.

No Person shall be a Representative who shall not have attained to the Age of twenty five Years, and been seven Years a Citizen of the United States, and who shall not, when elected, be an Inhabitant of that State in which he shall be chosen.

[Representatives and direct Taxes shall be apportioned among the several States which may be included within this Union, according to their respective Numbers, which shall be determined by adding to the whole Number of free Persons, including those bound to Service for a Term of Years, and excluding Indians not taxed, three fifths of all other Persons.][282] The actual Enumeration shall be made within three Years after the first Meeting of the Congress of the United States, and within every subsequent Term of ten Years, in such Manner as they shall by Law direct. The Number of Representatives shall not exceed one for every thirty Thousand, but each State shall have at Least one Representative; and until such enumeration shall be made, the State of New Hampshire shall be entitled to choose three, Massachusetts eight, Rhode Island and Providence Plantations one, Connecticut five, New York six, New Jersey four, Pennsylvania eight, Delaware one, Maryland six, Virginia ten, North Carolina five, South Carolina five and Georgia three.

When vacancies happen in the Representation from any State, the Executive Authority thereof shall issue Writs of Election to fill such Vacancies.

The House of Representatives shall choose their Speaker and other Officers; and shall have the sole Power of Impeachment.

SECTION 3. The Senate of the United States shall be composed of two Senators from each State, [chosen by the Legislature thereof,][283] for six Years; and each Senator shall have one Vote.

Immediately after they shall be assembled in Consequence of the first Election, they shall be divided as equally as may be into three Classes. The Seats of the Senators of the first Class shall be vacated at the Expiration of the second Year, of the second Class at the Expiration of the fourth Year, and of the third Class at the Expiration of the sixth Year, so that one third may be chosen every second Year; [and if Vacancies happen by Resignation, or otherwise, during the Recess of the Legislature of any State, the Executive thereof may make temporary Appointments until the next Meeting of the Legislature, which shall then fill such Vacancies.][284]

No person shall be a Senator who shall not have at-

---

282 Changed by Section 2 of the Fourteenth Amendment.
283 Changed by the Seventeenth Amendment.
284 Changed by the Seventeenth Amendment.

tained to the Age of thirty Years, and been nine Years a Citizen of the United States, and who shall not, when elected, be an Inhabitant of that State for which he shall be chosen.

The Vice President of the United States shall be President of the Senate, but shall have no Vote, unless they be equally divided.

The Senate shall choose their other Officers, and also a President pro tempore, in the absence of the Vice President, or when he shall exercise the Office of President of the United States.

The Senate shall have the sole Power to try all Impeachments. When sitting for that Purpose, they shall be on Oath or Affirmation. When the President of the United States is tried, the Chief Justice shall preside: And no Person shall be convicted without the Concurrence of two thirds of the Members present.

Judgment in Cases of Impeachment shall not extend further than to removal from Office, and disqualification to hold and enjoy any Office of honor, Trust or Profit under the United States: but the Party convicted shall nevertheless be liable and subject to Indictment, Trial, Judgment and Punishment, according to Law.

SECTION 4. The Times, Places and Manner of holding Elections for Senators and Representatives, shall be prescribed in each State by the Legislature thereof; but the Congress may at any time by Law make or alter such Regulations, except as to the Place of Choosing Senators.

The Congress shall assemble at least once in every Year, and such Meeting shall be [on the first Monday in December,][285] unless they shall by Law appoint a different Day.

SECTION 5. Each House shall be the Judge of the Elections, Returns and Qualifications of its own Members, and a Majority of each shall constitute a Quorum to do Business; but a smaller number may adjourn from day to day, and may be authorized to compel the Attendance of absent Members, in such Manner, and under such Penalties as each House may provide.

Each House may determine the Rules of its Proceedings, punish its Members for disorderly Behavior, and, with the Concurrence of two-thirds, expel a Member.

Each House shall keep a Journal of its Proceedings, and from time to time publish the same, excepting such Parts as may in their Judgment require Secrecy; and the Yeas and Nays of the Members of either House on any question shall, at the Desire of one fifth of those Present, be entered on the Journal.

Neither House, during the Session of Congress, shall, without the Consent of the other, adjourn for more than three days, nor to any other Place than that in which the two Houses shall be sitting.

SECTION 6. The Senators and Representatives shall receive a Compensation for their Services, to be ascertained by Law, and paid out of the Treasury of the United States. They shall in all Cases, except Treason, Felony and Breach of the Peace, be privileged from Arrest during their Attendance at the Session of their respective Houses, and in going to and returning from the same; and for any Speech or Debate in either House, they shall not be questioned in any other Place.

No Senator or Representative shall, during the Time for which he was elected, be appointed to any civil Office under the Authority of the United States which shall have been created, or the Emoluments whereof shall have been increased during such time; and no Person holding any Office under the United States, shall be a Member of either House during his Continuance in Office.

SECTION 7. All bills for raising Revenue shall originate in the House of Representatives; but the Senate may propose or concur with Amendments as on other Bills.

Every Bill which shall have passed the House of Representatives and the Senate, shall, before it become a Law, be presented to the President of the United States; If he approve he shall sign it, but if not he shall return it, with his Objections to that House in which it shall have originated, who shall enter the Objections at large on their Journal, and proceed to reconsider it. If after such Reconsideration two thirds of that House shall agree to pass the Bill, it shall be sent, together with the Objections, to the other House, by which it shall likewise be reconsidered, and if approved by two thirds of that House, it shall become a Law. But in all such Cases the Votes of both Houses shall be determined by Yeas and Nays, and the Names of the Persons voting for and against the Bill shall be entered on the Journal of each House respectively. If any Bill shall not be returned by the President within ten Days (Sundays excepted) after it shall have been presented to him, the Same shall be a Law, in like Manner as if he had signed it, unless the Congress by their Adjournment prevent its Return, in which Case it shall not be a Law.

Every Order, Resolution, or Vote to which the Concurrence of the Senate and House of Representatives may be necessary (except on a question of Adjournment) shall be presented to the President of the United States; and

---

285 Changed by Section 2 of the Twentieth Amendment.

before the Same shall take Effect, shall be approved by him, or being disapproved by him, shall be repassed by two thirds of the Senate and House of Representatives, according to the Rules and Limitations prescribed in the Case of a Bill.

SECTION 8. The Congress shall have Power **[1.]**[286] To lay and collect Taxes, Duties, Imposts and Excises, **[2.]** to pay the Debts and provide for the common Defence and general Welfare of the United States; but all Duties, Imposts and Excises shall be uniform throughout the United States;

[3.] To borrow money on the credit of the United States;

[4.] To regulate Commerce with foreign Nations, and among the several States, and with the Indian Tribes;

[5.] To establish an uniform Rule of Naturalization, **[6.]** and uniform Laws on the subject of Bankruptcies throughout the United States;

[7.] To coin Money, regulate the Value thereof, and of foreign Coin, **[8.]** and fix the Standard of Weights and Measures;

[9.] To provide for the Punishment of counterfeiting the Securities and current Coin of the United States;

[10.] To establish Post Offices and Post Roads;

[11.] To promote the Progress of Science and useful Arts, by securing for limited Times to Authors and Inventors the exclusive Right to their respective Writings and Discoveries;

[12.] To constitute Tribunals inferior to the supreme Court;

[13.] To define and punish Piracies and Felonies committed on the high Seas, and Offenses against the Law of Nations;

[14.] To declare War, grant Letters of Marque and Reprisal, and make Rules concerning Captures on Land and Water;

[15.] To raise and support Armies, but no Appropriation of Money to that Use shall be for a longer Term than two Years;

To provide and maintain a Navy;

[16.] To make Rules for the Government and Regulation of the land and naval Forces;

[17.] To provide for calling forth the Militia to execute the Laws of the Union, suppress Insurrections and repel Invasions;

To provide for organizing, arming, and disciplining, the Militia, and for governing such Part of them as may be employed in the Service of the United States, reserving to the States respectively, the Appointment of the Officers, and the Authority of training the Militia according to the discipline prescribed by Congress;

[18.] To exercise exclusive Legislation in all Cases whatsoever, over such District (not exceeding ten Miles square) as may, by Cession of particular States, and the acceptance of Congress, become the Seat of the Government of the United States, and **[19.]** to exercise like Authority over all Places purchased by the Consent of the Legislature of the State in which the Same shall be, for the Erection of Forts, Magazines, Arsenals, dock-Yards, and other needful Buildings;

[20.] And To make all Laws which shall be necessary and proper for carrying into Execution the foregoing Powers, and all other Powers vested by this Constitution in the Government of the United States, or in any Department or Officer thereof.

SECTION 9. The Migration or Importation of such Persons as any of the States now existing shall think proper to admit, **[1.]**[287]shall not be prohibited by the Congress prior to the Year one thousand eight hundred and eight, but a tax or duty may be imposed on such Importation, not exceeding ten dollars for each Person.

[2.] The privilege of the Writ of Habeas Corpus shall not be suspended, unless when in Cases of Rebellion or Invasion the public Safety may require it.

[3.] No Bill of Attainder or ex post facto Law shall be passed.

[4.] No capitation, or other direct, Tax shall be laid, unless in Proportion to the Census or Enumeration here in before directed to be taken.[288]

[5.] No Tax or Duty shall be laid on Articles exported from any State.

[6.] No Preference shall be given by any Regulation of Commerce or Revenue to the Ports of one State over those of another: nor shall Vessels bound to, or from, one State, be obliged to enter, clear, or pay Duties in another.

[7.] No Money shall be drawn from the Treasury, but in Consequence of Appropriations made by Law; and a regular Statement and Account of the Receipts and Expenditures of all public Money shall be published from time to time.

[8.] No Title of Nobility shall be granted by the

---

286 *Editors' Note:* The 20 Congressional powers are listed in Article I, Section 8, clauses 1–18. **The bracketed numbers** are added as a reference tool and are not part of the original Constitution.

287 *Editors' Note:* Limits on Congress are listed in Article I, Section 9, Clauses 1–8. **The bracketed numbers** are added for clarity and as a reference tool, and are not part of the original Constitution. The last clause contains two separate restrictions—the restriction on titles of nobility **[8.]** that prevents setting one citizen above another, is a *domestic* concern (for example, George Washington rejected being called "His Excellency"). And the restriction on accepting gifts or titles from overseas hosts **[9.]** prohibits American representatives from receiving things that can and do easily corrupt, making this a *foreign* concern.

288 Changed by the Sixteenth Amendment.

United States: [9.] And no Person holding any Office of Profit or Trust under them, shall, without the Consent of the Congress, accept of any present, Emolument, Office, or Title, of any kind whatever, from any King, Prince or foreign State.

SECTION 10. No State shall [1.]²⁸⁹ enter into any Treaty, Alliance, or Confederation; [2.] grant Letters of Marque and Reprisal; [3.] coin Money; [4.] emit Bills of Credit; [5.] make any Thing but gold and silver Coin a Tender in Payment of Debts; [6.] pass any Bill of Attainder, ex post facto Law, or Law impairing the Obligation of Contracts, [7.] or grant any Title of Nobility.

No State shall, without the Consent of the Congress, [8.] lay any Imposts or Duties on Imports or Exports, except what may be absolutely necessary for executing its inspection Laws: and the net Produce of all Duties and Imposts, laid by any State on Imports or Exports, shall be for the Use of the Treasury of the United States; and all such Laws shall be subject to the Revision and Control of the Congress.

No State shall, without the Consent of Congress, [9.] lay any duty of Tonnage, [10.] keep Troops, or Ships of War in time of Peace, [11.] enter into any Agreement or Compact with another State, or with a foreign Power, [12.] or engage in War, unless actually invaded, or in such imminent Danger as will not admit of delay.

ARTICLE II.

SECTION 1. The executive Power shall be vested in a President of the United States of America. He shall hold his Office during the Term of four Years, and, together with the Vice-President chosen for the same Term, be elected, as follows:

Each State shall appoint, in such Manner as the Legislature thereof may direct, a Number of Electors, equal to the whole Number of Senators and Representatives to which the State may be entitled in the Congress: but no Senator or Representative, or Person holding an Office of Trust or Profit under the United States, shall be appointed an Elector.

[The Electors shall meet in their respective States, and vote by Ballot for two persons, of whom one at least shall not lie an Inhabitant of the same State with themselves. And they shall make a List of all the Persons voted for, and of the Number of Votes for each; which List they shall sign and certify, and transmit sealed to the Seat of the Government of the United States, directed to

the President of the Senate. The President of the Senate shall, in the Presence of the Senate and House of Representatives, open all the Certificates, and the Votes shall then be counted. The Person having the greatest Number of Votes shall be the President, if such Number be a Majority of the whole Number of Electors appointed; and if there be more than one who have such Majority, and have an equal Number of Votes, then the House of Representatives shall immediately choose by Ballot one of them for President; and if no Person have a Majority, then from the five highest on the List the said House shall in like Manner choose the President. But in choosing the President, the Votes shall be taken by States, the Representation from each State having one Vote; a quorum for this Purpose shall consist of a Member or Members from two-thirds of the States, and a Majority of all the States shall be necessary to a Choice. In every Case, after the Choice of the President, the Person having the greatest Number of Votes of the Electors shall be the Vice President. But if there should remain two or more who have equal Votes, the Senate shall choose from them by Ballot the Vice-President.]²⁹⁰

The Congress may determine the Time of choosing the Electors, and the Day on which they shall give their Votes; which Day shall be the same throughout the United States.

No person except a natural born Citizen, or a Citizen of the United States, at the time of the Adoption of this Constitution, shall be eligible to the Office of President; neither shall any Person be eligible to that Office who shall not have attained to the Age of thirty-five Years, and been fourteen Years a Resident within the United States.

[In Case of the Removal of the President from Office, or of his Death, Resignation, or Inability to discharge the Powers and Duties of the said Office, the same shall devolve on the Vice President, and the Congress may by Law provide for the Case of Removal, Death, Resignation or Inability, both of the President and Vice President, declaring what Officer shall then act as President, and such Officer shall act accordingly, until the Disability be removed, or a President shall be elected.]²⁹¹

The President shall, at stated Times, receive for his Services, a Compensation, which shall neither be increased nor diminished during the Period for which he shall have been elected, and he shall not receive within that Period any other Emolument from the United States, or any of them.

---

289 *Editors' Note:* Limits on the States are listed in Article I, Section 10, Clauses 1–3. **The bracketed numbers** are added as a reference tool and are not part of the original Constitution.
290 Changed by the Twelfth Amendment.
291 Changed by the Twenty-Fifth Amendment.

Before he enter on the Execution of his Office, he shall take the following Oath or Affirmation:

"I do solemnly swear (or affirm) that I will faithfully execute the Office of President of the United States, and will to the best of my Ability, preserve, protect and defend the Constitution of the United States."

SECTION 2. The President shall be Commander in Chief of the Army and Navy of the United States, and of the Militia of the several States, when called into the actual Service of the United States; he may require the Opinion, in writing, of the principal Officer in each of the executive Departments, upon any subject relating to the Duties of their respective Offices, and he shall have Power to Grant Reprieves and Pardons for Offenses against the United States, except in Cases of Impeachment.

He shall have Power, by and with the Advice and Consent of the Senate, to make Treaties, provided two thirds of the Senators present concur; and he shall nominate, and by and with the Advice and Consent of the Senate, shall appoint Ambassadors, other public Ministers and Consuls, Judges of the supreme Court, and all other Officers of the United States, whose Appointments are not herein otherwise provided for, and which shall be established by Law: but the Congress may by Law vest the Appointment of such inferior Officers, as they think proper, in the President alone, in the Courts of Law, or in the Heads of Departments.

The President shall have Power to fill up all Vacancies that may happen during the Recess of the Senate, by granting Commissions which shall expire at the End of their next Session.

SECTION 3. He shall from time to time give to the Congress Information of the State of the Union, and recommend to their Consideration such Measures as he shall judge necessary and expedient; he may, on extraordinary Occasions, convene both Houses, or either of them, and in Case of Disagreement between them, with Respect to the Time of Adjournment, he may adjourn them to such Time as he shall think proper; he shall receive Ambassadors and other public Ministers; he shall take Care that the Laws be faithfully executed, and shall Commission all the Officers of the United States.

SECTION 4. The President, Vice President and all civil Officers of the United States, shall be removed from Office on Impeachment for, and Conviction of, Treason, Bribery, or other high Crimes and Misdemeanors.

ARTICLE III.

SECTION 1. The judicial Power of the United States, shall be vested in one supreme Court, and in such inferior Courts as the Congress may from time to time ordain and establish. The Judges, both of the supreme and inferior Courts, shall hold their Offices during good Behavior, and shall, at stated Times, receive for their Services a Compensation which shall not be diminished during their Continuance in Office.

SECTION 2. The judicial Power shall extend to all Cases, in Law and Equity, arising under this Constitution, the Laws of the United States, and Treaties made, or which shall be made, under their Authority; to all Cases affecting Ambassadors, other public Ministers and Consuls; to all Cases of admiralty and maritime Jurisdiction; to Controversies to which the United States shall be a Party; to Controversies between two or more States; [between a State and Citizens of another State;][292] between Citizens of different States; between Citizens of the same State claiming Lands under Grants of different States, [and between a State, or the Citizens thereof, and foreign States, Citizens or Subjects.][293]

In all Cases affecting Ambassadors, other public Ministers and Consuls, and those in which a State shall be Party, the supreme Court shall have original Jurisdiction. In all the other Cases before mentioned, the supreme Court shall have appellate Jurisdiction, both as to Law and Fact, with such Exceptions, and under such Regulations as the Congress shall make.

The Trial of all Crimes, except in Cases of Impeachment, shall be by Jury; and such Trial shall be held in the State where the said Crimes shall have been committed; but when not committed within any State, the Trial shall be at such Place or Places as the Congress may by Law have directed.

SECTION 3. Treason against the United States, shall consist only in levying War against them, or in adhering to their Enemies, giving them Aid and Comfort. No Person shall be convicted of Treason unless on the Testimony of two Witnesses to the same overt Act, or on Confession in open Court.

The Congress shall have power to declare the Punishment of Treason, but no Attainder of Treason shall work Corruption of Blood, or Forfeiture except during the Life of the Person attainted.

---

292 Changed by the Eleventh Amendment.
293 Changed by the Eleventh Amendment.

ARTICLE IV.

SECTION 1. Full Faith and Credit shall be given in each State to the public Acts, Records, and judicial Proceedings of every other State. And the Congress may by general Laws prescribe the Manner in which such Acts, Records and Proceedings shall be proved, and the Effect thereof.

SECTION 2. The Citizens of each State shall be entitled to all Privileges and Immunities of Citizens in the several States.

A Person charged in any State with Treason, Felony, or other Crime, who shall flee from Justice, and be found in another State, shall on demand of the executive Authority of the State from which he fled, be delivered up, to be removed to the State having Jurisdiction of the Crime.

[No Person held to Service or Labour in one State, under the Laws thereof, escaping into another, shall, in Consequence of any Law or Regulation therein, be discharged from such Service or Labour, But shall be delivered up on Claim of the Party to whom such Service or Labour may be due.][294]

SECTION 3. New States may be admitted by the Congress into this Union; but no new States shall be formed or erected within the Jurisdiction of any other State; nor any State be formed by the Junction of two or more States, or parts of States, without the Consent of the Legislatures of the States concerned as well as of the Congress.

The Congress shall have Power to dispose of and make all needful Rules and Regulations respecting the Territory or other Property belonging to the United States; and nothing in this Constitution shall be so construed as to Prejudice any Claims of the United States, or of any particular State.

SECTION 4. The United States shall guarantee to every State in this Union a Republican Form of Government, and shall protect each of them against Invasion; and on Application of the Legislature, or of the Executive (when the Legislature cannot be convened) against domestic Violence.

ARTICLE V.

The Congress, whenever two thirds of both Houses shall deem it necessary, shall propose Amendments to this Constitution, or, on the Application of the Legislatures of two thirds of the several States, shall call a Convention for proposing Amendments, which, in either Case, shall be valid to all Intents and Purposes, as part of this Constitution, when ratified by the Legislatures of three fourths of the several States, or by Conventions in three fourths thereof, as the one or the other Mode of Ratification may be proposed by the Congress; Provided that no Amendment which may be made prior to the Year One thousand eight hundred and eight shall in any Manner affect the first and fourth Clauses in the Ninth Section of the first Article; and that no State, without its Consent, shall be deprived of its equal Suffrage in the Senate.

ARTICLE VI.

All Debts contracted and Engagements entered into, before the Adoption of this Constitution, shall be as valid against the United States under this Constitution, as under the Confederation.

This Constitution, and the Laws of the United States which shall be made in Pursuance thereof; and all Treaties made, or which shall be made, under the Authority of the United States, shall be the supreme Law of the Land; and the Judges in every State shall be bound thereby, any Thing in the Constitution or Laws of any State to the Contrary notwithstanding.

The Senators and Representatives before mentioned, and the Members of the several State Legislatures, and all executive and judicial Officers, both of the United States and of the several States, shall be bound by Oath or Affirmation, to support this Constitution; but no religious Test shall ever be required as a Qualification to any Office or public Trust under the United States.

ARTICLE VII.

The Ratification of the Conventions of nine States, shall be sufficient for the Establishment of this Constitution between the States so ratifying the Same.

Done in Convention by the Unanimous Consent of the States present the Seventeenth Day of September in the Year of our Lord one thousand seven hundred and Eighty seven and of the Independence of the United States of America the Twelfth. In Witness whereof We have hereunto subscribed our Names.

G. Washington
President and deputy from Virginia

---

294 Changed by the Thirteenth Amendment.

AMENDMENTS

AMENDMENT I (1791)

Congress shall make no law respecting an establishment of religion, or prohibiting the free exercise thereof; or abridging the freedom of speech, or of the press; or the right of the people peaceably to assemble, and to petition the Government for a redress of grievances.

AMENDMENT II (1791)

A well regulated Militia, being necessary to the security of a free State, the right of the people to keep and bear Arms, shall not be infringed.

AMENDMENT III (1791)

No Soldier shall, in time of peace be quartered in any house, without the consent of the Owner, nor in time of war, but in a manner to be prescribed by law.

AMENDMENT IV (1791)

The right of the people to be secure in their persons, houses, papers, and effects, against unreasonable searches and seizures, shall not be violated, and no Warrants shall issue, but upon probable cause, supported by Oath or affirmation, and particularly describing the place to be searched, and the persons or things to be seized.

AMENDMENT V (1791)

No person shall be held to answer for a capital, or otherwise infamous crime, unless on a presentment or indictment of a Grand Jury, except in cases arising in the land or naval forces, or in the Militia, when in actual service in time of War or public danger; nor shall any person be subject for the same offence to be twice put in jeopardy of life or limb; nor shall be compelled in any criminal case to be a witness against himself, nor be deprived of life, liberty, or property, without due process of law; nor shall private property be taken for public use, without just compensation.

AMENDMENT VI (1791)

In all criminal prosecutions, the accused shall enjoy the right to a speedy and public trial, by an impartial jury of the State and district wherein the crime shall have been committed, which district shall have been previously ascertained by law, and to be informed of the nature and cause of the accusation; to be confronted with the witnesses against him; to have compulsory process for obtaining witnesses in his favor, and to have the As-sistance of Counsel for his defence.

AMENDMENT VII (1791)

In Suits at common law, where the value in controversy shall exceed twenty dollars, the right of trial by jury shall be preserved, and no fact tried by a jury, shall be otherwise re-examined in any Court of the United States, than according to the rules of the common law.

AMENDMENT VIII (1791)

Excessive bail shall not be required, nor excessive fines imposed, nor cruel and unusual punishments inflicted.

AMENDMENT IX (1791)

The enumeration in the Constitution, of certain rights, shall not be construed to deny or disparage others retained by the people.

AMENDMENT X (1791)

The powers not delegated to the United States by the Constitution, nor prohibited by it to the States, are reserved to the States respectively, or to the people.

AMENDMENT XI (1795/1798)

The Judicial power of the United States shall not be construed to extend to any suit in law or equity, commenced or prosecuted against one of the United States by Citizens of another State, or by Citizens or Subjects of any Foreign State.

AMENDMENT XII (1804)

The Electors shall meet in their respective states and vote by ballot for President and Vice-President, one of whom, at least, shall not be an inhabitant of the same state with themselves; they shall name in their ballots the person voted for as President, and in distinct ballots the person voted for as Vice-President, and they shall make distinct lists of all persons voted for as President, and of all persons voted for as Vice-President, and of the number of votes for each, which lists they shall sign and certify, and transmit sealed to the seat of the government of the United States, directed to the President of the Senate;—The President of the Senate shall, in the presence of the Senate and House of Representatives, open all the certificates and the votes shall then be counted;—The person having the greatest Number of votes for President, shall be the President, if such number be a majority of the whole number of Electors appointed; and if no person have such majority, then from the persons having the highest numbers not exceeding three on the list of those voted for as President, the House of Representatives shall choose immediately, by ballot, the President. But in choosing the President, the votes shall be taken by states, the representation from each state having one vote; a quorum for this purpose shall consist of a member or members from two-thirds of the states, and a majority of all the states shall be necessary to a choice. And if the House of Representatives shall not choose a President whenever the right of choice shall devolve upon them, before the fourth day of March next following, then the Vice-President shall act as President, as in the case of the death or other constitutional disability of the President—The person having the greatest number of votes as Vice-President, shall be the Vice-President, if such number be a majority of the whole number of Electors appointed, and if no person have a majority, then from the two highest numbers on the list, the Senate shall choose the Vice-President; a quorum for the purpose shall consist of two-thirds of the whole number of Senators, and a majority of the whole number shall be necessary to a choice. But no person constitutionally ineligible to the office of President shall be eligible to that of Vice-President of the United States.

Amendment XIII (1865)

Section 1. Neither slavery nor involuntary servitude, except as a punishment for crime whereof the party shall have been duly convicted, shall exist within the United States, or any place subject to their jurisdiction.

Section 2. Congress shall have power to enforce this article by appropriate legislation.

Amendment XIV (1868)

Section 1. All persons born or naturalized in the United States, and subject to the jurisdiction thereof, are citizens of the United States and of the State wherein they reside. No State shall make or enforce any law which shall abridge the privileges or immunities of citizens of the United States; nor shall any State deprive any person of life, liberty, or property, without due process of law; nor deny to any person within its jurisdiction the equal protection of the laws.

Section 2. Representatives shall be apportioned among the several States according to their respective numbers, counting the whole number of persons in each State, excluding Indians not taxed. But when the right to vote at any election for the choice of electors for President and Vice President of the United States, Representatives in Congress, the Executive and Judicial officers of a State, or the members of the Legislature thereof, is denied to any of the male inhabitants of such State, being twenty-one years of age, and citizens of the United States, or in any way abridged, except for participation in rebellion, or other crime, the basis of representation therein shall be reduced in the proportion which the number of such male citizens shall bear to the whole number of male citizens twenty-one years of age in such State.

Section 3. No person shall be a Senator or Representative in Congress, or elector of President and Vice President, or hold any office, civil or military, under the United States, or under any State, who, having previously taken an oath, as a member of Congress, or as an officer of the United States, or as a member of any State legislature, or as an executive or judicial officer of any State, to support the Constitution of the United States, shall have engaged in insurrection or rebellion against the same, or given aid or comfort to the enemies thereof. But Congress may by a vote of two-thirds of each House, remove such disability.

Section 4. The validity of the public debt of the United States, authorized by law, including debts incurred for payment of pensions and bounties for services in suppressing insurrection or rebellion, shall not be questioned. But neither the United States nor any State shall assume or pay any debt or obligation incurred in aid of insurrection or rebellion against the United States, or any claim for the loss or emancipation of any slave; but all such debts, obligations and claims shall be held illegal and void.

Section 5. The Congress shall have power to enforce, by appropriate legislation, the provisions of this article.

Amendment XV (1870)

Section 1. The right of citizens of the United States to vote shall not be denied or abridged by the United States or by any State on account of race, color, or previous condition of servitude.

Section 2. The Congress shall have power to enforce this article by appropriate legislation.

Amendment XVI (1913)

The Congress shall have power to lay and collect taxes on incomes, from whatever source derived, without apportionment among the several States, and without regard to any census or enumeration.

AMENDMENT XVII (1913)

The Senate of the United States shall be composed of two Senators from each State, elected by the people thereof, for six years; and each Senator shall have one vote. The electors in each State shall have the qualifications requisite for electors of the most numerous branch of the State legislatures.

When vacancies happen in the representation of any State in the Senate, the executive authority of such State shall issue writs of election to fill such vacancies: Provided, That the legislature of any State may empower the executive thereof to make temporary appointments until the people fill the vacancies by election as the legislature may direct.

This amendment shall not be so construed as to affect the election or term of any Senator chosen before it becomes valid as part of the Constitution.

AMENDMENT XVIII (1919)

SECTION 1. After one year from the ratification of this article the manufacture, sale, or transportation of intoxicating liquors within, the importation thereof into, or the exportation thereof from the United States and all territory subject to the jurisdiction thereof for beverage purposes is hereby prohibited.

SECTION 2. The Congress and the several States shall have concurrent power to enforce this article by appropriate legislation.

SECTION 3. This article shall be inoperative unless it shall have been ratified as an amendment to the Constitution by the legislatures of the several States, as provided in the Constitution, within seven years from the date of the submission hereof to the States by the Congress.

AMENDMENT XIX (1920)

The right of citizens of the United States to vote shall not be denied or abridged by the United States or by any State on account of sex.

Congress shall have power to enforce this article by appropriate legislation.

AMENDMENT XX (1933)

SECTION 1. The terms of the President and Vice President shall end at noon on the 20th day of January, and the terms of Senators and Representatives at noon on the 3d day of January, of the years in which such terms would have ended if this article had not been ratified; and the terms of their successors shall then begin.

SECTION 2. The Congress shall assemble at least once in every year, and such meeting shall begin at noon on the 3d day of January, unless they shall by law appoint a different day.

SECTION 3. If, at the time fixed for the beginning of the term of the President, the President elect shall have died, the Vice President elect shall become President. If a President shall not have been chosen before the time fixed for the beginning of his term, or if the President elect shall have failed to qualify, then the Vice President elect shall act as President until a President shall have qualified; and the Congress may by law provide for the case wherein neither a President elect nor a Vice President elect shall have qualified, declaring who shall then act as President, or the manner in which one who is to act shall be selected, and such person shall act accordingly until a President or Vice President shall have qualified.

SECTION 4. The Congress may by law provide for the case of the death of any of the persons from whom the House of Representatives may choose a President whenever the right of choice shall have devolved upon them, and for the case of the death of any of the persons from whom the Senate may choose a Vice President whenever the right of choice shall have devolved upon them.

SECTION 5. Sections 1 and 2 shall take effect on the 15th day of October following the ratification of this article.

SECTION 6. This article shall be inoperative unless it shall have been ratified as an amendment to the Constitution by the legislatures of three-fourths of the several States within seven years from the date of its submission.

AMENDMENT XXI (1933)

SECTION 1. The eighteenth article of amendment to the Constitution of the United States is hereby repealed.

SECTION 2. The transportation or importation into any State, Territory, or possession of the United States for delivery or use therein of intoxicating liquors, in violation of the laws thereof, is hereby prohibited.

SECTION 3. This article shall be inoperative unless it shall have been ratified as an amendment to the Constitution by conventions in the several States, as provided in the Constitution, within seven years from the date of the submission hereof to the States by the Congress.

AMENDMENT XXII (1951)

SECTION 1. No person shall be elected to the office of the President more than twice, and no person who has held the office of President, or acted as President, for more than two years of a term to which some other person was elected President shall be elected to the office of the President more than once. But this Article shall not apply to any person holding the office of President, when this Article was proposed by the Congress, and shall not prevent any person who may be holding the office of President, or acting as President, during the term within which this Article becomes operative from holding the office of President or acting as President during the remainder of such term.

SECTION 2. This article shall be inoperative unless it shall have been ratified as an amendment to the Constitution by the legislatures of three-fourths of the several States within seven years from the date of its submission to the States by the Congress.

AMENDMENT XXIII (1961)

SECTION 1. The District constituting the seat of Government of the United States shall appoint in such manner as the Congress may direct:

A number of electors of President and Vice President equal to the whole number of Senators and Representatives in Congress to which the District would be entitled if it were a State, but in no event more than the least populous State; they shall be in addition to those appointed by the States, but they shall be considered, for the purposes of the election of President and Vice President, to be electors appointed by a State; and they shall meet in the District and perform such duties as provided by the twelfth article of amendment.

SECTION 2. The Congress shall have power to enforce this article by appropriate legislation.

AMENDMENT XXIV (1964)

SECTION 1. The right of citizens of the United States to vote in any primary or other election for President or Vice President for electors for President or Vice President, or for Senator or Representative in Congress, shall not be denied or abridged by the United States or any State by reason of failure to pay any poll tax or other tax.

SECTION 2. The Congress shall have power to enforce this article by appropriate legislation.

AMENDMENT XXV (1967)

SECTION 1. In case of the removal of the President from office or of his death or resignation, the Vice President shall become President.

SECTION 2. Whenever there is a vacancy in the office of the Vice President, the President shall nominate a Vice President who shall take office upon confirmation by a majority vote of both Houses of Congress.

SECTION 3. Whenever the President transmits to the

President pro tempore of the Senate and the Speaker of the House of Representatives his written declaration that he is unable to discharge the powers and duties of his office, and until he transmits to them a written declaration to the contrary, such powers and duties shall be discharged by the Vice President as Acting President.

SECTION 4. Whenever the Vice President and a majority of either the principal officers of the executive departments or of such other body as Congress may by law provide, transmit to the President pro tempore of the Senate and the Speaker of the House of Representatives their written declaration that the President is unable to discharge the powers and duties of his office, the Vice President shall immediately assume the powers and duties of the office as Acting President.

Thereafter, when the President transmits to the President pro tempore of the Senate and the Speaker of the House of Representatives his written declaration that no inability exists, he shall resume the powers and duties of his office unless the Vice President and a majority of either the principal officers of the executive department or of such other body as Congress may by law provide, transmit within four days to the President pro tempore of the Senate and the Speaker of the House of Representatives their written declaration that the President is unable to discharge the powers and duties of his office. Thereupon Congress shall decide the issue, assembling within forty-eight hours for that purpose if not in session. If the Congress, within twenty-one days after receipt of the latter written declaration, or, if Congress is not in session, within twenty-one days after Congress is required to assemble, determines by two-thirds vote of both Houses that the President is unable to discharge the powers and duties of his office, the Vice President shall continue to discharge the same as Acting President; otherwise, the President shall resume the powers and duties of his office.

AMENDMENT XXVI (1971)

SECTION 1. The right of citizens of the United States, who are eighteen years of age or older, to vote shall not be denied or abridged by the United States or by any State on account of age.

SECTION 2. The Congress shall have power to enforce this article by appropriate legislation.

AMENDMENT XXVII (1992)

No law varying the compensation for the services of the Senators and Representatives shall take effect, until an election of Representatives shall have intervened.

THE THIRTY-FIVE OBJECTIONS BY THE ANTI-FEDERALISTS

An *Impartial* Address to the Citizens of the City and County of Albany: Or

The 35 Anti-Federal OBJECTIONS REFUTED.

By the Federal Committee of the City of Albany [New York], April 1788, selections[295]

We have lately seen, with no small degree of surprise, a publication intended to be dealt out in a private, underhanded way, by designing persons, a few days previous to the Election [of delegates to New York's ratifying convention]; with a view to prejudice the ignorant and uninformed citizen against the true interest of his country, and at so critical a time, that his prejudices might not be removed before he had given his final vote to condemn the new Government: but its having been accidentally exposed, has caused it to be circulated earlier than was intended.—We shall just observe, that it contains not only a variety of the most palpable improprieties but also a number of sentiments which, if admitted, must strike at the root of all government whatever, and leave us nearly in a state of nature.—We well know that the gentlemen who style themselves 'Anti-Federalists,' are in direct opposition to the Union of the States; but we cannot help expressing a great degree of pain on seeing them condescend to such low and designing arts on a subject so sacred as that of the establishing a Constitution for three millions of their countrymen.— The Federalists have, at their own expense, circulated many thousand copies of the New Constitution, in three languages,[296] with no other view than that every man may judge for himself.—The Anti-Federalists present publications, which express their private prejudices only, without pretending to offer a better system for the government of our country— Had their thirty-five objections been founded on truth and reason, ought they not to have circulated them publicly, and defied us to contradict them?—instead of which, they have attempted to impose them upon the public, at so late a period as, in some measure, to preclude the opportunity of obviating in time, the false prejudices they might occasion.—We shall take them up and state replies to each.

[1] OBJECTION. That the Convention who were appointed to revise the old Constitution, have made a new one.

ANSWER. Whether the proposed Constitution be entirely new or only amended, is of very little consequence at present, as the Convention do not undertake to establish it, but send it to us for examination: if we think it good we can accept of it, if we do not approve of it, we can reject it. But the old Confederation of the States, be it good or bad, was adopted and confirmed, without being submitted to the great body of the people for their approbation.

[2] OBJECTION. That it is not a federal, but a consolidated government; repugnant to the principles of a republican government, and destructive of the state governments.

ANSWER. It is consolidated only as to national purposes, and is founded on pure republican principles – deriving all powers from the people, the only criterion of a republican government. It expressly guarantees the same kind of government to each state in the Union; and if the state governments are destroyed, the Continental system must fall—as the several state legislatures have the sole power of appointing senators, and of directing the manner of appointing electors to choose the President.

[3] OBJECTION. Nine states ratifying the New Government, it is to be binding on the states so ratifying, which will dissolve the old Confederation.

ANSWER. States in an empire are so far like individuals in a state, that the majority must govern: the voice of three fourths of the states are here made necessary —A strong proof of the republican spirit of the New System—But the remaining

295 Complete text from a digital scan of the original 1788 pamphlet, courtesy of *Gale – Sabin Americana Print Editions 1500-1926*; see gale.com.
296 English, Dutch, German.

states may continue independent if they please; though policy must dictate all of them eventually to join the Union.

[4] OBJECTION. The great powers of the New Government over the lives and property of the citizens.

ANSWER. This objection is an address to the passions, and not an appeal to reason, and is aimed at no particular part of the proposed system; of course, it cannot receive a direct answer.—The powers in the New Government are well balanced with each other, and properly checked.

[5] OBJECTION. These powers not defined, and may be interpreted to arbitrary purposes.

ANSWER. This objection will stand equally good against the government of this state, and all other republican forms whatever, as it tends to destroy that degree of confidence in our rulers, without which no government, but an absolute monarchy, can exist.

[6] OBJECTION. Their laws to be the supreme laws of the land—Called a sweeping clause, that subjects everything to the control of the New Government.

ANSWER. The words "made in pursuance of the Constitution," which are fully expressed in the form of government submitted to us, are willfully omitted by the objectors, to deceive the people into a belief that the New System of Government will have power to make laws in all cases whatsoever; whereas they very well know that the New Government can make such laws only as will respect the United States: and should they not have this power, the small state of Rhode Island might, on every occasion, obstruct the most important national measures.

[7] OBJECTION. The small number of members who are to compose the National Legislature, and to pass laws to govern the Continent.

ANSWER. The new Congress will consist of upwards of ninety members. The present Congress who are, by the Articles of Confederation, vested with powers in many cases equally extensive, can legally transact the most important concerns of the nation with only eighteen members; which under the New Government must require at least forty-six—a great acquisition on the part of the people. Their laws will only respect Continental matters: the administration of justice between citizens of the same state, must and will remain the same as at present.

[8] OBJECTION. The members of the Senate are to be chosen by the Legislatures and not by the people. This will make them act like masters and not servants.

ANSWER. The members of the present Congress are chosen in the same way, and they never yet have been charged with acting as masters or betrayers of their country. The Chancellor, Judges of the Supreme Court, and other great officers of our state [New York], are chosen by the Council of Appointment, who are a remove from our Legislature, and generally make their appointments by only three persons; yet these wise observers will not pretend to say that our state officers have ever acted corruptly.—However, under the New System, the rights of the people will be perfectly well secured, as no law can be made by the Senate unless their Representatives agree to it.

[9] OBJECTION: That slaves are computed in apportioning Representatives.

ANSWER. Agreeable to the New System, taxation and representation must go together. These objectors should have been so candid as to add that all direct taxes must be laid, on each state, in proportion to the number of its inhabitants; that by this computation five slaves will pay taxes equal to three free men; which will be a great advantage to New York and the eastern states, who have very few slaves.

[10] OBJECTION: The power to regulate the times and places of holding elections.

ANSWER: Every Government must have the power of supporting its existence within itself, or it can have no stability; consequently, if the General Government cannot direct individuals of each state to elect their Representatives for Congress, on their state's neglecting or omitting to do it, it would be in the power of any little state to destroy the General System, and bring confusion into the Government, by neglecting to pass election laws. The Convention of Massachusetts have recommended an explanation of this clause, and we wish our Convention to do the same.

[11] OBJECTION: The power to lay poll taxes, duties, imposts and other taxes.

ANSWER: All Governments must have the right of taxation; which power, including that of laying a poll tax, is now vested in our state Government; but we have every security that reasonable beings can possibly ask, by the Constitution no tax or revenue law can be passed in Congress, but what must originate or have its beginning in the lower House, who are elected by the people at large. A poll tax has never been laid by this state nor by any of the southern states, and we have every reason to believe never will, as by the Constitution five slaves must pay as large a poll tax as three white men; and, consequently the southern states must ever be opposed to poll taxes. The principal and only sure dependence for the New Government, must be the impost or duty on trade, which will be paid by the merchant who imports foreign merchandise, and the wealthy citizen, and will be scarcely felt by the poor inhabitants of the country.

[12] OBJECTION: The power to appoint continental officers to collect those taxes.

ANSWER: Whatever revenues are granted to Congress for our national benefit must be collected by persons who are amenable to Congress for their conduct—should not this privilege be granted to the General Government, it would remain, in a very essential point, in the same situation it is at present. It is a sufficient security for the people at large that, should Congress make improper appointments or laws, on this or any other occasion, it must disgust the state so injured and of course tend to the dissolution and destruction of the United Government.

[13] OBJECTION: That the net produce of all duties on imports and exports laid by the several states, shall be for the benefit of the United States.

ANSWER. That Congress should have the benefit of the impost on all foreign goods imported into the United States, no one can object to, who wishes for a Union of the States, and has a sufficient share of common honesty to admit, that we ought to attempt to repay France and Holland the monies lent us in the court of the late war, and who would wish for the Government of our Country to have the means of protecting and defending us from all foreign foes and invaders;—for all must know, that the impost on trade, is the only solid dependence the United States can have for raising a revenue for our general benefit.

[14] OBJECTION That none of the states can coin money or emit bills of credit [print paper money].

ANSWER. The emitting of a paper currency by the different states, has occasioned many difficulties and much confusion between their citizens, as the funds on which it has been emitted, have been more or less adequate to its redemption:[297]—In many of the states, formerly as well as latterly, it has opened a door to fraud, villainy and discord—in Rhode Island it is at present a lawful tender, though going at twelve for one—in Pennsylvania and Jersey it is also going at a very large discount—in this state, although its credit has been tolerably well supported, so much has been counterfeited that many poor men have been thereby greatly injured and distressed. It is therefore, high time that the wicked and fraudulent system of paper money be checked, in order that those who have gold and silver laying by them, may be induced to bring it into circulation, without the fear of having a depreciated, counterfeit paper tendered in its stead.

[15] OBJECTION. The power of supporting a standing army in time of peace.

ANSWER. The words "time of peace" are not in the Constitution, but are made use of, on this occasion, as a scarecrow, to frighten people. The authority must be vested in every Government to raise troops to defend the country, and this power must be discretionary, to be used by the Government whenever it may be necessary; and, when it can only be used by our immediate Representatives, it can be attended with no possible danger—our present Congress, not only have this power, but have actually several hundred men in pay, on the back parts of Virginia and elsewhere. Our frontiers must be garrisoned in time of peace; and, should Congress not have power to hire men to do this duty, the militia must be dragged from their families for the purpose.

[16] OBJECTION. The power to call forth the militia to any part of the Continent, without limitation as to time or place.

ANSWER. What would have been the fate of our state in the late war, had not Congress called forth the militia of other states to defend us? and was it not through the assistance of Massachusetts, Connecticut, and New Hampshire, that [British General] Burgoyne with his army were captured? As our situation makes us a frontier to four or five states, we do not know how soon we may stand in need of assistance against savage and other enemies, though in all probability those states may never stand in need of assistance from us.

[17] OBJECTION. Men conscientiously scrupulous of bearing arms, made liable to perform military duty.

ANSWER. Those citizens who have conscientious objections against bearing arms, have ever been carefully attended to by the laws of their country, and there can be no doubt whatever, but the same generous attention will be paid to them by the laws of the New Government.

[18] OBJECTION. The power of the New Government to establish the salaries for their own services.

ANSWER. Is not this the case with our own and all the other state governments, and with every government in existence? and what superior power can possibly exist in a government that can regulate the salaries of persons who hold the governing powers?

[19] OBJECTION. The power of payment of the salaries of judges, which cannot be diminished.

ANSWER. To enable judges to be just, they must be independent. This principle has wisely induced the framers of the

---

297   The Articles of Confederation did not give Congress power to force the States to pay taxes or contribute revenue to the cause of the War for Independence. To keep the nation's economies running during that time both Congress and the States printed a great deal of paper money. After the war, this worthless paper led to massive debt and distrust of printed money, causing terrible inflation and an economic depression.

Constitution to put the judges in office during good behavior, and to put it out of the power of government to lower their salaries, lest it might deter them from doing their duty with firmness against men in power.

[20] OBJECTION. The power relating to the migration or importation of foreigners.

ANSWER. It is well known, that this clause principally reflects the importation of slaves into any of the United States. It is probable the eastern states in Convention wished to prohibit this infamous traffic immediately but that the southern states retained the privilege of importing slaves till the year 1808; but admitted of a tax or duty of ten dollars upon each, which is expressly mentioned to be on *such importation* and consequently alludes to slaves, as the word migration can only allude to freemen coming into our country.

[21] OBJECTION. The not securing the rights of conscience in religious matters.

ANSWER. How weak and idle is this observation? No powers that can interfere with the rights of conscience are to be given to the New Government; consequently they can make no laws that will interfere with those rights: and shall we not then be contented with the retaining the privilege of worshipping our Maker according to the free and uncontrolled dictates of our own consciences—or would we wish to have one sect of religion established over all others, this has been done by all the nations of Europe, and has caused more bloodshed than even the wicked ambition of princes.

[22, 23, 24] OBJECTIONS. The vast power vested in one man, not elected by the people, who has power equal to many European kings; and who, though elected for four years, may be again elected and continued for life.

ANSWER. The President is to be chosen by Electors appointed in such manner as the different Legislatures shall direct, and his power ceases of course at the end of four years, which is only one year longer than the time for which the Governor of this state is elected. It is true he may then be re-elected for the same time, and so may our Governor. His power does not extend to rejecting a single law that two thirds of the Legislature think proper to pass, which power answers directly to that of the Council of Revision in our own state. He cannot touch a shilling of money unless a law is passed for the purpose.—He can make no treaty, no permanent appointment to offices, nor, in fact, do anything whatever but by and with the consent of the Senate; except receiving Ambassadors and the common official powers that are vested in the Governor of our state by our Constitution—and in general, his powers are so far from being superior to a European king that, on many occasions, they are inferior to the Governor of our state.

[25] The trial by jury not provided for in civil cases.

ANSWER. The Continental Court, as far as private citizens of different states may be concerned, is a Court of Appeals, and may, perhaps, in some instances ,be compared with our Chancery Court, as well as to the Courts of Law in many of the other states, where no jury is called; and as nothing is said to prevent a jury on cases of appeal to the Continental Court, it must remain to be established by the future laws of our Representatives in Congress. The Massachusetts Convention have proposed an explanation of this section, and we have no doubt but our Convention will do the same: but all trials, between citizens of this state, must and will be conducted in future, just as at present, and determined by a jury as usual.

[26, 27, 28] OBJECTIONS. The great powers of the Continental Supreme Court, extending to all cases in law and equity—allowing the court original jurisdiction in some cases, and granting appeals to that court on both law and fact.

ANSWER. This court is confined to these cases only, which arise under the Constitution—all transactions between citizens that live in the same state must be determined, in future, just as they are at present, that is, by jury and the laws of their own state. The Continental Court is intended to try all cases that respect Ambassadors and other public Ministers, and where a whole state may be a party, it therefore must have the right of original jurisdiction in all such cases—and on cases of appeal from partial state Courts, by citizens who live in, or claim lands under grants of different states; it must have a right to determine on law, equity and fact, or it can never answer the necessary purposes: but that it will in the most distant manner enable the rich to oppress the poor, or that it has a power in all cases, arising in law and equity, is a false and groundless insinuation, only made to answer party purposes; for every other matter of dispute that can be brought into this court, must subsist between inhabitants of different states, who will, in all probability, be men of property, merchants or great landholders, and not poor men.

[29] OBJECTION. The power to constitute Inferior Courts in every state.

ANSWER. The clause here alluded to is, that Congress may constitute tribunals inferior to the Supreme Court. This will be attended with conveniency, but that it can be a grievance no one can suppose, as such tribunals must be inferior to the Supreme Court, whose powers are explained in the foregoing article, and who can have no control over citizens residing in the same state.

[30] OBJECTION. No provision is made to prevent placemen and pensioners.[298]

ANSWER. No Government can make universal provision in such cases, without doing injury to the common feelings of humanity. Would anyone wish to put it out of the power of our Representatives, to save the old soldier who is wounded and maimed, in fighting the battles of his country, from starving, or begging on his crutches from door to door? We think not— This is therefore, one of those powers which must be left to the caution and discretion of those men whom we shall in future appoint to make laws for us.

[31] OBJECTION. Nor for the liberty of the press.

ANSWER. The Continental laws can have no control over the internal regulations of the states; consequently, powers of this nature must remain where they are at present, that is, with the different state Legislatures. The Convention of Massachusetts has recommended a general explanation of all those state rights and privileges, and we have no doubt but our Convention will follow their example.

[32] OBJECTION. The power of appointing as many Continental officers as they shall think proper, in every state, and thereby extending their influence.

ANSWER. Every regular Government must have the privilege to appoint such inferior officers as may be necessary— their numbers must differ as circumstances occur and cannot be particularly defined.—it is a sufficient security, that we have the power of electing the persons who will make such appointments, and whenever they conduct improperly we will elect others in their stead and bring them to punishment for their malconduct.

[33] OBJECTION. The great expense of the New Government, and the additional taxes which will be thereby occasioned.

ANSWER. It is an undoubted fact, that the expense of supporting a Federal Government will not in any degree stand in competition with the great advantages which will be derived therefrom.—our trade and navigation will undoubtedly be greatly increased—foreign markets will be opened to our vessels, which must serve to raise the price of our produce—the Western Posts with the extensive Fur Trade will undoubtedly be given up to our Government, soon after it is established.

[34] OBJECTION. That the General Government guarantees to the several states the form, not the substance, of a republican government.

ANSWER. The words of the Constitution are that *the United States shall guarantee to each state in the Union a republican form of government, and shall protect each of them against invasion,* and what more can the Government do? Should they dictate in what particular form each state Constitution should be made? A republican form of government is that which derives all its powers from the people—but the particular manner in which the people are to use that power, must remain with themselves, or they would not be free. In short, this objection appears to have been introduced with no other intention but to swell up the number [of those against the Constitution].

[35] OBJECTION. It is not expressed that the several states retain the powers not given to the General Government, and that there is no bill of rights.

ANSWER. By the first section of the Constitution it is declared that all legislative powers therein granted, shall be vested in the Congress of the United States, consequently the powers not granted remain with the people of the different states.—Bills of rights are grants by absolute sovereigns to the great body of the people to secure, their privileges from encroachments or power; but in republican governments, where all power is derived from the people, the Constitution of the country, which gives certain privileges from the people to men whom they appoint as temporary law-makers, is to all intents and purposes, a bill of rights, granted or surrendered by the people, who are sovereigns in all republican countries. However, as Massachusetts' Convention have recommended an explanation on this subject, we expect our Convention will do the same.

They likewise add, "*is it for the sake of the poor and common people, that the rich and well-born are so indefatigable? Or is it because they and their friends expect lucrative offices under the New Government?*"

We answer, that when the general welfare of our country is at stake, when a peaceable, happy and united Government stands on one hand, and nothing but poverty, discord and confusion on the other.—as honest and sincere well-wishers to our common country, we step forth, with no other views than to counteract false prejudices, and to state the principles of the Constitution with truth and candor—that the great and important subject may be impartially investigated.—If there are men who think as we do, that have more property and more good sense than the general run of the opposers, we trust that no honest man will object to the system only on that account; for all must know that upon the principles of the New Government, the poor man's vote is as important as the rich man's, and when taxes are to be collected the rich man's estate must pay a large sum when the poor man will pay very little or nothing.

---

298 *placemen* and *pensioners:* An unelected friend of the king or of Parliament who was given a public office for private profit as a reward for political support was called a *placeman*. A *pensioner* is retired and is given a salary by the British government.

It is further said, in order to hold up a view the enormous expenses of the New Government, that Congress will run into the most ridiculous and unheard of expense, of building a federal town, ten miles square—erecting stately palaces, fitting out rooms with the most elegant furniture, decking their tables with the most costly plate, etc, as if our Representatives, the moment the New System is established, must begin to act like mad men and fools, and all at the expense of our poor country. Here the gentlemen have been wandering a very considerable distance "in the flowery fields of invention:" That part of the Constitution, from whence only all this absurdity can be conjectured, is in their words, "The Congress shall have the power to exercise exclusive jurisdiction, in all cases whatsoever, over such district (not exceeding a ten miles square) as may, be cession of a particular state, and the acceptance of Congress, become the seat of government of the United States." The whole amount of which is, that in whatever state the Congress shall sit, such district as the Legislature of that state shall assign to Congress, which may not exceed ten miles, and probably will not be one, shall be subject to the laws of Congress. Must not the resentment of every well-meaning man, rise against a set of men who, from this small yet necessary privilege to be granted to Congress, by the voluntary cession of any state, can wantonly and wickedly conjure up flaming ideas that are not only void of truth but even of probability.

Though we are inclined to believe the system, with very few exceptions, as good as can be obtained in a country like this, where there are a variety of people, states, and climates: we do not suppose it perfect, for we know perfection of wisdom is not with man; but, we are most assuredly convinced that should we now reject this system on account of those few imperfections of which as a single state, we should not allow ourselves to be the sole judges, particularly after its ratification by six states, we shall never get so far as we are at present on any other system whatever; and the consequence must be anarchy, confusion, and ruin to our country. Amendments, like the Constitution itself, must be previously arranged and agreed upon, by the united wisdom of the Continent, and not by any particular state; otherwise instead of a General Government capable of defending and protecting the Union, each state will eventually have a separate system, and the whole business after all, end where it began, without an other effect than banishing, perhaps for ever, the prospect of obtaining a General Government, unless usurped by violence—Massachusetts has led the way in recommending amendments, which will be considered as standing instructions to their Representatives until Congress in their wisdom, meet the wishes of their constituents.

A Convention could no doubt be easily obtained to agree upon amendments after the adoption of the system, whenever three fourths of the states should unite in calling one for the purpose; but we have no reason to believe that if the proposed plan should be rejected or adopted with amendments, which amounts to the same things, and is but another expression of a total rejection, that we, in such case, could obtain a new Convention. Georgia, Delaware, New Jersey and Connecticut, and have adopted it with an unanimity before unheard of, and the minority in Massachusetts, have expressed the most noble sentiments of giving it their support: These states, therefore, would reluctantly yield to a new Convention, in compliment to New York. And even granting the states would agree to another Convention, of whom would it be composed most surely of the partisans who, with warmth, have either opposed or defended the system now under consideration—would unanimity be expected form such a Council would not each member feel obligations to support the views of those by whom he was honored? Could that calm, dispassionate spirit of inquiry, which pervaded the former Convention, be expected to prevail in a new one formed under such circumstances? Beware, the, that under the specious and plausible idea of previous amendments, you are not led to an act which will, eventually defeat a system which you shudder at the thought of wholly rejecting. Experience will be the surest guide to what amendments are really necessary, and the Constitution has pointed out a mode of making them without hazarding our national existence. Be not deceived with the threadbare comparison of the New Government to a *private contract*, a contract, true it is, of the most solemn nature, but remember there are not less than THIRTEEN parties, SIX of whom have already sealed and delivered; how can we expect the other twelve will submit to receive alterations from one, and that one too which has already shewn no friendly disposition to her neighbors—THE GRAND AMERICAN UNION has already encircled us, except on the one side, where our haughty enemy still bleeds with the wounds of our conquest; and on the other a defenseless seacoast invites the avarice of an adventitious invader: our neighbors and friends extend their arms to embrace us—UNITE then, ye lovers of our common county; betray no unmanly jealousies of those who have fought your battles and guided your counsels with success, and by one rational act convince the world, that AMERICANS, as in war, they have been firm and intrepid, so in peace they will be UNITED and HAPPY.

By Order of the Federal Committee, ROBERT McCLALLEN, Chairman.

Members of the Committee.

Stephen Lush – Daniel Hale – Thomas Hun – John D.P. Ten Eyck – Cornelius Glen – Theodorus V.W. Graham – James Caldwell – Richard Sill – Philip Van Rensselaer – Leonard Gansevoort JR, – Jeremiah Lansingh – Stephen Van Rensselaer – James Bloodgood – Thomas L. Witbeek

HISTORICAL DOCUMENTS

Before the Constitutional Convention was called to order on May 25, 1787, it was first formally called into action by an act of Congress (#1 below).

When the delegates to the Constitutional Convention completed their work, they dispatched the proposed US Constitution to Congress in New York City on September 20, 1787. Their full report included Washington's letter of transmittal (#2 below) and a resolution given to Congress (#3 below). Also displayed is the resolution of the Continental Congress when it submitted the Constitution to the States for ratification (#4 below).

[1.] ACT OF CONGRESS

Calling for a Convention of Delegates
February 21, 1787

Whereas there is provision in the Articles of Confederation & perpetual Union for making alterations therein by the assent of a Congress of the United States and of the legislatures of the several States; And whereas experience hath evinced that there are defects in the present Confederation, as a mean to remedy which several of the States and particularly the State of New York by express instructions to their delegates in Congress have suggested a convention for the purposes expressed in the following resolution and such convention appearing to be the most probable mean of establishing in these states a firm national government.

Resolved that in the opinion of Congress it is expedient that on the second Monday in May next a Convention of delegates who shall have been appointed by the several states be held at Philadelphia for the sole and express purpose of revising the Articles of Confederation and reporting to Congress and the several legislatures such alterations and provisions therein as shall when agreed to in Congress and confirmed by the states render the federal constitution adequate to the exigencies of Government & the preservation of the Union.

[2.] WASHINGTON'S LETTER OF TRANSMITTAL
Philadelphia, September 17, 1787

To the President of Congress

"Sir. We have now the Honor to submit to the Consideration of the United States in Congress assembled that Constitution which has appeared to us the most advisable.

"The Friends of our Country have long seen and desired that the Power of making War Peace and Treaties, that of levying Money & regulating Commerce and the correspondent executive and judicial Authorities should be fully and effectually vested in the general Government of the Union. But the Impropriety of delegating such extensive Trust to one Body of Men is evident—Hence results the Necessity of a different Organization.

"It is obviously impracticable in the federal Government Of these States to secure all Rights of independent Sovereignty to each and yet provide for the Interest and Safety of all—Individuals entering into Society must give up a Share of Liberty to preserve the Rest. The Magnitude of the Sacrifice must depend as well on Situations and Circumstances as on the Object to be obtained. It is at all Times difficult to draw with Precision the Lines between those Rights which must be surrendered and those which may be reserved. And on the present Occasion this Difficulty was increased by a Difference among the several States as to their Situation Extent Habits and particular Interests.

"In all our Deliberations on this Subject we kept

steadily in our View that which appears to us the greatest Interest of every true American the Consolidation of our Union in which is involved our Prosperity Felicity Safety perhaps our national Existence. This important Consideration seriously and deeply impressed on our Minds led each State in the Convention to be less rigid on Points of inferior Magnitude than might have been otherwise expected. And thus the Constitution which we now present is the Result of a Spirit of Amity and of that mutual Deference & Concession which the Peculiarity of our political Situation rendered indispensable.

"That it will meet the full and entire Approbation of every State is not perhaps to be expected. But each will doubtless consider that had her Interests been alone consulted the Consequences might have been particularly disagreeable or injurious to others. That it is liable to as few Exceptions as could reasonably have been expected we hope and believe That it may promote the lasting Welfare of that Country so dear to us all and secure her Freedom and Happiness is our most ardent wish.

With great respect, We have the honor to be, Sir,

Your Excellency's most Obedient and humble Servants,

George Washington, *President.*
By Unanimous Order of the Convention."

[3.] RESOLUTION

"In Convention Monday September 17th 1787:

"Present The States of New Hampshire, Massachusetts, Connecticut, Mr Hamilton from New York, New Jersey, Pennsylvania, Delaware, Maryland, Virginia, North Carolina, South Carolina and Georgia.

"Resolved, That the preceding Constitution be laid before the United States in Congress assembled, and that it is the Opinion of this Convention, that it should afterwards be submitted to a Convention of Delegates, chosen in each State by the People thereof, under the Recommendation of its Legislature, for their Assent and Ratification; and that each Convention assenting to, and ratifying the Same, should give Notice thereof to the United States in Congress assembled.

"Resolved, That it is the Opinion of this Convention, that as soon as the Conventions of nine States shall have ratified this Constitution, the United States in Congress assembled should fix a Day on which Electors should be appointed by the States which shall have ratified the same, and a Day on which the Electors should assemble to vote for the President, and the Time and Place for commencing Proceedings under this Constitution. That

after such Publication the Electors should be appointed, and the Senators and Representatives elected: That the Electors should meet on the Day fixed for the Election of the President, and should transmit their Votes certified, signed, sealed and directed, as the Constitution requires, to the Secretary of the United States in Congress assembled, that the Senators and Representatives should convene at the Time and Place assigned; that the Senators should appoint a President of the Senate, for the sole Purpose of receiving, opening and counting the Votes for President; and, that after he shall be chosen, the Congress, together with the President, should, without Delay, proceed to execute this Constitution.

By the unanimous Order of the Convention

Go: Washington President

W. Jackson Secretary."

[4.] RESOLUTION OF THE CONTINENTAL CONGRESS
Submitting the Constitution to the Several States

Friday Sept 28. 1787

Congress assembled present New Hampshire Massachusetts Connecticut New York New Jersey Pennsylvania, Delaware Virginia North Carolina South Carolina and Georgia and from Maryland Mr Ross

Congress having received the report of the Convention lately assembled in Philadelphia

Resolved Unanimously that the said Report with the resolutions and letter accompanying the same be transmitted to the several legislatures in Order to be submitted to a convention of Delegates chosen in each state by the people thereof in conformity to the resolves of the Convention made and provided in that case.

SIGNIFICANT DATES IN THE FOUNDING OF AMERICA

1756-1763 Seven Years' War leaves Britain deeply in debt. They turn to the American colonies for revenue.

1764 Sugar Act is imposed—a duty on colonial sugar and other goods to raise revenue.

1765-1766 Stamp Act (November 1, 1765) is imposed—the first internal tax levied by Britain on the American colonists. Issue of taxation without representation is raised.

1765-1770 Quartering Act (May 15, 1765)—Required colonial authorities to provide food, drink, quarters, fuel and transportation to British forces.

1766 Stamp Act repealed—After widespread mob action against the local British stamp distributors, Parliament repealed the Act.

1767 Townshend Acts (1767-1768) were five British acts to raise revenue, control the colonies, punish New York, and set a precedent that British Parliament could tax the colonies.

1770 Boston Massacre (March 5, 1770) resulted in five colonists killed and six wounded.

1773 Tea Act (May 10, 1773) is imposed, restricting and taxing tea.

1773 Boston Tea Party (December 16, 1773)—About one hundred Sons of Liberty dump forty-five tons of tea (worth $1 million today) into Boston Harbor.

1774 Intolerable (Coercive) Acts (March 31-Jun. 22, 1774) comprised four laws: close the Boston Harbor; replace elected local council with appointed heads and forbidding town meetings; allow British officials charged with capital crimes to be tried only in England; and force colonists to house and provide for British troops.

1774 First Continental Congress (September 5–October 26, 1774)—delegates from twelve of the thirteen colonies gather to react to Intolerable Acts.

1774-1789 The Continental Congress served as government of thirteen American colonies.

1775 Second Continental Congress (May. 10, 1775–March 1, 1781)—Convened to manage the American Revolutionary War; Washington chosen as commander in chief of the army.

1775-1783 Revolutionary War (April 19, 1775–September 3, 1783) Eight years, four months and fifteen days.

1776 Colonies create State constitutions, starting with New Hampshire January 5, 1776. State constitutions replaced royal charters.

1776 Independence declared—The resolution for independence passed the Second Continental Congress on July 2, 1776, by a vote of twelve yes and one abstention (New York). A final revised version of the Declaration of Independence was approved on July 4, 1776.

1777 Articles of Confederation created (November 15, 1777) were sent to the States by Congress. Even though the Articles had not been legally ratified, it was the governing document for most of the war.

1781 Articles of Confederation ratified (March 1, 1781).

1783 Paris Peace Treaty (September 3, 1783) formally ending the war.

1785 Mt. Vernon Compact (March 28, 1785)—Washington invited reps from Virginia and Maryland to his Mt. Vernon home to negotiate their waterways as "a common Highway Free for use."

1786   **Annapolis Convention** (September 11–14, 1786)—Twelve delegates from five States met to deal with the States' protectionist trade barriers. They called for a national Convention in Philadelphia beginning May 14, 1787, to consider the same.

1786-1787 **Shays' Rebellion** (August 29, 1786–February 1787), among other disturbances, rose up to resist unfair taxation—a dangerous sign the Articles needed serious and immediate correction.

1787   **Congressional Act** (February 21, 1787) formally called for a convention of delegates to revise the Articles as needed.

1787   **Constitutional Convention** (May 25–September 17, 1787) convenes in Philadelphia with George Washington presiding, to revise the Articles.

1787   **The Northwest Ordinance** (July 13, 1787) outlaws slavery in any new States of that region, and encourages the teaching of "Religion, morality and knowledge" in all schools.

1787   **Constitution is completed** (September 17, 1787) and sent to Congress to be considered, and then sent to the States for ratification.

1787   **Federalist Papers** (October 27, 1787–May 28, 1788), urging ratification of the new Constitution begin appearing in New York newspapers starting on October 27, 1787.

1788   **Constitution ratified** (June 21, 1788) with the approval of the ninth State, New Hampshire.

1788   **The last Federalist paper**, No. 85, is published in local newspapers on August 16, 1788.

1789   **First Federal Congress** (March 4, 1789) convenes.

1789   **George Washington inaugurated** as president (April 30, 1789)

1790   **Constitution fully ratified** by all thirteen States when Rhode Island ratified the Constitution on May 29, 1790.

1791   **Bill of Rights ratified** December 15, 1791.

1797   **George Washington retires** from office March 3, 1797.

1799   **George Washington dies** December 14, 1799.

Answers to Review Questions

Paper 1

1. "Whether societies of men are really capable or not of establishing good government from reflection and choice, or whether they are forever destined to depend for their political constitutions on accident and force." (1:2)
2. Fire and Sword (1:7–8)
3. Supports (1:13)
4. (1) Importance of the Union, (2) Failure of Articles/Confederacy, (3) need of an energetic (empowered) government, (4) how well the Constitution conforms to republican principles, (5) how the Constitution compares to NY's constitution, (6) additional protections of liberty missing from Articles (1:16)
5. Yes (1:18)
6. Dismemberment, dissolution (1:19)

Paper 2

1. Natural rights (2:2)
2. Firmly united (2:4, 22-24)
3. One connected, fertile, wide-spreading country with navigable waters for commerce and communications (2:7–8)
4. Same ancestors, same language, same religion, same principles of government, same manners and customs, fought the war for Independence (2:9)
5. Design of Providence that the people not break apart into confederacies but unite under the new Constitution. (2:10-11)
6. Articles were written in haste without deep consideration (2:12–13)
7. To repair the serious flaws in the Articles of Confederation (2:14)
8. Patriotic, virtue, wisdom, unoccupied by other subjects, loved of country (2:15)
9. Recommended (2:16)
10. Dissolution, and farewell to all my greatness. (2:23-26)

Paper 3

1. Single Union (3:1)
2. First priority is safety and peace (3:3)
3. Union, not confederacies (3:4–5)
4. Best men (3:8–9)
5. States (3:17)
6. The strength and order needed to fend off foreign invaders is formed, financed, and controlled by the same means that apply to putting down factions and insurrections that individual States are not equipped to handle.

Paper 4

1. Yes (4:1)
2. Monarchs start wars for glory, revenge, ambition, aggrandize families or partisans (4:3)
3. Form a union and strong government (4:12)
4. Draw on all national resources (4:14)
5. Foreign nations (4:21–22)
6. They would see a prosperous and strong nation sufficiently stabilized and organized with which to form friendships and safely trade (4:25)
7. Britain, France, Spain (4:26)

Paper 5

1. Security of religion, liberty, property, animosities and jealousies. Stronger strength, riches, trade. Calmness, unanimity, happiness. (5:2)
2. Dangers from abroad (5:4)
3. No (5:6)
4. No, very different (5:13, 18)
5. One another (5:20)

Paper 6

1. Domestic factions and convulsions (See 6:1)
2. Human nature's tendency toward greed, power and violence as shown from the lessons of the ages (6:2)
3. That it has a tendency to soften the manners of men and encourage peace (6:13)
4. Love of wealth (6:18)
5. Athens, Carthage, Venice, Holland, Britain, Austria, Bourbon, Spain (6:19–28)
6. No (6:29–30)
7. Hostilities, enemies, (6:32–33)

Paper 7

1. Territorial disputes (7:3–2)
2. Granted lands, crown lands, Western territory, Indian lands (7:5)
3. An umpire, common judge, or ruling authority found only in a Union (7:9-10)
4. No (7:11)
5. Not at all. (7:22–31)
6. Divide et impera, divide and command; Yes (7:34)

Paper 8

1. Existing armies and forts (8:2–5)
2. Freedom (8:7)
3. Standing armies (8:8–10)
4. Central authority requiring immediate action would have to make sudden demands for survival and override objections from the legislature (8:11)
5. Other States respond in kind by arming themselves until an arms race is underway (8:12–13)
6. Military becomes priority, rights are weakened in preference to national security. (8:21–22)
7. Yes (8:28)
8. Trivial (8:30)
9. The coming devastation if the States don't form a strong Union (8:29–30)

Paper 9

1. Tyranny and anarchy (9:2)
2. Republican government and civil liberty (9:4)
3. Distribution of powers into distinct departments, legislative balances and checks, courts with judges in office for life, representatives chosen by the people, (9:6–8)
4. An assemblage of societies, association of States into one state where separate organization of the members is not abolished (9:14–26)
5. By senators they choose (9:27)
6. A State can no longer choose its representative to carry State interests to the federal level. Today the senator is chosen according to the ebb and flow of public passions that align with anybody running for that office. (9:27; See Const. Amendment 17)
7. Lycian Confederation (9:28)

Paper 10

1. A group of people seeking power over the rights of others and the interests of society (10:7)
2. Destroy liberty and force obedience, or force everyone to think the same (10:9)
3. No (10:10–11)
4. To protect rights of property and processes to acquire it (10:12)
5. No (10:13)
6. Yes (10:14)
7. Religion, partisanship, power, property, debt, biased judges, land owners (10:15–17, 19–23, 49)
8. No (10:25)
9. Yes; Yes (10:27–28)
10. Either the same passion existing in the majority must somehow be prevented, or prevent the majority from carrying out their scheme. (10:29)
11. No (10:30–33)
12. Small number of citizens who assemble and administer the government in person; Where the majority rules, even to the detriment of the minority. (10:31–32)
13. Government by representation (10:34)
14. A republican form of government (10:34)
15. Democracy is a small group of people in a local area directly involved in the governing processes. A republic has elected representatives who seek what is good for the people, and work to retain their trust to earn re-election. In democracies the leaders seek what will keep them in power at the expense of the minority or of others—See 10:31. (10:35-36)
16. Yes, the greater the number of citizens, variety of parties, interests, and size of land, the harder for factions to form. (10:44–47)
17. Republican form as established in the new Constitution (10:51)

Paper 11

1. Trade and shipping power (11:2)
2. European cabinets of ministers (11:3–4)
3. Bid against each other (11:6)
4. Power to exclude Great Britain, negotiate trading terms to our favor, more influence in West Indies, reduce prices worldwide (11:7–14)
5. A navy or merchant marine (11:15–16)
6. Ability to be neutral (11:18–19)
7. Helps with national defense, interstate commerce, and to train seamen (11:25–26)
8. Different components would come from different locations: Southern States—tar, pitch, turpentine, wood; Middle States—iron; Northern States—more qualified seamen (11:27–30)
9. Greater variety and quantity of goods created and sold, leaving surplus to send overseas (11:31–32)
10. By the use of arms, negotiations, force, and fraud; Europe, Africa, Asia, America (11:36)
11. Bring balance, dictate trade terms between the old and new (11:39–40)

Paper 12

1. Strong Union and free market (12:1–2)
2. Increases them (12:4–5)
3. Pay more taxes (12:7–8)
4. No (12:9–10)
5. Smuggling (12:16–21)
6. Consumption or indirect taxes such as imposts, excises, duties (12:11, 25–26)
7. The farmers and landholders (12:27–29)

Paper 13

1. Makes it less costly (13:1)
2. Three confederacies: four northern States, four middle States, five southern States. (13:2)

3 Every part (13:4)
4 One (13:10)
5 Economy, tranquility, commerce, revenue and liberty (13:11)

Paper 14

1 Government by representatives (republic) or by the whole (democracy) (14:4)
2 The flaws of a democracy were attributed to civilizations that were falsely or inaccurately declared republics (14:5–7)
3 A better form of republican government that is unmixed and extensive (14:8)
4 The distance from the central point where all citizens can conveniently assemble to carry out their civic duties (14:9)
5 The distance from a central point where all the representatives of the people can conveniently assemble to carry out their civic duties (14:10-11)
6 About 868.75 miles by 750 miles (651,562.5 square miles) (14:12–13)
7 No (14:16)
8 Only those objects that concern all members of the nation that no State could otherwise provide (14:16)
9 All others not specifically assigned to the federal government (14:17)
10 Private rights (14:29)
11 No (14:30–31)
12 All Americans (14:31)
13 Pursued a new and noble course which had no parallel in history, creating from scratch a new and vastly improved government (14:31)

Paper 15

1 Yes (15:4–7)
2 Can't pay our debts, can't enforce the peace treaty, foreign occupation continues, can't access the Mississippi as allowed in peace treaty, poor public credit, can't resist foreign encroachment, land values dropping, poor private credit, there is disorder and poverty (15:9–18)
3 Conferring requisite powers that give such energy (15:21)
4 On States (15:24–25)
5 Only recommend (15:26)
6 Yes; No (15:28–31)
7 Yes (15:31-32)
8 Yes (15:33)
9 Yes (15:34)
10 No (15:38)
11 No (15:46)
12 Yes (15:49–52)

Paper 16

1 No (16:2–3)
2 Anarchy (16:3)
3 Large army (16:4)
4 Ineffectual, bloody wars, civil war (16:16)
5 Courts of justice (16:17–18)
6 Citizens (16:23)
7 No; Court of law 16:23–25; 26)
8 General government (16:29)
9 Civil War (16:30)

Paper 17

1 Commerce, finance, negotiation, and war (17:3)
2 Private justice, agriculture, police, courts. All things of a local jurisdiction (17:4–5, 13)
3 When State governments are fair and prudent, the people will trust them the most, including if there is a clash of powers between the two levels (17:7–10)
4 Local; poorly run local government sends people looking for relief from a higher level (17:10–11)
5 The feudal system involved a chieftain or monarch over a whole nation who granted land to inferior classes to work the land. Each inferior class had a leader and sense of independence, as do the States under the Articles. Infighting was severe and the monarch was typically too weak, like Congress under the Articles, to control or prevent the warring factions from conquering each other. 17:17–21)
6 The writers didn't pay enough attention to the lessons to be learned from the histories of past failed confederate governments (17:25)

Paper 18

1 Amphyctionic council in ancient Greece (18:1)
2 The members retained their total independence, and there was no superior central authority. Their connection to one another was by oath, which, like a treaty is hard to enforce and easily broken. (18:2–8)
3 Inefficiency, ambition, jealousy; Can't unify the country for a strong defense; internal fighting weakens it; stronger states overpower weaker states (18:6–11)
4 The necessity of a strong union among the members of its council (18:12)
5 Instead of uniting, the two cities became rivals and then enemies leading up to the Peloponnesian war; Yes (18:13)
6 Internal dissensions weaken the nation and external forces take advantage (18:14)
7 Another Grecian society of republics with local control but united with same laws, customs and mediums of commerce, and a popular government. (18:17–25)
8 The general authority and laws of the confederacy were strong enough to intervene in troubles (18:25)

9 Anarchy, especially between member states (18:37)

Paper 19

1 German confederacy, Polish, Swiss (19:1, 27, 30)
2 Charlemagne (19:3)
3 Feudal system with princes ruling over their vassals (19:3–6)
4 The feudal system (19:7-8)
5 Many powers including right to make laws, veto laws, name ambassadors, confer titles on others, fill vacancies, start universities, tax and spend, and oversee self defense (19:12)
6 Wars between emperor, princes and states; strong oppressing the weak; foreign intrusions; requests for supplies from the members to support a national defense went ignored; imbecility, confusion, and misery (19:15)
7 No (19:19)
8 Either the districts did nothing or conquered their neighbor with the horror and the bloodshed of civil war. (19:21)
9 Religious strife (19:32–34)

Paper 20

1 Lessons showing failure for the same reasons in other confederacies as presented in prior papers (20:1)
2 The seven sovereign states and their cities (20:2)
3 By point of bayonet (20:19)
4 Yes (20:21–22)
5 The propitious concord (agreement between people or groups) in the Constitution (20:28)
6 Experience (20:31)
7 Governing governments instead of governing individuals, such as the Congress trying to govern the legislatures and governor of each State, instead of the citizens of those States. (20:32)
8 Destructive coercion, sword (20:32)

Paper 21

1 No, there was no power to force obedience and punish disobedience (21:2)
2 Article II (21:3)
3 No (21:7–9)
4 Shays' Rebellion (21:10)
5 No, there is no way to measure and tax wealth (21:15–17)
6 National, States, Counties (21:17–19)
7 Consumption taxes including imposts, excises, duties (21:24–26)
8 Indirect consumption taxes (21:28)

Paper 22

1 Highlights the flaws (22:1–48)
2 No (22:2)
3 Nations didn't dare sign trade agreements lest the US change the law, or any particular State change its own trade law (22:3–4)
4 No; no one wants to trade with a country where its member states could change their laws at any time, and relations and regulations are not the same among the many States. (22:4–7)
5 Their disagreements created doubt and suspicion about stability of international law with America; competing and infighting let Britain take advantage of the chaos to further its own gain (22:5–7)
6 A variety of taxes on imported goods that were accumulated over several collecting agencies ended up strangling its trade to the point its very waterway transportation systems were rendered underused and useless. (22:8)
7 Requisitions for troops failed miserably; competition between the States inhibited active help; it became an auction for men, outbidding until prices grew too high (22:10–12)
8 Enthusiasm of liberty (22:12)
9 Those nearest the battles supported the most, those furthest away the least (22:13–14)
10 Seven of the States, a majority, do not equal even a third of the total population (NH, RI, NJ, DE, GA, SC, MD); it is not fair, there is not equal suffrage under the Articles (22:16–19)
11 A holdout State could extort favors to give a deciding vote; it ignores future growth (22:20–22)l
12 Yes (22:30)
13 The differences are diluted across more voices and more difficult to sway in a 51% majority versus the pressures that grows when the numbers are more fragile at 66% or 75% (22:31)
14 The Articles provided no judiciary (22:38)
15 Could be as many final determinations as there are courts (22:40)
16 No because its core features and critical characteristics are inherently underpowered and shortsighted (22:43)
17 The State legislatures; The people; The legislatures might feel empowered to later repeal the Constitution, and the legislatures are unlikely to vote to lose some of their powers (22:46–48)

Paper 23

1 Government must have all necessary political, taxing and enforcement power to fulfill its assigned tasks (23:1–2, see footnote)
2 Common defense, public peace, regulation of commerce, foreign relations (23:3)

3   It is impossible to predict the extent and variety of national needs should war break out (23:5–6)

4   It means to give govt. the resources and power necessary to do the job, and where the needs for war is unknown, the limit or required means is also unknown, so make it limitless (23:7)

5   Yes (23:9)

6   The States could not be forced to obey and provide the "unlimited" means demanded of them. "Good will" wasn't strong enough to compel the States to obey. Congress needed the means to force obedience, and that's the crux of the whole problem with the Articles. (23:9–10).

7   Individual citizens (23:10)

8   For the same reasons as self defense: sufficient means to accomplish the ends. (23:13–16)

Paper 24

1   He addresses the false claim that there are not enough protections against the abuse of military power (24:1)

2   No, only Congress can do that (24:3-4)

3   Yes, its continued existence is controlled by Congress, which must renew its funding every two years (24:5)

4   Yes (24:6-7)

5   Two, Pennsylvania and North Carolina cautiously mention standing armies (24:7)

6   No (24:8–9)

7   Western frontier (24:19-23)

8   No, militia members are tied too closely to the people to perform those full-time duties (24:20)

Paper 25

1   That would transfer national defense duty to the States, creating uneven burdens among the States for a danger they all share in common (25:1–3)

2   The demolition of the national authority, settling State disputes with force (15:4–6)

3   When the means of injuring their rights are in the possession of those of whom they entertain the least suspicion (25:9)

4   Yes; People don't worry very much about their State's defenses which are so close to home. But an army in the hands of the federal government raises all kinds of worrisome red flags, and the people will be watching much more closely for infractions or collusions, thereby protecting their liberties more effectively. (25:9)

5   The term "keeping them up" was never cleanly defined or given a time frame (25:11–13)

6   Fabrications of approaching danger, Indian hostilities, imminent danger from Spain or Britain or other foreign powers (25:15–16)

7   Providing national defense (25:17)

8   Receive the blow before we could even prepare to return it (25:18)

9   Lacks regular training, professional army needs against professional foes (25:20–22)

10   Ignoring weak law gives leeway to violating other laws until the rule of law is fully corrupted (25:25–28)

Paper 26

1   Yes. Historically, rebelling people usually descend into anarchy. (26:1)

2   State government, sovereignty, and local control. The people were already passionately dependent and supportive of their States, and wanted those preserved. (26:1)

3   Nothing can improve on the Constitution now before us for consideration (26:1)

4   Yes, they didn't want to replace the king and Parliament with another oppressive central government (26:1)

5   No (26:2)

6   He meant the critics are failing to see the greater danger of foreign invasion that would happen if they put too much restraint on Congress's war powers in the name of liberty. (26:3)

7   Although people fear a government with too much power, it is even more dangerous to conclude that preventing it from defending the nation is safer for everyone. (26:4)

8   Because an abusive government remains the people's greatest defense against an enemy. Defeat, on the other hand, that disaster of being conquered by a foreign enemy, destroys any hope or power to correct the abusive government. (26:4)

9   Yes, they can see with their own eyes and sufferings that government is sorely lacking in authority, control, organization—in short, Energy. (26:7)

10   The history of England gave ample proof of the problems (26:8–10, 13)

11   1688 (26:9)

12   Parliament held the controls (26:9–10)

13   The king. Parliament needed power to defend the country, so no restraints were considered needful (26:11–12)

14   Yes, they took wariness too far and put too many restrictions on their representatives under the Articles (26:13–16)

15   Yes, the controls were more cautionary than prohibitory (26:17)

16   Yes (26:18)

17   The senators (26:22)

18   The Seventeenth amendment (26:22 footnote)

Paper 27

1   Military force (27:1)

2   No (27:3, 7)

3   Goodness or badness of its administration of the laws (27:3)

4   The options and choices for leaders will be greater (27:5)

5   The legislatures will choose from among them true leaders to best represent their State's interests (27:6)

6   Because the Articles could only operate on the States as entities, not the individual citizens (27:14)

7   It extends its authority to individual citizens and can use the local governments and court systems to gain obedience (27:14)

8   Yes (27:17)

9   Yes (27:15–16)

Paper 28

1   Yes; seditions, insurrections (28:1–2)

2   Yes (28:5)

3   Raise troops (28:6)

4   Massachusetts and Pennsylvania (28:7)

5   No (28:11–12)

6   Representatives of the people (28:13)

7   That where formidable powers are balanced, as between the States and the federal, each can serve as a check on the other due to lawful and logistical resources held by each (28:17–20)

8   The States have representatives to spy out conspiracy, they have access to the intimate resources to overpower a coup. The country is too large to easily conquer more than one State at a time, giving the rest of the States time to rise up as a check (28:20–23)

Paper 29

1   Federal control of the militia (29:1)

2   Their reliability as uniformly trained and outfitted units makes them more agreeable to working with the professional army, and a better stand-alone fighting unit if needed (2:2)

3   The States reserve the right to appoint militia officers and train them according to standards set by Congress. Local officers are more inclined toward loyalty to their State than the federal should such a confrontation arise. (29:3)

4   Yes, under those circumstances not requiring a larger mobilization (29:6)

5   Latin for "power of the county"; A body of men called up by a local sheriff to help enforce the law (29:7 footnote)

6   That the federal govt. intends to use the army as its main instrument to enforce legislation (29:7–8)

7   The Necessary and Proper clause (29:9–10)

8   It would pull people from their jobs for extended periods, disrupting society; (29:14)

9   Once or twice a year, at most (29:14)

10   Yes (29:16)

11   Sons, brothers, neighbors, fellow citizens; Yes (29:19)

12   The States (29:21)

13   Yes; Yes (29:29)

Paper 30

1   To raise and equip armies, pay the civil list (employees, expenses, buildings, infrastructure, so forth), pay national debts, and so forth (30:1–3)

2   Pillaging of the citizens—taking what is needed without mercy (30:6-7)

3   States were legally required to pay taxes but often neglected or refused; there was no federal power of compulsion to force them to pay (30:8–11)

4   No (30:12–13)

5   This would give the States undue power over the federal by withholding funds in exchange for favors; and the States proved themselves unreliable as providers of revenue under the Articles (30:13–14, 18–19)

6   Public projects would be left undone, credit would suffer, lenders would cover the risk with obscenely-high interest rate (30:20–25)

Paper 31

1   Enough to accomplish its responsibilities (31:11)

2   No; it is impossible to predict the defense needs of the future and future expenses (31:12)

3   Emergencies and availability of resources (31:13)

4   Power to procure revenue to provide defense and services (31:14)

5   Taxing individuals instead of trying to tax the States as entities (31:14–15)

6   Structure of government, not the extent of its powers (31:23)

7   The States; The strength is always on the side of the people and on their local governments. People respect those closest and most familiar to them more than any other so long as their rights are respected and protected. (31:25)

Paper 32

1   All authority, unlimited except for duties as noted (32:1–2)

2   Charging duties on imports or exports (32:2)

3   Where the Union has exclusive authority; Where the States are prohibited from exercising an authority; Where an authority is granted to the Union that would be contradictory if the State exercised the same authority (32:4)

4   Concurrent: Existing or happening at the same time (32:5)

5   Repugnancy: A contradiction or inconsistency within the law (32:5)

6   Legislation over Washington DC; Can lay duties on imports and exports; Establish rules for naturalization to the United States (32:7–10)

7   Yes, except those few places where forbidden (32:13, 16, 19)

8   Negative pregnant: A misleading or confusing denial that proves one point by admitting to a lesser but related point (32:15, and footnote)

9   No, both entities must have that power (32:20)

Paper 33

1. First, Article I, Section 8, Clause 18, and second, Article 6, Clause 2. (33:1, and the US Constitution)
2. Yes, they declare a truth that already exists, so the alarm over these is pointless (33:3)
3. Power to do something, the means to do it, the legislative power to compel it, thus, all laws necessary and proper (33:4–6)
4. A term given the "necessary and proper" clause by the Anti-Federalists (33:7 footnote)
5. As an additional protection of the Union's authority against erosion by the States (33:8–9)
6. The government (33:11–12)
7. Appeal to the standard, the Constitution, and remedy or set right the injury done (33:13)
8. Supremacy (33:16)
9. A treaty; dependent on good faith (33:17)
10. No, national laws are supreme only when they are in accordance with the Constitution (33:18–19)

Paper 34

1. Duties on imports (34:1)
2. Rome, where two legislatures were coequal and coexisting for ages (34:3–4)
3. Union needs are unlimited, States' needs are moderate (34:6)
4. Remote futurity or future contingencies, not existing exigencies or immediate necessities (34:7–8)
5. Folly (34:10)
6. No (34:16)
7. Speculations of lasting tranquility (34:17)
8. Wars and rebellions (34:18)
9. Posterity (34:24)
10. The power of the Union would be sacrificed to the States, and we'd be back where we started with the Articles and the States obeying the national laws only if they felt like it (34:31)

Paper 35

1. Shortfalls in revenue needs would fall on States and individuals differently, some carrying a larger load than the rest (35:1)
2. Smuggling (35:2–3)
3. When the consumers have stopped buying, especially if the prices are too high due to high duties (35:4–5)
4. Importing States would pay more tax, States not importing much would pay less or none (35:7–8)
5. Each class would be more inclined to vote in favor its own interests instead of the nation's best interests (35:13–16)
6. Highly educated (doctors, lawyer, theologian, engineer, and so forth) (35:19 footnote)
7. Their trustworthiness and those in whom the people have the most confidence (35:22)
8. Landholders, merchants, those of the learned professions (35:23–24)
9. Political economy and taxation; Such individuals would be more fair and less likely to manipulate the system for a particular advantage (35:29)

Paper 36

1. Proprietors of land, merchants, learned professions (36:1)
2. Fill in the blank: door, open, all (36:3)
3. Strong minds from every walk of life who have earned merit (36:3)
4. The merchants; they have the power to both buy and sell while all the others only sell (36:4)
5. In the same way county representatives bring such information to the legislature, so will the States' representatives bring that local knowledge to Washington DC. (36:7–8)
6. Yes; Experts in taxation are best equipped to consider and agree on the major points without triggering endless debates in larger bodies (36:9–10)
7. Taxes on items of consumption; taxes that are passed along to the consumer by raising the normal price of an item or service just enough to cover the tax (36:12)
8. Yes; When the States find the Union forcing taxpayers to pay without the State legislature's ability to prevent it, the States will rise up against it (Until the 16th Amendment was passed) (36:24)
9. No; If the federal level needs it, the States won't try to take it from the same source. The exception is an excise tax such as on tobacco, alcohol, and gasoline where both entities take a tax. (36:34)
10. No, the Union can use State resources to accomplish its needs (36:29–30)
11. A tax of a fixed amount levied on all persons in a described area (36:38 footnote)
12. He dislikes them but agrees they are necessary in case of a major emergency that requires quick revenue (36:40–41)

Paper 37

1. No (37:1)
2. Yes (37:6–7)
3. Sincere students of freedom, not biased critics (37:10)
4. False or fallacious principles (37:13)
5. Avoid the errors of the past, and invent the rest (37:14)
6. To combine the needed stability and energy while preserving liberty and the representative form of government (37:15)
7. Short terms, power spread out among many hands, frequent elections, execution power in one person (37:20–21)

8. Separating powers in the right way and place (37:23)
9. Separating the various abilities of the human mind, the kingdoms of nature from unorganized matter (37:24–25)
10. Yes; No (37:26)
11. Privileges and powers of the three branches of government (37:27); limits and boundaries of law and courts of law (37:28–30); human words and terms (37:31–33)
12. Yes (37:34)
13. Blurred boundaries between separate objects: imperfection in the eyes, ears, and mind; failure of the mediums of communications (37:35)
14. Trying to set the boundary between federal and State jurisdictions (37:36)
15. Yes (37:37–42)
16. Not at all, it was unexpected (37:44)
17. No (37:44)
18. No (37:44)
19. No (37:44)
20. Yes (37:44)
21. The delegates were free from partisan politics so they could view things with less party bias or loyalty; their interests were for the country as a whole, not to promote private interests (37:47–48)

Paper 38

1. An individual citizen of wisdom and integrity (38:1)
2. Minos, Zaleucus, Theseus, Draco, Solon, Romulus, Numa, Tullius Hostilius, Brutus, Amphictyon, Achaeus, Aratus, Lycurgus (38:2–7)
3. Probably the fear of discord and disunion among the members should a committee handle it (38:10)
4. The Convention improved the mode of preparing and establishing plans for government; Any flaws won't be from lack of careful study (38:14)
5. Trial period will point them out (38:14)
6. No (38:15–17)
7. While the doctors (the Convention) found an agreeable remedy, others (Anti-Federalists) raised concerns but couldn't agree on their reasons or solutions (38:19–22)
8. Seventeen (38:22–40)
9. No (38:41–44)
10. No (38:45–47)
11. Yes; Yes (38:60–66)

Paper 39

1. If the form of government created by the Convention was truly republican (39:1–2)
2. Republican (39:2–3)
3. Yes (39:8)
4. Derives powers directly or indirectly from the people; It is administered by people elected to office for limited time or during good behavior (39:9–14)
5. People elect representatives; People indirectly appoint senators and President; Judges reflect people's choice of President and senators who appoint justices; terms are defined; no titles of nobility; new States guaranteed republican form. (39:15–20)
6. Assent and ratification by the people acknowledging it as the supreme law of the land (39:32)
7. It is federal because the States acted as sovereign bodies when they ratified the Constitution (39:35)
8. It is national because the House of Representatives derives powers from the people (39:37)
9. Federal (39:38)
10. Neither national nor federal but a composition of both (39:56–61)

Paper 40

1. If the Convention was properly authorized to create the Constitution (40:1)
2. September 1786; To call on representatives to discover what changes are needed to make the federal government useful and how to invite approval of these changes by Congress and the States. (40:3, see Timeline)
3. February 1787 (40:2, see Appendix: Significant Dates in the Founding of America)
4. (1) To stabilize the government, (2) to give it sufficient power, (3) to alter it and provide additions as necessary, (4) to establish a form of proper ratification (40:5–10)
5. No; The terms are ill-defined and the critically needed alterations are not possible in some instances (40:15–19)
6. Fix the problems: Create adequate government, change the name, alter the body, add new provisions, retain old provisions that were based on true principles of republican government. (40:17–22)
7. State sovereignty (40:26), Senate appointed by States (40:27), Union will act on States and people (40:28), Union power can operate on persons (40:29), Power to tax (40:30), regulation of Commerce (40:31), residual power retained by States (40:32)
8. More of an expansion and enlargement, including new inventions and innovations in the science of politics (40:33)
9. Articles are so feeble (no proper energy) and confined (violates republican principles) that enlarging on these to make the process more efficient gives the Constitution the appearance of something totally new (40:33)
10. Ratification comes not from the State legislatures as required in Article XIII of the Articles of Confederation, but from the people themselves. Secondly, only nine instead of unanimous thirteen States were required for ratification, another violation of Article XIII. (40:34)
11. No, it was only advisory and recommended (40:40)
12. Its merits (40:56–58)

Paper 41

1. The sum or quantity of power given the Union, and the structure of government to manage that power (41:1)
2. The first, the quantity of power (41:2)
3. Yes (41:6–7)
4. National defense, regulation of commerce with foreign nations, peace between the States, general needs of the country, prevent interstate quarrels, the power to carry out these duties (41:8)
5. Yes (41:16–17)
6. A united America (41:23)
7. Yes (41:38)
8. Article I Section 8 Clause 1 (41:49)
9. No, the list gives limited permissions to the government (41:52)
10. A semicolon instead of a colon (41:52)
11. To summarize the overall goal and to introduce what follows (41:53–54)
12. Yes (41:54, 57)
13. No (41:56–57)

Paper 42

1. Foreign relations and interstate commerce (42:1)
2. Importation of slaves to be banned after twenty years, in 1808; A duty of $10 per person imported for slavery, all as a means of discouraging slavery. (42:1)
3. 20 years (42:17-18)
4. Yes, "Happy would it be for the unfortunate Africans, if an equal prospect... of being redeemed from the oppressions of their European brethren!" (42:18)
5. Allowing twenty years was tolerating illicit slavery, and discouraging immigration to America (42:16)
6. Postponement was better; Had slavery been eliminated (no compromise made) the slave States would have formed their own confederacy of probably five or more States, slavery would have continued there, and those States would have invited Spain or France to help them secure their border against the rest of the United States. European-style skirmishes and wars would commence. Foreign nations would not respect or lend or cooperate for lack of cohesion and strength in the Union. (42:17 footnote)
7. Coin money, establish monetary values, punish counterfeiting, fixed standards of weights/measures, rules of naturalization, bankruptcy, keeping public records, post offices, and so forth (42:22)
8. Serious interruptions would take place (42:22)
9. States would start adding import and export duties (42:24-25)
10. The status of Indians as free inhabitants, citizens, naturalized aliens, or "people of each State" was not resolved. Each designation brings with it conflicts with other provisions. (42:31–32, 42:31 footnote; 42:37-41)

Paper 43

1. The States could extort, influence or disrupt the proceedings of the national government (43:6)
2. So the State cannot interfere with federal activities (43:9)
3. See Article 3, Section 3, Clauses 1–2 (43:11-12)
4. No (43:16)
5. No (43:25)
6. Yes (43:39–42)
7. To save the Constitution from being too changeable (mutable) whereby mistakes will be avoided and rash decisions are forced to be given deeper consideration (43:45)
8. No; Yes (43:54)
9. With utmost respect and good relations because they might one day join the Union, and that friendship will be welcomed (43:57)

Paper 44

1. Restrictions on the States (44:1)
2. Activities that involve or extend to other States and Nations (44:2-18)
3. There would be as many different currencies as States, foolishly impeding commerce between the States (44:8)
4. One violation opens the door to many more until eventually the whole structure unravels (44:14)
5. Pointless, powerless, a dead letter (44:21)
6. They could have copied Article II that prohibits powers not expressly delegated; Made a list of permissions given the Union; Made a list of denials of power; Said nothing, leaving it to Congress to figure out (44:23-27)
7. "Expressly"; The word is not well defined or clarified (44:28-30)
8. The means to accomplish the end (44:37)
9. No (44:55)

Paper 45

1. No, all of the federal responsibilities are aimed at the people's happiness, a state of affairs not possible if States' sovereignty is destroyed (45:1-3)
2. To establish peace and happiness (45:5-6)
3. What is the supreme object the government must pursue? The public good, the real welfare (45:6)
4. The States intruding (45:9-10)
5. Few, defined (45:27)
6. Numerous, indefinite (45:28)
7. External and national objects such as war, peace, foreign commerce, taxation (45:29)

8. Internal objects, day-to-day lives, liberties and properties of the people; order and prosperity of the State (45:30)
9. Energizes or invigorates the original powers (45:33)

Paper 46

1. The people (46:1)
2. Agents, trustees, powers, purposes (46:2)
3. State (46:4)
4. No, it was not popular with them (46:7)
5. States (46:11-17)
6. Their own home States (46:11-13)
7. All States would be alarmed; every legislature would formally object to it; the country would be united against federal; communication between the States would begin in earnest; people would go to arms (46:19-24)
8. If properly armed, yes (46:25-27)
9. Right to bear arms (46:29-30)
10. No (All of No. 46)

Paper 47

1. To discuss the separation of powers (47:1)
2. The three branches are not totally separated from each other (47:2)
3. Accumulation of all political powers, legislative, executive and judiciary, into the same hands (47:5)
4. Where the judge becomes part of the legislative or executive branch (47:20-21)
5. 1689-1755 (47:8)
6. The value of the separation of the three branches of government (47:7-8)
7. England's (47:9)
8. The king and the legislative branch (47:11, 17, 19); The king and the judiciary (47:12); The legislature and the judiciary (47:13-14, 18); see also 47:20-21.
9. Montesquieu meant that the three branches should have partial agency in each other, not the whole power residing in one person or one branch itself. Without partial involvement with each other there could be no check or balance (see heading for 47:3) (47:15, 22)
10. No (47:23); See examples in New Hampshire (47:24-26); Massachusetts (47:27-30); New York (47:32-34); New Jersey (47:35-36); Pennsylvania (47:37-38); Delaware (47:39-41); Maryland (47:42); Virginia (47:43-44); North Carolina and South Carolina (47:45-47); Georgia (47:48)

Paper 48

1. No, the control from checks and balances can't function if the three branches exist as impervious silos of solo power, totally immune from external controls (48:2)
2. Directly, completely (48:3)
3. No; Legislative branch (48:6-7)
4. By taking advantage of emergencies, either real or fabricated (48:9)
5. Yes (48:13)
6. Its powers are more extensive and less susceptible to limits, making it easier to mask its activities. (48:11)
7. Their jobs are simpler, more defined, and more public. Corruption is easier to detect. (48:12)
8. "All the powers of government, legislative, executive, and judiciary, result to the legislative body." (48:16)
9. Divided, balanced, several, transcend, restrained (48:17)

Paper 49

1. A draft of a constitution for Virginia (49:1-2)
2. That a constitutional convention be called whenever two branches of government desire it to change the Constitution or correct any violation in it. (49:3-4)
3. Call a convention whenever government strays from the Constitution to enlarge, diminish or refine the powers of government (49:5)
4. Yes; The appearance of frequent corrections destabilizes the Constitutions legitimacy and creates distrust (49:8-9, 13-14)
5. Opinion rules most because it is easily fortified by popularity and precedent, even if not based on truth (49:10-12)
6. No, it's pointless because human nature to obey leader's opinions usually outweighs truth (49:11-12)
7. Yes (49:13-14)
8. A crisis in the midst of danger (49:15)
9. Passion instead of reason (49:24)
10. No; Pitting power against power is the built-in corrective that runs without outside interference. The Supreme Court's job is to pull back a branch that goes straying outside of the Constitution (49:26)

Paper 50

1. Jefferson's idea of periodic review of the three branches and their betrayal of boundaries (50:1-2)
2. Corruption is easy to hide under the shades of passing time (50:4)
3. React; Abuses take time to discover, and once in place that inertia and machinery of human nature tends to adopt it, increasing resistance to changing things from the way they are (50:5-6)
4. That their council wasn't neutral, and its members were parties to the illegal encroachments; Debates were ruled by passion not reason; Pennsylvania's constitution was misinterpreted for private gain; Legislature refused to take correction from the Council (50:7-16)

5   No, anyone elected to the Council would no doubt have party alliances, and perhaps support for their election from a factious group (50:18)

Paper 51

1   Structure, relations, proper, places (51:1)
2   Judiciary (51:3)
3   No, their actions could be coerced, punished or rewarded, thus destroying their independence (51:4)
4   A bulwark of opposing ambitious men (51:6)
5   Angels, angels; That men are imperfect and so are governments, so an abundance of caution and control is necessary in government to prevent usurpers finding ways to destroy liberty to serve their own selfish interests (51:7)
6   No (51:7)
7   A check on each other (51:8)
8   No; Congress/legislature (51:9)
9   Dividing, different, election, action (51:9)
10 The President could be wrong or corrupt, and like a king, could compel all to obey him against the peoples' will. (51:10)
11 All delegated power is surrendered to a single government divided into separate compartments. A compound republic is a structure where the people's delegated powers are divided over many layers and departments—first, between State and federal; second, subdivided many times in each of those, each division placed in opposition to the others. (51:13)
12 Oppression by rulers; oppression by majority against a minority (51:14)
13 First, creating a universal will that stands above any majority that might form; Second, dividing up society into so many parts, interests and classes, that minority rights can never be targeted by determined combinations of the majority (51:15-16)
14 Yes (51:17)
15 Justice for all (51:19-22)
16 Large; federal principle (51:23)

Paper 52

1   How the Constitution sets out the election of members of the House of Representatives (52:1)
2   So the States couldn't disrupt the national government's proceedings by withholding representatives or replacing them at disruptive times (52:3-4)
3   Must by twenty-five years old, a citizen for seven years, must live in the States he represents, can't hold any other political office (52:6)
4   Yes (52:8)
5   Short (52:19)
6   Yes, and that is the genius of biennial (every two years) elections (52:21)

Paper 53

1   No, the idea of "where annual elections end, tyranny begins" is a myth (53:1, 8)
2   No (53:2)
3   They can't amend or alter the Constitution by themselves (53:5)
4   Gives time for experience and knowledge to develop (53:11-18)
5   Main points:

a. The original design was that senators were chosen out from among a State's most experienced people, two people who were familiar with the laws and needs of that particular State.

b. It was thought that most often they would be chosen from among the ranks of the State legislature (see 56:10).

c. From such service their political trustworthiness and wisdom had already been proven by first winning their local election, and then experiencing the heat of State legislative action. This is where raw experience in the political processes served to train them, reveal their true character, and expose them to the intimate details of caring for the interests of others.

d. When such legislators arrived as senators in Washington DC, they were to that degree already matured and seasoned, making them more aware of the intricacies, cautions, and lessons that the national office would present to them—and, therefore, better suited as America's best statesmen.

e. The popularly elected representatives on the other hand typically would not come from those experiences and were deemed less seasoned for the role of statesmen.

f. The Seventeenth Amendment removed that refining process by making the senators popularly elected instead of being carefully vetted by the State legislature. Today, most senators arrive in office just as untried and just as unproven as the 2-year Reps.

Paper 54

1   Using population to decide how many representatives a State can have (54:1)
2   Should slaves be counted toward the 30,000 number for a representative? If yes, slave States would have more pro-slavery congressmen; If slaves are counted then they should be taxable; slave States didn't want to pay taxes because they viewed slaves as property; Constitution protects both property and persons; A compromise was needed to prevent the slave States from forming their own confederacy and dividing the nation while still keeping slavery alive. (54:4-24)
3   Property, according to the North (54:4)

4   By law, slaves had to be protected "in his life and in his limbs" against violence from others (54:6)
5   Yes (54:6)
6   No, it's an anti-slavery compromise—by reducing the slave count to 3/5ths, the slave States would have a harder time reaching the number needed to get a pro-slavery representative in Congress, but have an easier time paying taxes on slaves (54:4 and footnote; 54:14; 54:24 and footnote)
7   He assumes the voice of a Southern advocate or "brethren" (54:5-23)
8   The more people a State has the more representatives it may have. This entices them to exaggerate their census numbers high. The more people a State has the more taxes they must pay. This entices them to understate their census numbers low. In general, these off-setting incentives encourages honesty in the census. (54:25)

Paper 55

1   The size of the House of Representatives (55:1)
2   Too few members to protect the public's trust; members won't know enough; members will be narrow and biased; it will be inadequate as the population grows (55:3-6)
3   30,000 (55:18)
4   Three million (55:19)
5   Yes; Yes (55:28-30)
6   Yes; chains of despotism (55:36)

Paper 56

1   If the House of Representatives is too small to grasp the needs of the entire nation (56:1)
2   No, only those issues pertaining to the job (56:3)
3   To better assess national needs in the areas of commerce, taxation, and militia (56:4)
4   To make informed decisions for the whole country (56:16)
5   Yes, general issues will tend toward the same; Internal affairs will grow more localized and complex (56:17)
6   Britain (56:19-20)
7   The king and his ministers (56:21)
8   The king's (56:21)
9   Yes (56:22-23)
10 Very well, safely, and with competence (56:24)

Paper 57

1   That only the elite classes will be represented; that Congress will seek after self-aggrandizement (57:1)
2   Extraordinary (57:2)
3   Wisdom, discernment, virtue, interests of the nation at heart (57:3)
4   The strength and determination to stand up for what is right and defend it (57:3 footnote)
5   No (57:6)
6   Genius of the Constitution, the nature of the laws, and the vigilant and manly spirit which nourishes freedom (57:15)
7   Duty, gratitude, interest, ambition (57:17)

Paper 58

1   The charge that the number of representatives won't be increased as the country grows (58:1)
2   Temporary; In three years (58:3)
3   The States (58:5)
4   Too many people can fall prey to the leadership of just a few (58:22); Passion tends to reign over reason (58:23); too many members creates a body of ill-informed and weak leaders, a group vulnerable to single orators (58:24-25); ignorance and passion in a large group will lead to its domination by an oligarchy (58:26)
5   Making decisions on a 49-51 percent basis is less risky than seeking 66 percent or 75 percent majorities because in those higher margins a single State can extort more easily in exchange for its support of one side or the other. (58:27-28)

Paper 59

1   Article I Section 4 Clause 1 (59:2 footnote)
2   Places of choosing senators (59:2)
3   The power and necessity of preserving itself (59:4)
4   They could prevent federal officers from being elected and bring the federal government to its knees (59:9-11)
5   By controlling the appointment of senators to the federal government they can impact the fulfillment of federal duties. (59:14-20)
6   It would be difficult because even if a few States tried to prevent the election of senators, only a third of the Senate is up for reelection every two years, and it could continue functioning because a quorum is only 51%, a quantity sufficient to conduct business (59:21-22)
7   Yes, with thirteen States in the Union, that's 26 senators with 14 to be a simple majority. No other combination of States during the ratification period resolves the number 16. (59:21)
8   With elections every two years the States could shut down the House, or threaten to, at every election cycle, injecting chaos and inefficiency in government. (59:24)

Paper 60

1   That the federal government would use regulation of elections to the House to build a class of elites and wealthy and exclude low income voters (60:1-3)
2   With an immediate revolt of the people, headed by the State governments (60:4)
3   Fill in the blank: people, State legislatures, electors, people (60:7)
4   No, not at all, the States are very jealous of that power (60:8)

5   It is unlikely that partiality will exist; Landed class dominates the nation already; The damage from elevating one class above the other would not be worth the attempt (60:16-19)

6   Fill in the blank: confined, miraculous instinct, common, towns, cities (60:22)

7   No (60:24-28)

8   Military force (60:24)

9   Recall elections, rebellion in the streets, civil war (60:28)

Paper 61

1   No (61:1-2)

2   No (61:4-5)

3   No (61:7-9)

4   Total demolition of the old House and total renewal of the new House all at one time; or in other words, a fresh start (61:16)

5   It stops the perpetuation of bad ideas, bad policies, and diseases of faction from the old House to the new (61:16, 18)

6   No; legislature (61:20-21)

7   No. A set time might become inconvenient for everyone and it would take an amendment to change it. That's why the matter is better left to the legislature of each, the States and the federal, to sort out. (61:22)

Paper 62

1   Qualification of senators; appointment by legislatures; equality; number of senators; powers of Senate (62:2)

2   To bring together the best possible people measured by age, maturity, experience, priorities, and perspective to deal with international affairs, potential blunders by the House, resisting popular sentiment in lawmaking, and resisting foreign influence (62:3-7)

3   The Senate plays a key role in many core processes of the federal government and by Constitutional mandate must be composed of equal representatives from each State. (62:13)

4   A law or resolution must be passed by a majority of the people (the House) and a majority of the States (the Senate) (62:14-17)

5   Yes; Yes (62:19)

6   The influence of sudden and violent passions led by factious leaders; keeping its numbers smaller with a longer tenure in office, an environment where the ills of large assemblies are harder to gain a foothold (62:20)

7   By the voluminous quantity of repealing, explaining, and amending the laws it passed (62:24)

8   Monuments of deficient wisdom (64:24)

9   Fidelity to the happiness of the people, and knowledge of how to obtain that happiness (62:25)

10 Without stability and trustworthiness no one can trust the government to keep the same laws tomorrow that it passed today; international respect and confidence is lost for the same reasons of instability (62:29-33)

11 Fill in the blank: prey, nation, speculating, fluctuating (62:33)

12 Fill in the blank: voluminous, read, incoherent, understood, repealed, revised, changes, no man, will be (62:35)

13 A rule of action (63:36)

14 No (62:36)

15 By possessing a certain portion of order and stability (62:42)

Paper 63

1   It's instability naturally creates distrust in the eyes of nations abroad, and lacks the ability to properly correct itself and become more respectable (63:1)

2   1) International activities should appear the fruits of careful planning and honorable considerations; 2) International norms can help form policies for a nation still too young to know right from wrong (63:2-5)

3   A numerous and changeable body is too fluid and mutable to be trusted by others; Madison attributes Rhode Island's current calamities to a lack of calmer, more seasoned thinkers to review the actions of its lower house (63:6-7)

4   James Madison, first used it in 63:8 (63:8 footnote)

5   Those objects within the power of the responsible party (63:9-10)

6   To enact measures that have an immediate impact; to enact measures that have a gradual and perhaps unobserved long-term impact (63:11)

7   A calmer, supervising body, namely, the Senate (63:15-16)

8   Stimulated by irregular passion, seeking some illicit advantage, or misled by artful misrepresentations (63:18)

9   Fill in the blank: Reason, justice, and truth (63:19)

10 Fill in the blank: infection, violent, passions (63:21)

11 Sparta, Rome, Carthage (63:23)

12 No because it has defined terms of six years, and limited roles (63:39-40)

13 First, corrupt itself (63:41); corrupt the State legislatures (63:41); corrupt the House of Representatives (63:42); finally corrupt the people at large (63:42)

14 The House of Representatives (63:56)

Paper 64

1   The power of the president to make treaties with the consent of two thirds of the Senate (64:2)

2   Highest security, by best qualified men, suited to the nation's good (64:3)

3   The most enlightened and respectable citizens (64:6)

4   Reps don't have the experience or access to information necessary to properly measure treaties, and they're always rotating in and out of office (64:10)

5   Sufficient time to be become well acquainted with national concerns (64:11)

6   Only a minority of one third rotates every two years in the Senate whereas in the House the entire structure is up for election every two years (64:12)

7   The President and Senate (64:16-18)

8   No, they have the force of law but must remain immune from legislative change and the fickle rotations in Congress (64:22-23, 24-25)

9   Honor, oaths, reputations, conscience, love of country, family affections and attachments (64:31)

10 Fill in the blank: talents, integrity, advantageous; Yes (64:31)

Paper 65

1   Participating in executive treaty-making and appointments to office, and acting as a court for the trial of impeachments (65:1)

2   They deal with misconduct, abuse or violation of public trust, and doing injuries to society itself and will be viewed through partisan eyes. (65:3)

3   By the strongest party (65:4)

4   As judges in a political activity the Court is not equipped to deal with so broad a swath of political questions; if criminal or civil violations also took place, and the impeached president appealed lower-court decisions, how could he expect a fair trial when his appeal moves up to the Supreme Court, that very same body that found him guilty of the impeachment? (65:12-18)

5   Impanel a jury; Combining Supreme Court with Senate; Create a court of non politicians; Enlarging the Supreme Court for just this occasion (65:20-26)

6   Fill in the blank: Anarchy, desert (65:30)

Paper 66

1   The separation between the different departments of power (66:2)

2   Yes (66:3)

3   Making treaties; appointing people to offices in the executive branch (66:10-11)

4   Originating money bills, instituting impeachments, be the umpire in all elections of the President (66:14-17)

5   No (66:20)

6   Fill in the blank: pride, virtue (66:31)

Paper 67

1   Gross distortions, creations beyond a king, beyond fiction, greater than Britain's monarch, surrounded by minions and mistresses, and so forth (67:1-4)

2   The supposed power of the President to fill vacancies in the Senate (67:9)

3   Yes (67:13; Art. II, Sec. 2, Clause 2)

4   The Senate's (67:11)

5   Yes (67:12)

6   NO (67:13)

7   Art. II, Sec. 2, Clause 3; The phrase "...President shall have power to fill up all vacancies that may happen during the recess of the Senate" implies that ALL vacancies must include any vacancies in the Senate. (67:12)

8   The Legislature (67:18)

9   The State executive or governor (67:18)

10 No (67:18-19)

Paper 68

1   How to elect the President (68:1)

2   Can't involve politicians who are already "pre-established"; chosen by the people; wise men capable of analyzing qualities; small number; selected by fellow citizens from the general population; most likely to understand and be discerning (68:2-3)

3   A national meeting at one time in one place would expose the electors to persuasions that might steer or threaten or persuade them astray (68:4)

4   Politicians might have biases, close ties to the President or a candidate, or have subjected themselves to foreign influences (68:5-7)

5   A man popular in a State must prove his integrity and talent to other States where he is not known, a task not easily faked beyond his own State borders if he is not already a man "pre-eminent for ability and virtue" (68:13)

6   The Twelfth Amendment (68:16)

Paper 69

1   Saying he is not much different than the king of Britain (69:1-2)

2   President must be elected then reelected to four-year terms; the king is in office for life (69:3)

3   By impeachment; king can't be removed, he answers to no one (69:4)

4   Congress may override the President's veto with two thirds majority in each house; in Britain, the king is the last word and has total and irreversible veto power (69:5-6)

5   No; Yes (69:15-17)

6   Yes (69:20)

7   Levying war against US or adhering to enemies of the US, giving aid and comfort (69:23)

8   Length of term, veto power, military leadership, treaty making, political appointments, managing commerce, religious freedoms (69:37-44)

Paper 70

1   The objectives of republican government depend on a strong and forceful executive to get the job done (70:1-2)

2   Without private property the end purpose of government (justice for all) is destroyed. What is justice except to prevent those "high-handed combinations" from violating rights to property? Hamilton prioritizes rights to property higher than securing liberty. His list: (1) National defense, (2) Steady administration of the law, (3) Protection of property, (4) Securing liberty against assaults and anarchy. (70:2)

3   A strong executive backed by a numerous legislature to deliberate and guide best fulfills the efficiency of decisions, activities, secrecy, and expeditious fulfillment of needs (70:8-10)

4   Infighting for power, development of opposing factions, delay of time-critical decisions, divides the country into camps (70:10-19)

5   They weren't included in planning it (exclusion hurt their pride); it was planned by their political enemies (personal pursuits become superior to what's good for country); if they disapprove, they won't accept and support, but will fight it as a matter of honor (they fail to see how harmony and "country first" should be first priority) (70:20-22)

6   Although delaying forward action it forces debate and arguing, and examination and consideration of facts that otherwise might not be considered (70:24)

7   Circumstances often require swift action; once Congress decides the executive helps the country the most by executing the plan immediately; it is best to leave the slow deliberations to the legislatures (70:25-26)

8   Blame-shifting takes place all the time; blame must be placeable to know where corrections are needed (70:32-34)

9   The power of public opinion to restrain the executive from doing something selfish and foolish; The ability to pinpoint the misconduct of individuals to punish or remove from office (70:38-39)

10 No, it provides a proxy to blame for foolish error (70:40-44)

11 Actions can be watched more carefully without having to guess who did what (70:46-48)

12 Such executives could conspire, form a cabal, and more effectively cloak their faults from public scrutiny (70:50-51)

Paper 71

1   Having enough time in office to become acquainted and familiar with powers, responsibilities, and opportunities so that the office's fullest potential can be considered and pursued (71:4-5)

2   It's not his job to react to "the sudden breeze of passion" which, in the past, has led the nation into making mistakes; he must be a guardian of the people's interests, not their inclinations (71:7-11)

3   So that when the inclinations of the people drive the legislature to bad law the President can steer them back to safety (72:12-14)

4   Answer: subordinate, dependent, comports (71:15)

5   Any shorter of a term would probably dampen enthusiasm to take the job at heart; Any shorter would make him reticent to make bold proposals that could cost him reelection because some proposals would take time to prove themselves a good thing for the country (71: 21-14)

Paper 72

1   To help the president carry out his assigned duties as he best sees fit (72:3-5)

2   No incentive for good behavior (72:10); No incentive of reward (72:11); Can't finish projects (72:12); Temptations to build nest egg (72:13); Ambition to act regardless of good or harm (72:15-16); Unhappy ex-presidents' harmful influence on society (72:17)

3   Presidential experience and wisdom (72:18-19)

4   Those of greatest experience would be eliminated from coming to help. Changing leadership in the middle of war could be disastrous (72:21-22)

5   Yes, the disgruntled people might rise up to amend away the one-term limit for the President. Yes, it is better to let the voters decide how many terms in office a leader has earned according to his good deeds and hard work. (72:31-33)

Paper 73

1   By reducing his salary and emoluments by famine (no salary, no support) or tempting him by largesses (promising a raise or other benefits) (73:1-2)

2   Support, will (73:3)

3   The President's compensation shall neither be increased nor diminished during his term of office, and emoluments shall remain unchanged (73:5)

4   Two thirds of the House and two thirds of the Senate (73:9)

5   Gradually or in one fell swoop strip away his authorities; bring the two branches under the control of one, the legislative branch (73:11-12)

6   Bad law, dangerous action of factions, rash decisions not well considered (73:15-16)

7   Congress is encouraged to re-think its actions; to act with less haste and passion; to keep ever-present the consideration of the how the President might react (73:18, 28, 31)

8   Protect against an immediate attack on the constitutional rights of the executive, and for defending the rights of Americans (73:26, 31)

Paper 74

1   To serve as commander-in-chief of the armed forces and militia, and to grant reprieves and pardons (74:1, 4)

2   Single; A body of men is more likely to encourage each other to be rigid, less agreeable to mercy or pity; A single person is better at balancing compassion without the biases of partisanship or gainsaying that hardens groups of people against the merciful purpose of a pardon (74:5-8)

3   Yes (74:6, 8; see Art. II, Sec. 2, Clause 1)

4   Yes (74:10 and footnote)

Paper 75

1   Neither; Congress makes laws to regulate society, the executive executes those laws, especially for national defense. Treaty-making is neither but draws from both, so sharing it seems the safest place (75:8-9)

2   Yes; Good faith (75:10)

3   A political figure in and out of office in four or more years might make treaties to improve his own place instead of doing what's best for the nation (75:12-15)

4   Sovereigns have confidence and respect in face-to-face negotiations with sovereigns, not bodies of men (75:16-19)

5   Two thirds of senators present because if more than one third of the total were absent, passage of treaties would be stalled until more arrived in town. (75:22-24)

6   Under the Articles it was one vote per State, so if a State had one representative only, it had no vote. With each senator being able to vote, partial presence still permits a State to be represented, and helps ensure enough votes overall for the two thirds majority to approve treaties (75:29; see Articles of Confederation Art. V clause 2 and 4)

Paper 76

1   Nominate officers or temporary replacements in the executive branch, foreign representatives, federal judges and the Supreme Court; No, he cannot appoint without the consent of the Senate, and if the Senate is in recess, he can make temporary appointments to fill vacancies (76:1)

2   Groups are likely to be biased by cabal and intrigue (76:4); One man is a better judge of character than a group (76:5-8); partisan bickering will delay and pollute the process (76:10)

3   Not easily, there is enough separation and virtue to resist such pressure tactics (76:19-23)

4   No additional appointments or emoluments or salary increases may be granted to bribe or entice members of the Senate (76:24)

Paper 77

1   Helps keep the government stable and functioning through transitions or upheavals (77:1)

2   By conferring a benefit on a person (77:7)

3   No; If the Senate found a way to bribe or extort the President it would rarely succeed (77:7)

4   Such councils always give rise to a factious spirit, to cabal and intrigue that eventually blossoms and takes over; each member would have friends and influences and connections that would bias and corrupt the process; it would not be independent enough (77:17-20)

5   No. While appointments by the President are open to scrutiny and praise or blame, in New York the council of appointment was cloaked in secrecy and people suspected the worst—it was highly suspected by the public to be a nesting place for cabal, intrigue, favoritism, and corruption. (77:10-16)

6   Because it's too big and bogged down by infinite delays and entangling embarrassments (77:22)

7   Election every four years; elected by people chosen to elect him; always liable to impeachment, trial, and dismissal from office, unable to run for other offices, and possibly suffering consequences of criminal activity (77:29)

8   Yes (77:27)

Paper 78

1   How to staff and organize it, and how great its powers should be (78:2-6)

2   Because it has the least capacity to annoy or injure such rights; sword or purse (78:12-15)

3   Take on the role of the legislature and pass new law through judicial findings (78:18)

4   No (78:25)

5   The judicial branch (78:27)

6   To keep Congress within its Constitutional bounds; Yes (78:28)

7   The Judiciary (78:29)

8   The Constitution (78:32)

9   Adhere to the Constitution and void or disregard the law in violation (78:37)

10 Never exercise its own partisan or private will, only judgment (78:39)

11 Go through the formal amending process according to Article V; No, not at all, the Constitution must never be arbitrarily changed by the courts. (78:42-43 footnote)

12 That the law they pass today that is a gainer might turn against them in a different form tomorrow (78:47)

13 Temporary terms hurt independence because threats or bribes could impact a judge's application of the law. And, there might not be enough incentive or time to learn the complexities of the law. (78:49-52)

14 No, not many (78:53)

Paper 79

1   With power of his subsistence (salary) (79:1)

2   No; The Constitution forbids it because that power would be used to force judges to rule in a partisan fashion (79:3-5)

3   Yes, if found in violation of "good behavior," by the impeachment process outlined in Article I, Sections 2 and 3 (79:9)

4   No; No (79:10-12)

Paper 80

1   (1.) Cases involving federal law; (2.) involving the Constitution; (3.) involving the US government as a party in the case; (4.) cases involving the "peace of the confederacy;" (5.) cases involving maritime issues (80:3-7)

2   No (80:9-11)

3   Thirteen States, thirteen different interpretations and rulings (80:12-13)

4   If left to the States, one State could plunge the entire nation into war. "The peace of the whole ought not to be left at the disposal of a part," Hamilton says (80:15-16)

5   It brought order and peace (80:20)

6   No; land grants (80:28-29)

7   Cases where relationships of trust are broken, cases of give and receive such as loans, financial obligations, fraud, accident, trust, or hardship. This is separate from legal jurisdiction, that is, where laws are broken. (80:43-44)

8   In equity cases that involve many States, foreigners, and land disputes between the States (80:45-46)

9   Where citizens claim lands given to them under grants from different States (80:52)

10   Congress can choose whether to pass laws or grant authorities to the court that would resolve the problem (80:54–55)

Paper 81

1   Whether the Supreme Court should remain an independent body or be a branch of Congress (81:4)

2   Answer: construing, spirit, mould (mold) (81:7)

3   Thomas Jefferson; The court is irresponsible, meaning, answers to no one, and would gradually move all government under one head until State sovereignty was destroyed and it would be as venal and oppressive as Britain's king from whom they had just won independence (81:7 footnote)

4   No; The so-called "spirit" is ill-defined and open to any interpretation or definition imaginable, thus allowing the court to alter and ultimately destroy the Constitution (81:8)

5   No. It's job is to see if the controversy has a solution inside the boundaries of the Constitution, and if no relief is found, the case should revert to the States or the people for resolution (80:8-10)

6   Yes (81:8-9)

7   No (81:13)

8   No; Set new rules (81:20)

9   It can't support itself with force, only declare its rulings; Judges are always subject to impeachment (81:22-23)

10   States are not neutral; States would be deciding national law; Can't predict the impact of local bias; States would be tempted to rule in favor of themselves (81:27-31)

11   To determine if and how a law applies to a crime or action. A man in a rage shoots a neighbor who just assaulted his wife. With what law can he be charged, homicide? Murder? Justifiable homicide? These are matters of law. (81:47 footnote)

12   A trial of fact is a jury's job to determine the facts, if something existed or some event occurred. Did anyone witness the man shoot his neighbor? Was the man on medications—or missed a dose? Did he own a gun? Was he there at the time of the shooting? These are matters of fact presented to a jury to weigh if the man is guilty of the charge against him (81:47 footnote)

13   No; Trying facts is the job of juries and if retrying a fact was important in a Supreme Court case, Congress could set rules and regulations for these exceptions, thereby preserving the lower court jury systems from being reworked into insignificance and annihilation (81:61)

Paper 82

1   Yes; Cases where exclusive authority to the Union is granted; Where both State and federal share an authority; Where authorities come in conflict (82:4-8)

2   When both State and federal courts may try cases (82:3 footnote)

3   No; The States can be involved if it was involved prior to the new Constitution being ratified, but it can't have jurisdiction over the new areas denied them by the Constitution; Denying the States a role in the new areas cannot be considered a reduction of jurisdictions because such cases didn't exist before the Constitution was ratified. (82:13)

4   Fill in the blanks: one whole (82:17)

5   No; Where it is expressly prohibited the States do not have concurrent jurisdiction (82:17)

6   The power of appeal; Citizens not happy with their State court decisions can turn to the federal courts and appeal for relief (82:18-23)

7   Yes; Appealing to the federal system allows a case to rise to the Supreme Court. This option is important because in matters of national concern only the Supreme Court sets national standards, not the States (82:20-24)

8   This reduces the federal government's incentive to create more inferior federal courts (82:30-31); Allows most cases to be resolved in the lower levels of the judicial system without bogging down the Supreme Court (82:31-32)

Paper 83

1   5,707 words; Trial by jury for civil cases (see introductory paragraph; 83:1-3)

2   No (83:4-5)

3   "A specification of particulars is an exclusion of generals," and, "The expression of one thing is the exclusion of another" (83:6)

4   No; Congress may decide when juries in civil cases are appropriate (83:12-13)

5   No (83:22-24)

6   Juries protect against tyrannical judges or government, against judicial despotism (83:27:30)

7   Juries can't influence the amount of taxes or the objects taxed but they can affect the mode of collection and the conduct of tax collectors (83:31-35)

8   Those issues have so many variables, a jury would help to sort them out, but granting the parameters for land-dispute juries in the Constitution is still too complex to attempt (83:44-45)

9   Yes (83:63); Juries not competent in international law (83:64-65); Juries not competent in treaties and prize cases (seizing vessels on open seas) (83:66); State jury systems not the right place to manage national/federal laws (83:67)

10   These courts seek remedies not damages; juries would be focused on massive financial penalties instead of fairness and equity (83:68-70)

11   There would be jealousy and infighting to promote the adoption of each other's State form (83:85-88)

12   (A) Connecticut; (B) Yes; (C) Yes, most certainly (83:102)

Paper 84

1   Yes; There is no Bill of Rights (84:1-2)

2   The protection of individual rights is already written into the State constitution (84:4-5)

3   Power to impeach and remove from office (84:7); Writ of habeas corpus (84:8); Attainder and ex post facto laws (84:9); No titles of nobility or foreign emoluments (84:10); Trial by jury (84:11); Issues of treason and punishment not extending to relatives or property (84:12-13))

4   Because the Constitution gives no power to the federal government over these rights (84:25-26)

5   He means that the very act of listing a lot of restrictions alters the Constitution from being a list of permissions—what the government can do—to a list of restrictions, all the things government may not do. And where the restriction is not specific, all manner of machinations will be applied to get around the restriction. The danger is that if something is not on that list then the government may presume it has power to go do it. This intent was debated for decades until it was finally settled by the Supreme Court in the Butler case discussed in 41:49 footnote. See United States v. Butler, 297 US 1 (1936) (84:28-29)

6   Yes; It declares and specifies political privileges (84:38); It defines immunities and modes of proceeding (84:39) (84:36-40)

7   Yes; Many parts in the new Constitution are already being paid for under the Articles, and additional costs will be insignificant (84:53-56)

8   More than half the time in session by the States' legislatures is used for national issues. This burden will be lifted and carried by Congress. The tasks of 2,000+ legislators will now be done by 65 or fewer Congressmen. (84:70-72)

Paper 85

1   Yes and no—Paper 85 was published in a book on May 28, 1788, just three weeks before New Hampshire became the ninth State to ratify (June 21, 1788), making the Constitution official. However, the last eight papers, Nos. 78-85, had not yet been published in the local newspapers. These later newspaper dates give the impression they were not written until after ratification.

2   Re-eligibility of the executive; Lack of an executive council; No bill of rights; No protection of liberty of the press (85:4-6)

3   Restraints on factions and insurrections due to a stronger Union (85:7); Corrosive influence of foreign intrigue (85:8); Prevention of standing armies in each of the States (85:9); Guarantee of a republican form of government in each State (85:10); Exclusion of titles of nobility (85:10); Elimination of haphazard standards of coin, weights and measures (85:11)

4   It is the best the scholars of his generation could produce and superior to any other (85:19)

5   No (85:20)

6   Accommodating the great variety of particulars, interests and opinions of thirteen States created very different blocks of support or opposition (85:28)

7   Because the whole Constitution consisting of many different issues and points must first be decided up or down. Afterwards individual amendments can be considered in light of that starting place, the newly ratified Constitution (85:30-31)

8   No new powers should be granted, only corrections to the Constitution's grants on organization and efficiency. The Bill of Rights that came a couple of years later granted new powers by declaring a restriction of them. The Bill of Rights implied the new powers, and the federal government has been turning over every pebble and crumb to find ways around the restrictions—with much success. Hamilton warned against this. (85:33)

9   A convention of States may safely combine to propose amendments that Congress otherwise had not considered or refused to consider. For such a convention of States the several State legislatures would and can erect barriers against encroachments of the national authority or encroachments by that very convention to destroy liberty. (85:35-37)

10   "We may safely rely on the disposition of the State legislatures to erect barriers against the encroachments of the national authority" or any other authority for that matter (85:37)

11   To ratify it (85:38)

12   A "prodigy," meaning "so extraordinary as to excite wonder or astonishment" (Noah Webster's American Dictionary of the English Language, 1828) (85:42)

HOW TO USE THE INDEX

Paragraphs not pages: The index is created to pinpoint ideas according to individual sentences or paragraphs instead of general locations by page number. The references are Paper/Paragraph (example: 37:44). Some page numbers are provided, but for the first references only.

Concentration points: The authors' ideas are usually concentrated in one place, but there are hundreds of exceptions. Readers are encouraged to skim the adjoining paragraphs for additional comments and related information.

Abbreviations of longer words and terms are used frequently to conserve space.

Scope: This index is not meant to be a complete concordance of all words and topics. Discussion points that have dozens or hundreds of references are represented with several of the most expressive or clarifying examples.

Paper or paragraph? We use "No." (number) to mean the sequential number of an entire Federalist paper, for example, "No. 84" means that entire paper start to finish. Or, "Nos. 10-12" means the entire text of papers 10, 11, and 12.

Advisory: This term is used to alert readers of special cases or exceptions in the index such as definitions, helpful notes, or there being too many references to track.

ABBREVIATIONS

Amend. — Amendment to Constitution	fed. — federal
appt. — appointment	govt. — government
Articles — Articles of Confederation	House — House of Representatives
Const. — US Constitution	Indep. — Independence
const. — State or sundry constitutions	No. — Sequential number of a *Paper*
Const. Conv. — Constitutional Convention	Nos. — Plural Federalist papers
Decl. of Indep. — Declaration of Independence	reps. — representatives
esp. — especially	Sec. — Section of the Constitution

Index of Principles, Concepts, and Ideas

NY trial by jury processes (83:47), 343

CIVIL LIST. *DEFINED* **(SEE 30: 1 FOOTNOTE),**

CIVIL RIGHTS. *SEE* **"RIGHTS"**

CIVIL SOCIETY
Blessings of stability in a civil society (37:17), 140
Changing political form doesn't dissolve its moral obligations (43:10), 179
Factions caused by differences in society (10:14-17), 33
Justice is the end of govt. in civil society (51:19), 213
Liberty is not confined to any point of time (53:2), 219
Self-defense is an object of civil society (41:10), 163

CIVIL WAR
Consequence of trying to govern States (16:3, 30), 59
Even the Const. can't do impossible and stop civil war (16:30), 62
German confederacies created constant (19:16-18), 71

CLASSES---SOCIAL
Aristocracy as a ruling class (39:7-14; 85:10-11), 357
Conflicts between various classes (37:40-42; 43:35), 143
Fair representation of all classes (51:13-23), 213
Governments must be built on all classes (39:9-14), 151
Human nature creates many classes (10:14-18), 33
Impossible to represent all classes (35:15-27), 131
Influence of classes on representation (57:22), 236
Influence of classes on taxing powers (36:36-37), 137
Landed interests push for lowest taxes (35:20-21), 132
Learned professions as a class (35:19-20), 132
No path for elite to uniformly rise (60:22-23), 248
Not all are represented (35:23-24), 132
Poor and rich can run for office (57:7), 234
Poor class conserves, rich class spends (21:24; 36:36-37), 80
Ratios and proportions for representation (55:12-14, 23), 227
Reps. are impartially selected (57:5-10), 234
Reps. oversee three general types of social classes (35:23-27), 132
Senate appointed indirectly won't become its own class (63:39-40), 262
Slaves joining a faction can create a strong class (43:35) 178

COAST GUARD
Smuggling controlled with a Coast Guard (12:20),. *See* "Navy" "Trade"

COERCIVE ACTS AGAINST AMERICANS
See Significant Dates in the Founding of America, 387

COIN MONEY
Foreign coins and foreign powers intersect better with a Union (44:9-10), 182
Power to coin is not a State duty (42:22, 34, 44:5-8), 181

COLONIES---AMERICAN
Articles didn't provide for new States (43:14), 176
Congress was trusted before War by the colonies (52:16-17), 218
Elections before and during the War (52:17), 218

COLONIES---FOREIGN
European colonies near America are a threat if we're disunited (8:27-28), 26
Europe seeks to stymie American commercial expansion (11:2-3), 38
Settlements surrounding the States are a growing threat (24:15-17), 93

COMMANDER IN CHIEF
Articles of Confederation: Article IX, Clause 6, 367
Constitution: Art. 2, Sec. 2, Clause 1 373
President's role as Commander in Chief (69:7, 16), 283
Single hand best in emergency (74:2), 304
States and their commanders in chief (69:17), 283

COMMERCE. *SEE ALSO* **"CONGRESS"**
American commerce in this hemisphere is strong (4:9), 10
America's roads, rivers, and communications facilitate healthy (14:20-21), 50
Ancient republics fought over commerce (6:19-23), 17
Articles failed to regulate commerce (42:23-26), 171
Britain domination of commerce will cease if States united (11:5-40) 38
Competition among States is good for commerce (7:15-18), 21
Competition causes wars (4:6-11; 6:4, 15-18; 7:12-18), 10
Disunited States have differing concerns over commerce (5:17), 14
Disunited States won't respect trade laws (7:18), 21
Navy helps secure free trade (No. 11; 34:13), 38
Peace through commerce is a myth, won't work (6:29-30), 18
Revenue from commercial activity (21:23-28), 80
Roads will be multiplied to support commerce (14:20), 50
Self-sufficiency will decrease need for imports (41:48), 167
Source of conflict and war (6:3-4), 16
State commerce under Articles (42:23-24), 171
States charging import duties on each other (7:18-21), 21
States united will prosper in commerce (No. 12), 42
Trade won't guarantee peace (6:13-18) 17

COMMERCE CLAUSE
Const. Art. I, Sec. 8, Clause 2, #4 371
Federal and State responsibilities in commerce (45:27-32), 190
Federal authority to regulate commerce (22:2-5; 56:4-6), 81
Foreign commerce is a federal responsibility (42:16), 171
Regulation of commerce requires knowledge (53:15; 56:5), 231
States can't regulate interstate commerce (32:8-9; 44:17-19), 120

COMMON LAW. *SEE* **"LAW"**

COMMON SENSE DECREES THE FOLLOWING:
Militia, especially local units, need not be feared (29:19-25), 111
Most truths are easily self-evident (31:1-10), 116
One national court is better than thirteen State courts (80:1, 12-13), 324
Pardons best handled by one person not a group (74:5), 304
Perfect govt. not possible (85:20-23), 358
Plurality of executives always fails (70:17), 288
State leaders are best eyes on federal govt. (84:47-48), 353

COMPEL
Articles gave Congress no power to compel the States (23:9), 89
Can't be compelled to incriminate self (Const. Amend. V), 375
Contracts are binding according to good will (81:43), 333
Each House can compel attendance (Const. Art. I, Sec. 5, Clause 1), 370
Govt. of natural law less prone to military compulsion (27:12), 104
Political power is ability to make laws to compel obedience (33:4-5), 123
States cannot compel each other (54:20), 225
Under despotism, military force needed to compel the people (60:24), 248

COMPROMISE. *SEE* **"CONSTITUTION, COMPROMISES"**
Compromising made the Convention a success (37:37-39, 46-48), 143
Equal representation of States is compromise (62:9), 254
President's reversible veto power is a compromise (73:28-31), 302
Principle of compromising is wise politics (62:11), 254
Slave importation ban is brilliant compromise (42:17-18), 171
States' conflicting demands solved by a compromise (37:37-42), 142
Three Great Compromises: Slavery (42:17-18), Representation (37:37-39), Commerce (42:22; 56:4-5), 171
Wrong to side with a bad compromise (22:28), 84

COMPULSION
Govt. acting in accord with natural laws is less prone to force (27:12),. *See* "Government"; "Law"; "Violence"

CONCEIT
Conceited leaders sacrifice national interests for vanity (70:21-22), 289

CONCESSION
Friends of the Const. concede it's not perfect (85:20-21), 358

CONCURRENT JURISDICTION
State and federal courts (No. 82, esp. 82:2-8), 335
Taxation authority is a concurrent jurisdiction (No. 33) 125
Taxes shared by State and Federal (No. 32; 34:29-31) 121
Treaties by the Exec. and Senate (66:8; 69:36; 77:25) 272

CONFEDERACY
Contrasted with federal union (9:23-29), 30
Cost more for its members than forming one Union (13:3), 46
Dangers of a confederacy (5:7-22), 13
Defined (see Introduction; 9:23), xvi
Historical examples of failed confederacies (Nos. 18, 19, 20), 66
How many feasible if States don't unite? (2:23-24; 4:20, 26; 5:7-22; 13:5-9), 47
Lycian confederacy (see 9:29 Editors' Note), 31
Number: Three or four most likely to form (4:26), 12
Violence between members is sure to happy (6:2), 15

CONFEDERACY---FLAWS AND WEAKNESSES
America will be destroyed by confederacies (2:25), 6
Articles founded on false principles (37:13), 140
Confederacies won't unite in common defense (5:15), 14
Defense is weakened under a confederacy (4:20-24), 12
Extensive discussion (Nos. 16-20), 66
Force needed instead of power of law in a confederacy (27:13) 105
Members eventually will become enemies (5:16-22), 14
Neighbors are natural enemies in confederacies (6:2, 33; No. 7; 8:1), 19
Obedience can't be forced in a confederacy (27:8) 105
Quarreling will be constant between confederacies (5:4-8), 13
Revenue harder to raise in a confederacy (No. 13), 46
States can't be governed in a confederacy (15:24), 55
Utility of the Confederacy to control factions (9:9-13), 28
War is always the eventual outcome of confederacies (No. 5), 13

CONFEDERATE REPUBLIC
Definition (9:26-29), 30
Montesquieu describes (9:16-21, 28), 30

I

O

OATH

All govt. officers bound to support Const. (see Const. Art. VI, Clause 3), 374
An oath is not enough to hold a union together (18:4-5), 66
Elected officers bound by the sanctity of an oath (27:15), 105
Every influence to secure fidelity is listed (64:31), 267
Fed. officers bound to Const. by oath (44:49-52), 185
President's oath of office (Const. Art. II, Sec. 1, Clause 6-7 [last clause]), 373

OBEDIENCE

Articles couldn't force States' into obedience (21:2-6), 77

OBSCURE

Anti-Federalists obscure truth with fear (36:33), 137
Articles left US relations with Indians too obscure (42:31), 172
Definitions of words made obscure by three sources (37:35), 142
God's own messages are dimmed by obscure words (37:34), 142
Govt. workings are cloaked by obscurity (37:26-27), 141
Indian commerce regulations are rendered obscure by Articles (42:31), 172
Laws and ideas can be obscured by ambiguous words (37:28-30), 142
Morals and politics don't have the same certainty (31:8), 117
Words and terms are often obscured (37:31-33) 142

OBSTINACY

Politicians neglect what's good for country for personal vanity (70:21), 289

OLIGARCHY

Defined (see 58:26 footnote), 240
Elites trying to take over using military force would cause war (60:24-28), 248
Examples of oligarchies in ancient history (63:35-38), 261
Republican govt. prevents oligarchies (57:3), 234
Too many Reps. engender a spirit of oligarchy (58:26), 240

OPINION

Convention delegates sacrificed private opinion for public good (37:48), 144
Man's opinion is timid when alone, but firm in large numbers (49:10), 206

ORATOR

Majority vulnerable to shrewd orator (58:25), 240

P

PARCHMENTS

Laws not conforming to public interests are ignored (25:25), 98
Parchment delineation of the branches' boundaries not enough (73:10), 300
Poorly constructed constitutions don't protect the weak (48:6, 31), 201
War can't be stopped by parchment when obligations ignored (7:33), 23
Written protection alone is not enough control (49:26), 208

PARDONS

Executive has authority to grant pardons (74:4-11), 304
Pardons by a group won't be fair (74:7-9), 305
President's power to issue pardons (69:18-19; 74:4-11), 283
Treason can be pardoned (74:6), 304
Whiskey Rebellion, 1794, shows wisdom of pardons (see 74:10 footnote), 305

PARIS PEACE TREATY

See Appendix, Significant Dates in the Founding of America, 388

PARTISANSHIP. *SEE ALSO* "PARTY, POLITICAL," "PUBLIC GOOD"

Actions good for America often opposed by partisanship (70:20-22), 289
Appointments ignite passions of (76:9-10), 310
Judges are also subject to (79:11), 323

PARTY---POLITICAL

Appointments made complicated by spirit of party (76:9-10), 310
Beware of obstinate adherence to political party (85:18), 357
Conspiracies started and supported by political parties (26:23-27), 101
Const. Convention was insulated from political parties (37:47), 144
Dangers of political parties (1:4-11), 1
Judges' qualifications and abilities tainted by political party (79:11), 323
Judiciary can be tainted by political parties (81:16), 330
Liberty allows freedom to form political parties and factions (10:15), 33
Liberty dies when parties are extinguished (50:17), 210
Pardons process corrupted by bias in political parties (74:7-10), 305
Parties are natural but also have seeds of destruction (10:7-51), 32
Party discord forces slow deliberation that checks excesses (70:24), 289
Passion not reason forms political parties (49:2-26), 207
Political parties in conflict will always exist (50:17), 210
Spirit of political party infects all political bodies (26:21-22), 101
Violent parties ruled by violent feelings (50:12-13), 210

PARTY---SPIRIT OF

All political bodies are infected by spirit of party (26:21), 101
Anti-Federalists urged on by applause and spirit of party (67:10), 277
Appointing-process rife with spirit of party (76:9-10), 310
Convention enjoyed relief from impact of party spirit (37:47), 144
Direct election of senators would be fraught with spirit of party (64:5), 264
Extinction of party is end of liberty (50:16-17), 210
Party animosities often suppressed in times of danger (49:15), 207

PASSION

Conventions not driven by reason but by passion (49:24-25), 208
Pres. shouldn't fall in with every transient impulse (71:8), 293
Public passions hurry persons into excesses they'd avoid in private (15:42), 57
Too many Reps. bury reason under passion (58:22-23), 240
War often started by passions of pride, ego, and arrogance (3:20, 6:5-10) 9

PATENTS

Patents provided for only limited duration (43:2-4),. *See also* Copyrights

PATRIOTISM

Articles' flaws condemned most by those of strong patriotism (20:27), 76
Const. brings hope to strong patriots (1:3), 1
Convention composed of men of great patriotism (2:15, 19), 5
Federal usurpation is best prevented by people's patriotism (46:24), 194
Good character ensures good treaties because of patriotism (64:31) 267
Laws are evaluated best by people of great patriotism (10:36), 35
Patriots don't sacrifice interests of society to vanity (70:20-22), 289
People can be deceived by hyper-patriotism and zeal (64:7), 265
Press attacked Congress and Convention's patriotism (2:18), 6
Principles that protect liberty include patriotism (58:19) 240
Senate's influence improves patriotism and foreign respect (63:1-7), 258

PEACE

Federal force is inevitable to maintain public peace (28:1-4), 106
Govt. needs revenue and power to ensure peace (62:25-42), 256
Never measure our future needs by the present peace (34:8-13), 127
Revenue required to maintain peace (31:11-14), 118
States not reliable to set terms for national peace (80:15), 324
Union can better preserve the peace than competing confederacies (3:5, 21), 9
Union properly armed ensures the peace (21:12-14) 79

PEACE THROUGH COMMERCE. *SEE* "COMMERCE"

PEACE THROUGH STRENGTH

Can't predict hostilities of others so better to be ready (41:16-18), 164
Expecting lasting tranquility is foolish (34:17), 128
Federal govt. is tasked with maintaining the peace (No. 25), 95
History shows wisdom of peace through strength (41:19-20), 164
National survival depends on a policy of military strength (28:1-4), 106
Not preparing and receiving the blow before preparation is foolish (25:18), 97
Standing armies in times of peace necessary for safety (25:17-19), 97
Wise nations prepare and sacrifice for peace through strength (41:22-24), 164

PELOPONNESIAN WAR

Example of failed confederacies (18:13-16; 25:26), 67
Pericles started this ruinous war (6:6-7), 16

PENNSYLVANIA

Constitution's weaknesses and violations (48:20-31), 203
Council of Censors in Pennsylvania (48:20; 50:7-18), 203, 209
    Decisions made by passion not reason (50:12-13), 210
    Excluding politicians from a council won't help (50:18), 210
    Failed because such councils can't cultivate unbiased wisdom (50:16), 210
    Members biased toward status quo (50:9-11), 209
    Misconstrued the NY const. (50:14), 210
Dispute with Conn. over Wyoming Valley (6:31; 7:10-11), 19
Election of exec. and the separation of branches (47:37-38), 199
Impeachments in Pennsylvania (see 66:7 footnote), 272
Judiciary is an independent branch (81:18), 330
Juries and equity courts lack uniformity (83:49-50, 75), 343
Limits placed on legislature to provide armed defense (26:4), 99
Militia not enough for some uprisings (28:7), 106
Ratification of Constitution (see Introduction), viii, xvii
Representatives ratio set at 1 to 4,000-5,000 (55:10), 227
Speculation: Which confederacy would it likely join? (13:6-9), 47
Standing armies not forbidden but discouraged (24:7 footnote), 92
Standing army raised during peacetime (25:23), 97
Voting districts and representation (57:29-30), 237
Wealth can't be compared to other States (21:18), 79

PEOPLE---CHARACTER

High expectations by the people for their federal govt. (21:1-5), 103
High expectations by the people for the Union (3:1-3), 7
Republican principles govern the people (71:7-12), 293

PEOPLE---CONSENT. *SEE* "POWER, FOUNTAIN OF"

Const. rights and powers are granted by people's consent (23:19-20), 90

R

GLOSSARY

Vocabulary words (original spelling) footnoted in the text, plus other names and terms.

ABBE MABLY – French philosopher, historian and write, 1709-1785.

ABBE MILOT – French Jesuit and historian, 1726-1785.

ABOLITION – The act of officially ending or stopping something; abolishing a system, practice, or institution.

ACHAEAN pronounced "a-KEY-un."

ADVERT – To turn our attention to.

AMPHICTYONIC COUNCIL (pronounced "am-FIC-tea-on-ic") – A religious "league of neighbors" among neighboring city-states in ancient Greece formed to protect their religious, cultural, and political union. Founded around 1100 BC, it reached its peak of power around 500 BC.

ANIMADVERSION – A harsh, critical remark.

APOTHEGM – A terse statement; concise saying or maxim.

APPELLATE COURT – Also called an "appeals court" that can review the trial record sent up by a lower court to judge if the law was correctly applied.

ARCHON – A chief magistrate in ancient Athens.

AULIC COUNCIL (pronounced "OWL-ic," or "ALL-ic") was an executive organ of the Holy Roman Empire from 1407–1806. This was an official counsel of paid, permanent members who handled petitions to the emperor, and served as the private court of the emperor.

AVARICE – Covetousness or insatiable desire for gain; greed is the selfish desire for more than is needed.

BAILAGE – A duty imposed upon the delivery of goods, (See Oxford English Dictionary, 1913 ed., Vol. 1 (a–b), James A. H. Murray, et al., eds., p. 625).

BELGIC CONFEDERACY – A group of the northern provinces of the Netherlands that united to resist Spanish domination in 1579.

BILL OF ATTAINDER – A formal act of the government passed by majority vote that declares a specifically named person instantly guilty of a capital crime—without a trial—and simultaneously having his civil rights canceled, all property confiscated, and putting him in jail.

BILL OF CREDIT – A promissory note backed by the State (not a bank) to be circulated among the people as real money and redeemable on a future day.

BULWARK – A strong means of defense, support, or protection.

CABAL – A secret political faction or clique.

CALLICRATES – ("Ca-lick-ra-tease") Achaean politician (died 149 BC) who helped Rome infiltrate Greek states. He betrayed Polybius who was a prominent Greek historian, and 1,000 other nobles, whom he identified to be transported to Rome as hostages.

CALUMNIATED – To speak about falsely with malicious intent to defame and damage.

CANTON – a small territorial district or state of a larger country or confederation.

CAVIL – To grumble, carp, complain, and make petty and unnecessary objections; to find fault over trivial matters.

CAVILLING – To argue or find fault over trivial matters.

CHIMERICAL – Imaginary, vainly conceived, can have no existence except in thought.

CIVIL CASE is a legal dispute between two or more people.

CRIMINAL CASE is a legal examination of a person's conduct in relation to the laws of the land.

CIVIL LIST – A list of expenses budgeted annually for the support of the civil government (judges, secretaries, civil servants).

COLOR. Used twenty times as both positive and negative to caste doubt or to establish the validity or meaning of a claim. Instances include "What colorable (plausible) reason could be assigned," or, "pretenses to color" (validity), or, "had some color" (legitimacy), or "too highly colored" (exaggerated), and "destitute of color" (not legitimate)."

COLORABLE – Plausible; giving the appearance of being right.

COMITIA CENTURIATA – A military assembly that decided on war, passed laws, elected consuls, and considered appeals.

COMITIA TRIBUTA – A nonmilitary civilian assembly that did most of the legislating and dealt with the most serious public offenses.

CONCORD – Agreement or harmony between people or groups.

CONCURRENT JURISDICTION – Two or more courts, or a federal court and a State court permitted to try the same case.

CONCURRENT – Existing, happening, or done at the same time.

CONDUCE – Help bring about a desirable result.

CONFEDERACY – A group of states that unite by agreement into a league or alliance.

CONFEDERATE REPUBLIC: An assemblage of societies, or an association of two or more states into one state.

CONFORMABLY – Similar in form, consistent.

CONFORMITY – Compliance with standards, laws, and rules.

CONNIVE: conspire to do something considered wrong, immoral, or illegal.

CONSTRUE – To interpret a word in a particular way to give meaning that might not have been intended.

CONTUMACY – Stubborn resistance to authority; refusal to obey or comply with a court order or summons.

CORRUPTION OF BLOOD – This is a consequence of a bill of attainder. It involves punishing the innocent relatives of a felon. The punishment comes in the form of not allowing property to be inherited by the felon, owned by the felon, or passed along by the felon to his descendants. Also, any relative benefiting from the felon's reputation, inheritance, government position, or prestige would be stripped of those advantages.

CRONYISM – Appointing friends to positions of authority without proper regard to their qualifications.

DECEMVIRS – Ten men in ancient Rome who prepared 10 tables of law to settle differences between the rich landed class and the small farmers in 451 BC.

DECLAMATION – Passionate, emotional speech

DEFALCATION – Another word for embezzling, when a trusted person in charge of funds misappropriates those funds.

DEMAGOGUE – A political leader seeking people's support by appealing to their desires rather than rational arguments.

DEROGATE – To detract or deviate from; to lessen the importance of something that no longer needs to be considered.

DESIDERATUM – Something that is needed, wanted, or required.

DESPOTIC GOVERNMENT – All the powers of government, legislative, executive, and judiciary, result to the legislative body. The concentrating these in the same hands, is precisely the definition of despotic government.

DIET – An ancient Greek/Latin term meaning "an assembly." In politics it's used to mean a deliberative assembly, a gathering of members who make political decisions.

DILATE – To relate at large, to tell copiously or diffusely (Noah Webster, American Dictionary of the English Language, 1828.)

DILATORY – Slow to act, drawing out or extending the time; deferring action.

DISQUISITION – A formal inquiry or investigation of a subject, often in writing.

DIVIDE ET IMPERA – Divide and command by conquering a people and ruling by dividing them into manageable provinces.

DUCAT – A gold or silver trade coin, sometimes diluted or coated to deceive, traded in Europe beginning in the 1100s AD.

DUTIES – Taxes collected by customs on imports, exports or the consumption of goods. An impost on land or other real estate, or on the stock of farmers in not called a duty, but a direct tax. (From Webster's American Dictionary of the English Language, 1828.

EFFICACY – The power to produce effects.

ELECTORAL COLLEGE: The Framers didn't use the term "Electoral College." *College* was used in those days to mean groups of people with a common purpose or duty, but was not attributed to the American election process until decades later. A State choose a number of electors equal to its representatives in the House and Senate. These electors studied the candidates and cast their votes for President. This indirect process was meant to prevent bullying by the large States and avoid the tendency of the mass of voters to vote according to passion instead of reason.

ELECTORS – This is anyone who elects – The masses of the people, the electors choosing the president, representatives as electors, and senators as electors. It is confusing in places, so a careful reading in context helps reveal which particular elector is being referenced.

EMBARRASS – This is not like being ashamed but rather is used to mean hinder, entangle, confuse, or to make intricate – "Our public affairs are embarrassed."

ENAMOURED – British form of enamored; filled with a strong feeling of love.

ENCOMIUMS – A speech or writing that praises something or someone.

ENERGETIC – Powerful. A frequently used term meaning that the government must have all the necessary political, enforcement, and taxing power to fulfill its assigned tasks. The Articles of Confederation did not grant this power, so the government was not energetic.

ENERGY – Having sufficient political power to execute laws and perform the assigned duty.

EQUITY – A court of law must follow laws on the books, good or bad. A court of equity considers the issues of fair and equal. Stealing bread is a crime in the King's court of law, but a court of equity would consider the fact the king had already taken all of the man's bread.

EX-POST-FACTO LAW – A law that criminalizes conduct that was legal when originally performed.

EXECUTIVE AUTHORITY – Directing common strength in war.

EXCISE TAXES – Taxes put on the manufacture, sale or consumption of articles that are consumed by the family such as soap, coffee, candles, gas, alcohol, tobacco, and so forth.

EXCRESCENT – An abnormal, excessive, or useless outgrowth.

EXECRABLE – Extremely bad, wretched, or unpleasant.

EXIGENCIES – Urgent needs and demands of a particular situation that require immediate relief.

EXPRESSLY – For a specific purpose. That word created havoc because it was too open to interpretation and argument.

FACTION – This refers to a dissenting group that rises up against the whole. A faction can be politicians within a government assembly, a group within a State, a whole State, or several States.

FEDERAL – Latin, pertaining to a treaty, compact, contract, or agreement to unite independent entities or states.

FELONY – Any serious crime warranting prison or death. From the feudal period where a vassal failed in his fidelity to the lord by committing an offense for which he loses his feud or stewardship, such as being traitor or rebellious.

FLANDERS OF AMERICA – This makes reference to an independent feudal state in the European Low Countries. It was famous for textile production and enjoyed independence and prosperity for many centuries — but it was vulnerable to invasion. When regional fighting ended in the late 1500s Flanders was split between the Dutch-held north (the leading province of the Netherlands), and the Spanish-held south.

FORTITUDE – That strength or firmness of mind or soul which enables a person to encounter danger with coolness and courage."

GIVING EFFICACY – Producing the desired result.

GOOD GOVERNMENT – Energy in the Executive is a leading character in the definition of

GOOD GOVERNMENT – Energy essential to that security against external and internal danger, and to that prompt and salutary execution of the laws

HABEAS CORPUS – A legal order demanding a detained person be brought into court, and that the government show cause for the imprisonment.

HOUSE OF BOURBON was a European dynasty of French origin that held thrones in Spain, Sicily, Naples, and Parma (in northern Italy).

HUGO GROTIUS – A Dutch jurist, politician, theologian, and scholar in natural law and international law (1583-1645).

IGNIS FATUUS – Latin for "foolish fire," or a deceptive goal or misleading in one form or another.

IMBECILITY – The state of behaving very stupidly, foolishly, feebly, or incapably.

IMPERIAL CHAMBER COURT was founded by Maximilian I in 1495 as the Holy Roman Empire's permanent high court. The court helped calm regional quarrellings in imperial Germany.

IMPERIUM IN IMPERIO – An empire within an empire, like a two-headed monster.

IMPROVIDENCE – Without foresight or adequate consideration; rash; acting on mistaken assumptions.

IMPUNITY: free from punishment; exemption from the injurious consequences of an action.

INEXPEDIENT – Not practical, suitable, judicious, or advisable.

INFLUENCE – The power to confer a benefit on someone.

INJUDICIOUS – Unwise, showing lack of judgment. Hamilton here issues a warning that a minimum standard of good behavior is necessary for the new Constitution.

INSUPERABLE – Impossible to overcome, insurmountable or overwhelming.

INVEIGLING – Persuasion by deception or flattery.

JANIZARIES were the Sultan's personal guard in medieval Turkey. A **SERAGLIO** was the place where the wives and concubines resided in a harem.

JUDICIAL DESPOTISM – When the judiciary rules with absolute power.

LACEDAEMON (pronounced "LASSA-demon"; Lacaedaemonians pronounced "LASSA-dee-moan-ians") – A prominent city-state in ancient Greece with Sparta as its main settlement. Sparta's social system and constitution promoted military preparedness as part of its culture, making it the dominant and uniting military power in Greece.

LANDED INTEREST (or landholders) – Landowners who makes a living off the land or rents it out to others.

LAW is defined as a rule of action

LAW OF DESCENT – How property is inherited by another when the original owner dies.

LEARNED PROFESSIONS – Skilled vocations requiring a high degree of education (doctor, lawyer, theologian, engineer, and so forth.).

LEGERDEMAIN – Trickery, cunning, sleight of hand.

LETTERS OF MARQUE – Written authority granting a private person license to plunder the enemy. If captured, laws of war then apply. Without such a letter the person could instead be treated as a pirate and executed on the spot.

LEX LOCI – Latin for the "law of the place." The law of the nation, state, county, or place where a crime is committed.

LOUIS D'OR – A French gold coin first struck in 1640 and issued until the French Revolution in 1789.

MAGNA CARTA – Latin, "great charter." The great charter obtained by English barons from King John, AD 1215. "Charta" is pronounced with a hard "k" sound. At the end of the 18th century, English speakers were mispronouncing Charta with a "ch" sound. The spelling began changing to drop the "h" to "Carta" to encourage correct pronunciation. Both spellings are correctly pronounced with a hard "K" sound – KAHR-tuh.

MANUFACTURING – Using raw materials to create finished goods.

MATTERS OF FACT – The existence of facts or occurrence of events.

MATTERS OF LAW – How the law applies, the definition of a law.

MENSURATION – The act of measuring the dimensions.

MERCHANTS – Those buying and selling raw materials.

MULCTS – A fine or compulsory payment.

MUTABILITY – Changeableness, inconsistency; capability to change; variability.

NEGATIVE: Used to mean veto or cancel; the power or right vested in one part of government to cancel or postpone decisions or enactments of another.

NEGATIVE PREGNANT – Also called a pregnant denial, is being intentionally misleading and ambiguous. It is when a person makes it difficult to determine if a fact is being denied, or if the qualification of the fact is being denied. Denying part of an assertion implies that the rest of the assertion is admitted. Example – "I deny selling him cocaine on Tuesday" implies he did sell him cocaine on another day. The better denial is, "I never sell illegal drugs." Another – "I deny the existence of a birth certificate." But being the baby's father was not denied.

NOBILITY – A class of people who receive privileges at the expense of the rest of the people.

NUGATORY – Of no value or importance; of no force or consequence.

OBDURACY – State of being unmoved by persuasion or pity, hardened against good. The opposite is tenderness, flexibility, and amenability.

OBSEQUIOUS – Excessive eagerness to please; a fawning attentiveness.

OLIGARCHIC, OLIGARCHY – Small group of people having control of a country; rule by factions.

OLIVER CROMWELL – An English general and statesman famous for his leadership skills, 1599–1658,.

PALLADIUM – A safeguard or protective measure.

PALLIATE – Hide the seriousness of something.

PAROXYSM – A sudden outburst, attack, violent expression, or exacerbation of an emotion or activity.

PARSIMONY – Extreme frugality, excessive caution, stingy.

PATRICIAN – An aristocrat or nobleman.

PERSPICUITY – Penetrating discernment; ability to see clearly with understanding and insight.

PERTINACIOUS – Determined, dogged, persistent, tenacious, stubborn.

PLEBIAN – A commoner or general citizen.

PLENIPOTENTIARY – Person with full power of independent action on behalf of their government.

PLIANCY – The state of being easily persuaded.

POLL TAX – A tax of a fixed amount levied on everyone in a described area, sometimes as a condition of voting.

POPULAR – This term means pertaining to the common people as in popular voice, popular vote, popular government.

POSSE COMITATUS – (Latin for "power of the county") was a town's able-bodied males over age fifteen who could be mobilized by the local sheriff to keep the peace or catch a culprit. While the militia was trained for police or military action, the posse comitatus was not. It included anyone the sheriff might call, regardless of their role in the militia.

POWERS FEDERAL – The powers delegated by the proposed Constitution to the federal government are few and defined

POWERS STATES – Delegated to States are numerous and indefinite

PREPOSSESSIONS – Attitudes or impressions formed beforehand, usually more positive than negative as in "prejudice."

PRIZE CAUSES – Ships and cargo that are taken from an enemy in war, seized by force as spoil or plunder

PRODIGY – Something so extraordinary as to excite wonder or astonishment (from Noah Webster's American Dictionary of the English Language, 1828).

PROROGUE – Put off, delay, or end a legislative session, but not dissolve the assembly.

PURSUANT – In accordance with a law or legal document or resolution.

QUADRATE – To conform with other elements, or cause to conform – "a values system that would quadrate with his morality."

RECIPROCALITY – A formal political or social agreement of mutual benefit, dependence, or influence.

RECUR – Go back to something in thought or speech.

REFERENDUM – A direct and universal vote by citizens who may vote for or against an act brought before the legislature before it becomes law.

REMARKING – Redesigning.

REMEDY – The guarantee that a right will be defended. The Constitution assigns the satisfaction of that guarantee in Congress to make proper laws protecting a right, and in the judicial system to grant relief when a right is violated.

REPROBATED: To express or feel disapproval of.

REPUBLIC – a government which derives all its powers directly or indirectly from the great body of the people, and is administered by persons holding their offices during pleasure, for a limited period, or during good behavior.

REPUGNANCY – Contradiction or inconsistency between clauses of the same document or contract.

RESPONSIBILITY – This word was coined by James Madison, appearing for the first time in No. 63:8. For more than a century it was wrongly believed Hamilton wrote No. 63, but research since then accurately attributes it to Madison.

SALUTARY – producing good effects; beneficial.

SANGUINE – Eager hopefulness; confidently optimistic.

SIGNAL OR SIGNALLY – Eminently, remarkably, memorably, in a distinguished manner.

SOCIAL COMPACT – An unofficial agreement between the States to cooperate on issues that work best if shared in common, such as basic laws and rules of trade.

SUFFRAGE – The right to vote, a fundamental article of republican government

SUPERADDED – To add, especially in a way that magnifies an effect.

SUPERANNUATED – Deemed obsolete because of age.

SUPINENESS – Negligence, inattentiveness, heedlessness.

SWEEPING CLAUSE – Anti-Federalists called the "The Necessary and Proper Clause" the "Sweeping Clause" to imply that it allowed all loose ends and unidentified needs to be swept up into a little pile of unrestricted power.

TAUTOLOGY – Needless repetition using different words. Examples – global pandemic, dry desert, dead corpse.

TEMERITY: Audacity, excessive confidence or boldness.

TRACTABLE – Easy to control or influence.

TRANSMUTATION – The process of changing one thing into something completely different.

TREASON – Levying war upon the United States, and adhering to their enemies, giving them aid and comfort"

TYRANNY – The accumulation of all powers, legislative, executive, and judiciary, in the same hands, whether of one, a few, or many, and whether hereditary, self appointed, or elective,

UMBRAGE – A feeling of resentment, offense, or annoyance.

VENALITY – Ability to be bribed; being influenced by money; corruptibility.

VENDIBLE – Capable of being sold or traded; marketable.

VENERATION – Great respect or reverence.

VIRTUE – The word virtue here means the strength and determination to stand up for what is right and defend it.

VIVIFY – enliven or animate.

WEAL – The well-being, prosperity or happiness of a people or person.

WONDER – Feeling of surprise mingled with admiration.

YEOMANRY – Small landowning family farmers.

ABOUT THE EDITORS

Paul B. Skousen is a student of the Constitution, author, college professor, former analyst at the CIA, and was an intelligence officer at the Reagan White House. He holds a journalism degree from Brigham Young University, and an MA in national security studies from Georgetown University. He wrote *The Naked Socialist* and *How To Read the Constitution and the Declaration of Independence*, among other books. To clarify many of the difficult messages in the *The Federalist*, Paul subdivided the text into more than three thousand individual segments, and added paragraph headings, summary statements, and review questions to highlight and preview the important ideas of each paragraph. He prepared an extensive index for direct access to the many principles and ideas contained in this book. Paul is the son of W. Cleon Skousen.

Dr. W. Cleon Skousen (1913–2006) was a constitutional scholar, historian, biblical scholar, college professor, author, popular speaker, chief of police in Salt Lake City, FBI agent, and an administrator of the FBI communications section under J. Edgar Hoover. He wrote *The Naked Communist*, *The 5000 Year Leap*, and more than forty other books. He received his law degree from George Washington Law School. One of Dr. Skousen's research and teaching devices was underlining key words and phrases. Dr. Skousen taught his college students this technique to aid them in pulling out important points from complex writings. The underlines and margin notes from Dr. Skousen's six personal copies of *The Federalist* were painstakingly duplicated into this single master copy. His copious margin notes are reproduced in footnotes or in the subheadings of the paragraphs.

SOURCES FOR PAGE *i*, "WE DECLARE"

The statements on page *i* are consolidated from the quotes provided below.

HAMILTON: "It has been frequently remarked that it seems to have been reserved to the people of this country, by their conduct and example, to decide the important question, whether societies of men are really capable or not of establishing good government from reflection and choice, or whether they are forever destined to depend for their political constitutions on accident and force. (*The Federalist Papers Made Easier*, No. 1:2)

MADISON: "Ambition must be made to counteract ambition. The interest of the man must be connected with the constitutional rights of the place. It may be a reflection on human nature, that such devices should be necessary to control the abuses of government. But what is government itself, but the greatest of all reflections on human nature? If men were angels, no government would be necessary. If angels were to govern men, neither external nor internal controls on government would be necessary. In framing a government which is to be administered by men over men, the great difficulty lies in this: you must first enable the government to control the governed; and in the next place oblige it to control itself. (*The Federalist Papers Made Easier*, No. 51:6) A dependence on the people is, no doubt, the primary control on the government; but experience has taught mankind the necessity of auxiliary precautions. (*The Federalist Papers Made Easier*, No. 51:7)

JAY: "Providence has in a particular manner blessed it with a variety of soils and productions, and watered it with innumerable streams, for the delight and accommodation of its inhabitants." (*The Federalist Papers Made Easier*, No. 2:8) "With equal pleasure I have as often taken notice that Providence has been pleased to give this one connected country to one united people—a people descended from the same ancestors, speaking the same language, professing the same religion, attached to the same principles of government, very similar in their manners and customs, and who, by their joint counsels, arms, and efforts, fighting side by side throughout a long and bloody war, have nobly established general liberty and independence." (*The Federalist Papers Made Easier*, No. 2:8–9)

SOURCES FOR PAGE *ii*, "FIVE-STAR REVIEWS"

The statements on page *ii* are consolidated from the quotes provided below.

JEFFERSON: "With respect to the Federalist, the three authors had been named to me. I read it with care, pleasure and improvement, and was satisfied that there was nothing in it by one of those hands, and not a great deal by the second. It does the highest honor to the third, as being, in my opinion, the best commentary on the principles of government which was ever written. In some parts it is discoverable that the author means only to say what may be best said in defense of opinions in which he did not concur. But in general it establishes firmly the plan of government." Jefferson to Madison, 18 November 1788, *The Papers of Thomas Jefferson*, Julian P. Boyd, Editor, Princeton University Press, 1950, Volume 14:188.

WASHINGTON: "Upon the whole I doubt whether the opposition to the Constitution will not ultimately be productive of more good than evil; it has called forth, in its defence, abilities (which would not perhaps have been otherwise exerted) that have thrown new lights upon the science of Government, they have given the rights of man a full and fair discussion, and have explained them in so clear and forcible a manner as cannot fail to make a lasting impression upon those who read the best publications on the subject, and particularly the pieces under the signature of Publius." George Washington to John Armstrong, 25 April 1788.

WASHINGTON: "As the perusal of the political papers under the signature of Publius has afforded me great satisfaction, I shall certainly consider them as claiming a most distinguished place in my library. I have read every performance which has been printed on one side and the other of the great question lately agitated (so far as I have been able to obtain them) and, without an unmeaning compliment, I will say that I have seen no other so well calculated (in my judgment) to produce conviction on an unbiased mind, as the Production of your Triumvirate. When the transient circumstances & fugitive performances which attended this crisis shall have disappeared, that work will merit the notice of Posterity; because in it are candidly discussed the principles of freedom & the topics of government, which will be always interesting to mankind so long as they shall be connected in Civil Society." George Washington to Alexander Hamilton, 28 August 1788.

ALEXIS DE TOCQUEVILLE: French political commentator, writing in 1835, "'The Federalist' is an excellent book, which ought to be familiar to the statesmen of all countries, although it especially concerns America." *Democracy in America*, chapter 8, footnote 7, 1835

MADISON to Jefferson, February 8, 1825, "The "Federalist" may fairly enough be regarded as the most authentic exposition of the text of the federal Constitution, as understood by the Body which prepared & the Authorities which accepted it. Yet it did not foresee all the misconstructions which have occurred; nor prevent some that it did foresee. And what equally deserves remark, neither of the great rival parties have acquiesced in all its Comments. It may nevertheless be admissible as a School book, if any will be that goes so much into detail. It has been actually admitted into two Universities, if not more, those of Harvard & Rh. Island; but probably at the choice of the Professors, without an injunction from the superior authority." *The Papers of James Madison, Retirement Series*, vol. 3, 1 March 1823–24 February 1826, ed. David B. Mattern, J. C. A. Stagg, Mary Parke Johnson, and Katherine E. Harbury. Charlottesville: University of Virginia Press, 2016, pp. 471–473.

JOHN STUART MILL, 1861, *Considerations on Representative Government*, Chapter XVII: Of Federal Representative Governments.

JOHN ADAMS: William Cunningham in a letter to John Adams dated December 9, 1809 makes reference to Adams' complimenting *The Federalist*. "You spoke of the papers signed Publius, which were published under the general titles of the Federalist. You acknowledged them to have been well written ...." See: Founders Online, National Archives, https://founders.archives.gov/documents/Adams/99-02-02-5479.

CHANCELLOR JAMES KENT, *Commentaries on American Law*, p. 241, 12th ed. 1873.

JOSEPH STORY, *Commentaries on the Constitution of the United States*, 1833, preface.

Made in the USA
Middletown, DE
10 September 2024

60668061R00256